50 Years of Community Development Vol II

This 50th anniversary publication provides a comprehensive history of community development. Beginning in 1970 with the advent of the Community Development Society and its journal shortly thereafter, *Community Development*, the editors have placed the chapters in major themed areas or issues pertinent to both research and practice of community development.

The evolution of community development as an area of scholarship and application, and the subsequent founding of the discipline, is vital to capture. At the 50-year mark, it is particularly relevant to revisit issues that reoccur throughout the last five decades and look at approaches to addressing them. These include issues and themes around equity and inclusion, collective impact, leadership and policy development, as well as resilience and sustainability. Community change over time has much to teach us, and this set will provide a foundation for fostering understanding of the history of community development and its focus on community change.

The chapters in this book were originally published in the journal *Community Development*.

Norman Walzer is Senior Research Scholar at the Center for Governmental Services, Northern Illinois University, DeKalb, USA.

Rhonda Phillips is Dean, Purdue University Honors College, West Lafayette, USA.

Robert Blair is Professor of Public Administration and Urban Studies at the College of Public Affairs, University of Nebraska, Omaha, USA.

The Community Development Research and Practice Series

Volume 13
Series Editor: Rhonda G. Phillips, Purdue University, USA

Editorial Board:
Mark Brennan, Pennsylvania State University, USA
Jan Flora, Iowa State University, USA
Gary P. Green, University of Wisconsin, USA
Brian McGrath, National University of Ireland
Norman Walzer, Northern Illinois University, USA
Patricia A. Wilson, University of Texas, Austin, USA

As the series continues to grow with the ninth volume, it is our intent to continue to serve scholars, community developers, planners, public administrators, and others involved in research, practice and policymaking in the realm of community development. The series strives to provide both timely and applied information for researchers, students, and practitioners. Building on a long history since 1970 of publishing the Community Development Society's journal, *Community Development* (www.comm-dev.org), the book series contributes to a growing and rapidly changing knowledge base as a resource for practitioners and researchers alike. For additional information please see the series page at http://www.routledge.com/books/series/CDRP/.

The evolution of the field of community development continues. As reflected in both theory and practice, community development is at the forefront of change, which comes to no surprise to our communities and regions that constantly face challenges and opportunities. As a practice focused discipline, change often seems to be the only constant in the community development realm. The need to integrate theory, practice, research, teaching, and training is even more pressing now than ever, given rapidly transforming economic, social, environmental, political and cultural climates locally and globally. Current and applicable information and insights about effective research and practice are needed.

The Community Development Society, a nonprofit association of those interested in pushing the discipline forward, is delighted to offer this book series in partnership with Routledge. The series is designed to integrate innovative thinking on tools, strategies, and experiences as a resource especially well-suited for bridging the gaps between theory, research, and practice. The Community Development Society actively promotes continued advancement of the discipline and practice. Fundamental to this mission is adherence to the following core Principles of Good Practice. This book series is a reflection of many of these principles:

- Promote active and representative participation towards enabling all community members to meaningfully influence the decisions that affect their lives.
- Engage community members in learning about and understanding community issues, and the economic, social, environmental, political, psychological, and other impacts associated with alternative courses of action.
- Incorporate the diverse interest and cultures of the community in the community development process; and disengage from support of any effort that is likely to adversely affect the disadvantaged members of a community.

- Work actively to enhance the leadership capacity of community members, leaders, and groups within the community.
- Be open to using the full range of action strategies to work towards the long-term sustainability and well-being of the community.

We invite you to explore the series, and continue to do so as new volumes are added. We hope you will find it a valuable resource for supporting community development research and practice.

Other books in the series:

Knowledge Partnering for Community Development
Robyn Eversole

Social Capital at the Community Level
An Applied Interdisciplinary Perspective
John M. Halstead and Steven C. Deller

Arts and Community Change
Exploring Cultural Development Policies, Practices and Dilemmas
Max O. Stephenson Jr. and Scott Tate

Community-Built
Art, Construction, Preservation, and Place
Katherine Melcher, Barry Stiefel, Kristin Faurest

Using Collective Impact to Bring Community Change
Norman Walzer and Liz Weaver

Addressing Climate Change at the Community Level in the United States
Paul R. Lachapelle and Don E. Albrecht

The Heart of Community Engagement
Practitioner Stories from Across the Globe
Patricia A. Wilson

Culture, Community, and Development
Rhonda Phillips, Mark A. Brennan, Tingxuan Li

Community Capacity and Resilience in Latin America
Paul Lachapelle, Isabel Gutierrez-Montes, Cornelia Butler Flora

50 Years of Community Development Vol I
A History of its Evolution and Application in North America
Norman Walzer, Rhonda Phillips and Robert Blair

50 Years of Community Development Vol II
A History of its Evolution and Application in North America
Norman Walzer, Rhonda Phillips and Robert Blair

50 Years of Community Development Vol II

A History of its Evolution and Application in North America

Edited by
Norman Walzer, Rhonda Phillips and Robert Blair

LONDON AND NEW YORK

First published 2021
by Routledge
2 Park Square, Milton Park, Abingdon, Oxon, OX14 4RN

and by Routledge
52 Vanderbilt Avenue, New York, NY 10017

Routledge is an imprint of the Taylor & Francis Group, an informa business

© 2021 Community Development Society

All rights reserved. No part of this book may be reprinted or reproduced or utilised in any form or by any electronic, mechanical, or other means, now known or hereafter invented, including photocopying and recording, or in any information storage or retrieval system, without permission in writing from the publishers.

Trademark notice: Product or corporate names may be trademarks or registered trademarks, and are used only for identification and explanation without intent to infringe.

British Library Cataloguing-in-Publication Data
A catalogue record for this book is available from the British Library

ISBN13: 978-0-367-43994-1

Typeset in Times New Roman
by codeMantra

Publisher's Note
The publisher accepts responsibility for any inconsistencies that may have arisen during the conversion of this book from journal articles to book chapters, namely the inclusion of journal terminology.

Disclaimer
Every effort has been made to contact copyright holders for their permission to reprint material in this book. The publishers would be grateful to hear from any copyright holder who is not here acknowledged and will undertake to rectify any errors or omissions in future editions of this book.

Printed in the United Kingdom
by Henry Ling Limited

Contents

Citation Information x
Notes on Contributors xiii

Introduction: An Overview of 50 Years of Community Development:
A History of Its Evolution and Application in North America 1
Norman Walzer, Robert Blair, and Rhonda Phillips

SECTION 1
Leadership Development Introduction 17

1 Local Self-Development Strategies: National Survey Results 21
 Gary P. Green, Jan L. Flora, Cornelia Flora, and Frederick E. Schmidt

2 Defining the Role of Nonprofit Corporations in Community
 Economic Development 40
 Keith Snavely and Roger Beck

3 Ten Basic Principles of Leadership in Community Development
 Organizations 56
 Jerry W. Robinson, Jr.

4 "People First": Factors that promote or inhibit community transformation 61
 Mary Ellen Brown and Birgitta L. Baker

5 Assessing factors influencing political engagement in local communities 79
 Cecil Shelton and Lori Garkovich

SECTION 2
Justice, Inclusion, and Participation 103

6 Community Development as Social Movement: A Contribution
 to Models of Practice 108
 John J. Green

7	Incorporating social justice in tourism planning: racial reconciliation and sustainable community development in the Deep South *Alan W. Barton and Sarah J. Leonard*	121
8	An ethical principle for social justice in community development practice *Ru Michael Sabre*	146
9	People-Centered Community Planning *John Michael Daley and Julio Angulo*	154
10	Strategies for Citizen Participation and Empowerment in Non-profit, Community-Based Organizations *Donna Hardina*	170
11	Creating Great Places: The Role of Citizen Participation *Lynn Richards and Matthew Dalbey*	184
12	The Racial Bifurcation of Community Development: Implications for Community Development Practitioners *James D. Preston and Graves E. Enck*	199
13	Caught in the Middle: Community Development Corporations (CDCs) and the Conflict between Grassroots and Instrumental Forms of Citizen Participation *Robert Mark Silverman*	209

SECTION 3
Healthy and Resilient Communities Introduction   227

14	Applying innovative approaches to address health disparities in native populations: an assessment of the Crow Men's Health Project *Paul R. Lachapelle, Tim Dunnagan and James Real Bird*	231
15	The role of community-based strategies in addressing metropolitan segregation and racial health disparities *Malo André Hutson and Sacoby Wilson*	246
16	The Economic and Fiscal Impacts of the Elderly on a Small Rural Region *Martin Shields, Judith I. Stallmann and Steven C. Deller*	264
17	Bowling Alone but Online Together: Social Capital in E-Communities *James K. Scott and Thomas G. Johnson*	286

18 Can community interventions change resilience? Fostering perceptions of individual and community resilience in rural places 305
Marianna Markantoni, Artur Adam Steiner, and John Elliot Meador

19 Community Development and Community Resilience: An Integrative Approach 322
Alex Zautra, John Hall, and Kate Murray

20 Healthy Communities: The Goal of Community Development 340
Alvin S. Lackey, Robert Burke and Mark Peterson

Index 357

Citation Information

The following chapters were originally published in various issues of *Community Development*. When citing this material, please use the original page numbering for each article, as follows:

Chapter 1
Local Self-Development Strategies: National Survey Results
Gary P. Green, Jan L. Flora, Cornelia Flora, and Frederick E. Schmidt
Community Development, volume 21, issue 2 (1990) pp. 55–73

Chapter 2
Defining the Role of Nonprofit Corporations in Community Economic Development
Keith Snavely and Roger Beck
Community Development, volume 24, issue 2 (1993) pp. 213–228

Chapter 3
Ten Basic Principles of Leadership in Community Development Organizations
Jerry W. Robinson, Jr.
Community Development, volume 25, issue 1 (1994) pp. 44–48

Chapter 4
"People First": Factors that promote or inhibit community transformation
Mary Ellen Brown and Birgitta L. Baker
Community Development, volume 50, issue 3 (2019) pp. 297–314

Chapter 5
Assessing factors influencing political engagement in local communities
Cecil Shelton and Lori Garkovich
Community Development, volume 44, issue 4 (2013) pp. 469–491

Chapter 6
Community Development as Social Movement: A Contribution to Models of Practice
John J. Green
Community Development, volume 39, issue 1 (2008) pp. 50–62

Chapter 7
Incorporating social justice in tourism planning: racial reconciliation and sustainable community development in the Deep South
Alan W. Barton and Sarah J. Leonard
Community Development, volume 41, issue 3 (2010) pp. 298–322

Chapter 8
An ethical principle for social justice in community development practice
Ru Michael Sabre
Community Development, volume 11, issue 1 (1980) pp. 15–22

Chapter 9
People-Centered Community Planning
John Michael Daley and Julio Angulo
Community Development, volume 21, issue 2 (1990) pp. 88–103

Chapter 10
Strategies for Citizen Participation and Empowerment in Non-profit, Community-Based Organizations
Donna Hardina
Community Development, volume 37, issue 4 (2006) pp. 4–17

Chapter 11
Creating Great Places: The Role of Citizen Participation
Lynn Richards and Matthew Dalbey
Community Development, volume 37, issue 4 (2006) pp. 18–32

Chapter 12
The Racial Bifurcation of Community Development: Implications for Community Development Practitioners
James D. Preston and Graves E. Enck
Community Development, volume 20, issue 2 (1989) pp. 49–58

Chapter 13
Caught in the Middle: Community Development Corporations (CDCs) and the Conflict between Grassroots and Instrumental Forms of Citizen Participation
Robert Mark Silverman
Community Development, volume 36, issue 2 (2005) pp. 35–51

Chapter 14
Applying innovative approaches to address health disparities in native populations: an assessment of the Crow Men's Health Project
Paul R. Lachapelle, Tim Dunnagan and James Real Bird
Community Development, volume 42, issue 2 (2011) pp. 240–254

Chapter 15
The role of community-based strategies in addressing metropolitan segregation and racial health disparities
Malo André Hutson and Sacoby Wilson
Community Development, volume 42, issue 4 (2011) pp. 476–493

Chapter 16
The Economic and Fiscal Impacts of the Elderly on a Small Rural Region
Martin Shields, Judith I. Stallmann and Steven C. Deller
Community Development, volume 34, issue 1 (2003) pp. 85–106

Chapter 17
Bowling Alone but Online Together: Social Capital in E-Communities
James K. Scott and Thomas G. Johnson
Community Development, volume 36, issue 1 (2005) pp. 9–27

Chapter 18
Can community interventions change resilience? Fostering perceptions of individual and community resilience in rural places
Marianna Markantoni, Artur Adam Steiner, and John Elliot Meador
Community Development, volume 50, issue 2 (2019) pp. 238–255

Chapter 19
Community Development and Community Resilience: An Integrative Approach
Alex Zautra, John Hall, and Kate Murray
Community Development, volume 39, issue 3 (Nov 2009) pp. 130–147

Chapter 20
Healthy Communities: The Goal of Community Development
Alvin S. Lackey, Robert Burke and Mark Peterson
Community Development, volume 18, issue 2 (1987) pp. 1–17

For any permission-related enquiries please visit:
http://www.tandfonline.com/page/help/permissions

Contributors

Julio Angulo School of Social Work, Arizona State University, Tempe, USA.

Birgitta L. Baker Department of Recreation, Park and Tourism Management, Pennsylvania State University, USA.

Alan W. Barton Social Sciences, Delta State University, Cleveland, USA.

Roger Beck Department of Agribusiness Economics, Southern Illinois University, Carbondale, USA.

Robert Blair is Professor of Public Administration and Urban Studies at the College of Public Affairs, University of Nebraska, Omaha, USA.

James Real Bird Crow Indian Reservation, Crow Agency, USA.

Mary Ellen Brown School of Social Work, Arizona State University, Tucson, USA.

Robert Burke Department of Community Development, University of Missouri-Columbia, USA.

Matthew Dalbey Development, Community, & Environment Division (DCED), U.S. Environmental Protection Agency, Washington, D.C., USA.

John Michael Daley School of Social Work, Arizona State University, Tempe, USA.

Steven C. Deller Department of Agricultural and Applied Economics, University of Wisconsin-Madison, USA.

Tim Dunnagan College of Health Sciences, Boise State University, USA.

Graves E. Enck Department of Sociology, Memphis State University, USA.

Cornelia Flora Department of Sociology, Virginia Polytechnic Institute and State University, USA.

Jan L. Flora Department of Agricultural Economics, Virginia Polytechnic Institute and State University, USA.

Lori Garkovich Community and Leadership Development, University of Kentucky, Lexington, USA.

Gary P. Green Division of Applied Research, University of Georgia, USA.

CONTRIBUTORS

John J. Green Institute for Community-Based Research, Division of Social Sciences, Delta State University, Cleveland, USA.

John Hall School of Public Affairs, Arizona State University, Tempe, USA.

Donna Hardina Department of Social Work Education, California State University, Fresno, USA.

Malo André Hutson Department of City and Regional Planning, University of California at Berkeley, USA.

Thomas G. Johnson Truman School of Public Affairs, University of Missouri-Columbia, USA.

Paul R. Lachapelle Department of Political Science, Montana State University, Bozeman, USA.

Alvin S. Lackey Department of Community Development, University of Missouri-Columbia, USA.

Sarah J. Leonard The College Board, Chicago, USA.

Marianna Markantonia SRUC, Edinburgh, UK.

John Elliot Meador SRUC, Edinburgh, UK.

Kate Murray Psychology Department, Arizona State University, Tempe, USA.

Mark Peterson Community Development Specialist, Warrenton, USA.

Rhonda Phillips is Dean, Purdue University Honors College, West Lafayette, IN, USA.

James D. Preston Department of Sociology, Memphis State University, USA.

Lynn Richards Development, Community, & Environment Division (DCED), U.S. Environmental Protection Agency, Washington, D.C., USA.

Jerry W. Robinson, Jr. Department of Sociology, University of Illinois, Urbana-Champaign, USA.

Ru Michael Sabre College of Agriculture, Pennsylvania State University, USA.

Frederick E. Schmidt Rural Studies, University of Vermont, Burlington, USA.

James K. Scott Truman School of Public Affairs, University of Missouri-Columbia, USA.

Cecil Shelton Agricultural Economics, Sociology and Education, Pennsylvania State University, USA.

Martin Shields Department of Agricultural Economics and Rural Sociology, Pennsylvania State University, USA.

Robert Mark Silverman Department of Urban and Regional Planning and the Center for Urban Studies, University at Buffalo, USA.

Keith Snavely Department of Political Science, Southern Illinois University, Carbondale, USA.

Judith I. Stallmann Department of Agricultural and Applied Economics, University of Missouri, USA.

Artur Adam Steiner Glasgow Caledonian University, Scotland, UK.

Norman Walzer is Senior Research Scholar at the Center for Governmental Services, Northern Illinois University, DeKalb, USA.

Sacoby Wilson Maryland Institute for Applied Environmental Health (MIAEH) and Department of Epidemiology and Biostatistics, School of Public Health, USA.

Alex Zautra Department of Psychology Arizona State University, Arizona, USA.

INTRODUCTION: AN OVERVIEW OF 50 YEARS OF COMMUNITY DEVELOPMENT

A History of Its Evolution and Application in North America

Norman Walzer, Robert Blair, and Rhonda Phillips[1]

This two-volume set presents a wide range of topics and issues covered over five decades in the journal, *Community Development* (*CD*), the journal of the Community Development Society, published since 1970. By doing so, attention is drawn to both the complexity and relevance of community development as a field of study and practice. There can be little question that community development has changed during this time period, with many issues and challenges emerging.

An especially important aspect of *CD* as a publication is that it provides outlets for interactions between academic researchers and practitioners with definite advantages to each group. In fact, this interaction is often mentioned in discussions at Community Development Society (hereafter referred to as the "Society") meetings as a major reason for continued participation. For example, it is often the case that practitioners identify topics that need additional study and researchers apply scientific methods in identifying and evaluating potential strategies to address them. This teamwork contributes to effective practices and improvements in quality of life in communities. Interactions along these lines are what motivated launching the *Journal of Community Development* in 1970. It has continued for 50 volumes and, in the process, grew to the current five issues per year spanning a broad range of topics.

To create this book set on the history and evolution of community development, numerous articles were selected across several categories to illustrate the importance and impact of community development research and practice. While many contributions from around the globe have contributed to community development scholarship, the focus of these books is on North American practices and research. During the past several years, the authors (past editors of *CD*) compiled a list of articles published with the aim to generate a collection of representative contributions that the journal has made to the literature over five decades. Key researchers were surveyed, and presentations with discussions were held at Community Development Society conferences along with download counts in recent years. These efforts produced a list of articles by decade and topic that provide an overall picture of how issues changed, as seen by journal authors and contributors. The books are organized into two volumes, the first containing two sections: Community history and theory, and planning and policy development. The second volume presents three sections: Leadership development; justice, inclusion, and participation; and healthy and resilient communities. Each section includes an introduction.

The coverage by the journal reflects an aspect that community development as a discipline has had to address. The early focus was on rural development issues with the major focus in the early 1970s on this area as a priority. The range of topics soon moved from economic development to much broader topics such as poverty, housing, health, and other social issues that community leaders in both rural and metro areas had to address. Especially important is the recognition that these issues are intertwined and require collaboration among practitioners, public leaders, and academics trained in many disciplines. The journal continues to provide an outlet for these discussions making the editing process somewhat complex.

The journal remains broad enough in coverage to include contributions from disciplines that might not be included in outlets with a narrower and more focused coverage. Consequently, this broader and interdisciplinary perspective sometimes made it more difficult for community development to earn recognition as an independent academic and professional field of study by both scholars and practitioners. The Society still wrestles with this issue and is working to define topics and a field of study that should be covered in academic programs designed to train practitioners. Likewise, a debate continues whether a professional certification is appropriate, and, if so, what topics should be included to maximize the value to practitioners.

Throughout these discussions, *Community Development*[2] *(CD)* as a journal promoted the credibility and expertise of community development professionals and helped them guide communities to select policies based on tested theories and approaches used elsewhere. Because *CD* is a peer-refereed publishing outlet, it can command respect by scholars and its articles are cited in many other journals so is able to advance the knowledge on community development issues. As an outlet for interdisciplinary research and discussions, *CD* created its niche and continues to be used by a variety of both academics and practitioners. Practitioners identify relevant issues and concerns while scholars explore and document contributing factors and potential remedies. This teamwork provides direction to community development practices and boosts the credibility of community developers as they address a myriad and changing set of issues in their practices.

CHANGING COMMUNITY DEVELOPMENT TOPICS

Time and space do not permit an intensive discussion of these myriad changing topics; rather, several topics are discussed in the following sections along with references to articles during specific time periods to illustrate how ideas progressed. Defining community development precisely is difficult but a suitable place to start is with the Principles of Good Practice (POG) endorsed by the Community Development Society that sponsors the publication of *Community Development*. These principles include the following:

- Promote active and representative participation toward enabling all community members to meaningfully influence the decisions that affect their lives.
- Engage community members in learning about and understanding community issues, and the economic, social, environmental, political, psychological, and other impacts associated with alternative courses of action.
- Incorporate the diverse interests and cultures of the community in the community development process, and disengage from support of any effort that is likely to adversely affect the disadvantaged members of a community.
- Work actively to enhance the leadership capacity of community members, leaders, and groups within the community.

- Be open to using the full range of action strategies to work toward the long-term sustainability and well-being of the community (CDS, 2020, p. 1).

The Principles encompass a broad range of research and practice topics in *CD*. For many reasons, this breadth of topics has enabled *CD* to be a platform for active discussions among Society members – scholars as well as practitioners. The topics covered have changed with both community development issues and interests by scholars/practitioners in researching these topics.

Rural Development. The journal began in an era that focused on addressing rural concerns through regional solutions. For example, the Appalachian Rural Development Act (1965) recognized concerns in many low-income areas and funded agencies to address them. The U.S. Economic Development Administration, under the Public Works and Economic Development Act (1965), took a broader approach to rural issues in general and with financial assistance for regions to design overall economic development strategies. These and other issues motivated early discussions by both Society founders and researchers, and affected the types of topics published in the journal.

Thus, during the 1970s and 1980s, much research and interest by practitioners centered on issues facing rural areas including those resulting from the farm crises in that period (Pulver, 1989). Rural planning approaches with a more organized and consistent set of strategies were also researched in attempts to manage some of the rural concerns addressed. These concerns brought research that was reported in *CD* on a variety of rural-related planning issues (Blakely & Bradshaw, 1982).

Research on these topics was stimulated further by passage of the federal Rural Development Act (1972) that promoted efforts to find ways to help rural areas design a new future. Grant funds and technical assistance by federal agencies such as the U.S. Department of Housing and Urban Development provided opportunities, often with funding for local agencies in rural areas to expand planning and other efforts to address local issues and concerns. These strategies were sometimes based on research published in *CD* as federal financial support enhanced the need for solid research and a theoretical base for planning efforts in both rural and metro areas.

The topics published were expanded as the Society's clientele and interests broadened into finding new ways to address both urban and rural concerns and as community development became more accepted as a discipline based on solid research with a theoretical base and documented practices (Shaffer, 1990). The latter 1970s and early 1980s brought articles that integrated research with local development programs, examined participatory evaluation as a tool to bring community members into finding solutions, and looked for new approaches to long-term solutions (Goudy & Tait, 1979).

Consistent through these discussions was a need to focus on finding solid theoretical foundations that explain the inner workings of community development to continue enhancing its respect and acceptance as a discipline to study and pursue (Bhattacharyya, 2003). This basic direction for *CD* continues as is true of most scholarly outlets that try to link scholarship and practice.

Journal at 25 Years. A useful way to trace the changing topics in community development, especially in the early years of the journal, is to examine issues summarized 25 years ago by Blair and Hembd for the 25th anniversary volume. The editors at that time intended the volume to "reflect on and gauge the progress made in community development." The theme of the 25th volume – "What We Have Learned" – was a way to "reflect on the past and build for the future in community development...[providing] a forum to share important insights gained by people participating in community development the past quarter century." While many submitted manuscripts focused on theory, most emphasized practice. This emphasis reflects the ongoing purpose of *CD*: "to disseminate information on theory, research and practice" of community development. Manuscript reviewers for the special edition included practitioners, researchers, and community development educators. The reviewers emphasized the reflective nature of the 25th anniversary. The articles selected by the reviewers and editors were grouped into three broad categories: the community as an entity, the changing practice of community development, and development of small or rural communities.

It is an enlightening exercise to compare the three general themes of 25 years ago to community development in the 21st century. Community development, for instance, increasingly has taken an urban and neighborhood focus. The community, as the building block of society, which is part of the Society's Mission Statement, was examined in the first set of articles in the special edition. This emphasis has not changed in the subsequent 25 years. Authors explored the nature and structure of community development as a collective and inclusive collaborative process of the community residents.

The second set of articles examined both the practice and the process of community development, focusing on the facilitative role of community development practitioners. It is safe to conclude that the role of the community developer changed in the community development process with the growth in professionalism and knowledge of practices.

While the POG maintain their relevance, community development has become more complex. Several authors in the 25th edition anticipated that controversy would increasingly impact the practice of community development, as is clearly the case in the current environment. Other articles discussed ways that the profession of community development could be improved. The last general topic in the special edition addressed rural and small community development, a continued focus of the profession in its diamond anniversary. As we know, that is now the case with recent population declines and economic stagnation in many rural areas challenging their continued viability.

The 25th edition editors concluded from the scope of the articles that the theory and practice of community development had made significant strides from the birth of the Community Development Society (1969) to 1995, but admittedly more progress was needed in several areas. While much has been learned about community development since 1995, the scope of the profession has expanded to addressing urban issues and challenges, and the quality of community development research has contributed to a more robust set of applied theories of community development. However, essentially the same conclusion can be reached: We need to keep working and learning about community development.

Community and Economic Development. The early economic development literature devoted much attention to job creation and especially the use of financial incentives to lure manufacturing and other high-paying industries. These jobs, in turn, have local multiplier efforts that would stimulate local development. Of increasing importance was investing in workers (human capital) through education programs and workforce development to increase their capacity and make an area more attractive to private investment.

However, it also became clear that effective development practices required a strong community development focus, namely, how to build and strengthen broader community participation and contributions to finding remedies (Green, 2008). The many links between community and economic development capacities, factors, and functions emerged as increasingly important to both process and achieving desired outcomes (Pittman et al., 2009).

Equally clear was that society had changed as shown in discussions by Putnam in *Bowling Alone* in 1995. Residents now engaged in different types of activities, and membership/participation in traditional organizations was declining. Key to local development was to find new ways to engage these groups in community decision-making practices and betterment programs. With technology changes, residents spent less time in traditional group activities but, nevertheless, participated in other endeavors with special interest. In some respects, this scenario had contributed to a centralized decision-making "top-down" environment. This environment has begun to change more recently with more use of social media in community development.

Inclusion. Community development practitioners recognized that under-engaged populations such as minorities, females, and other groups were important contributors to local decision-making. Residents were shifting in how they interacted with groups so new ways to engage these residents in decisions about community issues and projects were discussed in more detail as an essential component of the community development process to enhance social well-being.

During the 1980s, *CD* articles described ways to better engage females and other groups in these processes (Lackey & Burke, 1984; Scott & Johnson, 2005). Much attention has been paid to approaches, tools, and techniques for resident or stakeholder participation. Given community development's roots in social change, issues around inclusion, participation, social justice, and related continued to evolve throughout the past five decades.

Small Business Emphasis. In addition, economic development thinking shifted from focusing mainly on attracting large plants to communities through incentives to finding ways to help local investors launch new businesses. Interest grew in finding ways to stimulate these efforts by focusing on entrepreneurship, small business finance, and related approaches (Lichtenstein, Lyons, & Kutzhanova, 2004). These initiatives were supported by federal agencies such as the Small Business Administration and were part of a national focus and local initiatives.

Local Leadership. The growing professionalism of community development recognized that effective local leaders are key to community sustainability and prosperity. *CD* contained an active discussion (1990s and later) of how to generate local leaders as well as the effects or outcomes when it does not exist. Issues were discussed such as the existence of community lifecycles, and ways to alter it through aggressive external and local intervention via active leadership.

Importance of the Capitals. Social capital grew in importance as an essential ingredient of community development which was crucial to effective local development – both business and industrial development. The five capitals such as financial, natural, produced, human, and social were recognized as elements that could be actively built and maintained in communities and, in fact, are essential for sustainability. Discussions of ways to engage a broad participation by residents in a community became an important part of effective community development (Emery & Flora, 2006). Strategies to deal with these issues were developed and empirically tested under different scenarios. Building and maintaining social capital are critical to community development, and these topics were an important part of discussions in *CD* during the 2000s.

The foundational concepts provided by the community capitals, especially in the context of asset-based community development, also helped in developing scholarship regarding sustainable, healthy, and resilient community approaches and applications. Resilience builds on assets to respond to shocks to community systems, such as those promulgated by natural or human-made disasters. A special issue on resilience provided resources for exploring the connection between sustainability, community development, capitals, and resilience (Cafer, Green, & Goreham, 2019; Kirkpatrick, 2019).

Measuring Outcomes. Measuring the outcomes from community development practices became increasingly important in discussions with both academics and practitioners as necessary to enhance the credibility of community development. The multi-dimensional nature of community issues complicates measuring outcomes but without solid information regarding effectiveness of strategies it is more difficult for practitioners to select and implement effective approaches. Thus, *CD* published many articles documenting the effects of development strategies to learn in which circumstances and scenarios they are effective and how they have a sound theoretical basis (Brennan & Brown, 2008).

Successful and lasting community change has been difficult to measure as well as to document successful strategies. This concern has been pursued by academics, practitioners, and agencies such as foundations that for many years invested in local groups interested in bringing about community change (Blanke & Walzer, 2013). The growth in Collective Impact and similar approaches that provide a framework to bring lasting change was an outcome of these discussions. The debate on measuring community change and factors that are important will continue as new approaches are formulated and implemented by community leaders in efforts to make desired and sustained community improvements. These discussions are at the heart of overall community development practice and are key to maintaining the credibility that community development practices have earned over the years.

THEMES IN THE 50TH ANNIVERSARY COLLECTION

Five major themes are explored in the two-volume book set. As previously mentioned, there are myriad topics, issues, challenges, and opportunities to discuss in community development but these five were selected via scan of articles present in *CD* since 1970. The following discussions provide information and insights about these areas: community history and theory; planning and policy development; leadership development; justice, inclusion, and participation; and healthy and resilient communities. Surely, other topics could have been included, and it is the editors' intention to encourage more exploration, scholarship, and application of these and many more areas of interest.

Community History and Theory

Community development evolved during the past 50 years both as a theoretical discipline and an important field of practice as the need for a better understanding of ways to enhance quality of life and living conditions grew. This evolution was even more complex because multiple academic and professional disciplines are involved in research about the importance of critical issues and best practices. Thus, a challenge facing community development involves incorporating research in each discipline and forging it into a comprehensive set of programs or tools to help improve quality of life and promote economic development vital to the future of an area.

Early discussions focused on economic development and creating employment using successful best practices in the past. As the study of development issues advanced, there was a better understanding that quality of life and living conditions are essential to business attraction and investment – both from internal and external sources. The shift from direct employment generating strategies to providing a conducive investment climate brought a need for a discipline that helps both explain and improve living conditions. Quality of life helps make an area attractive not only to current or potential residents but also entrepreneurs interested in starting or expanding businesses.

Understanding how local governance and strategies make the difference between prosperous and stagnant communities became more important. But was there a theory, or set of theories, to help explain how these conditions develop? More was known about industrial location factors or other economic development considerations than about determinants of quality of life and the importance of what is now termed social capital. This focus continued to change with discussions of community capitals that can be used to monitor and evaluate community change processes.

At the same time, there was growing interest in how Federal programs could help local government agencies create strategic plans with strong potential for development including job creation. This interest went beyond job creation only. It also recognized the need to work with populations disadvantaged in ways that prevented them from participating effectively in development efforts and to bring them more actively into local decision-making processes.

Poverty and housing issues gained more attention, and Federal programs offered technical assistance and incentives to local agencies for housing plus helped provide opportunities for disadvantaged residents to build skills through education and training programs. Some of these efforts might be considered more under the realm of community development than economic development, but they all are vital to the growth and prosperity of communities.

One outcome of this evolution was a better understanding that research on these activities was underway in many disciplines including sociology, economics, housing, and political science or others, but those literatures were not readily accessible to policymakers and even scholars working on a specific issue. In essence, there did not yet exist a clear discipline called community development.

The Community Development Society was an outgrowth of the need to incorporate the research and practice from related disciplines and to host discussions among representatives from each field around issues facing communities. Early discussions often focused on rural communities with limited technical expertise that were losing populations and facing economic stagnation. However, during the 1960s and 1970s, social unrest in large cities reinforced an understanding that neighborhoods in these areas function much like a community and must be better understood to design policies to alleviate some of the conditions. While many policies and practices differed from those used in smaller rural areas, the principles often were similar and based on the current research efforts.

The Society laid out a set of principles and practices, described previously, that could be applied to community development efforts in different scenarios. It also started a journal allowing scholars and practitioners to test their research findings in applications. Practitioners, in turn, can share their findings and further stimulate scholarly research. This multi-disciplinary approach was relatively unique because it reaches a more diverse audience while, at the same time, providing a peer-refereed outlet to evaluate work to add to the literature. The interaction between scholars and practitioner is invaluable in the growth and understanding of community development as an accepted academic discipline that trains future practitioners. The discipline continues to change as conditions in community development evolve.

Articles included in the community history and theory section highlight major contributions that advanced our understanding of important community formation and development components. Central to the early discussions was a need for a solid theoretical foundation that could give the discipline of community development credibility. The fact that diverse academic disciplines contribute to this body of knowledge complicated the development and understanding of this literature but strengthened the outcomes as scholars from multiple disciplines evaluated the work.

Especially noteworthy in advancing community development as a discipline and policy tool was recognizing the importance of "community" in addressing both rural and urban social needs (Pulver, 1989). A community is not necessarily a locality; rather, it is a group of people pursuing a common goal as noted by Brennan and Israel (2008). Understanding the role of the community casts a different perspective on policy formation. Likewise a focusing on outcomes or results became more important as a policy issue (Bhattacharyya, 2004). Top-down leadership may not always yield the most effective results. A broad cross-section of residents must engage in finding solutions that will work in the community. This participation in building or finding the solution is essential to make it work.

Another major contribution to community development thinking was viewing community as having as set of capitals that can be managed somewhat as in a business venture (Emery & Flora, 2006). The capitals, unless maintained, can reduce the sense of community and contribute to the decline of an area. Recognizing the importance of social capital, for instance, has spawned extensive research and many discussions regarding ways in which this component of community development can be advanced. Policies changed in approach because of this research.

Perhaps even more important is a widespread recognition of social capital as a necessary ingredient in a healthy community. It builds on previous work which differentiated community from a geographic location. This understanding enabled community development to embrace the work of several academic disciplines and opened the doors to new policies addressing social issues. Community development took a more holistic approach with scholars applying cutting-edge research in their separate disciplines.

The professional literature also emphasized the importance of internal communication within a community regarding policy issues. Informed constituents are more effective in leadership positions and in policy selection and implementation. The journal contributes to this communication process by providing information about policy options and issues at a professional, as well as academic level to help advance effective local decisions with lasting positive outcomes.

While poverty reduction continues as a major issue in community development discussions, the topics broadened to include housing, job creation, workforce training, transportation, and others that directly affect welfare of residents. Many of these issues interact and policies to address them must be coordinated. Community development as a field of study made serious contributions to policy development, and *CD* is a vehicle to share research and best practices on these initiatives by providing interactive discussions. In this way, it remains a reservoir of best practices along with theoretical bases for their effectiveness.

Because of these contributions, community development is on a par with economic development in creating livable communities where people want to live and work. Policies to improve quality of life and investment are in play around the world, and many factors leading to effective policy development have been discussed in the journal.

Planning and Policy Development

As noted, community development processes include a set of interconnected activities designed to improve a community and enhance the quality of life of its residents. These activities may include community demographic and economic information, analyses of trends, identification of community assets and challenges, formulation of sustainable development strategies, and the creation and an action plan implemented by area residents and entities. This is a time-consuming and strenuous undertaking involving a range of community stakeholders. Essential to this process are the planning and development of strategies and policies for the betterment of the community.

Articles in the planning and policy development section of this volume connect the principles, practices, and theories of planning and policy development to the process of community development. Not only do these articles provide a conceptual foundation to the art and craft of community development, they emphasize a critical component of the Community Development Society, namely, the importance of engaging residents in the community development process. The POG advocates that the community developer needs to facilitate meaningful engagement by promoting participation, involving community members, incorporating diverse interests, and enhancing community leadership, and be open to a full range of development strategies.

Meeting the objectives of the POG is not an easy task. However, the articles in the section on planning and policy development provide community developers with a range of tools, methods, and perspectives consistent with the Principles. At the same time, the guidance and information in this set of articles provide community developers with the practical and realistic skills required to assist the residents in the complex process of community development.

While articles in this section clearly address the community and resident engagement dimension as the foundation to the community development process, they also furnish valuable insights and cutting-edge research on other aspects of the process. Perhaps most importantly, the authors give community developers the ability to perform various aspects of their professional orientation and responsibility: a facilitator, a technical expert, and a community advocate.

On the other hand, because of the diversity of communities, the authors in this section note that there is no perfect approach to community development. Adaptability, then, becomes a key operating principle, as many obstacles and challenges will present themselves. Unfortunately, not every community development initiative meets with success, and the process of community development takes time and effort, as the articles discuss.

In addition to advocating community engagement as the foundation to the community development process, several key themes arise in the articles. Arguably, one key theme in several articles is the notion that community development includes a range of strategies and policies. This idea promotes a more comprehensive and holistic view of community development at a time when researchers began to question the viability of targeted and specific industrial development strategies. Working with community developers, then, residents have a range of development choices. The Community Capitals Framework provides residents with the ability to evaluate and select viable and diverse development strategies. Several articles provide guidance on this aspect of community development.

Organizational collaboration is another key theme discussed in several articles. The authors provide community developers with the ability to craft regional collaborative structures and partnerships among a range of public, private, and nonprofit entities. A community needs a number of partners to succeed in crafting and implementing development strategies.

Finally, several articles give the readers of *CD* insights into innovative approaches to the community development process. Authors address emerging community development issues and challenges, such as sustainability and urban sprawl, while others offered new information on improving community development tools of interactional techniques, collaborative strategies, and program evaluation.

The articles in the section on planning and policy development demonstrate that *CD* in the past 50 years has offered critical guidance on this important aspect of the community development process. *CD*, as an interdisciplinary journal, provides support not only to the community development profession, but also to other groups devoted to improving the quality of life in communities, such as planners, city managers, economic developers, public administrators, and developers of public policy.

Leadership Development

Local leadership is prominent throughout discussions of community development and change. It is essential in both identifying important issues and selecting among policies that will generate lasting results. Creating effective leadership can be difficult even when opportunities exist because it involves engaging a broad cross-section of residents, many with little or no past leadership experience. In some cases, a lack of sufficient credibility may hinder acceptance by others with more vested interests or experiences.

Leadership within a community often involves a process where long-time residents or groups experienced in past initiatives or investments in the community are elected or appointed to leadership roles. Self-interest, in some cases, may encourage a willingness to serve. While this model is fairly common, it can lead to status quo development approaches with less inclination to consider new development approaches or directions. It also can tend to overlook the needs or opportunities of groups not active in discussions or, for other reasons, are overlooked in the community.

A distributed leadership approach, for many reasons, can be more effective but it is also harder to implement. Finding highly qualified or motivated residents with the confidence to take leaderships roles is often difficult. In some instances, they also may not have the time and resources or be able to spend time away from work to participate in leadership roles. Without positive past leadership experiences, they may lack confidence to run for office or apply for appointed positions. The result is that significant groups in the community or development opportunities are overlooked or dismissed.

Important to understand is that community development projects are more likely to succeed when they have been built by and involve broad groups of residents. Residents must accept both the goals and strategies to commit and participate effectively. Without this support, local efforts are less likely to achieve strong results. A main leadership issue, then, is finding ways to engage diverse groups in determining objectives and projects that the community can achieve in light of resources available.

The leadership section in this volume begins with an article reporting types of local self-development strategies used across the US. High on the list of strategies implemented were tourism and cultural activities, business expansion and retention, industrial development, and historic preservation and restoration projects. Locally organized development groups complemented efforts by more traditional economic development organizations. This collaboration and focus on cultural activities and historic preservation and restoration enhances quality of life and living conditions as well as stimulates job creation.

The importance of a holistic approach to community and economic development justifies time spent working with groups in a locality to guide their collaborative efforts to reach community goals. Many different groups and organizations must be brought to the table with significant roles to play. Sometimes overlooked in leadership discussions are the roles played by nonprofit organizations. They provide essential services to both residents and business so are important to success. At the same time, however, these organizations assemble groups around key social issues and give them a voice in community discussions. They also can create less threatening leadership opportunities for residents who might otherwise be overlooked or ignored. Thus, the supportive roles played by nonprofits are key to leadership successes.

Much attention has been paid to ways to build local leadership and qualities that make it function. Robinson (1994) identified 10 basic principles or opportunities for leadership development. At the core, he suggests leadership opportunities exist in most organizations, but it is a matter of matching opportunities with people who have both the ability and interest. This highlights the importance of finding people who traditionally have not participated in these opportunities even though they may have had the potential.

Identifying potential leaders is the first step but equally important is to build support within the community for them to succeed. While they often have knowledge about a specific issue or have support from small groups of residents, they may not have sufficient experience or exposure to be accepted community-wide. Helping them succeed in a distributed leadership approach requires commitment from many players and may be one of the more difficult aspects of local leadership development. When it works well, though, it may create a positive contagion effect within the community that encourages others to be involved in discussions.

The literature on leadership also provides analyses about which approach is most likely to succeed. Top-down approaches often occur automatically on some issues, and this approach may work because leaders are focused on specific outcomes or directions. In other instances, though, a broader-based leadership model offers opportunities for community involvement in both setting goals and designing approaches to address specific issues. Thus, operationally, specific issues and circumstances are important in selecting the most suitable leadership approach for successful outcomes. At the very least, building leadership opportunities and engaging broader population groups are likely to enhance both interest and engagement in successful community development outcomes.

The political establishment plays an especially important role(s) in leadership development. While elected leaders have support from many groups, they cannot always commit residents to actions on specific issues. What they can provide, however, are opportunities to appoint knowledgeable residents who have not been active in these discussions in the past. Thus, elected leaders not only are responsible for designing and implementing effective community development policies, they also can build an active infrastructure for leadership engagement in the future.

An article in the section on leadership studied attitudes of minority residents regarding key factors that are considered important in community development decisions. These groups sometimes have not actively participated in past discussions. The findings from focus group discussions reveal that minorities, an often overlooked group in communities, place trust in program outcomes as highest in motivating people to participate. In other words, the program must have credibility that positive outcomes will happen in order to be accepted by these groups.

Also important is that development process and outcomes are driven by residents further supporting the importance of community engagement processes. Sense of community was also highly rated because greater acceptance of a project and engagement by residents lead to longer-lasting involvement and increase the prospects for success.

The importance of effective leadership in community development projects and outcomes cannot be overstated. Equally important to understand is that while leadership opportunities exist, they also must be developed and nurtured to engage broad-based support within the community. This sometimes means a concerted effort by elected leaders to actively engage affected residents even those with little past experience and established credibility.

The literature on leadership development is extensive and continues to growth as new opportunities arise and strategies are found. The articles in the leadership section are only the beginning but can help guide readers to find ways to stimulate and maintain community development projects.

Justice, Inclusion, and Participation

As noted, community development evolved from deep roots in social change, so issues of justice, inclusion, and participation have long been an important focus. This section of the book set recognizes the need to include all members of a community, especially those who are underrepresented. As part of the need to be more inclusive, much attention has been paid to approaches, tools, and techniques for resident or stakeholder participation. Both inclusion and participation may help foster better social justice processes and outcomes in community development.

The history of development is laced with responses to oppression and social ills; many examples exist where an injustice is the motivating factor to embark on the path of social change making. There is also an underlying foundational concept in community development that has existed since its earliest efforts and that is participation. As discussed previously, participation is a way for residents of a community to engage in decision-making. It represents more too – the idea and opportunity for people to be free to express themselves and participate in their own governance (Phillips & Kraeger, 2018).

Social justice is often discussed in efforts to enhance community development. Less clear is how it translates into processes and approaches for effecting desirable changes. In many cases, a sense of normative (or what should be) imperative may fuel desire for addressing social injustices directly. This normative standard is something to strive for in community development applications. It can also be thought of as a way of "giving voice, or agency, to the unrepresented (as)...a vital function of community development" (Phillips & Kraeger, 2018, p. 3).

Paul Davidoff was an urban planner and social justice and equity activist. He describes the need to rouse the nation to rectify racial and other social injustices, describing social inequalities and the need for greater inclusion in planning and development decision-making. He wrote of this need 55 years ago, and it still holds true today. Davidoff described a world in upheaval around the distribution of resources of nations and the inequities this was causing. While many things have changed since the 1960s, some have remained – by some metrics, there is more unequal distribution than ever before, with widening gaps between the richest and poorest people across the globe.

How then are scholars and practitioners of community development to respond? Given the enormity of the situation where structural barriers exist that divide people along social, economic, political, and other lines, how can communities move forward? Again, the underlying foundations of participation and inclusion are central. By more accessible decision-making and residents being a part of the processes for decisions that impact their lives, issues around social justice have a better chance of being addressed. In other words, inclusion and participation can aid in improving situations for residents. If community development processes are striving to be inclusive, then more people are represented across differences.

An example that can illustrate the connection between participation, inclusion, and striving for social justice improvements can be found in the arts. Artists may be among the first to call attention to social injustices or oppression in communities or societies. Indeed, social justice movements have arisen from efforts first initiated by artists calling attention and fueling desire for change. Culture is also an element influencing community connection that is so central to achieving desirable community development outcomes. It is often seen as "a motivating factor in the creation of social identity and serves as a basis for creating cohesion and solidarity," and these elements are crucial for connecting and enabling community members to take action (Brennan & Phillips, 2020, p. 5). Arts, artists, and culture are indeed a motivating force and are seen throughout the journal's history with both theoretical and applied works.

There are many at work in communities striving for improvements in quality of life and to foster a more just and inclusive environment. With works spanning 50 years, our hope is that the articles included in the section on justice, inclusion, and participation will inspire more attention to these crucial components of community development.

Healthy and Resilient Communities

Since the 1990s especially, ideas about healthy communities have been included in discussions of community development. It is an outgrowth of the desire to make improvements in quality of life, and since health is a major determinant, it is a well-deserved area of study. Health at the individual and collective, or community, level should be a central consideration of community development practices as it relates to health of the natural environment (water and air quality, for example), fresh food supply, and supporting infrastructure such as access to health care.

There is also a connected concept, that of community well-being, that is rapidly gaining more attention. Because well-being of communities is deeply and intricately connected with community development, it would be difficult to imagine that well-being at the collective or community level can be achieved without effective and just practices in community development. Community well-being typically describes a state of conditions, or assessment of health and related aspects. Health and resilience both are domains that connect community development and community well-being, and, as such, are important to include.

As mentioned, efforts began in the 1990s to make health a featured consideration of development processes. The World Health Organization launched the Healthy Cities Program, including indicators such as air quality, access to medical care, and nutrition. One of the first responses to this call to action in the US at the community level was that of Hampton, Virginia. With their Healthy Families Partnership, the city focused on improving parenting skills of residents, including prenatal and postnatal health and education to encourage healthy childhood experiences (Phillips, 2003). The results were impactful and helped to improve health outcomes in the community; these efforts were connected to other community development programs as well.

A second area of interest in this section is that of resilient communities. This is an area that continues to be of high interest, given the many anthropogenic and natural disasters that strike communities. With climate change bringing more incidences, resilience is a focus of many communities located in areas of high risk. This aspect of community development will continue to gain momentum and scholarship as need increases, it is often deeply connected with the disaster management and risk assessment field.

Resilience provides some contextual grounding for connecting to community development. For example, communities that are more prepared will be able to respond more quickly and efficiently. Often, indicators are used as part of the tool set in resilience planning, such as those for quality of life and for identifying, measuring, and monitoring conditions. Indicators and other tools can help communities expand or develop capacity to effectively plan for and respond to need; those communities with social capacity are better able to respond to need (Phillips, 2015). In many ways, resilience can be thought of as social community capacity as it influences adaptability and ability to recover.

As noted in the section on healthy and resilient communities in this volume, there are many aspects to consider, ranging from isolation and loneliness, to access to health care and education, to how to build ability to recover from disaster. Certainly, these aspects will play an even bigger role in community development in the future.

SUMMARY

*Community Development: Journal of the Community Development Society (*now known as *"Community Development"*) continues to provide an outlet for researchers on many aspects of community development. Growth from two issues per year to five issues increased its status as a research journal but it still faces challenges as it works to gain an even higher ranking among other journals as measured by number of citations and other factors. Achieving this status will attract additional authors and increase the flow and quality of submissions to *CD*.

At the same time, *CD* must cater to interests of both academics and practitioners in a diversity of associated disciplines. Meeting the needs and interests of diverse markets will continue to be a challenge but addressing the core market for a journal such as *CD* is essential in meeting its market niche. The range of topics included in *CD* will widen in the future as new topics gain importance. This trend is likely to make managing *CD* more difficult yet rewarding as future needs and challenges unfold.

Community development is a growing field of interest as the complexity of managing projects increases. Workforces adjusting to demographic changes with an aging population; housing market changes as well as shrinking retail markets due to internet competition; the inclusion and impact of rapidly evolving technology; overall community well-being and quality-of-life concerns; and changes in transportation demands are only a few of the issues community developers will face in the future.

CD also must adjust to competition from electronic publishing outlets that can respond to interest in specific topics quickly and inexpensively. Many, if not most, major journals offer electronic access to publications. A growing number of private outlets can offer a quicker turnaround. If they are accepted in university or business promotion and advancement schemes, they will represent competition for journals such as *CD*.

Nevertheless, community development is growing in professionalism and relevance for public policy development. *CD* has a definite market niche in serving both academics and practitioners. Combined with an annual conference that attracts an international audience, the future looks bright for both *CD* and the Society as an organization that offers a ready source of information about current effective policies and practices. This two-volume set on the history of community development via the lens of the journal, *CD,* hopefully will deepen the understanding of both research and practice. By doing so, a new generation of practice and scholarship will be informed by learning from the past 50 years.

NOTES

1. Walzer is Senior Research Scholar, Center for Governmental Studies, Northern Illinois University, and served as *CD* co-editor from 2005 to 2007. Blair is Professor of Public Administration and Urban Studies, University of Nebraska at Omaha, and served as *CD* editor from 1992 to 1997. Phillips is Professor of Agricultural Economics and Dean of the Honors College at Purdue University and served as *CD* editor from 2007 to 2012, transitioning publication to Taylor & Francis.

2. In 2006, the *Journal of Community Development* was renamed *Community Development: Journal of the Community Development Society* to reduce confusion by rating agencies with the *Community Development Journal* published in the UK.

REFERENCES

Bhattacharyya, J. 2004. Theorizing community development. *Journal of the Community Development Society* 34(2): 5–34, DOI: 10.1080/15575330409490110

Blakely, E.J. & Bradshaw, T.K. 1982. New roles for community developers in rural growth communities. *Journal of the Community Development Society* 13(2): 101–120, DOI: 10.1080/15575330.1982.9987154

Blair, R. & Hembd, J. 1994. What we have learned: A community development symposium. *Journal of the Community Development Society* 25: 1–4.

Blanke, A. & Walzer, N. 2013. Measuring community development: What have we learned? *Community Development* 44(5): 534–550, DOI: 10.1080/15575330.2013.852595

Brennan, M.A. & Brown, R.B. 2008. Community theory: Current perspectives and future directions. *Community Development* 39(1): 1–4, DOI: 10.1080/15575330809489737

Brennan, M.A. & Israel, G.D. (2008). The Power of Community. *Community Development.* 39(1).

Brennan, M. & Phillips, R. 2020. Culture, community, and development: A critical interrelationship. In R. Phillips, M. Brennan & T. Li (eds.), *Culture, Community and Development*, pp. 15–27. London: Routledge.

Cafer, A., Green, J., & Goreham. G. 2019. A community resilience framework for community development practitioners building equity and adaptive capacity. *Community Development* 50(2): 201–216, DOI: 10.1080/15575330.2019.1575442

Community Development Society (CDS). 2020. Principles of good practice. Retrieved 20 January from: https://www.comm-dev.org/about/principles-of-good-practice.

Darling, D., Rahman, H., & Pillarisetti, J.R. 1994. Measuring and monitoring change with a community life cycle model. *Journal of the Community Development Society* 25(1): 62–79, DOI: 10.1080/15575339409489895

Davidoff, P. (1965). Advocacy and pluralism in planning. *Journal of the American Institute of Planners* 31(4): 331–338.

Emery, M. & Flora, C. 2006. Spiraling-up: Mapping community transformation with community capitals framework. *Community Development* 37(1): 19–35, DOI: 10.1080/15575330609490152

Goudy, W.J. & Tait, J.L. 1979. Integrating research with local community-development programs. *Journal of the Community Development Society* 10(2): 37–50, DOI: 10.1080/15575330.1979.9987091

Green, J. 2008. Community development as social movement: A contribution to models of practice. *Community Development* 39(1): 50–62, DOI: 10.1080/15575330809489741

Hustedde, R. & Ganowicz, J. 2002. The basics: What's essential about theory for community development practice? *Journal of the Community Development Society* 33(1): 1–19, DOI: 10.1080/15575330209490139

Kirkpatrick, S.J.B. 2019. Using disaster recovery knowledge as a roadmap to community resilience. *Community Development* 50(2): 123–140, DOI: 10.1080/15575330.2019.1574269

Lackey, A.S. & Burke, J.L. 1984. Women in community development 1970–1980: A decade of change. *Journal of the Community Development Society* 15(1): 99–114, DOI: 10.1080/15575338409490077

Lichtenstein, G., Lyons, T.S., & Kutzhanova, N. 2004. Building entrepreneurial communities: The appropriate role of enterprise development activities. *Journal of the Community Development Society* 35(1): 5–24, DOI: 10.1080/15575330409490119

Phillips, R. 2003. *Community Indicators*. Planning Advisory Service, Report Number 517. Chicago, IL: American Planning Association.

Phillips, R. 2015. Community quality-of-life indicators to avoid tragedies. Pp. 293–304 in R. Anderson (ed.), *World Suffering and Quality of Life*. Dordrecht, The Netherlands: Springer.

Phillips, R. & Kraeger, P. 2018. General Introduction. Pp. 1–12 in R. Phillips & P. Kraeger, (eds.), *Community Planning and Development*, Volume 1. London: Routledge.

Pittman, R., Pittman, E., Phillips, R., & Cangelosi, J. 2009. The community and economic development chain: Validating the links between processes and outcomes. *Community Development* 40(1): 80–93, DOI: 10.1080/15575330902918956

Pulver, G.C. 1989. Developing a community perspective on rural economic development policy. *Journal of the Community Development Society* 20(2): 1–14, DOI: 10.1080/15575338909489979

Robinson, J. 1994. Ten basic principles of leadership in community development organizations. *Journal of the Community Development Society* 25(1): 44–48, DOI: 10.1080/15575339409489893

Scott, J. & Johnson, T.G. 2005. Bowling alone but online together: Social capital in e-communities. *Community Development* 36(1): 9–27, DOI: 10.1080/15575330509489868

Shaffer, R. 1990. Building economically viable communities: A role for community developers. *Journal of the Community Development Society* 21(2): 74–87, DOI: 10.1080/15575339009489962

Section 1
Leadership Development Introduction

Building a sense of community has been high on the list of important issues in community development as was summarized in a previous section. Self-development approaches are key to successes in community development but often are unique to local circumstances. At the same time, they are accomplished through local support and collaboration by many players supported by community leaders.

Leadership is provided by individuals and organizations involving residents from many sectors. Distributed leadership includes networks and associations that offer opportunities and encourage participation from diverse local groups, and this leadership model is important in creating a healthy community. Opportunities to lead often arise unexpectedly but specific practices and principles can foster leadership growth.

Solid and well-informed leadership is crucial to successful community building and was stressed throughout community development discussions in previous sections. Developing local leaders is a complex, time-consuming process that is not always well-understood. *Community Development* has actively contributed to these discussions with several representative articles addressing these topics. Articles in this section illustrate how the leadership development concepts evolved.

Green, Flora, Flora, and Schmidt (1990) report on a national survey of local self-development strategies, their types, and how they affect overall economic development. This article is one of the early systematic examinations of how community groups took charge in trying to supplement traditional business attraction efforts. Contacts were made with 600 key informants in 46 states, and surveys generated 105 verified local self-development projects. The self-development projects complemented other industrial and business attraction programs underway in the community.

Identified projects engaged many groups in the communities as well as assistance from external groups such as state, Federal, and regional agencies. The efforts included tourism and cultural activities, business retention and expansion, locally controlled industrial development projects, and historic renovation and preservation efforts. Of special interest is that they elicited disproportionate involvement by farmer and farm organizations as well as other private groups not always directly involved in development efforts.

The projects generated positive employment returns with a high percentage of the positions obtained by residents in the area which is less common in traditional industrial or business recruiting efforts. At the same time, however, the self-development projects typically generated fewer jobs than business recruiting programs. Nevertheless, the higher proportion of employment benefits to residents can make these projects useful in building community capacity and leadership along with economic viability. The authors cite the importance of involvement by nonprofit organizations in local self-development projects.

Snavely and Beck (1993) analyzed the potential roles that nonprofit corporations play in promoting community development efforts. First, they provide essential services used as inputs in businesses but these services also offer other jobs and incomes that contribute directly to economic development. Second, they provide cultural amenities and other programs that improve local quality of life making the area a more attractive place to live. Third, they assemble groups of people from across the community in a setting where they can network and interact in decision-making processes, many involving development issues.

Thus, given the importance of community development as a prerequisite to economic development, engaging nonprofits is an essential, but sometimes overlooked, task. Nonprofit agencies that provide access to health care or social services are especially important in improving quality of life that attracts both business investment and new residents. In areas with blighted conditions or limited opportunities for private investment, these third-sector agencies provide services that otherwise might be unavailable some of which are used by businesses in daily operations.

Effective leadership is essential to successful community development as has been documented by many authors. Robinson (1994), for example, presents ten basic principles of leadership in community development organizations based on many years of working with these agencies. He makes several especially important points. Leadership potential exists within most organizations but it must be identified and developed. This point is crucial in trying to create a pluralistic leadership scenario. Some groups have not played leadership roles in past decisions so those with leadership potential must be encouraged to step forward, be trained on appropriate skills, and then be encouraged to pursue collective agendas.

Equally, or even more, important is that these newly formed leaders must be supported and guided to minimize discouragement or failure. They are more likely to succeed when they have participated in creating an action agenda. This experience not only motivates their actions but also allows them to incorporate past experiences and see more clearly how the actions or results affect others in the community. In other words, leaders from previously underrepresented groups can have a contagion effect that stimulates others to take leadership roles on issues in which they have interest. Nearly everyone has expertise on some issue, and it is important to identify and engage this potential while working on community development items.

There are many misconceptions about effective leadership models, and democratic leadership is not always the most effective approach, especially in situations involving considerable disagreement and discord among some groups. A strong leader with the ability to direct the actions may be needed to achieve the best outcomes for the community. During the process, however, leadership opportunities arise and new leaders can emerge when they are encouraged and the development of leadership capacity and credibility is important in the overall community development process.

Growth in leadership occurs most often in an appropriate atmosphere and structure. This indicates that flexibility in approaches is important when working through the development process. Likewise, there must be adequate encouragement for those who step up to leadership positions, along with protections that minimize possibilities of failure. Broad-based leadership, as described previously, greatly enhances community development.

The political sector is important in community development decisions where many local groups and agencies are involved. Election to political positions gives individuals credibility, acceptance, and control over important decisions. At the same time, they must gain trust and acceptance in discussions of important issues within a community. This need can cause residents to become better informed and interested in positive outcomes.

The importance of effectively engaging residents in local decision-making processes in meaningful ways is well-recognized. Less well-understood, however, are the perceptions by hard-to-reach residents regarding how community change decisions are made and their effectiveness. Brown and Baker (2019) examined attitudes of minority residents in a neighborhood of approximately 5,000 residents regarding key factors involved in bringing about positive community change. They used a semi-structured focus group setting where residents could react to a neighborhood development plan and then identify five themes considered important to bringing about significant changes.

The first theme identified is the importance of developing trust among participants, especially those not traditionally involved in development processes. Second is that the process must be resident-driven to succeed. Third, building a sense of community and cohesion around specific approaches is crucial to both in engaging residents and in bringing about lasting community changes. Fourth, continuing collaboration and engagement by residents is necessary to motivate residents to embrace the projects and stay involved in the process. Fifth, the ability to make residents open to changes and transformation in the community is needed for effective change to happen.

Not all office-holders are trained or skilled leaders, yet they can influence or set an agenda for many decisions that affect or determine community development. Shelton and Garkovich (2013) examine factors that influence political engagement and the potential effects on outcomes. A large literature exists on factors associated with voting patterns, but less is known about how these characteristics determine other forms of political activity including leadership. What is clear, however, is that the sense of trust in the community and whether residents feel their actions have positive effects can be important motivations. This finding highlights the importance of leaders' ability to create an environment that builds this trust and encourages residents to participate in the process by playing leadership roles.

Shelton and Garkovich examine four types of political engagement including using data from a study in Kentucky. The options include the following: worked on a campaign; signed a petition for local candidate or issue; contacted a local public official; and attended any local rallies, protests, boycotts, or marches. While not all of these activities indicate a leadership role, they nevertheless shed light on factors in the community that encourage engagement and provide leadership opportunities. They also show characteristics of residents most likely to predict various levels of engagement. Differences between metro and rural areas are especially interesting. Further work is needed on this issue given the importance of creating an environment that encourages participation in the leadership process.

By all accounts, leadership is a crucial component of the community development process and articles on this topic in the Journal can help practitioners better understand the types of scenarios or pursuits that can promote successful leadership development and engagement. Broad-based leadership and creating community consensus around development issues are key, and subsequent articles can help foster an environment that encourages these efforts. While there are many opportunities for research to increase the understanding of how leadership evolves and operates, the collection of articles in *Community Development* clearly laid a solid basis for additional work to come.

LOCAL SELF-DEVELOPMENT STRATEGIES: NATIONAL SURVEY RESULTS

By Gary P. Green, Jan L. Flora,
Cornelia Flora, and Frederick E. Schmidt

ABSTRACT

This paper evaluates local self-development strategies among nonmetropolitan communities. It analyzes the characteristics of these projects, their benefits and costs, and the obstacles facing self-development communities. Based on a survey of more than one hundred communities, it was found that most self-development projects in the 1980s were initiated because of the depressed rural economy. Self-development efforts do not appear to replace traditional rural economic development activities; instead, they appear to complement them. Self-development activities produce a wide variety of jobs that are taken primarily by local residents. Informants reported that the cost and availability of credit are major obstacles for self-development projects. In terms of benefits, local business/industrial development projects tend to produce the most jobs and to produce them at the least cost.

INTRODUCTION

The decade of the 1980s was a period of economic restructuring and decline for most nonmetropolitan communities in the United States. Several factors contributed to this turnaround in the fate of rural America (see Henry et al. [1986] for an excellent review). The farm crisis, produced by a conjuncture of declining land values and commodity prices and substantial increases in interest rates and debt, had negative consequences not only for the farm population but also for businesses in rural communities dependent on the farm economy.

Gary P. Green is an associate professor and head of the Division of Applied Research at the University of Georgia; Jan L. Flora is a professor in the Department of Agricultural Economics and Cornelia Flora is a professor in the Department of Sociology, both at Virginia Polytechnic Institute and State University; and Frederick E. Schmidt is an associate professor in the Center for Rural Studies at the University of Vermont.

This project was supported by the Economic Research Service, United States Department of Agriculture, Cooperative Agreement No. 58-3AEN-8-00082. The authors appreciate the assistance of Eddie Gale, Jim Chriss, Kate Inman, and Tsz Man Kwong and the comments of Dave Sears.

Internationalization of the economy led an increasing number of manufacturing firms dependent upon low-wage workers to move their operations overseas (Falk & Lyson, 1988). The new federalism and increased military spending decreased the relative share of government spending in many rural communities (Dubin, 1989). Deregulation in several industries (e.g., transportation, communication, and banking) tended to benefit urban areas more than it benefitted rural areas (Moore, 1987).

In response to the changing relationship between capital and community in nonmetropolitan America, many localities have responded by stepping up their efforts to promote economic development through industrial recruitment. Industrial recruitment strategies are most often based on adopting an arsenal of financial incentives and tax policies. Research on the effectiveness of these local economic development incentives, however, is inconclusive (Wilson, 1989). Also, research on rural industrialization suggests that recruitment does not benefit those in the community who are most in need, such as the unemployed, underemployed, and poor (Summers et al., 1976). Given the realities of industrial recruitment as an economic development strategy in rural communities, many academicians and policy analysts have become increasingly critical of this approach to local economic development and have advocated that rural communities consider alternative strategies.

This paper evaluates self-development efforts among nonmetropolitan communities. Local self-development strategies stand in contrast to traditional local economic development strategies based on attracting new firms or branch firms from outside the community.

Definition of Self-Development

For purposes of this paper, self-development is defined as the implementation of a project or the creation or expansion of a firm that increases income to the community and/or generates a net increase in jobs (see Reid [1987]). In addition, a self-development project must include the following three characteristics: (1) involvement by a local organization (in most cases, a local government); (2) investment of substantial local resources (this does not preclude the use of outside resources); and (3) local control of the enterprise or activity. In addition to these criteria, only self-development projects implemented since January 1980 were included in the study.

Self-development, as defined here, does *not* include industrial recruitment. It does *not* include the establishment of businesses by local entrepreneurs unless there is broader community involvement (in terms of finance and/or an organizational effort leading to the establishment or expansion of the firm); it does *not* include recruitment of a federal or state facility—such as a prison or job-training facility—because the facility is not locally controlled. Improvements in the quality of life that may attract additional residents and, therefore, indirectly create jobs or increase incomes are also beyond the scope of this study's definition of self-development.

There were several instances where a community held a fair or festival to generate jobs and income. These cases were included as part of the sample only if the events were recurrent. Activities related to the retention and expansion of existing businesses and downtown revitalization were considered self-development projects if a significant proportion of the firms retained were controlled locally and a genuine organizational effort occurred in the process. For example, if downtown revitalization activities were directed at making downtown retail stores more competitive vis-a-vis suburban malls, then they would not be considered self-development efforts. Similarly, retention and expansion activities focusing on providing additional services or training to branch plants would not fall under the definition of self-development.

Several projects in a formative stage were identified, but they had not yet generated income or jobs in the community. These cases were not included in the sample.

METHODOLOGY

To locate instances of self-development in nonmetropolitan communities, a national inventory was conducted that utilized existing bibliographies and listings of economic development efforts. One of the prime secondary sources was Thomas (1988). Shaw and Rubin (1986) and University of Missouri (1986) also proved useful in locating potential self-development cases. Publications from regional and state organizations (such as the North Carolina Rural Development Center) were helpful in identifying potential self-development cases. Newspapers and journals were also searched for case studies of self-development.

A variety of organizations (e.g., the National Association of Towns and Townships, the National Association of Development Organizations, and Building Our American Communities) were contacted as well. In addition, key informants in each state were requested to identify innovative self-development activities. Key informants included individuals associated with state departments of economic development, the Cooperative Extension Service, Economic Development Administration University Centers, and regional planning commissions. Finally, a large number of community development experts were contacted.

More than six hundred key informants were identified through the various primary and secondary sources. Potential cases of self-development were identified by sending key informant questionnaires to these same rural community development specialists from across the country. The questionnaire included a definition of self-development and brief examples of what does and does not constitute self-development. The specialists were asked to identify cases they believed fit the description, identify local contact persons involved in each project, and list some basic characteristics (and a description, if possible) of each project. This procedure yielded 249 cases that, on the surface, met the criteria for self-development projects. At least one potential self-development activity each was reported in forty-six states. The four states not reporting any self-development activity were Connecticut, Maryland, Nevada, and New Jersey. (New Jersey has no nonmetropolitan counties, and Connecticut has only two.) In a limited number of cases, communities were identified as having more than one self-development project. These multiple projects were often actually initiated and developed by or under a single umbrella organization.

A questionnaire was sent to all 249 of the projects identified by key informants or through secondary sources. The survey focused on the characteristics of the project, key actors in the development of the project, benefits and costs associated with the project, and obstacles facing self-development activities. Three weeks after the initial mailing, a follow-up postcard was sent to communities that had not responded to the survey. Finally, each of the communities that had not responded to either mailing was phoned and asked to complete the survey.

This procedure produced 160 cases that appeared—at this stage—to meet the criteria for self-development.[1] In addition, 41 other cases out of the original 249 were ultimately determined not to be self-development activities. It was impossible to determine whether or not the remaining 48 cases were actually instances of self-development.

Through additional phone calls and mailings, 105 of the 160 cases were verified as meeting all of the criteria for self-development. These

---

[1] The self-development project, not the community, was the unit of analysis in this study. There were a few instances where more than one self-development project was identified in a community.

Table 1. Types of Self-Development Projects

Type of Project	Percent of Total Reported in Category*
Tourism/arts, craft fairs, or recreational/cultural activity	38
Business retention and expansion/downtown revitalization	31
Locally controlled industrial development	21
Historic renovation or preservation	15
Incubator/small business assistance center	15
Community-owned enterprise	14
Value-added firm (processing local primary products)	14
Worker-controlled enterprise	12
Community financial institution/revolving loan fund	11
Agricultural marketing organization	11
Community-based service firm	5

* Sum of column is greater than 100 percent because some projects fit or were reported in more than one category.

105 cases form the basis of the following analysis. These cases are not the only self-development projects in the country; in fact, several projects that appeared to meet the criteria did not respond to the survey. It is impossible, therefore, to assess how representative the sample is.

FINDINGS

Characteristics of the Projects

Self-development projects were categorized in terms of their major activities.[2] Tourism and cultural activities were the most frequent, followed by the retention and expansion of existing businesses, locally controlled industrial development, and historic renovation and preservation. (See Table 1 for the complete list of project types and their associated frequencies.)

The largest share—47 percent—of the self-development projects were community-based, 21 percent were countywide, and 25 percent were multicounty projects. The remaining 8 percent of the projects were either statewide or regional in orientation.

The majority of the self-development projects were located in the North-Central states. Using the census definition of regions (U.S. Department of Commerce, 1982), 7 percent of the projects were in

---

[2] These categories are not mutually exclusive. In a few self-development cases, the project could be simultaneously categorized as a locally controlled industrial development, an income-generating cultural activity, and historical preservation.

the Northeast, 51 percent in the North-Central states, 23 percent in the South, and 20 percent in the West. Given the findings reported below that most self-development projects were in response to the recession of the early 1980s, it is not surprising to find that the North-Central states were the most active in terms of self-development programs.

Initiation of the Projects

Although all self-development projects begun since 1980 were considered, most of the projects—65 percent—had been initiated since January 1985. This finding may be a sign that self-development projects have a short life span or that there has been increased interest in this approach to economic development.

In more than half the cases (54 percent), self-development projects were initiated due to a specific event in the community or area. The two most frequently cited events leading to the creation of a self-development project were a plant closing (39 percent) and a downturn in the local economy (44 percent). Only 9 percent cited the farm crisis. Thus, there appears to be evidence that self-development strategies were adopted by nonmetropolitan communities influenced by the recession in the early 1980s, the exodus of manufacturing and other firms, and the stagnating economy of these areas throughout the 1980s.

Self-development strategies often involve local government units. Respondents were asked to identify which level of government, if any, was actively involved in the creation of the self-development project.[3] In 24 percent of the cases, no local government unit was involved in the initiation of the project. In 56 percent of the cases, the city or town government was active in the promotion of the self-development project. In almost 38 percent of the self-development cases, a county government was involved in the development of the project.

Respondents were asked to identify the three most active groups in the initiation and implementation of the self-development project and the three groups or organizations most critical of self-development strategies (see Table 2). Among the various groups and organizations considered, private business interests (e.g., chambers of commerce) and city governments were reported most often as initiating and implementing self-development activities. Private business inter-

---

[3] The total of the percentages reported for this question in the following sentences does not equal 100 percent because more than one level of government was involved in the initiation of some of the self-development projects.

Table 2. The Roles of Various Community Groups in Self-Development Projects

Group	Percent of Total Projects Where Group Was Active in Initiation or Implementation	Percent of Total Where Group Was Critical of Project
Private business	39	13
City government	28	13
Local development organization	27	11
Local media	20	4
County extension agent	19	7
Farmers or farm organization	14	5
State government	14	8
County government	13	8
Retirees	10	9
Federal government	13	5
Local university or community college	9	2
Labor organization	4	—
Other community organizations	23	14

Note: Respondents were provided with a list of community groups and asked to identify those groups that were the most active in the initiation and implementation of the project and those that were the most critical of the self-development project. Respondents could check the three groups most active in each project.

ests were indicated by 39 percent of the respondents and city government by 28 percent. A local development corporation or committee was central in initiating the project in 27 percent of the self-development cases. Unlike city governments, county governments were seldom reported as being central in the initiation of projects. Labor organizations and local universities or community colleges were the least likely to be reported as active in the initiation and implementation of self-development projects.

Among the groups and organizations considered, private business, a local development corporation or committee, and city government were reported as most likely to be critical of self-development activities. It is interesting to note that these three groups were identified as the most important actors in the initiation of self-development projects as well as the groups most critical of these same activities. These data support other findings in the literature which suggest that communities where the local government is the lead actor in economic development are more likely to be involved in a wide range of development activities (Robinson, 1989). These findings may also suggest, however, that when local governments or local business interests are not involved in the projects, they may take a critical stance toward these activities.

Respondents were most likely to report that one of four methods was used to develop the local self-development strategy. Nineteen percent of the respondents indicated that an individual instigated the self-development strategy. In 17 percent of the cases, open meetings/public hearings were used to choose the strategy adopted by the self-development project. A private sector advisory group, such as a chamber of commerce committee, was used in 14 percent of the cases. In 11 percent of the cases, the strategy was chosen chiefly through consultation with an outside agency. It was less likely that respondents would indicate the strategy was based on one of the following: a consultant's study, an initiative of the economic development director, a local official, or any other community organization.

Local leaders relied on federal, state, or regional agencies for important assistance in ninety-three of the cases. The outside agency most relied on was the Small Business Development Center. Of those indicating an important role for state or regional organizations, almost one-third reported that a Small Business Development Center had played an important role in initiating the self-development activity. A significant number of respondents—29 percent—stated that a regional or state extension specialist was involved in the project. In 18 percent of the cases a regional planning commission played an important role in the self-development project; in the other 18 percent of the cases a state economic development agency played an important role.

Respondents were asked whether there had been local efforts made since 1980 to attract absentee-owned firms or branches to the community. Forty-one percent of the respondents indicated that no effort had been made to attract branch plants to the community. Twenty-eight percent of the respondents reported that an effort had been made but that it had been unsuccessful. Thirty-one percent of the respondents indicated that an effort had been made to attract new industry and that it had been successful. Therefore, it appears that self-development activities are not a substitute for industrial recruitment but are considered a complementary strategy. Furthermore, it would appear that self-development communities that attempt to recruit outside industries are unusual in terms of their success rate.

Among those communities in the study that successfully recruited new industries, the mean number of jobs created by the largest firm was 143 and the median was 83. There was a wide variation in the number of jobs created by these firms—ranging from 3 to 750.

Benefits and Costs of Self-Development

Self-development activities yield both benefits and costs to the community or region. Benefits may be in the form of jobs created or saved, new leadership, diversification of the local economy, or additional dollars in the local economy. Examples of costs to communities include additional demands for government services, revenue foregone due to tax abatements or credits, external costs borne by the community (e.g., air or water pollution), and a loss of revenue for existing businesses in the community. Much of the existing literature suggests that the costs of industrialization often exceed the benefits (Summers et al., 1976). The following is an attempt to assess this issue in the case of self-development activities.

An average of fifty-one jobs were created or saved by the self-development efforts in this study. This figure is somewhat deceiving because of a few outliers. The median number of jobs produced or saved by the self-development projects was twenty-five. For the average project, about 30 percent of the jobs created or saved were unskilled, and 46 percent were skilled. Thus, self-development projects tend to generate a wide range of job opportunities that are not concentrated in unskilled positions.

Much of the literature on rural industrialization suggests that attracting branch plants to a community produces few benefits for the local residents because the jobs created are taken by inmigrants (Logan & Molotch, 1987; Summers & Branch, 1984). In order to assess whether local residents benefitted from self-development activities, respondents were asked to estimate the percentage of jobs created or saved that were taken by workers who already lived in the project area. On an average, 91 percent of the jobs were taken by residents living in the area. Over half of the respondents reported that 100 percent of the jobs generated by the self-development project were filled by local residents.

The self-development activities in this study generated a mean gross sales of $1,054,019 for the year in which the respondents had information. The median gross sales generated was $150,000.

Funding for self-development projects was categorized into four types: public-local; public-nonlocal; private-local; and private-nonlocal. Public-local funding averaged $300,654 (median = $25,000), and public-nonlocal funding averaged $450,873 (median = $80,000). Among the sources of public funding used for the largest projects were federal programs (29 percent), state government (18 percent), and local government (11 percent). Among the federal programs or agencies most often used were the Tennessee Valley Authority, the Small Business Administration, and the Economic Development Administration. Although there were significant cuts in federal spending for rural and community development during the 1980s, these data suggest that the federal government continued to be a major source of capital for community economic development activities. It may be reasonable to assume that if there had been more federal dollars available in the 1980s, there would have been more self-development activities occurring in nonmetropolitan areas.

Informants were asked to estimate the total amount of private funds devoted to the project and to indicate the sources of these funds. Only fifteen projects relied on private-nonlocal sources of funding. The mean amount of private-nonlocal funds devoted to self-development projects was $1,059,524, and the median amount was $25,000. The majority of the private-nonlocal funds were provided by foundations (14 percent), individuals (29 percent), and businesses (29 percent). Sixty-five projects relied on private-local funds. The average amount of private-local funds devoted to a project was $610,300, and the median amount was $80,000. Private-local funds were usually provided by individuals (50 percent) or local businesses (20 percent). Only 10 percent of the private funds were provided by banks.

The costs of economic development projects may be indirect, resulting from revenue foregone by the government. In most cases, the local government did not forego any revenue (e.g., tax abatements and credits) to support the self-development project. In only 16 percent of the projects did a local government forego any revenue. When local governments did forego revenue, it was not for a large amount. Five out of the ten cases indicating lost revenue estimated that the amount was $1,000 or less. On an average, these ten local governments were willing to forego revenue for four years to support the project.

In only 10 percent of the cases did a state forego revenue for the self-development project. State governments were also willing to forego revenue for an average of four years to support the self-development project.

In addition to foregoing revenue, many local governments provide in-kind benefits to support self-development projects. In 34 percent of the self-development projects, in-kind costs were borne by the local government. When local governments provide in-kind benefits to support self-development activities and projects, they tend to be one of three types: (1) a service, (2) a building, or (3) some form of labor. Other types of in-kind costs borne by the local government included equipment, infrastructure, and insurance.

Respondents were asked to report the effects—negative, positive, or none—that their self-development project had on various aspects of community life. It could be assumed that self-development, like other types of economic development activities, produces a variety of indirect benefits and costs that cannot be measured in monetary terms.

Of the fourteen facets of community life considered, self-development was reported to have had the strongest positive impact on job creation. Ninety-three percent of the respondents indicated that their project had a positive impact on job creation. Ninety percent of the respondents indicated that the self-development activity had a positive impact on community satisfaction. Eighty-one percent of the informants indicated that their self-development project had a positive impact on local economic stability.

Informants reported that self-development projects were least likely to have positive impacts on residents who are on fixed incomes (e.g., retired persons), the demand for public services, and the fiscal situation of the local government. These data do not permit a comparison of the impacts of traditional economic development activities with those of self-development activities. It does appear, however, that self-development projects were perceived by respondents to have many of the same types of effects as those associated with traditional economic development activities. For example, few respondents felt there were positive impacts on either the poor or residents who are on fixed incomes.

Obstacles to Self-Development

Because self-development strategies rely to a much greater extent on local resources and organizations than do traditional economic development approaches, it is reasonable to expect that a lack of resources or support may hinder the development of these programs. At the same time, a dependency on local resources and organizations may produce innovative approaches to overcoming these obstacles. Respondents were asked to indicate the degree—none, some, or great—to which various obstacles hindered or complicated the implementation of self-development strategies in their rural community.

Among the obstacles considered, informants reported that the availability and cost of capital were the greatest hindrances or complications to self-development projects. For 31 percent of the self-development cases, availability of capital was considered a great hindrance; in 52 percent of the cases, it was considered some hindrance. Among 19 percent of the self-development cases, the cost of capital was considered a great problem; in 52 percent of the cases, it was perceived to be some problem.

These findings regarding the cost and availability of credit as constraints on self-development activities are inconsistent with recent research on economic development. This research suggests that access to public or external private sources of financing is not an important obstacle to firms' investment decisions in rural areas (Rosenfeld et al., 1988). Local self-development projects, however, may face a completely different set of constraints and obstacles than do traditional economic development projects.

None of the other possible obstacles listed in the questionnaire were perceived to be as important as the availability and cost of capital. The lack of capable management was considered a great obstacle by 13 percent of the respondents, 10 percent considered the lack of skilled labor to be a great obstacle, and the lack of technical assistance was perceived to be a great problem by 12 percent of the respondents. Only 2 percent of the respondents indicated that the opposition of retired persons or others on fixed incomes, farmers or farm groups, or labor groups were great hindrances.

Type of Project

To further evaluate the effectiveness of local self-development strategies, an assessment by type of project was undertaken. To simplify the analysis, self-development projects were categorized into three groups. First, tourism projects (recreational developments, art festivals, craft fairs, and other income-generating cultural activities) and historic renovation or preservation projects were combined. The second category, defined as community-based development, included community finance institutions (e.g., revolving loan funds and community credit unions), community land trusts, community-owned enterprises, worker-owned enterprises, community-based service firms (e.g., health facilities and cable TV systems), and agricultural marketing organizations (including farmers' markets). The third category, referred to as local business and industrial development, included locally controlled industrial developments, programs for the retention and expansion of local business (including downtown revitalization efforts), value-added activities (processing locally produced agriculture, forestry, petroleum, or mineral products), business incubators, and small business assistance centers.

The three different categories of self-development projects are compared in Table 3 with regards to the actors most involved in initiating the projects. There are several statistically significant dif-

Table 3. Community Groups Active in Project Initiation by Type of Self-Development Project[1]

Group	Tourism and Historic Preservation N = 32	Community-Based Development N = 28	Local Business and Industrial Development N = 37	Chi-Square
	Percent of Projects Where Group Was an Initiator			
City government	31.3	21.4	36.1	1.64
County government	15.6	3.6	19.4	3.57
State government	25.0	3.6	13.9	5.53*
Federal government	9.4	7.1	19.4	2.61
Local development organization	18.8	17.9	41.7	6.21**
Private business	59.4	32.1	33.3	6.20*
Local newspapers	28.1	17.9	8.3	4.55*
University/community college	12.5	7.1	5.6	1.42
County extension agent	31.3	17.9	8.3	5.86*
Farmers/farm organization	12.5	32.1	2.8	11.07**

* $p < .1$.
** $p < .05$.

[1] Respondents were provided with a list of community groups and asked to identify those that were the most active in initiating and implementing the self-development project. Respondents could check the three groups most active in each project.

ferences among the three categories. In almost 42 percent of the local industrial development projects, a local development organization was actively involved in initiating the project. On the other hand, in only 18 percent of both the tourism and historic preservation cases and the community-based development projects were local development organizations identified as critical actors. This finding makes intuitive sense because the promotion of local industrial projects is a key activity for most local development organizations.

One of the most interesting findings shown in Table 3 is that farmers and farm organizations were disproportionately active in promoting community-based development projects—at the same level as was the case for private business involvement. City government activity was less in this category—but not at a statistically significant level—than it was for the other two types of projects. The most-often-reported initiator for tourism and historic preservation projects was private business (in over 59 percent of the cases). Cooperative extension agents were also disproportionately active in promoting this type of self-development project (in over 31 percent of the cases).

Table 4. Obstacles to Projects by Type of Self-Development Project[1]

Obstacle to Project	Tourism and Historic Preservation N = 32	Community-Based Development N = 28	Local Business and Industrial Development N = 37	Chi-Square
	Percent of Projects Where Obstacle Reported as "Great"			
Availability of capital	10.7	57.1	33.3	16.09**
Cost of capital	21.4	32.1	11.1	7.24
Lack of skilled labor	21.4	7.1	5.7	7.56
Lack of professional labor	10.7	7.1	5.7	5.24
Lack of capable management	10.3	25.0	8.6	10.97**
Lack of technical assistance	3.6	17.9	16.7	11.63**
Opposition of local government	3.6	7.1	2.9	3.95
Opposition of private sector	7.1	3.6	—	2.65
Lack of community leadership	13.8	10.7	—	10.35**
Lack of local government capacity to provide assistance	10.7	14.3	5.7	13.36**

* p < .1.
** p < .05.

[1] Respondents were asked to indicate which obstacles hindered or complicated the implementation of self-development projects. Possible responses included "none," "some," and "great." The percentage of respondents reporting "great" for each obstacle is reported in this table.

The major obstacles faced by communities in the implementation of self-development strategies are compared with respect to type of project in Table 4. The availability of credit was primarily a problem for community-based development projects and not an important obstacle for tourism and historic preservation projects. Community-based development projects generally have much less government involvement and, therefore, would have more difficulty gaining access to credit than would be the case for the other types of projects.

Interestingly, the lack of capable management was an additional problem for community-based development projects. There were also statistically significant differences among the three categories of projects with respect to lack of community leadership and lack of local capacity to provide assistance. These two obstacles were not important at all for local business and industrial development projects but were moderately important for the other two types of projects.

Finally, it is important to note the differences with respect to the

Table 5. Project Benefits by Type of Self-Development Project

Benefit	Tourism and Historic Preservation N = 32	Community-Based Development N = 28	Local Business and Industrial Development N = 37	Eta Squared
Number of jobs per project	36.0	38.2	86.9	.082*
Percent jobs unskilled	29.6	36.0	22.6	.028
Percent jobs skilled	38.8	37.6	48.8	.022
Percent jobs clerical	7.0	7.1	9.2	.004
Percent jobs professional	13.0	3.9	12.4	.038**
Percent jobs managerial	6.81	15.6	6.9	.068
Percent jobs filled by local citizens	92.9	92.6	85.7	.037
Cost to produce one job (thousands of dollars)	99.2	42.0	15.8	.026*

* $p < .1$.
** $p < .05$.

lack of technical assistance as an obstacle to self-development projects. Technical assistance (or the lack thereof) was not a problem for tourism and historic preservation projects, but it was a moderately important problem for the other two categories of projects. Obviously, if the managerial, technical, and community support problems noted above were important obstacles with respect to successful projects, they were likely causes of failure for the unsuccessful projects as well.

To assess the benefits derived from the various types of projects, the number and types of jobs created were compared (see Table 5). On average, a larger share of the jobs produced by tourism and historic preservation projects were classified as professional jobs than were the jobs produced by projects in the other two categories. In the case of community-based development projects, only 4 percent of the jobs created were professional jobs.

Different patterns existed in terms of the number of jobs created and the average cost of producing a job (see Table 5). Local business and industrial development projects produced an average of 87 jobs, community-based development projects created an average of 38 jobs, and tourism and historic preservation projects created an average of 36 jobs. Local business and industrial development projects produced the largest number of jobs among the three categories and created them at the lowest cost per job. This contrasted with tourism and historic preservation projects where it cost six times as much to produce a job as it did in local business and industrial development projects.

SUMMARY AND CONCLUSIONS

This research on self-development efforts reveals that a large number of these projects were initiated over the past five years. Many of the projects were developed because of the depressed rural economy during the period under study or because of specific events such as plant closings. Self-development efforts do not appear to be a replacement for traditional economic development activities and may complement these activities. Many communities engaging in self-development activities have been relatively successful in attracting new industry to their community.

Self-development projects did not generate as many jobs, on average, as were produced through the successful attraction of absentee-owned firms or branches to the community. It is important to remember, however, that only about one-third of the communities had engaged in a successful effort to attract such a firm or branch plant. In addition, jobs created as a result of industrial recruitment activities often have direct and indirect costs that outweigh their benefits.

In contrast to the types of jobs typically associated with industrial development projects in rural areas, a relatively low percentage of the jobs created by self-development projects were unskilled jobs. Furthermore, 91 percent of the jobs created and/or saved were taken by local residents in the area. The benefits of self-development activities were significant, and most of the benefits were realized by those in the local community. However, self-development efforts did not appear to benefit the poor or those on fixed incomes any more than did industrial recruitment efforts.

The costs of self-development activities appeared to be relatively low. In most cases, the local government did not forego any revenue (e.g., tax abatements and credits) to support the self-development project. In only one-third of the cases were in-kind costs borne by the local government.

Among the set of obstacles possibly hindering the implementation of self-development strategies in rural communities, informants reported that the cost and availability of credit was a major problem. This is consistent with another finding reported here indicating that commercial banks were not an important funding source for self-development activities. Commercial banks may perceive self-development activities as too risky, thereby forcing communities to seek other private and public sources of credit for their projects.

Tourism and historic preservation projects, which were most frequently initiated by private business interests (e.g., business organizations and local newspaper publishers) or the local extension agent, tended to directly generate more professional jobs than did the other two types of development. The investment per job, however, was six times as great for this type of project as it was for community-based and local industrial and business development projects. Although some of the tourism and cultural projects may have indirectly generated jobs and income, such benefits are hard to measure.

Tourism and historic preservation projects were least likely to have had problems in terms of obtaining capital or experiencing a lack of technical assistance. The lack of capital problems for these projects relates, in part, to a ready means of taxation—the entertainment or so-called "bed tax" that captures dollars principally from outsiders—and the availability of state and national government funds for historic preservation.

Local industrial and business development projects created the greatest number of jobs per project. Not surprisingly, these projects were typically initiated by a combination of local business and government interests. Unlike the results for the other two types of projects, none of the respondents perceived lack of leadership as being a problem for local industrial and business development projects.

The community-based development projects were more likely than the other two types of projects to have faced shortages of capital, limited technical and political assistance, and managerial difficulties. They were also the only type of self-development project in which farmers and farm organizations played a significant role in terms of project initiation.

These data provide a broad framework for understanding self-development activities. Many of the details regarding the initiation and processes of self-development can only be provided through in-depth case studies. The survey data also raise some important questions that need to be addressed in future research. Why do some communities respond to economic stress by developing an alternative development strategy while others intensify their traditional economic development activities? How do the costs and benefits of self-development activities compare to those associated with industrial recruitment? Why are the cost and availability of capital the most important obstacles to self-development—especially for community-based development projects? How important is participation by the local government in the success of a self-development project? Why, of the three types of self-development projects, do community-based development projects garner the least local and outside assistance?

Lessons for Practitioners

Self-development—the mobilization of local resources to generate locally controlled growth—is possible through the cooperation of the public sector with private sector groups. Projects work best when there is a general local conviction that the community shares a major economic problem. Early practitioner efforts in self-development should build on the local definition of the problem; at the same time, possible solutions to the problem should be explored and kept salient.

In organizing self-development projects, practitioners should focus on individuals who are already entrepreneurs in one way or another. Practitioners need to carefully identify groups or entities that have previously pursued economic development activities within the community and build on existing skills and organizations.

Practitioners involved in self-development efforts are most effective when they can link local organizations to different local and nonlocal sources of capital. Building a local revolving loan fund that combines local funds with community development block grants is one effective way to do this. Practitioners involved in self-development efforts need to work with both private and public sources of local capital and educate them regarding the advantages of local investment and the best ways to manage such investment.

Practitioners should provide management training to participants at an early point in the self-development process. Mechanisms for financial and managerial oversight by the community should be built into the organization formed. Practitioners can help identify key decision points in the self-development process and link local project managers to the types of information and expertise needed to make informed decisions on the investment of resources. Working with community groups to help them understand the different types of investments that are necessary is a key factor in developing the management skills of self-development project participants. Practitioners should be particularly attuned to when project management should shift from volunteer to paid status. They can help the community accept the need for paid management and work with the project managers to help them develop the same commitment to the project that the community has demonstrated.

Practitioners can be effective in assisting local self-development efforts. By concentrating on building effective public-private organizations and linking the local community to key resources, the special expertise of the community development practitioner can be mobilized to empower local communities as they decide on their own futures.

REFERENCES

Dubin, Elliot J. *Geographic Distribution of Federal Funds in 1985.* Washington, DC:
1989   Agriculture and Rural Economy Division, Economic Research Service, U.S. Department of Agriculture.

Falk, William W. & Lyson, Thomas A. *High Tech, Low Tech, No Tech: Recent Industrial*
1988   *and Occupational Change in the South.* Albany, NY: State University of New York Press.

Henry, Mark, Drabenstott, Mark & Gibson, Lynn. A changing rural America. *Economic*
1986   *Review* 71(7):23–41.

Logan, John R. & Molotch, Harvey L. *Urban Fortunes: The Political Economy of Place.*
1987   Berkeley: University of California Press.

Moore, T. U.S. airline deregulation: Its effect on passengers, capital, and labor. *Journal*
1987   *of Law and Economics* 29(1):1–28.

Reid, J. Norman. Increasing the effectiveness of local government institutions. Paper
1987   prepared for presentation at the Symposium on the Great Plains of the Future, November, Denver, CO.

Robinson, Carla Jean. Municipal approaches to economic development. *Journal of the*
1989   *American Planning Association* 55(3):283–295.

Rosenfeld, Stuart A., Malizia, Emil E. & Dugan, Marybeth. *Reviving the Rural Factory:*
1988   *Automation and Work in the South.* Research Triangle Park, NC: The Southern Technology Council of the Southern Growth Policies Board.

Shaw, Linda & Rubin, Sarah. *Broadening the Base of Economic Development: New Approaches*
1986   *for Rural Areas.* Chapel Hill, NC: MDC, Inc.

Summers, Gene F. & Branch, Kristi. Economic development and community social
1984   change. *Annual Review of Sociology* 10:141–166.

Summers, Gene F., Evans, Sharon D., Clemente, Frank, Beck, E. M. & Minkoff, Jon.
1976   *Industrial Invasion of Nonmetropolitan America.* New York: Praeger.

Thomas, Margaret G. *Profiles in Rural Economic Development.* Kansas City, MO: Midwest
1988   Research Institute.

U.S. Department of Commerce. *Census of Population and Housing, Technical Documen-*
1982   *tation.* Washington, DC: U.S. Government Printing Office.

University of Missouri. *Alternative Economic Development Ideas: Tool Kit.* Computerized
1986   data base. Columbia, MO: Community Development Extension.

Wilson, Roger. *State Business Incentives and Economic Growth: Are They Effective? A Review*
1989   *of the Literature.* Washington, DC: Council of State Governments.

DEFINING THE ROLE OF NONPROFIT CORPORATIONS IN COMMUNITY ECONOMIC DEVELOPMENT

By Keith Snavely and Roger Beck

ABSTRACT

In this paper we outline the unique nonmarket and market functions nonprofit corporations perform in the local economy that are important to community economic development. Their key nonmarket functions include the provision of cultural and environmental amenities, stimulus of community development and entrepreneurial activity in the most economically distressed communities, and delivery of numerous human welfare services. Each of these functions enhances the quality of life factors for its residents. A positive spinoff is that as the community becomes a more desirable place to live, location decisions of households and business enterprises are influenced. As for market functions, nonprofit corporations supply essential services which are treated as inputs into the business production process, attract income into the community or region through sales of services to residents outside the community, attract grants and loans that contribute to the circular flow of income in the community, and facilitate secondary employment and income expansion outside the nonprofit sector. Given these significant market and nonmarket economic and social functions, communities should intentionally include support and stimulus of nonprofit corporations in their economic development plans.

INTRODUCTION

Recent data compiled by the organization, Independent Sector, demonstrate that nonprofit corporations are a growing, significant element of the national economy (Hodgkinson et al., 1992). Often referred to as the "third sector" because of its comparatively small size in respect to government and private for-profit businesses, the nonprofit corporate sector generates a considerable amount of economic activity. In 1990, nonprofit organizations' income (the total of

---

Keith Snavely is Associate Professor, Master of Public Administration Program, Department of Political Science, Southern Illinois University, Carbondale, Illinois. Roger Beck is Associate Professor, Department of Agribusiness Economics, Southern Illinois University, Carbondale, Illinois.

wages and salaries paid plus an estimate of the value of volunteer labor) totaled nearly $315 billion, equaling 6.8 percent of total national income. Employment in charitable (501(c)(3)) and social welfare (501(c)(4)) organizations alone equaled 10.4 percent of the total U.S. employment, and employee earnings represented 7.8 percent of the total for all workers (Hodgkinson et al., 1992, p. 35).

Nonprofit corporations are a vital segment of the national and regional economies as these data demonstrate. From a purely economic accounting point of view as providers of jobs and income, it is important for community development practitioners, as participants in local economic development planning, to understand how nonprofit corporations fit into the development process, in direct contribution to job and income generation, and also in enhancement of factors that facilitate community economic development. This is in sync with the broadened perspective of economic development articulated in recent years which recognizes the significance of community factors beyond land, labor and capital.

For example, Glen Pulver (1989) illustrates the more encompassing approach to rural economic development by highlighting five variables crucial to location of goods and service producing enterprises: access to knowledge, access to capital, access to telecommunications, access to transportation, and access to a high quality living environment. Similar key location variables are also examined in Beck (1981). Nonprofit corporations perform a central role in provision of education (schools, research, training, consultation) and community services (social services, recreation, libraries, arts), and also are instrumental in supplying access to capital to certain community populations. Their potential role in economic development is quite broad. Yet, nonprofit corporations, with a few notable exceptions like community development corporations, have been little examined as instruments of economic development and, as McNamara and Green (1988) found, are given scant attention by local economic development planners.

The purpose of this paper is to sketch the theoretical outlines of the economic functions of nonprofit corporations in the development process. We consider nonprofit corporations a very important component of community economic development, and believe community development practitioners and community leaders should give them much more consideration in formulating their economic development policies. Our analysis applies specifically to the Internal Revenue Service classified 510(c)(3) charitable and 501(c)(4) social welfare organizations, which constitute the heart of the nonprofit sector.

In the following discussion we will begin first with a definition of community economic development which reaches beyond job and income creation to include broad quality of life factors for all community members. This definition suggests the potential role of nonprofit corporations in economic development. Two economic functions—market and nonmarket—are examined in our analysis.

ECONOMIC FUNCTIONS OF NONPROFIT CORPORATIONS

Ron Shaffer offers one of the most intriguing, thoughtful definitions of economic development.

> Economic development is the sustained, progressive attempt to attain individual and group interests through expanded, intensified, and adjusted use of available resources . . . Economic development can also be defined as those activities which lead to greater resource productivity, a wider range of real choices for consumers and producers, and broader clientele participation in policy formation . . . Human welfare (well being) is the end product of the development process. It is a value laden concept that affects the economic efficiency and equity (social justice) dimensions that pervade definitions of economic development. Human well-being includes health, interpersonal relationships, physical environment, housing, education, the arts, and numerous other aspects of life. (Shaffer, 1989, p. 7)

Shaffer's definition draws attention to the importance of community amenities and the "bundle of attributes" of a community termed agglomeration economies (Richardson, 1973) in the community economic development process. This bundle of attributes can be allocated to both market and nonmarket functions. Let us define market functions to include those functions for which the market can distinguish between purchasers of the good or service by the exclusionary principle on the basis of price, and those beneficiaries of the good or service for whom exclusion is difficult to maintain on the basis of price.

The latter part of Shaffer's definition, with its emphasis on social justice and human well-being, speaks to the role of amenities. An amenity has been defined as a "location specific good" or service (Diamond & Tolley, 1982). Each community offers its own specific mix of goods and services like education, recreation, cultural programs, sports, health care, public services, libraries, and social services that influence the location decisions of households. Both businesses and households make location decisions based in large part on the amenities communities offer to them, thus amenity goods and services affect the community's business environment in the current time frame and through the location activity of the future business environment.

Amenities also influence the market component of business location decisions. Some amenities—for instance, transportation services—figure into the economic portion of the calculations of business location decisions, but as regional economist Harry Richardson (1978) has demonstrated, non-economic variables also influence those decisions. Business people desire an attractive community environment for their employees and therefore will look beyond strict profit maximization variables. Moreover, regional development policies, which affect business location decisions, integrate equity goals intended to distribute welfare among citizens. As Richardson points out, these goals are "a social rather than strictly economic concern" (p. 201).

Nonprofit corporations figure prominently in the supply of community amenities. They are of course particularly active in the realm of social services (counseling programs, health services, crisis intervention, etc.), but also supply amenities in art, education and recreation. If household and business location decisions are in fact strongly affected by the supply of amenities, then nonprofit corporations responsible for delivery of essential goods and services must be cultivated.

Shaffer's reference to "expanded, intensified and adjusted use of available resources" suggests the significance of the bundle of market and nonmarket factors called agglomeration economies in economic development. As a community's economy develops, services available to businesses and households expand, which in turn invites further and intensified use of community resources. A location becomes more attractive to a business because of the concentration of suppliers, financial institutions, markets, labor and business services. The concentration or agglomeration of such factors in a community offers benefits to businesses in the form of cost savings, increased availability of inputs, and easy access to inputs. In addition to business agglomeration economies, there are also household and social agglomeration economies (Richardson, 1973). Households benefit from a wider array of amenity choices, and society as a whole benefits through efficiency of production in public services.

Nonprofit corporations affect the overall community environment in important ways. As participants in the competitive marketplace, certain nonprofits like hospitals and nursing homes draw income into the community and stimulate job and income growth. They can thus be counted as part of the base economy. Other nonprofit corporations like educational institutions and research institutes help create a more skilled work force and introduce new technology, thus supplying important producer services to for-profit enterprises and expanding the community's pool of valued resources. Still other nonprofit corporations provide attractive consumer services that bring income into the community. Each of these nonprofit corporations plays an integral role in the market economy, contributing importantly to business expansion. In addition, nonprofit corporations are important to household agglomeration economies. As the community economy develops and income grows, amenity offerings supplied by nonprofit corporations expand, thereby enhancing the attractiveness of the community to households.

In sum, nonprofit corporations sustain both nonmarket and market economic development functions. They contribute to the community in important ways and in a reciprocal fashion their viability is ensured with economic activity. The nonprofits' nonmarket functions encompass the various community amenities they supply, while their market functions include their offering of producer and consumer services and direct contributions to employment and income growth. We turn now to a discussion of these economic functions, addressing nonmarket functions first.

NONMARKET FUNCTIONS OF NONPROFIT CORPORATIONS

The major nonmarket function of nonprofit corporation is their supply of community amenities. The amenities they produce address the human welfare needs of all socio-economic groups, but especially the most needy and distressed community residents. Nonprofits engage in community amenity development in at least three unique ways: (1) enhancing community cultural and environmental amenities; (2) devising and carrying out redevelopment projects; and (3) implementing social welfare/redistributive programs.

Nonprofit corporations supply many of the desired cultural and environmental amenities. Art galleries, museums, symphonies, and performance theaters are typically operated by nonprofit enterprises. Other activities include historical preservation, preserving special natural habitats, supporting libraries, offering outlets for social interaction and community service, and provision of recreation programs. Many if not most of these programs are by financial necessity established under a nonprofit corporation. For instance, few communities can support a profit making performance theater. Instead, performances are supported through a combination of ticket sales, grants and donations. According to one survey of 113 nonprofit theaters in the 1976–1977 time period, 45.8 percent of their revenue came from earned income, while 51.6 percent was labeled unearned (donations, grants) income (National Endowment for the Arts, 1981).

If cultural and environmental amenities are indeed considered one central element in economic development plans, then local governments, business and community groups will have to act to cultivate nonprofit corporations that supply amenities. There is evidence that this occurs. Whitt and Lammers (1991) found in their study of Louisville that business development leaders take an active interest in promoting the arts as part of an overall development strategy. That development leaders' promotion of cultural attractions may be productive has some empirical support. Availability of museums, zoos, symphonies, dance and performance theaters has been found to affect households' intercity choices of location (Clark and Kahn, 1988).

A second nonmarket amenity role for nonprofits is in conducting redevelopment activities. These encompass tasks including housing rehabilitation, tenant management training, recreation and arts programs, community organizing, and job training. Programs of this type begin with addressing basic quality of life improvements and proceed with attempts to build a sense of community and empowerment. Benefits resulting from mitigation of social problems accrue not only to neighborhood residents but to the whole community.

Community development corporations (CDCs) are among the most well-known mechanisms for engaging neighborhood residents in tackling redevelopment projects. Among community development corporations, housing rehabilitation, construction and management are the most common redevelopment projects (Vidal & Komives, 1989).

Redevelopment projects often include what appears to be a more market-like function, business development, but that activity is incorporated here into the discussion of nonmarket activities. Business development programs in distressed areas are conceived in the context of a larger redevelopment project that is nonmarket in function. They are often a small portion of those projects.

More importantly, it is appropriate to include many of the business development activities in the discussion of nonmarket functions because of the nature of risk involved in business investment and expansion in poor, economically distressed locations. Because of the economic nature of poor communities, nonprofits have to approach business development in fairly unconventional ways that lie outside the strictures of the market place. If the market place determines that investment in distressed communities is unprofitable, then special mechanisms have to be established to obtain needed capital. Businesses must be granted a longer than average period of time to show a profit, and a network of support services is needed to aid inexperienced entrepreneurs.

Local governments have shown a reluctance to invest financial resources in such risky business. For instance, two very popular tax incentive programs—tax increment financing and enterprise zones—

have been portrayed as urban redevelopment programs, but typically neither type of district has been located in blighted urban areas where rates of poverty and unemployment are high (Paetsch & Dahlstrom, 1990; Wolf, 1990). Instead, they are more often found in suburban cities and even rural areas in locations where business potential is great. Risk averse officials are more likely to site a TIF district where there is a relatively high probability that they can recoup property tax increments sufficient to pay off bonds (Davis, 1989; Paetsch & dahlstrom, 1990).

In locations of high poverty and unemployment, nonprofit organizations are apt to be in a better position than local governments to take the risks associated with redevelopment and to intercede in the marketplace on behalf of prospective enterpreneurs, providing them with the resources and protection they need to succeed. Community development corporations have been especially instrumental in stimulating for-profit business development in impoverished areas. One Chicago CDC set up a construction company in an area of the city where no dependable construction company was present, and in another identified market niche and helped organize a printing business (Wiewel & Mier, 1986). CDCs have also served as effective conduits to supply badly needed capital. Where they have a well established record of working with community residents, CDCs can serve as brokers between financial institutions and community entrepreneurs, or, with initial outside grants, operate a loan fund made available to those who have been unable to secure loans from established financial institutions (Wiewel & Weintraub, 1990). For example, with financial aid from the Ford Foundation and the nonprofit Southern Development Bankcorporation, a special loan program called the Good Faith Fund was established in rural Arkansas for the purpose of issuing loans to newly developing, high risk small businesses (Thomas, 1991).

Bank CDCs are another important financial resource. These institutions, which can organize as nonprofits, are permitted to make investments regular banks are denied, such as equity investments in real estate and business ventures (Sower & Milkman, 1991). Investments must be directed to moderate- and low-income neighborhoods and individuals.

The accomplishments of CDCs are significant. A recent survey of 1,160 community-based development corporations revealed the CDCs produced over 87,000 low-income housing units in the 1989–1991 time period, assisted in creating and retaining 90,000 jobs over a five year span, and contributed to development of 17.4 million square feet of industrial and commercial space (Greene, 1992, p. 16).

Support of nonprofit capitalization and small business development projects fits well within the scope of what Eisinger (1988) has called the "entrepreneurial state." Eisinger maintains that states and local governments are gradually moving away from the supply-side tax and financial incentive programs, to demand-sides policies. Among the demand-side policies are various venture capital programs like development credit corporations and venture loan programs. Since demand-side programs attempt to create and discover opportunities rather than intervene "after an opportunity has been identified," government experiences a higher degree of risk (Eisinger, 1988, p. 228). Product development corporations (PDCs), established to produce new products and capitalized with public funds, are one such risk. Many new products simply do not make it to the market or do not attract sales. In authorizing its PDC, Connecticut determined that success should not be measured in terms of profits, but in jobs created (Fisher, 1990). Some of that risk and reasoning could justifiably be extended. Nonprofit corporation can contribute in areas of marginal economic viability by assuming some of the economic risk and uncertainty of entrepreneurial ventures and investment activities not justified by strict accounting criteria.

A third nonmarket function of nonprofit corporations is the implementation of social welfare or redistributive programs. While social welfare programs have little direct impact on job creation or stimulus of economic activity, they do not serve purposes that benefit a community's social and economic environment. Lending assistance in maintaining social stability, building self-esteem among individuals, creating a sense of belonging to the community among disadvantaged populations, and improving the life situation of people striving to make the transition to gainful employment are but a few of the community development–related services charitable organizations are skilled at supplying. Charitable nonprofit organizations help attain the social welfare goals of economic development in ways that private enterprise and sometimes government cannot. Profit making businesses are not good at nor interested in finding emergency shelter for the homeless or setting up food pantries for the hungry. But, if there is any sense of philanthropic obligation, they are willing to work through nonprofits that support these activities.

Private citizens and businesses may also be supportive of the transfer of some government social services to nonprofit organizations, if in fact nonprofit corporations can provide those services with greater efficiency and effectiveness (social agglomeration economies). Government avoids building a new bureaucracy and minimizes red tape, and benefits from the lower personnel costs of nonprofits which rely on volunteers, pay lower salaries, and are not constrained by civil service regulations (Wolch, 1990). Nonprofit organizational activity also supplements the service activities of local governments. Police forces, for example, find that in cases of rape and domestic violence they can conduct their investigations more effectively when victims receive the counseling services of a women's crisis center. It is also possible to envision that social service nonprofits depress the costs of negative externalities to business. To the extent that housing and food services, juvenile programs, drug counseling and other intervention programs reduce crime, nonprofit corporations have helped lower the cost of doing business.

MARKET FUNCTIONS OF NONPROFIT CORPORATIONS

We turn now to an examination of market functions and the potential of nonprofits to stimulate employment and income growth. In this section the service sector—of which nonprofits are a part—and its export functions are examined.

Economic base theory is employed here to explain the occurrence of community and regional economic growth. This theory posits that "the development of a community depends on the vigor of its export industries" (Shaffer, 1989, p. 29). Economic base theory has commonly considered agriculture, forestry, mining and manufacturing as basic industries, because they export products out of the region, and thus import funds to pay for these exports which eventually end up as income to resource suppliers. These resources suppliers spend that income locally, contributing to the community's income. Producer services, such as finance, insurance, real estate, accounting and legal advice, originally were conceived as inputs into the production process and thus were thought to have no independent effect on economic growth (Harmston, 1983). However, conception of the role of services in economic development has changed. That change, of course, is due in part to the growing dominance of service industry jobs. To illustrate the dominance of the service sector, by 1988 75.9 percent of all nonfarm jobs in the nation were in service industries, a figure projected to rise to 79 percent by the year 2000 (Personick, 1989).

Service industries, especially producer services, create the potential for further economic growth through such means as expanding the division of labor and introducing technological innovations. Regarding the division of labor, Hansen (1990) points to the close interrelations between basic industries and producer services. As corporations become larger and their structures more complex, they become increasingly reliant on a broad array of management services (e.g., engineering, personnel management, computing, insurance). Industry actually helps stimulate an absolute increase in the number of service industry jobs, and does not just transfer their own service positions to independent businesses (Tschetter, 1987). However, producer services have a reciprocal influence on industry. For example, research institutes develop new technology that changes products and the production process, and education institutions expand information and help enlarge the pool of intelligent, skilled labor. Producer services are therefore in a position to influence job creation through their attraction of new industries to a region, creation of new production processes, and development of skilled, well-educated labor.

Service industries stimulate income and job growth through their sales of services to extra-regional clients and import substitution. While perhaps depending on local base industries, the regional service sector may become increasingly independent of those industries as they expand. Producer services can grow to establish markets outside the region, and consumer service industries (e.g., retail, entertainment, food service) attract extra-regional customers. In this way, service enterprises become an established part of the export sector. Furthermore, an import substitution function can occur as service industries expand to fill the needs of local customers. Service enterprises outside the region decline in importance as local suppliers.

Like other service enterprises, nonprofit corporations enhance the environment for additional economic development and facilitate community income and employment growth. For instance, as suppliers of producer services, colleges, universities and technical schools supply business and industry with an educated, skilled workforce, with consulting services, and with research that leads to practical application. Additionally, education institutions bring money into the community through research grants, donations, student payment of tuition and fees, and student and staff consumer purchases. Likewise, hospitals and nursing homes can serve large areas so that money is imported into the community. The more consumer oriented services such as camps and recreation centers, theaters and symphonies, and museums and historical sites potentially draw customers from a large geographical area.

There has been little evaluation of the export functions and multiplier effects of nonprofit corporations, but a few studies are suggestive of their effects. Using the Department of Commerce RIMS II input-output model and 1977 national census data, Wolch estimated that nonprofit corporation spending created an additional 5.78 million jobs outside the sector with earnings of $45.6 billion (1990, p. 56). Bringing the analysis to the local level and using the same 1977 census data, it was estimated that in Los Angeles County the nonprofit sector employed approximately 5 percent of the regional workforce and generated 151,000 additional service sector jobs (Wolch

& Geiger, 1986). The authors of the Los Angeles study concluded that because of their share of resources and job opportunities, nonprofit organizations "should not be excluded in the analysis of privatization policy" (p. 16). Another study estimated the employment and income impacts of the Stratford Festival in Ontario, Canada. According to the researchers' estimates the festival generated a 1.6 employment multiplier, adding 451 tourist jobs to the community (Mitchell & Wall, 1989).

These case studies are of course more suggestive than conclusive. There is much work to be done to document the precise economic functions of nonprofit corporations. Yet the proposition that some nonprofit corporations, like many for-profit service industries, help facilitate employment and income growth is reasonable.

The growing dependence of nonprofit corporations on self-generated revenues will likely lead to expansion of their market functions. The flow of federal dollars, upon which social service nonprofits greatly depend, was dramatically reduced during the 1980s. Between 1977 and 1987 government funds as a percent of the total of all funds received by social service nonprofits, declined form 53.9 percent to 41.4 percent (Bailey, 1990, p. 4). Private contributions were insufficient to replace lost federal funds so nonprofits have had to increase revenues, in part through enterprise activities. Social welfare organizations find their enterprise options limited, but they have been able to raise money through sales of products made by clients, contracting out the professional advisory services of their staff, or selling the services of clients who have been trained in job skills (Crimmins & Kiel, 1990). Some nonprofits are able to exploit very obvious and very profitable program related products and services (Skloot, 1987). Art museums sell art reproductions and books, symphonies sell calendars, music and shirts, and both types of operations open cafeterias or sell snacks to their customers.

Nonprofits have also been able to spin off for-profit businesses. To cite one example, the California Human Development Corporation, which has developed a number of low income housing projects, created a for-profit management firm to oversee its management complexes (Voight, 1988). The Internal Revenue Service has pledged to monitor more closely nonprofit corporations, particularly in regards to their business activity (Williams, 1992). Closer scrutiny could lead to creation of more such for-profit businesses in order to escape the unrelated business income tax restrictions, rather than to a shrinking back from enterprise activity. Nonprofit organizations gain from the profits that are fed back into the organization while at the same time contributing to small business creation.

Two cautionary remarks are appropriate at this point. First, following Shaffer's advice, we must recognize that internal or local markets "do not just follow the export base," but that they are strongly shaped by spatial relationships as predicted by central place theory (1990, p. 80). This theory's concept of a regional hierarchy of central places (communities) producing goods and services applies well to the size and distribution of nonprofit corporations. Large cities, because of their wealth of human and financial resources, can sustain a richer mix of nonprofits than places of smaller size. These factors especially constrain development of organizations specializing in nonmarket functions, but affect also the more commercial service enterprises. Economic development experts thus need to give careful consideration to the kinds of nonprofits that could be developed, given a community's social and economic characteristics.

Secondly, it is important in distinguishing the market functions of nonprofit corporations not to lose sight of their charitable, nonmarket services. Indeed, one of the greatest advantages of nonprofit corporations is that they can simultaneously supply economic and social welfare benefits. Many hospitals maintain charitable functions that are at the core of their original missions. Hospitals located in some of the most deprived urban neighborhoods have acted to revitalize their communities by working with community organizations and philanthropies to initiate health related job training programs, and establish low interest loan programs (Pallarito, 1992). One hospital in the Bronx has been described as a community's "economic anchor," not only because it is the major employer for the neighborhood but also because it has led a broad-based community redevelopment project (p. 62). This case illustrates the often dual functions of individual nonprofits as producers of human welfare services (amenities) and as generators of economic activity.

COMMUNITY ACTION AND REACTION TO SUPPORT OF NONPROFIT CORPORATIONS

The analysis presented here calls upon economic development planners to recognize the relevance of nonprofit corporations to community development planning as initiators of their own economic activity, contributors to the economic activity of other businesses, and as providers of essential community social services. Communities should therefore contemplate providing support for nonprofit corporations just as they provide support and incentives for profit making businesses. For instance, communities can offer financial support to nonprofits through the awarding of grants and subsidies, issuing low interest loans, and contracting with nonprofit corporations for delivery of services. They can supply human resources to nonprofit organizations by lending local government staff expertise and offering other personnel the opportunity and encouragement to volunteer their time. Communities can also accumulate wage, salary and other data on nonprofit corporations and add this information to their economic analyses, in order to better understand the economic influences and impacts of nonprofit corporations.

Community development practitioners can expect that objections will be raised to investment in nonprofit sector development. A common argument is that nonprofit organizations already have an unfair advantage in the marketplace resulting from federal and state tax exemptions. Small businesses are disadvantaged, it is argued, because they work at such a small profit margin (Rose-Ackerman, 1990). When forced to compete in the same area of business with a nonprofit (e.g., recreation or entertainment), it is much harder to succeed because the nonprofit can set lower prices. Thus government adds to the misery of small businesses and undermines economic development.

As a further argument, one might take up the reasoning of Paul Peterson (1981) that local government investment in redistributive programs is harmful. These programs are costly to middle and upper income taxpayers, thereby discouraging their location and investment in the community. Thus redistributive programs implemented by some nonprofits and which are reliant on local government funding work at cross purposes to economic development.

The former argument is emotionally charged, making it hard to convince opponents that the profit making business activities of nonprofit corporations are in fact highly regulated by state and federal laws, and that nonprofit business activities in recent years have been undergoing more stringent oversight by the Internal Revenue Service and by state courts (Bookman, 1992; Williams, 1992). Local officials will have to give attention to identifying the few instances where there is for-profit/nonprofit competition, and take pains not to disadvantage either.

The redistributive policy objection is in part answered by Salamon's (1987) concept of the symbiotic relationship between government and the nonprofit sector. He posits that in the era of the welfare state, government has adopted a "third party government" style of service delivery whereby it often turns to private organizations for actual service implementation. Nonprofit organizations represent a significant part of the network of government contracting and grant and subsidy allocation. They become a preferred mechanism for implementation because they offer more personal service delivery, less bureaucracy, and competition in service delivery. Since local officials cannot realistically ignore redistributive programs because of mandates and citizen demands, they can turn to the nonprofit sector for program implementation. In doing so, communities might very well join the twin goals of effecting cost savings through private nonprofit service delivery and support of nonprofit corporations as one means to advance economic development. Community investment in the nonprofit sector thereby is integrated into the broader scope of public policy, and is not conceived solely as an economic development tool.

CONCLUSION

The economic contributions of nonprofit corporations in the form of jobs and income are easily understood, but the interplay between social welfare and charitable activities and economic development is less well recognized. The connection is best understood when economic development is conceived as a holistic approach to enhancing the quality of life of all community residents, including the economic environment within which businesses must operate. When understood in these terms, the role of nonprofits as producers of human welfare and locational amenities becomes clearer. Nonprofit corporations with strong roots in distressed communities are able to mobilize people to change their home environments for the better, can initiate business development, and can help these people communicate to development planners their particular needs. Other nonprofit organizations assist people in coping with life stresses, while still others help develop the cultural and environmental attractiveness of the community.

While the benefits received by communities from nonprofit corporations are not always as dramatic or as obvious as those contributed by for-profit enterprises, this sector of the economy should not be ignored by development planners. Nonprofit corporations can accomplish economic and social tasks at which government often fails and in which businesses are not interested. Economic development plans should therefore include nonprofit agents of economic and social production.

REFERENCES

Bailey, A. L. 1980's giving boom not matched by growth for many groups. *Chronicle of Philanthropy* 2 (January 9):4.
1990

Beck, R. *New Approaches to Economic Development Research in Rural Areas.* Ithaca, NY: Northeast Center for Rural Development.
1981

Bookman, M. *Protecting Your Organization's Tax-Exempt Status.* San Francisco: Jossey-
1992   Bass.

Clarke, D. E. & J. R. Kahn. The social benefits of urban cultural amenities. *Journal of*
1988   *Regional Sciences* 28(2):363–377.

Crimmins, J. C. & M. Kiel. Enterprise in the nonprofit sector. Pages 315–327 in D.
1990   L. Gies, J. S. Ott & J. M. Shafritz (eds.), *The Nonprofit Organization.* Pacific
        Grove, CA: Brooks/Cole.

Davis, D. Tax increment financing. *Public Budgeting and Finance* 9(1):63–73.
1989

Diamond, Jr., D. B. & G. S. Tolley. The economic role of urban amenities. Pages 1–
1982   23 in D. B. Diamond, Jr. & G. S. Tolley (eds.), *The Economics of Urban*
        Amenities. New York: Academic Press.

Eisinger, P. K. *The Rise of the Entrepreneurial State.* Madison: University of Wisconsin
1988   Press.

Fisher, P. S. Connecticut's new product development corporation. Pages 101–122 in
1990   R. D. Bingham, E. W. Hill & S. B. White (eds.), *Financing Economic Devel-*
        opment. Newbury Park, CA: Sage.

Greene, S. G. Community-based development groups found to gain broad private
1992   support. *Chronicle of Philanthropy* 4(January 14):16.

Hansen, N. Do producer services induce regional economic development? *Journal of*
1990   *Regional Sciences* 30(4):465–476.

Harmston, F. K. *The Community as an Economic System.* Ames: Iowa State University
1983   Press.

Hodgkinson, Virginia A., Murray S. Whitzman, Christopher M. Toppe & Stephen M.
1992   Noga (eds.), *Nonprofit Almanac: 1992–1993.* San Francisco: Josey Bass.

McNamara, K. T. & G. Greene. Local and regional economic development planning
1988   and the role of community development practitioners. *Journal of the Com-*
        munity Development Society 19(2):42–55.

Mitchell, C. A. & G. Wall. The arts and employment: A case study of the Stratford
1989   Festival. *Growth and Change* 20(Fall):31–40.

National Endowment for the Arts. *Conditions and Needs of the Professional American*
1981   *Theater.* Washington, DC: National Endowment for the Arts.

Paetsch, J. R. & R. K. Dahlstrom. Tax increment financing: What it is and how it
1990   works. Pp. 63–73 in R. D. Bingham, E. W. Hill & S. B. White (eds.),
        Financing Economic Development. Newbury Park, CA: Sage.

Pallarito, K. Providing more than just care to neighborhoods. *Modern Healthcare*
1992   22(August 22):59–64.

Personick, V. A. Industry output and employment: A slower trend for the nineties.
1989   *Monthly Labor Review* 112(November):25–41.

Peterson, P. *City Limits.* Chicago: University of Chicago Press.
1981

Pulver, G. C. Developing a community perspective on rural economic development
1989   policy. *Journal of the Community Development Society* 20(2):1–13.

Richardson, H. *Regional Growth Theory.* New York: John Wiley and Sons.
1973

Richardson, H. *Regional Economics.* Urbana: University of Illinois Press.
1978

Rose-Ackerman, S. Unfair competition and corporate income taxation. Pp. 91–108
1990   in D. L. Gies, J. S. Ott & J. M. Shafritz (eds.), *The Nonprofit Organization.*
        Pacific Grove, CA: Brooks/Cole.

Salamon, L. M. Partners in public service: The scope and theory of government-
1987   nonprofit relations. Pp. 99–117 in W. W. Powell (ed.), *The Nonprofit Sector.*
        New Haven, CT: Yale University Press.

Shaffer, R. *Community Economics*. Ames: Iowa State University Press.
1989

Shaffer, R. Building economically viable communities: A role for community devel-
1990 opers. *Journal of the Community Development Society* 21(2):74–87.

Skloot, Edward. Enterprise and Commerce in Nonprofit Corporations. In Walter W.
1987 Powell (ed.), *The Nonprofit Sector*. New Haven, CT: Yale University Press.

Sower, John & Beverly L. Milkman. "The bank community development corporation:
1991 An economic development tool for the '90s." *Economic Development Quarterly* 5(Feb):3–8.

Thomas, Karen M. "Fund Gives Community a Bootstrap." *Chicago Tribune* December
1991 22:3.

Tschetter, J. Producer service industries: Why are they growing so rapidly? *Monthly*
1987 *Labor Review* 110(December):31–40.

U. S. Bureau of the Census. *1987 Census of Service Industries*. Washington, DC: Gov-
1989 ernment Printing Office.

Vidal, A. C. & B. Komives. Community development corporations: A national per-
1989 spective. *National Civic Review* 78(May–June):168–177.

Voight, J. California dreamin'. *Planning* (December):10–14.
1988

Whitt, J. A. & J. C. Lammers. The art of growth: Ties between development organiza-
1991 tions and the performing arts. *Urban Affairs Quarterly* 26(1):376–393.

Wiewel, W. & R. Mier. Enterprise activities for not-for-profit organizations: Surviving
1986 the New Federalism. Pp. 205–225 in E. M. Bergman (ed.), *Local Economies in Transition*. Durham, NC: Duke University Press.

Wiewel, W. & J. Weintraub. Community development corporations as a tool for eco-
1990 nomic development finance. Pp. 160–176 in R. D. Bingham, E. W. Hill & S. B. White (eds.), *Financing Economic Development*. Newbury Park, CA: Sage.

Williams, F. IRS steps up enforcement of laws on charities. *Chronicle of Philanthropy*
1992 4(May 19):25–27.

Wolch, J. *The Shadow State*. New York: The Foundation Center.
1990

Wolch, J. &. R. K. Geiger. Urban restructuring and the not-for-profit sector. *Economic*
1986 *Geography* 62(January):3–18.

Wolf, M. Enterprise zones: A decade of diversity. Pp. 123–141 in R. D. Bingham, E.
1990 W. Hill & S. B. White (eds.), *Financial Economic Development*. Newbury Park, CA: Sage.

TEN BASIC PRINCIPLES OF LEADERSHIP IN COMMUNITY DEVELOPMENT ORGANIZATIONS

By Jerry W. Robinson, Jr.

INTRODUCTION

After working for more than 25 years as an educator, researcher and consultant with more than 2,000 community organizations, I have learned ten valuable lessons about leadership. The purpose of this brief paper is to describe and justify ten basic theoretical, operational and philosophical principles which guide my behavior as I work with leaders and managers in community and economic development organizations. These ten principles are based on my philosophy of organization development, human resource development, leadership development and community development. Most of the principles *can not* stand alone, instead each should be understood and practiced in relation to the other nine and in relation to the members of the group and situation in the community organization (Bass, 1985; Fielder & Chemers, 1984; Hersey & Blanchard, 1993).

Managers and volunteers in community organizations are interested in leadership. Why? Perhaps their success usually depends on their ability to enable others to get things done. There is demand for excellence in leadership in all types of community and economic development organizations—in both private and public sector groups. However, all managers or leaders do not agree on a definition of leadership.

What is leadership? *Leadership is the behavioral process of influencing the activities of an individual or group to accomplish goals in a given situation. Leadership is a learned behavioral skill which includes the ability to help others achieve their potential as individuals and as team members* (Robinson & Clifford, 1991).

PRINCIPLES OF LEADERSHIP

1. Everyone Is a Leader. Group members do not have equal knowledge and skill (Bennis, 1989), but each person can excel in some as-

---

Jerry W. Robinson, Jr., is Director of the Laboratory for Community and Economic Development and Professor of Sociology and Rural Sociology at University of Illinois at Urbana–Champaign.

pect of organizational or community leadership. Managers must know their staff and volunteers well enough to discover the abilities of each person, even if abilities and skills are limited, and then enlist and support their efforts. Beware of the tendency for "educated" persons to underestimate the potential leadership contributions of the unexperienced, uneducated or novice.

2. **Leadership Behavior is a Learned Skill.** Leaders aren't born, they are developed or made! Leaders usually evolve (Stogdill, 1974). We learn leadership by copying role models, by trial, error and experience, and by study. Crises in a community organization are usually fertile ground for "creating" new leaders (Robinson & DiFonso, 1992). For example, persons with specific knowledge or skill may come to the forefront with solutions to a critical problem. Regardless of who you are, you can become a better leader by studying, practicing new behaviors and asking for constructive feedback from your work group (Fielder & Chemers, 1984).

3. **For Effective Team Work, Remember—People Support Actions, Programs and Goals Which They Help Create.** Involving others in planning, program development, delivery and evaluation is the key to teamwork in a community development organization. Morale and production usually decreases when people are given a plan and *told* what to do (Bass, 1985; Bennis, 1989). Leaders of successful community development organizations usually involve, involve and continue to involve others.

4. **Atmosphere and Structure Should Permit Every Team Member to Lead at Some Time.** The leader cannot know all the answers to every problem in a community development organization. One person does not have enough energy or time to solve all the problems faced in community organizations, especially those organizations working in economic development (Blake & Mouton, 1985). Excellence in community and economic development requires intelligent and informed group decision making. Delivering technical information and fostering economic development requires many skills and much know-how from many experts (Drucker, 1974). To succeed, community and economic development leaders must depend on others. When one individual monopolizes power, resources and time, and takes all the credit, failure is imminent.

5. **"Everyone Is, in Some Capacity, My Superior."** Dr. Samuel Johnson, 18th century English writer, originated this axiom. You may have to look closely to find something which someone can contribute to a specific project, but something is there. Look around and you will discover that many people have skills and abilities which you do not possess (Bennis & Nanus, 1985; Nanus, 1992; Terry, 1993). The person

who is willing and able to follow through on the most mundane, routine tasks may end up making a valuable contribution to the team—if only the leader frees up the time to spend in creative thought.

6. Democratic Leadership is Not Permissive Leadership! There's a common myth that team leadership is permissive and autocratic persons are especially prone to believe this myth. While democratic leadership is more flexible, it is not unstructured. *When the management team is in charge, that's not permissive leadership!* (Robinson & Silvis, 1993) Many studies have shown that peer or work groups have more influence than the boss over the behavior of their fellow workers (Stogdill, 1974).

There is much more organizational structure in democratic or team-shared leadership; that's why it may be harder for some folks to understand team management or to become team leaders (Bass, 1990). In democratic groups, the communication systems are much more complex and require more skill to manage. Sometimes, democratic leadership is more difficult because more time, accommodation to divergent ideas and more "people" skills are required (Fielder, 1967; Fielder & Chemers, 1984). Democratic leadership is developmental leadership because, through this system, it's easier to develop new leaders in a community or economic development organization.

7. In Spite of Many Virtues, Democratic or Team-Centered Leadership is Not Always Best! When a crisis arises, such as a fire in a building, there is no time to call a committee meeting. Someone must make decisions and do something, quickly! Democratic teams should develop policy as a group, then leader or manager can be charged with implementing the policy (Blake & Mouton, 1985). Sometimes it's o.k. to be the boss (Robinson & Silvis, 1993)! The leader cannot accommodate everyone or do everything by committees or through groups. For example, sometimes managers encounter irresponsible people who must be told what to do, when and how (Hersey & Blanchard, 1993). The next principle helps explain why democratic leadership is not best for all people or in all situations.

8. Autocratic Leadership is Not Always Bad! Some situations require "the leader" to take charge decisively—to exhibit and use authority and power (Hersey & Blanchard, 1993). This is especially effective when you are initiating an activity with people who are immature, irresponsible, disloyal or incorrigible. It's unfortunate, but some people only understand and respond to power. Some individuals have never been exposed to democratic team work, and they don't know how to follow a developmental, team-center leader (Bass, 1985). In other situations, employees may be in a dispute among themselves over work assignments. In such situations, the leader or manager should use authority to bring the group together to discuss administrative policies which facilitate the development of a more flexible team-center style, then use his or her authority and power to enforce the rules developed by the work group to accomplish the task (Blake & Mouton, 1985; Drucker, 1974; Robinson & Clifford, 1991; Robinson & Silvis, 1993).

9. The Leader's Knowledge and Behavior, a Particular Situation and the Expectations and Experience of Others Determine Leadership. We are social and emotional beings. Many of us conform to the expectations of others—to the "power of the group." If a group expects authority in a crisis, the leader will frequently respond as a power actor. However, if a group is talented, loyal and expects to be involved in solving the problem in a crisis, a skilled team leader should quickly respond by involving members of the group in creative planning and teamwork (Hersey & Blanchard, 1993).

10. Leaders Must be Flexible! Leaders and managers must adjust their behavior to meet the levels of experience, the knowledge, the skills, and the expectations of group members in every situation which faces the community development organization (Stogdill, 1974). A dictator will destroy morale of a loyal and productive staff by trying to control everything they do (Robinson & Silvis, 1993). Leaders who are abdicators, always totally shaped by the demands of others or the fear of change, will discover that morale and productivity suffer. Developmental activators will become transformational leaders (Bass, 1990) because they will discover that *employees and volunteer leaders will support goals and action strategies which they help create* (Robinson & Silvis, 1993). Managers and leaders of community organizations must be many things to many people. One style of leadership will not be adequate in every situation.

SUMMARY

What is leadership? It is the ability to influence, guide or shape the attitudes, expectations and behavior of others to achieve goals. Leadership is largely a behavior skill, and new behaviors can be learned! Superb and sometimes complex leadership skills are required for leading contemporary community organizations, especially if community and economic development is the goal. Knowledge, experiential training and practice can help improve leadership skills. The effective community development professional must be a leadership role model and use a flexible framework for collaborative teamwork to be effective in today's community and economic development arena.

REFERENCES

Bass, Bernard. 1985. *Leadership and Performance Beyond Expectations*. New York: The Free Press.

Bass, Bernard. 1990. From transactional to transformational leadership: Learning to share the vision. *Organizational Dynamics*. 18:19–36.

Bennis, Warren. 1989. *Why Leaders Can't Lead: The Unconscious Conspiracy Continues*. San Francisco: Jossey-Bass.

Bennis, Warren & Burt Nanus. 1985. *LEADERS: The Strategies for Taking Charge*. New York: Harper and Row Publishers.

Blake, Robert R. & Jane S. Mouton. 1985. *The Management Grid*. Houston: Gulf Publishing.

Drucker, Peter F. 1974. *Management: Task, Responsibilities, Practices*. New York: Harper and Row.

Fielder, Fred E. 1967. *A Theory of Leadership Effectiveness*. New York: McGraw Hill.

Fielder, Fred E. & M. M. Chemers. 1984. *Improving Leadership Effectiveness: The Leader Match Concept*. New York: Wiley and Sons.

Hersey, Paul & Kenneth H. Blanchard. 1993. *Management of Organizational Behavior: Utilizing Human Resources*. 6th Edition, Englewood Cliffs, NJ: Prentice Hall.

Nanus, Burt. 1992. *Visionary Leadership: Creating A Compelling Sense of Direction for Your Organization*. San Francisco: Jossey-Bass.

Robinson, Jerry W., Jr., & Roy A. Clifford. 1991. *Leadership Roles in Community Groups*. Publication A.E. 4672-3, RURAL PARTNERS®/Kellogg Program. Urbana, IL: University of Illinois Laboratory for Community and Economic Development.

Robinson, Jerry W., Jr., & Louis DiFonso. 1992. *Conflict Management in Community Groups*. Publication A.E. 4672-6, RURAL PARTNERS®/Kellogg Program. Urbana, IL: University of Illinois Laboratory for Community and Economic Development.

Robinson, Jerry W., Jr., & Anne Heinze Silvis. 1993. *Maintaining Participation in Community Organizations: Motivating Others to Achieve Objectives*. Publication A.E. 4672-10, RURAL PARTNERS®/Kellogg Program. Urbana, IL: University of Illinois Laboratory for Community and Economic Development.

Stogdill, Ralph M. 1974. *Handbook of Leadership: A Survey of Theory and Research*. New York: The Free Press.

Terry, Robert W. 1993. *Authentic Leadership: Courage in Action*. San Francisco: Jossey-Bass Publishers.

"People first": Factors that promote or inhibit community transformation

Mary Ellen Brown and Birgitta L. Baker

ABSTRACT
Residents are key assets in community change. Despite this, little is known about residents' perspectives regarding factors that facilitate or inhibit successful planning for neighborhood transformation. We conducted focus groups with residents of a low-wealth community involved with a neighborhood planning initiative and examined a planning document to elicit lived experience perspectives. Using Colaizzi's approach to phenomenology, the following themes emerged: (1) trust; (2) resident-driven transformation; (3) sense of community and cohesion; (4) engagement and collective action; and (5) openness to transformation. Attending to the factors identified by neighborhood residents can inform community development planning and practice.

Places where people live have profound effects on their health, economic, and social outcomes. Deep inequities exist between neighborhoods, leading to shorter life expectancies, lower educational attainment, and higher incarceration rates in communities of concentrated disadvantage (Blackwell, 2012; Cheezum et al., 2013). Historically, federal policies have exacerbated the plight of urban communities of color (Van Vliet, 1997). Redlining, exclusion of domestic and agricultural workers from labor protection laws, and separate but equal educational policies exclusively or disproportionately disadvantaged people of color resulting in a widening wealth and opportunity gap (Katznelson, 2005). Despite an emphasis on resident engagement in community planning, citizen engagement in government funded community change efforts has largely been given lip service for more than a century. A lack of guidelines for engagement, oversight, accountability, and sustained inclusion contributed to this issue (Price, 2011). Power differentials and politics have, more often than not, relegated community voices to the margins from the Progressive Era to the War on Poverty and into the current era.

As resident involvement is deemed essential in launching a sustainable neighborhood revitalization initiative (Brueggemann, 2014; Hyman, 2002; Price, 2011; Van Vliet, 1997), resident engagement should be an integral part of the early stages of planning (Chaskin, 2001; Derr & Kovacs, 2017; Fudge, 2011; Hyman, 2002). Despite the recognition that resident participation and community empowerment are important strategies for community change (Christens & Inzeo, 2015; Dreier, 1996), much is left to be learned about what works, particularly from the perspective of the community members themselves (Sandoval & Rongerude, 2015). Therefore, the purpose of this study is to help to address this gap by examining the perspectives of community members concerning factors that promote or inhibit community change.

Community development and transformation

In the US today, the field of community development is primarily concerned with addressing poverty and stabilizing communities through comprehensive, place-based initiatives that address health, economic, environmental, and social concerns (Keita, Hannon, Buys, Casazza, & Clay, 2016; von Hoffman, 2012). Community transformation refers to efforts to develop, revitalize, and stabilize neighborhoods experiencing social, environmental, or economic issues that reduce opportunities for community members to improve their life circumstances. Contemporary community development theories maintain that strategically planned social interventions can bring about positive social change and improve social and economic welfare (Midgley & Livermore, 2005; Weil, 1996). Over the past century, the community development field has increasingly shifted from a planning orientation principally concerned with fixing problems to one concerned with building on community assets (Kretzmann & McKnight, 1996; von Hoffman, 2012). Successful community development is driven by a local agenda and promotes building up communities, strengthening assets, and cultivating partnerships (Cnaan & Rothman, 1995; Lindsey, Stajduhar, & McGuinness, 2001), as opposed to viewing the problems of people and places through a prescriptive, top-down lens (Kretzmann & McKnight, 1996; Midgley & Livermore, 2005).

Holistic community development often involves comprehensively addressing a number of challenges across multiple domains simultaneously. Responses to community-specific issues can include capacity building, interventions, and policy improvements at the individual, family, organizational, and community levels. Aligning stakeholders and leveraging resources across multiple sectors is often necessary to bring about the desired change. For positive transformation to take place, a key stakeholder group whose involvement is critical to achieving meaningful, sustainable change is the community members themselves (Rothman, 2008).

Facilitators of and barriers to community transformation

For decades researchers have sought insight into the processes and outcomes of effective planning and implementation of community transformation initiatives. Failure of community transformation has often been predicted by experiences of disenfranchisement, social isolation, and mistrust (Aiyer, Zimmerman, Morrel-Samuels, & Reischl, 2015; Geller, Doykos, Craven, Bess, & Nation, 2014). Rothman's (2008) model of capacity-centered community development charts a path for community building focused on empowerment, social cohesion, leadership development, and participation/engagement.

Empowerment is a fundamental technique in successful and sustainable community organizing initiatives (Maton, 2008; Sandoval & Rongerude, 2015). Collective empowerment refers to the development and promotion of a shared sense of identity and purpose of a group of people around a cause, and further, the group achieves awareness that if they work together and build capacity they can take action on addressing a common issue (Coleman, 1968; Maton, 2008). Pyles (2009) posits that the more empowered residents are in the process of affecting change, the more sustainable organizing initiative.

Community empowerment is a process whereby communities band together over time, strengthening their collective agency to facilitate social and structural improvements (Aiyer et al., 2015). Building and maximizing collective capacity to enact social change requires fostering social cohesion within a community group. Social cohesion has been described as "a core element of community empowerment that brings community members together to analyze, articulate, and demand" community change, and as "necessary for community mobilization and engagement" (Carrasco & Bilal, 2016, p. 128). Social cohesion facilitates a sense of belonging and promotes shared values among community members (Rothman, 2008). For community development initiatives to succeed, social cohesion and leadership skills within the community are essential components of a community's capacity for change (Rothman, 2000).

Leadership skills are central to community driven change (MacPhee, Forlenza, Christensen, & Prendergast, 2017), in which citizens make decisions and take action to shape the future of their communities (Maton, 2008). Shared leadership is a key facet of an empowering context that builds the capacity of residents (Maton, 2008). Leadership training can help citizens of under-resourced communities resist systemic discrimination and oppression (Douglas, Grills, Villanueva, & Subica, 2016) and can lead to more readily sustained community engagement (MacPhee et al., 2017). Community practitioners and organizers can offer leadership training and education for residents in strategic planning and political engagement and advocacy, cultivate open and reciprocal relationships and communication to build social networks, connect residents to resources and supports, and promote civic engagement that encourages residents to use their voices in advocating for issues and electing representative leadership (Ahsan, 2008).

Arnstein's ladder of citizen participation provides guidance for cultivating meaningful resident engagement and promoting empowerment strategies (Arnstein, 1969; Pyles, 2009). At the lower levels of *manipulation* and the misuse of *psychotherapy*, participation is non-existent or low; at the midlevel rungs of the ladder of *informing, consultation*, and *placation*, participation is regarded as tokenism; and as a neighborhood revitalization effort moves residents up the higher three levels of *partnership, delegated power*, and *citizen control* (with *citizen control* at the top), authentic citizen power and empowerment become possible (Arnstein, 1969; Pyles, 2009). In the upper rungs of *partnership* and *delegated power*, power begins to get authentically redistributed, and planning and decision-making is shared, with citizens taking over majority authority at the *delegated power* level. At the top rung, *citizen control*, the citizens are fully in charge with full authority and in control of the organization or program, with the ability to negotiate relationships and conditions with outsiders on their own terms (Arnstein, 1969).

Much as engaging residents and empowering individuals are key strategies in promoting successful, sustainable social and community-level change, disenfranchisement and social isolation are key factors in ensuring social stagnation (Aiyer et al., 2015; Wilson, 1987). Social isolation contributes to the perpetuation of cyclical poverty in the urban underclass (Wilson, 1987). Changing patterns of social isolation to patterns of social inclusion and empowerment is necessary to combat concentrated poverty and to nurture neighborhoods of choice and opportunity (Aiyer et al., 2015). Sustainable neighborhood revitalization for people living in impoverished communities marked by concentrated and chronic disinvestment cannot take place if there is a lack of trust between residents within the neighborhood and those outside of it with access to resources, power, and influence over policy to invest in transformation (Geller et al., 2014).

The literature regarding the mobilization and organization of the members of a community in a neighborhood revitalization initiative is clear: residents must be meaningfully engaged for a transformation to be successful and sustainable (Ahsan, 2008; Pyles, 2009). Given that community members are the lynchpin of successful community transformation, it is important that their perspectives inform approaches to community practice. Therefore, the purpose of this study is to examine the experiences of community members regarding factors that facilitate or impede community change.

Method

A constructivist paradigm shaped this research in a research context where the researchers are not members of the community but were embedded in the neighborhood as part of the larger planning process. The shared control characteristic of constructivism (Guba, Lincoln, & Lynham, 2017) enabled the researchers and participants to co-create a narrative of the lived experiences of participants, situated in the context of a particular time and place. The constructivist paradigm reflected the use of the results to shape action. We used a phenomenological approach to examine the lived experiences of the participants and the meanings they ascribed to these experiences (Colaizzi, 1978; Creswell, 2007). The phenomenon examined was the experience of participating in a revitalization planning process in a low-wealth neighborhood as described by neighborhood residents.

Procedures

Research context

This study was conducted as part of a larger neighborhood-transformation planning project design to create a neighborhood plan built on resident-identified assets and challenges. The planning initiative was federally funded through the U.S. Department of Housing and Urban Development and led by the city and the city's community development department. The research team comprised residents, other community stakeholders, and university personnel. Members of the research team collectively made decisions regarding the research design and execution. The shared expertise of community members and university personnel allowed the research team to develop an approach to data collection and analysis that balanced community authenticity with scientific rigor (Brown & Stalker, 2018). Community members and partners contributed in-depth knowledge of the culture, strengths, and challenges of the neighborhood to the research while university personnel contributed expertise in research methods, analysis, and resource acquisition. This research took place in a low-wealth neighborhood in a mid-sized southern US city. Of the approximately 5000 residents, over 99%

were Black or African American, and over 45% lived below the poverty line. The trajectory of this neighborhood was shaped by policies and laws that disproportionately impacted communities of color including redlining, exclusion of domestic workers from labor laws, and separate but equal education. Compared to similar white neighborhoods, residents in this predominantly Black neighborhood had fewer opportunities to own property, get paid for overtime, and access high quality education, resulting in less wealth and opportunity. This urban community was located adjacent to the City's central business district, and was characterized by blighted and abandoned properties, chronically low-performing schools, and high incidents of crime and victimization.

Participants

We recruited participants for the focus groups through word of mouth and fliers posted in civic centers, churches, convenience stores, and housing complexes in the neighborhood. We employed a purposeful sampling technique (Creswell, 2007) to recruit individuals who lived in the neighborhood and were of different ages and genders. All members of the focus groups lived in the two contiguous neighborhoods targeted for the revitalization planning effort. A total of 24 residents participated in three focus groups. Participants ranged in age from 33 to 76 years, and 14 identified as female and 10 identified as male. All participants identified as Black or African American. The facilitators of the focus groups were both white females.

Data collection

Data were collected through a series of three semi-structured focus groups (see Table 1 for guiding questions) and through examination of a planning document previously developed for this community. The purpose of the focus groups was to capture the residents' perceptions of what facilitated or impeded community change. Participation in the focus groups was voluntary and participants were not compensated. The previous planning effort emphasized a "People First" approach, soliciting input from neighborhood residents and stakeholders through meetings, retreats, and design charettes. The previous planning document included planning notes and quotes from these meetings (Mitchell, 2007).

To ensure accessibility, the focus groups sites were centrally located in the neighborhoods. Each focus group met for approximately 1.5 h, and the rooms were set up with chairs in a large circle and a table in the center. Information about the purpose of the research and the initiative was presented, and informed consent was read aloud and

Table 1. Focus group interview guiding questions.

Question 1: How would you describe your neighborhood? What are the most important things to you that currently make you proud of your neighborhood?
Question 2: What is missing in your neighborhood that you think would make your life better?
Question 3: How do you feel about a process to come up with a plan to make improvements in your neighborhood?
Question 4: What opportunities are there for getting involved with civic, faith-based, and social organizations? Others? What makes you want (or not want) to participate in these groups?
Question 5: What does "trust" mean to you? What people or groups do you trust most?

Table 2. Select significant statements of residents and formulated meanings.

Significant statement	Formulated meaning
Don't do "to" the community. Do "with" and "for" the community.	Residents want to be included as partners in planning and decision-making for their neighborhood.
Can the city be counted on to step up and improve infrastructure?	Residents question the commitment of the city to improving their neighborhood.
So little has been done for so long, without the best interests of the entire community at hand. Residents have a lack of hope and trust.	The community has been neglected and ignored. Residents are losing hope. Residents distrust the intentions of outsiders.
A plan is meaningless unless it is implemented. Identifying and nurturing leaders that understand and respect [the neighborhood]'s history as well as its future is essential to moving the plan forward.	No more plans without action. Build capacity of leaders from within the community. Need leaders who understand the potential of the neighborhood to create meaningful change.

signatures obtained prior to launching into the discussion. The IRB of the researchers' university approved the study procedures, and each focus group was audio-recorded and transcribed verbatim.

Data analysis

We followed Colaizzi's (1978) structured approach to phenomenology and used NVivo10 for data analysis. Focus group transcripts and the planning documents and appendices were read repeatedly before extracting significant statements (Colaizzi, 1978) related to the participants' perceptions of facilitators and barriers to neighborhood transformation. From the three focus groups and two planning documents, 254 significant statements were extracted. We examined these significant statements to construct their formulated meanings (see Table 2 for examples). These formulated meanings identified key meanings in the significant statements (Colaizzi, 1978), and these were condensed and arranged into clusters using nodes. Five themes emerged from the analysis and were developed into a narrative. This narrative was then reduced and the results were presented to participants and other residents for validation.

Credibility and trustworthiness

The criteria of credibility, consistency, and objectivity (Lincoln & Guba, 1985; Riddick & Russell, 2014) were used to address rigor and trustworthiness of this research process. Prolonged engagement with the community and many of the study participants; triangulation among data from the focus groups and documents from the previous planning process; and member and community checks strengthened credibility (Lincoln & Guba, 1985). During member/community checks, neighborhood residents – some of whom were focus group participants – reviewed the findings from the focus groups and validated the themes. Peer debriefing with colleagues familiar with qualitative research was used to address issues of consistency and objectivity and helped validate both the research process and the emerging themes (Lincoln & Guba, 1985).

Table 3. Five theme clusters with examples of associated meanings.

Theme 1: Trust and mistrust	Lack of trust in general
	Mistrust for outsiders and their intentions
	Need to nurture trust for residents to believe and have hope
	Need to build trust
	Lack of trust in political leadership
	Lack of trust in police
Theme 2: Resident-driven transformation	Nurture the skills of the residents to build a sustainable and prosperous neighborhood
	Focus on the people, and their skills and strengths
	People hold the power to rebuild and the ability to shape its future
	Need to help people recognize their own skills and power
	Need to empower and motivate residents
	People feel disempowered
	Lack of motivation from people who need support the most
	People need to be included
	Neighbors are strength of neighborhood
Theme 3: Sense of community and cohesion	Promote the character, history, and spirit of the neighborhood
	Build community pride and a sense of community
	Neighborhood events and activities create community Strategies must encourage building and nurturing relationships
	Neighbors value a strong sense of community
	Love of community and one another and connections between church, school, and friendship are characteristic of the neighborhood
	Residents are committed to their neighborhood
	Residents want a sense of community
	Residents value the soul and history of the neighborhood and that bonds them to one another
Theme 4: Engagement and collective action	Lack of participation and motivation
	Need for key leadership to motivate people
	Need for effective communication
	Need to move in positive direction
	Need effective strategies for ongoing collaboration
	Lack of collaboration among outside partners
	Lack of collaboration between residents and leaders
	Change is possible when residents work together for a common purpose
	Residents work together to build and improve community
Theme 5: Openness to transformation	Need to build hope in the future
	Spirit of hopelessness and helplessness among neighbors
	Need to respect history as well as future to move forward
	Skepticism about neighborhood improvements and its impact on the residents
	Feeling let down from broken promises from the past
	Belief in possibility of transformation
	Readiness for transformation

Findings

Five themes related to factors that facilitated or impeded neighborhood transformation emerged from the analysis (see Table 3 for themes and associated formulated meanings). The five themes were: (1) trust; (2) resident-driven transformation; (3) sense of community and cohesion; (4) engagement and collective action; and (5) openness to transformation.

Theme 1: Trust and mistrust

Concern about trust and mistrust was mentioned repeatedly, particularly with regard to outsider relationships. Trust in general was described as a community concern as one resident stated, "There is a lack of trust internally and externally," and another described the current conditions as a "spirit of hopelessness and lack of trust." Several residents expressed mistrust for planning processes that were focused on the neighborhood stating, "The lack of trust in the neighborhood is a threat" and "everyone's opinion must be included." Other residents also connected trust to relationships, engagement, and involvement, stating the need for project leaders to "help build trust," "build relationships and trust," and "provide existing residents with meaningful input to the plan." One resident suggested, "The way to build trust is to have open networks of communication." Several residents connected trust to the concept of empowerment. One example of this expressed in the words of a resident was "the people recognize that they have strengths, skills, and resources that can be drawn upon if trust is nurtured."

Along with trust in general, residents shared concerns about trust relationships with local law enforcement. One resident stated there was an "overwhelming presence of open crime and lack of cooperation from city officials and the police department." Resident trust in police by the community was mixed, as the recently initiated neighborhood policing program was described as "building trust," while others stated that the "relations between residents and police need improving," and there should be "regular meetings between neighborhood district police and residents." One resident stated, "We need police protection, and right now our police – unfortunately – you don't see them until after something happens."

Another sub-theme of trust that emerged was trust of local government and city officials. Several residents expressed concern over the city's commitment to their neighborhood, and the authenticity of any expressed commitment – that promises were made but investments in change have not been followed through with. Statements that captured these concerns included, "Can the city be counted on?," "The good 'ole [sic] boy political system is a threat," and from the previous planning document "A major concern raised in the planning process was a lack of trust – whether the plan will be followed by political leaders, whether a sufficient investment of money and time will be made, and whether the residents – at the grass roots level – will be involved when decisions that affect their lives are made." When speaking about the city council, one neighbor stated, "It has a lot to do with trust," and "I've gone to meeting after meeting after meeting. Filled out form after form after form. Did they turn around and do something?"

Theme 2: Resident-driven transformation

Focus group participants identified neighborhood residents as a key factor in both the current strengths of the neighborhood and in the process of community change. They indicated that successful neighborhood transformation would require building on neighbors' existing strengths and addressing current feelings of disempowerment and a lack of motivation among those who most need support. During the focus groups, residents discussed that to "nurture a better future," there was a need to recognize the "skills in [the neighborhood]" to "build people ... to improve [the community]." It was important for "the people who work and reside in the neighborhood to lead its rebuilding." It was shared there was a need "to get people to realize that the only power to change the neighborhood is held by them," and that "it will be the people that will rebuild the area." "The interests and needs of the people of [the neighborhood] –

people first – at its center," was a message shared by one neighbor, emphasizing the importance of capturing "the desires and priorities of the residents" in plans for neighborhood transformation.

Strategies to improve collaboration and promote a resident-driven transformation process that were suggested included a need for building "effective community between leadership" so that people "could work together [toward] a positive direction." One resident stated that "no one is an island," and "the sum of the whole is greater than its parts." Content analysis of the planning document uncovered the need for collaboration to build community as "leaders' working together empowers the neighborhood to act effectively." Mobilizing the community, including residents in planning, and building "consensus and movement in a positive direction" were important to residents regarding collaboration and building up the community; one neighbor shared that "they have to come together for a purpose, all the people that's connected – I know it can happen." One resident emphasized, "We've got to build the community back. The census from 1980 or 1990 – population was 17,000. By 2000 it was closer to 6 or 7,000, and that's actually going up a little now, but we've got to get people back in the community."

Theme 3: Sense of community and cohesion

The theme of *sense of community and cohesion* reflects both the importance of the existing sense of community in the neighborhoods and the need to further develop neighborhood pride and connections. Neighbors value their existing connections, rooted in the rich history of the neighborhoods, and look forward to creating more. Residents described numerous strengths of the neighborhood as "my neighbors," "friendship," "love," "connectivity between neighbors, schools and churches," and "the feeling of the familiar and all the memories my family has created." Residents felt it was important to "nurture connections" and to "build relationships that will allow us to work together" to enact meaningful change.

Focus group participants expressed that "neighborhood activities and events help to create and build community." The neighborhood transformation plan should be designed in such a way that establishes "meeting places for community" and facilitates "pride building, festivals, celebrate[s] skills and talents, old coming together with the young, cultural arts, athletics" and "where people from the neighborhood can participate." The planning document described the impact of engagement through "cultural and community events" as an opportunity to "strengthen a sense of community" and "build pride."

"A neighborhood is much more than the homes within its borders." In talking about their neighborhood, residents wanted a "simple life, a place for ordinary people" and a "sense of community and neighborhood, real common life." One resident said "[the neighborhood] is about people and community – focus on people first." Another described the neighborhoods as having "a soul – family and community where everyone knows everyone." Residents wanted to see a "spirit of family," with a "community, people focus." The planning document described residents' views of [the neighborhood] historically "as a place where neighbors knew each other and helped each other out." More recently, the community was concerned that "crime and lack of a sense of safety in the neighborhood keeps people closed – physically and spiritually." One resident stated the need for commitment "to community building, going door to door, helping out neighbors in need and becoming friends," and another "a neighborhood of people that care and want to change their lives and [their neighborhood]." Another resident stated "the culture" and "sense of community" was what makes the neighborhood unique.

Theme 4: Engagement and collective action

Neighbors indicated that their sense of community could create collective action that would generate change, but there are barriers to overcome. Translating the individual assets and sense of community into participation would require overcoming a lack of collaboration among outside partners and among residents and leaders, and a lack of empowerment and engagement among residents. Effective communication and effective strategies for ongoing collaboration would be key to overcoming these challenges. Residents said the planning process "requires collaboration" and suggested the need for "neighborhood groups that work together, care for each other" and have a "spirit of volunteerism." In a focus group, residents shared "we're trying to bring this neighborhood back," and the need was expressed for "action that is focused, committed, collaborative and inclusive." The planning document pointed to the need for leadership to "guide their conversations forward into doable actions." Residents did not want outsiders to come in and transform their community without their input and leadership, and one neighbor stated, "Don't do TO the community; do WITH and FOR the community" (emphasis from resident).

Patterns of empowerment were captured through language that conveyed the feeling of hopelessness experienced by some residents, and several residents stated they once had hope in the past but no longer do since "nothing has been done" and "so little has been done for so long." One resident said, "A lot of them think they don't have a voice. And it's not worth me coming." Many residents shared the concern that people felt disempowered and therefore were not motivated to participate in conversations regarding neighborhood transformation, and one noted that "this is what it takes [to improve the neighborhood] – it is just a shame this room is not crowded with concerned adults, and you know it's sad." Another neighbor said, "The problem is an overwhelming poverty rate and not much of a political voice and that's what I'm worried about." "If you don't have power behind your name, you're not gonna do stuff."

One resident said that "citizen involvement is the key" to building community. Several residents expressed concern that there was "very low turnout" in neighborhood and community events and meetings" and that "more people should be involved." "How many people [are] in this area? Over 100, right? 200? See the problem is – people who need the services the most are the ones that don't even bother to come." One resident said, "You gotta find some way to motivate folks to come in the first place," and another shared, "We live in a neighborhood where there are lots of people for some reason or other don't know the value of coming [to community meetings]."

> They've been programmed in a way – sorry to say it. I'm going to talk about my neighborhood and we all know it's true – but they've been programmed – some of them – they've

been programmed in a certain way that if there ain't nothing out here for us, personally, then it's not worth me coming [to community meetings].

Many residents cited a "need to get the parents involved" in "their kids' education," as "hardly any parents [come] out" for school events. Suggestions for improving participation and engagement included utilizing a "targeted effort to get the residents involved" because "if we're trying to improve the quality of life for people that live [here] then things have to be targeted." The churches in the community were discussed as a potential avenue for improving involvement, as one resident explained, "With 41 churches we have 41 ministers – they have flocks, and they need to reach their flocks; if we can motivate the leaders, we can motivate the flocks." Some other examples of the need for collaboration included the comment that "Resource agencies and organizations available inside or outside the neighborhood do not work together – there is a lack of collaboration," and a need "to improve collaboration between the 51 neighborhood churches and the programs and services they provide."

Residents spoke of the opportunities and services provided through the numerous neighborhood churches. Many viewed the churches as an asset to the community and a place that connected people, but shared that the experience was not the same for all residents in the neighborhood. One resident observed: "What we gotta do – it's complex. Look at the churches in the community who are doing things. But they can't do it alone. If they do then it's done in isolation. It creates an isolation effect." Another said, "If you're not a part of those churches – then they aren't connected – they won't use services, they don't think they are for them." "You know what it's all about – churches take care of their own. If you're in the church then you'll get taken care of, but that's not always the case. Because unless you pay your tithe, if you don't pay your tithe, then you are going to get overlooked."

Theme 5: Openness to transformation

When asked about openness to transformation and revitalization of their neighborhood, residents commonly responded by reflecting on experiences and feelings of both skepticism and optimism for the future. "Efforts are needed to lift up existing residents to build hope," one resident said. Participants revealed a mixture of hope, skepticism, and resignation about the future of the neighborhood, which was once "the heart of the black community" in the city. One resident wanted to see improvements to the area, but to "keep [the neighborhood name], [the neighborhood name]." Another asked, "A lot of the love once in [the neighborhood] is no longer there – how do we rehabilitate the people for new opportunities?" The planning document cited the sentiment that "so little has been done for so long … without the best interests of the community" that "residents have a lack of hope and trust in change in their neighborhood."

> Our neighborhood is better now than what it used to be. [The neighborhood] is like any other neighborhood. I think the reasons people don't want to be in our neighborhood is [sic] because of the shotgun houses and the people doing drugs. If we get rid of the people doing drugs we can have a better neighborhood.

Residents had questions about how neighborhood improvements would be possible "without driving out any of the current residents." As one neighbor said, "It's clear that improving the neighborhood will increase the cost of living." Skepticism for the future surfaced in comments such as "Don't let this plan follow so many others that displace existing residents" and "We want to know what is going on – we've been built up and built up and nothing has happened – change hasn't happened." Residents shared the need to promote the people in the neighborhood to realize meaningful change, and that there was a need for "people moving in a forward direction so that the community could also move forward." One resident described the need for community mobilization as, "I've seen this neighborhood going from good to, you know, now it's pretty much kind of bad – it's kind of up to us to do whatever it takes to help it get back where it was or even better than what it is." Some residents expressed "hope of a better future," and that they "would like to see it come back;" another resident saw "the potential in the community," so long as people were committed to "staying focused, committed, and open." One neighbor stated, "I have a real passion for what's happening and what's going to happen in the community." Another stated, "We have to share with the younger generations the legacy that was once here, the history. At one point in time it was the community of choice to live. And it can return to that."

Discussion

In this study, we examined facilitators and barriers to neighborhood change identified by residents in a low-wealth community engaged in a neighborhood planning process. The five themes of (1) trust and mistrust, (2) resident-driven transformation; (3) sense of community and cohesion; (4) engagement and collective action; and (5) openness to transformation reflect neighbors' insights into the planning and transformation process.

The first theme identified sources and consequences of *Trust and Mistrust*. Similar to previous research findings in low-wealth communities, participants in this study discussed a lack of trust within their neighborhood between and among residents, including a mistrust of external institutions and organizations, in particular law enforcement and political leadership. Participants identified reasons for this lack of trust and mistrust and presented various mechanisms to build trust. Lower levels of trust both among residents and of outsiders often characterize low-wealth neighborhoods. Social disorganization and isolation are cited as common characteristics of high poverty neighborhoods (Wilson, 1987), and low levels of trust within a community have been associated with social disorganization (Ross, Mirowsky, & Pribesh, 2001). Social disadvantage can further generate feelings of mistrust (Aiyer et al., 2015; Ross et al., 2001).

A history of discrimination, sense of powerlessness, and broken promises from outsiders in power and those who come to "rescue" the neighborhood can contribute greatly to generating mistrust (Geller et al., 2014). Previous studies have shown that perceived powerlessness is related to experiences of diminished social trust (Alesina & Ferrara, 2002; Ross et al., 2001). Residents in this study were understandably leery of outside individuals and groups who arrive with promises of improving the neighborhood and solving their problems. Scholars and revitalization planners should be cautious to not make promises that cannot be kept, as trust takes time to develop and is difficult to repair once broken. There was a collective desire for meaningful inclusion and partnership in community transformation efforts. Building trust within the community and effectively engaging residents in decision-making roles related to transformation is necessary to facilitate readiness for revitalization.

The second theme focused on *Resident Driven Transformation*. Residents of low-wealth, under-resourced communities are sometimes viewed as being in need of rescue by more powerful, "expert" outsiders (Rothman, 2008). Contradicting this, the participants in this study identified the existing strengths and skills of neighborhood residents and the importance of building on those assets to create sustainable change. Congruent with previous literature regarding the importance of community-based leadership in creating and sustaining change (MacPhee et al., 2017; Maton, 2008), residents explicitly stated that the power to transform the neighborhood and lead the process resided within the residents. They also highlighted the importance of community leadership and involvement in sustaining the initiative. Failing to recognize neighborhood residents as the key resources to their community, as experts regarding their community, and as partners for change will result in the inability to achieve success and sustainability in neighborhood improvement efforts.

In addition to identifying individual skills and strengths as assets, participants identified their existing *Sense of Community and Cohesion* as a primary strength and essential aspect of transforming the community. Participants in this study described the strong internal bonds and a lack of connections outside the neighborhood. They expressed the importance of further strengthening the bonds between neighbors and developing connections with key partners from outside the neighborhood. This finding was especially interesting as it contrasted with statements regarding a lack of trust among and between neighbors. One resident suggested getting rid of the "people doing drugs" would improve the community. Others suggested parents who did not come to meetings were not engaged in their children's education. This *us* versus *them* mentality could represent a bias in the participant sample, where harder to reach populations including residents working multiple jobs, single parents, and those engaged in certain types of substance use may not have been represented. The polarization of certain groups of residents by other residents can present detrimental roadblocks to advancing community change. Participants identified a lack of trust and inclusion of all voices of residents in change processes as the greatest potential barrier or "threat" to community transformation. Leadership of community transformation initiatives must be prepared to delve deep into the root causes of strained relationships among and between community groups to understand the various drivers (e.g. emotions, experiences, perceptions, beliefs) of these "othering" statements. Illuminating the root causes of these divides can allow for the creation of pathways toward communication, reconciliation, and healing that can contribute to building the community's capacity for readiness for change. Strategies that build particularized trust within and among community members can create cohesion across groups that are currently somewhat divided and reduce or eliminate the exclusion or "othering" that can occur.

Participants recognized the potential of their sense of community to generate *Collective Action and Engagement*. They highlighted the importance of that action in ensuring that any changes were responsive to the needs and desires of the community. Previous research has indicated that a community's perception of its own collective efficacy can result in positive, actionable change and foster resilient communities (Bandura, 2000). The residents identified challenges to collective action, including a sense of disenfranchisement among neighborhood residents. The mix of feelings regarding the potential for neighborhood change reflected the strengths and challenges of the neighborhood. As demonstrated in the findings, some participants expressed frustration that more of their neighbors were not coming to meetings and were not actively invested in the process to improve their community. The finger pointing by some participants toward others in the community may indicate the need for leadership development and capacity building training with a focus on empathy building. Certain voices in the community may not be heard in these types of planning processes because they are not often at the table for a variety of reasons. Leadership development efforts are needed that focus on intentionally recruiting residents from differing backgrounds to develop trust, cohesion, engagement, and openness to change among residents.

The final theme addressed the neighborhood's *Openness to Transformation*. Residents described openness to transformation as both a facilitator of transformation (e.g. when openness is present) and a barrier to transformation (e.g. when there is a need for it). Participants spoke of their desire to see positive changes in the neighborhood and hope that it could return to the vibrant area it had been historically. Residents expressed concern as to whether people with the greatest need for services, supports, and pathways to opportunities associated with transformation would be motivated to become involved in driving change for their community. At the same time, they expressed resignation to the potential that the neighborhood would continue to decline, and fears of displacement of existing residents if the area were improved. This fear of gentrification reflects the reality experienced by many under-resourced neighborhoods when positive changes occur (Marcuse, 2016), that if things improve they will be forced out of their own communities. These concerns illuminate the need to consider power dynamics in community development initiatives. Disempowerment inhibits positive community change and false promises from local leadership or outsiders leads to disempowerment and a sense of hopelessness for the future. Participants repeatedly expressed the viewpoint that change can only successfully be achieved if it begins from within – led by the people, building on the skills and strengths of the people – "people first."

As residents see themselves as the key facilitator of positive change, revitalization initiatives should allow for residents to be meaningfully engaged in leadership positions. Capacity building, leadership training, trust building, and training and support for those most in need in the community are critical steps toward shifting the power balance that will afford community members to fully participate and recognize their own power in shaping the future of their communities. When community members work together with a shared purpose and have developed the capacity and leadership skills necessary to take action, collective empowerment occurs (Aiyer et al., 2015; Coleman, 1968; Maton, 2008).

It is important to consider the findings of this study in the context of its limitations. This study addressed only one community. While it presents an in-depth examination of perceptions of facilitators of and barriers to change in these neighborhoods, experiences in other neighborhoods, even those with similar demographics, may be quite different. Additionally, while participants reflected the age and gender demographics of the neighborhood, variables including educational attainment, homeowner status, previous involvement in the planning effort, length of time in the neighborhood, and family status (e.g. partnered vs. single, children vs. no children) were not captured. Other residents in the neighborhood may have had different views and experiences. For example, those who chose to participate in the focus groups may have valued and participated in community engagement more than those who did not. Therefore, more research is needed to fully understand the process of change in neighborhoods undergoing transformation efforts.

Conclusion and implications

This study illuminates the importance of community empowerment, engagement, trust, cohesion, and leadership as essential factors necessary for successful neighborhood revitalization. It is critical to include the voices of residents in community change processes and research to understand the actions needed to facilitate positive community change. By centering the knowledge and opinions of residents at the core of place-based community development initiatives, communities will be more readily positioned to achieve change that is meaningful, realistic, and sustainable.

Based on findings from this study, it is important for community development practitioners, community organizers, and urban planners to invest time and effort in building trust within a community before planning for community improvements can take place. Some methods of cultivating outsider/insider trust include a focus on open communication and continuous dialog, recognizing and valuing the expertise that already exists within a community, keeping promises and following through, and creating inclusive processes. Even (and perhaps especially) in distressed communities, residents desire to be a partner in the process of collective decision-making about improvements for their own communities. In addition to building trust, building capacity through leadership development and strategies for fostering social cohesion facilitate a community's readiness to engage in meaningful change activities.

Scholars, community practitioners, and urban planners would benefit by recognizing the value that a resident-driven approach lends to the community change process; after all, residents are experts with lived experience on matters in their own community. Building the knowledge of local governments to understand the need for shifting power dynamics so that residents have a true voice at the table, and building capacity to embrace a community-driven agenda and recognize residents as experts with skills, knowledge, and expertise to contribute to the change process, can be a key catalyst for positive transformation. Enlisting residents as partners at the table guiding and participating in decision-making about the future direction of their neighborhood is the path to building the community up in a positive direction, toward a healthy, sustainable community.

More research should be conducted to understand facilitators of and barriers to neighborhood change to identify best practices to inform future practice and policy decisions. Community engagement is a loosely defined term and subject to the interpretation of local leadership. It is recommended that standards for authentic community engagement are established, and that these standards are established with meaningful input from residents in low-wealth neighborhoods that are targeted for place-based transformation. Future research should examine the polarization that can exist within marginalized communities among resident groups to understand more fully how this impacts community functioning, healing, and change. Additionally, as suggested in research recommendations, formalized measures for meaningful resident engagement should be derived to assist local leadership in evaluating the process and impact of engagement activities. Including residents in decision-making about establishing standards for policy and programming regarding authentic resident engagement, and in the development of instrumentation to evaluate the practice of resident engagement are important steps that would model meaningful community engagement practice in community development.

Acknowledgments

This work was supported in part by the U.S. Department of Housing and Urban Development, Office of University Partnerships, (Grant Number H-21640SG). Points of view or opinions in this document are those of the authors and do not necessarily represent the official position or policies of the U.S. Department of Housing and Urban Development.

Disclosure statement

No potential conflict of interest was reported by the authors.

Funding

This work was supported by the Office of University Partnerships [H-21640SG].

ORCID

Mary Ellen Brown http://orcid.org/0000-0002-1916-5863

References

Ahsan, N. (2008). *Sustaining neighborhood change: The power of resident leadership, social networks, and community mobilization*. Baltimore, MD: The Annie E. Casey Foundation.
Aiyer, S.M., Zimmerman, M.A., Morrel-Samuels, S., & Reischl, T.M. (2015). From broken windows to busy streets: A community empowerment perspective. *Health Education & Behavior*, 42, 137–147. doi:10.1177/1090198114558590
Alesina, A., & Ferrara, E.L. (2002). Who trusts others? *Journal of Public Economics*, 85, 207–234. doi:10.1016/S0047-2727(01)00084-6
Arnstein, S. (1969). A ladder of citizen participation. *Journal of the American Institute of Planners*, 35 (4), 216–224. doi:10.1080/01944366908977225
Bandura, A. (2000). Exercise of human agency through collective efficacy. *Current Directions in Psychological Science*, 9(3), 75–78. doi:10.1111/1467-8721.00064
Blackwell, A.G. (2012). America's tomorrow: Race, place, and the equity agenda. In N.O. Andrews & D.J. Erickson (Eds.), *Investing in what works for America's communities* (pp. 133–139). San Francisco, CA: Federal Reserve Bank of San Francisco.
Brown, M.E., & Stalker, K.C. (2018). Assess connect transform in our neighborhood: A framework for engaging community partners in CBPR research designs. *Action Research Journal*. doi:10.1177/1476750318789484
Brueggemann, W. (2014). *The practice of macro social work* (4th ed.). Belmont, CA: Brooks/Cole.
Carrasco, M.A., & Bilal, U. (2016). A sign of the times: To have or to be? Social capital or social cohesion? *Social Science & Medicine*, 159, 127–131. doi:10.1016/j.socscimed.2016.05.012

Chaskin, R.J. (2001). Building community capacity: A definitional framework and case studies from a comprehensive community initiative. *Urban Affairs Review*, 36, 291–323. doi:10.1177/10780870122184876

Cheezum, R.R., Coombe, C.M., Israel, B.A., McGranaghan, R.J., Burris, A.N., Grant-White, S., & Anderson, M. (2013). Building community capacity to advocate for policy change: An outcome evaluation of the neighborhoods working in partnership project in Detroit. *Journal of Community Practice*, 21, 228–247. doi:10.1080/10705422.2013.811624

Christens, B.D., & Inzeo, P.T. (2015). Widening the view: Situating collective impact among frameworks for community-led change. *Community Development*, 46, 420–435. doi:10.1080/15575330.2015

Cnaan, R.A., & Rothman, J. (1995). Locality development and the building of community. In J. R. Rothman, J.L. Erlich, & J.E. Tropman (Eds.), *Strategies of community intervention: Macro practice* (pp. 241–257). Itasca, IL: F. E. Peacock Publishers.

Colaizzi, P.F. (1978). Psychological research as the phenomenologist views it. In R.S. Valle & M. King (Eds.), *Existential-phenomenological alternatives for psychology* (pp. 48–59). New York: Oxford University Press.

Coleman, J.S. (1968). Community disorganization and conflict. In R.K. Mert (Ed.), *Contemporary social problems* (pp. 657–708). San Francisco, CA: Harcourt Brace Jovanovich.

Creswell, J.W. (2007). *Qualitative inquiry and research design: Choosing among five approaches* (2nd ed. ed.). Thousand Oaks, CA: Sage.

Derr, V., & Kovacs, I.G. (2017). How participatory processes impact children and contribute to planning: A case study of neighborhood design from Boulder, Colorado, USA. *Journal of Urbanism: International Research on Placemaking and Urban Sustainability*, 10, 29–48. doi:10.1080/17549175.2015

Douglas, J.A., Grills, C.T., Villanueva, S., & Subica, A. (2016). Empowerment praxis: Community organizing to redress systemic health disparities. *American Journal of Community Psychology*, 58, 1–11. doi:10.1002/ajcp.12101

Dreier, P. (1996). Community empowerment strategies: The limits and potential of community organizing in urban neighborhoods. *Cityscape*, 2, 121–159. Retrieved from https://www.jstor.org/stable/20868413

Fudge, K. (2011). Choice neighborhoods: History and HOPE. *Evidence Matters*, Winter, 1–7. Retrieved from https://www.huduser.gov/portal/periodicals/em/winter11/highlight1.html

Geller, J.D., Doykos, B., Craven, K., Bess, K.D., & Nation, M. (2014). Engaging residents in community change: The critical role of trust in the development of a promise neighborhood. *Teachers College Record*, 116(4), 1–42.

Guba, E., Lincoln, Y.S., & Lynham, S. (2017). Paradigmatic controversies, contradictions, and emerging confluences. In N.K. Denzin & Y.S. Lincoln (Eds.), *The SAGE handbook of qualitative research* (5th ed., pp. 108–150). Thousand Oaks, CA: Sage Publishing.

Hyman, J.B. (2002). Exploring social capital and civic engagement to create a framework for community building. *Applied Developmental Science*, 6, 196–202. doi:10.1207/S1532480XADS0604_6

Katznelson, I. (2005). *When affirmative action was white: An untold history of racial inequality in twentieth-century America*. New York: W. W. Norton & Company.

Keita, A.D., Hannon, L., Buys, D., Casazza, K., & Clay, O. (2016). Surrounding community residents' expectations of HOPE VI for their community, health, and physical activity. *Journal of Community Practice*, 24, 18–37. doi:10.1080/10705422.2015.1129005

Kretzmann, J., & McKnight, J.P. (1996). Assets-based community development. *National Civic Review*, 23–29. doi:10.1002/ncr.4100850405

Lincoln, Y., & Guba, E. (1985). *Naturalistic inquiry*. Beverly Hills, CA: Sage Publications.

Lindsey, E., Stajduhar, K., & McGuinness, L. (2001). Examining the process of community development. *Journal of Advanced Nursing*, 33, 828–835. doi:10.1046/j.1365-2648.2001.01722x

MacPhee, D., Forlenza, E., Christensen, K., & Prendergast, S. (2017). Promotion of civic engagement with the family leadership training institute. *American Journal of Community Psychology, 60*, 568–583. doi:10.1002/ajcp.12205

Marcuse, P. (2016). Gentrification, social justice, and personal ethics. *International Journal of Urban and Regional Research, 39*, 1263–1269. doi:10.1111/1468-2427.12319

Maton, K.I. (2008). Empowering community settings: *Agents of individual development, community betterment, and positive social change. American Journal of Community Psychology, 41*, 4–21. doi:10.1007/s10464-007-9148-6

Midgley, J., & Livermore, M. (2005). Development theory and community practice. In M. Weil (Ed.), *The handbook of community practice* (pp. 153–168). Thousand Oaks, CA: Sage.

Mitchell, K. (2007). *AllendaleONE: Part of the "total" commitment neighborhood initiative.* Shreveport, LA: MHSM Architects.

Price, H. (2011). A seat at the table: Place-based urban policy and community engagement. *Harvard Journal of African American Public Policy, 17*, 65–73.

Pyles, L. (2009). *Progressive community organizing: A critical approach for a globalizing world.* New York, NY: Routledge.

Riddick, C.C., & Russell, R.V. (2014). *Research methods: How to conduct research in recreation, parks, sport and tourism* (2nd ed.). Champaign, IL: Sagamore Publishing Co.

Ross, C.E., Mirowsky, J., & Pribesh, S. (2001). Powerlessness and the amplification of threat: Neighborhood disadvantage, disorder, and mistrust. *American Sociological Review, 66*, 568–591. jstor.org/stable/3088923

Rothman, J. (2000). Collaborative self-help community development: When is the strategy warranted? *Journal of Community Practice, 7*, 89–105. doi:10.1300/J125v07n02_05

Rothman, J. (2008). Multi modes of community intervention. In J. Rothman, J. Erlich, & J. Tropman (Eds.), *Strategies of community intervention* (7th ed., pp. 141–170). Peosta, IA: Eddie Bowers.

Sandoval, G., & Rongerude, J. (2015). Telling a story that must be heard: Participatory indicators as tools for community empowerment. *Journal of Community Practice, 23*, 403–414. doi:10.1080/10705422.2015.1091417

Van Vliet, W. (1997). *Affordable housing and urban redevelopment in the United States: Learning from failure and success.* Thousand Oaks, CA: Sage.

von Hoffman, A. (2012). The past, present, and future of community development in the United States. In N.O. Andrews & D.J. Erickson (Eds.), *Investing in what works for America's communities* (pp. 10–54). San Francisco, CA: Federal Reserve Bank of San Francisco.

Weil, M. (1996). Community building: Building community practice. *Social Work, 41*, 481–499. doi:10.1093/sw/41.5.481

Wilson, W.J. (1987). *The truly disadvantaged: The inner city, the underclass, and public policy.* Chicago, IL: University of Chicago Press.

Assessing factors influencing political engagement in local communities

Cecil Shelton and Lori Garkovich*

This article explores the relationship between perspectives on community leadership and both attitudes about political participation and actual political engagement. While there is a considerable body of scholarship focused on factors associated with political attitudes and engagement, there is little that addresses the link between views on community leaders and political behavior. This analysis is based on a statewide survey of a random sample of households in Kentucky that was conducted in the summer of 2009. The survey obtained information on several ways in which local people might evaluate their community leaders, as well as information on respondents' political perspectives and actual behavior. The analysis will include both a statewide assessment, as well as a comparison of rural and urban respondents.

Introduction

Democracy requires the participation of its citizens. Trends in political participation, as well as the factors that influence participation, have been the focus of considerable research over time (Caren, 2007; McDonald, 2002, 2012; McDonald & Popkin, 2001; Putnam, 2000; Teixeira, 1987; Verba & Nye, 1972; Zipp, Landerman, & Luebke, 1982; Zukin, Keeter, Andolina, Jenkins, & Delli Carpini, 2006). Two issues get little, if any, attention, though, and these are: differences in political participation by residence and the relationship between people's perceptions of the qualities of local leaders and their political participation. Indeed, Oliver (2000) points out that most of the studies on rural/urban differences in political participation are more than 30 years old, and so the effects of recent population trends on these relationships are relatively unknown.

This article assesses two factors that are missing from much recent scholarship on political participation. First, while there are some studies of local political participation, there is little known about similarities or differences in patterns of rural and urban political participations. Given a long history of research noting the influence of residence on attitudes, beliefs, and behaviors, it would seem that rural and urban residents would view their political leaders, their political attitudes, and their actions differently. Second, there is almost no consideration of how citizens' views on the performance of their leaders might be related to their interest in or willingness to participate in the political realm. This issue goes beyond trust to a broader set of concerns about openness of communication and decision-making, as well as effectiveness of leaders' actions.

---

*Corresponding author. Email: lgarkov@uky.edu

An overview of factors influencing political participation

There are many ways to think about political participation, but the most common is voter turnout. Indeed, Dalton (2008, p. 89) notes that other than voter turnout, there is surprisingly limited longitudinal data on other forms of political participation, either because these types of questions are not asked (e.g. American National Election Survey, Political Action/World Values Survey) or there is no consistency in how the questions are asked (e.g. Citizenship, Involvement, Democracy Survey). Hence, much of the discussion about trends in political participation focuses on voting.

Whether Americans are becoming more or less likely to vote and how these patterns might vary by local, state, or national elections is a point of continued discussion (Caren, 2007; Kornbluh, 2000; McDonald, 2010, 2012; McDonald & Popkin, 2001; Pew Research Center for the People and the Press, 2010). What we do know is that we lag far behind most other democracies in the proportion of citizens voting, and there has been a general decline in the likelihood of Americans engaging in any aspect of political life (See the *2012 Statistical Abstract for the US*, voting trends since 1930 – Table 397; by state since 2004 – Table 398; by US voter characteristics since 1996 – Table 399).

Individual characteristics, ranging from sociodemographic characteristics to attitudes and beliefs, also have been associated with political participation. For example, age, education, and income are positively related to likelihood of voting, as are marital status and residential stability (Binstock, 2006–2007; Gelman, Kenworthy, & Su, 2010; Gimpel, Morris, & Armstrong, 2004; Han, 2008; Martinson & Minkler, 2006; Straughn & Andriot, 2011). Solt (2010, p. 285), in a study of 144 gubernatorial elections, concludes that "citizens of states with greater income inequality are less likely to vote."

There seems to be considerable evidence that education is strongly related to political participation. For example, Han (2008, p. 62) found that "Among sociodemographic indicators, education counted the most in the 2000 presidential election," and that sociodemographic characteristics were stronger predictors of voter turnout than the use of new media. Similarly, Straughn and Andriot (2011, p. 576) find that "education greatly enhances commitment to active citizenship as a civic virtue, which in turn exerts a powerful influence on both grass-roots activism and electoral participation," and that

> commitment to active citizenship is itself a byproduct of other components of civic patriotism (political trust, rights consciousness), as well as political efficacy. With the exception of rights consciousness, all these sources of civic norms increase significantly with level of education.

But, Berinsky and Lenz (2011, pp. 357–358) raise the question of why if education in the USA has been increasing, the rate of voter participation has been declining. Their analysis finds that "education itself has little reliable causal effect on voter turnout."

Socioeconomic status (SES) also has been associated with beliefs and organizational traits that influence political participation (Hoffman & Appiah, 2008; Solt, 2010). For example, it is asserted that the social isolation of the poor and their sense of alienation lead to lower levels of participation (Brady, 2004; Solt, 2008, 2010; Verba & Nye, 1972). Brady, Verba, and Schlozman (1995) look at a variety of resources (i.e. time, money, and civic skills) that are related to political participation. Their research suggests that these resources are distributed differentially among groups based on their SES. Moreover, when they consider three different types of political activity (giving time, donating money, and voting), their analysis shows that each of these political behaviors requires a different configuration of resources.

What do we know about the relationship between residence and political participation? In a study of voter turnout in 332 local elections in 38 large cities from 1979 to 2003, Caren (2007) found that there is considerable variation in turnout between and within cities over the time period, and that voter turnout for mayoral elections averages about one half that for presidential elections over the 25-year period. As Caren (2007, p. 39) comments, "this turnout gap is somewhat counterintuitive" because local governments have the most direct (and daily) impact on voters' lives, while the decisions and actions of the federal government are remote in time, space, and impact.

Surprisingly, there is a limited amount of research on voting patterns of rural and urban residents, especially in the USA (Gimpel & Karnes, 2006; McKee, 2008). At an intuitive level, place of residence should account for differences in both voting and other forms of political engagement. We know that communities differ in political structure, age structure, educational attainment, and a host of attitudes, beliefs, and behaviors. Research also indicates that, "social capital is stronger in rural communities than in urban ones" (Beaudoin & Thorson, 2004, p. 381; Putnam, 2000). The very characteristics of rural communities – smaller population, stronger kinship ties, a tendency to longer durations of residence, and so, longer friendships – should all contribute to stronger community ties and so, a higher level of civic and social engagement.

These characteristics of rural communities should lead to higher levels of political participation. For example, because my rural community is smaller, and I have lived here for a long time, I probably see my elected officials more frequently and in more diverse contexts than if I lived in a larger place. In fact, I am more likely to be a friend, colleague, employee, or neighbor of an elected official if I live in a rural community, and so, it should be easier for me to reach out and talk to my elected officials, and I should have a greater sense of duty or obligation to vote. In other words, in rural communities, there are more and more easily accessible opportunities to be involved in local politics than in larger cities. Edlin, Gelman, and Kaplan (2007) provide another reason why people of smaller communities might be more politically active. From a rational choice perspective, they argue, in smaller communities my participation is more likely to make a difference in outcomes. A $100 contribution to a political campaign may be insignificant in a state or national election, but it will have a huge impact in a local election.

Others have found higher rates of civic and social engagement in rural communities. For example, Oliver (2000) finds that residents of larger cities are much less likely to contact officials, attend community or organizational meetings, or vote in local elections. What is especially interesting is that Oliver (2000, p. 371) finds that "the variations in political participation between the smallest and largest places are often greater than differences between high school and college graduates, homeowners and renters, or single and married people."

Attitudes, such as political efficacy or partisanship, may be explanatory factors in political participation, such that the greater the sense of efficacy or the stronger the sense of partisanship, the higher the voter turnout (Gastil & Xenos, 2010; Kwak, Shah, & Holbert, 2004; Zipp et al., 1982). In an analysis of the 2004 elections, Gastil and Xenos (2010, p. 318) conclude there is a "complex interaction between political and civic attitudes (internal and external efficacy and civic pride and faith) and a range of political and civic behaviors (voting, political action, media use, political/community talk, and group involvement." Anderson (2010) confirms that if an individual feels a sense of attachment or feels their views are valued, this leads to a sense of trust and a greater likelihood that the individual will participate in the political sphere.

Trust is an important component to social capital and has been linked to political attitudes, social capital, and political engagement (Anderson, 2010; Southwell & Pirch, 2003; Uslaner, 1998). Recent research on social capital and political attitudes and activity has focused on the influence of the Internet and other technological innovations on these relationships (Boulianne, 2009; Jennings & Zeitner, 2003; Johnson & Kaye, 2003; Mossberger, Tolbert, & McNeal, 2008; Scheufele & Nisbet, 2002; Wilkins, 2000) and the general conclusion is that

> social capital can be generated in multiple ways, and those mechanisms are changing with social, economic, and technological changes in America. Specifically, virtual civil society has the potential to be an important new source of social capital formation in the contemporary age. (Kittilson & Dalton, 2011, p. 642)

Oxendine et al. (2007, p. 31) examine the role of political context on civic engagement through a comparative analysis of "the influence of rural, local leadership in two Minnesota communities and policies that these elites have developed to bring Internet connectivity to their citizens." Their conclusion is that "context matters greatly. Not only can political context – in the form of governmental institutions, leadership or structural forces – shape the nature of civic activity, but it can also interact with civic activity to modify its effects" (Oxendine et al., 2007, p. 60). This may account for what Morris-Jones (2010, p. 35) found in a case study of a land use conflict. Morris-Jones notes that, "if government is perceived by citizens to be untrustworthy, whether or not the perception is deserved, involvement is not enough to overcome the impact of that perception." Morris-Jones (2010, p. 43) concludes, "Once distrust arises, it is very difficult to overcome."

Not only must one trust individuals within a society, but also they must have trust in institutions and their representatives (Zhang & Chia, 2006). Bowler and Karp (2004) demonstrate that when people have negative attitudes of politicians, these carry over to negative attitudes toward the government. Barisione (2009) argues that the critical question is under what conditions do our perceptions of and attitudes toward leaders make a difference in political behavior. Anderson (2010) notes the importance of political efficacy, or when an individual feels they personally can make an impact through some type of political activity and that the political system is capable of responding to that action. In this situation, individuals will feel empowered which will motivate them to participate in the political sphere. Finally, Piotrowski and Van Ryzin (2007, p. 320), in a study of factors influencing citizen attitudes toward government transparency, particularly at the local level, found that "The more confidence the public has in their local officials, the less they are interested in fiscal, principled, and good government transparency." Yet, they also found that type of community does not predict the demand for transparency. In many ways, Piotrowski and Van Ryzin (2007) explore many of the same factors as this study, but they focus on a different form of political engagement.

But, a recent Pew Research Center for the People and the Press (2010) study found considerable cynicism about the responsiveness of politicians to the views and concerns of "people like me." As a result, a significant number of respondents believe voters do not have much influence on what the government does. Yet, despite these views, a significant majority of respondents also believe in the power of voting with about 90% saying that voting is a "duty" (even though just half say, they actually "always" vote). Nearly 80% of respondents in the Pew survey assert that they are interested in local politics, and less than 30% say that issues discussed in Washington do not affect them.

This suggests that people's attitudes, beliefs, and other social factors may also be influencing political participation. This view reflects a Brookings Institute study (Macedo et al., 2005, p. 1) that concludes that the "erosion of the activities and capacities of citizenship" has left "our civic life impoverished."

Dalton (2008) argues that what is happening is a shift in citizenship norms from a pattern of duty-based citizenship to engaged citizenship. Citizenship norms, according to Dalton (2008, pp. 80–81) are a "shared set of expectations about the citizen's role in politics" that fall into two dimensions:

- Citizen duty, which primarily involves norms related to social order as well as the responsibility to vote; and,
- Engaged citizenship, which includes norms typically associated with solidarity, autonomy, and the other two participation norms.

Dalton (2008, pp. 83–84) suggests that while there has been an erosion of duty-based norms, which tend to be emphasized by older Americans, engaged citizenship norms are increasing in importance, especially among the young and the better educated (see also Hays, 2007). So, what is happening, Dalton (2008, p. 85) argues, is that people are not waiting for elections every four years to influence policy but instead "are seeking more direct means of influencing policy-makers such as working with public interest groups, direct contact, contentious political action, political consumerism and similar methods." Dalton reports data from several studies that show that voting and participation in two or more campaign activities has stayed relatively flat since the 1950s. But, engagement in a broader set of citizenship activities (e.g. membership in at least one public interest group, signed a petition, worked with a group on a local issue) has increased since the 1950s (Dalton, 2008, p. 90). Straughn and Andriot (2011, p. 577) confirm Dalton's analysis, saying,

> Although citizenship norms play a significant role in both types of participation, each also appears to be governed by domain-specific norms of active citizenship. Thus, individuals who regard voting as important for good citizenship need not feel the same way about activities like marching in protest demonstrations, joining online political discussions, or boycotting products for political reasons – and vice versa.

Finally, Dalton explores the relationships between these two norm sets and various types of political participation and the influence of key demographic characteristics (i.e. age, education, gender, and race). He finds that education is positively associated with nearly all types of political activity, while age is positively related to likelihood of direct political action (i.e. voting, donating to campaigns), but negatively related to political protests and Internet-based political activism.

This review of the literature indicates the following factors influence political participation, particularly voting. Socioeconomic characteristics, particularly age, education, and income have been linked to greater political participation. While less clear, intuitively, place of residence should also account for variations in political participation. There also is evidence that civic attitudes, political efficacy, and trust influence political participation. Yet, there are also questions as to how these different factors relate to not only voting, but other types of political activity as well. For the purposes of this study, we will be testing the relative importance of four variable clusters in predicting local political participation. Figure 1 provides a visual representation of these variable clusters.

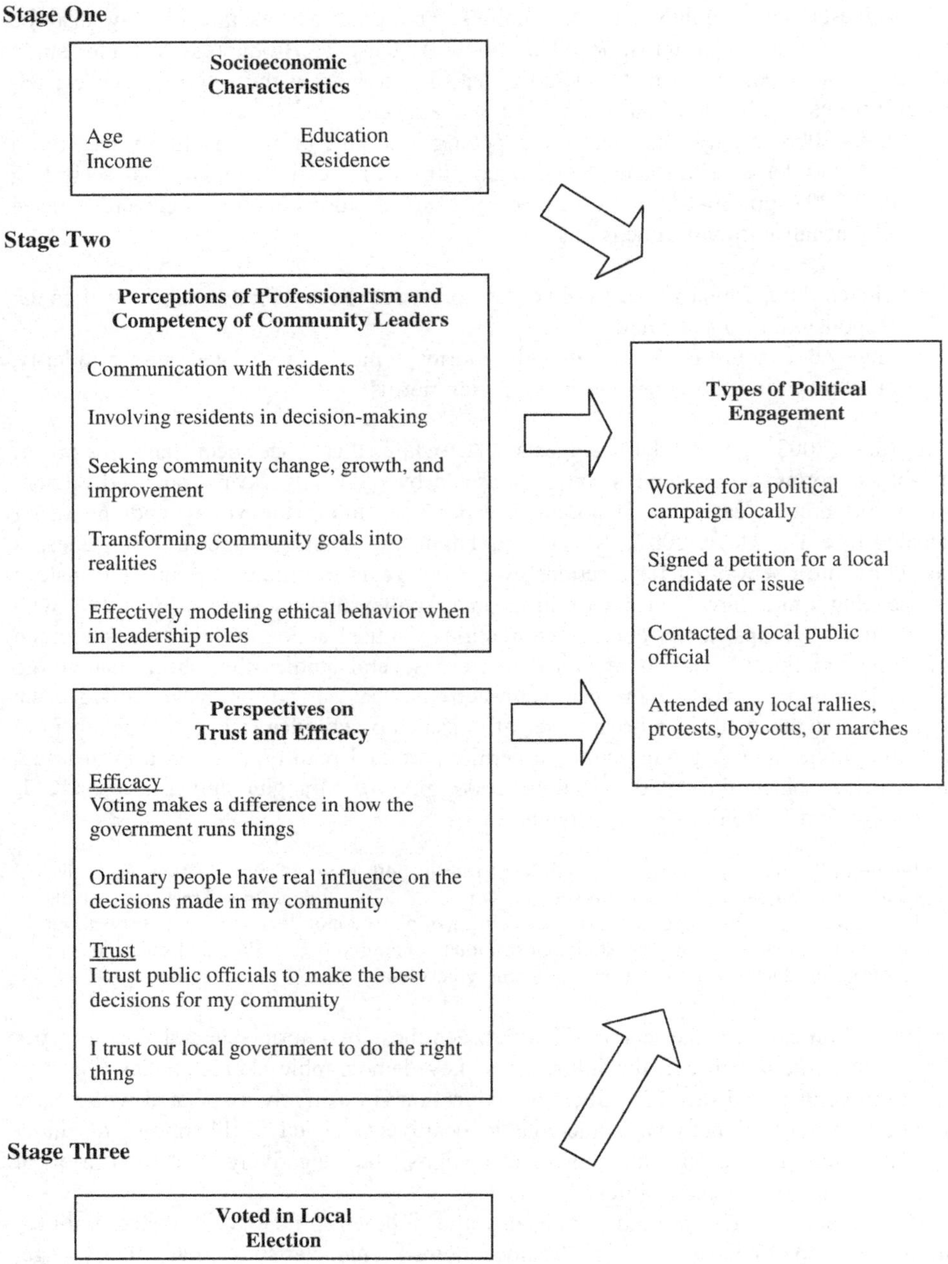

Stage One

```
    Socioeconomic
    Characteristics

Age           Education
Income        Residence
```

Stage Two

```
Perceptions of Professionalism and
Competency of Community Leaders

Communication with residents

Involving residents in decision-making

Seeking community change, growth, and
improvement

Transforming community goals into
realities

Effectively modeling ethical behavior when
in leadership roles
```

```
Types of Political
Engagement

Worked for a political
campaign locally

Signed a petition for a local
candidate or issue

Contacted a local public
official

Attended any local rallies,
protests, boycotts, or marches
```

```
Perspectives on
Trust and Efficacy

Efficacy
Voting makes a difference in how the
government runs things

Ordinary people have real influence on the
decisions made in my community

Trust
I trust public officials to make the best
decisions for my community

I trust our local government to do the right
thing
```

Stage Three

```
Voted in Local
Election
```

Figure 1. Proposed relationships among study variables.

The specific research question that we will focus on is: What is the relative influence of SES characteristics (e.g. age, income, education, residence) positive perceptions of the quality of community leaders, positive attitudes toward political engagement, and voting on four types of nonvoting political engagement? We will be using a forward stepwise logistic regression analysis to identify which of these factors has a significant influence on the model to predict nonvoting political engagement.

Methodology

The data used to answer these questions were collected through a statewide, mail-out survey in Kentucky. The survey was conducted by a university-based Survey Research Center, which used its sampling frame of households to draw a simple probabilistic, representative sample.

Initially, 4000 survey questionnaires were mailed between 6 and 10 March 2009. After that, 3666 follow-up post cards were mailed on 19 March 2009. Then, a second survey was mailed to 3123 non-respondents between 6 and 8 May 2009. The survey was closed on 23 June 2009, having received 1154 complete responses. Out of the 4000 residents, 184 were not eligible due to inaccurate address or no longer residing at the address. Therefore, the survey yielded a response rate of 30.2% based on 3816 eligible residents.

A descriptive statistical comparison of the respondents and the population of metro and non-metro areas in Kentucky were completed. The responding sample has a higher proportion of females and an older median age than the population, but these differences are not statistically significant. However, only 8.7% of the respondents in this study reside in non-metro places compared to 42% of Kentucky's 2010 population.

For the purposes of this analysis, residence is county-based and is a recoding of USDA's ERS rural-urban continuum codes.[1] We use county as the place of residence, because Kentucky has the highest number of counties per population of any state reflecting the combination of small geographic size and small population size that has historically meant that the county is the key political unit of community identity.

The measures of political efficacy, social trust, and political participation are similar to those used in prior studies (see Beaudoin & Thorson, 2004; Dalton, 2008; Lowndes, Pratchett, & Stoker, 2001; Oliver, 2000; Zhang & Chia, 2006 and are presented in Figure 1). The variables related to perceptions of professionalism and competency of community leaders and perspectives on trust and efficacy were recoded to create a summed score of positive perspectives in each variable section. In other words, if the respondent indicated that they agreed or strongly agreed with four of the five questions relating to perceptions of trust and efficacy, then they would have a score of four.

For this analysis, we begin with a descriptive analysis of the relationships among the variables. We then present three different logistical regression models using a forward stepwise approach, so that variables enter based on their contribution to the predictive value of the model. The first is a consideration of the influence of socioeconomic factors (age, education, income, and residence) on four different types of nonvoting political engagement (worked for a political campaign locally, signed a petition for a local candidate or issue, contacted a local public official, attended any local rallies, protests, boycotts, or marches). The second adds positive perceptions of professionalism and competency of community leaders and positive perspectives on trust and efficacy to assess the ability to predict nonvoting political engagement. The third adds voting in a local election to measure the model's ability to predict nonvoting political engagement.

Limitations of the study

A limitation of the study is that the sample is composed of only residents from Kentucky. Hence, the results may not be generalizable to other states or the nation due to different political, cultural, and social environments.

The measurement tool was a one-time, self-reported, mail questionnaire. Therefore, responses to questions on perceptions of community leaders and attitudes toward political engagement might be influenced by recent events in their community or the state, or reflect the particular circumstances of political engagement in their community.

Because this study is based on a mail survey, only a select few variables were used to draw conclusions about this topic. In other words, with regard to perceptions of community leaders, attitudes toward political engagement, and types of political engagement, a researcher could add many more variables, which might better explain the relationships under consideration.

Analysis of results

Overview of descriptive analysis

The basic demographic characteristics of the respondents to this survey are presented in Table 1, while the distribution of respondents on the components of perceptions of professionalism and competency of community leaders, perspectives on trust and efficacy, and all types of political engagement, including voting, are presented in Table 2.

A χ^2 analysis of the relationship between the sociodemographic variables and political participation shows the following (see Tables 3–5). For age, the oldest respondents are least likely to have been active in three (voting, worked for a local campaign,

Table 1. Selected demographic characteristics of respondents.

Variable	Frequency	Percent
Residence		
Metro	648	56.2
Urban adjacent	180	15.6
Urban non-adjacent	208	18.0
Rural adjacent	49	4.2
Rural non-adjacent	52	4.5
Missing	17	1.5
Age		
30 years old or younger	94	8.1
31–60 years old	741	64.2
61 years old and older	319	27.6
Missing	0	0
Education		
Less than high school or GED	122	10.6
Completed high school or equivalent	299	25.9
Some college or associate's	386	33.4
Bachelor's or higher degree	338	29.3
Missing	9	0
Income		
$24,999 or less	224	19.4
$25,000–$49,999	292	25.3
$50,000–$74,999	216	18.7
$75,000–$124,999	223	19.3
$125,000 or more	111	9.8
Missing	88	7.6

Table 2. Political perspectives and political engagement.

Perceptions of professionalism and competency of community leaders		
Item (% good, great)	Number	Percent
Communication with residents	221	19.5
Involving residents in decision-making	129	11.2
Seeking community change, growth and improvement	292	25.3
Transforming community goals into realities	206	18.4
Effectively modeling ethical behavior when in leadership roles	266	23.6
My community has good leaders	304	26.8

Perspectives on trust and efficacy		
Item (% strongly agree/agree)		
Voting makes a difference in how the government runs things	447	39.5
Ordinary people have real influence on the decisions made in my community	247	21.9
I trust public officials to make the best decisions for my community	194	17.1
I trust our local government to do the right thing	248	22.0
I trust others in my community to do what's best for the community	297	26.3

Types of political participation		
Item (% yes)		
Voted in a local election	1.05	88.5
Contacted a local public official	518	45.3
Signed a petition for a local candidate or issue	464	41.2
Worked for a political campaign locally	144	12.6
Attended any local rallies, protests, boycotts or marches	133	11.5

Table 3. Age and political engagement.

Item (% yes)	Under 30 years old	31–60 years old	61+years old
Voted in a local election; χ^2 (2)=17.88, $p<.05$	91.5 ($n=86$)	91.0 ($n=667$)	82.1 ($n=252$)
Contacted a local public official; χ^2 (2)=18.60, $p<.05$	33.0 ($n=30$)	50.5 ($n=369$)	38.8 ($n=119$)
Signed a petition for a local candidate or issue; χ^2 (2)=7.72, $p<.05$	30.1 ($n=28$)	40.5 ($n=295$)	45.9 ($n=141$)
Worked for a political campaign locally; χ^2 (2)=5.60, $p>.05$	16.5 ($n=15$)	13.8 ($n=101$)	9.1 ($n=28$)
Attended any local rallies, protests, boycotts or marches; χ^2 (2)=2.19, $p>.05$	13.0 ($n=12$)	12.6 ($n=92$)	9.5 ($n=29$)

Table 4. Education and political engagement.

Item (% yes)	Less than high school or no GED	Completed high school or GED	Some college or associates degree	Bachelor degree or higher
Voted in a local election; χ^2 (3)=45.54, $p<.05$	73.1 ($n=87$)	86.3 ($n=253$)	89.2 ($n=340$)	95.5 ($n=317$)
Worked for a political campaign locally; χ^2 (3)=34.14, $p<.05$	3.4 ($n=4$)	8.4 ($n=24$)	12.1 ($n=46$)	20.8 ($n=69$)
Signed a petition for a local candidate or issue; χ^2 (3)=45.91, $p<.05$	20.5 ($n=24$)	32.3 ($n=94$)	45.4 ($n=173$)	50.9 ($n=169$)
Contacted a local public official; χ^2 (3)=31.92, $p<.05$	29.1 ($n=34$)	38.8 ($n=113$)	48.4 ($n=184$)	55.3 ($n=184$)
Attended any local rallies, protests, boycotts or marches; χ^2 (3)=37.51, $p<.05$	6.0 ($n=7$)	5.5 ($n=16$)	11.1 ($n=42$)	20.2 ($n=67$)

and participated in a protest) of the five forms of engagement, but interestingly, they are most likely to have signed a petition. All of these are significant except for working for a local political campaign and attending a local rally. For education, there is a statistically significant positive relationship between educational attainment and the measures of political engagement. Our analysis of age and education patterns mirrors that of Dalton (2008), who also found that education is positively associated with nearly all types of political activity, while age is positively related to likelihood of direct political action (i.e. voting, donating to campaigns), but negatively related to political protests and Internet-based political activism. For income, there is a statistically significant relationship with all measures except working for a local political campaign. To a certain extent, this would be expected given that there is a statistically significant positive relationship between income and education.

How do participants in this study perceive the professionalism and competency of their community leaders? For all respondents, the assessments are rather modest, with those expressing approval ranging from a low of 11.1% for local officials involving residents in decision-making to a high of 25.3% saying that local leaders do a good job seeking community change, growth and improvement or being "good" leaders (26.8%) over all (Table 6). Although there has been little research on how residents perceive the

Table 5. Gross annual family income and political engagement.

Item (% yes)	$24,999 or less	$25,000–$49,999	$50,000–$74,999	$75,000–$124,999	$125,000 or more
Voted in a local election; χ^2 (4) = 39.01, $p<.05$	77.2 ($n=169$)	89.6 ($n=258$)	89.7 ($n=192$)	94.6 ($n=210$)	93.5 ($n=101$)
Worked for a political campaign locally; χ^2 (4) = 8.93, $p>.05$	9.8 ($n=21$)	10.8 ($n=31$)	12.1 ($n=26$)	16.7 ($n=37$)	18.5 ($n=20$)
Signed a petition for a local candidate or issue; χ^2 (4) = 36.61, $p<.05$	26.3 ($n=57$)	38.2 ($n=110$)	44.9 ($n=96$)	49.5 ($n=109$)	54.6 ($n=59$)
Contacted a local public official; χ^2 (4) = 28.77, $p<.05$	34.7 ($n=75$)	41.0 ($n=118$)	52.3 ($n=112$)	52.5 ($n=116$)	59.3 ($n=64$)
Attended any local rallies, protests, boycotts or marches; χ^2 (4) = 17.30, $p<.05$	8.4 ($n=18$)	8.3 ($n=24$)	12.2 ($n=36$)	16.3 ($n=36$)	20.4 ($n=22$)

Table 6. Residence and political engagement (total $n=1154$).

Item (% yes)	State	Metro	Urban adj.	Urban nonadj.	Rural adj.	Rural nonadj.
Voted in a local election; $\chi^2 (4)=1.57, p>.05$	88.5 ($n=988$)	88.1 ($n=560$)	86.9 ($n=152$)	89.9 ($n=186$)	91.7 ($n=44$)	90.2 ($n=46$)
Contacted a local public official; $\chi^2 (4)=1.94\ p>.05$	45.3 ($n=504$)	46.2 ($n=293$)	43.4 ($n=75$)	43.7 ($n=90$)	52.1 ($n=25$)	41.2 ($n=21$)
Signed a petition for a local candidate or issue; $\chi^2 (4)=1.90\ p>.05$	41.2 ($n=458$)	40.9 ($n=259$)	39.1 ($n=68$)	41.7 ($n=86$)	50.0 ($n=24$)	41.2 ($n=21$)
Worked for a political campaign locally; $\chi^2 (4)=5.61, p>.05$	12.6 ($n=140$)	13.4 ($n=85$)	14.2 ($n=25$)	9.3 ($n=19$)	16.7 ($n=8$)	5.9 ($n=3$)
Attended any local rallies, protests, boycotts, or marches; $\chi^2 (4)=5.05\ p>.05$	11.5 ($n=128$)	12.5 ($n=79$)	12.1 ($n=21$)	9.2 ($n=19$)	14.6 ($n=7$)	3.9 ($n=2$)

effectiveness of their local leaders, previous research (e.g. Beaudoin & Thorson, 2004; Oliver, 2000) on perceptions of political performance would suggest that types of communities should influence opportunities for residents to see and assess their leaders' performance. This is the case and there are some interesting differences by residence. For example, rural nonadjacent residents are most likely to say that their community has good leaders who communicate with local residents, but they are least likely to state that their leaders effectively model ethical behavior. But, only the statement "Ordinary people have real influence on the decisions made in my community" is statistically significant (χ^2 (8) = 21.52, $p < .05$).

In terms of perceptions of efficacy and trust, again, the levels of positive responses are rather modest. The proportion of respondents reporting either agree or strongly agree range from a low of 17.1% for "I trust public officials to make the best decisions for my community," to a high of 39.5% for "Voting makes a difference in how the government runs things." The highest level of trust is for "others in the community to do what's best" by those living in rural adjacent communities, and this is only one third of the respondents in these communities. Respondents in rural nonadjacent communities report the lowest levels of trust and are least likely to say that ordinary people have influence on decisions in their community. All of the differences in these measures of efficacy and trust are statistically significant except for "Voting makes a difference in how the government runs things."

Interestingly, however, there is wide divergence in reported political involvement. For example, while only about 12% reported that they had "Worked for a political campaign locally" or "Attended any local rallies, protests, boycotts or marches", more than 40% have "Contacted a local official" and "Signed a petition for a local official." Yet, 88.5% say that they have "Voted in a local election." In terms of place of residence, respondents living in rural adjacent places consistently indicate a higher level of political activity than do respondents in all other types of communities, yet none of the variation by residence is statistically significant.

It seems that voting itself has become something that one does because it is expected. This reflects what Dalton (2008) identifies as a set of political norms he calls "citizen duty" which includes the responsibility to vote. But there is a disconnection between this duty and what people believe will be the outcome of voting in terms of producing real consequences in their communities or even being "heard" by local leaders.

In Table 7, it is clear that having a positive evaluation of the professionalism and competency of community leaders does not increase the likelihood of voting or engaging in any other type of political activity. On the other hand, with respect to voting, 41% of those who agree that voting makes a difference also vote. But, on all the other measures of efficacy and trust, if a person does not feel that ordinary people can influence decisions or does not trust local public officials, local government, or others in the community, then they are more likely to have voted in a local election than someone who does trust. It is as if the lack of trust, leads us to become more involved politically to try and alter the landscape of who serves as local leaders.

Summary of logistic regression analysis

To explore in greater detail the relative influence of sociodemographic characteristics, perceptions of the professionalism, competency of community leaders, perspectives on efficacy, trust, and voting and the four nonvoting forms of political engagement, a series of forward stepwise regressions were completed (Tables 8–11). A forward stepwise

Table 7. Attitudes and perspectives related to political participation.

Perceptions of professionalism and competency of community leaders	Voted (yes)	Worked for campaign (yes)	Signed petition (yes)	Contacted public officials (yes)	Attended rallies (yes)
Communication with residents	18.0 ($n=199$)	3.2 ($n=35$)	7.9 ($n=87$)	9.2 ($n=102$)	2.7 ($n=30$)
% good	p.030	p.045	p-.027	p-.047	p.024
Involving residents in decision-making	10.2 ($n=112$)	1.8 ($n=20$)	4.8 ($n=53$)	5.6 ($n=61$)	1.9 ($n=21$)
% good	p-.012	p.035	p-.024	p-.035	p.062
Seeking community change, growth and improvement	23.9 ($n=262$)	3.7 ($n=41$)	11.4 ($n=124$)	12.5 ($n=137$)	4.0 ($n=44$)
% good	p.046	p.026	p.007	p.008	p.066*
Transforming community goals into realities	16.8 ($n=185$)	2.4 ($n=26$)	8.0 ($n=87$)	8.8 ($n=96$)	3.0 ($n=33$)
% good	p.039	p.003	p.003	p-.017	p.061*
Effectively modeling ethical behavior when in leadership roles	21.8 ($n=239$)	3.7 ($n=40$)	9.5 ($n=104$)	11.5 ($n=125$)	3.1 ($n=34$)
% good	p.029	p.037	p-.034	p-.015	p.012
My community has good leaders	24.4 ($n=271$)	3.9 ($n=43$)	10.6 ($n=117$)	11.5 ($n=127$)	3.8 ($n=42$)
% strongly agree, agree	29.0 ($n=233$)	4.1 ($n=45$)	14.0 ($n=155$)	17.1 ($n=189$)	3.5 ($n=39$)
% strongly disagree, disagree	p.044	p.024	p-.020	p-.070	p.041
Perspectives on trust and efficacy					
Voting makes a difference in how the government runs things	41.4 ($n=410$)	6.8 ($n=76$)	17.5 ($n=194$)	18.8 ($n=208$)	7.0 ($n=77$)
% strongly agree, agree	29.9 ($n=296$)	2.9 ($n=32$)	12.4 ($n=137$)	15.5 ($n=172$)	2.4 ($n=27$)
% strongly disagree, disagree	p.124*	p.107*	p.042	p-.009	p.133*
Ordinary people have real influence on the decisions made in my community	19.9 ($n=221$)	4.2 ($n=46$)	9.3 ($n=103$)	10.4 ($n=115$)	3.9 ($n=43$)
% strongly agree, agree	41.6 ($n=461$)	5.2 ($n=58$)	19.1 ($n=211$)	23.2 ($n=256$)	4.5 ($n=50$)
% strongly disagree, disagree	p.027	p.076*	p.018	p-.037	p.089*
I trust public officials to make the best decisions for my community	15.3 ($n=170$)	2.8 ($n=31$)	6.7 ($n=74$)	7.7 ($n=85$)	2.4 ($n=27$)
% strongly agree, agree	44.2 ($n=492$)	5.6 ($n=62$)	21.4 ($n=238$)	24.9 ($n=276$)	5.3 ($n=59$)
% strongly disagree, disagree	p-.017	p.049	p-.042	p-.072*	p.039
I trust our local government to do the right thing	19.9 ($n=221$)	3.0 ($n=33$)	8.1 ($n=90$)	8.9 ($n=98$)	2.9 ($n=32$)

(*Continued*)

Table 7. (Continued).

Perspectives on trust and efficacy	Voted (yes)	Worked for campaign (yes)	Signed petition (yes)	Contacted public officials (yes)	Attended rallies (yes)
% strongly agree, agree	40.4 ($n=446$)	5.4 ($n=60$)	20.7 ($n=229$)	24.0 ($n=265$)	5.2 ($n=57$)
	$p.022$	$p.023$	$p.075^*$	$p.113^*$	$p.022$
% strongly disagree, disagree	23.7 ($n=262$)	3.7 ($n=41$)	10.9 ($n=120$)	12.2 ($n=135$)	3.7 ($n=41$)
I trust others in my community to do what's best for the community					
% strongly agree, agree	27.0 ($n=299$)	3.3 ($n=36$)	12.7 ($n=140$)	16.1 ($n=178$)	3.8 ($n=42$)
	$p.028$	$p.041$	$p.001$	$p.053$	$p.018$
% strongly disagree, disagree					

*Pearson value is significant at $p<.05$.

Table 8. Coefficients related to logistic regressions – attended any local rallies, protest, boycotts or marches ($n = 1154$).

Included	B (SE)	Lower	Odds ratio exp (B)	Upper
Constant	−3.95 (.65)		.02	
Education (less than high school, no GED)				
Education (completed high school or GED)	.15 (.53)	.41	1.16	3.31
Education (some college or associates degree)	.70 (.50)	.76	2.02	5.36
Education (bachelors or higher degree)	1.33 (.50)	1.46	3.79	9.89
Did vote at least once in the past two years	1.03 (.53)	.99	2.80	7.87
Positive perspectives on trust and efficacy	.21 (.07)	1.06	1.23	1.42

Notes: $R^2 = .29$ (Hosmer & Lemeshow), .05 (Cox & Snell), .09 (Nagelkerke). Model χ^2 (5) = 44.58.

Table 9. Coefficients related to logistic regressions – worked for political campaign locally ($n = 1154$).

Included	B (SE)	Lower	Odds ratio exp (B)	Upper
Constant	−4.79 (1.14)		.01	
Education (less than high school, no GED)				
Education (completed high school or GED)	.54 (.57)	.56	1.72	5.29
Education (some college or associates degree)	1.09 (.55)	1.02	2.97	8.69
Education (bachelors or higher degree)	1.61 (.54)	1.73	5.01	14.50
Age (30 years or younger)				
Age (31–60 years old)	−.55 (.36)	.29	.58	1.16
Age (61 years old and older)	−1.05 (.40)	.16	.35	.77
Did vote at least once in the past two years	2.51 (1.01)	1.70	12.36	90.12

Notes: $R^2 = .92$ (Hosmer & Lemeshow), .05 (Cox & Snell), .10 (Nagelkerke). Model χ^2 (6) = 52.88.

Table 10. Coefficients related to logistic regressions – signed a petition for a local candidate or issue ($n = 1154$).

Included	B (SE)	Lower	Odds ratio exp (B)	Upper
Constant	−2.20 (.34)		.11	
Education (less than high school, no GED)				
Education (completed high school or GED)	.47 (.30)	.89	1.60	2.85
Education (some college or associates degree)	1.05 (.28)	1.64	2.87	5.01
Education (bachelors or higher degree)	1.22 (.29)	1.91	3.37	5.92
Did vote at least once in the past two years	1.09 (.26)	1.77	2.96	4.96

Notes: $R^2 = .81$ (Hosmer & Lemeshow), .06 (Cox & Snell), .08 (Nagelkerke). Model χ^2 (4) = 62.90.

regression starts with a model that contains no independent variables. SPSS software will begin adding one independent variable in each step testing to see if the addition of that variable improves the predictive power of the model. This process is repeated until the addition of new variables no longer improves the model. At the end of the analysis, there is a statistical model with the highest predictive power based on the variables of interest. Please note that we used all "low-first" categories as our reference point, in other words, as one increases education or income level "x" happens. Therefore, all first

Table 11. Coefficients related to logistic regressions – contacted a local public official ($n = 1154$).

Included	B (SE)	Lower	Odds ratio exp (B)	Upper
Constant	−1.92 (.38)		.15	
Income ($24,999 or less)				
Income ($25,000–$49,999)	.10 (.20)	1.10	.74	1.64
Income ($50,000–$74,999)	.52 (.21)	1.69	1.11	2.59
Income ($75,000–$124,999)	.52 (.21)	1.68	1.11	2.54
Income ($125,000 or more)	.77 (.26)	2.16	1.31	3.58
Age (30 years or younger)				
Age (31–60 years old)	.49 (.29)	1.63	.93	2.86
Age (61 years old and older)	.01 (.31)	1.01	.56	1.85
Did vote at least once in the past two years	1.25 (.29)	3.49	2.10	5.79

Notes: $R^2 = .90$ (Hosmer & Lemeshow), .07 (Cox & Snell), .09 (Nagelkerke). Model χ^2 (7) = 67.05.

level categories of independent variables are references and are blank lines in the tables. This discussion will move from the form of political engagement least likely to occur among our respondents to the most likely.

When asked whether they had ever attended any local rallies, protests, boycotts, or marches, only 11.5% of the sample indicated that they had done so. Table 8 presents the results of the logistic regression using attending any local rallies, protests, boycotts, or marches as the dependent variable ($R^2 = .29$, Model χ^2 (5) = 44.58). In the first step of the analysis, education is the only socioeconomic variable to enter the predictive model and the higher the education, the more likely it is that one has attended these types of political events. In the second step of the analysis, a positive sense of political efficacy is significant, such that the more one feels that they can make a difference, the more likely they are to attend one of these types of political events. However, education has a higher level of predictive ability than political efficacy. In the third step, education and a positive sense of political efficacy remain significant as explanatory factors even after considering whether someone voted in a local election. It is interesting to note that voting, although not significant, was included in this model, because it contributed to increasing its predictive ability.

When asked if they had ever worked for a political campaign locally, 12.6% of the respondents indicated that they had done so. Table 9 presents the results of the logistic regression using ever worked for a political campaign locally as the dependent variable ($R^2 = .92$, Model χ^2 (6) = 52.88). In the first step of the analysis, both education and age are significant predictors, but neither perceptions of community leaders nor efficacy and trust, enter as predictors in the second step of the analysis. Having voted in a local election is a significant predictor of working for a political campaign, and both age and education remain statistically significant, although to a lesser extent than in the prior models.

When asked if they had ever signed a petition for a local candidate or issue, 42.1% of the sample ever indicated that they had done so. Table 10 presents the results of the logistic regression using ever signed a petition for a local candidate or issue as the dependent variable ($R^2 = .81$, Model χ^2 (4) = 62.90). In the first step of the analysis, both education and income are significant predictors, and they remain the only significant explanatory variables in the second step. In other words, neither perceptions of community leaders nor efficacy and trust enter as predictors at this point. In the third step of this analysis, only "did you vote" and education remain as predictors of signing a petition. In other words, as suggested by the literature, education is a key factor in predicting political behavior.

When asked if they had ever contacted a local public official, 45.3% of the respondents stated they had done so. In the first step of the analysis, age, education, and income are statistically significant. Table 11 presents the results of the logistic regression using ever contacted a local public official as the dependent variable ($R^2 = .90$, Model χ^2 (7) = 67.05). Here, middle-aged persons are most likely to have contacted a local public official, while education and income are positively related to contacting a public official. In the second step of the analysis, income is no longer a significant factor, and neither perceptions of community leaders, nor efficacy, nor trust are significant; only age and education remain. In the third step, age, education, and whether someone had voted in a local election are significant factors in whether someone has contacted a local public official and prior voting is the most important factor.

Summary and conclusions

Education and having voted in a local election are consistent predictors of all four types of nonvoting political engagement considered in this study. But, perceptions of the professionalism and competency of community leaders and perspectives on trust and efficacy do not contribute significantly to explaining participation in three of four types of nonvoting behavior (signed a petition for a local candidate or issue, worked for a political campaign, and contacted a local public official). Perspectives on trust and efficacy did enter the model on attending local rallies, protests, boycotts, or marches. In this case, even after the influence of education and voting in a prior local election, a positive perspective on trust and efficacy increased the likelihood of participating in these types of nonvoting political behavior by 23%.

It is clear that only a small proportion of participants in this statewide survey have positive views on the performance of their community leaders, and only a small number feel empowered or that they can trust their community leaders. Yet, in the face of this lack of trust, there are still high levels of engagement in different types of political activities; an overwhelming majority of respondents vote, and many have also contacted a local leader or signed a petition. Interestingly, low levels of trust lead to higher levels of participation than does the presence of trust. Moreover, if people believe that voting makes a difference, they are more likely to vote and engage in other kinds of political activities but if people believe that ordinary people can have an influence on how decisions are made, they are less likely to vote or engage in other types of political activities. In the regression analysis, education and having voted in a local election are the only consistent predictors of other types of political activity.

Previous studies have tended to focus almost exclusively on voting as the measure of political engagement. Our results suggest that there is a basis for this assumption, at least with respect to involvement in one's community. Our results show that voting is a key predictor of whether or not someone engages in other types of political behaviors. This implies that we do not have to worry about capturing information on them, because voting is the best reflection of political engagement as a multidimensional concept. Yet, we also cannot ignore the enormous variation in these other types of political activity.

Our findings reflect those of Dalton (2008), in that there may be an emerging divergence in views of democratic citizenship. One perspective defines voting as the primary mechanism for involvement and participation in a democratic society. The other is more reminiscent of an "activist politics," where direct participation is the key to democracy. While our research suggests that rural nonadjacent counties fall into a view of political participation as a duty, it is the rural adjacent counties that reflect a more activist approach to political engagement. A question for future study is: what is it about living in rural adjacent counties that leads to a sense that political activism is a responsibility of citizens? These communities are at a point of transition between urban and rural lifestyles and scale of life. Perhaps residents in rural adjacent places feel that they must make democracy work if they are to have an influence over the future of their communities.

Rural adjacent places attract both ex-urbanites as well as rural residents who are moving closer to employment or services. These new residents mix with existing residents in a geographic space that is experiencing considerable changes in land use, the local economy, the composition of schools, churches, and other civic organizations, and the very meaning of community. In this context, multiple concerns may be driving the higher levels of political activism. For example, long-term residents may be politically active in an attempt to preserve the qualities of community life they cherish. Rural residents from more distant places may be politically active in an effort to re-establish the civic culture they left behind. Former urban residents may be politically active in order to re-gain the services and opportunities they left behind.

The failure of residence to appear as an explanatory variable in most of the bivariate analyses and in any of the regression models raises some interesting questions, especially given earlier studies suggesting attitude, value, and participation differences among communities. So how can we explain these results? While it is possible that the failure reflects a problem in our data, the results may also reflect a growing sociocultural homogeneity among places. Residential mobility and migration, urban and rural suburbanization, and new media may have created the mass society predicted in the 1950s.

This research also suggests that what we define as "good" or "effective" political leadership may vary depending on whether we are thinking about this at the local, state, or national level. Do our performance expectations differ depending on whether we are focusing on local or national leaders? What is the focus of trust in the context of politics and political engagement? Is it trust in the political system and the processes of decision-making, the institutions, or the individuals in politics that influence political participation? Cook and Gronke (2005, p. 789) found that "Confidence in institutions … seems very closely related to approval of institutions," and that confidence or lack of confidence in government is not the same thing as trust or lack of trust. From their perspective, trust is a continuum from active trust, to a lack of trust (skepticism), to active distrust. While we cannot determine if our respondents simply lack trust or actively distrust their local leaders, we believe that more research is needed to fully understand the factors that shape how people evaluate their community leaders.

Future research

One key area of future research is to continue to evaluate the relationships among actual political engagement, perceptions of community leaders, and attitudes toward political engagement. This study did highlight that these variables have a negative relationship (i.e. residents with negative perceptions of community leaders are more political engaged), but there were no measures that helped explain this relationship. Another area that needs to be researched, so a more complete understanding of the relationship between type of community and political engagement can be reached is: Why do residents in the rural-adjacent communities have higher engagement levels than those who are in the other types of communities?

Additionally, there are limited studies linking political engagement to type of community, and nearly all prior research focuses on voting as the measure of political engagement. More research needs to be done to explore a wider variety of types of political engagement (i.e. both formal and informal) in general, and specifically in different types of communities. Furthermore, what if residents in different types of communities are motivated to become politically engaged by different types of issues? In other words, what if political activism is not a generalized behavior but triggered by particular issues that resonate with the voter? The level and types of political engagement based on the type of issue is another area requiring additional research.

Implications for community development

This study appears to show that with few exceptions, type of community does not play a significant role in predicting political engagement. This may suggest that efforts should be focused on designing programs for increasing civic engagement that can be effective regardless of type of community.

With regard to the relationship between sociodemographic characteristics and political engagement, it is evident that more work needs to be done to make sure that community services and programs that relate to political engagement are reaching individuals of all backgrounds. This is essential to insure that all residents are better informed and equipped to participate in the political arena. This would ensure that all groups of people are having their voices heard regarding the decisions that leaders are making that could have a major effect on their lives.

Another implication from this study is that individuals who perceive their community leaders in a positive light are less likely to be politically engaged. Knowing this, intentional steps should be taken to engage these individuals so that they can contribute their thoughts and dialog to the political arena. This will allow community leaders and other residents to hear a different side of the political chatter. This may help to bring about some balance in the political sphere and allow for others to accurately gage the state of politics in a local community.

The American political landscape is complex, especially at the local level. This study suggests that the simplistic red state/blue state dichotomy that has come to dominate our views on political attitudes and participation does little to tease out the reality of the complex relationships among attitudes, beliefs, and practices. It is clear that place makes a difference. But fully understanding how and why will require more study.

Note

1. Residence codes are a recoding of Beale's USDA ERS rural-urban continuum codes. For a complete description of the codes see: http://www.ers.usda.gov/Briefing/Rurality/RuralUrb-Con/1 = Metropolitan (1, 2, 3) All metropolitan counties 2 = Urban adjacent (4, 6) Counties with an urban population of 20,000 or more, adjacent to a metro area and counties with an urban population of 2,500 to 19,999, adjacent to a metro area3 = Urban nonadjacent (5, 7) Counties with an urban population of 20,000 or more, not adjacent to a metro area and counties with an urban population of 2,500 to 19,999, not adjacent to a metro area4 = Rural adjacent (8) Completely rural or less than 2,500 urban population, adjacent to a metro area5 = Rural nonadjacent (9) Completely rural or less than 2,500 urban population, not adjacent to a metro area

References

Anderson, M. R. (2010). Community psychology, political efficacy and trust. *Political Psychology, 31*, 59–84. doi:10.1111/j.1467-9221.2009.00734

Barisione, M. (2009). So, what difference do leaders make? Candidates' images and the "conditionality" of leader effects on voting *Journal of Elections, Public Opinion and Parties, 19*, 473–500. doi:10.1080/17457280903074219

Beaudoin, C. E., & Thorson, E. (2004). Social capital in rural and urban communities: Testing differences in media effects and models. *Journalism and Mass Communication Quarterly, 81*. 378–399. Retrieved from http://www.sagepub.com/journalsIndex.nav#J

Berinsky, A. J., & Lenz, G. S. (2011). Education and political participation: Exploring the causal link. *Political Behavior, 33*, 357–373. doi:10.1007/s11109-010-9134-9

Binstock, R. H. (2006–2007). Older people and political engagement: From avid voters to "cooled out marks". *Generations*(Winter)24–30. Retrieved from http://www.generationsjournal.org/

Boulianne, S. (2009). Does Internet use affect engagement? A meta-analysis of research *Political Communication, 26*, 193–211. doi:10.1080/10584600902854363

Bowler, S., & Karp, J. A. (2004). Politicians, scandals and trust in government. *Political Behavior, 26*. 271–287Retrieved from http://www.springerlink.com

Brady, H. E. (2004). An analytical perspective on participatory inequality and income inequality. In K. M. Neckerman (Ed.), *Social inequality* (pp. 667–702). New York, NY: Russell Sage Foundation.

Brady, H. E., Verba, S., & Schlozman, K. L. (1995). Beyond SES: A resource model of political participation. *The American Political Science Review, 89*. 271–294. Retrieved from http://www.ssc.msu.edu/~apsr

Caren, N. (2007). Big city, big turnout? Electoral participation in American cities *Journal of Urban Affairs, 29*, 31–46Article first published online: February 5, 2007. doi:10.1111/j.1467-9906.2007.00321.

Cook, T. E., & Gronke, P. (2005). The skeptical American: Revisiting the meanings of trust in government and confidence in institutions. *Journal of Politics, 67*, 784–803. doi: http://dx.doi.org/10.1111/j.1468-2508.2005.00339 Published online: July 29, 2008

Dalton, R. J. (2008). Citizenship norms and the expansion of political participation. *Political Studies, 56*, 76–98. doi:10.1111/j.1467-9248.2007.00718

Edlin, A., Gelman, A., & Kaplan, N. (2007). Voting as a rational choice: Why and how people vote to improve the well-being of others. *Rationality and Society, 19*, 293–314. doi:10.1177/1043463107077384

Gastil, J., & Xenos, M. (2010). Of attitudes and engagement: Clarifying the reciprocal relationship between civic attitudes and political participation. *Journal of Communication, 60*, 318–343. doi: 10.1111/j.1460-2466.2010.01484

Gelman, A., Kenworthy, L., & Su, Y. (2010). Income inequality and partisan voting in the United States. *Social Science Quarterly, 91*(5), 1–17. doi:10.1111/j.1540-6237.2010.00728

Gimpel, J. G., & Karnes, K. A. (2006). The rural side of the urban-rural gap. *PS: Political Science and Politics, 39*. 467–472. Retrieved from www.apsanet.org or http://www.apsanet.org/imgtest/PSJuly06GimpelKarnes.pdf

Gimpel, J. G., Morris, I. L., & Armstrong, D. R. (2004). Turnout and the local age distribution: Examining political participation across space and time. *Political Geography, 23*, 71–95. doi: 10.1016/j.polgeo.2003.09.002

Han, G. (2008). New media use, sociodemographics, and voter turnout in the 2000 presidential election. *Mass Communication & Society, 11*, 62–81. doi:10.1080/15205430701587644

Hays, R. A. (2007). Community activists' perceptions of citizenship roles in an urban community: A case study of attitudes that affect community engagement. *Journal of Urban Affairs, 29*, 401–424. doi:10.1111/j.1467-9906.2007.00353

Hoffman, L. H., & Appiah, O. (2008). Assessing cultural and contextual components of social capital: Is civic engagement in peril? *The Howard Journal of Communications, 19*, 334–354. doi:10.1080/10646170802391755

Jennings, M. K., & Zeitner, V. (2003). Internet use and civic engagement: A longitudinal analysis. *Public Opinion Quarterly, 67*. 311–334. Retrieved from http://poq.oxfordjournals.org.

Johnson, T., & Kaye, B. (2003). A boost or bust for democracy? How the web influences political attitudes and behaviors in the 1996 and 2000 presidential elections *Press/Politics, 8,* 9–34. doi:10.1177/1081180X03008003002

Kittilson, M. C., & Dalton, R. J. (2011). Virtual civil society: The new frontier of social capital? *Political Behavior, 33,* 625–644. doi:10.1007/s11109-010-9143-8

Kornbluh, M. L. (2000). *Why America stopped voting. The decline of participatory democracy and the emergence of modern American politics.* New York: New York University Press.

Kwak, N., Shah, D. V., & Holbert, R. L. (2004). Connecting, trusting, and participating: The direct and interactive effects of social associations. *Political Research Quarterly, 57.* 643–652. Retrieved from http://www.poli-sci.utah.edu/PRQ1.htm.

Lowndes, V., Pratchett, L., & Stoker, G. (2001). Trends in public participation: Part 2 – citizens' perspectives. *Public Administration, 79,* 445–455. doi:10.1111/1467-9299.00264

Macedo, S., Alex-Assensoh, Y., Berry, J. M., Brintnall, M., Campbell, D. E., Fraga, L. R., ..., & Walsh, K. C. (2005). *Democracy at risk: How political choices undermine citizen participation, and what we can do about it.* Washington, DC: Brookings Institution Press.

Martinson, M., & Minkler, M. (2006). Civic engagement and older adults: A critical perspective. *The Gerontologist, 4.* 318–324. Retrieved from http://gerontologist.oxfordjournals.org.

McDonald, M. P. (2002). The turnout rate among eligible votes in the states: 1980–2000. *State Politics and Policy Quarterly, 2.* 199–212. Retrieved from http://www.sagepub.com/journals-ProdDesc.nav?prodId=Journal202001

McDonald, M. P. (2010). American voter turnout in historical perspective. In J. Leighley (Ed.), *Handbook of American elections and political behavior* (pp. 125–143). Cambridge: Oxford University Press.

McDonald, M. P. (2012, March 31). *United States Election Project.* Retrieved from http://elections.gmu.edu/Turnout_2008G.html

McDonald, M. P., & Popkin, S. (2001). The myth of the vanishing voter. *American Political Science Review, 95.* 963–974. Retrieved from http://www.ssc.msu.edu/~apsr

McKee, S. C. (2008). Rural voters and the polarization of American presidential elections. *Political Science and Politics, 41,* 101–108. doi:10.1017/S1049096508080165

Morris-Jones, D. (2010). The impact of trust (or lack thereof) on citizen involvement. *National Civic Review*(Spring)35–43. Retrieved from http://www.wiley.com.

Mossberger, K., Tolbert, C. J., & McNeal, R. S. (2008). *Digital citizenship: The Internet, society and participation.* Cambridge, MA: MIT Press.

Oliver, J. E. (2000). City size and civic involvement in metropolitan America. *American Political Science Review, 94.* 361–373. Retrieved from http://www.jstor.org/stable/2586017

Oxendine, A., Sullivan, J. L., Borgida, E., Riedel, E., Jackson, B., & Dial, J. (2007). The importance of political context for understanding civic engagement: A longitudinal analysis. *Political Behavior, 29,* 31–67. doi:10.1007/s11109-006-9016-3

Pew Research Center for the People and the Press. (2010). *Trends in political values and core attitudes: 1987–2009.* Full report. Retrieved from http://www.people-press.org/files/legacy-pdf/517.pdf. *Section 8: Politics and political participation.* Retrieved from http://people-press.org/2009/05/21/section-8-politics-and-political-participation/

Piotrowski, S. J., & Van Ryzin, G. G. (2007). Citizen attitudes toward transparency in local government. *The American Review of Public Administration, 37,* 306–323. doi: 10.1177/0275074006296777

Putnam, R. (2000). *Bowling alone: The collapse and revival of American community.* New York, NY: Simon and Schuster.

Scheufele, D., & Nisbet, M. (2002). Being a citizen online: New opportunities and dead ends. *Harvard International Journal of Press/Politics, 7,* 55–75. doi:10.1177/1081180X0200700304

Solt, F. (2008). Economic inequality and democratic political engagement. *American Journal of Political Science, 52,* 48–60. doi:10.1111/j.1540-5907.2007.00298

Solt, F. (2010). Does economic inequality depress electoral participation? Testing the Schattschneider hypothesis *Political Behavior, 32,* 285–301. doi:10.1007/s11109-010-9106-0

Southwell, P. L., & Pirch, K. D. (2003). Political cynicism and the mobilization of Black voters. *Social Science Quarterly, 84,* 906–917. doi:10.1046/j.0038-4941.2003.08404020

Straughn, J. B., & Andriot, A. L. (2011). Education, civic patriotism, and democratic citizenship: Unpacking the education effect on political involvement. *Sociological Forum, 26,* 556–580. doi:10.1111/j.1573-7861.2011.01262

Teixeira, R. A. (1987). *Why Americans don't vote: Turnout decline in the United States, 1960–1984.* New York, NY: Greenwood Press.
US Census Bureau. (2013). *The 2012 statistical abstract.* Washington, DC: US Government Printing Office. Retrieved from http://www.census.gov/compendia/statab/
Uslaner, E. M. (1998). Democracy and social capital. In M. Warren (Ed.), *Democracy and trust* (pp. 121–150). Cambridge: Cambridge University Press.
Verba, S., & Nye, N. (1972). *Participation in America.* New York, NY: Harper and Row.
Wilkins, K. G. (2000). The role of media in public disengagement from political life. *Journal of Broadcasting and Electronic Media, 44.* 569–580. Retrieved from http://www.tandf.co.uk/journals/HBEM
Zhang, W., & Chia, S. C. (2006). The effect of mass media use and social capital on civic and political participation. *Communication Studies, 57,* 277–297. doi:10.1080/10510970600666974
Zipp, J. F., Landerman, R., & Luebke, P. (1982). Political parties and political participation: A re-examination of the standard socioeconomic model. *Social Forces, 60.* 1140–1153. Retrieved from http://uncpress.unc.edu/
Zukin, C., Keeter, S., Andolina, M., Jenkins, K., & Delli Carpini, M. X. (2006). *A new engagement? Political participation, civic life, and the changing American citizen.* New York, NY: Oxford University Press.

Section 2
Justice, Inclusion, and Participation

Community development as a discipline arose from a need to address issues around justice and equity, and its origins can be traced to social movements of earlier times. Recalling the efforts of early advocates for communities such as Jane Addams, community development ethos and practice were forged in rather noble principles to help make situations better. These underlying principles were stated clearly when the Community Development Society was formed in the US in 1969 and refined through the years in its "Principles of Good Practice." These principles are listed as follows:

Promote active and representative participation toward enabling all community members to meaningfully influence the decisions that affect their lives.

Engage community members in learning about and understanding community issues, and the economic, social, environmental, political, psychological, and other impacts associated with alternative courses of action.

Incorporate the diverse interests and cultures of the community in the community development process, and disengage from support of any effort that is likely to adversely affect the disadvantaged members of a community.

Work actively to enhance the leadership capacity of community members, leaders, and groups within the community.

Be open to using the full range of action strategies to work toward the long-term sustainability and well-being of the community.

(CDS, 2020, p. 1)

Reading through the Principles of Good Practice is a reminder of the history and evolution of community development, generally in response to dire conditions or situations in human settlements. Indeed, throughout history of the profession or discipline, it has been very much shaped by its focus on social problems (Green & Goetting, 2010). And while community development is concerned with the entire spectrum of domains that influence collective well-being (the environment, certainly), its overriding focus is on improving the human condition. The emphasis on equity is a "common thread, given community development's origins in social advocacy and calls to social action....The need for social reform and social justice has always been present, and continues to be critical across communities globally" (Phillips & Pittman, 2015, p. 5).

Articles in this section focus on the vital underlying principles guiding community development – justice, inclusion, and participation. Eight articles have been selected, each discussing an important element around underlying values of community development research and practice. As was true in the early days of its origins, community development continues to focus on people who will be impacted by decisions made in the places they live.

This section begins with an exploration of community development as social movement. Green (2008) presents models of practice grounded in participation and collective impact. Moving beyond traditional models of self-help, technical assistance, and conflict models, the author calls for more action-oriented direction, as proposed by theories and models grounded in social movements. These models include "those focused on political-economic constraints and opportunities, resource mobilization and organization, and framing of grievances and collective action" (Green, 2008, p. 50). The call for a shift from typical approaches is reminiscent of the discipline's origins and practice per se as ways to improve conditions via direct and very intentional social change.

The models are framed around three areas: collective action and social movement as political-economic constraints and opportunities, mobilization and organization, and grievance and collective action. The article concludes by proposing that utilizing social movement models, community development practice and assessment need to be better understood to have more effective outcomes.

The next article provides a powerful case of how reconciliation tourism can provide the foundation for healing deep divides in communities. Barton and Leonard (2010) frame their discussion around tourism as a way to approach sustainable community development. The emphasis is on equity and social justice, and they discuss the very moving case of Emmett Till's murder and the Emmett Till Memorial Commission on Tourism in rural Mississippi. This commission worked across groups and divides to create a civil rights trail at sites where the murder took place as well as other venues as a mechanism to educate, inform, and heal.

As the authors note, tourism planning may help gain some level of reconciliation in communities where racial and other divides have separated them from each other. The idea of bringing together historically divided groups is indeed a powerful one and can serve to foster more desirable community development outcomes. They conclude with perspectives on what it takes for communities to use reconciliation tourism, finding it "requires a willingness to challenge people's perceptions and demand that people consider a civil rights perspective and a worldview that represents society's disenfranchised and marginalized members" (Barton & Leonard, 2010, p. 316).

Next, in an earlier article, "An Ethical Principle for Social Justice in Community Development Practice," Sabre (1980) positions community development most importantly as ways for residents to participate in changes impacting their communities. Ethics are not always an easily agreed-upon term, and currently, it seems just as difficult to reach agreement, over 40 years later. Essentially, ethics imply practices that have value terms such as good and bad, or right and wrong. The author proposes that community development practitioners "explicitly adopt a deontological ethic because it is consistent with an educational mission; serves as a guide to action in capacity building and technical assistance; and because it leads to social justice" (Sabre, 1980, p. 17). Deontological essentially implies one's duty, or that an action's rightness or wrongness is in the action itself.

Sabre explains that since community development practitioners engage in those activities, an ethical principle helps understanding of actions. Further, it would promote social justice, by focusing on the actions embedded within community development practices such as needs assessment or advocacy. A basic principle is presented to encourage, rather than suppress, any capability for persuasion of either one's own or another's capacity in question (Sabre, 1980, pp. 17–18). This principle focuses on fostering education and understanding, in a social justice context.

A decade later, Daley and Angulo (1994) explored the idea of people-centered community planning. Their discussion focuses on the problems inherent in the dominant method of planning, the rational model, citing problems with implicit values or approaches that may not include those impacted by decisions made using it. In other words, the dominant approach leaves out those without a voice or a seat at the table – the oppressed or disenfranchised – when decisions are made.

This article is relevant for several purposes, including bringing more attention to the idea that community planning and development that considers values and participation by all is important. It is the inclusion of people in the processes that impact their lives. The authors reiterate the need for inclusionary practices, with participation as a clear part of the planning process. They state, "the people to be served can and should be systematically involved in every aspect of the development, implementation, and evaluation of interventions because participation in this process, in itself, contributes to their dignity and empowerment" (Daley & Angulo, 1990, p. 93). The rational model (what some call "rational choice"), while functional and efficient, leaves out crucial aspects of the human element in development and planning; the people-centered approach the authors call for helps alleviate some of these shortcomings. This people-centered mindset was a precursor to asset-based development approaches.

Hardina explores citizen participation in the context of nonprofit, community-based organizations. Organizational structures highly influence development processes and outcomes. As nonprofits have been instrumental in development since the mid-20th century, this article is important in understanding the role of this sector. In this 2006 article, the author places great importance on participation and empowerment to serve community development.

Hardina proposes strategies for nonprofits to foster meaningful participation to influence both organizational and political decision-making. Strategies include working to connect citizens with public sector agencies,

> increasing the political power of the organization and the power of individuals to facilitate social change.... Such action increases the organization's access to resources and volunteers while helping local low income wage earners to develop skills and acquire resources (such as tangible services, social support, and informal networks) they need to improve their lives.
>
> (Hardina, 2006, pp. 13–14)

The article illustrates the rising importance of the social action themes, via participation and empowerment, as community development continues to evolve.

Participation is explored also in the next article. Richards and Dalbey (2006) consider smart growth strategies for fostering better outcomes across many spectrums of concern for community residents, including economic, environmental, and public health. (Note that terminology may change through time, whereas "citizen participation" may generally refer to resident, stakeholder, or simply just participation.)

In the 1990s, smart growth grew out of desire to improve quality of development; it essentially is a set of principles by the Smart Growth Network (Smart Growth Network, 2020), which is comprised of private, nonprofit, and public sector organizations. It became a rallying cry for community planning and development, and the Richards and Dalbey article explores it about ten years after its initial applications in context of participation. They propose that smart growth enhances "participation to create better community outcomes; provides for a process that is more predictable, democratic, and fair; and provides more tools and strategies for dialogue" (Richards & Dalbey, 2006, p. 29). Illustrating their premises with three short case studies, they state that smart growth's approaches widen participation, with such tools as charettes (design workshops).

Organizational structure and power relationships are crucial to understand in the community development context. In 1989, Preston and Enck explored racial bifurcation of community development, using a survey of leaders in a city with a large minority population. While community development is often considered as inclusive, their findings imply something far different – that black leaders are not included into overall community development leadership. Their work uncovered divisions along racial lines. Further, the authors present implications for practitioners in situations with built-in dissensus where contesting as opposed to collaborative approaches are used.

This article cites seminal studies from earlier decades, showing that progress has been elusive in terms of black leadership being in partnership in equitable ways with white leadership. This is referred to as the black subcommunity thesis, and the authors explain that the resulting contesting strategies of community development emphasize the relevance of the racial bifurcation of community leadership to community development practitioners working in communities with sizable minority populations. The role of minority leadership is critical "for both community development theory and practice and illustrates the need for research replication in other communities with large minority populations" (Preston & Enck, 1989, p. 56).

The final article in this section, by Silverman (2005), discusses the role of participation in community development corporations (CDCs) and, by doing so, brings together explorations of inclusion, grassroots or resident-driven efforts, and organizational structure of nonprofits. The author provides a review as well as survey results based on CDCs in Detroit.

Silverman reported that two fundamental changes must occur for grassroots activism and local nonprofit CDCs to partner more effectively:

> First, local nonprofits must become more proactive in their efforts to promote grassroots participation. In essence, more resources and time must be committed to community-organizing and capacity-building. Second, this renewed emphasis on community-organizing and capacity-building must be reinforced with stronger institutional mandates for grassroots participation in the policy process.
>
> (Silverman, 1989, p. 49)

A participation continuum tool is provided, as an aid for evaluating projects and approaches for developing programs and policies to expand resident control in decision-making.

These eight articles show the progression of thought around justice, inclusion, and participation during 50 years. While many volumes of books can be written on these topic areas, the selections included next provide an overview of some of the transitions in approaches and thinking about these vital aspects of community development. Without social reform or social change as an underlying ethos or principles, community development would not have evolved as it did. The future remains to be seen but hope holds that the discipline and practice will continue to evolve in ways that are even more just, inclusive, and participatory while addressing deep racial, social, economic, and other divides.

REFERENCES

Barton, A.W. & Leonard, S.J. 2010. Incorporating social justice in tourism planning: Racial reconciliation and sustainable community development in the Deep South. *Community Development* 41(3): 298–322.

Community Development Society (CDS). 2020. Principles of good practice. Retrieved 20 January from: https://www.comm-dev.org/about/principles-of-good-practice.

Daley. J.M. & Angulo, J. 1994. Understanding the dynamics of diversity within nonprofit boards. *Community Development* 25(2): 172–188.

Green, J.J. 2008. Community development as social movement: A contribution to models of practice. *Community Development* 39(1): 50–62.

Green, G. & Goetting, A. 2010. Lessons learned. Pp. 177–188 in G. Green, & A. Goetting (eds.), *Mobilizing Communities, Asset Building as a Community Development Strategy*. Philadelphia, PA: Temple University Press.

Hardina, D. 2006. Strategies for citizen participation and empowerment in non-profit, community-based organizations. *Community Development* 37(4): 4–17.

Phillips, R. & Pittman, R. 2015. A framework for community and economic development. Pp. 1–21 in R. Phillips, & R. Pittman (eds.), *Introduction to Community Development*, 2nd edition. London: Routledge.

Preston, J.D. & Enck, G.E. 1989. The racial bifurcation of community development: implications for community development practitioners. *Community Development* 20(2): 49–58.

Richards, L. & Dalbey, M. 2006. Creating great places: The role of citizen participation community development. *Community Development* 37(4): 18–32.

Sabre, R.M. 1980. An ethical principle for social justice in community development practice. *Community Development* 11(1): 15–22.

Smart Growth Networ. 2020. Retrieved 2 January from: https://smartgrowth.org/what-is-the-smart-growth-network/.

Community Development as Social Movement: A Contribution to Models of Practice

John J. Green

Community development practice includes the self-help, technical assistance and conflict models. Although instructive, this realm of practical theorizing might be reinvigorated by directing attention to the work that people engage in collectively to impact community life. Approaching community development from an action-oriented direction requires that we borrow from, synthesize and augment existing theoretical perspectives within the realm of social movements, including those focused on political-economic constraints and opportunities, resource mobilization and organization, and framing of grievances and collective action. This approach will help to inform researchers, community development practitioners and policymakers to better understanding the enterprise of intentional social change at the local level. Additionally, it holds promise for those scholars engaged in applied research with change initiatives who want to pursue a more critical assessment of community development work.

If it is to be used in informing practice, theory must help us to interpret and understand the world. Community theory may benefit from directing more attention to the work that people collectively do to shape community life. As one step in this direction, models of community development practice should be revisited to bring in and synthesize theory describing, interpreting and understanding people's strategic action. Approaching community development from this action-oriented direction requires consideration of existing theoretical perspectives within the realms of collective action and social movements, especially those focused on political-economic constraints and opportunities, resource mobilization and organization, and framing of grievances and collective action. These insights fit well with and add depth to the primary models of community development practice: the self-help, technical assistance and conflict approaches.

To begin this enterprise, the logic behind approaching community development as a form of social movement is outlined. This is followed with a brief overview of prominent

John J. Green: Assistant Professor of Sociology and Community Development, Director of the Institute for Community-Based Research, Division of Social Sciences, Box 3264, Delta State University, Cleveland, Mississippi 38733, Tel: (662) 846-4069, E-mail: jgreen@deltastate.edu. Acknowledgments: The author would like to thank the *CD* special issue editors – Mark Brennan and Ralph Brown – and the anonymous reviewers for their critical insights. Additionally, he acknowledges the contributions made by J. Sanford Rikoon, Elizabeth Barham, William Heffernan, Clarence Lo, Corinne Valdivia and Bernard Lewis to the early development of many of the ideas expressed in this article.

models of community development and a review of three theoretical frameworks in the social movement literature. The article ends with a discussion of the ways in which the proposed theoretical framework may help to inform researchers, community development practitioners and policymakers.

Conceptualizing Community Development

Theoretical frameworks are important for making sense of the world and people's actions within it, and community work provides an arena of study and critical reflection (Ledwith, 2001). There have been numerous attempts to construct theoretically informed approaches to better understand community and community development work. Conceiving of theory as a conversation within a discipline or field (Neitz, 1999), sense making (Knight, 2002), and providing orienting frames (Domahidy, 2003), it is useful to bridge multiple ways of thinking about and looking at community development, including consideration of literature from outside of the traditional community field.

It is necessary to provide a working definition of community development. Drawing from a wide variety of definitions, Christenson, Fendley and Robinson (1989, p. 14) define it as "a group of people in a locality initiating a social action process (i.e., planned intervention) to change their economic, social, cultural and/or environmental situation". As part of a critical review of community development theory, Bhattacharyya (2004) is more concise, defining community development as the "pursuit of solidarity and agency" (pp. 14, 25). For this article, the two definitions are combined to view community development as collective social action toward solidarity and agency focused on a particular locality.

Based on the insights from leading theorists in the field (Buechler, 2000; McAdam, 1999; McAdam, McCarthy & Zald, 1996), social movements are thought to build from collective social action to involve a wide combination of individuals, informal groups, formal organizations and networks across time and space. Social actors' work goes beyond specific ends to incorporate broader agendas. Efforts to define and implement the best means to achieve these goals are often contested, both from within and outside of the social movement. At this broader level, community development may be approached as *collective action for solidarity and agency in a particular place that often expands to involve a range of formal and informal groups working between and across places*.

In many communities there are people who are working together to "improve" the situation in which they and others live. They are engaged in the neighborhood through church, and operate through a wide variety of business and civic organizations. They clearly do not all agree on what this "improvement" should be. Used rather loosely, improvement, development and growth are contested concepts. Some people and groups might focus their attention on business recruitment of low-wage employers, while others attend to "living wage" jobs and corporate responsibility. There may be groups that try to recruit heavy industry, while others focus on conservation of natural areas or pursuing environmental justice. Groups attend to affordable housing, but there also are those who want to develop more expensive housing as a way of attracting wealthier families. Despite their differences, these are all representations of collective action toward some definition of development. The concept of development, however, is conflict-ridden and negotiated, and therefore part of their collective work is to construct definitions of development, mobilize and organize people around those definitions, and take action to achieve their goals, all in an environment of structural relations and unequal access to resources.

Action within any particular community does not take place in a vacuum. People are connected to other communities through their past experiences, families and organizations. Media tell them what is happening in other places, and this provides a broader context in which to assess their situation relative to more general standards. People are impacted by broader economic trends, policies and conflicts, ranging from the regional to national and global levels. This type of "messy" interaction results in the creation of dispersed social movements where social action may have spontaneously arisen in a few locales but is brought together toward larger agendas such as civil rights, access to health care, environmental protection, and downtown revitalization at the same time as legal reform, educational standards and business-friendly environments. Communities and their movements within them are influenced by the broader mass culture and ways of getting things done. For example, we see similar types of organizations pursuing development across the nation and world more broadly (e.g., churches, unions, nonprofits, cooperatives, nongovernmental organizations, credit unions and so on).

Here it is important to address the point that approaching community development as collective social action and social movement will emphasize strategic work on particular issues or problems rather than *the* community as an entity in and of itself. While many community theorists might argue that the focus should be on demarcating the boundaries of community, understanding people's sense of place, and so forth, the framework being proposed here assumes that people typically engage the community through the vehicles of specific issues and problems as they relate to a particular place. Thus, the broader issues are necessary but not sufficient to understanding concepts of development and action. This point is in no way novel. Wilkinson (1989, p. 341) makes a similar argument. He states that,

"In practice, community development means that people who are engaged in efforts to reach specific goals and solve specific community problems also pay attention to the community relationships involved in their efforts. . . . Ironically, however, community development rarely is the manifest purpose of the action. More often this purpose is secondary to such purposes as attracting jobs to the local area or solving some particular local problem. . . . Community development emerges typically as an assertion of community interest during the course of actions addressing other more specific goals."

Following Wilkinson's lead, this article will now turn to attempting just that, understanding when, where and how "community development emerges" through people's interests and action in pursuing goals.

Models of Practice

A starting point for considering community development as social action and social movement is the strong and robust tradition of work focused on models of practice in the field. In a general sense, there are three broad models or themes under which community development work takes place. They are the self-help, technical assistance and conflict approaches (Christenson, 1989; Green & Haines, 2008; Hardina, 2002). The self-help approach focuses on community residents working to pursue their own goals and further develop their capacity for action. The focus is on community building (Littrell & Hobbs, 1989). Professional community development practitioners may play a role in this, but it is typically in the form of a facilitator and/or resource person. The technical assistance approach concerns access to and provisioning of information, technical skills and expertise for development initiatives. These resources are seen as being needed by community residents to pursue their collective goals (Fear, Gamm, & Fisher, 1989). Typically attributed to the work of Alinsky (1972, 1969) but expanded through the wisdom generated by civil rights and anti-poverty movements, the conflict approach to community development focuses on mobilizing, organizing and advocating for change. It is more confrontational and power-focused than the other models (Robinson, 1989). Over the past few decades, theorizing has been expanded on participatory and empowerment approaches to development drawing from the work of Freire (1972). This model attends to building a sense of consciousness, addressing power inequalities and expanding access to resources for people to pursue their development agendas.

These are ideal types of community development practice. On the ground, it is likely that most development initiatives involve a combination of these models in multiple variant forms. These models are useful for categorizing development activities and analyzing subsequent strategies and techniques, but more consideration is needed to better understand how, why and to what ends people take these different approaches to community development. Social movement theory will help in this regard.

Social Movement Theories

Social action and social movements take place and are influenced by multiple levels of reality, and at each of these levels there are structures and cultural constructs that are created, re-created and transformed by social actors which in turn influence future action (Buechler, 2000). There are three primary and interconnected dimensions (Table 1): political-economic constraints and opportunities, mobilization and organization, and grievance and collective action frames (see: Buechler, 2000; McAdam, 1999; McAdam, McCarthy & Zald, 1996).

Table 1. Three Dimensions of Collective Action and Social Movements

Dimensions	Issues of Interest
Political-Economic Constraints and Opportunities	Broad political-economic characteristics of time and place Social actors as "insiders" or "outsiders" Perceived contradictions in structures and processes
Mobilization and Organization	Organizational infrastructure Access to and use of resources Organizational structures, rules and norms Communication networks
Grievance and Collection Action Frames	Social actors' understanding of prevailing structures and processes Claims and frames concerning what needs to/can be done Social actors' positions, roles and identities Comparison of views between social actors and broader "publics"

Political-Economic Constraints and Opportunities

Bhattacharyya (2004) maintains that community development is part of responses to broad historic processes of social change that have eroded solidarity and agency, including industrial capitalism, the nation-state and positivist reason. Augmenting this line of thought, attention is needed to how these responses shape and are shaped by the political-economic situation in which they take place. There are theorists who focus attention on the shifting political-economic constraints and opportunities that shape social movements (McAdam, 1999; Pellow, 2001; Tarrow, 1998). In addition to an understanding of broad contextual characteristics of the time and place of interest including the structure of the ruling regime, existence of some semblance of democracy and a free press, of particular concern is whether social actors are considered insiders or outsiders in decision-making processes. Comparable to this is Lo's call for theorists to look at the divide between the polity and challengers and to question how and why some groups move from being challengers to being a part of the polity while others do not (1992). Also, as Pellow points out, it is crucial not to be state-centric in this analysis, because corporate firms and quasi-governmental bodies are increasing their control over decision-making processes (2001). This is of particular concern in community development work, where nongovernmental organizations, private foundations, businesses and religious groups are all involved in shaping, implementing and deciding the future of programs and policies. Therefore, it is critical to investigate who/what is considered legitimate (insider/outsider) in a more expanded understanding of politics to include a broader set of institutions, mainly those operating within the state, economy and civil society. These factors may influence whether self-help, technical assistance or conflict models of development are utilized.

Important areas of focus are the extent to which participation in decision making is officially sanctioned, actually exists, and whether it is popularly practiced. For some movements the first battle might be for a disempowered group to gain recognition as a legitimate participant in a particular realm and then followed by attempts to actually participate in decision making. For instance, civil rights activists worked for decades in the United States to gain the acceptance of marginalized ethnic and racial groups in government decision-making circles. In doing so, they focused attention primarily, but not solely, on voting rights. After achieving "official" legally sanctioned recognition of the rights of Blacks and other minority groups, activists then sought to make participation a reality, addressing such issues as access to public institutions. As victories were achieved, the focus of attention shifted increasingly toward economic relations, where they continue to face great resistance. (For assessments of the Civil Rights Movement from social movement perspectives useful for community development, see: ; Dittmer, 1994; Green, 2002; McAdam, 1999; Payne, 1995).

Political-economic constraints and opportunities are also of interest in terms of social actors being able to identify and capitalize on perceived contradictions in social structures and processes which undermine the status quo (McAdam, 1999; Williams, 2001). As McAdam (1999, p. 41) argues,

"The point is that *any* event or broad social process that serves to undermine the calculations and assumptions on which the political establishment is structured occasions a shift in political opportunity. Among the events and processes likely to prove disruptive of the political status quo are wars, industrialization, international political realignments, prolonged unemployment, and widespread demographic changes" [emphasis in original].

According to the political process model, the influence of these factors is more indirect than direct (McAdam, 1999). Impact primarily results from the restructuring of power relations which are then conducive to specific forms of mobilization, organization and models of practice.

Examples of political contradictions and opportunities abound in histories of the American Civil Rights Movement. Starting with World War I and continuing through World War II, the Brotherhood of Sleeping Car Porters, led by A. Philip Randolph, contrasted Black emancipation from slavery, official citizenship granted with Amendments to the U.S. Constitution, participation in national defense, and contributions through economic activities to the continued existence of racial codes keeping Blacks from fully exercising their rights. The southern wing of the civil rights struggle also used the contradiction seen in fighting for freedom abroad while being denied the right to vote and access public facilities at home as one of its primary mobilizing messages in local, state and national campaigns (Bates, 2001; Dittmer, 1994; Payne, 1995). Recent work on the struggle of Black farmers in the American South tells a similar story (Green, 2002). Activists noted their participation in the production process and contributing to rural development, yet Blacks were systematically denied access to the programs and credit afforded to other farmers, thereby denying them basic fairness in public services. Utilizing both conflict and self-help models of practice, they used tactics to obtain acceptance by the U.S. Department of Agriculture as legitimate farmers parallel with efforts to organize a variety of self-help cooperative groups and credit unions.

Mobilization and Organization

Within the context of broader political-economic structures and opportunities and constraints, collective action and social movements take form through the activities of mobilization and organization (Payne, 1995). Mobilization concerns the processes by which leaders are able to inform and persuade others to commit to a cause and participate in activities ranging from direct protests such as sit-ins, marches and boycotts to fund-raising, public awareness campaigns, policy advocacy and even the creation of alternative institutions (e.g., cooperatives). Organization consists of the processes through which people interact over time to develop a deeper understanding of a movement and its goals and work toward those goals through a variety of informal and formal mechanisms (Payne, 1995). These are related processes, and both of them are necessary for social movements and their organizations.

In the attempt to better understand mobilization and organization, the insights provided in resource mobilization and political process literatures are especially helpful (McCarthy & Zald, 1977; Tilly, 1978; Zald & McCarthy, 1987), as is the work from community development and community practice within social work (Hardina, 2002). Beyond issues of identity (discussed below under "grievance and collective action frames"), one area of focus in this realm is the development, life-course and survival or demise of movements and their organizations. To start, the existence and strength of indigenous community organizations from other arenas, civic groups and churches are of interest. They often provide the foundation on which mobilization and organization occur. Again noting the example of the Civil Rights Movement, analysts have pointed to the critical role of the church in providing an organizational base and structure.

Another factor of concern – organizational infrastructure – is largely dependent on four basic resources: 1) participants' integration in community life, 2) established structures of incentives, 3) communication networks, and 4) recognized leadership (McAdam, 1999). Researchers have addressed access to various resources (e.g., money, labor, networks) and the strategic use of these resources by social actors in their attempts to create change (Zald & McCarthy, 1987). Results stress the existence of important relationships between the source and control of resources and the avenues utilized for achieving change. A primary issue in this regard is whether resources are derived from internally or externally based individuals and/or organizations. Sources of monetary funding, whether generated through membership dues, personal investments, public fund-raising events, private foundations or government grants, all have the potential to influence organizational structure and the types of activities that an organization may undertake. Although access to financial resources outside of the organization may be crucial to its longevity and participation in movement activities and broader networks, outside funders sometimes attempt to influence the direction of the organization in an often de-radicalizing way, changing the nature of its work from conflict to self-help and/or technical assistance models of practice.

Also of importance in the realm of mobilization and organization are the structural forms that exist in the movement, as well as the shape and extent of their networks. Based on social movement groups being the primary actors in pursuing change and the assumption that once formed, the continued existence of these groups is one of the many goals of action, the shape and structure of organizations are crucial to the success of a movement (Zald & McCarthy, 1987). Two of the most common organizational structures are federated organizations – horizontally organized networks of relatively autonomous groups – and isolated constituency organizations – hierarchically organized networks of individuals. There are numerous substantive organizational forms that follow ideal-type structures, often as a result of the rules set forth by regulatory bodies. Such organizations include nonprofits, community development corporations (CDCs) and cooperatives, to name just a few. Interestingly, a body of literature is being developed around the issue of the opportunities and constraints posed by the CDC as an organizational form (for example, see: Stoecker, 1997). Zald (1966) notes the importance of analyzing organizational structures, rules and procedures to better understand their place and influence within a movement.

Organizational form has both instrumental and symbolic value. Different structural forms may be more or less conducive to promoting organizational maintenance and/or influencing social change. Part of this effectiveness rests on what the particular organizational form symbolizes. This can be a tenuous relationship. Williams (2001) argues that blatantly hierarchical organizations with little in the way of participation mechanisms may be highly effective in mobilizing some resources, especially from traditional sources, but the legitimacy of such an organization in a democratic struggle may be limited from the perspective of both activists and the wider public (Williams, 2001).

Organizational mechanisms for participation are of major concern. Considering a continuum ranging from marginal to full participation in decision making, Williams provides a list of functional benefits to be gained from the latter end of the spectrum (2001). These include organizations being able to avoid selective repression within their own ranks, convince onlookers that the organization represents something that is alternative to prevailing structures, and to have a diverse repertoire of strategies at hand for advancing the movement. Assessing organizational structures on this basis requires a deeper focus than simply looking at the existence or nonexistence of formalized participation mechanisms. The actual use of such mechanisms, how they impact decision making and their relationship to more informal modes of interaction all need attention. And, as Arnstein (1969) points out, there is a continuum of participation from token inclusion to full involvement in decision-making processes.

Organizations are embedded in fields of multiple actors that overlap in numerous networks (Klandermans, 1992). They may be networked in a variety of ways, resulting from the possible and/or preferred level of participation and interaction among participants. Two prominent examples include networks of newly formed organizations and networks created through previously existing organizations, including, but not limited to, indigenous groups (Zald & McCarthy, 1987). There are also two primary levels of inter-organizational connections. With the first there is overlap between organizations in terms of joint activities, board members, staff and resources. As for the second, there are links between organizations through the multiple affiliations of individual members (Klandermans, 1992). Whatever their form, these networks serve as avenues through which information is diffused, group cohesion is developed and a variety of actions take place. They also represent space for participation beyond the internal relations of specific groups. Organizations that tend to work on similar issues with compatible constituencies are referred to as solidarity networks.

Occupying the typical focus of social movement analyses, solidarity networks are not the only ones in which social actors and their organizations are embedded. Networks include alliance and conflict systems, and both need to be taken into account (Fantasia, 1988; Klandermans, 1992; McAdam, 1999). In other words, besides solidarity networks, social movement organizations are embedded in oppositional networks that shape and are shaped by their action. One result of this interaction is the alteration of a proactive social movement attempt to gain, for example, greater social services for poor families, to one that is reactive where activists have to spend their time and energy on protecting those services already in place.

Insights from resource mobilization and organization theories fit well with, and are complemented by, contemporary asset-based frameworks widely used within the field of community development. Much of this work has taken place largely through "capitals" analysis (Flora, Flora & Fey, 2004; Green & Haines, 2008; Kretzmann & McKnight, 1993). Asset-based approaches to understanding and pursuing community development are concerned with the assets that individuals, groups and communities have to pursue their collective goals (Kretzmann & McKnight, 1993). These assets may be generally grouped in the following categories: human, social, financial/economic, political, cultural, physical, and environmental (Flora, Flora & Fey, 2004; Green & Haines, 2008). Among the many combinations of assets, local organizations, community institutions and networks are particularly important. Assets must be recognized, mobilized and organized for collective action. And, in cases where needed resources are not available locally, they must be accessed through extra-local networks. Also compatible with a focus on resource mobilization and organization research is the livelihood systems framework (Bebbington, 1999, 1996; De Haan, 2000; De Haan & Zoomers, 2005; Meert, 2000). Studies conducted in both veins demonstrate that a variety of assets provide capabilities for action.

Grievance and Collective Action Frames

Peet and Watts note that social movements are just as much about cultural struggles over meaning and identity as they are struggles over material conditions and resources (1996). Therefore, to better understand specific social movements and organizations, it is necessary to look at the multiple ways in which social actors understand the situation they face and believe that it can and should be changed. Compatible with approaches aimed at grasping processes of collective attribution (Ferree & Miller, 1985), the framing approach to social movements may be especially useful (Gamson, 1992; Goffman, 1974).

The framing approach involves a combination of taking "folk understandings" of the world and comparatively evaluating them (Lo, 1990). Building on the work of Goffman, the concept "frame" refers empirically to patterns of experiencing and perceiving events that shape social reality (Eder, 1996; Goffman, 1974). Frames are derived from "accounts" of particular and generalized situations and events, and they exist at multiple levels of abstraction. They include social actors' understanding of structural arrangements and processes, what they claim ultimately needs to be done about them, and how they see themselves as playing a role in the process. Frames are often strategically constructed so as to resonate with a specific membership base or broader audience. Additionally, they are part of the socialization process and are packed with cultural meaning.

With grievance and collective action frames, beliefs about structures and power relations serve to define collective activity in particular contexts (see: Snow and Benford, 1992). Grievances concerning social order may be framed in various ways (Buechler, 2000; Klandermans, De Weerd & Sabucedo, 1999; Snow & Benford, 1988). Diagnostic framing involves the identification of a problem and assigning blame or arguing causality. Such injustice frames provide movements with targets for their action. Prognostic framing involves the identification and articulation of how a problematic situation may be changed. Taken together, these framing processes translate dissatisfaction into calls for action (Buechler, 2000). Important to transforming these frames into a wider social movement are frame alignment processes which serve to bridge different frames in ways that shape more general social action (Buechler, 2000).

Framing takes places through interaction between actors in solidarity and conflict networks. It is when there is controversy and conflict over development initiatives that we hear and see frames most vividly. People and organizations vie for attention from each other, policymakers, leaders and the general public.

The role of the general public, whether conceived of in narrow interest group terms or more broadly as citizens, consumers or constituents, should not be discounted in analysis of collective action and social movement. Put simply, the state relies on the public for legitimacy, businesses need consumers for purchases, and civil society organizations must have members for their time, money and voluntary support. Social movement actors and their opponents make claims about what "most people think." This constructed legitimacy is in large part the currency or capital of collective action. As analysts, it is critical to know what people at the community level think. What are their perceptions and frames of the issues at hand? How does this fit with the characterizations offered by leaders? What are the similarities and differences?

Identity and solidarity are factors in need of attention in understanding grievance and collective action frames. One might ask how actors identifying themselves as members of a particular class, ethnic/racial group or gender view the world differently than those who identify themselves in other ways. Furthermore, it is necessary not only to look at actors' understanding of the world at-large or a particular segment of it, but also to assess whether their frames promote or limit collective definitions and action. In conducting such assessment, it is crucial not to divorce the issues of identity or consciousness from the action being undertaken (Fantasia, 1988). It is important not to define specific identity attributes, such as class, ethnicity or race, as all-encompassing to action *a priori*. It may be the case that these categories represent just one segment of identity among many others. Identities might even be contested as part of the conflict.

This is an area where new social movement theoretical approaches may prove insightful, especially those strands that focus attention on identity (Habermas, 1989; Melucci, 1989; Touraine, 2001, 1981). Theorists from this perspective maintain that the relationship between collective identity and collective action in the form of social movements has been under-explored. Collective identity is viewed as processual and rooted in the lived experiences of social actors and their relation to each other. Collective identities, it is argued, are most likely to develop around shared experiences in a particular context. Collective action and movements are made possible when social actors as a group are able to recognize the effects of their actions and attribute outcomes to their endeavors.

New social movement theorists view many contemporary collective struggles as being primarily based on the terrain of cultural identity and demands for cultural rights as opposed to the classical movements seen as concerning material conditions (Touraine, 2001). This so-called cultural battle is not just the case, however, for "post-industrial" countries or middle-class groups within such countries. In extrapolating findings and theory, it is necessary to move away from the Western, middle-class bias of many new social movement theories and conceive of identity more broadly (Buechler, 2000). Following Gramsci's (1999) line of thought, power struggles always incorporate both material and cultural elements. This holistic understanding is crucial when considering marginalized groups in terms of class or ethnicity/race whose material livelihoods are directly tied to their cultural identity and where both are threatened (Bebbington, 1996; Escobar, 1992; Pulido, 1996). Pulido notes that while researchers only recently acknowledged the role of identity in social movements, it has surely played an important part since long before this recognition.

Synthesis for Exploring Community Development as Social Movement

This article has presented an argument in favor of conceiving of community development work as social action and broader social movements. This framework has much to offer understanding of community development models of practice. Considering the self-help, technical assistance and conflict models as ideal types of strategic community work, the proposed framework sheds light on maintenance and change of prevailing community structures and processes while taking broader social, political, economic and cultural forces into account. The purpose is to better describe and interpret "community work" and how social actors' efforts fit in with the construction of community. Approaching community development from this direction, there are several questions that an analyst might want to address. These include, but are not limited to, the following:

- What are the social, political-economic, cultural and/or ecological characteristics of the communities in which an issue or problem has arisen? What are the opportunities and constraints for collective action?
- How is the issue defined and framed? Who (individuals and organizations) are involved in constructing this meaning?
- Do the frames and claims about the problem provide avenues for individual, collective and/or institutional responses? What are the proposed solutions offered by the various social actors? How are they similar, and how do they differ?
- Which models of community practice are pursued?
- What strategies and techniques are implemented? Who is involved? What are the outcomes from their actions?
- How and to what extent do particular combinations of problem definition, solutions and organized responses result in or inhibit the rise and strengthening of social interaction and networks that make for a more resilient community? Are assets further developed?

There are benefits to this social movement framework that are likely to contribute to understanding community development practice. It provides an avenue for critically assessing intentional social change, including perceptions, structures, constraints and opportunities, thus augmenting insights from the models of development practice. Furthermore, the framework emphasizes creativity and action in the development process, all while taking structural concerns into account. Within this action, both development practitioners and organizations are incorporated into the analysis. It also allows for assessment between levels of analysis from the micro to macro level, tracing specific issues and projects as well as the abstract.

This social movement framework of community development practice also is compatible with action and community-based approaches to applied research. It is useful to scholars who work directly with organizations engaged in community practice. The framework allows them to take a more grounded, reflexive approach to their work. For instance, an analyst might ask how community organization leaders, staff and volunteers define and act toward a situation, and then compare this to what other social actors are saying and doing. These others could include the general public, elites and policymakers. This information could then be used to evaluate development efforts, shape future practice, and mitigate conflict.

Clearly, there is more to the construction, maintenance and/or change of community than intentional action, constraints and opportunities. However, addressing these issues will help in construction of a more thorough and penetrating understanding of community and community change. To end, it is important to place this argument in the larger context of sociological and community organizational discourse. This is best done by Zald (1966, p. 56) in his address delivered more than forty years ago to social workers engaged in community practice. He states,

"The interdependence of subject matter in the fields of community organization and sociology has long been recognized by teachers and practitioners. Possibly to a greater extent than with any other segment of social work, the problems of this field of practice are grist for the mill of the student of society and the community. And yet, there is no systematic sociology of community organization.... Such a sociology would include a social history of the emergence and growth of the field of practice, an analysis of its ongoing social system, and diagnostic categories and criteria for investigating community problems and structure."

Here it is contended that social movement theory adds to such a sociology of community organization and community development.

References

Alinsky, S. (1972). *Rules for radicals*. New York: Random House.
Alinsky, S. (1969). *Reveille for radicals*. New York: Random House.
Arnstein, S.R. (1969). A ladder of citizen participation. *Journal of the American Planning Association*, 35(4): 216-224.
Bates, B.T. (2001). *Pullman porters and the rise of protest politics in Black America, 1925-1945*. Chapel Hill, NC: University of North Carolina Press.
Bebbington, A. (1999). Capitals and capabilities: A framework for analyzing peasant viability, rural livelihoods and poverty. *World Development*, 27(12): 2021-2044.
Bebbington, A. (1996). Movements, modernizations and markets: Indigenous organizations and agrarian strategies in Ecuador. In R. Peet & M. Watts (eds.) *Liberation ecologies: Environment, development, social movements* (pp. 86-109). London: Routledge.
Bhattacharyya, J. (2004). Theorizing community development. *Journal of the Community Development Society*, 34(2): 5-34.
Buechler, S.M. (2000). *Social movements in advanced capitalism: The political economy and cultural construction of social activism*. New York: Oxford University Press.
Christenson, J.A. (1989). Themes of community development. In J.A. Christenson and J.W. Robinson, Jr. (eds.) *Community development in perspective* (pp. 26-47). Ames, IA: Iowa State University Press.
Christenson, J.A., Fendley, K. & Robinson, J.W. (1989). Community development. In J.A. Christenson and J.W. Robinson, Jr. (eds.) *Community development in perspective* (pp. 3-25). Ames, IA: Iowa State University Press.
De Haan, L.J. (2000). Globalization, localization and sustainable livelihood. *Sociologia Ruralis*, 40(3): 339-365.
De Haan, L. & Zoomers, A. (2005). Exploring the frontier of livelihoods research. *Development and Change*, 36: 27-47.
Dittmer, J. (1994). *Local people: The struggle for civil rights in Mississippi*. Urbana, IL: University of Illinois Press.
Domahidy, M. (2003). Using theory to frame community and practice. *Journal of the Community Development Society*, 34(1): 75-84.
Eder, K. (1996). *The social construction of nature: A sociology of ecological enlightenment*. London: Sage Publications.
Escobar, A. (1992). Culture, economics, and politics in Latin American social movements, theory and research. In A. Escobar & S. Alvarez (eds.) *The making of social movements in Latin America* (pp. 62-85). Boulder, CO: Westview Press.
Fantasia, R. (1988). *Cultures of solidarity: Consciousness, action and contemporary American workers*. Berkeley, CA: University of California Press.
Fear, F., Gamm, L. & Fisher, F. (1989). The technical assistance Approach. In J.A. Christenson and J.W. Robinson, Jr. (eds.) *Community development in perspective* (pp. 69-88). Ames, IA: Iowa State University Press.
Ferree, M.M. & Miller, F.D. (1985). Mobilization and meaning: Toward an integration of social psychological and resource perspectives on social movements. *Sociological Inquiry*, 55(1): 38-61.
Freire, P. (1972). *Pedagogy of the oppressed*. New York: Penguin Books.
Flora, C., Flora, J. & Fey, S. (2004). *Rural communities: Legacy and change*. Boulder, CO: Westview

Press.
Gamson, W.A. (1992). *Talking politics*. Cambridge, UK: Cambridge University Press.
Goffman, E. (1974). *Frame analysis: An essay on the organization of experience*. Boston: Harvard University Press.
Gramsci, A. (1999). *Selections from the prison notebooks*. New York: International Publishers.
Green, G. and Haines, A. (2008). *Asset building and community development*. Thousand Oaks, CA: Sage Publications.
Green, J.J. (2002). Community-based cooperatives and networks: Participatory social movement assessment of four organizations. Doctoral Dissertation, Department of Rural Sociology, University of Missouri-Columbia.
Habermas, J. (1989). *The theory of communicative action, Volume II. Lifeworld and system: A critique of functionalist reason*. Boston: Beacon Press.
Hardina, D. (2002). *Analytical skills for community practice*. Irvington, NY: Columbia University Press.
Klandermans, B. (1992). The social construction of protest and multiorganizational fields. In A.D. Morris & C.M. Mueller (eds.) *Frontiers in social movement theory* (pp. 77-103). New Haven, CT: Yale University Press.
Klandermans, B., De Weerd, M. & Sabucedo, J.M. (1999). Injustice and adversarial frames in a supranational political context: Farmers' protest in the Netherlands and Spain. In D. Porta, H. Kriesi & D. Rucht (eds.) *Social Movements in a Globalizing World* (pp. 134-147). New York: St. Martin's Press.
Knight, P. (2002). *Small-scale research: Pragmatic inquiry in social science and the caring professions*. London: Sage Publications.
Kretzmann, J. & McKnight, J. (1993). *Building communities from the inside out: A path toward finding and mobilizing a community's assets*. Evanston, IL: Center for Urban Affairs and Policy Research, Northwestern University.
Ledwith, M. (2001). Community Work as critical pedagogy: Re-envisioning Freire and Gramsci. *Journal of the Community Development Society*, 36(3): 171-182.
Littrell, D.W. & Hobbs, D. (1989). The self-help approach. In J.A. Christenson and J.W. Robinson, Jr. (eds.) *Community development in perspective* (pp. 48-68). Ames, IA: Iowa State University Press.
Lo, C. (1992). Communities of challengers in social movement theory. In A.D. Morris & C.M. Mueller (eds.) *Frontiers in social movement theory* (pp. 224-248). New Haven, CT: Yale University Press.
Lo, C. (1990). *Small property versus big government: Social origins of the property tax revolt*. Berkeley, CA: University of California Press.
McAdam, D. (1999). *Political process and the development of Black insurgency, 1930-1970*. Chicago, IL: University of Chicago Press.
McAdam, D., McCarthy, J.D. & Zald, M.N. (1996). *Comparative perspectives on social movements: Political opportunities, mobilizing structures and cultural framings*. Cambridge, UK: Cambridge University Press.
McCarthy, J.D. & Zald, M.N. (1977). Resource mobilization and social movements: A partial theory. *American Journal of Sociology*, 82: 1212-1241.
Meert, H. (2000). Rural community life and the importance of reciprocal survival strategies. *Sociologia Ruralis*, 40(3): 319-338.
Melucci, A. (1989). *Nomads of the present*. London: Hutchinson Radius.
Neitz, M.J. (1999). Course lecture in qualitative research methods. Columbia, MO: University of Missouri.
Payne, C.M. (1995). *I've got the light of freedom: The organizing tradition and the Mississippi freedom struggle*. Berkeley, CA: University of California Press.
Peet, R. & Watts, M. (1996). Liberation ecology: Development, sustainability, and environment in an age of market triumphalism. In R. Peet & M. Watts (eds.) *Liberation ecologies: Environment, development, social movements* (pp. 1-45). London: Routledge.
Pellow, D.N. (2001). Environmental justice and the political process: Movements, corporations, and the state. *Sociological Quarterly*, 42(1): 47-67.
Pulido, L. (1996). *Environmentalism and Economic justice: Two Chicano struggles in the Southwest*.

Tucson, AZ: University of Arizona Press.

Robinson, J.W., Jr. (1989). The conflict approach. In J.A. Christenson and J.W. Robinson, Jr. (eds.) *Community development in perspective* (pp. 89-116). Ames, IA: Iowa State University Press.

Snow, D.A. & Benford, R.D. (1992). Master frames and cycles of protest. In A.D. Morris & C.M. Mueller (eds.) *Frontiers in social movement theory* (pp. 133-155). New Haven, CT: Yale University Press.

Snow, D.A. (1988). Ideology, frame resonance and participant mobilization. In B. Klandermans, H. Kriesi & S. Tarrow (eds.) *International social movement research* (pp. 197-217). Greenwich, CT: JAI Press, Inc.

Stoecker, R. (1997). The CDC model of urban redevelopment: A critique and an alternative. *Journal of Urban Affairs*, 19(1): 1-22.

Tarrow, S. (1998). *Power in movement: Social movements and contentious politics*. NY: Cambridge University Press.

Tilly, C. (1978). *From mobilization to revolution*. Reading, MA: Addison-Wesley.

Touraine, A. (2001). *Beyond neoliberalism*. Cambridge, UK: Polity Press.

Touraine, A. (1981). *The voice and the eye: An analysis of social movements*. Cambridge, UK: Cambridge University Press.

Wilkinson, K. (1989). The future for community development. In J.A. Christenson & J.W. Robinson, Jr. (eds.) *Community development in perspective* (pp. 337-354). Ames, IA: Iowa State University Press.

Williams, H. (2001). *Social movements and economic transition: Markets and distributive conflict in Mexico*. Cambridge, NY: Cambridge University Press.

Zald, M.N. (1966). Organizations as polities: An analysis of community organization agencies. *Social Work*, 11(4): 56-65.

Zald, M.N. & McCarthy, J. D. (eds). (1987). *Social movements in an organizational society: Collected essays*. New Brunswick, NJ: Transaction Books.

Incorporating social justice in tourism planning: racial reconciliation and sustainable community development in the Deep South

Alan W. Barton* and Sarah J. Leonard

Tourism can serve as a vehicle for sustainable community development by contributing to equity and social justice. This happens as tourists learn about marginal groups through educational tourism, engage in development projects with host-area residents, undertake pilgrimages that bring greater meaning and cohesiveness to an ethnic identity, or encounter stories that transform their view of social injustice and spur further action to reduce inequities. Tourism planning can produce a sense of reconciliation when it brings historically divided groups together. An example is found in Tallahatchie County, Mississippi, where a group of white and African American residents are collaborating to develop tourism projects designed around a narrative of reconciliation, while they use the process of tourism planning to work towards racial reconciliation within their community. This case illustrates strategies tourism planners employ and challenges they face when they envision tourism as more than merely a means of economic growth.

The advantages of tourism to rural communities are generally painted as economic: developing a tourism industry brings in "fresh" dollars, provides jobs and offers opportunities for local entrepreneurship (National Agricultural Library, 2008; World Travel & Tourism Council, 2008). When tourism focuses on local heritage, cultural advantages can accrue as well, as local residents learn about, take pride in, and conserve their own stories (Barton, 2005; Howard, 2002; President's Committee on the Arts and the Humanities, 2005). A growing body of literature argues that tourism can also contribute to social equity and justice in rural communities, and that social and cultural factors are important elements in sustainable community development in many rural contexts (Higgins-Desbiolles, 2008; Moore & Jie Wen, 2009; Scheyvens & Momsen, 2008). Recently, the social justice aspects of tourism have received substantial attention in the media as well (see, e.g., Gentleman, 2006; Lancaster, 2007; Markey, 2007; Popescu, 2007; Rao, 2009; Weiner, 2008).

We consider one aspect of social justice, the case of racial reconciliation in the Deep South. The Civil Rights Movement that emerged in the mid-twentieth century

---

*Corresponding author. Email: abarton@deltastate.edu

in America made substantial progress in the extension of political rights to African Americans, but economic disparities and cultural differences continue to separate black and white residents in much of the region (Andrews, 1997; Austin, 2006; Edelman, 2005; Hill, 2007; US Commission on Civil Rights, 2001). We draw on a case study of a rural county in the Mississippi Delta to examine how tourism might contribute to or detract from equality and social justice in rural communities, and the challenges that community planners face when promoting tourism as a means of addressing ingrained racial disparities.

Sustainable community development

When assessing tourism as a community development strategy, community planners must consider how tourism will contribute in a sustainable way to community well-being (Haywood, 1988; Richards & Hall, 2000). The literature on sustainable development has emphasized three crucial dimensions: economic efficiency, environmental integrity and social equity and justice (Edwards, 2005; Klein-Vielhauer, 2009; World Commission on Environment and Development, 1987). Finding a balance among these factors that is appropriate in a given context increases the chances for sustainability, and distortions arise when one of these elements dominates the others. In the tourism industry, economic considerations frequently drive decisions, while the potential for negative impacts such as environmental deterioration and increased inequity are given less attention.

Sustainable tourism

Tourism has the potential to produce social inequities in a variety of ways. Mass tourism organized along industrial lines is largely a product of modern society (Eadington & Smith, 1992; Malkin, 1999), and like many industries, tourism produces core-periphery inequities (Frank, 1986; Murphy & Andressen, 1988; Sharpley, 2001). When tourists travel from an industrial/post-industrial region to a less industrialized region, they tend to exacerbate the economic differences. Host (tourist-receiving) areas benefit economically, as tourists spend money locally on entrance fees, food, gifts and transportation; locals obtain jobs in tourism-oriented businesses; and tourists often pay special taxes. But tourists also purchase services from providers based in core areas, such as airlines, cruise lines, chain hotels and chain restaurants. As a result, the host region does not benefit fully from its hospitality, and often there is a net transfer of value from host to home (tourist-sending) region. One dimension of inequity, then, is the gap between the host and home regions.

Tourism often leads to greater inequities within a host region as well (Thomas, 2009). Some residents are better positioned to capitalize on entrepreneurial opportunities and capture a larger portion of tourist dollars. Others are relegated to low-paying service jobs, and still others are excluded from the tourism industry entirely. An influx of free-spending tourists may drive up prices of basic commodities like food and increase property values, leaving residents outside the industry in a squeeze. Another dimension of inequity is the increasing differentiation within host communities.

The inequities produced by tourism are not solely economic, however, as tourists extract other intangible, often unquantifiable values as well. Heritage tourists take away knowledge and information from a unique museum; tourists on a pilgrimage to a sacred site feel an increased sense of pride in their culture; and tourists who work on a development project in a poor community experience a transformation in their worldview. Does the extraction of these non-monetary values ultimately benefit or harm the host community? Tourists can create relationships with host-area residents, which could lead to benefits to the peripheral area. Tourists who return year-after-year can create the basis for a sustainable local industry. But these factors are conditional, and difficult to quantify (Robinson, 2000). There is no systematic recipe for how a region can optimize its opportunities to capture intangible benefits or reduce intangible losses from tourism.

A similar dilemma arises with respect to culture. The tourism industry appropriates and packages cultural stories, often eroding their authenticity and cultural value (Robinson, 1999). All cultural stories are produced by winnowing through variation to create a meta-narrative (Hitchcock & King, 2003), but what criteria are used to produce that narrative? And whose interests are represented by the narrative that emerges? In industrial tourism, often the criteria and interests are commercial in nature, and the story that emerges is one that will sell to a mass public, bringing money to tourism providers (Cohen, 1988; Kirtsoglou & Theodossopoulos, 2004; Silver, 1993). A third form of inequity, then, is produced by how the tourism narratives are framed, benefiting cultural identities framed as mainstream, and sidelining or excluding others.

By increasing opportunities for local coordination and organization, tourism can build skills and capacities that can be applied in other areas. Organizational systems are a critical part of community development (Fischer, 1989; Flora and Flora, 2008). Tourism builds relationships, and under the right conditions, relationships can grow into institutions, which create the stability necessary for sustainability. Stable relationships and institutions are facilitated under circumstances of relative equality and justice.

Narratives in a tourism industry

The product that tourism providers and officials market is a narrative about the host community; this is the commodity that generates economic growth, as well as social and cultural meaning. The production of this narrative is a complex process of social construction, involving many voices (Edson, 2004). Inequities arise in the construction of the narrative, as some voices are better represented than others, and some may be excluded entirely (Porter & Salazar, 2005). As noted it is often the tourism industry that produces the dominant narrative for public consumption, driven by commercial interests. The narrative, as a result, is often a sanitary version of a much larger, more complex and possibly more uncomfortable story (Kelner, 2001; Kirtsoglou & Theodossopoulos, 2004; Silver, 1993). The distortions that arise from this process marginalize groups whose voices are ignored or underrepresented.

While the processes through which groups are marginalized are complex and context specific, the general process is one in which cultural identity is eroded. This may occur through homogenization into a broader commercial identity, loss of identification with a particular group, or a transformation of identity into something different (Brown, 2003; Edson, 2004).[1] Under some conditions, this refined story may take on new and empowering meaning to peripheral communities; under other conditions, it erodes cultural identity (Cohen, 1988).

Creating narratives of justice through tourism

Tourism contributes to equity and justice by increasing the wealth, power and/or prestige of marginalized groups, by raising awareness among privileged groups, and in some cases by challenging their sense of privilege and entitlement. Several models of tourism for justice have emerged. All are forms of alternative tourism, that is, tourism with a mission that is more than finding sun, sand and sea (Eadington & Smith, 1992).

One model is *Educational Tourism*, in which members of privileged core communities visit less privileged peripheral communities to learn about their reality. Tourists in peripheral regions often see poverty, but educational tourists intentionally visit impoverished areas with the specific goal of learning about them, and the impoverished people are organized to benefit from the tourists. Educational tourism allows marginal groups to tell stories from their own perspective, awakens awareness among members of core communities, clarifies misperceptions that privileged tourists may hold, and channels some money into marginal communities. One example of educational tourism is eco-lodges that take visitors to view the hospitals, schools and community centers that are sustained by their visits (Pearce, 1992). Another is visits to slum areas that have been organized to show visitors both the good and bad in their environment; the money they generate is then used for community development. This sort of tourism, dubbed "poorism," has been controversial, as some see it as exploitative (Lancaster, 2007; Weiner, 2008). Distinguishing community development from exploitation may be difficult, but generally depends on how much of the value created by tourism is controlled by the marginal community and how members of the marginal community view the overall enterprise. In the realm of civil rights, monuments to African American heroes are being erected around the southern US, to right historical wrongs and to take advantage of a growing interest in civil rights tourism (Parker, 2001). Monuments and historic sites provide tourists with opportunities to learn more about the South's civil rights stories. However, learning by itself does not lead to reconciliation nor even necessitate reflection.

A second model is *Development Tourism* in which privileged tourists visit less privileged groups to carry out community development projects together (Raymond & Hall, 2008). As they collaborate, they construct a narrative through interaction and working together, and become more equal as they partner for a common goal. While educational tourism is observational, development tourism involves more direct interaction, and as a result the narrative is not simply received by tourists, rather, the tourist participates in its construction (McIntosh & Zahra, 2007). One example of development tourism involves young people who participate in programs such as alternative spring breaks or "gap year" travel.[2] Another version is volunteers who travel to assist on a research project during their vacation (Clifton & Benson, 2006; Ellis, 2003). Despite its positive intentions, development tourism also generates controversy. Community development is a long-term enterprise, requiring extended commitment and a resiliency to failure. Idealistic youth may have good intentions, but lack the knowledge and skills necessary to accomplish something meaningful in a short time. Well-organized development tourism may generate personal and community benefits. But it may create a false sense of accomplishment among tourists, while members of the host community understand little will change when the tourist leaves. Development tourism may serve relief efforts well, however. Following Hurricane Katrina, a steady stream of volunteers traveled to the Gulf

Coast for short periods to assist in clean-up and recovery. Indeed, their labor made a significant difference in many people's lives.

A third model is *Pilgrimage Tourism*, in which members of defined groups travel to study and connect with their own story and heritage (Collins-Kreiner, 2006; Gatewood & Cameron, 2004; Hasty, 2002; Kelner, 2001). People engage in pilgrimages to experience first-hand places with sacred meaning, or because they feel a personal connection to a leader or story. Pilgrimage tourists are generally associated with religious groups (Povoledo, 2008), but non-religious pilgrims travel as well (Carrier, 2004). For example, African Americans carry out pilgrimages to visit their ancestors' homelands in Africa (Hasty, 2002; Pierre, 2009) and to visit meaningful sites in North America, including iconic sites in the Civil Rights Movement (Allman-Baldwin, 2006; Dewan, 2004; Grant, 2005). Cities with substantial African American populations, including Washington DC, Philadelphia PA and Atlanta GA have created African-American themed heritage trails, museums and other amenities to attract African American tourists (Carrier, 2004; Cobb, 2008; Grant, 2005). This approach to tourism can empower group members by extending a central narrative throughout a community, creating shared meaning even across large spaces, and by instilling a sense of transformation as group members connect to their roots in a deeper way.

A fourth model is *Reconciliation Tourism*, which involves using tourism as a means of reducing conflicts and constructing linkages between groups (Hemming, 1993; Higgins-Desbiolles, 2003, 2008). Conflict produced through stratification calls for reconciliation to ease differences and enable groups to construct a narrative that represents a wider range of voices. As such, reconciliation tourism frequently aims at providing transformational experiences to tourists (Hasty, 2002). For example, the United States Holocaust Memorial Museum in Washington, DC tells a tragic story "like it is," challenging visitors to think and act rather than sanitizing a narrative to make them more comfortable.[3] Examples from the American Civil Rights Movement include the National Civil Rights Museum in Memphis, TN (http://www.civilrightsmuseum.org/home.htm), and the Martin Luther King, Jr. National Historic Site in Atlanta, GA (http://www.nps.gov/malu/index.htm). Building tourism enterprises can also lead to reconciliation among those organized to provide the tourism services. For instance, Lang (2004) chronicles how the construction of the Gateway Arch in St. Louis, MO, led to a new social movement among African Americans who were displaced from their homes and excluded from the project's higher-paying jobs.

Method

This study began with informal discussions about racial reconciliation and its role in tourism development, which led us to conduct a formal literature review on the topic. A serendipitous series of events then connected us to the Emmett Till Memorial Commission (ETMC) in Tallahatchie County, Mississippi, an organization working to create racial reconciliation through tourism. Our observation began with a visit to one of the Commission's monthly meetings in early 2008, followed by a series of exchanges with ETMC leaders, and an invitation by one of the Commission's chairs to observe the next monthly meeting. At this meeting, we were introduced to the members of the ETMC, who agreed that we could continue to observe their activities as part of a formal research project.

Research questions

Our initial interest in the subject of racial reconciliation and tourism stemmed from current conditions in the Mississippi Delta. From its settlement, racial disparities have shaped the character of the Delta. Since the late 1970s racial roles have been changing, and opportunities have been opening for African Americans that historically were proscribed (Austin, 2006), particularly in politics and education. At the same time, the region's economy is shifting from agriculture and small industry to services. A substantial push towards tourism has been growing since the early 1990s (Austin & Middleton, 2006). Since 2003 heritage tourism has grown, focusing on the Delta's claim to be "the birthplace of the blues" (Barton, 2007). Efforts to promote other aspects of the Delta's heritage, including the role of Delta residents in the Civil Rights Movement, are in their early stages. In many Delta communities, tourism is still a cottage industry, but a stronger tourism industry is emerging in some of the larger towns, in the region and in the state.

From these circumstances, our initial question in this study was whether tourism could expand opportunities for social mobility among the region's African Americans, and provide a sense of healing in race relations. Our on-going study of the Emmett Till Memorial Commission has led us to question how reconciliation comes about and what reconciliation means, beyond simply healing fractured relationships.

Methodological approach

Our research uses an interpretative approach. Interpretive studies aim for contextual understanding, gaining insights about theoretical and policy issues from close attention to specific cases (Greene, 1990; Yin, 1984). Interpretive researchers generally rely on qualitative data, and follow an inductive path to discovery (Patton, 1990; Ragin, 1994). An interpretive approach is appropriate for case studies as its focus is on context rather than universal application, so data collection is fluid and researchers have flexibility to follow changing circumstances (Babbie, 1986). Interpretive research also allows for more depth of understanding and nuance, as researchers can observe attitude and expression in addition to content.

Interpretive research is useful in community settings, where relationships are more rooted in emotional than instrumental ties. Where science and technology form people's worldviews, quantitative methods may be more appropriate (Berg, 2004). In communities, where people know each other and establish personal bonds, the flexibility inherent in an interpretive approach allows researchers to shape and mold their understanding and account for inconsistencies and changes. The ETMC had been in existence for nearly three years when we began our observations, so we opted for a non-participant approach, and have resisted taking an action research stance so as not to interrupt the progress the Commission has made on its own.

Data collection

We have employed three techniques to gather data: observation of ETMC activities, a review of documents, and open-ended interviews with ETMC members. These are the three most commonly used forms of data collection in qualitative studies (Miles & Huberman, 1994).

Observation

Our observation has focused primarily on the monthly meetings of the ETMC. At least one of the authors has attended all of the Commission's monthly meetings since we initiated the study. We took detailed notes during the meetings and completed field notes following the meeting as a way of filling in details and additional information, including our perceptions.

In addition to the monthly meetings, we also observed other events carried out by ETMC members in Tallahatchie County communities. ETMC members have participated in events organized by our campus as well. For events that we could not observe directly, we have observed artifacts, such as the signs posted for the Emmett Till Trail, discussed below.

Document review

As part of the observation of artifacts, the authors reviewed documents produced by the ETMC and others related to the case. Principal among these were minutes of ETMC meetings that occurred before we began our study, which produced insight into the early days of the Commission. We also reviewed websites produced by the ETMC and by the William Winter Institute for Racial Reconciliation at the University of Mississippi, an ETMC collaborator. Also, we collected newspaper articles and other sources of information in the mass media pertaining to the ETMC, and to the Emmett Till case. Finally, we reviewed the Commission's organizational documents, such as by-laws.

Interviews

When we began our study the ETMC had 18 members, nine white and nine African American. The membership included co-chairpersons, one of each race. Other collaborators occasionally attended the group's meetings, including representatives from the William Winter Institute and an attorney who works with the ETMC.

Our goal was to interview all ETMC members and some collaborators. Commission members were personally contacted at the monthly meetings, and the authors explained the project and extended an invitation to participate in an interview. We completed interviews with fourteen Commission members and one knowledgeable partner. Interviews were conducted between April and September 2008. Two members declined to be interviewed; and two were unavailable during the interview period.

All interviews except one were conducted in person. An open-ended questionnaire was sent by e-mail to one informant who was unable to participate in a face-to-face interview; the informant used this questionnaire to respond in writing. We carried out one additional interview with two members, and later interviewed each individually. Face-to-face interviews typically took place in the respondent's home or office, with a few occurring in public places such as a park or City Hall. Interviews typically lasted about one hour.

Role of the researcher

Given the complicated nature of race and class relations in the Delta, the authors recognized that some interviewees might be less forthcoming than others. We are both white and represented universities at the time of the interviews, and neither of us is from the South. Going in, we recognized that African American informants might feel uncomfortable talking about race relations with white researchers and that white informants might try to demonstrate their open-mindedness; that informants might feel uncomfortable sharing cultural information with outsiders; and some might be hesitant to provide information to people who were university-affiliated. However, we found informants to be candid in their responses, speaking openly and (for the most part) on the record about their feelings, thoughts, and experiences. At the same time, these interviews only provide a snapshot of race relations in the Mississippi Delta. The issue runs much deeper, and a single interview with an individual only scratches the surface of the nuances that are so entrenched in the culture.

Data analysis

We recorded and transcribed all interviews, and independently reviewed each transcript to identify topics and themes in the conversations, then compared our individual results. In our discussions, we further developed the topics and themes, and drew in observational and documentary evidence to triangulate our interview findings. We then went through and coded the interview transcripts. We have extracted quotes that are illustrative of concepts pertaining to racial reconciliation and tourism, and built the description of our case study based on these quotes and themes.

Once we had completed the analysis, we shared the results with our informants and asked for feedback. Specifically, we asked them to assess whether the description of the case study accurately represented their perspective, and whether anything was omitted that should be included. We revised our analysis based on the comments provided by informants.

Case study: the Emmett Till Memorial Commission

Located in the Deep South, Tallahatchie County, Mississippi, has a stark, persistent and entrenched racial divide between the county's black and white residents (Austin, 2006). The pervasive effect of race on social structure and social interaction in the region is hard to overestimate. In 1955, Tallahatchie County gained international attention when a local jury acquitted two white residents accused of murdering a black teenager named Emmett Till, who was visiting relatives in the area from his home in Chicago.[4] The trial verdict left a pall of fear and shame on the county that continues to shape race relations today.

The context

Tallahatchie County is small, rural and remote. The western part of the county lies in Mississippi's "Delta" region, and the eastern portion is in the region known locally as the "Hills" (see Figure 1). These two regions have distinct cultures, and there is substantial competition between them (Adams & Gorton, 2006; Asch, 2008). As they described their community, the informants in this study took pains to distinguish themselves from "the other side." The distinction has immediate ramifications for the ETMC, related to the restoration of the Tallahatchie County Courthouse in Sumner, discussed below.

Countywide, nearly 60% of the population is African American, but in the western part of the county, almost 80% is black (see Table 1). Like most of the Mississippi Delta, Tallahatchie County reached its highest population in the 1920s and 1930s, surpassing 35,000 residents, but the numbers have steadily declined since (US Census Bureau, 2009a). The 2000 census counted 14,903 residents and today the population is estimated at slightly more than 13,000 (US Census Bureau, 2009b).

Politics in Western Tallahatchie County center around the Board of Supervisors, other county offices, and on the municipal governments of the region's four towns: Tutwiler, Sumner, Webb and Glendora. There are two county seats in Tallahatchie County, Charleston in the East (Hills) and Sumner in the West (Delta), each with its own functioning courthouse. The county offers a variety of services, but has

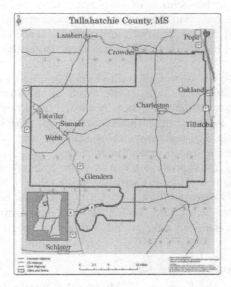

Figure 1. Tallahatchie County, Mississippi.

Table 1. Population and race in Tallahatchie County, Mississippi and its towns.

Place	Total population	White	Black
Tallahatchie County	14,903	5867 (39.4%)	8784 (58.9%)
Western Tallahatchie County (Census Tracts 9403 and 9404/Block 3)	5704	1106 (19.4%)	4491 (78.7%)
Eastern Tallahatchie County (Census Tracts 9401, 9402 and 9404/Blocks 1 and 2)	9199	4761 (51.8%)	4293 (46.7%)
Sumner Town	407	236 (58.0%)	158 (38.8%)
Tutwiler Town	1,364	160 (11.7%)	1186 (87.0%)
Webb Town	587	206 (35.1%)	360 (61.3%)
Glendora Town	285	13 (4.6%)	254 (89.1%)
Charlestown Town	2198	852 (38.8%)	1299 (59.1%)

Source: US Census, 2000.

relatively little in the way of public infrastructure. Up until the 1970s, all of the political offices were held by white residents, even though the majority of the population was African American. Beginning in the late 1970s, black residents have occupied more of the town and county offices. Today, the mayors in three of the four towns are African American, and several positions in the county are held by African Americans, including, since 1994, two of the five seats on the County Board of Supervisors.

Outside of agriculture, Western Tallahatchie County has little in the way of commerce. There are a few small businesses in the towns, but residents typically travel to one of the larger towns in adjacent counties to shop. There is no chamber of commerce, but there is a public Industrial Authority organized to attract business to Tallahatchie County. A private prison in the northwest corner of the county provides one of the largest sources of employment for residents, and a state prison in an adjacent county is another source of employment. A public Prison Authority, derived from the Industrial Authority, coordinates the prison. Landownership is a significant indicator of economic power, and in the absence of other institutions, a few churches, the local country club and a service organization function as the seats of economic power.

Social life is largely based on families and churches, and the pace of life is slow and rooted in personal relationships. Like much of the rural South, interaction between black and white residents is generally cordial but strained, and occurs in the context of substantial racial stratification (Schultz, 2007). African Americans often serve as laborers on white-owned farms, or as domestic help, much as they have for generations. Some black and white residents develop genuine friendships, but economic and cultural differences intercede in many cases. A small number of well-to-do African Americans do intermix with the white elite. A Habitat for Humanity chapter founded in 1984 created the county's first interracial board, largely through the efforts of its founder. Since 2005, the ETMC was created, and two of the county's historically white organizations have added African American members.

The Emmett Till Memorial Commission

The initial impulse for the Emmett Till Memorial Commission was to restore the Tallahatchie County Courthouse in Sumner, where the trail of Emmett Till's murderers was held. The County Board of Supervisors decided to create a biracial commission of concerned citizens to take on this task, bringing black and white residents together in a spirit of racial reconciliation. The supervisors and town mayors appoint members, who are diverse in age, gender, income, length of residence in the county and most notably race. One member who has lived in the county for several decades explained that this was the first time white and black residents have sat down to work together as equals. The ETMC has decided that the courthouse restoration should include a museum on the Emmett Till case, and have found other ways to use heritage tourism as a vehicle for racial reconciliation. This case illustrates some of the social justice benefits, as well as the challenges, of heritage tourism.

The ETMC started slowly. Few of the white residents who were appointed got involved in the beginning. Tallahatchie County operates on an informal basis, and some explained that they were not notified that they had been named to the Commission. Participation among black members fluctuated initially as well. After a few months, the ETMC formed a partnership with the William Winter Institute for

Racial Reconciliation at the University of Mississippi. The Winter Institute helped the ETMC develop goals and a working procedure. The ETMC settled on a racially balanced membership, and increased their numbers to nine white and nine black members. Participation stabilized. Staff and students from the Winter Institute brought expertise in reconciliation, as well as experience with other groups in the state who have similar missions. The ETMC was able to draw on the work of these other groups, reviewing by-laws and other documents to help craft their own. The Winter Institute has operated mostly "behind the scenes," however, and has not been directly involved in facilitating meetings.

Reconciliation and tourism projects

The project to restore the courthouse has grown into an effort to develop local tourism opportunities, primarily oriented around the story of Emmett Till and the Civil Rights Movement. This has been driven by an interest among local leaders to honor Emmett Till, by a still-small but growing demand from tourists, and by the growth of the tourism industry in the state. The ETMC is currently engaged in three tourism efforts. The first is the courthouse restoration of the Tallahatchie County Courthouse in Sumner; the second is the Emmett Till Interpretive Trail and driving tour, which was initiated with a Public Proclamation to the Till Family; and the third is the development of a tourism infrastructure in the county, including a tourism specialist housed within a newly created county Department of Recreation, Parks and Tourism.

Courthouse restoration

The Sumner courthouse is picturesque and historic. It was built in 1909 in the Richardsonian Romanesque style and in 1990 it was declared a state landmark by The Mississippi Department of Archives and History (Mississippi Department of Archives and History, 2009). However, the building is structurally deficient and inadequate for current administrative needs. Residents of Sumner are aware that the courthouse supports a legal profession and employs many residents. Residents fear that if the courthouse is shut down, even temporarily, they will lose their legal infrastructure to the courthouse in Charleston, and Sumner might slip into the same doldrums as other impoverished Delta communities. The ETMC has raised money and coordinated the courthouse restoration. Current plans are to configure the courtroom to look like it did during the 1955 trial, and to add a Civil Rights Museum to commemorate Emmett Till. The restoration would accommodate heritage tourists who want to visit the site of one of the most important incidents in the Civil Rights Movement.[5]

Restoring the courthouse is one step toward achieving racial reconciliation. The story of Emmett Till has been told many times, but owing to local residents' reluctance to discuss the topic, their voices have been muted in shaping how America understands this story. The courthouse and museum provide an opportunity to present these voices, crafted by a biracial commission. Thus, the ETMC's activities construct reconciliation tourism by contributing a local perspective on the wider narrative and meaning of the Emmett Till case in American society.

The value of this project toward reconciliation at a local scale is more complex. The project brings black and white ETMC members together to work on a common project, although as one member explained, the motivation of the two groups is probably different:

> In this instance, I think [reconciliation] specifically has to do with the fact that both races are trying to attain the same goal. Now, the motivation on each side might be different. I think for the white part of this Commission, probably the strongest motivation is saving the courthouse. And the black motivation is probably honoring or memorializing the Emmett Till trial.

Although the black and white members have different motivations for involvement in the courthouse restoration, according to some members the process of working together on the project engenders racial reconciliation as a by-product. One lifelong resident of Sumner said working together on the Emmett Till Memorial Commission has "enhanced mutual respect among the races," and this has led to a more positive tone in interracial interactions.

Not all members agree, however. Some believe the African Americans on the Commission are marginalized, and that interactions between black and white members follow the same stratified patterns that have long existed in the county. As one member said:

> The beginning of the Emmett Till Commission—it started out, basically, all African Americans, and there were a few Caucasians on the Board, about three or four and about eight or nine African Americans. The first or second meeting, it was proposed by a Caucasian member that the body should be fifty-fifty. We're talking about racial reconciliation and so forth, and we ought to be nine African Americans and nine Caucasians. And the body voted for that, and that's what took place. But, after that, no more participation by the African American community, as far as being open, and expressing whatever they talked about or wanted to see or was hoping for. Basically because, what happened was, when they changed the Commission, and brought on the additional members, everybody was from the affluent—everybody was the bossman.

This quote suggests that the structure of the Commission affects the level of trust felt by members. Because white residents historically have held virtually all power in Tallahatchie County, and continue to hold substantial economic power today, black members of the ETMC still feel like a minority, even if the membership is racially balanced (Gallardo & Stein, 2007).

Additionally, the emphasis on Emmett Till in local tourism development is not wholly supported by all ETMC members and other residents of the county. Some members believe the county is doing too much to honor Mr. Till, while others are uneasy because they believe their actions exploit a family tragedy (Jubera, 2007).[6] On the other hand, some members believe the name "Emmett Till" has come to transcend the personal tragedy of one 14-year-old boy, and carries an iconic status, particularly among African Americans. Outsiders will come to visit as educational, pilgrimage and reconciliation tourists, and the county should provide for their needs and tell the local version of the story. These contrasting views impose barriers to reconciliation that the ETMC must address.

Emmett Till interpretive trail

This driving tour consists of historical markers located at eight sites in the county, which chronicle events in the death of Emmett Till and the subsequent trial. Members worked with historians to ensure that the locations and the information on the signs were as accurate as possible. A ninth marker, erected by the State of Mississippi, commemorates the trial at the courthouse in Sumner. A brochure that describes the historical background of the Emmett Till murder and trial, with photos and descriptions of each site on the trail, is available on-line.[7] The interpretive trail was inaugurated in October, 2007 with a ceremony that included a public "Statement of Regret," expressing the county's regret to the Till family for the injustice committed fifty years earlier (Jubera, 2007). The text of the Statement of Regret was crafted with assistance from the Winter Institute, and it was signed by all members of the ETMC.[8] Surviving members of Emmett Till's family attended the event. Public statements like this are a common practice in reconciliation efforts. This was a significant step in racial reconciliation, as it broke a long-standing silence regarding the murder and unjust trial in Tallahatchie County.

The historical markers along the interpretive trail have generated interest from tourists, but have also produced controversy in the county. One marker was vandalized in October 2008, and the ETMC is responsible for replacing it (Associated Press, 2008). It is unknown if the vandalism was racially motivated. Another marker has generated a backlash for referring to the Ku Klux Klan; many local residents refute the claim that the KKK was ever active in Tallahatchie County. This is a source of pride for them, and they feel that to have alleged Klan activity publicly displayed on a sign projects an undeserved negative image.

Members of the ETMC feel the interpretive trail and the story it tells are important for a variety of reasons. "It's all trying to understand where we were and where we've come, how far we've come, and have we come very far at all? I really do think we've come a long way," one member commented. Another member explained how some sites on the interpretive trail have the potential to generate a sense of healing:

> It has been my experience [that] whenever we have [visited the site where Till's body was pulled from the river] it was a negative feeling but it was a positive, it was a healing, or it was a connection. And I think that each site is a connection to some part of each individual. Where the body was pulled out is the most negative [site on the trail], but it can be the most positive also, because that's the site that will make you think the most, make you feel the most. So if you're gonna get it, you're gonna get it there. You're gonna feel the loss, you're gonna feel the pain, and maybe that will inspire you—never again, never again.

These comments illustrate the idea that while reconciliation and healing are difficult, often painful processes, acknowledging and confronting that pain may be a way to move past it. While the driving tour is marketed to visitors, the process of discussing the sites and their meaning has brought greater understanding and healing to ETMC members as well.

Tourism planning

A third project, initiated at the beginning of 2009, is the creation of an administrative structure for tourism planning and management in the county. The County Board of Supervisors requested that the ETMC act as an advisory council on tourism development. During 2008, Tallahatchie County developed a parks and recreation program. The initial impetus was to provide after-school activities for the county's youth. The county acquired a building near Sumner as a headquarters and recreation center, named in honor of Emmett Till, and they hired a part-time recreation manager. In early 2009, the supervisors added tourism to the mission of this program. The County Administrator was named interim director of the Parks, Recreation and Tourism Department, and they began developing a means of recording tourist visits. They also began fundraising to hire a tourism professional to run the county office, and guides to take tour groups around the Emmett Till Interpretive Trail. These efforts are in their early stages.

One town in the county has been working to build a local tourism infrastructure as well, in conjunction with Mississippi Valley State University. Glendora has its own Emmett Till Museum, a park named in honor of Emmett Till and a small bed and breakfast, the county's only lodging. Glendora was where one of Emmett Till's murderers resided, and four of the eight markers on the Emmett Till Interpretive Trail are in Glendora. The town also recently inaugurated a marker on the Mississippi Blues Trail to honor Sonny Boy Williamson, a noted harmonica player who grew up on a plantation near Glendora (Barretta, 2009). However, Glendora is a very poor town; over 68% of the families live in poverty (US Census Bureau, 2009c). The shop fronts on its main street are mostly boarded up, and a visit to Glendora would likely appeal only to a select group of tourists.

Tourism as an engine of reconciliation

The Emmett Till Memorial Commission provides an interesting study of the relationship between tourism and reconciliation. The most compelling aspect is that the planners are not only developing a story of reconciliation as a tourism narrative, but as they do so they are also engaging in a process of reconciliation among their members and in their community. One example is the Statement of Regret the ETMC prepared and read in public. The statement itself opened a door for reconciliation between black and white Americans, as the Emmett Till story has national significance. But the process of crafting the statement also required ETMC members to confront various issues, think about definitions, and express their sentiments about Emmett Till and the trial. Certainly, this process did not resolve the issues that make race such a significant divide in Tallahatchie County, but black and white members did sit down and discuss the issues, something that was inconceivable not long ago in this context.

In many places in the US today, different racial groups working together may seem mundane, but in Tallahatchie County, with its long history of strict racial segregation and exclusion, residents consider it remarkable that black and white residents can hold equal positions on a public commission, and can sit down and work together in a climate of equality. The personal stories of some members illustrate this. Two of the African American members grew up on plantations owned by two of the white members. From subservient child to equal partner, this is truly a transition for these individuals and for this community. On the ETMC, black elected officials sit beside the landed white gentry, and all have an opportunity to shape how the county creates its story, to decide how it builds its tourism industry, and to engage in the processes by which reconciliation may occur.

During our interviews, some members expressed the positive repercussions the ETMC's work could have on reconciliation not only within the membership, but within the greater community.

I think that by restoring the Sumner Courthouse to its condition in 1955, creating the Emmett Till Interpretive Trail, and hopefully also creating a visitors center for potential tourists is a great step in the process of healing race relations in Tallahatchie County. For too long, the story of Emmett Till has been suppressed and neglected by the general population of Tallahatchie County. It is as if the people here have remained in denial about what happened, hoping that if it was ignored and not spoken of it would somehow disappear. The formation of the Emmett Till Memorial Commission has no doubt shown the people of Tallahatchie County that the murder of Emmett Till, and especially the injustice that followed, is not to be ignored. The Commission sends the message that not only is it time to accept this black spot on our county's history, but it's time to memorialize the name of Emmett Till to give him the respect he deserves.

As this member explains, telling the story of Emmett Till through heritage tourism has the potential for tourists and residents alike to experience reconciliation. Heritage tourism allows residents to tell their own story, and to share their experiences with others. Through this process, acknowledgement, acceptance, and healing can occur.

Challenges to reconciliation

While the ETMC has made some strides toward racial reconciliation, they still face several challenges. As previously noted, some members of the ETMC question the notion that the Commission operates on an equal playing field. The ETMC has tried to create a sense of racial equality on the Commission by maintaining a balance in the number of black and white members. However, this does not take into account the historically produced perceptions of the relative power held by each member. Several of the white members come from the elite ranks of Tallahatchie County, including families that have owned plantations for generations. Several of the black members hold important political offices, but all of them have risen to these positions relatively recently, as these positions were unavailable to African Americans in the past. Residents have become accustomed to particular codes of conduct that subtly and perhaps unintentionally enforce racial stratification in the county, and these rules do not fully disappear when the county supervisors create a commission. The statuses that have existed for generations outside the Commission continue to shape how people interact at ETMC meetings.

Other members have highlighted cultural preferences that impede reconciliation. One expression of cultural differences is in ideas about what reconciliation means. To some, reconciliation is produced through black and white members interacting with each other. Under this view, the racial divide was created because blacks and whites were raised differently, and thus have different cultures. The solution is to find ways to get to know each other and appreciate each other's cultures. As one member stated, "If I can't be around you, I can't get to know you." To other members, reconciliation is a by-product of working together toward common goals. Those who expressed this view believe that ETMC members need not focus explicitly on their differences, on building friendships or respect, or on openly discussing cultural differences. Rather, they need to take on common tasks and work together, and through these activities they will build common values and respect for each other. To illustrate this point, one member said, "I think the reconciliation is starting out with the [ETMC] board and I think that we're working together to get things done and I think we're going to get things done because of that working together."

For the most part, these distinct approaches represent cultural differences in the black and white communities. African American members of the ETMC are more likely to see reconciliation as happening through interaction and discussing racial issues openly, while the white members tend to see reconciliation as stemming from common work. These differences are also represented in other preferences expressed by ETMC members. For example, one topic raised in interviews was how their monthly meetings should be run. The African American members are comfortable with an informal meeting structure, in which everyone can talk and which covers a wide range of topics. One gets the sense that the product the black members wish to produce is as much a sense of community as specific outputs. The white members, on the other hand, demonstrate a clear preference for a business-like meeting, following procedures such as Roberts Rules of Order. Privately, some white members have expressed dismay at how the meetings ramble and stray off-topic, and during the meetings the white members are much more likely to enforce established procedures. It is white members, for example, who typically make motions to vote on matters, and who require that new business be formally submitted one month before it may be officially considered. Before there was a strong white presence on the ETMC, the black members ran the meetings in a much more fluid manner, admitting non-members to participate and even vote, and not taking into account set procedures to resolve issues.

In addition to differences in preferred and observed behavior, there are underlying tensions within the group regarding racial issues. Some white members of the Commission stated that they felt unfairly blamed, both at the time of Emmett Till's murder and subsequent trial, and now during the reconciliation process. They recounted how Tallahatchie County, though not the site of the kidnapping or murder, became known as a hotbed of racial tension, the site of a brutal murder where the Civil Rights Movement began. One member explained, "What we don't like is the fact that it was committed by two [men] who were citizens of Leflore County and [Emmett Till] was kidnapped in Leflore County, and Tallahatchie County got blamed for it." This idea of the community being blamed for such a gruesome act is in contrast with how some Commission members described Sumner, which may be why they feel the focus on their town paints it in an undeserved negative light. As one member commented, "Sumner is a wonderful, wonderful place. We have virtually no crime. It's just, you know, a pretty free place to raise children. [In the past] it was just Mayberry. I mean, the policeman really didn't have any bullets. He kept one in his glove compartment." Another Commission member explained what the community was like around the time of the trial, saying, "It was a very prosperous farming community with lots of people, lots of young people, lots of families, vigorous economy, and a lot of educated people. Sumner's always had a high percentage of people who were well-educated. That's always helped it."

So why was this seemingly idyllic community selected as the site for the murder trial? As one member explained the situation, Emmett Till's body was pulled from the Tallahatchie County side of the Tallahatchie River. When neighboring Leflore County, site of the kidnapping, refused to indict the suspects, authorities in Tallahatchie County stepped in. This member went on to explain that Tallahatchie County did not deserve the reputation is has acquired. "At least we indicted them. We didn't convict them, of course, but at least we indicted them and there was a trial, which we should get some credit for."

With regard to feelings of blame, some white members of the Commission also made attempts to remove themselves from any responsibility for wrongdoing. "As far as I know, nobody from Tallahatchie County was in any way remotely involved in that murder. Yet we inherited the stigma of being the place where it happened because the trial was held here," one member explained. Another commented that the trial, "absolutely tore this community apart. The white people felt like they were—I didn't live here then, but I've heard stories—the white people felt like they were unfairly blamed and the press was horrible and negative." The interruption about not living in Tallahatchie County at that time indicates that this member may feel separate from any repercussions that have resulted from the trial in the ensuing years as the community has struggled to redefine itself. Maintaining removal from the problem may make it difficult for this member to be part of reconciliation efforts.

Another member expressed the concept of blame in relation to the Statement of Regret that Tallahatchie County extended to the Till Family in October, 2007:

> I had problems with the first statement and then we had to kind of regroup. [A member of the Commission] took the statement and reworded it and then we discussed it in the meeting and really kind of picked it apart and changed some things and came up with the Statement of Regret. The first one was a Statement of Apology and all of the white people said, 'We're not going to apologize for something we did not do.' We regret very much that it happened, but I'm not going to say that I'm sorry for what happened. I wasn't even living here at the time.

Again, there is the idea of distance from the actual events removing all blame, when in reality there are systems and cultural norms embedded in Tallahatchie County and the Delta region that perpetuate racism to this day. An individual may not have directly been responsible for an act, but at the same time can benefit from and participate in systems that are racist and oppressive. This is why the focus on reconciliation through the ETMC becomes so important. If Tallahatchie County is to truly move beyond these horrible events and find some sense of peace and healing between the races, community members must recognize and transcend these systems that perpetuate oppression and segregation.

Conflicting goals and objectives among members is another challenge to the reconciliation process. Early on in the life of the ETMC, members determined a list of priority activities, which included restoring the courthouse, tourism initiatives, and creating a community center, among others. It became clear through these interviews, however, that many members are divided over what their priorities are or should be.

These conflicts seem to be divided primarily along racial lines. "I think that we both think we have different agendas and it's probably true," one member commented. White members showed a preference toward restoring the courthouse to ensure economic viability. "There's a lot of fear on some of the people that if we lose the courthouse we really will lose [our community]," one member explained. This member went on to add, "There's always something going on, it employs a lot of people, and it's sort of a symbol for the town. We want to have the courthouse redone and we want it to be a viable, working courthouse." Another echoed this sentiment, saying, "[I think] the reason the white people signed on is because of the restoration of the courthouse. And we see this Till thing as a way to get the funds to restore the courthouse, which it needs."

While recognizing the importance of restoring the courthouse, African American members tended to favor a commemorative focus through projects such as the interpretive trail, museum, or reconciliation activities. "Most things is about the restoration of the courthouse, but for me it's more about the museum and the community and the youth. It might even be further than that as far as relationships," explained one member. Another added, "At first they were just in terms of talking about the courthouse, but now we're working on civil rights, education, recreation, and everything that we can add in to help promote this county other than just the courthouse." Someone else suggested that telling the story as accurately as possible might be the most profitable outcome in terms of understanding. "I think Emmett Till, his life story, would be something good to help people see how important it is to value people and that type of thing. My priority is that we learn from history."

Recommendations for community planners

In part stemming from the publicity generated by the historical markers and driving trail, interest in tourism to Tallahatchie County has grown. While the number of visits remains relatively small, the supervisors and others have fielded telephone calls from groups interested in touring the Emmett Till Interpretive Trail and other landmarks. Members of the ETMC and other town residents lead the tours on an informal basis. Tallahatchie County stands on the cusp of taking tourism from a cottage industry to a diversified and professionalized enterprise. But getting to the next level requires planning.

Building tourism, building reconciliation

The most significant impediment to building a tourism industry, to date, has been a lack of understanding on the part of county residents as to the value of the story they can market to tourists. The Emmett Till story provides an opportunity for Tallahatchie County to create a sustainable tourism industry, based on its status as "ground zero in the Civil Rights Movement," if residents are willing to overcome the legacies of the past and take ownership of the story. The starting point is an honest accounting of the county's role in the Emmett Till case and the extent of injustice manifested by the verdict. The ETMC has started this process with the public Statement of Regret, but there remains a "culture of silence" in the county regarding the case, and reluctance, particularly among white residents, to acknowledge the iconic status that Emmett Till has in the struggle for civil rights in the US. The county's leaders and the ETMC have taken an appropriate step in linking tourism to reconciliation. In this case, though, reconciliation is not just the nature of the story the county is marketing, it is also necessary for the county to undergo a process of reconciliation before they can truly create a sustainable tourism industry.

Mississippi has recently undergone a similar story in relation to the blues. For a long time, the blues was viewed by many Mississippi residents, both black and white, as "the devil's music," and blues culture was seen as an embarrassment. Recently, however, Mississippi has created the Mississippi Blues Trail and has established a series of historical markers around the state, which have been widely supported by local residents as well as tourists. Today, many Mississippians, even if they are not blues fans, recognize this music's significance in American popular culture, and are proud to see its practitioners recognized. Many other Mississippians appreciate the markers because they attract tourism and build economic development at the local level. The story of Emmett Till could provide similar benefits to Tallahatchie County if the residents could come together and agree to honor Emmett Till and the Civil Rights Movement though open, honest dialogue about race. This could truly become a means of community development. The central need is for people to eradicate racial divisions and co-exist respectfully and appreciatively. Reconciling the pain and injustice is essential for this community and others like it to move beyond the past and embrace a collective future.

The ETMC probably missed an opportunity early in its existence to build a form of reconciliation in relationships on the Commission itself, for example, by sitting members down and having facilitated discussions that drew out the diverse perspectives in the room. Members likely would have benefited from taking time to understand each other, and particularly the various notions that members have about how to put reconciliation into practice. Instead, the Commission forged ahead with its projects, and by default, adopted one version of reconciliation, which is that it will emerge as a by-product of working together. This limits the potential for reconciliation, because it channels the activities of the ETMC away from visions of reconciliation that focus on healing through interaction and understanding, instead expressing a vision favored by white members of the Commission, reinforcing the existing power structure. An initial attempt at creating new relationships may have been strained in this context, however, since many of the members already knew each other well and had long-established patterns of interaction. One member thought an initial exercise was probably unnecessary, and said he was pleasantly surprised at how amicably the members were able to work together on the Commission. But without skillful facilitation and thoughtful reflection, efforts like the ETMC run the risk of simply reinforcing entrenched patterns of discrimination, and can deny a voice to the full range of perceptions and positions. In effect, this could delay or even impede reconciliation.

Of course, to truly benefit from this tourism program, Tallahatchie County has to build a tourism infrastructure, including lodging and food options. Right now, the county is only positioned for pass-through tourism, as visitors will have to stay and eat in adjacent counties. Nearby Tunica County provides an example of how a county can go from little infrastructure to a multi-million dollar tourism industry; through the 1980s, Tunica was one of the poorest counties in the US, but today it is a major gaming destination, with hotels, restaurants, and other amenities. Civil rights tourism in Tallahatchie County will probably not be as significant a draw as gambling in Tunica, but Tallahatchie does have a unique heritage resource. With vision and collaboration Tallahatchie County can develop its own tourism-based industrial development, and in the process contribute to how Americans view the extension of civil rights to all citizens.

Conclusion

Tourism for reconciliation is a relatively new idea and a difficult undertaking. It requires a cohesive narrative that can be marketed to a target audience. More importantly, and thornier, reconciliation tourism requires a willingness to challenge people's perceptions and demand that people consider a civil rights perspective and a worldview that represents society's disenfranchised and marginalized members.

To do so, tourism planners, managers, and providers, as well as residents in the host area may have to ask themselves hard questions. In the process, though, both the story and the process of reconciliation can lead to a transformative sense of healing to accomplish what Freya Higgins-Desbiolles (2003) defines as the task of reconciliation tourism: "tourism healing divided societies!"

Overall, Tallahatchie County has initiated a tourism effort that should contribute to reconciliation in the global sense—they have the means to tell a compelling civil rights story representing the local perspective. People who visit Tallahatchie County can view first-hand the environment that both produced the Emmett Till verdict, and that has resulted from that case. The Commission's actions may also lead to reconciliation at the local level, which is equally important in conveying the narrative of Emmett Till's legacy. Both elements of reconciliation contribute to equity and social justice in the county and in the nation, and as such build the foundation for a sustainable tourism industry in the Mississippi Delta.

Acknowledgments

The authors thank the members of the Emmett Till Memorial Commission of Tallahatchie County, MS for graciously collaborating on this research. We appreciate the helpful comments from Katie Kerstetter, Deborah Moore and two anonymous reviewers on a previous draft. We thank Subu Swaminathan and the Delta State University Center for Interdisciplinary Geospatial Information Technologies for their assistance.

Notes

1. Michaels (2006) argues that attention to culture comes at the expense of structure. A focus on diverse identities ignores the real issue, economic inequality. We do not mean to detract from the importance of economic equality, but we view equality as multifaceted, involving more than just economics.
2. In alternative spring breaks, common at many American universities, students forego a week on the beach to engage in community development projects (Bermudez, 2008). The gap year, a concept more common in Europe than North America, refers to a year of travel between high school and college, and some "gappers" are finding time to work on community development projects in lieu of or while backpack touring through places like Southeast Asia or South America (Simpson, 2004).
3. On the USHMM's webpage (http://www.ushmm.org/museum/mission/), part of the description of the museum's mission is: "With unique power and authenticity, the Museum teaches millions of people each year about the dangers of unchecked hatred and the need to prevent genocide. And we encourage them to act, cultivating a sense of moral responsibility among our citizens so that they will respond to the monumental challenges that confront our world." This call to action exemplifies the transformative experience that the museum seeks to provide for visitors.
4. For more information on the Emmett Till case, see Beauchamp (2005), Beito & Beito (2004), Huie (1956), Popham (1955), Russell (2006), Segall & Holmberg (2003), Sparkman (2005), and Whitfield (1988).
5. About three months after the verdict was handed down in the Emmett Till murder, Rosa Parks refused to give up her seat on a Montgomery, Alabama bus, which led to an extended bus boycott by the city's African Americans. Mrs. Parks' actions have been widely recognized as sparking the civil rights movement, but Mrs. Parks also acknowledged that she was inspired by Emmett Till as she remained seated on the bus (Segall & Holmberg, 2003).
6. One complaint we did not hear, but that was common during the 1950s and even part of the strategy used by the defense lawyers during the Emmett Till trial, was that the NAACP and other outside groups were using the murder of Emmett Till as a way of undermining "the Southern way of life" (Popham, 1955). While some residents are concerned about the appearance of exploiting Emmett Till's personal tragedy, the

notion that outsiders are exploiting it for political gain does not seem to be a prevalent view in the county today.
7. The brochure can be viewed at http://www.etmctallahatchie.com/pages/et-brochure.htm
8. The text of the statement can be viewed at http://www.etmctallahatchie.com/pages/news-archives.htm

References

Adams, J., & Gorton, D. (2006). Confederate lane: Class, race and ethnicity in the Mississippi Delta. *American Ethnologist, 33*(2), 288–307.
Allman-Baldwin, L. (2006, July 20). Ebony escapes! On African American heritage tours. *New York Amsterdam News, 97*(30), pp. 24, 31.
Andrews, K.T. (1997). The impacts of social movements on the political process: The Civil Rights Movement and black electoral politics in Mississippi. *American Sociological Review, 62*(5), 800–819.
Asch, C.M. (2008). *The senator and the sharecropper: The freedom struggles of James O. Eastland and Fannie Lou Hamer.* New York: The New Press.
Associated Press. (2008, October 27). Vandals destroy sign marking Emmett Till murder site. *USA Today.* Retrieved November, 2008 from http://www.usatoday.com/news/nation/2008-10-27-emmett-till_N.htm
Austin, S.D.W. (2006). *The transformation of plantation politics: Black politics, concentrated poverty, and social capital in the Mississippi Delta.* Albany, NY: State University of New York Press.
Austin, S.W., & Middleton, R.T. (2006). Racial politics of casino gaming in the Delta: The case of Tunica County. In D. von Herrmann, *Resorting to casinos: The Mississippi gambling industry* (pp. 47–66). Jackson, MS: University Press of Mississippi.
Babbie, E. (1986). *Observing ourselves: Essays in social research.* Prospect Heights, IL: Waveland Press.
Barretta, S. (2009, March 2). Sonny Boy marker erected, Bronzeville blues, Blues Hall of Fame inductees announced. *Highway 61 Radio.* Retrieved March, 2009 from http://www.highway61radio.com/?p=1392
Barton, A.W. (2005). *Attitudes about heritage tourism in the Mississippi Delta: A policy report from the 2005 Delta Rural Poll.* Cleveland, MS: Center for Community and Economic Development, Delta State University.
Barton, A.W. (2007). *Visitation to heritage tourism sites by residents of the Mississippi Delta.* Cleveland, MS: Center for Community and Economic Development, Delta State University.
Beauchamp, K. (2005, February). The murder of Emmett Louis Till: The spark that started the Civil Rights Movement. *Black Collegian, 35*(2), 88–91. Retrieved March, 2008 from http://www.black-collegian.com/african/till2005-2nd.shtml
Beito, D.T., & Beito, L.R. (2004, April 26). Why it's unlikely the Emmett Till murder mystery will ever be solved. *George Mason University's History News Network.* Retrieved March, 2008 from http://hnn.us/articles/4853.html
Berg, B.L. (2004). *Qualitative research methods for the social sciences* (5th ed.). Boston, MA: Allyn and Bacon.
Bermudez, C. (2008). Working vacation. *Chronicle of Philanthropy, 20*(9), 1.
Brown, M.F. (2003). *Who owns native culture?* Cambridge, MA: Harvard University Press.
Carrier, J. (2004). *A traveler's guide to the Civil Rights Movement.* Orlando, FL: Harcourt, Inc.
Clifton, J., & Benson, A. (2006). Planning for sustainable ecotourism: The case for research ecotourism in developing country destinations. *Journal of Sustainable Tourism, 14*(3), 238–254.
Cobb, C.E., Jr. (2008). *On the road to freedom: A guided tour of the civil rights trail.* Chapel Hill, NC: Algonquin Books.
Cohen, E. (1988). Authenticity and commoditization in tourism. *Annals of Tourism Research, 15*(3), 371–386.
Collins-Kreiner, N. (2006). Graves as attractions: Pilgrimage-tourism to Jewish holy graves in Israel. *Journal of Cultural Geography, 24*(1), 67–89.

Dewan, S.K. (2004, August 10). Civil rights battlegrounds enter world of tourism. *New York Times*. Retrieved October, 2007 from http://www.nytimes.com/2004/08/10/us/civil-rights-battlegrounds-enter-world-of-tourism.html?sec=travel&&scp=1&sq=civil%20rights%20battlegrounds&st=cse

Eadington, W.R., & Smith, V.L. (1992). Introduction: The emergence of alternative forms of tourism. In V.L. Smith & W.R. Eadington (Eds.), *Tourism alternatives: Potentials and problems in the development of tourism* (pp. 1–14). Philadelphia: University of Pennsylvania Press.

Edelman, P. (2005). Where race meets class: The 21st century civil rights agenda. *Georgetown Journal on Poverty Law and Policy, 12*(1), 1–12.

Edson, G. (2004). Heritage: Pride or passion, product or service? *International Journal of Heritage Studies, 10*(4), 333–348.

Edwards, A.R. (2005). *The sustainability revolution: Portrait of a paradigm shift*. Gabriola Island, BC, Canada: New Society Publishers.

Ellis, C. (2003). When volunteers pay to take a trip with scientists—Participatory environmental research tourism (PERT). *Human Dimensions of Wildlife, 8*(1), 75–80.

Fischer, M.A. (1989). The practice of community development. In J.A. Christensen & J.W. Robinson, Jr. (Eds.), *Community development in perspective* (pp. 136–158). Ames, IA: Iowa State University Press.

Flora, C.B., & Flora, J.L. (2008). *Rural communities: Legacy and change* (3rd ed.). Boulder, CO: Westview Press.

Frank, A.G. (1986). The development of underdevelopment. In P.F. Klaren & T.J. Bossert (Eds.), *Promise of development: Theories of change in Latin America* (pp. 111–123). Boulder, CO: Westview Press.

Gallardo, J.H., & Stein, T.V. (2007). Participation, power and racial representation: Negotiating nature-based and heritage tourism development in the rural South. *Society and Natural Resources, 20*(7), 597–611.

Gatewood, J.B., & Cameron, C.M. (2004). Battlefield pilgrims at Gettysburg National Military Park. *Ethnology, 43*(3), 193–216.

Gentleman, A. (2006, May 7). Slum tours: A day trip too far? *The Observer*. Retrieved January, 2009 from http://www.guardian.co.uk/travel/2006/may/07/delhi.india.ethicalliving/print

Grant, E. (2005). Race and tourism in America's first city. *Journal of Urban History, 31*(6), 850–871.

Greene, J.C. (1990). Three views on the nature and role of knowledge in social science. In E.G. Guba (Ed.), *The paradigm dialog* (pp. 227–245). Newbury Park, CA: Sage Publications.

Hasty, J. (2002). Rites of passage, routes of redemption: Emancipation tourism and the wealth of culture. *Africa Today, 49*(3), 46–76.

Haywood, K.M. (1988). Responsible and responsive tourism planning in the community. *Tourism Management, 9*(2), 105–118.

Hemming, S.J. (1993). Camp Coorong—Combining race relations and cultural education. *Social Alternatives, 12*(1), 37–40.

Higgins-Desbiolles, F. (2003). Reconciliation tourism: Tourism healing divided societies! *Tourism Recreation Research, 28*(3), 35–44.

Higgins-Desbiolles, F. (2008). Justice tourism and alternative globalisation. *Journal of Sustainable Tourism, 16*(3), 345–364.

Hill, M. (2007, December). The economic status of African-Americans in Mississippi. *Mississippi Economic Review and Outlook, 21*(2). Retrieved February, 2008 from http://www.mississippi.edu/urc/economics.html

Hitchcock, M., & King, V.T. (2003). Discourses with the past: Tourism and heritage in South-East Asia. *Indonesia and the Malay World, 31*(89), 3–15.

Howard, P. (2002). The eco-museum: Innovation that risks the future. *International Journal of Heritage Studies, 8*(1), 63–72.

Huie, W.B. (1956, January 24). The shocking story of approved killing in Mississippi. *Look, 20*(2), 46–50.

Jubera, D. (2007, October 2). Decades later, an apology: Once an icon of racism, town plans to say it's sorry near where Emmett Till's killers were freed. *Atlanta Journal Constitution*. Retrieved March, 2008 from http://www6.lexisnexis.com/publisher/EndUser?Action=User DisplayFullDocument&orgId=574&topicId=100020422&docId=1:678257167&start=15

Kelner, S. (2001). Narrative construction of authenticity in pilgrimage touring. Paper presented to the 96th annual meeting of the American Sociological Association, Anaheim, CA.

Kirtsoglou, E., & Theodossopoulos, D. (2004). 'They are taking our culture away': Tourism and culture commodification in the Garifuna community of Roatan. *Critique of Anthropology, 24*(2), 135–157.

Klein-Viehhauer, S. (2009). Framework model to assess leisure and tourism sustainability. *Journal of Cleaner Production, 17*(4), 447–454.

Lancaster, J. (2007, March). Next stop, squalor. *Smithsonian, 37*(12), 96–105. Retrieved January 2009 from http://www.smithsonianmag.com/people-places/squalor.html

Lang, C. (2004). Between civil rights and black power in the Gateway City: The Action Committee to Improve Opportunities for Negroes (ACTION), 1964–75. *Journal of Social History, 37*(3), 725–754.

Malkin, R. (1999, July/August). The pioneers. *The UNESCO courier, 52*(7), 24–25. Retrieved February, 2009 from http://www.unesco.org/courier/1999_08/uk/somm/intro.htm

Markey, E. (2007, July 20). Tourism with a conscience. *National Catholic Reporter, 43*(32), 12.

McIntosh, A.J., & Zahra, A. (2007). A cultural encounter through volunteer tourism: Towards the ideals of sustainable tourism? *Journal of Sustainable Tourism, 15*(5), 541–556.

Michaels, W.B. (2006). *The trouble with diversity: How we learned to love identity and ignore inequality*. New York: Metropolitan Books/Henry Holt and Company.

Miles, M.B., & Huberman, A.M. (1994). *Qualitative data analysis: An expanded sourcebook* (2nd ed.). Thousand Oaks, CA: Sage Publications.

Mississippi Department of Archives and History. (2009). *Review board makes Nat'l Register recommendations*. Retrieved January, 2009 from http://mdah.state.ms.us/admin/news/preservation.html

Moore, S., & Jie Wen, J. (2009). Tourism employment in China: A look at gender equity, equality, and responsibility. *Journal of Human Resources in Hospitality & Tourism, 8*(1), 32–42.

Murphy, P.E., & Andressen, B. (1988). Tourism development on Vancouver Island: An assessment of the core-periphery model. *Professional Geographer, 40*(1), 32–42.

National Agricultural Library. (2008). *Promoting tourism in rural America*. Baltimore, MD: National Agricultural Library, Agricultural Research Service, U. S. Department of Agriculture. Retrieved February, 2009 from http://www.nal.usda.gov/ric/ricpubs/tourism.html#tourismdevelopment

Parker, S. (2001, June 20). African American's heritage set in stone. *Christian Science Monitor*. Retrieved March, 2009 from http://www.csmonitor.com/2001/0620/p3s1.html?s=widep

Patton, M.Q. (1990). *Qualitative evaluation and research methods* (2nd ed.). Newbury Park, CA: Sage Publications.

Pearce, D.G. (1992). Alternative tourism: Concepts, classifications, and questions. In V.L. Smith & W.R. Eadington (Eds.), *Tourism alternatives: Potentials and problems in the development of tourism* (pp. 15–30). Philadelphia: University of Pennsylvania Press.

Pierre, J. (2009). Beyond heritage tourism: Race and the politics of African-diasporic interactions. *Social Text, 27*(1), 59–81.

Popescu, R. (2007, October 15). A boom in 'poorism.' *Newsweek, 150*(16), 12. Retrieved February, 2009 from http://www.newsweek.com/id/42482

Popham, J.N. (1955, September 23). Mississippi jury acquits 2 accused in youth's killing. *New York Times*. Retrieved March, 2008 from http://www.nytimes.com/packages/pdf/magazine/till4.pdf

Porter, B.W., & Salazar, N.B. (2005). Heritage tourism, conflict, and the public interest: An introduction. *International Journal of Heritage Studies, 11*(5), 361–370.

Povoledo, E. (2008, September 7). Searching for the roots of a deep faith. *New York Times*. Retrieved September, 2008 from http://www.nytimes.com/2008/09/07/travel/07journeys.html

President's Committee on the Arts and the Humanities. (2005). *A position paper on cultural heritage tourism in the United States.* Washington, DC: U.S. Department of Commerce. Retrieved February, 2009 from http://www.pcah.gov/pdf/05WhitePaperCultHerit Tourism.pdf

Ragin, C.C. (1994). *Constructing social research: The unity and diversity of method.* Thousand Oaks, CA: Pine Forge Press.

Rao, K. (2009, March 11). 'Slumdog' success calls attention to tours in Mumbai. *New York Times.* Retrieved March, 2009 from http://globespotters.blogs.nytimes.com/2009/03/11/slumdog-success-spawns-tours-in-mumbai/?scp=2&sq=slumdog%20tours&st=cse

Raymond, E.M., & Hall, C.M. (2008). The development of cross-cultural (mis)understanding through volunteer tourism. *Journal of Sustainable Tourism, 16*(5), 530–543.

Richards, G., & Hall, D. (2000). The community: A sustainable concept in tourism development? In G. Richards & D. Hall (Eds.), *Tourism and sustainable community development* (pp. 1–14). London: Routledge.

Robinson, M. (1999, July/August). Is cultural tourism on the right track? *The UNESCO courier.* Retrieved February, 2009 from http://www.unesco.org/courier/1999_08/uk/somm/intro.htm

Robinson, M. (2000). Collaboration and cultural consent: Refocusing sustainable tourism. In B. Bramwell & B. Lane (Eds.), *Tourism collaboration and partnerships: Politics, practices and sustainability* (pp. 295–313). Clevedon, UK: Channel View Publications.

Russell, M.M. (2006, Spring). Justice delayed: Reopening the Emmett Till case. *Santa Clara Magazine.* Retrieved March, 2008 from http://www.scu.edu/scm/spring2006/justice.cfm

Scheyvens, R., & Momsen, J.H. (2008). Tourism and poverty reduction: Issues for small island states. *Tourism Geographies, 10*(1), 22–41.

Schultz, M. (2007). *The rural face of white supremacy: Beyond Jim Crow.* Urbana, IL: University of Illinois Press.

Segall, R., & Holmberg, D. (2003, February 3). Who killed Emmett Till? *The Nation.* Retrieved March, 2008 from http://www.thenation.com/doc/20030203/segal

Sharpley, R. (2001). Tourism in Cyprus: Challenges and opportunities. *Tourism Geographies, 3*(1), 64–86.

Silver, I. (1993). Marketing authenticity in Third World Countries. *Annals of Tourism Research, 20,* 302–318.

Simpson, K. (2004). 'Doing development': The gap year, volunteer-tourists and a popular practice of development. *Journal of International Development, 16*(5), 681–692.

Sparkman, R. (2005, June 21). The murder of Emmett Till: The 49-year-old story of the crime and how it came to be told. *Slate.* Retrieved March, 2008 from http://www.slate.com/toolbar.aspx?action=print&id=2120788

Thomas, P. (2009). The trouble with travel. *Geographical, 81*(2), 50–52.

US Census Bureau. (2009a). *Mississippi: Population of counties by decennial census: 1900 to 1990.* Retrieved February, 2009 from http://www.census.gov/population/cencounts/ms190090.txt

US Census Bureau. (2009b). *County quickFacts: Tallahatchie County, Mississippi.* Retrieved February, 2009 from http://quickfacts.census.gov/qfd/states/28/28135.html

US Census Bureau. (2009c). American Factfinder: Glendora Village, Mississippi. Retrieved March, 2009 from http://factfinder.census.gov/servlet/SAFFFacts?_event=Search&geo_id=&_geoContext=&_street=&_county=glendora&_cityTown=glendora&_state=04000US28&_zip=&_lang=en&_sse=on&pctxt=fph&pgsl=010&show_2003_tab=&redirect=Y

US Commission on Civil Rights. (2001). *Racial and ethnic tensions in American communities: Poverty, inequality, and discrimination—Volume VII: The Mississippi Delta report.* Washington, DC: U.S. Commission on Civil Rights. Retrieved May, 2004 from http://www.usccr.gov/pubs/msdelta/pref.htm

Weiner, E. (2008, March 9). Slum visits: Tourism or voyeurism? *New York Times.* Retrieved March, 2008 from http://www.nytimes.com/2008/03/09/travel/09heads.html?_r=1&scp=1&sq=slum%20visits&st=cse

Whitfield, S.J. (1988). *A death in the Delta: The story of Emmett Till.* Baltimore, MD: Johns Hopkins University Press.

Woods, M. (2000). *Diversifying the rural economy: Tourism development.* Mississippi State, MS: Southern Rural Development Center. Retrieved February, 2009 from http://srdc.msstate.edu/publications/woods.pdf

World Commission on Environment and Development. (1987). *Our common future*. New York: Oxford University Press.
World Travel & Tourism Council. (2008). *World Travel & Tourism Council: Progress and priorities, 2008/09*. London, UK: WTTC. Retrieved February, 2009 from http://www.wttc.org/bin/pdf/original_pdf_file/progress_and_priorities_2008.pdf
Yin, R.K. (1984). *Case study research: Design and methods*. Beverly Hills, CA: Sage Publications.

AN ETHICAL PRINCIPLE FOR SOCIAL JUSTICE IN COMMUNITY DEVELOPMENT PRACTICE

By Ru Michael Sabre

ABSTRACT

This paper presents considerations which recommend an ethical principle to help guide community development practice towards consciously achieving social justice. Here community development is defined as the activity of participating in community responses to changes in its internal or external environment which help insure the survival of or enhance the quality of life for those living in the community. Community development practitioners are those engaged in that activity and thus would include those individuals who reside in the community and those who come from the "outside." An ethical principle would provide a standard for practitioners and observers by which to judge such activities. Justice is defined in terms of fairness and recognition of inequality not implying inequity. The goal is to provide an ethical principle for community development practice which brings about social justice.

This paper presents considerations which recommend an ethical principle to help guide community development practice towards consciously achieving social justice.[1] Here community development is defined as the activity of participating in community responses to changes in its internal or external environment which help insure the survival of or enhance the quality of life for those living in the community. Community develop-

---

Ru Michael Sabre is a Research/Extension Specialist in the College of Agriculture at The Pennsylvania State University. The author wishes to thank Professor Henry W. Johnstone, Jr. (Philosophy Department, PSU) for allowing him to use material from the manuscript of "Toward an Ethics of Rhetoric." Professors Walter Freeman (Division of Community Development, PSU) and Robert Price (Philosophy Department, PSU) were also very helpful.

---

[1] Practioners and researchers have been aware of ethical problems in community development and related practice. Blizek and Cederbloom [1973] present Rawl's principles as a basis for a *normative* view of community development practice, but do not make the connection between those principles and community development practice. Howe and Kaufman [1979] surveyed professional planners and in summarizing their findings one could say that for many planners the need to achieve some *end* tends to compromise their ethical standards. The present paper examines the origin and nature of the standard and hopefully talks directly and realistically to what it is to deviate from that standard.

ment practitioners are those engaged in that activity and thus would include those individuals who reside in the community and those who come in from the "outside." An ethical principle would provide a standard for practitioners and observers by which to judge such activities. Justice is defined in terms of fairness and the recognition of inequality not implying inequity. The goal is to provide an ethical principle for community development practice which brings about social justice.

To date I have been able to isolate three basic functional areas of community development practice. Community development may be seen as public affairs education (Bevins, 1978), as capacity building (Koneya, 1978) and as technical assistance (Gamm, 1979). Briefly, public affairs education means providing citizen groups and elected and appointed officials with the information they need to address problems that these groups deem important. Such information would include problem solving skills, organizational knowledge and value clarification methods to help them function more effectively as problem solving groups. By capacity building is meant the assistance provided to a set of concerned citizens to help them create an organized group in order to address some problem they feel is confronting them. Technical assistance is generally associated with the informational support for a specific community functional area which allows for some physical change in a community such as building a community swimming pool or hospital. Each of these three areas of community development is not distinct from the other and combinations are common.

The term "ethics" is derived from *ethos* or "folk ways." It connotes practices which are judged by value terms such as right and wrong, good and bad. While there is no agreement among philosophers about there being one overall ethical system, ethical systems can be divided into two basic classes of theory about ethical standards. These are teleological ethics and deontological ethics (Frankena, 1963).

A teleological ethic assigns the rightness or wrongness of an action in accordance to a goal which is external to and a result of the action. There are various sorts of teleological ethics which are differentiated by the end. Some examples of ends are the greatest good for the greatest number, happiness, and pleasure which are, respectively, utilitarian ethics, eudaemonian ethics and hedonism. In the case of utilitarian ethics, an action is judged as right when it leads to the greatest good for the greatest number of people. The standard criticism of this and other such positions is that the end does not provide a sufficient explanation for some of the problems caused by adopting certain means to those ends.

With deontological ethics, the rightness or wrongness of an action is in the action itself, which is to say, doing or failing to do one's duty.

Knowing one's duty becomes central, for action is not judged by its consequences, pleasant or otherwise. Knowing one's duty involves the conformity of the action to some formal moral criterion. In the history of ethics, there have been three recurrent standards offered: the authority of God, conscience and the categorical imperative. The categorical imperative does not directly appeal to divine revelation nor does it become entangled in the cultural relativism of the content of conscience.

Immanuel Kant offered the first formulations of the categorical imperative as the criterion for ethical choice as duty (Kant, 1949). The two most commonly used forms of the categorical imperative are: (1) act in such a way that the maxim of your action can become universal law and (2) never act as to treat people as means to an end but as ends in themselves.

An example of the first formulation can come about if a person takes a contemplated course of action and asks if that action could be generalized so as to become a general law. Such a generalization can occur if the law is consistent, but if a contraction arises, that action is not our duty. Suppose I consider breaking a promise to someone. Can I generalize promise breaking to all situations? The answer is no, because the concept of keeping a promise loses its meaning, if one will never keep promises.

The second formulation sheds light on the first, for in breaking a promise we are not treating that person as an end in him or herself (that is, as a person), but as a means to an end, generally, our own advantage. We are saying that this person should operate on misinformation about our intentions in the promise situation and we thus undercut that person's ability to make individual, responsible and effective decisions.

My position is that community development practitioners should explicitly adopt a deontological ethic because it is consistent with an educational mission, serves as a guide to action in capacity building and technical assistance and because it leads to social justice. The remainder of the paper develops this point in the following manner. I first discuss how an educational stance is a deontological stance and present a Basic Principle for community development practice. I then present and discuss the problems which come about because capacity building and technical assistance suggest a teleological standard of moral judgment. Next, I show how the Basic Principle helps us judge the wrongness of certain kinds of means, and as with any ethical consideration, *recommending* in this case a deontological ethics for community development practice. Finally, I show how the application of the Basic Principle is consistent with Rawl's interpretation of justice as fairness.

COMMUNITY DEVELOPMENT AS AN EDUCATIONAL PROCESS

As an educational stance, community development addresses community issues or needs with the position that what people need is information and the ability to interpret it, and then they can make up their own minds as to what to do or not do. Education enhances the capacity of individuals and groups to be persuaded *and* to persuade in specific subject areas and in human situations in general. Education is *not* simply changing behavior. As I will specify below, what makes this stance particularly interesting is that it embodies a deontological position.

In a recent article Bevins (1978) presents a discussion of community development and public affairs education. Here the situation of public affairs education is characterized as a decision situation on public policy "based on both facts and value." Differences in values entail differences of opinions over courses of action. Because of the latter, Bevins appends Mauch's philosophy of education in public policy:

1. Clearly define the problem so controversial issues are thoroughly understood.
2. Set forth the goals or objectives of those affected by the decision.
3. List all important alternatives that should be considered.
4. Analyze each alternative in light of its social and economic impact on producers, consumers, taxpayers, international relations and all other important areas of our society.
5. Leave decisions to the people. Decision making is not a proper function of the educator....(p. 83)

Bevins then lists the objectives or the desired state of affairs in people's behavior:

1. A more active interest in public affairs problems.
2. A better understanding of the issues and principles involved.
3. Increased ability to make judgments on the basis of a critical examination of the evidence and logical thinking.
4. Increased desire to participate effectively in the solution of public affairs problems. (p. 84)

In effect the educational process creates a state of affairs where individuals and groups are open and can be persuaded and yet still have the capacity to be resolute in holding a position. In essence, the educational stance allows people to both be persuaded and to persuade. What I am putting forward is that an educational approach to an individual or group embodies the following Basic Principle: *so act in each instance as to encourage, rather than suppress, the capacity to persuade and to be persuaded, whether the capacity in question is yours or another's.*[2]

"Persuasion" is used because it includes rational as well as nonrational means of getting a point across, with the Basic Principle qualifying this so that at the end of the interaction both you and the other(s) are on equal positive footing. We are to behave towards others as if they are ends in themselves, and not means to an end. As such, we preserve our own autonomy as well as theirs. It is a person's duty never to deprive another person of the capacity to perform his/her duties. An educational approach to community development avoids this by helping to give persons the capacity to make individual and responsible choices.

CAPACITY BUILDING AND TECHNICAL ASSISTANCE AS TELEOLOGICAL

Generally speaking, a community is in need of development when citizens begin to experience deprivations which could be addressed by the prudent or proper use of collective resources, but for a variety of reasons these resources are not being brought to bear. Community development practitioners assume that there is more than one "need" and begin logically enough by attempting to assess and prioritize these needs. The needs assessment whether carried out by a key informant procedure, social report, or a statistical survey has as its outcome the targeting of a set of needs which can be transformed into goals of activity. These activities are either capacity building or technical assistance as defined above.

However, at this point some problems occur. Evaluation of community development and the funding of community development from external sources are tied to tangible results. These evaluators and funding sources want a connection between process, and bricks and mortar. The need to produce these results reinforces the community development practitioner's tendency to equate meeting community needs with *attaining goals*. What *can* and often does enter the picture is the maxim, the end justifies the means, that is, teleological ethics. There is a tendency to become "broad-minded" about means.

The broad-mindedness includes coming to a sympathetic understanding with means which are known to be questionable. These means include

---

[2] This is the formulation as presented in Professor Johnstone's paper. In discussion with him, he thought that referring to the principle as the K-Principle had the advantage of associating the principle with Kant. I recommend this usage, but for the sake of expositional convenience refer to it simply as the Basic Principle in this paper.

(1) creating or fixing the public agenda, (2) conflict of interest, (3) co-optation, (4) advocacy and (5) assuming leadership. Brief definitions of these are helpful. Some people claim that any sort of needs assessment creates or fixes a public agenda which in turn orchestrates the expenditure of public funds and available time. Conflict of interest arises when an individual is involved in an issue in which two contending groups are depending on that individual for defense or testimony. Cooptation occurs when people are made into participants in an activity which is not in their best interest if they could define those interests. Advocacy entails giving one group or individual a special advantage over another group or individual when all individuals or groups have an equal claim over the practitioner's abilities. Assuming leadership means taking on the problem of making a group dependent upon the practitioner's expertise.

STRIKING A BALANCE

The Basic Principle makes us sensitive to the wrongness of these activities and pinpoints what is wrong. For example, by creating or fixing a public agenda we preclude some courses of action and deprive some community groups of the ability to fully debate courses of action. Their resoluteness is not firmly based. Conflict of interest violates the Basic Principle in that one group's capacity to have its case heard is unfairly diminished. Cooptation is wrong because people are acting under the false impression that they are pursuing their own best interests. When advocating for one group against another, when both have a claim on that practitioner's efforts, one group has not been treated as an end in itself. In assuming leadership the individual is taking from the group its capacity to exercise its own autonomy in diminishing its capacity to persuade or be persuaded in that particular situation and subsequent situations.

SOCIAL JUSTICE AS FAIRNESS

It is evident that each of the five ethically questionable practices defined above indicate common situations in community development practice. Just as the Basic Principle sheds light on wrong practice, so it helps us see right practice or activity.

• Needs assessment can be designed in such a way that they are reasonably representative of a community's problems, and their limitations can be pointed out. Bias in a social survey, for example, can be mitigated by nominal group procedures in selecting the set of social categories to be assessed.

- Conflict of interest can arise out of the normal course of events, particularly with institutes having technical expertise which is attractive to both community groups and industry. But, it is possible to monitor these two areas and make sure that (say) soil tests performed for community groups are not affected by the needs of the land-application-of-sludge industries.
- Cooptation need not occur if the community developer has in mind and intention the up-grading of the group's understanding of the issue area they are being led into as with a demonstration project. Recall that education in principle asks students to suspend their judgment in order to be able to carry out rigorous mental exercises and achieve a state of insight and understanding they can only understand once they have been through the process.
- Advocacy can be positive if the group being advocated for has an extreme disadvantage compared to a comparable group or groups which are in competition for local funding.
- Assuming leadership can be positive if the community developer does not make the group dependent upon his/her leadership but attempts to create a replacement from the group.

The thread which runs through the five examples is that when a social policy is implemented, the least advantaged are to gain something and not lose as a result of that policy, satisfying one half of Rawls' two criteria of justice as fairness. Rawls' other criterion is that everyone should contribute to social policy when it is formulated and *implemented* [Rawls 1971, 302]. Thus the Basic Principle above guides community development practice so that equal opportunity has more of a chance to be realized.

SUMMARY

I have presented an argument which shows how community development as an educational process embodies an ethical principle, and that that principle when applied to the analysis of community development practices promotes justice (understood as fairness). The position argued is that if the Basic Principle is made a part of community development practice, then that practice will promote social justice.

REFERENCES

Bevins, R. J. "Cooperative extension's public affairs tradition in community development." *Journal of the Community Development Society of America* 9(2):76–85.

Blizek, W. L. and Cederbloom, J. "Community development and social justice." 1973 *Journal of the Community Development Society of America* 4(2).

Frankena, W. K. *Ethics.* Englewood Cliffs, N.J. Prentice-Hall, Inc.
1963

Gamm, L. and Fisher, F. "The technical assistance approach to community de-
1979 velopment." manuscript. The Pennsylvania State University, University Park, Pennsylvania.

Howe, E. and Kaufman, J. "The ethics of contemporary planners." *Journal of the*
1979 *American Planning Association* 45(3):243–55.

Johnstone, H. W., Jr. "Toward an ethics of rhetoric." 65th Annual Speech Com-
1979 munication Association Meeting, San Antonio, Texas, Nov. 12.

Kant, I. *Critique of Practical Reason and Other Writings in Moral Philosophy.*
1949 L. W. Beck (trans. and ed.), Chicago.

Koneya, M. "Citizen participation is not community development." *Journal of the*
1978 *Community Development Society of America* 9(2):23–30.

Rawls, J. A. *A Theory of Justice.* Cambridge: Harvard University Press.
1971

PEOPLE-CENTERED COMMUNITY PLANNING
By John Michael Daley and Julio Angulo

ABSTRACT

Citizens, scholars, and planners have criticized various aspects of planning practice. The traditionally dominant approach, rational synoptic planning, has been characterized as overly rational, simplistic/reductionistic, elitist, and essentially supportive of existing power relationships in societies, organizations, and communities. Critiques have focused on the implicit values of this planning model, its consequences for less-powerful groups, and the problems encountered during plan implementation.

People-centered community planning is proposed as an alternative to rational synoptic planning. People-centered planning borrows liberally from other approaches, especially Friedmann's (1973) transactive planning, Dunn's (1971) social learning, and Habermas's (1976) critical theory. People-centered planning unites participatory planning with population-specific planning.

INTRODUCTION

Citizens, scholars, and planners have criticized the ideology, theory, and practice of synoptic planning.[1] Nonetheless, synoptic planning remains relatively unrevised as the dominant approach to many community planning efforts (Hudson, 1979). This paper incorporates common elements from various critiques into an outline for an alternative approach: people-centered community planning. This alternative offers promise for effective community planning that is consistent with the values of democracy, self-determination, human dignity, empowerment, and social justice. Although a description of the application of people-centered planning to a specific population is beyond the scope of this paper, people-centered planning can po-

---

[1] Synoptic planning "stresses a rational approach . . . with decisions made after setting of objectives, identification of alternatives, evaluation of each alternative by means of sophisticated analytical tools, and selection of those alternatives shown to be most efficient for attaining the goals" (Johnson, 1989, p. 102). Synoptic planning usually encompasses a broad range of human needs and has a long-range (perhaps 10 to 20 years) time perspective (Johnson, 1989).

John Michael Daley is a professor and Julio Angulo is a clinical assistant professor, both in the School of Social Work at Arizona State University.

tentially be applied to any oppressed group—including ethnic groups, the aged, women, the disabled, and low-income groups. Selections from the critical literature developed by Hispanics and women are used to illustrate the views of oppressed groups.

Planning is a broad concept and a diverse field of professional practice. It encompasses societal, community, and organizational attempts to shape the future of human institutions. A subfield, community planning, focuses on societal, community, and organizational efforts to address unmet or emerging community needs. Planning practice differs in accordance with the level of application. For example, legislative reform may call for different strategies than those that might be employed to restructure a human service agency. Yet the principles of a given planning model remain largely invariant and, thus, applicable across all levels of practice—forms of synoptic planning are applied at societal, community, organizational, and program levels.

The community planning field is broad and heterogeneous. Planning efforts may reflect the rational synoptic approach (or the people-centered planning approach) to different degrees in different institutional areas (e.g., physical, human service, and health) and in different communities. This paper contributes to the development of community planning practice by first synthesizing the critiques of rational synoptic efforts that have been articulated by diverse groups and by subsequently synthesizing elements of alternatives that have been proposed by critics of the dominant rational synoptic efforts.

CRITICISMS OF THE SYNOPTIC APPROACH TO PLANNING

The intellectual and moral development of planning has evolved in response to diverse stimuli, including planners' experiences with earlier approaches or models, the emerging political aspirations and power of groups and communities, and scholarly trends (Alexander, 1984; Brandwein, 1981; Bricker-Jenkins & Hooyman, 1986). This paper draws primarily from the critiques directly advanced or influenced by critical theorists, Hispanics, and women. One implication of these critiques is to energize a planning practice model by replacing one core metaphor—technical, value-free man—with another—historically grounded, value-oriented human beings. The conceptual work involved, however, is not free of pitfalls. Precautions must be taken so that the newly envisioned *homus historicus* does not turn out, literally, to be male, white, or both. The revitalization of planning practice needs to be considered not exclusively in the context of mainstream culture and concepts but also with reference to notions conceived by women and ethnics.[2]

Citizens, scholars, and planners have challenged synoptic planning—the historically dominant approach to community planning (Johnson, 1989; Hudson, 1979). The synoptic or rational comprehensive approach is in paradigmatic crisis (Alexander, 1984; Kraushaar, 1988) since it is now judged as overly rational, simplistic/reductionistic, elitist, and essentially supportive of the status quo. Critiques have focused on the implicit values of its underlying model, its consequences for less-favored or less-powerful groups in an organization, community, or society, and the problems encountered during plan implementation.[3]

Essentially, critics have challenged the ideological relationships between planning, the social sciences, and the dominant groups or interests in society. A number of troubling themes have been identified. First, the development of a knowledge base for planning practice is not an objective, technical enterprise. Knowledge development is socially and politically determined. Social science and practice paradigms reflect the historical experiences and aspirations of the dominant groups in a society (Sampson, 1977).

Second, the production of knowledge for planning is tied to the intentions and interests of a given group or class. Theories or facts are never value free; they are normative. Bricker-Jenkins and Hooyman (1986, p. 16) state that "the process of defining problems is always subjective, shaped by values, interests and ideologies" (see also Bolan [1980], Dunn [1971], and Forester [1980]). Instrumental rationality, the root of synoptic planning, largely reflects and maintains the values, beliefs, and influence of traditional power structures (Habermas, 1976). In the United States, this ideology asserts the power of white men over women and people of color.

---

[2] These critiques cut to the heart of planning practice. They question what we know about the community groups to be served and planning theory and practice and how we obtain and use this knowledge. Readers not familiar with the intellectual and moral themes and substance of these critiques may wish to review the works of Angulo and Arguelles (1985), Bricker-Jenkins and Hooyman (1986), Habermas (1976), Kraushaar (1988), and Rendon (1971). For an overview of planning theory and practice, see Alexander (1984), Bolan (1983), Forester (1980), Hudson (1979), and Johnson (1989).

[3] A different type of critique is articulated by Lindblom and others. Applied to administrative decision making or policy development, these critiques (Lindblom & Braybrooke, 1970; Etzioni, 1973; Etzioni, 1978) tend to view the rational synoptic approach as techically limited rather than ideologically and politically flawed. In subsequent work, Lindblom and Cohen (1979) begin to explore the ideological implications of the rational synoptic approach.

Third, the existing literature that is used to educate professionals often contains negative appraisals of the lives of the less powerful or less favored and leads to erroneous understandings as well as ineffective or even harmful interventive practices (Angulo & Arguelles, 1985; Brandwein, 1981). The less influential have been ignored, oppressed, stereotyped, and victimized; the resulting phenomenology of intergroup relationships espoused by dominant groups is adversarial—"us versus them" (Padilla et al., 1975; Alvarez, 1973).

Finally, the marriage of convenience between planning practice and empirical science produces a practice that is based on an ahistorical, acontextual view of social phenomena that distrusts subjectivity and favors universal categories of understanding and intervention (nomothetic) over unique and specific ones (idiographic). Practice approaches, so conceptualized, increase their internal, theoretical validity at the expense of ecological, practical validity (e.g., they may appear elegant conceptually and work in the laboratory but become problematic in the field).

ALTERNATIVES TO SYNOPTIC PLANNING

The themes outlined above have challenged citizens, scholars, and planners to articulate alternatives that address the problematic aspects of synoptic planning. In essence, as suggested by the critiques, these alternatives entail making explicit the connections between ideology and theory (or model building). More concretely, practitioners must recognize that practice models and theories are always normative (Bolan, 1980; Forester, 1980; Klosterman, 1983; Sampson, 1977). They must see that espoused theory (theory that practitioners say they use) and theory in use may differ significantly (Bolan, 1980) and that the logic of empirical science (prediction/control) and the logic of action/practice (understanding and choice) differ. Knowledge metaphors rooted in the empirical, physical sciences may be of limited value to planners who must operate in the politically and historically defined world (Klosterman, 1983).

Planners must also appreciate the phenomenology of the planning episode, including the context in which it occurs and the vectors crossing it (e.g., history, values, interests, ideologies, needs, intentions, and interpretive schemas). Planning can be viewed as essentially drama—a communicative, attention-shaping, political activity (Bolan, 1980; Forester, 1980). In this context, planners must do the following: adhere to the pragmatics of effective communication; seek intersubjective agreement (e.g., cooperation and mutuality) between planner and audience(s); accept object-subject, fact-social value, means-ends, and expert-audience dialectical tensions; and recognize the influences of language in the development of the concepts of problem and solution(s).

The planning process must be viewed as being composed of two interwoven elements: the analytical and the interpersonal. Brandwein (1981) suggests that in recent years the analytical component has been overemphasized, resulting in elegant, analytical models that suffer from a lack of attention to the human elements of planning.

Devotees to the logical positivist school focused on what were labeled "key" factors in the planning process. They often concentrated on easily observed and measured elements (e.g., the numbers of consumers on policy boards) while neglecting other elements of the situation that posed problems of observation, measurement, or analysis (e.g., the influence exercised by consumers on policy boards). These (mis)labeled "key" factors were seen in isolation from their historical, social, psychological, economic, and political determinents and consequences. The logical positivist framework can become simplified to the point of being reductionistic. For example, the emphasis placed on data processing technology often has been excessive and without proper appreciation of its limits. The "hardness" and, therefore, widespread acceptability of a computer printout has disarmed the critical capacity of many planners, politicians, and citizens.

Alternative approaches to planning require new power relationships among citizens, scholars, and planners and explicit new value sets. Oppressed groups, including women and ethnics, must reject or be critical of dominant forms of "knowledge," consciousness, ideology, and rationality. The less powerful must engage in the articulation of their own history, values, and self-view (Atencio, 1983; Brandwein, 1981). Less-influential groups must challenge and transform, from within, the mainstream view of their lives. This entails a transformation of the manner in which the "definer" interacts with the "defined." The less powerful need to enter the ranks of the "definers" in such areas as academia and the professions (Bricker-Jenkins & Hooyman, 1986; Forester, 1985). Women and ethnics need to develop sensitive, people-serving social provisions (resources and services) that include services they themselves plan and operate (Casas, 1976; Malgady et al., 1987; Gibson, 1983). These social provisions must have as central purposes the raising of consciousness and the empowerment of professionals and citizens who are members of less-powerful or less-favored groups (Parker, 1988; Freire, 1972).

People-centered community planning is an approach that offers the potential for addressing the problems identified with the rational synoptic approach to planning. People-centered planning stays attentive to the themes outlined above and also borrows liberally from other approaches, especially Friedmann's (1973) transactive planning, Dunn's (1971) social learning, and Habermas's (1976) critical theory. People-centered planning is characterized by the marriage of participatory and population-specific planning.[4]

PEOPLE-CENTERED COMMUNITY PLANNING

People-centered planning is an approach to designing professional interventions to respond to the problems, needs, issues, or opportunities of a specific group of people (or population in the public health sense). All community planning entails consideration of the clients, consumers, citizens, or population to be impacted. Often these identified recipients of benefits are not engaged in the planning process itself. Their life circumstances and aspirations are not fully appreciated, and their interests are subordinated to the interests of others (dominant groups) during the planning process. In contrast, people-centered community planning includes actively involving the recipients in the planning process, making them the central focus of the planning episode, and being committed to their interests, needs, and aspirations.

People-centered community planning views the people to be served as ideological and historical beings. They are seen as possessing a unique understanding about their own lives, hopes, aspirations, goals, and preferences and about the manner in which resources should be provided or services should be designed and delivered. Further, the people to be served can and should be systematically involved in every aspect of the development, implementation, and evaluation of interventions because participation in this process, in itself, contributes to their dignity and empowerment.

With people-centered community planning, the relationship between professionals (including planners) and persons to be served is based on mutual respect. Their interactions constitute mutual learning—each is both teacher and learner and contributes unique expertise to the planning process (Dunn, 1971; Friedmann, 1973; Freire,

---

[4] Participatory planning emphasizes the central role of citizens and community groups in the community planning process—planning with, rather than for, citizens and community groups (Bricker-Jenkins & Hooyman, 1986; Dunn, 1971; Friedmann, 1973). Population-specific planning entails the specification of the human system(s) or groups that will be the focus of an episode of planned community change. Once the community groups have been identified, their history, traditions, aspirations, and related characteristics can be considered as part of the planning process (Kettner et. al., 1985).

1972). The relationships developed transcend the more-segmented professional-client relationships found in other approaches (Morris, 1970). Planners become involved with various aspects of community life. In turn, citizens come to know planners not simply as distant objective experts but as flesh-and-blood persons who have histories, values, and aspirations. The quality of this relationship is vital to the process. Segmented or superficial relationships between professionals and the people to be served will limit the mutual respect and learning central to people-centered community planning. This is a most-demanding aspect of this approach for both the professional and the citizen.

ELEMENTS OF PEOPLE-CENTERED COMMUNITY PLANNING

People-centered community planning consists of a set of integrated elements: ideology and values as metacontext; knowledge base (about the people and the planning process); and skills (people/interpersonal and technical/analytical).

Ideology and Values

People-centered community planning explicitly embraces a specific ideology and set of values. As Alexander (1984) noted, "Adopting a definite social ideology as a guiding framework for planning is a valid response to [synoptic] paradigm breakdown" (p. 67). Ideology constitutes the "essential glue" of the approach. It is the signature or essence of people-centered community planning. In the most general sense, ideology refers to the preferred ideas, values, and beliefs held by a given social group at a particular time (Atencio, 1983). A preferred world view can aim to maintain and support existing social arrangements or contemplate reform or radical change in social norms (Atencio, 1983; Bricker-Jenkins & Hooyman, 1986).

The world view and values of people-centered community planning include notions about the nature of the human condition, the relationships that affect the individual, the family, the community, and society, and the nature of the community planning process. The human condition is viewed as highly complex, a mosaic comprised of historical, physical, biological, social, economic, spiritual, cultural, political, and other elements (Kraushaar, 1988). Understanding the human condition entails the use of quantitative and qualitative, objective and subjective, and general and specific modes. People-centered planning holds an essentially positive view of humanity. Individual, family, and community strengths are stressed rather than focusing exclusively on individual, family, or community problems. Natural helping systems are viewed as crucial community strengths that can be used to meet human needs (Whittaker & Garbarino, 1983). Family and community integrity is valued.

In concert with Judeo-Christian social values, the individual and society are viewed as sharing mutual rights and responsibilities that include the right and obligation to both help and be helped. People are assumed to know what is best for themselves and to have the right to be involved in decisions that will shape the form and content of their lives. People have a unique expertise concerning their lives, needs, hopes, aspirations, and preferences that should be respected. All persons should be valued for their intrinsic worth. Social justice dictates that social provisions be made to meet the basic human needs of all citizens.

Within the people-centered approach, the planning process is essentially a socially defined, normative enterprise that reflects the values of both its environment and its participants. Planning is a deliberate effort to shape a desired future state or condition. Planning should support human growth and dignity. During each planning episode, people-centered planning includes all groups with a vested interest in the possible outcomes. A vested interest exists whenever a planning process will potentially influence a group's future life environment or opportunities. The planning process itself is both a growth and an empowering process for those involved. Mutual learning between professionals and citizens is anticipated as an integral element of the planning process (Dunn, 1971; Friedmann, 1973). Both a theory of planning and theory in planning (substantive knowledge of human behavior, social problems, or policy in an area such as housing or health care) are needed for theoretically sound planning practice. Finally, the planning process recognizes and values the participation of diverse individuals and groups in a manner that acknowledges and respects all of their views.

Knowledge Base

Knowledge of and by the People

Peoples' knowledge is the foundation upon which people-centered planning operates. Simply stated, there is no substitute for a solid appreciation of the life conditions, aspirations, and preferences of the people to be served. Both professionals and the people to be served contribute to the understanding of these life circumstances.

A comprehensive understanding develops as the result of a holistic approach that takes into account the rich contextual elements of life—as opposed to a more-focused approach or image that fails to place the person or group in its historical context.

In contrast to planning and intervention models that focus exclusively on a few "key" behaviors or conditions (such as the rate of employment or substance abuse), people-centered planning seeks the richer texture of each group's life. One step in this process locates the group of people in relation to larger groupings. Obviously, this demanding task is an ongoing one. The true picture of any group's experiences, understandings, hopes, fears, and other characteristics can only be approximated. Therefore, the understandings achieved in the planning process are treated as incomplete and provisional notions that need to be tested—leading to progressively more-refined understandings.

History. The people-centered approach retains a sharp focus on the people to be served and incorporates aspects of their history, including an appraisal of present needs and definitions, in the context of their cultural history, language, religion, and traditions (Gibson, 1983). As presently conceptualized, this alternative asserts that the professional episode is eminently historical. Individuals and social groups generate goals and objectives with reference to a story or vision of themselves that has been forged, in many cases, over the course of generations of struggle. As a derivative notion, people-centered planning holds that the episode is essentially an ideological encounter. It is a drama involving the planners and the planned, wherein both attempt to assert their own preferred set of values, ideas, or beliefs— their intentionality.

Planning must place the people to be served in a historical context to appreciate where these people have been, where they are now, and where they hope to go or think they will go in the future. As Heilbroner (1960) forcefully argued, history has a significant subjective component. A group defines its own history. At the same time, a group may have competing histories imposed upon it by other more-powerful groups. Each group will recognize and believe its own version. Multiple histories of a single group may be identified and considered.

People-centered planning involves the group in reconsidering and redefining its history. This may entail specifying the group's subjective understandings or myths about itself and recognizing the distinct historical understandings and myths others hold with regard to the group. A group's own history may be influenced by the histories attributed to it by others. Although it is necessary to understand the implications of competing histories, it may not be possible to reconcile them.

One key element of a group's history is its sense of being able to shape or control the essential circumstances within which it lives. If a group knows that it can exercise influence over its life conditions and can shape its own future, it will be inclined to become involved in environmental change efforts (Sower et al., 1957). If the group does not see itself as empowered in such matters, it may ignore or even resist efforts to reshape environmental conditions. A group's history and traditions are powerful molders of its hopes and expectations.

Sources of data and insight. Planners and groups members can use a variety of sources of population-specific information. Generic data sets (from the Census Bureau, government planning bodies, voluntary planning bodies, and private sector planning offices) may provide data breakouts of significance to the group. The group to be served may be a part of a larger group for which data are available. Caution and careful creativity are needed, however, when extrapolating in this manner.

Local colleges and universities may have conducted (often unpublished) studies on the specific population or its environment. Local newspapers, radio reports, or television specials may shed light on particular aspects of the group's life. Agency statistics may be available. In sum, written information and other physical evidence (for example, how well kept are public spaces or how many people attend meetings) from various sources may prove useful (Webb et al., 1981). Persons who are not group members can also contribute to an understanding of the group. Business operators, professionals, civil servants, religious leaders, politicians, and journalists serving the group can provide valuable insights.

Mutual learning. Participant observation is a key means by which the professional can gain a grounded understanding of the group and its ways. Group members contribute their unique expertise to the education of professionals within the mutual learning framework. Coupled with the use of group members as collaborative "guides," participant observation provides direct access to group life. An agreement between professionals and group members to discuss the subjective meanings attached to shared activities provides some safeguard that the professional will not draw distorted interpretations of observed and experienced group activities.

Additionally, it is through mutual learning that the professional and the group to be served become teamed. Each can enrich the understanding of the other in mutually respectful encounters. The objective of this collaborative effort is a firm grounding for both sides in the realities of the group's life as the basis for the content of the planning process—it is the vital anchor that sustains the group to be served as the focus of planning.

To fulfill the logic of the people-centered approach, community workers and persons from the group to be served embark on a process of mutual learning. The results of this process include trusting relationships and common understandings of the life complexities of the group and of the planning process. These same relationships and common understandings are always in the process of development. Like gardeners, people-centered planning participants constantly look for new developments and use new understandings as the basis for further nurturing the growth process.

The process of mutual learning is a two-way street. The professional is responsible for helping the group members to understand the planning process and the culture of planning (Bolan, 1983). This process of gaining appreciation can draw upon multiple means: written materials, shared experiences, and discussions between planners and group members. Without this mutuality, the process would simply be the uncritical socialization of the group members to the "proper" way to do planning—as defined by the planners.

Knowledge of the Planning Process

Members of the group to be served enter a planning episode as experts about their lives, needs, and aspirations. The planner, on the other hand, is usually the one that is more knowledgeable about initiating and facilitating the planning process. Just as a group of people must be understood within ideological and historical contexts, the planning process itself must be appreciated as ideologically, historically, and contextually shaped. Planners, members of planning agencies and organizations, and planning practitioners are, to a large degree, creatures of their world views, past experiences, current needs, interests, aspirations and fears, and knowledge and technology base.

People-centered community planning uses a critical approach to the knowledge base of community planning, an approach that views peoples' lives and the planning process as too complex to be reduced to a few factors that are asserted to be "key" to understanding and action. Technology is viewed as a tool to be used where it can facilitate the exploration-and-action process. To that end, both quantitative and qualitative and objective and subjective elements of reality are valued. Finally, the people-centered approach places value on a contextual understanding, an appreciation of the total environment of the target population and planning process. For example, the ecology of a life situation or planning episode would include an understanding of the historical realities of the situation, the values involved, and the social, political, and economic forces influencing the situation. This brief description is intended to be suggestive of the rich milieux of peoples' lives and planning processes.

Skills

Interpersonal Skills/People Skills

Interpersonal and analytical skills are needed to engage in people-centered planning. Interpersonal skills include people skills and the ability to work effectively with diverse groups through the use of a wide variety of planning roles, including those of facilitator/enabler, expert, advocate, communicator, organizer, and educator (Morris, 1970; Bolan, 1980; Forester, 1980; Brandwein, 1981).

It is beyond the scope of this paper to discuss incentive systems that seem promising in terms of motivating all types of previously uninvolved groups. Daley et al. (1989) and Widmer (1987) discuss in some detail a set of incentives and planning options that may motivate members of ethnic groups. Involving members of community groups that have historically suffered a forced exclusion from civic affairs is a challenge that will test the commitment, persuasiveness, negotiating skills, and patience of professionals and civic leaders.

Interpersonal skills must be particularly attuned to the ways of the people to be served by the planning process. This suggests the need to reframe community planning practice in order to accommodate the culture(s) of the participants—including groups that have not been involved with traditional planning efforts. Similar to Jenkins' (1980) description of the "ethnic agency," a planning process can be designed to encourage the involvement of specific groups via culturally focused adaptations to the planning process. Tropman et al. (1979) and Widmer (1987) briefly propose tactics to involve new groups in the committee process, which is a crucial element of the overall planning process. At times, the planner and the planning process must prove to be trustworthy before the process can proceed (Tropman et al., 1979).

It seems reasonable to expect that groups excluded from, manipulated by, or poorly served by earlier planning efforts will not enter into subsequent efforts without some firm evidence that they will be treated fairly and that their involvement will produce valued results (Daley et al., 1989). This suggests the need for planners to design specific strategies to involve these previously uninvolved or ill-served groups. Evidence of good faith might include planning topics or objectives that are valued by the new participant group or a planning process that clearly respects the views of new participants. Specific sets of incentives can be offered to make participation reasonable, valued, and comfortable. For example, if the new group suffers from poor educational programs, the planning process might focus on visible, short-term, educational benefits as part of its educational agenda. The establishment of trusting relationships is a key task that needs to be undertaken early in the planning episode and that requires the investment of time and other resources.

Community planners and civic leaders will need to deal with intergroup conflicts as the interests of traditional influentials—who historically have been involved in civic life—clash with the interests and needs of new participants. Daley and Kettner (1981) and Fisher and Ury (1981) describe in detail the bargaining and negotiating approaches that are consistent with community development values and that appear to offer promise in terms of resolving community conflicts in a manner that is both effective and perceived as fair by participants. It is vital that conflict resolution be viewed as a fair and just process, especially by groups that are new to civic affairs and that may have suffered historically from exclusion or exploitation. Early, visible victories in the competition for scarce resources can provide a strong incentive for newly involved groups to stay involved in the long-term political process that characterizes American civic life.

Analytical Skills

A highly developed critical stance toward such topics as the world as it is, the motivational characteristics of human behavior, and knowledge building, knowledge utilization, and planning as social processes are needed in order to practice people-centered planning (Habermas, 1976). Multiple paradigms are used flexibly and creatively in people-centered planning, and theories are continuously tested against the subjective realities of the parties engaged in the planning process.

Critical theory[5] can enlighten the communications central to the planning process (Forester, 1980). A critical analysis of communication can help the planner understand the meaning of communications in a planning episode. Through an appreciation of the setting,

---

[5] Critical theory provides a context within which to understand social and political thought and action. This context itself is useful in understanding the manner in which knowledge is developed and communicated and the relationships among thought, public discourse, and social and political choices and actions (Bernstein, 1978).

content, and intention(s) of communications, critical theory provides a framework within which the planner can shape the planning process via the deliberate design of communications. For example, the planner can influence the timing of communications, the manner in which messages are phrased, and the individuals and groups that will originate or receive specific information. In even this brief description, the inherent interrelatedness and inseparability of the interpersonal and analytical skill elements can be seen. While it is possible to separate these elements for discussion, in the real world of planning they are a single piece of cloth.

CLOSING COMMENTS

This paper argues for people-centered community planning—as an alternative to synoptic planning—for oppressed populations. Almost a quarter of a century has elapsed since both critical theory and critical visions of the ethnic and women's movements echoed in academia. Further, planners have already issued revised versions of synoptic rational models. In community development, however, this integrative effort has yet to take place. This paper presents the views of advocates for the oppressed, or the oppressed themselves, and provides an approach to planning with, rather than for, oppressed peoples. The intent is not to describe, in detail, the elements of a new model of community planning. Rather, the description of the complex and demanding people-centered approach is intended to spark discussion among policymakers, community workers, and oppressed people and to provide, in synthesis, the basis for new planning efforts.

REFERENCES

Alexander, E. R. After rationality, what? *Journal of the American Planning Association*
1984   50(1):62–69.
Alvarez, R. The unique psycho-historical experiences of the Mexican-American peo-
1973   ple. Pp. 45–55 in R. Rosaldo, R. Calvert and J. Seligman (eds.), *Chicano: The Evolution of a People*. Minneapolis, MN: Winston Press.
Angulo, A. & Arguelles, L. Chicano social work: A critical analysis. *Journal of Sociology*
1985   *and Social Welfare* 12(1):95–112.
Atencio, T. Ideology in social work: The perspective of Chicanos. Pp. 22–39 in G.
1983   Gibson (ed.), *Our Kingdom Stands on Brittle Glass*. Silver Spring, MD: National Association of Social Workers.
Bernstein, R. J. *The Restructuring of Social and Political Theory*. Philadelphia, PA: Uni-
1978   versity of Pennsylvania Press.
Bolan, R. S. The practitioner as theorist: The phenomenology of the professional
1980   episode. *American Planning Association Journal* 46(3):261–274.

Bolan, R. S. Community decision behavior: The culture of planning. Pp. 209–224 in
1983   R. M. Kramer and H. Specht (eds.), *Readings in Community Organization Practice.* 3d ed. Englewood Cliffs, NJ: Prentice-Hall.

Brandwein, R. A. Toward the feminization of community and organizational practice.
1981   *Social Development Issues* 5(2/3):180–193.

Bricker-Jenkins, M. & Hooyman, N. R. A feminist world view: Ideological themes
1986   from the feminist movement. Pp. 7–22 in *Not For Women Only.* Washington, DC: National Association of Social Workers.

Casas, J. Applicability of behavioral model in serving the mental health needs of
1976   Mexican Americans. Pp. 61–65 in M. Medina (ed.), *Psychotherapy with the Spanish Speaking: Issues in Research and Service Delivery.* Monograph No. 3. Spanish Speaking Mental Health Research Center, University of California, Los Angeles.

Daley, J. M., Applewhite, S. & Jorquez, J. Community participation of the Chicano
1989   elderly: A model. *The International Journal of Aging and Human Development* 29(2):133–148.

Daley, J. M. & Kettner, P. M. Bargaining in community development. *Journal of the*
1981   *Community Development Society* 12(2):25–38.

Dunn, E. S., Jr. *Economic and Social Development: A Process of Social Learning.* Baltimore,
1971   MD: The Johns Hopkins Press.

Etzioni, A. Mixed scanning: A "third" approach to decision making. Pp. 217–229 in
1973   A. Faludi (ed.), *A Reader in Planning Theory.* New York: Pergamon Press.

Etzioni, A. (ed.). *Policy Research.* Leiden, The Netherlands: E. J. Brill.
1978

Fisher, R. & Ury, W. *Getting to Yes: Negotiating Agreement Without Giving In.* Boston:
1981   Houghton-Mifflin.

Forester, J. Critical theory and planning practice. *American Planning Association Journal*
1980   46(3):275–286.

Forester, J. *Critical Theory and Public Life.* Cambridge, MA: MIT Press.
1985

Freire, P. *Pedagogy of the Oppressed.* New York: Herder & Herder.
1972

Friedmann, J. *Retracking America: A Theory of Transactive Planning.* New York: Anchor
1973   Doubleday.

Gibson, G. (ed.). *Our Kingdom Stands on Brittle Glass.* Silver Spring, MD: National
1983   Association of Social Workers.

Habermas, J. *Legitimation Crisis.* London: Heineman Educational Books.
1976

Heilbroner, R. L. *The Future as History.* New York: Grove Press.
1960

Hudson, B. Comparison of current planning theories: Counterparts and contradic-
1979   tions. *Journal of the American Planning Association* 45(4):387–399.

Jenkins, S. The ethnic agency defined. *Social Service Review* 54(2):249–261.
1980

Johnson, W. C. *The Politics of Urban Planning.* New York: Paragon House.
1989

Kettner, P., Daley, J.M. & Nichols, A.W. *Initiating Change in Organizations and Com-*
1985   *munities.* Monterey, CA: Brooks Cole.

Klosterman, R. Fact and value in planning. *Journal of the American Planning Association*
1983   49(2):216–225.

Kraushaar, R. Outside the whale: Progressive planning and the dilemmas of radical
1988   reform. *Journal of the American Planning Association* 54(1):91–100.

Lindblom, C. E. & Braybrooke, D. *A Strategy of Decision.* New York: Free Press.
1970

Lindblom, C. E. & Cohen, D. K. *Usable Knowledge: Social Science and Social Problem*
1979   *Solving.* New Haven, CT: Yale University Press.

Malgady, R. G., Rogler, L. H. & Constantino, G. Ethnocultural and linguistic bias in
1987   mental health evaluations of Hispanics. *American Psychologist* 42(3):228–234.

Morris, R. The role of the agent in the community development process. Pp. 171–
1970   194 in C. J. Cary (ed.), *Community Development as a Process.* Columbia, MO: University of Missouri Press.

Padilla, A. M., Ruiz, R. A. & Alvarez, R. Community mental health services for the
1975   Spanish-speaking/surnamed population. *American Psychologist* 30(9):892–905.

Parker, W. *Consciousness Raising.* Springfield, IL: Charles C. Thomas.
1988

Rendon, A. *Chicano Manifesto.* New York: Macmillan.
1971

Sampson, E. Psychology and the American ideal. *Journal of Personality and Social Psy-*
1977   *chology* 35(11):767–782.

Sower, C., Holland, J., Tiedke, K. & Freeman, W. *Community Involvement.* Glencoe, IL:
1957   Free Press.

Tropman, J. E., Johnson, H. R. & Tropman, E. J. *The Essentials of Committee Management.*
1979   Chicago: Nelson-Hall.

Webb, E. J., Campbell, D. T., Schwartz, R. D., Sechrest, L. & Grove, J. B. *Nonreactive*
1981   *Measures in the Social Sciences.* Boston: Houghton-Mifflin.

Whittaker, J.K. & Garbarino, J. *Social Support Networks: Informal Helping in the Human*
1983   *Services.* New York: Aldine.

Widmer, C. Minority participation on boards of directors of human service agencies:
1987   Some evidence and suggestions. *Journal of Voluntary Action Research* 16(4): 33–44.

Strategies for Citizen Participation and Empowerment in Non-profit, Community-Based Organizations

Donna Hardina

In community development, there is a consensus that citizen participation, empowerment, and linking community residents and clients of organizations to the political system are important goals. There is also a great deal of empirical evidence that verifies the effectiveness of empowerment in community-based organizations. However, little of this literature explicates the actual activities that are required to implement this approach. This paper examines strategies that can be used by non-profit, community-based organizations to encourage participation in organizational and political decision-making. A conceptual model is described that links citizen participation with specific outcomes associated with empowerment-enhancing activities in community-based organizations.

The literature on empowerment in community-based non-profit organizations generally focuses on enhancing the power of staff members or clientele to make policies or design programs (Bowen & Lawler, 1995; Gutierrez, GlenMaye, & DeLois, 1995). However, some proponents of empowerment in organizations argue that community-based organizations should also serve as "mediating institutions" linking low-income community residents, informal networks, local organizations, and government (Berger & Neuhaus, 1977). The purpose of empowerment-related activities in these organizations should be to increase civic participation among participants, decrease their sense of alienation from mainstream society, and facilitate the development of political influence to affect social change. Increasing citizen participation is an important and essential function for non-profit organizations. According to Putnam (2000), most forms of political participation in American society decreased by over 25 percent during the period between 1973-1974 and 1993-1994.

Craig (2002) defines empowerment in the community development context as "the creation of sustainable structures, processes, and mechanisms, over which local communities have an increased degree of control, and from which they have a measurable impact on public and social policies affecting these communities" (pp. 125-126). Although

---

Donna Hardina is a professor in the Department of Social Work Education, California State University, Fresno, 5310 Campus Drive, Fresno, CA, 93722. E-mail: donna_hardina@csufresno.edu.

there is a general consensus about the meaning of the term, the literature on empowerment in community-based, non-profit organizations is often limited to general discussions that examine motives behind efforts to increase citizen participation (Arnstein, 1969). This literature gives limited guidance to community developers or organization administrators who wish to provide opportunities to enhance the political influence of organization constituents (Pigg, 2002). The acquisition of political power is of special concern in these organizations because of the unique nature of their constituency base. The term "constituent" can be used to describe board members, community residents, clients of social or health services, staff members, and others who either benefit from the organization's activities or are involved with the organization in some decision-making capacity.

In this paper, the author addresses these gaps in the literature by examining the historical development of the term "empowerment" and recent efforts to document the use and effectiveness of empowerment-oriented community development practice. The author also describes common organizational practices identified in the literature as associated with civic participation and the empowerment of members of low-income communities and other marginalized groups. A conceptual model is described that links the activities of community-based organizations with specific outcomes associated with empowerment in community-based organizations.

A Brief History of the Linkage between Citizen Participation and Empowerment in Community-Based Organizations

The term "empowerment" most likely has its roots in government-mandated anti-poverty programs implemented in the 1960s. Although the actual term "empowerment" did not appear in the professional literature until the mid-1970s, efforts to involve consumers explicitly in the management of social service organizations were referred to as "citizen participation" (Arnstein, 1969). Some program planners and researchers viewed the purpose of citizen participation as a mechanism for ensuring the effectiveness of service delivery and making these services more responsive to people in need (Gulati, 1982). The participation of service beneficiaries in community-based organizations was intended to train community leaders as political activists and provide a greater sense of inclusion in mainstream society for low-income people (Gittell, 1980).

Involving citizens in community planning efforts was viewed as a mechanism for social reform (Marris & Rein, 1982). The inclusion of low-income people in organization decision-making was to be used as a tool to alleviate poverty. Community Action projects, funded by private foundations and the federal Office of Economic Opportunity (OEO), were operated through non-profit organizations. Some of these organizations fulfilled government requirements for "maximum feasible participation" by placing residents of marginalized and disadvantaged communities on their boards of directors.

According to Marris & Rein (1982), OEO program planners made it clear that in addition to low-income community residents, other constituency groups (such as religious leaders, business persons, entrepreneurs, and mayors) were to be given prominent roles in the decision-making process. However, engagement in social protest and scattered efforts to challenge local political elites by some of the Community Action agencies reduced public and governmental support for the programs. In 1967, Congress cut funds and attempted to limit the role of OEO-funded programs to job creation (Moynihan, 1969).

References to the "empowerment approach" for delivering services to members of marginalized groups first started to appear in the social work and social psychology literature in the 1970s and 1980s (Solomon, 1976; Rappaport, 1984). Barbara Solomon defined empowerment as "a process whereby persons who belong to a stigmatized social category throughout their lives can be assisted to develop and increase skills in the exercise of interpersonal influence and the performance of valued social roles" (p. 6). Empowerment-oriented strategies for involving service recipients in organization decision-making, self-advocacy, and program evaluation were intended to help individuals see themselves as having the power to resolve their own problems and to influence political change (Rose & Black, 1985). Zimmerman and Rapport (1988) specifically linked empowerment to citizen participation, arguing that inclusion of community residents in organization decision-making and social change activities had therapeutic effects, helping participants develop leadership skills. Skill development and participation in social change activities were expected to reduce feelings of oppression and increase each individual's sense of personal self-efficacy. What was not addressed in this literature was the role of the community-based organizations in facilitating these changes. However, Berger and Neuhaus (1977) advocated that non-profit organizations should take explicit action to help low-income people gain power. These organizations could link residents of low-income neighborhoods to community-based institutions and government agencies. Such alliances were expected to alleviate poverty and bring marginalized groups into the political process.

During the 1990s, the term empowerment came to encompass non-profit and for-profit management approaches. The goal of empowerment-oriented management strategies is to involve staff members in organizational decision-making. Such approaches are thought to improve the quality of service, increase worker productivity, stimulate innovation, and improve interpersonal relationships between staff members and administrators (Bowen & Lawler, 1995; Shera & Page, 1995; Spreitzer, 1996).

Theory Development: Documenting if Empowerment "Works"

Theories help us connect assumptions about the impact of specific activities or behaviors and the outcome produced as a consequence of these actions. Models of practice can be differentiated from theories in that models generally consist of several sets of theoretical assumptions as well as additional principles or guidelines for action. For example, most people involved in community work would agree that citizen participation in organization and government decision-making is an ethical imperative. Just as theories are tested empirically, models of practice are evaluated to determine their effectiveness. Although there is some skepticism in the literature about whether empowerment is either a theory or a model of practice (Reid, 2002), social psychologists have conducted numerous studies to verify the effectiveness of applying empowerment theory and related participatory management activities in non-profit organizations.

Many studies have found that participatory management and worker autonomy have positive influence on the psychological empowerment, improving feelings of personal self-efficacy among workers in community-based social service organizations (Foster-Fishman, Salem, Chibnall, Legler, & Yapchai, 1998; Wallach & Mueller, 2006). A small, but growing, body of literature also documents increases in psychological empowerment among people served by organizations that use an empowerment-oriented approach to deliver services (Franze, Foster, Abbott-Shim, McCarty, & Lambert, 2002; Leslie & Holzab, 1998; Littell, 2001; Maton & Salem, 1995; Parsons, 1999). In addition, qualitative studies confirm a link between staff and client empowerment; to engage in activities to help clientele and community residents gain a sense of personal mastery over their environment, staff members must feel empowered as well (Bartle, Couchonnal, Canda, & Staker, 2002; Boehm & Staples, 2002; Cohen & Austin, 1997; Cohen, 1998). Some studies document the effect of involving constituents in organization decision-making and political action. Such strategies are effective in increasing personal feelings of self-efficacy and empowerment (Checkoway & Zimmerman, 1992; Itzhaky & York, 2002; Speer & Peterson, 1995). These studies primarily replicate research conducted by Zimmerman and Rappaport (1988) who confirmed a linkage between citizen participation and feelings of self-efficacy and psychological empowerment among community activists.

Other than psychological empowerment, there is limited research that verifies whether organization or community-level outcomes are produced using empowerment-oriented approaches. Saegert and Winkel (1996) argue that empowerment should be measured by looking at whether participation in decision-making has improved the quality of life for low-income individuals and families. Peterson and Zimmerman (2004) distinguish between *empowering* organizations that facilitate increases in psychological empowerment among participants and *empowered organizations* that generate sufficient political power that they can successfully influence community and legislative change. Speer and Hughey (1995) note that "a reciprocal relationship exists between the development of power for community organizations and individual empowerment for organization members" (p. 729), suggesting that it is imperative that efforts to increase personal and political power take place at multiple levels in an organization.

According to Peterson and Zimmerman (2004), empowered organizations share three key features:
1. internal characteristics such as a supportive leadership and employee and constituent participation in decision-making;
2. inter-organizational linkages with community residents and groups as well as formal linkages with coalition groups, organizations, and local institutions; and
3. extra-organizational power or the ability to mobilize resources (people, money, information, and political support) to influence social change.

Although this approach is well articulated in the theoretical and research literature, few specifics are given about how to implement it. The next sections of this paper describe these specific practice activities and the outcomes that they are expected to produce.

Activities for Increasing Constituent Empowerment

The literature in community development, social work, and urban planning identifies a number of actions that the managers of community-based non-profit organizations can take to increase citizen participation in organizational decision-making or to empower clients and constituents of the organization. Some of this material identifies outcomes associated with these activities.

At minimum, an organization should work to recruit and maintain a board of directors with decision-making capacity. To accomplish this task, the organization should adopt specific administrative practices that support client and resident inclusion in organization decision-making. Such action should include, but not be limited to, seats on boards of directors and advisory panels. In addition, an empowerment-oriented organization should make on-going efforts to consult with and empower organizational staff members so that they are supportive of efforts to empower clients and other organization constituents. Effective efforts to increase participation among clients, constituents, and staff require that the organization becomes culturally competent, understanding how to recruit diverse individuals and involve them in decision-making. Members of the organization should attempt to strengthen and maintain informal community networks and to serve as a mediating institution to link residents with local institutions and government agencies to increase organization capacity and respond to local needs. The organization should prepare to use participatory evaluation techniques to assess the effectiveness of citizen participation efforts and programs and services. Such preparation will increase the participants' sense of inclusion in the organization and improve the organization's delivery of services. Finally, the organization should take action to increase the political power of constituents by engaging in and promoting actual participation in political action among organizational participants. Each of these activities requires administrators, board members, and staff members to take a specific set of actions.

Recruit and Maintain a Board of Directors with Decision-Making Capacity

Most boards of directors consist of middle- and upper-income individuals, often of European American descent. However, including low-income individuals and marginalized persons of color on community boards is an essential component of empowerment-oriented management (Daley, 2002). According to Rappaport (1984), involving low-income and marginalized community residents in decision-making decreases feelings of alienation from the dominant culture, increases the psychological empowerment of participants, helps individuals develop a capacity for collective action, and contributes to the development of a diverse sense of "community" or responsibility for and ability to resolve local problems.

According to Zimmerman and Rappaport (1988), people become psychologically empowered through participation in social change-oriented activities. The actual involvement in organizational decision-making of those who receive services from an organization is believed to be an essential component of this process. The purpose of involving clients is to decrease personal feelings of powerlessness and to improve the quality of and access to services (Iglehart & Becerra, 2000; Rose & Black, 1985).

Seats on boards of directors, advisory panels, or simple partnerships with organizers in planning direct actions are mechanisms typically used to empower low-income consumers. However, research indicates that in many situations, organizational or political elites continue to retain primary control of decision-making processes unless the organization takes unequivocal precautions to prevent such control (Julian, Reischl, Carrick, & Katrenich, 1997; King, Feltey, & Susel, 1998; Tauxe, 1995). According to Silverman (2003), members of marginalized groups can experience further oppression if they receive token roles on decision-making boards. Staff and middle- or high-income board members often attain professional degrees that serve to increase their power advantage vis-à-vis representatives of low-income or other marginalized groups (Hardina & Malott, 1996). Consequently, knowledge of the status of other board members may intimidate some low-income constituents.

Oppressed groups lack resources to ensure political power (money, social contacts, political influence, media coverage, politicians, and social status), which further limits their ability to bargain with professional staff and government officials (Winkle, 1991). O'Neill (1992) argues that representatives of low-income and other marginalized groups are more effective on boards when they represent powerful community constituencies. Such groups obtain power through membership (strength in numbers), ability to influence the media, and linkages with community institutions.

Adopt Practices to Include Clients and Residents in Organizational Decision-Making.

Often successful empowerment of clients in organizations is a function of whether or not administrators provide opportunities for clients and staff to participate in organizational operations (Hardina & Malott, 1996). Administrators must make sustained efforts to increase access to services for clientele and increase program responsiveness (Cohen, 1998). Paul, Niehoff, and Turnley (2000) identify some characteristics of leaders who foster empowerment in organizations: conveying charisma, exhibiting deep concern for people, providing intellectual stimulation, offering inspirational motivation, and helping staff members achieve goals that are important to them.

Empowerment-oriented administrators can undertake some specific actions to increase a sense of empowerment among staff. Executives and managers can provide in-service training and access to conferences and workshops for staff members who can transfer new skills to agency clientele and constituents to foster empowerment. The administrator should look for opportunities for employees to develop programs and professional skills in relation to their own interests. Peer supervision and staff support systems can be developed to foster feelings of staff inclusion and to minimize burnout and stress. In addition, administrators can attempt to improve the pay, benefits, and working conditions for staff (Gutierrez, et al., 1995; Shera & Page, 1995).

Make On-Going Efforts to Empower Organizational Staff

Participatory decision-making structures in organizations should have a dual function: to empower both service users and staff members. Staff members develop their own skills, learn to change organization policies, and consequently gain a sense of mastery over their own work environments. Accordingly, as they become better motivated and rewarded, they increase productivity (Paul et al., 2000).

Empowerment within organizational structures often involves giving employees more autonomy or control over how they do their jobs and allowing them to solve problems (Bowen and Lawler, 1995). Administrators can effect strategies for increasing decision-making among workers ranging from decisions that affect the individuals own work to direct participation in organizational policy-making. Staff members should be encouraged to advocate for better services to clients and for policy changes that will enhance the organization's capacity for the delivery of quality services (Bowen & Lawler, 1995; Gutierrez et al., 1995).

In addition to improving service delivery to clients, managers can increase workers self-perceptions of their ability to perform work as well as their ability to influence organizational decision-making (Spreitzer, 1996). Psychological empowerment is believed to benefit the organization because it increases employee commitment to the job (Paul, et al., 2000). However, Cohen and Austin (1997) argue that full autonomy to make decisions can create service fragmentation and conflict among workers. Instead, they advocate approaches, such as teamwork, that encourages collaboration among staff members.

Create a "Culturally Competent" Organization

Solomon (1976) explicitly describes empowerment as an approach to working with persons of color and a mechanism for overcoming feelings of alienation from and oppression by the dominant culture. The best way to overcome feelings of powerlessness and reduce racism is to participate in activities designed to develop skills and foster social change (Zimmerman & Rappaport, 1988). However, to assist clientele, staff members must become culturally competent, tailoring activities to fit the values and practices of program beneficiaries. Some methods may increase the cultural competency of organizational staff including on-going dialogue with ethnic or diverse group members, ethnographic research into cultural norms and practices, providing appropriate training for organizational staff, designating seats for ethnic group members on organization boards, and hiring staff members who are members of the ethnic group served (Gutierrez, Parsons, & Cox., 1998; Iglehart & Becerra, 2000). Kahn (1991) believes that organizations become culturally competent by developing formal organizational structures to foster equity in resource sharing, administration, and leadership. Such organizations provide on-going education about ethnicity, "race," and cultural issues to both staff and constituents. Cultural and social activities designed to maintain the organization and sustain participation should be culturally appropriate and inclusive.

Strengthen and Maintain Informal Community Networks

Communities consist of patterns of social interaction or networks. Informal networks are comprised of members of one's primary group: relatives, friends, and neighbors.

Members of such a group can provide friendship, mutual support, nurturance, health care for a sick relative or friend, child care, child rearing tips, financial support, transportation, housing, or food. Informal networks can help individual members find work, transition off welfare, provide information about public programs and services, or help mitigate the effects of substance abuse (El-Bassel, Chen, & Cooper, 1998; Jackson, 1998; Stack, 1974; Wilson, 1996).

Many programs offered by community-based non-profit organizations and public agencies rely on informal networks to "get the word out" about their services or link up with existing networks to provide services. In some cases, local organizations hire "natural helpers" or community leaders to provide health care information and other services to friends and neighbors (Lowe, Barg, & Stephens, 1998; Muquiz, 1992). Community organizations use informal networks to recruit volunteers and organize social action campaigns. Community development efforts often focus on creating strong informal networks as a means for reducing feelings of alienation among community residents and increasing neighborhood ability to address community problems such as unemployment, red-lining by financial institutions, educational inequities, and crime (Krumholz, 2006; Venkatesh, 1997; Wilson, 1996). Consequently, empowerment-oriented community-based organizations should link up with existing local networks to increase access to individuals who can bring skills, volunteer time, and other resources to the organizations.

Local networks can recruit new clients and constituents for the organization to increase the organization's ability to mobilize residents for lobbying and other types of political action. According to Speer and Hughey (1995), organizing efforts are more powerful and sustainable over time when they involve people with established interpersonal ties and shared values in the community, rather than simply involve individual support or opposition to public initiatives.

Using the Non-profit Organization as a Mediating Institution

Communities can be distinguished from one another because of their linkages with local organizations such as churches, schools, and hospitals (Figueira-McDonough, 2001). Backman and Smith (2000) observe that non-profit organizations are essential components of community networks because the organizations are able to link members of the community together through volunteer activities and programs. These organizations can link residents with institutions such as city governments, the health care system, schools and universities, jobs, and lending institutions. However, Backman and Smith warn that such linkages may result in a decrease in social action-oriented activities as members of alienated communities and isolated organizations are integrated within more established social service networks.

Community-based organizations can play a critical role in developing and maintaining these networks (Berger & Neuhaus, 1977). Local institutions can "mediate" between the individual and government to facilitate changes in public policy. Individuals who participate in organizational decision-making and the public policy debate will be "empowered" and consequently feel less alienated from government.

Use Participatory Evaluation Techniques to Assess Programs

A basic premise of empowerment in managing community-based organizations maintains that organizational clientele, staff, and other participants should become involved in needs-assessment, program planning, and evaluation activities (Balsam & Daewoo, 2002; Forester, 1999; Rose & Black, 1985). Many organizations provide formal roles for clientele as well as constituents and staff in such processes. "Empowerment evaluation" is the term often used to describe the process for bringing clients or community residents into the process of program assessment (Fetterman, 1996). Empowerment evaluation is used to document community needs, conduct agency evaluations, and assess the outcome of projects that involve community-based collaboration. Empowerment evaluation techniques are believed to be preferable to the more traditional evaluation model that is often conducted by objective, professional evaluators. A primary rationale for using the empowerment approach is that using expert knowledge may sustain and even enhance traditional power imbalances between privileged and underprivileged groups. The information produced will be relevant to the needs of participants; the findings are more likely to benefit the community (Coombe, 1998). Through engagement in program evaluation, participants are "empowered" with technical skills, knowledge, and access to data (Rapp, Shera, & Kishardt, 1993). Inclusion in evaluation helps to ensure that culturally-competent programs and approaches to evaluation are developed (Padilla, Lein, & Cruz, 1999).

Engage in Voter Registration and Education

One of the critical activities needed to empower low-income communities is voter registration. With turnouts in recent campaigns at about 40 to 50 percent, less than 30 percent of all U.S. adults actually vote. Voters are substantially more likely to be of European American descent, older, more educated, and have more income than non-voters (Jackson, Brown, & Wright, 1998; Verba, Schlozman, & Brady, 1997). The limited participation of low-income individuals and communities is part of the legacy of the pre-civil rights era literacy tests and poll taxes designed to suppress voting and political participation among African American citizens. These citizens were prohibited from voting or running for office. Requirements that people re-register after moving or that they must provide identification cards (often a barrier for non-drivers) have a disproportionate impact on people with income limitations (Piven & Cloward, 2000). Other factors that discourage members of marginalized groups from actually voting include the limited availability of ballots in languages other than English, ballot wording that may confuse elderly or inexperienced voters, and the limited number of polling places that are fully accessible to disabled individuals (Constitution Project, 2002, League of Women Voters, 2002; NAACP, 2002; U.S. Commission on Civil Rights, 2001; U.S. General Accounting Office, 1998).

In addition, some demographic groups are systematically excluded from voting. Two million persons are incarcerated in the United States. At least 13 percent of African American men are denied voting rights. They are incarcerated, on parole, or on probation often because of disparities in drug-sentencing laws (King, 2006). Consequently, the voting power of the African American community continues to be severely compromised. Voter suppression efforts in Florida during the 2000 presidential election and in Ohio in 2004 also systematically targeted communities of color (Kennedy, 2006; U.S. Commission on Civil Rights, 2001).

The League of Women Voters (2002) and the National Association of Colored People (NAACP-2002) maintain that low rates of participation exist because of limited efforts to educate potential voters about the electoral process and voting rights. They advocate training about voting rights for citizens and poll workers. Empowerment-oriented community-based organizations can play an important role in conducting voter registration drives and educating their constituents about the voting process and their choices at the polls.

Promote Actual Participation in Political Action among Organization Participants

Leadership roles within the organization prepare people to become political activists and provide low-income people with a greater sense of inclusion in mainstream society (Checkoway & Zimmerman, 1992; Pigg, 2002; Zachary, 2000). According to Reisch, Wenocur, and Sherman (1981), the ultimate goal of empowerment is "the liberation" or "dis-alienation of those without privilege or power" (p. 115). This goal is to be accomplished through political action and the creation of local organizations. Social activism (involvement in protests and petition drives, participation in voting and political campaigns, and lobbying by organization constituents) provides a powerful constituency for the organization that can be easily mobilized to advocate for policies and funding allocations that will benefit the organization and its clients (Burke, 1983; Checkoway & Zimmerman, 1992).

A Conceptual Model for Empowerment: Linking Action to Outcomes

The activities described above can construct a conceptual model of activities in empowerment-oriented citizen participation that administrators can adopt in non-profit organizations. This model links these activities with specific, interrelated outcomes for the organization and the constituents and communities it serves (see Figure 1). The activities can be summarized: education, mobilization, political participation, outreach, worker inclusion, evaluation, and voter registration and education.

Figure 1. A conceptual model of empowerment-oriented participatory practices for community-based organizations and the outcomes they produce.

	EMPOWERMENT ACTIVITIES:		EMPOWERMENT OUTCOMES:
E	Provide on-going **EDUCATION** and training on advocacy, decision-making, leadership, and other skills.	R	Increases the **RECRUITMENT** of constituents and resource acquisition.
M	Find appropriate methods to **MOTIVATE** and **MOBILIZE** for skill development and political action.	E	The **EFFECTIVENESS** of services is improved.
P	Increase **PARTICIPATION** in **POLITICS**.	S	The **SKILLS** of constituents and staff members increase.
O	Conduct **OUTREACH** to local constituents, informal networks, and institutions.	O	**ORGANIZING** efforts strengthen informal networks and increase links between residents and local institutions. Institutional oppression is reduced.
W	Provide opportunities to staff **WORKERS** for participation in organization decision-making in order to improve worker perceptions of personal self-efficacy and commitment to the workplace.	L	**LEADERSHIP** skills are acquired by constituents.
E	Provide opportunities to **EVALUATE** service outcome, processes and quality on a regular basis with significant input from clients, constituents, and workers.	V	**VOTER** participation and local political power increase.
R	**REGISTRATION** of voters and voter education and training.	E	Constituents increase feelings of personal **EFFICACY** and **EMPOWERMENT**.

The organization should proactively make efforts to provide on-going education and skills training for clients, community residents, staff members, and other constituents in many areas: education, advocacy, voting rights, decision-making, and leadership. Appropriate methods should be found to motivate and mobilize constituents to develop skills in effective political action. Efforts should be made to increase the participation of clients, constituents, and staff in local, state, and national politics. The organization should engage in multi-level outreach efforts, recruiting new constituents, and establishing strong relationships with informal networks, local organizations, and institutions that can improve services and increase the organization's political power. To provide effective services to constituents, organizations must make efforts to empower staff members, offering opportunities to participate in organization decision-making and increase skills and feelings of personal self-competency. In addition, organizations should evaluate empowerment efforts as well as service delivery. Such an assessment should include clients, constituents, and employees and focus on program outcomes, processes, and quality. Participatory evaluation methods provide an excellent opportunity for organizations to develop skills among constituents and to improve programs and services. Finally, the organization should aggressively engage in voter education and registration; providing information and assistance to ensure that local residents are able to make their voices heard in the political process.

Empowerment theory indicates that these activities should improve client and worker skills and feelings of self-efficacy, organizational resources, service delivery, and political power, better linkages among organizations, constituents, and local institutions, the acquisition of political power by constituents, and ultimately political change that will benefit organization constituents. These activities can produce measurable outcomes to benefit the organization at multiple levels.

Empowerment activities should produce immediate benefits for constituents and the organization. Efforts to stimulate citizen participation and empowerment should recruit volunteers, board members, and constituency group members who can bring new skills, resources, and political clout to the organization. Involvement in organizational decision-making will help these new constituents acquire leadership, community organizing, and political skills (Beresford & Croft, 1993). Through acquiring these skills, clients and constituents can resolve personal problems and develop an improved sense of self-efficacy (Gutierrez et al., 1998; Zimmerman & Rappaport, 1988). These new constituents will provide a strong base of support for the organization, helping to recruit other volunteers, raise funds, and lobby for the organization (Burke, 1983).

Some intermediate outcomes will promote non-profit organizations that engage in empowerment efforts. Outreach efforts and coalition-building will build strong linkages to community networks and institutions (Backman & Smith, 2000; Brenton, 2001). Such linkages will help the organization acquire information, funds, and other resources and consequently be in a better position to respond to clients' needs. This acquisition should enhance service effectiveness, quality, and client access. Improvements in service delivery are critical to motivate staff members, increasing workers sense of personal self-efficacy and empowerment. Motivated workers are likely to increase productivity and seek out opportunities to improve their own skills (Gutierrez et al., 1995; Spreitzer, 1996).

In addition, some long range outcomes are associated with empowerment-oriented management in non-profit organizations. A primary benefit involves securing political power to lobby for programs and services and increase participation in voting (Checkoway & Zimmerman, 1992). Mobilizing politically powerful constituents increases the organization's ability to influence local, state, and federal legislation and policies. Political power should improve the quality of the life of the community and the lives of its residents (Itzhaky & York, 2002). As noted by Solomon (1976), the ultimate goal of power is that the political oppression of clients and organizational constituents is reduced, giving low-income or otherwise marginalized groups greater access to education, employment, and community resources.

CONCLUSIONS

Organizations need empowerment-oriented administrative practices to counteract the decline in civic participation noted by Putnam (2001) as well as voter alienation from the political process. Non-profit organizations can work to link citizens with governmental agencies, increasing the political power of the organization and the power of individual participants to facilitate social change. Such action increases the organization's access to resources and volunteers while helping local low income wage earners to develop skills and acquire resources (such as tangible services, social support, and informal networks) they need to improve their lives.

Effective empowerment-oriented approaches to operate non-profit, community-based organizations should include some activities such as leadership skills training, inclusion of local residents and clientele on boards of directors, empowerment or participatory evaluation techniques, the political involvement of constituents, and voter registration and education. The use of informal networks and formal linkages with other local institutions is important. In addition, administrators should include staff members in evaluating services and operations. An empowerment-oriented administrator must be ideologically committed to give power to clientele, constituents, and staff and to take concrete action to help the organization and its members increase personal and political power.

Additional research should be conducted in a variety of settings, among community volunteers of different social and economic class, age, gender, and ethnic backgrounds to verify citizen participation in social action increases the political power of organizational participants and the power and influence of the organization to achieve change. However, it may be impossible to standardize outcome measures because efforts to change policies, improve services, or reduce oppression will vary by organization and community. Scholars and practitioners must understand the circumstances in which organizational structures and initiatives such as membership in social action-oriented self-help groups or participation on advisory boards impede or enhance feelings of empowerment. Additional measures of effective participation across organizations and communities can be developed. For example, scholars and administrators should measure actual increases in the number of volunteers, skill development, and quality or effectiveness of service delivery.

Evaluation should focus on whether participation actually improves quality of life for individuals involved. An empirically-tested and validated model of empowerment-oriented participatory practices in community-based organizations will be a valuable asset for non-profit managers and organizational constituents, helping to find effective methods to include low-income constituents in organizational planning and the political process.

REFERENCES

Arnstein, S. (1969). A ladder of citizen participation. *Journal of the American Institute of Planners*, 35(4), 216-224.

Backman, E., & Smith, S. R. (2000). Healthy organization, unhealthy communities. *Non-profit Management and Leadership*, 10(4), 355-373.

Balaswamy, S., & Dabeloko, H. (2002). Using a stakeholder participatory model in a community-wide needs assessment. *Journal of Community Practice*, 10(1), 55-70.

Bartle, E., Couchonnal, G., Canda, E., & Staker, M. (2002). Empowerment as a dynamically developing concept for practice: Lessons learned from organizational ethnography. *Social Work*, 47, 32-43.

Beresford, P., & Croft, S. (1993). *Citizen Involvement: A Practical Guide for Change*. London: Macmillan.

Berger, P., & Neuhaus, R. (1977). *To Empower People: From State to Civil Society*. Washington, D.C.: American Enterprise Institute.

Boehm, A., & Staples, L. (2002). The functions of the social worker in empowering the voices of consumers and professionals. *Social Work*, 47, 337-480.

Bowen, D., & Lawler, E. (1995). Empowering service employees. *Sloan Management Review*, 36 (4), 73-84.

Brenton, M. (2001). Neighborhood resiliency. *Journal of Community Practice*, 9(1): 21-36.

Burke, E. (1983). Citizen participation: Characteristics and strategies. In R. Kramer and H. Specht (Eds.), *Readings in Community Organization Practice*. Englewood Cliffs, NJ: Prentice-Hall.

Checkoway, B., & Zimmerman, M. (1992). Correlates of participation in neighborhood organizations. *Administration in Social Work,* 16 *(3/4),* 45-64.

Cohen, B. & Austin, M. (1997). Transforming social service organizations through the empowerment of staff. *Journal of Community Practice,* 4 (2), 35-50.

Cohen, M. (1998). Perceptions of power in client/worker relationships. *Families in Society,* 79 (4), 433-443.

Coombe, C. (1999). Using empowerment evaluation in community organizing and community-based health initiatives. In M. Minkler (Ed.), *Community Organization and Community Building for Health.* New Brunswick, NJ: Rutgers University Press.

Constitution Project. (2002). *Election reform briefing: Voter identification.* Retrieved August 9, 2002, from: http://www.electiononline.org

Craig, G. (2002). Toward the measurement of empowerment: The evaluation of community development. *Journal of the Community Development Society,* 33(1), 124-146.

Daley, J. (2002). An action guide for non-profit board diversity. *Journal of Community Practice,* 10(1), 33-54.

El-Bassel, N., Chen, D., & Cooper, D. (1998). Social support and network profiles among women on methadone. *Social Service Review,* 72(3), 379-401.

Fetterman, D. (1996). Empowerment evaluation: An introduction to theory and practice. In D. Fetterman, S. Kaftarian, & A. Wandersman (Eds.), *Empowerment Evaluation: Knowledge and Tools for Self-assessment and Accountability.* Thousand Oaks, CA: Sage.

Figueira-McDonough, J. (2001). *Community Analysis and Praxis: Toward a Grounded Civil Society.* Philadelphia: Taylor and Francis.

Forester, J. (1999). *The Deliberative Practitioner: Encouraging Participatory Planning Processes.* Cambridge, MA: Massachusetts Institute of Technology.

Foster-Fishman, P., Salem, D., Chibnall, S., Legler, R., & Yapchai, C. (1998). Empirical support for the critical assumptions of empowerment theory. American *Journal of Community Psychology,* 26, 507-536.

Franze, S., Foster, M., Abbott-Shim, M., McCarty, F., & Lambert, R. (2002). Describing head start family service workers: An examination of factors related to job satisfaction, empowerment, and multiculturalism. *Families in Society,* 83, 258-264.

Gittell, M. (1980). *Limits to Citizen Participation: The Decline of Community Organization.* Beverly Hills, CA: Sage.

Gulati, P. (1982). Consumer participation in decision-making. *Social Service Review,* 55, 403-422.

Gutierrez, L., GlenMaye, L., & DeLois, K. (1995). The organizational context of empowerment practice: Implications for social work administration. *Social Work,* 40(2), 249-258.

Gutierrez, L., Parsons, R., & Cox, E. (1998). *Empowerment in Social Work Practice: A Sourcebook.* Pacific Grove, CA: Brooks/Cole.

Hardina, D., & Malott, O. (1996). Strategies for the empowerment of low-income consumers on community-based planning boards. *Journal of Progressive Human Services,* 7(2), 43-61.

Iglehart, A., & Becerra, R. (1995). *Social Services and the Ethnic Community.* Boston: Allyn & Bacon.

Itzhaky, H., & York, A. (2002). Showing results in community organization. *Social Work,* 47(2), 125-131.

Jackson, A. (1998). The role of social support in parenting for low-income single, black mothers. *Social Service Review,* 72 (3): 365-378.

Jackson, R., Brown, R. & Wright, G. (1998). Registration, turnout, and the electoral representativeness of U.S. state electorates. *American Politics Quarterly,* 26(3), 259-272.

Julian, D., Reischl, T., Carrick, R., & Katrenich, C. (1997). Citizen participation-lessons from a local United Way planning process. *Journal of the American Planning Association,* 63, 345-355.

Kahn, S. (1991). *Organizing: A Guide for Grassroots Leaders.* Washington, D.C.: National Association of Social Workers.

Kennedy, R. (2006). *Rolling Stone Magazine.* Was the 2004 election stolen? Retrieved December 9, 2006, from: http://www.rollingstone.com/news/story/10432334/was_the_2004_election_stolen

King, C., Feltey, K., Susel, B. (1998). The question of participation: Toward authentic public participation in public administration. *Public Administration Review,* 58(4), 317-327. 75.

King, R. S. (2006, October). A decade of reform: Felony disenfranchisement policy in the United

States. Retrieved December 9, 2006, from: http://www/sentencingproject.org/pdfs/FVR_Decade_Reform.pdf

Krumholz, N. (2006). The long-term impact of CDCs on urban neighborhoods: Case studies of Cleveland's Broadway-Slavic Village and Tremont neighborhoods. *Community Development: Journal of the Community Development Society*, 37(4), p. 40.

League of Women Voters. (2002). *Election reform survey*. Retrieved July 7, 2002, from http://www.lwv.org

Leslie, D., & Holzab, C. (1998). Measuring staff empowerment: Development of a worker empowerment scale. *Research on Social Work Practice*, 8: 212-223.

Littell, J. (2001). Client participation and outcomes of intensive family preservation services. *Social Work*, 25(2), 103-113.

Lowe, J., Barg, F., & Stephens, K. (1998). Community residents as lay health educators in a cancer prevention program. *Journal of Community Practice*, 5(4), 39-52.

Marris, P., & Rein, M. (1982). *Dilemmas of Social Reform*. Chicago: University of Chicago Press.

Maton, K., & Salem, D. (1995). Organizational characteristics of empowering community settings: A multiple case study approach. *American Journal of Community Psychology*, 23, 631-656.

Moynihan, D. (1969). *Maximum Feasible Misunderstanding*. New York: Free Press.

Muquiz, G. (1992, September/October). Oregon programs reach farmworker families and elderly farmworkers through two new outreach models. *Migrant Health Clinical Supplement*, 1-2.

National Association for the Advancement of Colored People. (2002). *Defending the vote: Holding officials accountable – NAACP 2001 election report*. Retrieved July 30, 2002, from: http://www.naacp.org/news/releases/ElectionReformJuly02.pdf

O'Neill, M. (1992). Community participation in Quebec's health system. *International Journal of Health Services*, 22(2), 287-301.

Padilla, Y., Lein, L., & Cruz, M. (1999). Community-based research in policy planning: A case study addressing poverty in the Texas-Mexico border region. *Journal of Community Practice*, 6(3), 1-22.

Parsons, R. (1999). Assessing helping processes and client outcomes in empowerment practice: Amplifying client voice and satisfying funding sources. In W. Shera & L. Wells (Eds.). *Empowerment Practice in Social Work* (pp. 390-417). Toronto: Canadian Scholar's Press.

Paul, R., Niehoff, B., Turnley, W. (2000). Empowerment, expectations, and the psychological contract—managing the dilemmas and gaining the advantages. *Journal of Socio-Economics*, 29, 471-485.

Peterson, N. A., & Zimmerman, M. (2004). Beyond the individual: Toward a nomological network of organizational empowerment. *Journal of Community Psychology*, 34(1-2), pp. 129-145.

Pigg, K. (2002). Three faces of empowerment: Expanding the theory of empowerment in community development. *Journal of the Community Development Society*, 33(1), 107-124.

Piven, F., & Cloward, R. (2000). *Why Americans Still Don't Vote*. Boston: Beacon Press.

Putnam, R. (2001). *Bowling Alone*. New York: Touchstone.

Rapp, C., Shera, W., & Kishardt, W. (1993). Research strategies for consumer empowerment of people with severe mental illness. *Social Work*, 38(6), 727-736.

Rappaport, J. (1984). *Studies in Empowerment: Steps toward Understanding and Action*. New York: Haworth.

Reid, W. (2002). Knowledge for direct social work practice: An analysis of trends. *Social Service Review*, 76: 6-33.

Reisch, M., Wenocur, S., & Sherman, W. (1981). Empowerment, conscientization and animation as core social work skills. *Social Development Issues*, 5, 108-120.

Rose, S., & Black, B. (1985). *Advocacy and Empowerment*. Boston: Routledge & Kegan Paul.

Saegert, S., & Winkel, G. (1996). Paths to community empowerment: Organizing at home. *American Journal of Community Psychology*, 24 (4), 517-551.

Shera, W., & Page, J. (1995). Creating more effective human service organizations through strategies of empowerment. *Administration in Social Work*, 19(4): 1-15.

Silverman, R. 2003. Citizens' district councils in Detroit: The promise and limits of using planning advisory boards to promote citizen participation. *National Civic Review*, 92(4), 3-13.

Solomon, B. (1976). *Black Empowerment: Social Work in Oppressed Communities*. New York: Columbia University Press.

Speer, P., & Hughey, J. (1995). Community organizing: An ecological route to empowerment and power. *American Journal of Community Psychology*, 23, 729-748.

Speer, P., & Peterson, N. A. (2000). Psychometric properties of an empowerment scale: Testing cognitive, emotional, and behavioral domains. *Social Work Research*, 24(2), 109-118.

Spreitzer, G. (1996). Social structural characteristics of psychological empowerment. *Academy of Management Journal*, 39, 483-504. Stack, C. (1974). *All Our Kin*. New York: Harper & Row.

Tauxe, C. (1995). Marginalizing public participation in local planning: An ethnographic account. *Journal of the American Planning Association*, 61(4): 471-482.

Venkatesh, S. (1997). The social organization of street gang activity in an urban ghetto. *Social Service Review*, 103, 82-111.

Verba, S., Schlozman, K. L., & Brady, H. E. (1997). The big tilt: Participatory inequality in America. *The American Prospect*, May/June (32): 74-80.

Wallach, V., & Mueller, C. (2006). Job characteristics and organizational predictors of psychological empowerment among paraprofessionals with human service organizations: An exploratory study. *Administration in Social Work*, 30(1), 95-115.

Wilson, W. (1996). *When Work Disappears*. New York: Vintage Books.

Winkle, C. (1991). Inequity and power in the non-profit sector. *Non-profit and Voluntary Sector Quarterly*, 20, 312-328.

U.S. Commission on Civil Rights. (2001). *Status report on probe of election practices in Florida during the 2000 Presidential campaign*. Retrieved July 30, 2001, from http://www.usccr.gov/pubs/vote2000/florida.htm

U. S. General Accounting Office. (1998). *Voters with disabilities: Access to polling places and alternative voting methods*. Retrieved December 9, 2006, from: http://www.gao.gov/new.items/d02107.pdf

Zachary, E. (2000). Grassroots leadership training. *Journal of Community Practice*, 7(1), 71-94.

Zimmerman, M., & Rappaport, J. 1988. Citizen participation, perceived control, and psychological empowerment. *American Journal of Community Psychology*, 16(5): 725-750.

Creating Great Places:
The Role of Citizen Participation

Lynn Richards and Matthew Dalbey

Smart growth strategies can help ensure that development projects yield better community, economic, environmental, and public health outcomes. A principle component of these strategies is meaningful stakeholder participation in development decision-making. This paper (1) discusses how increased and meaningful participation can lead to better projects and a more predictable and fair development process, and (2) outlines some of the tools the public and private sector have begun to use. Within the development process, community members need information about a range of possible alternatives before voicing choices or concerns. Under most citizen participation processes, only a small portion of the community engages in decision-making because of socioeconomic, linguistic, or educational class barriers. To better engage all residents, local governments and the development community can get creative in identifying and using new methods for soliciting, responding to, and sharing information. Reaching out and working with community residents in a meaningful and enduring process will allow communities to realize their vision for where and how to grow next.

Our regions, cities, towns, and neighborhoods are growing. Every day, new buildings or houses are proposed, planned, and built. Local governments, working with planners, citizens' groups, and developers, are thinking about where and how this new development can enhance existing neighborhoods and also protect the community's natural environment. They are identifying the characteristics of development that can build vibrant neighborhoods, rich in natural and historic assets, with jobs, housing, and amenities for all types of people. They are accommodating growth by directing investments to existing places, which is a fiscally-responsible strategy that grows on a community's previous investments in its buildings and infrastructure.

Growth can create great places to live, work, and play—if it responds to a community's sense of how and where the community wants to grow. Articulating this vision, however, can be a challenge because the vision should reflect the needs of a wide range of stakeholders and community members. But this challenge presents an opportunity because this process allows stakeholders to develop creative solutions to the most troublesome problems.

Lynn Richards and Matthew Dalbey are senior policy analysts at the Development, Community, & Environment Division (DCED) of the U.S. Environmental Protection Agency in Washington, D.C. Richards joined the division in 2000, and Dalbey joined in 2004.

Ultimately, community and stakeholder collaboration can create a sound basis for creative, speedy resolution of development conflicts, which can help make development decisions more timely, cost-effective, and predictable.

However, in most communities, the current development process satisfies neither citizens, developers, nor local government officials. Often, a lengthy, exhausting visioning process can leave citizens frustrated and disillusioned when the plans, codes, and development they collaborated on never materialize. This stalemate can be time-consuming, frustrating, and expensive, leaving all stakeholders disillusioned with the process and sometimes, the final product.

The purpose of this paper is to discuss why and how to increase citizen participation beyond the traditional processes of public involvement to a process in which a wide range of stakeholders is engaged and the final product is better because of their involvement. This paper discusses (1) what smart growth approaches are and why communities are implementing them, (2) how citizen participation practices in land use decision-making evolved through much of the twentieth century, and (3) how a smart growth approach to citizen participation can promote effective strategies:

1. creating better development projects and enhancing a community's economy, quality of life, public health, and the environment;
2. providing a process that is more predictable, democratic, and fair, thereby making the public process more meaningful and result-oriented; and
3. making available more tools and strategies for civic engagement that can create better development projects.

The paper concludes with three case studies that demonstrate strategies of early and significant citizen involvement from nationally recognized projects. The examples demonstrate how citizens added value and helped build strong constituencies for the projects.

The paper is based on the authors' work in the U.S. Environmental Protection Agency's Development, Community, and Environment Division (DCED).[1] The EPA's mission is to protect human health and the environment, and where and how communities grow and develop have significant environmental and public health implications (U.S. EPA, 2001). The DCED implements this mission by promoting development patterns and practices that benefit the economy, the community, public health and the environment. In our work, we have found many examples of participatory processes that are inclusive, allowing an open exchange of ideas and making the development process more efficient—all of which can ultimately create better communities.

SMART GROWTH APPROACHES TO DEVELOPMENT

The impact of development in communities across the country is enormous. Nearly two million homes were built in 2004, and over 756 million square feet of commercial space were constructed. This activity represents 17.5 percent of our national gross domestic product.[2] Much of this new development is occurring where suburbs meet agricultural and undeveloped land. A recent U.S. Department of Agriculture study notes that approximately 80 percent of new homes are being built on the urban fringe, and of those, more than 90 percent are on lots of one acre or more (Heimlich & Anderson, 2001, p. 14). However, research shows that this type of development pattern is costly—both in terms of environmental and economic costs (Burchell, et al., 2002; U.S. EPA, 2001). In addition, this type of dispersed development pattern forces residents to drive longer distances to jobs, shops, and leisure activities, which can cause significant increases in traffic (U.S. EPA, 2001a; U.S. EPA, 2001). Finally, this type of edge development contributes to the population decrease in some downtown areas—leaving scores of abandoned buildings, schools, shops, and other costly infrastructure (Burchell, et al., 2002; International City/County Management Association, ICMA, 1998).

Although they want growth, communities are rethinking the economic costs of abandoning brownfields and infrastructure in older communities while developing open space and prime agricultural lands at the suburban fringe, which damages our environment. Residents are looking for alternatives to spending more time in traffic, paying higher taxes, driving long commutes, and having neighborhoods where walking and playing are unsafe (ICMA, 2002).

Communities want to enjoy the benefits of growth and also minimize impacts to environment, reuse existing infrastructure and investments, reclaim historic buildings and abandoned properties, and protect natural areas. Communities are looking for development approaches that achieve multiple benefits to help increase local economies and improve the quality of life. Communities are looking for approaches to development that allow its residents choices on how to get around—walk, bike, drive, and take transit as they live, work, shop, and play. Community outcomes to these types of development approaches include spending less time in traffic, enjoying higher tax bases, increased public health, decreased air emissions by reducing time spent in cars, less stormwater runoff and associated pollutants, and reduced land development pressures at the urban edge.[3]

Often, the development approach that seeks to meet multiple community objectives is referred to as smart growth, which is a development approach based on ten principles (See Figure 1).[4] These principles were developed in 1996 by the Smart Growth Network, which is a group of private, public, and non-governmental organizations working together to improve the quality of development in neighborhoods, communities, and regions across the United States. The principles are based on the characteristics and experiences in existing communities that are often thought of as thriving, diverse, and successful communities. The principles have since been adopted by the 38 network partners, 50 units of government, 40 non-governmental organizations, and 13 private-sector groups. These principles help guide growth and development in communities that have a vision of what they want their future to be and of what they value in their community (Smart Growth Network).

Figure 1. Smart Growth Principles

1	Mix land uses.
2	Take advantage of compact building design.
3	Create a range of housing opportunities and choices.
4	Create walkable neighborhoods.
5	Foster distinctive, attractive communities with a strong sense of place.
6	Preserve open space, farmland, natural beauty, and critical environmental areas.
7	Strengthen and direct development towards existing communities.
8	Provide a variety of transportation choices.
9	Make development decisions predictable, fair, and cost effective.
10	Encourage community and stakeholder collaboration in development decisions.

For more on these principles, see the Smart Growth Network, www.smartgrowth.org

In cities and older suburbs, smart growth approaches invest time, attention, and resources in restoring community and vitality. New development is generally more town-centered, transit and pedestrian oriented, and has a greater mix of homes, offices, shops, and other uses. Often too, more open space and other environmental amenities are preserved or enhanced. Communities use smart growth techniques to try to improve development's environmental, economic, social, public health, and fiscal effects (ICMA, 2003; ICMA, 2002).

Examples of these approaches can be found in many large and small communities throughout the United States. Since 2002, the EPA has given 24 communities a "National Award for Smart Growth Achievement," for demonstrating exemplary development practices in built projects, policies, and community outreach. In addition, the EPA and the International City/County Managers Association released in 2006, *This is Smart Growth*, which highlights over 40 communities and their approaches to development. At *Smart Growth Online*, viewers can read numerous case studies in "Smart Growth in Action." These are just a few resources that highlight successful development strategies in *Smart Growth Online*.

The Belmar neighborhood in Lakewood, Colorado, demonstrates many smart growth principles. Lakewood is a close-in suburb and its older, under-used Villa Italia shopping center was transformed into a mixed-use, compact, walkable neighborhood named Belmar. Numerous Lakewood residents had a strong attachment to the old mall, and they were concerned about losing all connection with it. On the other hand, Lakewood lacked a physical downtown. The developers worked with the City and residents to reuse adaptively some pre-existing buildings and added in a grid that provides a physical center of the redevelopment. Now, Belmar is the walkable downtown that this inner suburb lacked; it contains new stores, meeting places, and housing options. It created jobs and increased municipal revenues. Estimates from Lakewood indicate that by the time it is completed, the project will bring in 7,000 new jobs and add $952 million to the local economy. At build-out, Belmar will have 1,300 new housing units and 700,000 square feet of office space (EPA, 2005). Samantha Bales, a Belmar homeowner, observed, "Everything about it is just fabulous. The whole design, the concept, the whole look of the area. It's the new downtown Lakewood" (EPA, 2005).[5]

Citizen Participation in the Post-World War II Era

As used in this article, "citizens" and "public" are catch-all terms for people, residents, advocacy groups, and vested individuals and/or groups (land owners, investors, etc.) who have an interest or stake in decisions related to development patterns and the use of land. "Stakeholders" is another way to describe these participants in the development decision-making process. Bill Lennertz from the National Charrette Institute (NCI) describes stakeholders as:
- decision-makers,
- people who will be affected by the outcome of any project or projects,
- people who have the power to promote the project, and
- people who have the power to block the project (National Charrette Institute).

Getting all stakeholders involved in planning not only produces better plans but also can make it easier to implement the plan (Burby, 2003, p. 33) and lead to better development.

The nature, methods, and theory of citizen participation in government decision-making are much discussed in the broad academic and practitioner literature. The literature describes participation as a fundamental part of an idealized democratic tradition, yet our form of governing is a "representative democracy" that inherently removes citizens from the place where many decisions are made. How citizens participate in decision-making has evolved over time in the United States. It was not until the early twentieth century that legislative decision-making began to incorporate input from citizens outside of elected representatives (Gil & Lucchesi, 1979). Even at this point, though, there wasn't much citizen participation in land use decision-making. In the first third of the twentieth century, the planning profession supported the formation of planning commissions made up of good-government advocates, technical experts, and civic leaders. These commissions were meant to prevent the local political machine from controlling the decision-making process;

they incorporated a broad variety of viewpoints and allowed some citizens—primarily the business elite—to exercise more control.

A survey of the literature indicates that not until the 1960s and early 1970s was broader-based citizen participation tolerated in local land use decision-making (Day, 1997, p. 421; Gil & Lucchesi, 1979, p. 553; Kelly & Becker, 2000, p. 112; Burby, 2003, p. 33; Brody et al., 2003, p. 245). Early state-enabling legislation for local planning activities required public notification and public hearings to solicit comments in response to proposals. According to Kelly and Becker (2000), in the 1970s, planning agencies and local governments tried to ensure that their hearings and decision-making processes included the maximum number of contacts with people, rather than ensuring that these contacts represented broader interests or added substance to the process. In the citizen participation section of ICMA's updated *The Practice of Local Government Planning*, Klein (2000) argues that the public hearing process was not about getting citizens to participate in the planning process, as much as it was about ensuring that citizens had a chance to *hear* about that process.

The most recent literature on citizen participation reveals that participation methods are unevenly implemented and fail to achieve stated objectives such as better plans and better implementation (Burby, 2003, pp. 34-35; Baker et al., 2005, pp. 490-491). Citizen participation strategies exist to produce better plans and increase the likelihood that those plans will be implemented—good goals that require strong, evenly applied methods of engaging stakeholders.

Current citizen participation practices often limit public input to hearings typically held on weeknights or during the day (when planning commissions or boards have work sessions). Details related to plans and development projects are often negotiated with the planning staff, developers, and key decision-makers. Results are then presented to the public in hearings. Public hearings are structured in a way that lacks the nuance and detail intrinsic to land development debates. Citizens speak either for or against plans, projects, or pending decisions. One consequence of this structure is that citizen participation often devolves into a "growth vs. no growth" argument. Framing the debate over how and where to grow as "growth vs. no growth" stifles conversation, limits public input, divides communities, and contributes to development patterns that do not benefit the community as a whole. Citizen groups are left exercising the only power they perceive they have—the power to say "no." David Goldberg of Smart Growth America describes the practice this way:

> Because development ideas so rarely arise from a shared vision of what the community wants and needs, nearly every development decision results in conflict. Neighborhood residents are taken by surprise by projects they couldn't have foreseen, and rise up in anger. By the same token, responsible developers who submit proposals based on existing plans and zoning can find themselves engulfed in expensive, bitter, and time-consuming battles. Local governments, for their part, are in a constant scramble to find the money to keep up with roads, sewer and water lines, police and fire protection, parks, libraries and other services AFTER development occurs (Goldberg, 2005, p. 1).

Smart growth approaches aim to make development decisions fair to everyone and provide a market climate that encourages the development of vibrant, diverse, and safe neighborhoods.

Moving Citizen Participation Forward: How Smart Growth Approaches Expand Opportunities

Population is increasing. The development of land is required to accommodate population growth. How and where this growth occurs has fiscal, environmental, social, and community consequences. Any new development—whether it produces new houses, shops, or offices—brings change to a community. Treating all stakeholders impacted by new development fairly requires a predictable, inclusive process.

The more that stakeholders are involved in decision-making, the more predictable and fair the development process can be. Too often, developers and local government officials work together on a new development, leaving out stakeholders. Development is typically the result of minutely-detailed zoning plans, governmental policies, and regulations that few laypersons fully understand. Once the plans are almost fully developed, the local government will invite public comment through an open meeting format in which each speaker is allocated two to three minutes to speak. Within this format, speakers can do little more than say a few words supporting or opposing the project as it is presented. This type of public comment offers the community little opportunity for comprehensive dialogue on the site's design, components, uses, layout, or any other details that can make a new development outstanding. Because of this non-inclusive process, the resulting development, if approved, can often fail to contribute to a healthy, vibrant neighborhood fabric or perhaps not serve the multiple purposes it may otherwise serve. If the development is not approved in local elections, the developer often has to begin the design and approval process again.

A smart growth approach to development differs from less inclusive methods because more stakeholders are involved in more steps of the development process. This collaboration often produces better results for both the community and the developer because each stakeholder comes to understand the needs, desires, and concerns of the other participants. For example, when the town of Davidson, North Carolina,[6] adopted new policies that required a charrette or workshop for new development plans, developers initially balked. Once the requirement was implemented, though, the development community recognized the benefits. One Davidson developer, Frank Jacobus, said that the charrette helped "me to come up with a new plan that was better than the original" (U.S. EPA, 2004). Citizen participation represents more than just a means toward creating new and better plans; it's about creating better places.

A more open and collaborative stakeholder process offers an alternative to conventional public involvement processes because it challenges developers and local government officials to engage stakeholders early and often. Doing so can cultivate the following outcomes:
1. creating better development projects and enhancing a community's economy, quality, of life, public health, and the environment;
2. providing a process that is more predictable, democratic, and fair, thereby making the public process more meaningful and result oriented; and
3. making available more tools and strategies for civic engagement that create better development projects.

The three sections below discuss each of these themes in greater detail.

Creating Better Community Outcomes

Development projects can either contribute to the fabric of the neighborhood or detract from it. Arguably, projects that contribute to the quality of the neighborhood are the ones that serve a variety of community purposes. Often, the prevailing participatory process in many communities in the United States does not provide a forum for an exchange of ideas about the characteristics of a development, usually characterized by tense exchanges between supporters and opponents. The discussion of how and where development occurs is excluded. What happens if the public is involved in the design of a project, from the very first conceptual idea through to the time when the project is built out and becomes a contributing asset to the community? For one thing, the project can gain a better and more informed constituency that will support it through the entire approval process and will feel a sense of ownership and pride in the completed project (Burby, 2003). For example, in discussing redevelopment plans along the Blackstone River in Pawtucket, Rhode Island, Mayor James E. Doyle cited the public involvement process as the reason for the redevelopment's success:

> In the mid-1990s, we started using a grass-roots approach and created a Riverfront Commission that spent countless hours meeting with abutters and other parties to come up with a plan that made sense. The plan still has the backing of the public because it's their ideas that we are using (Dujardin, 2005).

In addition to building a stronger constituency, the public engagement ensured that development would perform better for the economy, environment, and residents' quality of life.

The Southside neighborhood in Greensboro, North Carolina,[7] demonstrates how involving the public in the development process can lead to a better built project. The Southside neighborhood was a blighted ten-acre parcel with several brownfields. The city wanted to revitalize an area that was a three- to five-minute walk from the central business district. The planning process for Southside began in 1993 with the formation of a steering committee comprised of residents from the Southside neighborhood and surrounding neighborhoods, historic preservation groups, the financial community, and the Norfolk Southern Railroad. This steering committee, along with city staff, engaged in an intensive two-year planning process that solicited community participation through design workshops, community forums, and working meetings. This inclusive process yielded a plan that represented the community's vision for Southside (US EPA, 2004a).

The results speak for themselves. Not only did all the rehabilitated and new homes sell, but the tax base for the neighborhood increased from $400,000 before revitalization to over $20 million at build out. A new resident captures one reason the redevelopment was a success: "Southside was the type of neighborhood we were looking for—it provides us with the sense of community we crave, within walking distance of all the services and amenities downtown has to offer" (Schwartz interview).

Another example of better development resulting from improved public participation is represented by Atlantic Station, located in midtown Atlanta, Georgia. It comprises a $2 billion, mixed-use, live, work, and play neighborhood on the former 138-acre Atlantic Steel brownfield. The conceptualizing and planning for Atlantic Steel's redevelopment demonstrates how involving more stakeholders leads to better results. The Georgia Conservancy hosted a 13-week planning workshop at the start of the project, involving citizens in the community adjacent to the site (Goldberg, 2005, p. 59). This early involvement generated priorities that drove the rezoning process and set the stage for additional stakeholder involvement. Indeed, participants in the process felt it was invaluable to the development's final design. One resident commented, "There are parts of the plans [for Atlantic Station] you can point to and say, 'that change is a direct result of one neighbor's suggestion at on particular Saturday session'" (Goldberg, 2005, p. 60).

Officially opened in October 2005, Atlantic Station offers a range of housing types, choices of transportation, and a mix of shops and offices. The environmental and economic benefits of the project are numerous: clean-up of an old industrial property; separation of sanitary and storm sewer systems; reduction of auto emissions by giving people options in transportation; and creation of jobs and economic development where infrastructure already exists. The developer estimates that the tax base will increase from $300,000 when the property was purchased to over $100 million when build-out is complete (Watson, 2005). Atlantic Station is a new neighborhood in the center of Atlanta that is good for the environment, fiscally sound, and a place that people want to live, work, and play. As one resident, who chooses to walk to work, remarks, "I don't have a car, and I walk for groceries—I love it" (Gogoi, 2006).

Creating a Process that is More Predictable, Democratic, and Fair

Stakeholders need to be engaged at or near the beginning of the process. When community members are brought in late, they mistrust the development plans because they feel that specific decisions have already been made and any attempt to solicit public comment signifies an insincere effort to meet some requirement. An effective citizen participation process is predictable, comprehensive, seeking input from a wide range of stakeholders, and, in the end, fair—that is, offering "the greatest good to the greatest number."

A timely and predictable approval process, complete with citizen participation elements, can allow developers to take into account the concerns of nearby residents and businesses. Citizens expect new development that is consistent with the community's vision and does no harm. It is also the responsibility of citizens to work constructively with local government and developers on development proposals. Local government establishes development policies and priorities that use tax dollars wisely and balance the needs of residents and developers. A smart growth development process embraces teamwork: it takes many ideas from the developer, local government, neighborhood businesses, community development practitioners, and community members to create lasting and enduring places.

The example of Vienna, Maryland, demonstrates this teamwork. On Maryland's Eastern Shore, two hours from Washington, D.C., Vienna is a small town of approximately 300 people. Like many small towns adjacent to a metropolitan area, the town is facing significant pressures from growth. Compounding these pressures is its location along the Nanticoke River and nearby Chesapeake Bay, which provide the town beautiful landscapes and coastal amenities. To ensure that the expected population growth and associated economic opportunity benefit the entire community, the local elected leaders of Vienna and the surrounding communities worked together to create a vision for Vienna and the area around it (Brinsfield, 2005).

It was critical to the crafters of the *Vienna Community Vision Plan* that the process involving the public was broad, transparent, and fair. They realized they were facing a critical juncture in determining where and how their town could grow. Surveys were sent to all residents, asking for their opinions about current development patterns, their likes and dislikes related to existing social and economic opportunities, and how they thought growth in the area could occur. In addition, the authors of the plan analyzed the undeveloped land around the existing town to determine places best suited for development. They assessed the current road network, existing facilities, and regulatory structure. The surveys and assessments identified opportunities and challenges for future development. Through a series of workshops and town meetings, residents discussed, debated, and refined the proposed scenarios. The early and meaningful public input made the entire process—visioning, consensus building, implementing the plan, and identifying a developer—more efficient and more likely to succeed. (Brinsfield, 2005; *Vienna Community Vision Plan*, 2003)

Of course, "fair" guarantees neither unanimity of opinion nor consensus. It should mean, though, that all stakeholders have a chance to express their concerns, that there's an ability to consider a development's impact on the community as well as individuals, and that the prospect of negative consequences are addressed. Ideally this fairness means that the participatory process is transparent and that the development project will meet multiple goals agreed upon by the members of the community.

Providing More Tools and Strategies for Civic Engagement

As discussed, the typical process to encourage citizen participation generally involves residents speaking for two to three minutes at an evening public comment session or county or planning board meeting. This "presentation then reaction" process offers limited opportunity for meaningful dialogue and does little to inspire creative solutions. A smart growth approach to development, however, offers local governments, developers, residents, and other stakeholders a wide range of tools and opportunities to engage more meaningfully on the proposed development project. Indeed, new tools to assess a project's impact and to tap into stakeholders' creativity are constantly being developed. State-of-the-art tools and technologies, such as a visual preference survey or computer assisted design programs that can illustrate a proposed project in its setting, have enabled developers to create interactive, virtual models of proposed plans for development. Such tools can help developers create design elements that benefit both the community and the project.

Increasingly, planning offices and development consulting firms are using computer imaging to engage citizens in planning workshops. Computer visualization can depict radical changes in a streetscape—such as the addition of new buildings or the incorporation of transit—in just seconds. It can show how a proposed multi-family development would look, giving community members a more tangible way to assess it rather than using vague planning concepts such as "higher-density construction." Alternative-future scenarios can model the growth of a region over a given time frame and can respond in real time to different variables suggested by a live audience. This rapid response helps facilitators to reach consensus more quickly and efficiently. In other exercises, local stakeholders might be able to vote on design scenarios, comment on different designs of a proposed project, or speak directly with designers and architects.

For example, in Chattanooga, Tennessee, after the East Gate Mall failed, the community came together with strong ideas about future uses of the outmoded shopping center. Members of the community were tired of large, single-use developments and wanted to see a village center consistent with the scale of surrounding neighborhoods. Since it was not feasible to redevelop the entire site at once, community members worked with computer simulation programs to provide input on the form of the new development and how development would be phased-in over several years, according to market conditions. This simulation let citizens visualize how new buildings would be sited in outlying parking areas, eventually replacing the mall itself. This work formed the basis for a plan that will guide development and help shape the neighborhood's character in future years (ICMA, 2002).

Engaging the community to create a vision for its future can be a time-consuming process that may take months or years. Charrettes, which are intense four- to seven-day design workshops, are geared to help the community develop a plan that can be built. They indicate one tool that many communities have used to reach consensus on where and how a development could be built. All interested citizens are invited to participate. Working with maps, drawings, and other tools, participants learn how to evaluate what their community needs and can accommodate; how to share their vision of their neighborhoods and their concerns and dreams for the future; and how to work with each other and professional designers to create, critique, and collaborate on options. This shared achievement creates a sense of "buy-in" that gives a project a better chance of successfully navigating the numerous political, economic, and environmental obstacles it may face (National Charrette Institute).

Charrettes allow participants to address a variety of needs, from reaching consensus on long-term visions for town development to finding workable agreements on single projects. They can identify short-term and long-term problems, opportunities, needs, and issues that are important to residents and business leaders. Charrettes permit community members to build both immediate and long-term solutions by outlining short-term steps. They may offer strategies to implement policies and principles for future decision-making and development. Brainstorming and negotiating during a charrette can change minds and create unexpected concepts or solutions to problems. As a result, the number and variety of solutions and ideas generated and considered are far greater than those developed under conventional planning methods, which would normally take months to achieve (National Charrette Institute).

Putting It All Together: Three Case Studies

Citizen and community participation is a core value now idealized in our society, and indeed, our country. There are many places in the world and in our nation where ideas and ideals can be expressed freely—although the technology and practice of participation are often lacking. Where and how our neighborhoods will improve indicates one area in which many people have something to say. Of course, it's unrealistic to believe that everyone in a community will agree on how and where growth occurs. Differing views and perspectives need to be heard, however, and it's the responsibility of local governments to harness the ideas, concerns, inspirations, and energy of their constituents into a productive and constructive process.

As we've discussed, smart growth approaches can effectively engage the public in development projects. This section highlights case studies that demonstrate how these approaches enhance citizen participation to create better community outcomes, provide a more predictable, democratic, and fair process, and use more tools and strategies.

The cases selected for this section show how practitioners in communities across the United States have changed the typical process of engaging the public and improved development in their neighborhoods. Each case emphasizes one of the three themes discussed above; however, the themes overlap significantly.

Creating Better Outcomes: Arlington, Virginia

Development in Arlington County, Virginia's Rosslyn-Ballston (R-B) corridor,[8] shows how effective public participation can benefit the community. To the west of Washington, D.C., the R-B corridor (the area that straddles Metrorail's Orange Line) is one of the earliest community-wide efforts to link land use and transportation decisions. Beginning in the late 1970s, Arlington County officials decided to direct the Metrorail underground through an underdeveloped area of the R-B Corridor.

The county's Department of Community Planning, Housing, and Development worked with residents to identify areas around the five Metro stops where higher-density development would be accommodated. In exchange for the higher-density development in the transit corridor, the county agreed to lower densities in neighborhoods of single-family homes and other areas outside of the R-B corridor. With the community on board from an early stage, Arlington's implementation of this plan has been exemplary—92 percent of the county's commercial development is in the R-B corridor, consuming only 7 percent of the total land area. (Leach, 2004, p. 148; Goldberg, 2005, p. 56)

Started several decades ago (before the term smart growth was commonly used), the citizen participation process continues today. Community partnerships, such as the Ballston Partnership, Clarendon Alliance, and Rosslyn Renaissance, help ensure full and active participation by citizens and businesses in nearly all public and private development and policy decisions. In addition, the county solicits citizen input through more than 40 board-appointed county commissions and nearly 60 neighborhood civic associations. Arlington uses a comprehensive site plan review process that includes public meetings with staff, citizens, county supervisors, and developers. The result, as of 2003, is a planning approach that places dense, mixed-use, infill development at five Metro stations and then tapers down to lower-density neighborhoods made up mostly of detached, single-family homes. The area is home to more than 21 million square feet of office, retail, and commercial space, 3,000 hotel rooms, and 22,500 homes, which all help to create vibrant "urban villages" where people live, shop, work, and play using transit, walkways, bicycles, and cars. (U.S. EPA, 2002)

This development approach allowed Arlington County to collect its tax revenues over a mix of uses, which allowed the county to keep its overall property tax rate below that of most of the neighboring localities. The corridor itself is an economic engine for the county, generating 33 percent of the county's real estate tax revenue. The corridor also performs well environmentally. The same amount of development in the two square-mile Rosslyn-Ballston Corridor would consume more than 14 square miles if built at typical suburban densities. Accommodating growth in the Rosslyn-Ballston corridor—rather than in the suburbs—provides for the region's air, land, and water resources.[9] In addition, almost half of the corridor's residents commute by transit, significantly decreasing regional air emissions (Leach, 2004, pp. 132 *ff*). Arlington County used a strong community involvement process as part of an overall land use and transportation strategy to create great places that offer significant environmental, economic, and quality of life benefits.

Providing a More Predictable, Democratic, and Fair Process: Davidson, North Carolina

Local governments can ensure a democratic and predictable public involvement process in development decision-making. This is what happened in Davidson, North Carolina. To the residents of Davidson, located 20 miles from Charlotte, the essence of their small town derives from its great neighbors, great neighborhoods, and its college-town feel. Like Vienna, Maryland, the town's proximity to a major metropolitan area and its high quality of life are attracting development. To preserve and enhance Davidson's character and ensure appropriate citizen participation, the town adopted the *Davidson Land Plan* in 1995 and the innovative *Planning Ordinance* in 2001.

The Planning Ordinance in particular seeks significant public involvement for all new development projects. According to the ordinance, public involvement is scaled to reflect the community-wide impact of the proposed project. For instance, minor subdivisions with three or fewer lots require public workshops, although developments of more than 100 acres require a charrette of at least 40 hours (Town of Davidson, 2001). These charrettes and workshops allow the developer and the community to understand each other's goals, ensuring that development projects meet the vision that the community adopted. In addition, the workshops and charrettes provide developers with the predictability they need to invest time and resources for incorporating citizen concerns into development projects.

The plan and ordinance clearly articulate the town's vision for its future, which, in turn, makes developers active partners in implementing the community's vision of connected, walkable neighborhoods that maintain Davidson's legacy as a traditional small town. The plan and ordinance allow Davidson to build on its strengths while accommodating new growth. For example, the old Davidson Cotton Mill complex was transformed into offices, condominiums, and a restaurant. (U.S. EPA, 2004a)

Davidson's leaders recognize that growth and development could and should improve the community. By ensuring the community's vision provides the basis for the regulations and ordinances that determined the pattern of development and by clearly articulating the process by which community input is integrated into decision-making, Davidson has made the development process fair and predictable to all stakeholders.

More Tools and Strategies for Civic Engagement: Sacramento, California, Region Blueprint: Transportation and Land Use Study

The Sacramento Blueprint Project[10] is an example of how a community used a wide range of tools and strategies to engage, and engage in a more meaningful manner, a broader range of stakeholders. The Sacramento, California, region is expected to double in population over the next 50 years. To determine how best to accommodate this growth and how best to respond to the needs of its residents, the Sacramento Council of Governments (SACOG) launched the Sacramento Region Blueprint Transportation and Land Use Study. Through the Blueprint Project, SACOG expected to accomplish three goals: (1) link transportation and land use policy to manage congestion; (2) involve the public and incorporate citizen input into the study's recommendations; and (3) use the best available technology to improve decision-making. (Zwas, 2005)

Blueprint began in 2003 with a base-case scenario that showed citizens how the expected population growth would affect the region under current regulations. Over the ensuing months, 5,000 residents, elected officials, and business leaders participated in a series of workshops, regional conferences, Web-based dialogues, and surveys. The extensive outreach, including public workshops for Spanish speakers and distribution of information written in different languages, was successful, in part, because of the collaboration of 30 agencies and private businesses.

SACOG partnered with Valley Vision, a nonprofit organization, to develop a broad community outreach program. The outreach program included neighborhood, community, and regional workshops in which citizens had the opportunity to propose different development scenarios. Using state-of-the art simulation technology, Blueprint Project organizers could quickly and efficiently model the estimated effects of those scenarios on transportation infrastructure, air quality, and the economy. Through these outreach efforts and use of the information generated in the workshops, Blueprint Project organizers presented four build-out scenarios (including the base case) showing different development patterns in each scenario, but keeping the population accommodated in each scenario constant. Participants then rated each scenario using ten economic, environmental, and transportation indicators. Finally, they were asked to vote for the scenario that best matched their own vision for the region (U.S. EPA, 2004a). The scenario garnering the most votes called for accommodating growth through reinvesting in existing places, increasing densities, and allowing for a greater mix of uses. In contrast, the base-case scenario received very little support (Zwas, 2005).

The Blueprint Project changed how the Sacramento region approaches growth—it educated and engaged the public and gave participants the tools to help them design the future they wanted (U.S. EPA, 2004a). In addition, the Blueprint Project demonstrated how technology could help raise awareness of the challenges created by growth as well as the opportunities. Clearly, the strong involvement by citizens in the Sacramento region can only help as SACOG implements the study's findings.

CONCLUSION

Public participation can be time-consuming and "messy." The prospect of managing different personalities, agenda, and preferred issues often drives developers and local governments to tightly structured and limited public participation. By doing so, however, they miss opportunities to improve public dialogue and find creative new ideas about where and how a community could grow. A community taking a smart growth approach to citizen participation embraces the opportunity to hear the ideas, dreams, and hopes its residents have for their community. In this way, smart growth enhances citizen participation to create better community outcomes; provides for a process that is more predictable, democratic, and fair; and provides more tools and strategies for dialogue.

Citizens need information about possible alternatives before they voice their choices or concerns. Often, however, only a small portion of the community engages in decision-making because of socioeconomic, linguistic, or educational class barriers. To engage all residents, local governments can get creative in identifying and using new methods for soliciting, responding to, and sharing information. Every community needs to develop its own range of methods to reach all of its residents as it is the community members who are the greatest resource needed to create a great place. Reaching out and working with community residents in a meaningful and enduring process will allow communities to realize their vision for where and how to grow next.

NOTES

1 The Development, Community, & Environment Division (DCED) is part of the U.S. EPA's Office of Policy, Economics, and Innovation. Many smart growth-related documents cited in this paper can be downloaded from the DCED Website: www.epa.gov/smartgrowth.

2 These data were compiled by the DCED staff using sources including the U.S. Census, the National Association of Home Builders Website (www.nahb.org), and the U.S. EPA *Sector Strategies Performance Report* 2004.

3 See, for example, U.S. EPA, 2001, *Our Built and Natural Environment*, U.S. EPA, 2006, *Protecting water resources with Higher-Density Development*, Frank, et al., *Health and Community Design*," and Muro and Puentes, *Investing in a Better Future: A Review of the Fiscal and Competitive Advantages of Smarter Growth Development Patterns*.

4 See www.smartgrowth.org for further discussion of the 10 principles and the Smart Growth Network.

5 In November, 2005, the City of Lakewood and the Lakewood Reinvestment Authority won the National Award for Smart Growth Achievement Built Project category for their work on the Belmar neighborhood.

6 The Town of Davidson received a 2004 National Award for Smart Growth Achievement in the Overall Excellence category for its development planning and implementation. Davidson's workshop and charrette process is described in more detail in the case study section of this paper.

7 The city of Greensboro, Department of Housing and Community Development, received a 2004 National Award for Smart Growth Achievement in the Built Projects category for the redevelopment of the Southside neighborhood.

8 Arlington County received a 2002 National Award for Smart Growth Achievement in the Overall Excellence category for the Rosslyn-Ballston corridor. See U.S. EPA 2002.

9 See, for example, U.S. EPA documents *Protecting Water Resources with Higher-Density Development* and *The Transportation and Environmental Impacts of Infill Versus Greenfield Development: A Comparative Case Study Analysis*.

10 The Sacramento Area Council of Governments (SACOG) received a 2004 National Award for Smart Growth Achievement in the Community Outreach and Education category for the Blueprint Project.

REFERENCES

Arnstein, S. R. (1969). A Ladder of Citizen Participation. *AIP Journal*, 35(4), 216-229.

Baker, W. H., Addams, H. L., & Davis, B. (2005). Critical Factors for Enhancing Municipal Public Hearings. *Public Administration Review*, 65(4), 490-499.

Brinsfield, R. (2005, November 17). Vienna, MD, Community Vision Plan. Slide presentation at the University of North Carolina-Charlotte.

Brody, S. D., Goldshalk, D. R., & Burby, R. J. (2003). Mandating Citizen Participation in Plan Making: Six Strategic Planning Choices. *APA Journal*, 69(3), 245-263.

Burchell, R. W., Lowenstein, G., Dophin, W. R., Galley, C. C., Downs, A., Seskin, S., Still, K. G., & Moore, T. (2002). *Costs of Sprawl—2000: TCRP Report 74*. Washington, D.C.: Transportation Research Board.

Burby, R. J. (2003). Making Plans that Matter: Citizen Involvement and Government Action. *APA Journal*, 69(1), 33-49.

Day, D. (1997). Citizen Participation in the Planning Process. *Journal of Planning Literature*, 11(3), 421-434.

Dujardin, R. C. (2005, August 3). Leaders vow cooperation on waterfront development. *Providence Journal*.

Ewing, R., with Hodder, R. (1998) *Best Development Practices: A Primer for Smart Growth*. Smart Growth Network, Washington, D.C.

Frank L. D., Engelke P. O., & Schmid, T. L. (2003). *Health and Community Design. The Impact of the Built Environment on Physical Activity.* Island Press: Washington, D.C., 2003.

Gil, E., & Lucchesi, E. (1979). Citizen participation in planning. In F. S. So, I. Stollman, F. Beal, & D. S. Arnold (Eds.), *The Practice of Local Government Planning* (2nd ed.). Washington, D.C.: ICMA.

Gogoi, P. (2006). Bringing the community to the city. *BusinessWeek Online.* Retrieved February 16, 2006, from: www.businessweek.com/innovate/content/feb2006/id20060202_200657.htm

Goldberg, D. (2005). *Choosing our Community's Future.* Smart Growth America, Washington, D.C.

Heimlich, R. E., & Anderson, W. D. (2001). *Development at the Urban Fringe and Beyond: Impacts on Agriculture and Rural Land.* Economic Research Service, U.S. Department of Agriculture. Agriculture Economics Report No. 803, Washington, D.C.

International City/County Management Association (ICMA) /Smart Growth Network. (2002). *Getting to Smart Growth: 100 Policies for Implementation.* ICMA, Washington, D.C.

ICMA/Smart Growth Network. (2003). *Getting to Smart Growth II: 100 More Policies for Implementation.* ICMA, Washington, D.C.

ICMA/Smart Growth Network. (2006). *This Is Smart Growth.* ICMA, Washington, D.C.

ICMA with Anderson, G. (1998). *Why Smart Growth: A Primer.* ICMA, Washington, D.C.

Kelly, E. D., & Becker, B. (2000). *Community Planning: an introduction to the Comprehensive Plan.* Island Press, Washington, D.C.

Klein, W. R. (2000). Building Consensus. In C. J. Hoch, L. C. Dalton, & F. S. So, (Eds.), *The Practice of Local Government Planning* (3rd ed.). ICMA: Washington, D.C.

Lail, M. (2004). Greensboro and Davidson honored with Smart Growth National Awards. North Carolina League of Municipalities. Retrieved February 17, 2006, from www.nclm.org/A1%20Center%20Page%20News/Archived%20News%20stories/smartgrowth_greensboro_davidson.htm

Leach, D. (2004). Rosslyn-Ballston Corridor. In H. Dittmar & G. Ohland (Eds.), *The New Transit Town.* Washington, D.C.: Island Press, 132-153.

Local Government Commission/National Association of Realtors. (2003). *Creating Great Neighborhoods: Density in Your Community.* National Association of Realtors, Washington, D.C.

Molotch, H. (1976). The City as Growth Machine: Toward a Political Economy of Place. *The American Journal of Sociology,* 82(2), 309-332.

Muro, M., & Puentes, R. (2004). *Investing in a Better Future: A Review of the Fiscal and Competitive Advantages of Smarter Growth Development Patterns.* Washington, D.C.: Brookings.

National Charrette Institute (NCI). (2006). National Charrette Institute. Retrieved February 1, 2006, from www.charretteinstitute.org

Schwartz, S. (2004, November 17) Director of Neighborhood Development, City of Greensboro, North Carolina. Interview with author, L. Richards.

Smart Growth Network. (2006). *Smart Growth Principles* Retrieved February 1, 2006, from www.smartgrowth.org

Smart Growth Online. (2006) *Smart Growth in Action.* Retrieved September 16, 2006, from www.smartgrowth.org/library/projects.asp

Town of Davidson, NC. (2001). *Planning Ordinance (as amended 2003).* Davidson, North Carolina.

Town of Vienna, MD. (2006). Homepage. Retrieved February 15, 2006, from: www.viennamd.org

U.S. Census Bureau. (2004).

U.S. Environmental Protection Agency. (2006) *Protecting Water Resources with Higher-Density Development.* U.S. EPA, Washington, D.C.

U.S. Environmental Protection Agency. (2005) *National Award for Smart Growth Achievement, 2005.* U.S. EPA, Washington, D.C.

U.S. Environmental Protection Agency. (2004a) *National Award for Smart Growth Achievement, 2004.* U.S. EPA, Washington, D.C.

U.S. Environmental Protection Agency. (2004b) *Sector Strategies Performance Report 2004.* U.S. EPA, Washington, D.C.

U.S. Environmental Protection Agency. (2003) *National Award for Smart Growth Achievement, 2003.* U.S. EPA, Washington, D.C.

U.S. Environmental Protection Agency. (2002a) *National Award for Smart Growth Achievement, 2002.* U.S. EPA, Washington, D.C.

U.S. Environmental Protection Agency. (2002b). EPA-Atlantic Steel. Retrieved September 23, 2005, from: www.epa.gov/projectxl/atlantic/1098.htm

U.S. Environmental Protection Agency. (2001). *Our Built and Natural Environments.* U.S. EPA. Washington, D.C.

U.S. Environmental Protection Agency. (2001a). *Comparing Methodologies to Assess Transportation and Air Quality Impacts of Brownfields and Infill Development.* U.S. EPA: Washington, D.C.

U.S. Environmental Protection Agency. (1999). *The Impacts of Infill vs. Greenfield Development: A Comparative Case Study Analysis.* U.S. EPA, Washington, D.C.

Vienna Community Vision Plan. (2003). Prepared by The Conservation Fund and the Town of Vienna. Retrieved February 1, 2006, from: www.viennamd.org.

Watson, J. (2005). 30363: One hot zip code. Retrieved February 16, 2006, from: www.llalive.com/news/news_article.aspx?storyid=70775

Zwas, A. (2005). Alternative Futures: Scenario Planning in Transportation. *The Heinz School Review*, 2(1), 1-10.

THE RACIAL BIFURCATION OF COMMUNITY DEVELOPMENT: IMPLICATIONS FOR COMMUNITY DEVELOPMENT PRACTITIONERS

By James D. Preston and Graves E. Enck

ABSTRACT

Consensus and dissensus models of development, and the underlying assumptions of each approach, are presented and discussed. The findings of a reputational leadership survey conducted in a metropolitan area with a large minority population are then outlined. They indicate that the minority population leadership represents more of a subcommunity than part of an overall, integrated leadership structure. Implications of the survey results for practitioners in communities where leadership is divided along racial lines are discussed. These practitioners may face built-in dissensus situations where contesting, rather than collaborative, strategies of purposive change are present.

INTRODUCTION

Community theorists and community development practitioners, reflecting an understandably pragmatic interest in problem solving, have long emphasized consensus models of purposive change. These models have typically been applied to issues about which agreement is relatively easy to obtain (Miller, 1952; Ross, 1955; Kaufman, 1959; Warren & Hyman, 1966; Wilkinson, 1972; Warren, 1978; Christenson & Robinson, 1980). Based on the assumption of a single community public interest, these models prescribe a process of collaboration and consensus building that enables all important groups in the community to define and pursue their common purposes. Community participants meet and discuss what is best for the overall community and then work toward attaining their goals. Community development is viewed, therefore, as being confined primarily to non-controversial issues. It is maintained that the community's welfare is identical to the welfare of all groups within it. Collaborative strategies are assumed to be appropriate for finding and implementing the best

---

James D. Preston is a professor and Graves E. Enck is an assistant professor, both in the Department of Sociology at Memphis State University.

interests of the community. Given the assumption that consensus can be created both on the specific change issue and on the legitimacy of the final outcome, controversial issues were dismissed as relating only to special, segmented, selfish interests rather than to community interests (Warren, 1978).

Concurrently, a minority of community development theorists has long emphasized the necessity of dissensus models of purposive change (Alinsky, 1941, 1965, 1969, 1970). These theorists view the community as differentiated and fragmented, with multiple and potentially competing levels of social participation. They share Coser's (1971) emphasis on conflict as a means for dissatisfied groups to restructure themselves and deal with dissatisfaction in ways that may alter society (Robinson, 1980). Pointing to such controversial issues as inadequate housing, differential treatment of the poor, and systematic racism, these theorists have challenged the fundamental assumption of consensus models and the belief that there is a single public interest that people can agree on (Warren, 1978). These issues, they argue, cannot be dealt with adequately within the confines of collaborative strategies. They require, instead, the recognition of contesting strategies if different interests are to be represented in decision making (Warren, 1978). These issues, compounded by such factors as community diversity, changes in population composition, and power structures that ignore the interests of minorities, have convinced some community development theorists that conflict management is the most appropriate role for the community development practitioner. Conflict is seen as inevitable (Robinson, 1980), and the practitioner needs to be able to creatively cope with it.

Community theorists and community development practitioners share a common interest in discovering and defining those community characteristics that can potentially lead to or result in dissensus situations. This paper is intended to contribute to that understanding by focusing on the racial bifurcation of community leadership as a potential context for dissensus. It illustrates the contribution of a traditional community research methodology—the reputational leadership survey—in defining the characteristics of such a leadership structure. Research was conducted in a large, southern, metropolitan city with a 1980 population of slightly over 600,000, approximately 48 percent of which was black. The identity of the community and the specific year in which the research was conducted are not given as confidentiality and anonymity were promised to all respondents.

METHOD OF INVESTIGATION

Data on community leadership was collected using a traditional two-step reputational method. This approach identifies individual community leaders by relying on the designation and ranking of leaders by informants. The first step consisted of enlisting two community "knowledgeables" who were longtime community residents and active in community affairs. They developed a list of "key informants" in the following institutional areas of community life: government, media, religion, business, law, social agencies, and education. The resulting list consisted of the names of 72 persons and included both black leaders and white leaders. The question that guided the construction of this list was: "In the community there are often people whom one would find in positions of leadership time and again on many types of issues. Who in your opinion are the general leaders in this community?" This approach ignored race in eliciting the nominations for leadership, thereby avoiding any assumption that blacks either would or would not be nominated.

The second step consisted of field interviews, beginning with the initial list and then continuing through use of a chain-referral procedure. Individuals whose names were not on the original list but who received ten or more leadership nominations during the course of the interviewing were also interviewed. This procedure was continued until the interviews began to contain more duplications of previous nominations than new names. Moreno (1960) referred to this as the "socio-dynamic effect." It is based on the assumption that additional interviews would have yielded the same proportion of multiple nominations for the top leaders and few nominations for those seldom chosen. Other researchers, conducting similar studies of community power, have accepted the procedure as valid (Bonjean, 1963; Preston, 1969). The 74 interviews resulted in 816 leadership nominations distributed among 167 individuals. The nominations tended to cluster around a relatively small number of individuals (see Table 1).

A leader was defined as an individual receiving more than the mean number of nominations for all nominees. This procedure has been utilized extensively in previous research (Preston, 1969; Preston et al., 1972). Because they received only one nomination each, seventy-one individuals were deleted from the list. These deletions were made to control for single nominations resulting from inaccuracies in respondents' memories, self-nominations, and nominations on the basis of friendship. The mean number of general leadership nominations was then calculated for those individuals receiving two or more nominations. The resulting mean of 7.76 was used as the cutoff point, with twenty-eight individuals identified as general reputational leaders. There was no assumption made that all individuals playing leadership roles in the community had been identified. Instead, it was assumed that if a leadership group did exist, the identified persons

Table 1. Ranking of General Reputational Leaders

Nominee	Rank	Number of Nominations	Percent of Total Nominations
Manufacturer A	1	38	4.66
College President	2.5	33	4.04
Officer of Bank A	2.5	33	4.04
Manufacturer B	4	32	3.92
Attorney A	5.5	28	3.43
School Board Member A	5.5	28	3.43
City Council Member A	7	27	3.31
President of Company A	8	26	3.19
Officer of Bank B	9.5	25	3.06
Officer of Bank C; Court Squire A	9.5	25	3.06
President of Company B	11	21	2.57
University President	12	16	1.96
City Council Member B	13.5	15	1.84
President of Company C	13.5	15	1.84
Attorney B	15.5	14	1.72
Industrialist	15.5	14	1.72
Officer of Bank C	17	13	1.59
Realtor	18.5	12	1.47
Officer of Bank D	18.5	12	1.47
School Board Member B	21	11	1.35
Court Squire B	21	11	1.35
Criminal Court Judge	21	11	1.35
Court Squire (retired), Former Mayor	23	10	1.22
Mayor	25	9	1.10
Religious Official	25	9	1.10
Newspaper Editor	25	9	1.10
City Council Member C	27.5	8	.98
Court Squire C	27.5	8	.98

were part of it and would meet with less resistance than nonleaders were they to engage in efforts to either initiate community action or reach solutions to community problems (Bonjean, 1963; Preston, 1969).

FINDINGS

Of the twenty-eight general leaders identified in this study, six were black. Table 2 presents selected characteristics of the black leaders and their ranks in the total leadership group. Four of the black leaders were ranked above the eleventh leadership position, and four were incumbents in elected positions of authority in the community.

The identification of individual leaders through designation and ranking by informants does not distinguish whether those identified act singly, as aggregates, as members of competing factions, or as a

Table 2. Black Leaders by Rank and Selected Characteristics

Nominee	Rank	Education (Years)	Age	Sex
College President	2.5	19	44	M
School Board Member A	5.5	17	43	F
City Council Member A	5.5	16	39	M
Officer of Bank C; Court Squire A	9.5	17	54	M
Officer of Bank C	17	18	64	M
Criminal Court Judge	21	20	36	M

group. One way of approaching these distinctions is through the use of two sociometric techniques developed by Moreno (1960) to measure group cohesiveness—ratio of interest and ratio of attraction.

The ratio of interest is the proportion of in-group choices to the total number of choices made by the leaders. It measures the extent to which community leaders nominate each other as leaders. Possible ratio values constitute a continuum, ranging from 1.00, indicating the existence of a group structure, to .00, indicating an aggregate of individuals. The twenty-eight leaders directed 151 of their total 239 choices to each other, yielding a ratio of interest of .63. This tendency to nominate one another was significantly greater than would have been expected by chance alone, because they could have, theoretically, nominated 239 different individuals.

The ratio of attraction measures perception of group structure and is reflected in the nominations made by the remainder of the panel of informants—those designated as nonleaders. It is the proportion of nonleader nominations of members of the leadership group to the total number of choices made by the nonleaders. Of the total of 577 choices made by nonleaders, 340 were directed toward the identified leaders, yielding a ratio of attraction of .59. The nominations of nonleaders concentrated on the leadership group.

Using Moreno's (1960) measures of group cohesiveness in combination with a sociogram yields some important insights on the cohesiveness of the six black leaders identified in the group of twenty-eight general leaders. Implied in the idea of sociometric structure is the notion that likes and dislikes are differentially and systematically distributed among members of a group (Smelser, 1988). Figure 1 depicts the pattern of sociometric choices of the black leaders. With the exception of the black leader who tied for fifth-highest rank in the leadership group, the black leaders did not confine their nominations for general leaders to other black members. Of the twenty-two white leaders identified as general leaders, fifteen were nominated by the black leaders at least once. Of the forty-eight choices that black

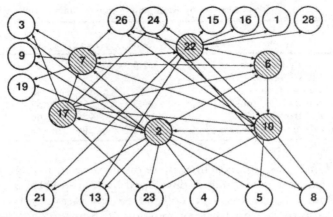

Figure 1. Sociometric choices of black leaders (shaded).

leaders directed to the leadership group, nineteen were to other black leaders, yielding a ratio of interest of .40. This indicates that the black leadership group is less cohesive than the total leadership group, which had a ratio of interest of .63, and would seem to imply that the six black leaders function as a rather loosely knit group within the total leadership group. A ratio of attraction was computed using the nominations of the twenty-eight general leaders. Of the 115 total choices, only 20 were directed to the black leaders, generating a ratio of attraction of .17. This extremely low ratio indicates that the black leaders were not highly recognized as leaders by members of the top leadership group.

In an effort to determine more explicitly the source of the nominations that placed black leaders in the general leadership group, the ratio of attraction was recalculated in two ways using the nominations of the remainder of the panel of informants (nonleaders). They made 577 leadership choices, with 136 going to the black leaders. This yields a ratio of attraction of .24. Using only the leadership nominations of the nine black respondents among the nonleaders, however, yields a ratio of attraction of .57, a figure much closer to the group segment on the continuum.

Several inferences can be made from these data. First, the black leadership group falls within the middle range of the aggregate-group continuum with a ratio of interest of .40. The black leaders are not recognized by the other general leaders, however, as indicated by the ratio of attraction for them among the general leadership group of .17. Recognition of the six black leaders as community leaders appears to derive, to some extent, from the relatively concentrated choices of the black nonleadership group in the panel of informants. Finally, the black leaders appear to have attained high ranks in the leadership group due to the existence of a relatively small cohort of black leaders in the community. Their nominations were concentrated on a smaller number of individuals than was the case for the white leadership group.

DISCUSSION AND IMPLICATIONS

The findings are striking in their consistency with the black subcommunity thesis that runs throughout the literature on community power (Pfautz, 1962; Pfautz et al., 1975; Hunter, 1953, 1980; Bullard, 1987). The basic premise of this thesis is that, to date, in most communities, black leaders are not integrated into the inner power structure of the overall community but instead are recognized by and act as leaders of blacks within the community. The six black general leaders in this study have community visibility, occupy positions of authority, and are knowledgeable about the community leadership structure, all of which suggest changes in the status of blacks in the overall community leadership area. In keeping with the black subcommunity thesis, however, the black leaders were not recognized as leaders by other general leaders but derived their recognition instead from the concentrated choices of the black informants in the nonleader group. These data suggest that the six black leaders are representative of a subcommunity rather than the general community.

These findings are consistent with Hunter's (1953) classic and ground-breaking study in Atlanta, which concluded that "None of the leaders in the Negro community may operate in the same echelons of power as the top leaders in the total community, and herein lies a basic difference between the power wielded by the top Negro leaders and the top leaders in the general community" (p. 139). Hunter's (1980) follow-up study found that the situation had not changed much since 1950 in terms of black participation and effectiveness in Atlanta (see, especially, pp. 72 and 84).

Hunter's (1953, 1980) work has been confirmed in subsequent community power studies on the roles of black leaders. These efforts have concluded that black leaders are representative of black subcommunities. For example, Pfautz (1962) depicted the black leadership as representative of a subcommunity that was monolithic in terms of power structure, with a small, articulate leadership at the top and an undifferentiated and inarticulate mass at the bottom. In a follow-up study, Pfautz et al. (1975) reported that although black leaders had a greater orientation to the black community and that there was a decline in community consensus regarding reputed leadership, the basic notion of treating black leaders as leaders of a subcommunity remained unchanged.

The most telling implication of the black subcommunity thesis, which our data illustrate and support, is for those who continue to believe in the appropriateness of consensus models of community change. In communities with large minority populations, if black leaders are recognized as leaders only by their black constituents, there is, as Warren (1978) points out, little reason to believe that blacks will gain important concessions from a white-dominated leadership structure simply by supplying small bits of minority-group input. Instead, such a structure of community leadership is ripe for dissensus models that emphasize the necessity of a black power base supporting a black point of view that represents, not the public good, not the public interest, and not the common good but, the interests of a black constituency. Such an emphasis provided the ideational basis of the black power movement in the 1960s: "... the goal [should be] to build and strengthen the black community ... [which] must win its freedom while preserving its cultural integrity" (Carmichael & Hamilton, 1967, pp. 54–55). Twenty years later, an extensive community study of the nation's fourth-largest city closes by emphasizing precisely the same point:

> The key to future black civil rights victories and effective black political empowerment is the presence of a well-organized, independent, and highly disciplined community structure. This organized political structure must work to elect not only black candidates but also candidates sympathetic to its interests, to develop a plan of action (an agenda), and to work with its candidates and other representatives to convert agenda items into workable policy. Conversely, the absence of economic muscle or clout mitigates the development of disciplined black political organizations that are not bashful about maximizing political power. Too often blacks have gone to great lengths to assure their adversaries that they do not wish to take over but merely to participate in the decision-making process (Bullard, 1987, p. 137).

The persistence of the black subcommunity thesis and the resulting contesting strategies of community development emphasize the relevance of the racial bifurcation of community leadership to community development practitioners working in communities with sizable minority populations. That relevance points directly to the value of joint research between community development practitioners and university-based community researchers using reputational leadership surveys. Such surveys are valid diagnostic tools for analyzing the structure and dynamics of community power and can therefore potentially predict the likelihood of dissensus situations for specific community projects. Through their use, the community development practitioner gets an objective map of the leadership structure and can choose a strategy appropriate to the program being implemented, the groups affected, and the resources available.

This paper raises crucial issues for both community development theory and practice and illustrates the need for research replication in other communities with large minority populations. In-depth analyses of several community action programs should be added to these studies in order to examine the role of minority leadership in these programs and to analyze the models (consensus versus dissensus) and strategies (collaborative versus contesting) that characterize them. The outcomes of these projects, in terms of task acomplishment, the effects of such accomplishments on community structure, and, specifically, the community's capacity to deal with similar problems in the future should be examined. In addition, practitioners who have been involved in such programs need to be urged to publish their observations and findings.

REFERENCES

Alinsky, S. Community analysis and organization. *American Journal of Sociology* 46(6):
1941   797–808.
Alinsky, S. The war on poverty—political pornography. *Journal of Social Issues* 21(1):
1965   41–47.
Alinsky, S. *Reveille for Radicals.* Chicago: University of Chicago Press.
1969[1946]
Alinsky, S. Citizen participation and community organization in planning and urban
1970   renewal. Pp. 216–266 in F. M. Cos, J. L. Erlich, J. Rothman and J. E. Tropman (eds.), *Strategies in Community Organization.* Itasca, IL: F. E. Peacock.
Bonjean, C. M. Community leadership: A case study and conceptual refinement. *American Journal of Sociology* 68(6):672–681.
1963
Bullard, R. D. *Invisible Houston. The Black Experience in Boom and Bust.* College Station,
1987   TX: Texas A&M University Press.
Carmichael, S. & Hamilton, C. V. *Black Power.* New York: Vintage Books.
1967
Christenson, J. A. & Robinson, J. W., Jr. (eds.). *Community Development in America.*
1980   Ames, IA: Iowa State University Press.
Coser, L. A. *The Functions of Social Conflict.* Glencoe, IL: Free Press.
1971
Hunter, F. *Community Power Structure.* Chapel Hill, NC: University of North Carolina
1953   Press.
Hunter, F. *Community Power Succession.* Chapel Hill, NC: University of North Carolina
1980   Press.
Kaufman, H. F. Toward an interactional conception of community. *Social Forces* 38(1):
1959   8–17.
Miller, P. A. The process of decision-making within the context of community organization. *Rural Sociology* 17(2):153–161.
1952

Moreno, J. L. *The Sociometry Reader.* Glencoe, IL: Free Press.
1960
Pfautz, H. M. The power structure of the Negro sub-community: A case study and
1962 comparative view. *Phylon* 23(Summer):156–166.
Pfautz, H. M., Huguley, H. C. & McClain, J. W. Changes in reputed black community
1975 leadership, 1962–72. *Social Forces* 53(3):460–467.
Preston, J. D. The search for community leaders: A re-examination of the reputational
1969 technique. *Sociological Inquiry* 39(1):39–47.
Preston, J. D., Spiekerman, D. & Guseman, P. The identification of leadership in two
1972 Texas communities: A replication of the Bonjean technique. *Sociological Quarterly* 13(4):508–515.
Robinson, J. W., Jr. The conflict approach. Pp. 73–95 in J. A. Christenson and J. W.
1980 Robinson, Jr. (eds.), *Community Development in America.* Ames, IA: Iowa State University Press.
Ross, M. G. *Community Organization: Theory and Principles.* New York: Harper.
1955
Smelser, N. J. Social structure. Pp. 103–129 in N. J. Smelser (ed.), *Handbook of Sociology.*
1988 Beverly Hills, CA: Sage Publications.
Warren, R. L. *The Community in America.* 2d ed. New York: Rand McNally.
1978
Warren, R. L. & Hyman, H. H. Purposive community change in consensus and dis-
1966 sensus situations. *Community Mental Health Journal* 4(4):293–300.
Wilkinson, K. W. A field-theory perspective for community development research.
1972 *Rural Sociology* 37(1):42–52.

Caught in the Middle: Community Development Corporations (CDCs) and the Conflict between Grassroots and Instrumental Forms of Citizen Participation

Robert Mark Silverman

This article examines the role of citizen participation in community development corporations (CDCs). It is argued that CDCs are caught between two distinct forms of participation: instrumental participation that focuses on activities that support project and program activities of CDCs, and grassroots participation that focuses on expanding the role of citizens in local decision-making processes. A continuum based on these two forms of citizen participation is introduced. It is suggested that CDCs are often in the middle of the continuum where they must balance pressures to expand the scope of grassroots participation against the need to use citizen participation techniques to facilitate project and program implementation. The article is based on a series of in-depth interviews with the executive directors of CDCs in Detroit, Michigan. Recommendations growing out of the research focus on how the tendency toward conflicts between the instrumental goals of CDCs and the long-standing value of grassroots activism can be managed better.

INSTRUMENTAL AND GRASSROOTS PARTICIPATION

This article examines the role of citizen participation in community development corporations (CDCs). The purpose of the analysis is threefold. First, the analysis will be used to synthesize existing theories and develop a citizen participation continuum. Second, the data will be used to highlight the conflict between grassroots and instrumental forms of participation in Detroit's CDCs. Finally, I will discuss how the citizen participation continuum can be used by CDC executive directors, their staff, and others in the community development field to expand the scope of citizen participation. These issues are of particular concern given the growing interest in implementing public policy through community-based organizations like CDCs, since they are considered to be more responsive to grassroots constituencies than institutions traditionally involved in the formulation and implementation of local public policy.

This article draws from past research to develop a continuum based on two distinct forms of citizen participation: instrumental and grassroots participation. This continuum encompasses two extreme forms of citizen participation, or ideal-types. It is argued that neither type of

---

Robert Mark Silverman is at the Department of Urban and Regional Planning and the Center for Urban Studies, University at Buffalo, New York. Phone: 716-829-2133 x227. E-Mail: rms35@ap.buffalo.edu. An early version of this article was presented at the 2002 Urban Affairs Association Annual Meeting in Boston, Massachusetts. The author would like to thank Ted Bradshaw, Laura Reese, Randy Stoecker, June Thomas, and three anonymous reviewers from the *Journal of the Community Development Society* for their comments on previous drafts of this article.

citizen participation in its pure form is found in an organization. Instead, the scope of citizen participation in most community-based organizations tends to fall at an intermediate point between the continuum's two extremes. The application of this continuum to the analysis of citizen participation in community-based organizations expands our understanding of how nonprofits and other groups shape the dialogue concerning neighborhood revitalization, and it provides those interested in expanding citizen participation with a tool to form strategies to expand grassroots participation in institutionally-oriented organizations. In essence, this study argues that it is important to understand where organizations fall along the citizen participation continuum in order to chart a course for expanding citizen input in community development activities.

It is further argued that CDCs represent a unique case to examine, since they are located near the center of the citizen participation continuum. This is a place where the conflict between instrumental and grassroots forms of participation is the most intense. In essence, CDCs are caught in the middle of participatory techniques used to facilitate program implementation and the long-standing value of grassroots activism. How CDCs respond to these pressures illuminates potential strategies to reform community-based organizations and enhance citizen participation in the future.

A Continuum of Citizen Participation

The citizen participation continuum helps to define the range of potential grassroots activities a community-based organization can pursue and the participatory outcomes they can produce. At one end of the citizen participation continuum is a type of participation identified as instrumental participation. This type of participation is argued to be task-oriented, with a focus on the completion of specific projects or programs in which a community-based organization is engaged. Accordingly, instrumental participation is predicted to be driven by community-based organizations that are administering specific projects and programs. Organizational representatives drive this type of participation in order to inform and consult residents about upcoming project and program activities.

At the other end of the citizen participation continuum is the type of participation identified as grassroots participation. It is argued to emerge in response to neighborhood threats, which residents perceive because of disinvestment, institutional neglect, or the development of noxious facilities in their communities. Unlike instrumental participation, grassroots participation is driven by local residents interested in increasing the visibility of perceived neighborhood threats and defending their turf. As a result, residents often take action when neighborhood threats are highly salient, and they utilize grassroots participation to influence the agenda of community-based organizations.

Conceptualizing citizen participation as a continuum that encompasses instrumental and grassroots forms has a number of theoretical and practical advantages. Viewing citizen participation through the prism of a continuum allows several dimensions of participation to be considered in an integrated framework. This approach to examining citizen participation also allows for greater integration of prior scholarship on citizen participation. The development of a continuum for citizen participation is an extension of past research that focused on categorizing voluntary organizations in terms of their functional orientation. Scholars who examine this dimension of participation argue that community-based organizations can be expressive or instrumental in nature (Gordon & Babchuk 1959, Jacoby & Babchuk 1963, Woodard 1986, Stoll 2001). From this perspective, expressive organizations like athletic clubs and fraternal societies focus on enhancing social and recreational opportunities for members, while instrumental organizations like political and civic associations tend to be task-oriented. Jacoby and Babchuk (1963), and more recently Stoll (2001), point out that these tendencies are part of an ideal type, and that many organizations serve both expressive and instrumental functions in society. Although this body of scholarship has focused on the orientation of various types of community-based organizations, other scholars, such as Smock (2004) have developed similar categories to describe the nature of community organizing and citizen participation within organizations.

Figure 1: The Citizen Participation Continuum

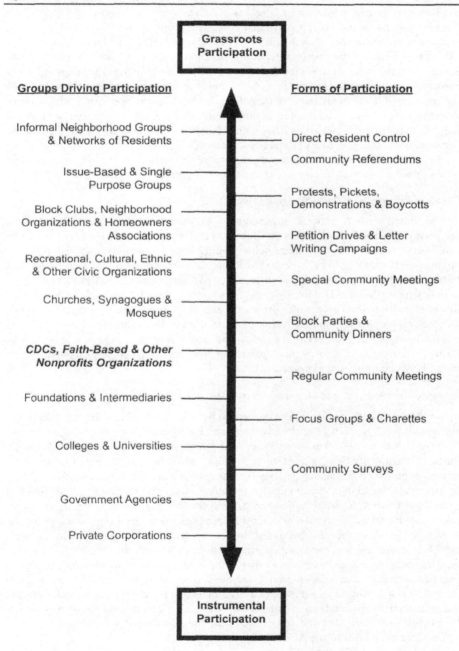

Groups Driving the Participation Process

The continuum introduced in this article begins to identify the types of organizations and groups that would be associated with various levels of instrumental and grassroots participation. In some respects, this approach builds on the work of Simonsen and Robbins (2000) who categorize citizen participation in relation to the types of organizations that sponsor it. They distinguish between participation sponsored by governmental and grassroots organizations. This distinction focused on power relations in the citizen participation process and on who sets the agenda of grassroots organizations. This distinction is developed further in Figure 1. On the left side of this figure, formal societal level organizations such as private corporations and government agencies are associated with instrumental participation, although informal parochial level organizations such as block clubs and informal neighborhood groups are associated with grassroots participation. In addition to predicting which types of organizations would be located at the extremes of the continuum, this framework predicts that organizations like CDCs would fall in an intermediate position along the continuum. In other words, community-based organizations and other nonprofits are predicted to face conflicting pressures to balance the necessity of using instrumental forms of citizen participation against demands for greater grassroots participation.

Forms of Participation Used by Organizations

As noted earlier, another advantage of viewing citizen participation through the prism of a continuum is that it allows several dimensions of participation to be considered simultaneously. Along with gaining greater insights into the types of organizations that would be expected to fall at different points of the continuum, this framework allows us to predict what forms of participation organizations would tend to use. This is illustrated on the right side of Figure 1. This figure places expert-driven forms of participation like survey research and charettes at the instrumental end of the continuum, while populist forms of participation like community boycotts and referendums fall at the grassroots end of the continuum. A number of intermediate forms of participation, such as block parties and letter writing campaigns, are predicted to fall between these two extremes.

Applying Citizen Participation Theory to the Continuum

At another level of analysis, prior conceptual frameworks for citizen participation can be elaborated upon by applying them to the citizen participation continuum. For example, Alinsky (1969) and Arnstein (1969) make seminal statements about the types of citizen participation found in community-based organizations. Alinsky discusses citizen participation in the context of grassroots organizing, arguing that true participation stems from the development of indigenous leadership, community-led initiatives, and confrontational tactics. Building upon these themes, Arnstein argues that participation often assumes less extreme forms, since it is shaped by the degree of control citizens have over local organizations and the institutions in which they are embedded. In her "ladder of citizen participation" Arnstein identifies several levels of participation that reflect the degree of control residents have over local agendas. In essence, she argues that without direct control over community-based organizations, participation is reduced to varying degrees of tokenism and manipulation. In the bullets below, Arnstein's ladder of citizen participation is elaborated upon and applied to the continuum. In this iteration, an extension of Arnstein's ladder is presented with grassroots forms of participation listed first, followed by instrumental forms of participation:

- Citizen Control of the Agenda
- Delegation of Power to Citizens

- Partnership with Citizens
- Citizen Advisory Role in Decision-Making
- Placation of Citizens
- Consulting Citizens
- Informing Citizens
- Therapy to Citizens
- Manipulation of Citizens

The integration of Arnstein's model with the continuum for citizen participation reveals additional nuances of the participation process. This extension of existing theory concerning participation allows connections to be drawn between organizational types, forms of citizen participation, and the scope of participation. By rotating the lens used to view citizen participation, one gains greater insights into how different dimensions of participation are interrelated.

Using the Continuum to Promote Change

When one considers each of the dimensions of citizen participation together, it becomes possible to imagine how social change can be promoted by emphasizing one end of the continuum over another. In essence, the citizen participation continuum provides organizations and groups with a road map for evaluating programs that promote change in society. The citizen participation continuum also helps organizations and groups understand the source of conflicts between different types of citizen participation. In this article, these issues are elaborated upon through an examination of the degree to which instrumental and grassroots forms of participation are manifested in a unique type of community-based organization, the CDC.[1] Through this discussion, conflicts between instrumental and grassroots participation will be identified and strategies to address them will be recommended.

CDCs and Citizen Participation

CDCs are ideal organizations to focus upon in this analysis, since they were initially envisioned to encompass physical redevelopment and community organizing[2] within the scope of their activities (Perry 1972, Perry 1987, Stoutland 1999, Peterman 2000). Some scholars believe that the neighborhood orientation and limited scale of CDCs act as inducements to expand collaborative activities at the grassroots level. For instance, Clavel, Pitt, and Yin (1997) argue for the implementation of federal and local urban policy through CDCs to promote a bottom-up approach to urban revitalization. Rubin (2000) expands upon this idea in his analysis of community-based organizations. He argues that nonprofit networks serve as a mechanism for infusing grassroots interests in the community development process. Similarly, Goetz and Sidney (1995) argue that CDCs are able to pursue activism through such networks.

Others are more cautionary in their assessment of the influence of community-based organizations on the local policy process. For instance, Gittell and Vidal (1998) indicate that successful networking and collaborative activities between CDCs and local government require the support of institutional actors. Bockmeyer's (2000) analysis of the Empowerment Zone (EZ) process in Detroit expands this critique. In this analysis, she argues that CDCs had little impact on the EZ process since they had fewer resources to draw from when compared to governmental and private sector organizations. Bockmeyer concludes that inequalities in the availability of resources led to less effective participation. It should be noted that Bockmeyer, as well as many of the others cited above, frame participation in the context of CDC activities in the policy process. Although this body of research contributes significantly to our understanding of the role that community-based organizations fill in inter-organizational relations, CDCs are treated as a proxy for citizens in the participation process.[3]

The issues identified by Vidal and Bockmeyer are developed further in other scholarship that focuses more directly on participation as it pertains to residents in communities where CDCs operate. In part, this critique has been informed by observations concerning the role of fiscal retrenchment on the evolution of CDCs. For instance, Vidal (1997) argues that the agendas of contemporary CDCs are being transformed by a decline in the level of resources available for community development. Similarly, Blakely and Aparicio (1990), Marquez (1993), and Silverman (2003) identify fiscal constraints associated with the institutional structures in which CDCs are embedded as potential impediments. On a broader scale, Swanstrom (1999) and Bockmeyer (2003) warn that changes in the structure of housing policy in the United States and the growing role of nonprofits in the delivery of community development projects and programs have led to a decrease in activism and advocacy at the local level. In response to funding barriers and other institutional changes, the manner in which CDCs have balanced physical redevelopment and community organizing needs has varied over time. For instance, Robinson (1996) indicates that CDCs reduced their emphasis on community advocacy and focused on service provision in reaction to funding constraints that emerged during the last two decades. Similarly, Stoecker (1997) argues that contemporary CDCs lack the capacity to manage both physical redevelopment and community organizing because of these constraints. In the wake of these concerns, scholars like Glickman and Servon (1998) have re-emphasized the need for citizen participation in CDCs, and organizations that fund CDCs have increasingly identified the need for community organizing and citizen participation (Sirianni & Friedland 2001, 62-63).

DATA AND METHODS

Given the scope and context in which participation has been discussed in past literature, this article proposes a method for interpreting citizen participation in community-based organizations. Specifically, the role of citizen participation in Detroit's CDCs will be examined in order to understand the tension between instrumental and grassroots participation better. This examination will be followed by a discussion of ways in which executive directors of CDCs, their staff, and others in the community development field can use this continuum to address the conflicts between these two forms of citizen participation in community-based organizations.

The data for this article come from a series of in-person interviews with executive directors of CDCs in Detroit. This approach to data collection was selected since executive directors serve as gatekeepers in the community development process. They are attuned to the daily operations of a CDC, and they determine the degree to which an organization will pursue citizen participation and advocacy activities. Given their position in the community development process, the perspective of executive directors is critical to understanding the rationale for how citizen participation is approached by CDCs.

Interviews were conducted between February 2001 and July 2001. During the interviews, informants were asked a series of open-ended questions about the institutional networks they accessed and the role of citizen participation in their organizations. The questions were drawn from an interview guide that consisted of 17 items and 22 probes. This research instrument focused on a core set of questions that related to the theoretical issues under examination. Of particular interest to this article were elements of the research instrument that focused on the role of citizen participation in these organizations and their decision-making processes. In addition to this information, data were collected concerning the demographic characteristics of each organization's staff. Each interview was administered at a given informant's organization during normal operating hours. The interviews ranged from 30 minutes to two hours in length. In addition, secondary data were collected from each of the organizations to supplement the interviews. These data included pamphlets, brochures, newsletters, annual reports, and other materials printed by the CDCs.

The larger study from which this research is drawn focuses on the structure of organizational networks and the scope of citizen participation in Detroit's CDCs. Detroit is of interest because it has a relatively large number of CDCs that target their services to low-income neighborhoods with sizable minority populations. In addition, all of the CDCs in this study focus on developing projects and programs in neighborhoods with built environments that have been impacted by decades of abandonment and physical decline. Therefore, factors related to community characteristics and location are controlled for in the research design. Similarly, factors related to the scope of CDC projects and programs are considered in the research design. For example, the CDCs examined in the study are engaged in community organizing, housing, neighborhood beautification, economic development, crime prevention, culture and the arts, youth and social programs, historic preservation, and workforce development.

Efforts were made to conduct interviews with all of the CDCs in the city to ensure that organizations with all types of program focuses were included in the study. To accomplish this, a systematic methodology employing grounded theory and theoretical sampling techniques were used during data collection and analysis to ensure representativeness such as those described by Glaser and Strauss (1967), and Strauss and Corbin (1998). In addition, executive directors of CDCs from the entire city were interviewed to ensure that unique attributes of specific neighborhoods did not distort the data. In total, a population of 23 CDCs was identified in Detroit. The executive director of each CDC was approached for an interview, and 21 of these individuals agreed to be interviewed. Several attempts were made to schedule interviews with the executive directors of the two remaining CDCs, however they were unavailable.

Characteristics of Detroit's CDCs

The characteristics of the CDCs that were examined are summarized in Table 1. Several dimensions of Detroit's CDCs are illuminated in this table. For example, the first and second element of Table 1 reports information concerning the race and gender composition of the executive directors and staff of Detroit's CDCs. Table 1 indicate that 71 percent of the CDC executive directors in the city were women and 72 percent of the staff in these organizations were women. In contrast, only 47 percent of Detroit's population was identified as female in the 2000 Census. Table 1 also indicates that 48 percent of the executive directors of CDCs in Detroit were African American, while 74 percent of the staff members of these organizations were African American. Yet, 82 percent of the population in the city was identified as African American in the 2000 Census.

Information pertaining to the tenure, geographic territory, and duration of leadership in CDCs is also reported in Table 1. This information provides some insights into the context in which these organizations operate. In general, Table 1 indicates that most of the CDCs in Detroit were formed after 1980, the period Stoutland (1999) associates with the third-generation of CDC growth. Table 1 also indicates that these CDCs focused on a relatively small geographic area, and they had stable leadership. These features have the potential to increase the likelihood of Detroit's CDCs being accessible to grassroots groups. In part, the combination of relatively new organizations with stable leadership raises the possibility for greater accessibility to residents and a heightened level of responsiveness to grassroots concerns. This potential is furthered since many of Detroit's CDCs have not been in place

Table 1: Characteristics of CDCs (N=21)

	Frequency	Percent
Executive Directors		
Gender:		
Female	15	71
Male	6	29
Race:		
Black	10	48
White	11	52
Staff		
Gender:		
Female	96	72
Male	38	28
Race:		
Black	99	74
White	27	20
Latino	4	3
Other	4	3
Year CDC Established		
1970 - 1979	2	10
1980 - 1989	8	38
1990 - 1997	11	52
Census Tracts in CDC Boundaries*		
1 - 5	14	67
6 - 10	1	5
11 - 15	3	14
16 or more	3	14
Years CDC Under Current Executive Director		
1 - 5	6	29
6 - 10	13	61
11 or more	2	9
Project and Program Areas of CDC**		
Community Organizing	20	95
Housing	17	81
Neighborhood Beautification	13	62
Economic Development	6	29
Crime Prevention	4	19
Culture and the Arts	4	19
Youth and Social Programs	4	19
Historic Preservation	2	10
Workforce Development	2	10

* This estimate is based on 2000 census tract boundaries.

** Each director identified two or more (ϕ=3.5) project and program areas focused on by their CDC.

long enough to have their grassroots focuses threatened by increased professionalism and institutionalization. However, these observations should be tempered somewhat, since the formation of some CDCs in Detroit has been influenced by local foundations and intermediary organizations that have helped to define the program and project areas of CDCs. Unless sponsoring organizations emphasize community organizing and citizen participation during the developmental stages of new CDCs, accessibility to grassroots groups is not guaranteed.

Finally, information concerning the project and program areas that CDCs focus on is reported in Table 1. These data indicate that each of the organizations focused on two or more project and program areas. On average, CDC executive directors indicated that their organizations were active in 3.5 project and program areas. Typically, a CDC would work on some aspect of community organizing, housing, neighborhood beautification, and another small project area. Notably, 95 percent of the executive directors indicated that their CDCs were engaged in some form of community organizing. This percentage clearly illustrates the conflict that CDCs face because of their position on the citizen participation continuum. These organizations face regular pressure to use instrumental forms of citizen participation when implementing projects and programs, while simultaneously facing demands to pursue grassroots community organizing.

Regardless of its scope, citizen participation was identified as a dimension of the activities of virtually all of the organizations in Detroit. Moreover, the identification of citizen participation by virtually all of the organizations is of interest, since Detroit's CDCs tended to be geographically concentrated. For example, Table 1 indicates that 67 percent of the organizations confined their activities to 1 - 5 census tracts. This concentration means that the typical CDC focused on a geographic area with a population that ranged from 1,320 to 6,600 persons. This estimate is based on the mean population ($\mu = 1,320$) for census tracts in the City of Detroit. This calculation was based on 2000 Census data from the STF1A file. The relatively parochial character of the geographic boundaries of most CDCs and the frequency of identifying community organizing as a core activity makes inquiry critical concerning the role of instrumental and grassroots forms of participation in these organizations.

Although the characteristics of CDCs in Detroit parallel those of CDCs nationally, some distinctions exist that are important to later parts of this analysis. For instance, the median staff size of CDCs in Detroit is four, although the most recent national census of CDCs reported a median staff size of six (National Congress for Community Economic Development 1999, p. 7). In terms of tenure, the median age of CDCs in Detroit was twelve years, while the median age of CDCs nationally was fifteen years (National Congress for Community Economic Development 1999, p. 7). In essence, the CDCs in Detroit are slightly newer and smaller than those identified at the national level. In addition, there is no national data reporting the gender and racial composition of CDC staffs. However, some emerging research indicates that local demographics and job cues influence the racial and gender composition of CDC staff (Silverman 2001, Gittell, Ortega-Bustamante & Steffy 2000, Silverman 2003). Despite these discrepancies, the program activities of CDCs in Detroit paralleled those identified by the National Congress for Community Economic Development (1999) and Stoutland (1999, p. 216) as characteristic of these organizations.

CITIZEN PARTICIPATION IN DETROIT'S CDCS

The executive directors of CDCs in Detroit identified community involvement as a component of their organizations' activities. At the most elementary level, each executive director considered their organization's designation as a "community development corporation" to be evidence of a grassroots orientation. As one executive director stated, "We're totally independent, a community development corporation, the word 'community' says it all." Others made similar observations. For instance, the executive director of a large CDC made the following observation.

If you call yourself a community development corporation, the most important word in that is "community." So if you really don't have the input or the investment of the people that live and work in the neighborhood, you might be a nonprofit, you might be doing wonderful work, but you're not really a community development corporation.

The need for some level of community input in project and program planning was identified by all of the CDC executive directors. However, views about the optimal level of community input varied across organizations. A small minority of executive directors, roughly ten percent, saw citizen participation as a "necessary evil." At the other extreme, roughly twenty percent of the executive directors had a broad commitment to expanding the scope of grassroots involvement. More typically, executive directors were instrumental in their approach to citizen participation, and they felt it was part of their organization's "operating procedures to do things that involve the community." Although there was no clear consensus on an optimal level of participation, most executive directors agreed that, at a minimum, citizens should be consulted before an organization put a new project or program in place.

Instrumental Goals of Citizen Participation

Consulting citizens served a number of pragmatic purposes. Paramount among them was the use of citizen participation in an instrumental manner to build support for projects and programs. For example, one executive director discussed how her organization increased its level of community outreach in response to neighborhood resistance to the CDC's proposed projects. When referencing this predicament, she remarked about the importance of citizen participation.

We [now] consult the community on a regular basis with regard to our development initiatives, because what we don't want to have happen is there's a project that we put together, investing time and money into it, and the neighborhood's opposed to it. It just doesn't make sense. It's an inefficient use of resources.

To this executive director, regularizing contact with residents was instrumental in keeping the development process on track. In this case, participation occurred at an intermediate point on the citizen participation continuum. This disposition toward citizen participation fits into Arnstein's (1969) conceptualization of citizen participation as a form of "tokenism," since the practice was adopted in an effort to placate residents. Despite pragmatic motives for increasing opportunities for citizen participation, the result was that the organization expanded its networks with local residents and neighborhood associations. More regularized contact between the CDC and residents improved the chances that residents could voice concerns to the executive director and could drive community action through the organization. However, since the focus of participation tended to be on the instrumental goals of the CDCs, only a small number of residents turned out for regular meetings and other events organized by CDCs.

During interviews, executive directors identified a number of modes of participation that were used to incorporate citizens into the planning and development process. Most of these modes of participation fell at an intermediate point on the citizen participation continuum. Among these activities, residents were invited to public meetings, asked to fill out surveys, and included in focus groups and charettes. A common motivation for organizing each of these activities was the connection between participation and the instrumental goals of the organizations. For example, one executive director pointed out, "We do call public meetings whenever we're moving forward on anything in housing." In other instances, CDC executive directors identified citizen participation as a useful tool for determining if their proposed projects and programs were marketable. For example, two executive directors described how small numbers of residents were included in focus groups to discuss floor plans for units in a proposed housing project. In other cases, CDC executive directors discussed how small groups of leaders from local churches and neighborhood-based organizations were consulted in an ad hoc manner. These impromptu focus groups served an advisory role in the planning process, and they were used as a proxy for more direct forms of citizen involvement in decision-making. During earlier stages of project development, CDC executive directors used citizen surveys to gather basic demographic information about their communities. This information was used to supplement grant applications and to determine if there were a potential market for specific housing and social services that were being developed for a community.

Blending Grassroots and Instrumental Goals?

In addition to using citizen participation as a tool to realize the instrumental goals and objectives of an organization, executive directors indicated that other forms of participation were used to promote a sense of community among residents. Again, these forms of participation fell at an intermediate point on the citizen participation continuum. Typically, this type of citizen participation was organized around block parties and community dinners. On the surface, these types of activities represented a diversion for residents and entailed few opportunities for grassroots involvement beyond eating and celebrating. When executive directors discussed block parties and community dinners, they characterized them as "social" events and not as a form of "activism." These events were considered to be popular among residents because they were "non-threatening" and often included "free food." In essence, block parties were small community fairs where CDCs would "bring in a moon walk for the kids to play in, get the barbecue pits out, do hot dogs and hamburgers, get the music playing, and get the volleyball nets up." Notwithstanding their recreational benefits, block parties and community dinners also assisted CDCs in achieving their instrumental goals and objectives. For this reason, these types of activities remain closer to the end of the citizen participation continuum representing instrumental forms of participation. For instance, one executive director made the following comment about how block parties fit into the broader goals and objectives of her organization.

> Sometimes there are people who close off the street, [open] the fire hydrants, and have a block party for the children, and that sort of thing. But, that's usually at the end of an activity that we've done, either a spring cleanup or at the end of a project that we've completed, and we're opening it up so that the neighbors can see what we've done before the people move in. That sort of thing.

In this way, CDCs were able to blend activities that promote social engagement with their instrumental goals and objectives. A variety of other strategies complemented the use of block parties and community dinners to entertain residents while informing them of a CDC's accomplishments and future plans for a community. For example, CDC executive directors organized raffles, garage sales, and annual dinner meetings designed to attract residents to venues where they could get information about the organization and its activities. As one executive director put it, "They're coming because there's something in it for them, so we have to hook-em." Once citizens were pulled in with food and entertainment, they could be informed and consulted via a circumscribed participation process. Although these activities entailed some elements of grassroots involvement, they were still driven by CDCs' instrumental goals, and they concentrated on informing and consulting residents. This type of participation differs from other forms that emanate from the grassroots level.

WICKED PROBLEMS AND INCREASED TENSION BETWEEN GRASSROOTS AND INSTRUMENTAL PARTICIPATION

Citizen participation driven by CDCs tended to focus on instrumental goals and objectives. Moreover, meetings and events organized by CDCs for such purposes tended to have erratic attendance. Typically, a core group of residents and institutional stakeholders would interact with a CDC on a regular basis. Despite their focus on instrumental goals and modest turnout, the executive directors pointed out that these same activities were not totally under their control since the activities inevitably exposed them to unanticipated community concerns. For example, executive directors indicated that residents often voiced concerns about neighborhood conditions during focus groups, community dinners, and through community surveys. In addition, CDC executive directors were made aware of grassroots concerns through direct contacts from residents, informal exchanges at community events, and interactions with representatives of block clubs, homeowners associations, local churches, and other neighborhood-based organizations. Many of these concerns focused on parochial issues. For example, residents would identify property abandonment, pollution, illegal dumping, trash pick-up, prostitution, topless bars, and other issues as highly salient. CDC executive directors described these issues as "wildcards," since they often focused on things that were outside of their organizations' core project and program focus.

The types of issues that CDC executive directors referred to as wildcards were synonymous with what Roberts (2004) identifies as "wicked problems." According to Roberts, wicked problems involve threats to the quality of life in communities, hard questions about budget cuts, citing of noxious facilities, pollution remediation, and other questions that relate to the equitable distribution of costs and benefits in society. Roberts argues that these problems manifest themselves with increased frequency in modern society, and as a result, calls to address them have proliferated from the grassroots. Roberts maintains that it is necessary for society to expand the level of participation and provide residents and disenfranchised groups with greater access to decision-making processes in order to address wicked problems. In essence, these types of problems are a source of pressure to adopt grassroots forms of participation identified on the citizen participation continuum.

When confronted with wildcard or "wicked" issues, executive directors of CDCs attempted to leverage organizational resources in order to assist residents and neighborhood-based groups. For instance, one executive director commented about her organization's efforts to address residents' complaints about accumulated trash on local streets.

> Where are we going to get the resources so it doesn't look so trashy? That was important to them. On our list of development priorities, that probably isn't on the top of the list. Frankly, because people just tend to dirty it back up. But, nonetheless, because of the importance to the community, we put a lot of time and effort toward it, because that's what they want to do, and so it's like, "okay." And, it's a good thing and we have some expertise we can blend to the process and give them some resources. So we do that with all of them, and we try to follow their agenda to the extent possible.

The degree to which CDCs were responsive to grassroots concerns was, in part, restricted by their emphasis on other project and program areas. In addition, the organizations had limited resources and staff, which reduced their ability to manage a number of issues simultaneously. However, CDCs were often caught off-guard by grassroots issues that seemed to emerge spontaneously. When residents were able to voice their concerns about salient issues, CDCs attempted to broker remedial solutions to these problems to clear the way to resume work on their core projects and programs. These solutions tended to apply forms of participation that were in an intermediate position on the citizen participation continuum, rather than moving the organization toward more grassroots-oriented forms of participation.

Bringing Grassroots Problems into the Fold

CDC executive directors identified a number of times in which their organizations were drawn into issues by groups of residents who had "banned together" for protection against threats to the neighborhood. In some cases, the CDCs placated these groups by supporting them "in name" without committing organizational resources to resolve problems. In other cases, they temporarily diverted staff and funding to assist community groups. For example, one executive director discussed how his CDC ended up joining a coalition to keep unwanted businesses out of a community.

> The community got together on a gas station someone wanted to build in the neighborhood, but the community didn't want them to build it. The government, well it just so happened that they had to rezone it, and if they didn't have to rezone it, they could have built it without

coming to the community. But because they had to rezone it, then the community was notified and the community [got] united [and went] down to the government and protested the building of this gas station . . . Well, we help them and we worked together. They could have done it by themselves, but we're glad to be there to be alert to the situation, and we came in and organized the group, by joining the community group.

There were other examples of CDCs' agendas being captured by groups organized at the grassroots level. For instance, other executive directors described how their organizations had become involved in local grassroots efforts to address water pollution, factory emissions, topless bars, and prostitution. In most cases, CDCs agreed to assist with grassroots concerns since they shared a mutual interest in removing a specific threat from a community, or because a particular concern dovetailed with existing CDC activities. For example, one executive director pointed out that her organization was able "to be activist" when residents voiced concerns about prostitution since the problem threatened the CDC's efforts to promote neighborhood revitalization, and it fit into an existing neighborhood watch program. However, the CDC's activism did not eclipse existing program activities. When asked about specific things the CDC did to combat prostitution in the community, the executive director responded, "We've had the vice squad come into our neighborhood meetings a couple of times." Despite the interest in incorporating some grassroots concerns into a CDC's agenda, organizations remained focused on instrumental approaches to addressing community problems that were within the domain of existing program activities. In this way, organizations were able to respond to grassroots concerns by drawing residents into instrumental forms of participation that were in an intermediate position on the citizen participation continuum.

CAUGHT BETWEEN INSTRUMENTAL AND GRASSROOTS PARTICIPATION

The dilemma of being caught between instrumental and grassroots approaches to addressing community concerns was clearly articulated by the executive director of a large CDC in a discussion of her organization's strategy for dealing with community protests about the closing of a local hospital. In this case, resident activism grew out of community meetings initiated by the CDC to discuss the organization's strategy for reusing the site where the hospital was located. Residents who disagreed with the CDC's strategy decided to pursue a different course of action and to protest the closing of the hospital. In the following passage, the executive director describes how her organization was caught between the grassroots activities of this group of community activists and the CDC's instrumental goals.

When the campus of General Hospital shut down, up here on Southeast Street, the residents we were working with, their agenda was to protest the closing of the campus. They were angry, and they needed to be angry. And their decision was, they were going to create a series of actions, organizing actions, to embarrass the owners of that campus for not trying to keep it open. The analysis of our board and staff was that the campus was closing no matter what anyone said, and we needed to simultaneously make sure that the reuse of the campus met the priorities of the residents. So once again, you had a situation where potentially there was schizophrenia. Our organizers were helping residents conceive of organizing actions to protest the closing and trying to get the owners of the campus to change their minds, while our development staff was working to influence how the campus was going to be reused. At one point in time the health system that owned the campus came to me as said, "will you call those people off," meaning the residents that were organizing. What we said to them was, "if you want to send that message, you have to talk directly to the residents, because we don't control the residents' agenda. Now if you want to talk to the development staff about the reuse of the campus that's fine, but we are not going to be the intermediary for you to tell the residents to go away, it's not our choice." So there's another potential conflict. So, sometimes it creates that kind of dichotomy.

The multiple roles that the CDC assumed during the conflict over the hospital closure illustrate how organizations are caught in the middle of conflicting demands for instrumental and grassroots participation. However, this type of organizational "schizophrenia" is not always easy to manage. In this case, the CDC was able to pursue instrumental goals and negotiate with the hospital while it supported residents engaged in grassroots activism. The CDC benefited from this type of positioning since it was able to form alliances with all groups that engaged in the dispute over the hospital closure. Maintaining multiple alliances gave the CDC an advantage when negotiating with the hospital; however, it also compromised the organization's ability to speak for protesters at the grassroots level.

Although the CDC's community organizers were in a position to give aid and comfort to protesters at the grassroots level, the organization's focus remained in the hands of its development staff. In the long-run, instrumental goals prevailed, and the immediate assistance the CDC provided to residents involved in local activism was not linked to a more comprehensive community-organizing strategy focused on expanding grassroots control of the organization's agenda. In essence, participatory strategies used by the organization remained at an intermediate position on the citizen-participation continuum. This outcome was linked to a number of interrelated factors. For example, the CDC had to walk a fine line between the protesters and its own organizational goals, since open opposition to residents would raise questions about the legitimacy of the CDC. In addition to being involved at the community level, this organization was embedded in a number of institutional and professional networks that reinforced instrumental goals. The CDC was dependent on governmental and nonprofit funding for its survival. It had to appear cooperative in the eyes of local interests in the public and private sectors. And, it needed to appear professional in the eyes of peers in the community development field. Moreover, the organization was divided internally between a small group of community organizers and the larger development staff that dealt with the CDC's core projects.

In spite of these apparent shortcomings and institutional constraints, the degree to which this CDC was able to manage the conflict between instrumental and grassroots participation was both praiseworthy and somewhat anomalous. Unlike other organizations, this CDC benefited from a high degree of organizational capacity. As a result, this organization was able to assign full-time staff members to work with residents engaged in local activism, while maintaining a fully staffed development team. In contrast, most CDCs in Detroit lack the organizational resources to pursue community development projects and local activism simultaneously. Subsequently, smaller CDCs tended to curtail community organizing activities in order to maintain existing projects and programs. Constraints linked to organizational capacity and the institutional structure that CDCs were embedded in, led to a heavier emphasis on instrumental forms of citizen participation.

NEXT STEPS—EXPANDING GRASSROOTS PARTICIPATION

Participation in Detroit's CDCs had a tendency to fall at an intermediate point along the citizen participation continuum. These organizations tended to use intermediate forms of participation such as focus groups, block parties, and regular community meetings to involve residents in organizational decision-making processes. This participation was primarily aimed at informing and consulting residents about core activities of CDCs. The purpose of such participation was to comply with institutional mandates for participation, and to facilitate project planning, resource mobilization, and task completion. In instances where grassroots issues were brought to the attention of CDCs, there was a tendency to reframe them in the context of an organization's instrumental goals. In the short-term, demands for grassroots participation were balanced with instrumental participation. In the long-term, CDCs returned to an intermediate position on the citizen participation continuum.

In order for CDCs and organizations like them to move in the direction of institutionalizing greater grassroots participation, two fundamental changes must occur. First, local nonprofits must become more proactive in their efforts to promote grassroots participation. In essence, more resources and time must be committed to community-organizing and capacity-building. Second, this renewed emphasis on community-organizing and capacity-building must be reinforced with stronger institutional mandates for grassroots participation in the policy process. In other words, foundations, government agencies, and funding intermediaries need to increase funding levels for community-organizing and capacity-building activities. These institutions also need to require such activities as a condition to receive resources for project and program implementation. Strengthening external mandates for community-organizing and capacity-building activities will reinforce the long-standing value of grassroots participation within CDCs and other community-based organizations.

It should be noted that many of the reasons that CDCs do not pursue strategies for grassroots participation more aggressively are linked to limited organizational capacity. In large part, limited organizational capacity stems from the institutional structures in which CDCs are embedded. Consequently, the success of efforts to expand grassroots participation in CDCs and other community-based organizations will be heavily influenced by the creations of new mandates for participation and strengthened supporting structures in institutions that provide these nonprofits with resources. Calls for such reforms have come from scholars like Dreier (1996) who argues for intermediaries to place greater emphasis on supporting community-organizing and advocacy efforts in local nonprofits.

If it is backed with resources and mandates, the citizen participation continuum can assist efforts by local nonprofits and larger institutional actors to develop mechanisms to expand grassroots decision-making in the community development process. This continuum can be particularly useful to organizations like CDCs, in which citizen participation falls somewhere between purely instrumental and purely grassroots forms. For instance, the citizen participation continuum can be used by such organizations to identify a broader spectrum of groups to include in collaborative partnerships. Expanding the role of grassroots organizations in such partnerships can cultivate a more conducive environment for enhanced participation. Likewise, the citizen participation continuum can be used by CDCs and similar organizations to identify grassroots forms of participation that are compatible with empowering residents and expanding the scope of citizen control in decision-making.

The need for a more systematic focus on capacity-building and grassroots participation in community-based organizations is linked to the increased frequency of problems that Roberts (2004) labeled as "wicked." In the urban and rural communities where CDCs are located, the prevalence of these problems calls for expanded grassroots participation in local agenda-setting and decision-making. Despite the intensification of these problems, most CDCs remain small in size and limited in capacity. For instance, most of Detroit's CDCs had small staff and limited capacity, and they were relatively new organizations. These characteristics mirrored national trends in CDCs (National Congress for Community Economic Development 1999). At the same time, CDCs in Detroit and CDCs nationally focused on small geographic areas with identifiable populations and articulated an interest in making community-organizing a central focus of their activities. With added institutional support, CDCs can help to expand the scope of grassroots participation in society.

The citizen participation continuum provides CDCs and other community-based nonprofits with a road map for evaluating projects promoting change in society. It also provides larger institutions with a framework from which to develop policies and programs that are supportive of expanded citizen control in local decision-making processes. If used by local nonprofits and larger societal institutions in unison, the continuum could become a powerful tool to develop strategies for expanding the range of groups in local agenda-setting and decision-making, selecting grassroots forms of participation, setting the goals of participation strategies, and evaluation of participation in decision-making processes.

NOTES

1 In this analysis, CDCs are defined as community-based nonprofit organizations that focus on various combinations of activities related to community development, community organizing, affordable housing development, social service delivery, and other programs that are designed to assist low-income communities. Three important characteristics tend to set CDCs apart from other nonprofits that deliver similar programs and services. First, CDCs focus their activities within geographic boundaries that encompass distinct neighborhood boundaries within a larger municipality or jurisdiction. Second, CDCs attempt to adopt a multidimensional or comprehensive approach to community development. Rather than focusing on a single program or service area, CDCs attempt to implement programs and projects that address multiple community needs. Finally, CDCs anchor their organizations' legitimacy on the principle that they are accessible to residents. Consequently, community organizing and citizen participation are considered key components to the successful achievement of organizational goals.

2 For the purposes of this article, community organizing encompasses activities that focus on empowering residents and cultivating grassroots leadership. As a result, community organizing would go beyond social engagement and activism focused on accomplishing the short-term objectives of a community-based organization. In addition to activism, community organizing would promote the long-term goal of expanding the degree to which residents control the agenda and decision-making processes of community-based organizations.

3 Past scholarship has identified the role of residents' organizations, neighborhood institutions, and community-level agencies as a source of grassroots participation in the policy process. These works site incidences in which representatives from such organizations provide communities with a voice in broader policy debates. This article takes a more micro approach to examining participation within such organizations. This approach is adopted to determine if residents and individuals in the communities where such organizations operate have access to them. The underlying question of this analysis focuses on the degree to which community-based organizations are accessible to residents in the communities that they serve.

REFERENCES

Alinsky, S. (1969). *Reville for Radicals*. New York: Vintage Books.
Arnstein, S. R. (1969). "A Ladder of Citizen Participation." *Journal of the American Institute of Planners*, 35(4), 216-224.
Blakely, E. J. & Aparicio, A. (1990). "Balancing Social and Economic Objectives: The Case of California's Community Development Corporations." *Journal of the Community Development Society*, 21(1), 115-128.
Bockmeyer, J. L. (2000). "A Culture of Distrust: The Impact of Local Political Culture on Participation in the Detroit EZ." *Urban Studies*, 37(13), 2417-2440.
Bockmeyer, J. L. (2003). "Devolution and the Transformation of Community Housing Activism." *The Social Science Journal*, 40, 175-188.
Clavel, P., Pitt, J., & Yin, J. (1997). "The Community Option in Urban Policy." *Urban Affairs Review*, 32(4), 435-458.
Dreier, P. (1996). "Community Empowerment Strategies: The Limits and Potential of Community Organizing in Urban Neighborhoods." *Cityscape*, 2(2), 121-159.
Gittell, M., Ortega-Bustamante, I., & Steffy, T. (2000). "Social Capital and Social Change: Women's Community Activism." *Urban Affairs Review*, 36(2), 123-147.
Gittell, R., & Vidal, A. (1998). *Community Organizing, Building Social Capital as a Development Strategy*. Newbury Park: Sage Publications.
Glaser, B. G., & Strauss, A. L. (1967). *The Discovery of Grounded Theory: Strategies for Qualitative Research*. New York: Aldine De Gruyter.
Glickman, N. J., & Servon, L. (1998). "More than Bricks and Sticks: Five Components of Community Development Corporation Capacity." *Housing Policy Debate*, 9(3), 497-539.
Goetz, E. G., & Sidney, M. (1995) "Community Development Corporations as Neighborhood Advocates: A Study of the Political Activism of Nonprofit Developers." *Applied Behavioral Science Review*, 3(1), 1-20.

Gordon, W., & Babchuk, N. (1959). "Typology of Voluntary Associations." *American Sociological Review*, 24, 22-29.

Jacoby, A., & Babchuk, N. (1963). "Instrumental and Expressive Voluntary Associations." *Sociology and Social Research*, 47(4), 461-471.

Marquez, B. (1993). "Mexican-American Community Development Corporations and the Limits of Direct Capitalism." *Economic Development Quarterly*, 287-295.

National Congress for Community Economic Development. (1999). *Coming of Age: Trends and Achievements of Community-based Development Organizations*. Washington, D.C.: National Congress for Community Economic Development.

Perry, S. E. (1972). "Black Institutions, Black Separatism, and Ghetto Economic Development." *Human Organization*, 31(3), 271-278.

Perry, S. E. (1987). *Communities on the Way: Rebuilding Local Economies in the United States and Canada*. Albany: State University of New York Press.

Peterman, W. (2000). *Neighborhood Planning and Community-Based Development: The Potential and Limits of Grassroots Action*. Thousand Oaks, CA: Sage Publications.

Roberts, N. (2004). "Public Deliberation in an Age of Direct Citizen Participation." *American Review of Public Administration*, 34(4), 315-353.

Robinson, T. (1996). "Inner-city Innovator: The Non-profit Community Development Corporation." *Urban Studies*, 33(9), 1647-1670.

Rubin, H. J. (2000). *Renewing Hope within Communities of Despair: The Community-Based Development Model*. Albany: State University of New York Press.

Silverman, R. M. (2001). "Neighborhood Characteristics, CDC Emergence and the Community Development Industry System: A Case Study of the American Deep South." *Community Development Journal*, 36(3), 234-245.

Silverman, R. M. (2003). "Progressive Reform, Gender, and Institutional Structure: A Critical Analysis of Citizen Participation in Detroit's Community Development Corporations (CDCs)," *Urban Studies*, 40(13), 2731-2750.

Simonsen, W., & Robbins, M. D. (2000). *Citizen Participation in Resource Allocation*. Boulder, CO: Westview Press.

Sirianni, C., & Friedland, L. (2001). *Civic Innovation in America: Community Empowerment, Public Policy, and the Movement for Civic Renewal*. Berkeley: University of California Press.

Smock, K. (2004). *Democracy in Action: Community Organizing and Urban Change*. New York: Columbia University Press.

Stoecker, R. (1997). "The CDC Model of Urban Redevelopment: A Critique and an Alternative." *Journal of Urban Affairs*: 19(1), 1-22.

Stoll, M. A. (2001). "Race, Neighborhood Poverty, and Participation in Voluntary Associations." *Sociological Forum*, 16(3), 529-557.

Stoutland, S. E. (1999). Community Development Corporations: Mission, Strategy, and Accomplishments. Pp. 193-240 in *Urban Problems and Community Development*, edited by Ronald F. Ferguson and William T. Dickens. Washington, D.C.: Brookings Institute Press.

Strauss, A., & Corbin, J. (1998). *Basics of Qualitative Research: Techniques and Procedures for Developing Grounded Theory, Second Edition*. Thousand Oaks, CA: Sage Publications.

Swanstrom, T. (1999). "The Nonprofitization of United States Housing Policy: Dilemmas of Community Development." *Community Development Journal*, 34, 28-37.

Vidal, A. C. (1997). "Can Community Development Re-Invent Itself?: The Challenge of Strengthening Neighborhoods in the 21st Century." *Journal of the American Planning Association*, 63(4), 429-438.

Woodard, M. D. (1986). "Voluntary Association Membership Among Black Americans: The Post-Civil Rights Era." *The Sociological Quarterly*, 28, 285-301.

Section 3
Healthy and Resilient Communities
Introduction

Well-being of communities is deeply and intricately connected with community development. It is difficult to imagine that well-being at the collective or community level can be achieved without effective and just practices in community development. One definition of community well-being is that it is a "wide-ranging concept encompassing multiple dimensions related to people and their communities. .... (it) is also thought of as an overarching concept with related conceptions such as happiness, quality of life and community development often being mentioned jointly or interchangeably" (Phillips & Wong, 2017, p. xxix). Further, individual well-being can be considered to arise "in the context of society and social collectivity (McGregor, 2007, p. 318). This sounds very similar to the foundations of community development as social change and improvement.

Community well-being typically describes a state of conditions, or assessment of health and related aspects. It is not yet a discipline or a practice, per se, as is community development. At the same time, there is much interest in connecting the two areas of inquiry around community well-being and community development. As noted in this section, health and resilience both are domains that are garnering much more attention as reflected in scholarship and practice.

This section provides seven articles that explore domains of health and resilience in the context of community development. For example, the healthy communities approach emerged in the 1990s as a relevant and connected concept alongside community development. It has since grown in use within community development and vice versa. Public health programs have begun to incorporate more conceptions of community development and community well-being within the context of communities of place. There are other resources within *Community Development*, including a special issue on health with Volume 42, Number 2. These, along with growing numbers of articles, continue to serve as ways to promulgate and encourage stronger recognition of the links between overall collective health with that of community development practice and application.

The first selection in this section is by Lachapelle, Dunnagan, and Bird (2011) who discuss issues of men's health in "Applying Innovative Approaches to Address Health Disparities in Native Population: An Assessment of the Crow's Men's Health Projects." The authors found that by using a very participatory approach for the research, trust, and partnership building enabled more addressing of community needs and health problems. The community-based participatory research approach was endorsed by tribal leaders and elders, with data gathered via community meetings, focus groups, surveys, outreach, and related activities to generate support. The authors state that "the importance of genuine partnerships in health research and applied interventions is critical, particularly when addressing health concerns with a population that has a long history of neglect or mistreatment in terms of both health and academic research" (p. 252). This community development approach enabled building of relationships to achieve greater awareness of health issues.

Also in 2011, Hutson and Wilson examined racial health disparities. Racial and ethnic health disparities exist in communities, contributing negative impacts for economically disadvantaged and minority populations. The authors consider community and regional development strategies for improving situations of health disparities for those most impacted. They found that linking local community development efforts to larger macro-level metropolitan regional strategies can provide more holistic approaches for potential solutions. Their work centers on bridging gaps, and states a comprehensive framework is needed:

> that considers ecologic features of the built and social environment to enhance community development in unserved and underserved communities hurt by health disparities. .... (the) approach must focus on understanding how context, place, and local socioenvironmental conditions impact the health of populations and individuals. (p. 491)

Such place-based strategies build on strengths of community development practices while fostering better health outcomes for residents.

In 2003, Shields, Stallmann, and Deller (2003) examine impacts of retirees as a community development strategy for rural communities. The authors found that assumptions about increased costs for communities that pursue retirees did not hold – "while total healthcare costs increase because of population increase, we find no evidence to support the gray peril health care concern for local governments" (p. 101). They considered various groups of retirees by age and income and found all groups have positive economic benefits for the case study region. This finding that retirees provided positive net fiscal impacts for local governments is significant for community development practice, especially those that are pursuing development of retirement communities or attracting retirees to their areas.

"Bowling Alone but Online Together: Social Capital in E-Communications" looks at the influence of social media on community. Scott and Johnson (2005) provide a review of online communities, investigating relevance for community development theory and practice. This article was published rather early in the advent of social media. The authors found that these online communities were providing users with learning tools as well as ways for collective action to be actualized via extensive interaction (and notably, at the time, quite civil).

It is intriguing to see the nascent idea emerging around use of online communities to advance collective action and community development. Scott and Johnson propose online communities as offering "important opportunities to advance community development research—in terms of both theory and method. Community development scholars can pursue both qualitative and quantitative studies of the design, use, and effects of online communities for collective action" (pp. 22–23). During the intervening 15-year time period since this article was written, there is more use of online communities, although some of the intent and direction has certainly changed. Now, it would be hard to imagine not using online tools or access to individuals and groups for enabling community development research.

Resilience is a concept that emerged a bit later. Zautra, Hall, and Murray (2008), in "Community Development and Community Resilience: An Integrative Approach," explore ideas of how to quantify indicators of quality of life and community well-being to improve successes and understanding. They found the most important aspect to include is identification of an underlying model to guide community's work for resilience. The selection of meaningful indicators is dependent upon several factors including a process that stimulates meaningful involvement of community stakeholders, but the single most important is the identification of an underlying model to guide the work. Relationships between types of indicators as well as community approaches are explored, and the case of Phoenix, Arizona, is used. They state that:

> webs of social interconnection determine the extent of civic engagement and social capital. From the perspective of resilience, a key domain of interest is how communities further the capacities of their constituents to develop and sustain well-being, and partner with neighboring communities of location and interest to further the aims of the whole region. (p. 139)

Resilience continues to grow in importance, and this earlier work provides some contextual grounding for connecting community development and resilience, supporting use of indicators for building community relationships.

A more recent exploration of the topic by Markantoni, Steiner, and Meador (2019) is entitled, "Can Community Interventions Change Resilience? Fostering Perceptions of Individual and Community Resilience in Rural Places." Active community participation is a focus of this work, with governments taking on roles as facilitators to enable community members to be more active in improving resilience in their areas. The authors conclude that

> the process of moving toward resilient communities seems to require a set of appropriate mechanisms at the local level with the right support (financial and others) to build the capacity that enables communities to act and successfully complete their community projects. (p. 252)

They found that in order to enhance the resilience of rural communities, meaningful community participation must be present, even for those members that may be isolated or less accessible.

The section is concluded with a classic reading from 1987, "Healthy Communities: The Goal of Community Development" by Lackey, Burke, and Peterson that provides an overview of why health, at the community level, is crucial. Community health is proposed as the goal of community development and includes a rationale for why this should be attempted. Additionally, the authors present implications of the use of community health to measure program success.

Health is also considered as values and attitudes. The authors explain why it is critical to connect community health and development:

> The adoption of the concept of community health as a goal of community development has major implications for the profession. It implies that the success of a community development effort would be measured, in large part, by the extent to which the attributes of community health have been incorporated within a community. (p. 12)

They further explain that by people becoming vested in the health of their communities, they will better serve and protect it.

This is a wide-ranging section but connected by issues around health, healthy communities, and resilience or the ability to recover from shocks to communities (whether of human or natural origin). After examining these selections, there may be little doubt that these domains of health and related considerations are deeply interwoven into the well-being and development of communities.

REFERENCES

Lachapelle, P.R., Dunnagan, T. & Bird, J.R. 2011. Applying innovative approaches to address health disparities in native populations: An assessment of the Crow Men's Health Project. *Community Development* 42(2): 240–254.

McGregor, J.A. 2007. Research well-being: From concepts to methodology. Pp. 316–355 in I. Gough and J.A. McGregor (eds.), *Well-Being in Developing Countries: From Theory to Research*. New York: Cambridge University Press.

Phillips, R. & Wong, C. 2017. *Handbook of Community Well-Being Research*. Dordrecht, The Netherlands: Springer.

Scott, J.K. & Johnson, T.G. 2005. Bowling alone but online together: Social capital in e-communities. *Community Development* 36(1): 9–27.

Shields, M., Stallmann, J.I. & Deller, S.C. 2003. The economic and fiscal impacts of the elderly on a small rural region. *Community Development* 34(1): 85–106.

Markantoni, M., Steiner, A. A. & Meador, J. E. (2019). Can community interventions change resilience? Fostering perceptions of individual and community resilience in rural places. *Community Development*, 50(2): 238–255.

Applying innovative approaches to address health disparities in native populations: an assessment of the Crow Men's Health Project

Paul R. Lachapelle*, Tim Dunnagan and James Real Bird

Using a Community-Based Participatory Research approach, the Crow Men's Health Project is a partnership between university researchers and men of the Crow Indian Reservation to address health disparities, particularly cancer risk, screenings and treatments. The objective in using this approach is to establish trust, share power, foster co-learning, and ultimately address community-identified needs and health problems. However, application within the context of Native American communities has only recently been studied with only a paucity of evaluative research on the quality and outcome of partnerships. This research details the accomplishments to date of this partnership. The findings and implications of the research illustrate the importance of establishing support by tribal leaders, recognizing the time commitment and potential for conflict with timelines, the significance of creating a trusting environment for health discussions, and the critical role of an Advisory Council to ensure the active participation of the community.

Introduction

Many public health issues, including the incidence of cancer, are significantly higher for Native populations in the United States than other minority populations. Nationwide, the Indian Health Service reports that American Indian men's life expectancy is 2.4 years less than the US all races population (Indian Health Service, 2006). The state of Montana has a significant Native population; American Indian men in Montana exhibit the highest cancer incidence rates compared to American Indian women and white men and women, and mortality from all cancers are higher for American Indian men than for white men (Montana Cancer Control Coalition, 2006).

This paper describes a new partnership called the Crow Men's Health Project, between researchers at Montana State University and members of the Crow Indian Reservation (Apsáalooke Nation) in southeastern Montana. An innovative approach called Community-Based Participatory Research (CBPR) has been

*Corresponding author. Email: paul.lachapelle@montana.edu

implemented to address general health issues for Crow men and specifically to increase the participation of adult men from the Crow Tribe in preventative health screenings, particularly prostate, testicular, and colorectal cancer. CBPR is widely-recognized as a promising strategy for conducting public health research because it emphasizes partnerships and has the potential to empower communities that wish to address their health disparities in a culturally-relevant manner. Consequently, our objective, at this early stage of research, is to apply a descriptive and exploratory research design using a CBPR approach, while also providing some preliminary evaluative and analytical perspectives of this new health initiative.

This community-based approach is innovative in terms of research design, data collection and analysis, and ultimately program implementation and evaluation since community members, tribal organizational representatives, and researchers are equal partners in all components and phases of the research process and outcome. The approach is critically relevant to improving public health disparities amongst this population, improving relations both on the Reservation and with the university research community, and holds a good chance of success because of the collaborative approach used to address various community health issues.

Overview of community-based participatory research

The central premise of CBPR is active collaboration and power sharing amongst partners to collectively address and defined issues. Community members, tribal organizational representatives, and researchers are equal partners in all components and phases of the research process and outcome. The active involvement of all community stakeholders including tribal leaders, elders, various clan interests, and youth, is critical to forming strong partnerships and ensuring the success of a project.

In many Indian contexts across the United States, and internationally, a lack of trust has developed as a result of research conducted without proper consent, or with ensuing hidden agendas, financial profiting, exploitation of the population being studied, or failure to follow-up with research findings. Investing time to build trust and mutual learning in partnerships is critical in any collaborative project, particularly in Native American communities where community members have had many negative experiences with researchers and research processes, resulting in a valid apprehension to engage in research (Christopher, Watts, Knows His Gun McCormick, & Young, 2008; Holkup et al., 2009). Developing trust and maintaining successful community-based health partnerships is dependant on sharing information, responsibilities, power, and funding equitably among partners (Beil, Evans, & Clarke, 2009; Strickland, 2006). Critical to successful CBPR is recognizing and being cognizant of the diversity of cultural values and norms that exist within and between native populations as sovereign tribal governments with distinct needs and issues (LaVeaux & Christopher, 2009). Of particular importance is establishing mechanisms for formal and informal tribal oversight from both a practical and ethical standpoint (Baldwin, Johnson, & Benally, 2009; Fisher & Ball, 2003).

The CBPR approach is widely-recognized as an efficacious strategy for conducting research with American Indians because it emphasizes collaboration and has the potential to empower communities to address health disparities in a culturally-relevant manner (Mail, Conner, & Conner, 2006). In this sense, the CBPR approach can provide remedial action to both historical and continuing experiences of exploitation (Christopher, 2005; Foster & Stanek, 2007; Potkonjak, 2004). The integration of academic perspectives and skills with local experience, knowledge and resources allows more useful and credible interpretation and use of methods and results. In addition, a CBPR approach can build community capacity through community members' participation in project implementation (Cargo & Mercer, 2008).

There are many broad principles of CBPR that have been applied in general health contexts (Israel, Eng, Schulz, & Parker, 2005; Minkler & Wallerstein, 2003). However, application within the context of Native American communities has only recently been studied (see for example, Baldwin et al., 2009; Burhansstipanov, Christopher & Schumacher, 2006; Fisher & Ball, 2003). To date, there is only a paucity of research on effective strategies in the context of Native American communities and few studies provide detailed insights or evaluate the quality and outcome of the partnerships (Christopher et al., 2008; Holkup, Tripp-Reimer, Salois, & Weinert, 2004). Applying this innovative approach to the Crow Reservation has already shown signs of success in terms of fostering mutual learning and building trust, both with the current project, and recent unrelated research initiatives.

Crow Men's Health Project history and objectives

Several years ago, a number of Crow men approached faculty at Montana State University about a project devoted to men's health disparities, after seeing great success with improved rates of cervical cancer screening among Crow women on the Reservation using "Messengers for Health" or lay health advisors (Watts, Christopher & Smith, 2005). Initial meetings were arranged amongst the authors and tribal community members to engage Crow men in in-depth conversations about health issues and social, economic and cultural barriers to improving health status and addressing health disparities among them.

The first Crow Men's Health Project meeting, held in October, 2007, was attended by tribal members and key leaders in the community including individuals from Little Big Horn College, Indian Health Service, and the Crow Tribe governing bodies. The group established a five-member Crow Men's Health Project Advisory Council made up of Crow tribal members. Funding was provided by the Center for Native Health Partnerships (CNHP), an Exploratory Center of Excellence funded by the National Center on Minority Health and Health Disparities located at Montana State University. The purpose of the CNHP is to fund projects that bring together Native American community members and academic researchers to establish trust, share power, foster co-learning, and examine and address community-identified needs and health problems.

The Advisory Council determined there were four objectives in the short-term that could be accomplished through the CNHP funding;

(1) Identify relevant Crow men's health topics,
(2) Obtain baseline survey data,
(3) Increase an awareness of health, and,
(4) Pursue future funding.

Each of the objectives is described in more detail below but a brief explanation is provided here. First, a series of community meetings and focus groups would be held to begin to identify central themes and relevant topics of the Crow men's health project. This was done by establishing trust and building relationships in a safe environment where personal issues could be brought forward, discussed, and debated through in-depth conversations on health issues of concern to men. Second, the Council felt it was important to establish or gather a coherent baseline dataset on Crow men's health issues through community-based surveys and historical data. Third, the Council felt that establishing an education and outreach component of the project would be critical. Last, the Council determined that a longer-term funding source needed to be identified and secured.

As a result of the community meetings and focus groups (detailed below), the Crow Men's Health Project Advisory Council determined that the focus of the project would be on the health topic of prostate, testicular and colorectal cancer and factors that could contribute to low preventative screening rates; topics that have been repeatedly raised and discussed at community meetings.

Background on Crow Reservation and Crow men's health

The Crow Indian Reservation (Apsáalooke Nation), the largest in Montana (approximately 2.3 million acres), is located in a high plains prairie and Rocky Mountains environment of south central Montana. Eighty-five percent of the Apsáalooke Nation speaks Crow as their first language, but nearly all adults are fully bilingual with English. There are approximately 12,300 enrolled members of the Apsáalooke Nation, of whom about 3800 are adult men. Of these, approximately 2500–3000 live on or adjacent to the Reservation where they are eligible for treatment at Indian Health Service. The 2000 US Census found 42% of Crow families living below poverty (compared to the US rate of 9.2%). The Bureau of Indian Affairs estimates the unemployment rate for the Reservation at 47% in 2005. Primary employers for the Reservation are the Crow Tribe, the Indian Health Service, the Bureau of Indian Affairs, and Little Big Horn Community College.

As with many residents of Montana, most communities on the Reservation are remote and isolated. The health care provided through Indian Health Service, tends to be overtaxed. Lung/bronchus, colorectal and prostate cancer are the most common cancers among Crow men, and cancer is the second most common cause of death, after heart disease (Montana Department of Public Health and Human Service, 2008). Most cancer researchers realize that a complete cancer picture does not exist for American Indians, and reported estimates almost assuredly are lower than actual rates (Swan & Edwards, 2003). Proportionately to Whites, the American Indian population in Montana drops precipitously after age 44 (Montana Cancer Control Coalition, 2006). Some of the greater mortality may be due to later stage at diagnosis with corresponding poorer prognosis. For some cancers, American Indians have a slightly poorer survival experience at each stage of diagnosis than Whites. This may be due to less access to treatment and follow-up care (Montana Department of Public Health and Human Services, 2008). The actual reasons for these disparities are not clear and additional research is needed to identify the specific causes for these differences, nevertheless, they exist.

Increased early screening could reduce cancer mortality rates among American Indian men. For example, colorectal cancer screening can reduce colorectal cancer mortality by at least 60% (CDC, 2009). However, early screening appears to be extremely uncommon, at least among Crow men. Furshong and Wamsley (2009) show a difference in 2006 endoscopy rates for American Indians and Whites in Montana of less than 40% to more than 50% respectively. Differences are similar for various prostate cancer tests. However, reliable data about screening rates for the Crow population are unavailable as datasets of Apsáalooke Nation population are not large enough to provide reliable findings on Crow men's cancer screening behaviors from the Montana Behavioral Risk Factor Surveillance System (Carol Ballew, Epidemiologist/Program Manager for the MT Cancer Surveillance and Epidemiology Program, personal communication, October 6, 2009).

The Indian Health Service keeps data about the number of individuals who have sought cancer screening, but there are many inadequacies in this record-keeping. First, the reported rates pertain only to a count of the men who have visited Indian Health Service clinics. Partin, Rith-Najarian, Slater, Korn, Cobb, and Soler (1999) note that Indian Health Service data tend to underestimate cancer incidence in American Indian populations because not all individuals seek medical care or use IHS when ill. Another challenge to accurate screening rates, at least at the Crow IHS clinic, is poor coding practices regarding reasons for visits and diagnoses (David Mark, M.D. IHS Crow Agency, personal communication, October 17, 2009). Underreporting is also known to be a problem, and misclassification of race also occurs at all levels of the health care process, from health care provider observation or inappropriate classification options, to how individuals choose to classify themselves (Hampton, Keala, & Luce, 1996; Montana Department of Public Health and Human Services, 2008). Therefore, valid baseline data related to Crow men health behaviors does not exist.

Despite the problematic data related to health behaviors, it is clear that many American Indian men are not receiving screening at recommended ages or intervals. A study by Rhoades (2003) found that although American Indian/Alaska Native (AI/AN) males' death rates exceeded those for AI/AN females, males contributed only 37.9% of outpatient visits, and only 47% of hospitalizations. He concludes that AI/AN males suffer inordinate lack of utilization of health care services. Consistent with the Montana Comprehensive Cancer Control Plan (2006-2011), the first step toward increasing compliance with the American Cancer Society Cancer Detection Guidelines is to identify barriers to screening accessibility and utilization, which may include cost, geographic location, cultural factors, uneven distribution of resources, or care choices that lack standardization. Consequently, a major focus of the current project has been to identify these barriers and culturally-appropriate methods to address them.

The Crow Tribe currently has public health programs dealing with other health problems (diabetes, obesity and drug abuse, in particular, meth awareness), but no programs address cancer generally, or men's cancer risks in particular. Rhoades (2003) recommends more attention should be given to cancer among AI/AN men middle-aged and older, and done in conjunction with interventions that consider poverty, loss of self-esteem, loss of traditional roles, and depression. Burhans-stipanov (1998) has written that community-based and community-driven cancer prevention and cancer control projects can and will work in Native American communities. The input from the tribe and resulting sense of urgency reinforce the intervention.

The Crow Men's Health Project takes a holistic, community-based approach to address cancer in the context of embracing, celebrating and affirming men's whole health, enhancing resources available to them (both information and material resources), and affirming both traditional and nontraditional men's roles relative to gatherings, men's activities and cultural traditions.

Findings and implications

While findings of the research are still in the early stages, there are some preliminary conclusions and implications that are beginning to surface. With regard to the four major objectives of the Advisory Council, findings and implications are offered and discussed.

Objective 1. Identify relevant Crow men's health topics

Through the funding provided through CNHP, the project research team (university faculty and Crow tribal members) initiated 14 community meetings using a focus group approach involving 220 Crow men of all ages at different locations on the Reservation while bringing in health experts and introducing health data from existing sources. Detailed notes were taken at all meetings and results were presented to the Advisory Council to synthesize the many topics covered and to corroborate findings. Among the issues identified by meeting attendees have been cancer, obesity, alcohol-related diseases, diabetes, mental illness and heart disease.

Through the focus group discussions, the Advisory Council decided to focus on the health topic of prostate, testicular and colorectal cancer as these topics were repeatedly raised and discussed at community meetings as urgent and under-represented in terms of health education and treatment. The central objective of the focus groups was the identification of various barriers to health, wellness and health prevention and treatment for Crow men. Collaboratively, through the focus group process, seven distinct themes were identified that influenced or served as barriers to good health and wellness for Crow men.

Theme 1. Non-traditional lifestyle

A common theme identified by Crow men at the focus groups was the relatively recent non-traditional lifestyle that seemed to permeate the tribe, particularly with young Crow men and youth. In particular, descriptions of non-traditional food containing high amounts of sugar and fat were seen to be readily available throughout the Reservation and over-used and abused. The high consumption of soda and candy and other fattening foods were often described and seen to be having a harmful and in some cases, lethal impact for men on the Reservation. Coupled with this was a non-active lifestyle augmented by such issues as television and video games and lack of interest in traditional activities such as hunting, horsemanship, and drum circles and dancing. Great concern was expressed, particularly by elders, of the rapid changes they had seen with the younger generation, in terms of general obesity rates, sedentary lifestyles, and general lack of interest in traditional cultural knowledge and practice.

Theme 2. Lack of role models

Many men recognized the need for effective role models (particularly male role models) on the Reservation. A common theme was the lack of men who could provide good examples of a healthy lifestyle. Reasons for the lack of role models were varied and complex but were generally centered on the fact that many men were moving away from the Reservation for educational and employment opportunities, resulting in the "brain drain" of some of the "best and brightest" of the population.

In addition, the deteriorating condition of the cohesive family unit was often cited as a barrier to effective role models on the Reservation with divorce and domestic violence described as creating a cascading generational affect for Crow men.

Apart from identifying these many barriers, the men also described the importance of "cues to action;" the people or conditions that might persuade them to obtain screening tests. Many men discussed tribal members who had died from cancer, and relatives who had had colorectal cancer and this in turn led to considerable discussion of the benefits of screening. The men identified the importance of having these types of conversations and the role of elders and others in influencing their health behaviors. For example, often cited was one's "clan uncle" that has responsibility to assist or promote healthy behaviors. Family members, especially women, were also perceived as having great potential to influence behavior.

Theme 3. Quality of care

A great deal of the focus group conversations centered on the poor quality of care available to Crow men, creating disincentive to use local health services. In particular, Crow men reported a strong aversion to utilizing Indian Health Service (IHS) because of their negative experiences (individually and collectively). The main details to emerge about the health services available to Crow men were issues of efficiency, the quality of care that resulted, and confidentiality.

This information was corroborated with personal communications with those working at IHS and through secondary data. For example, the available documented and anecdotal evidence suggests that, despite the existence of a specific health agency to serve them (e.g. IHS), in general, Reservation residents are receiving sub-par medical care (Dixon & Roubideaux, 2001). This is due in part to the fact that IHS consistently runs out of funds by April or May of each fiscal year (October through September), and subsequently for at least half of the year, only life-threatening conditions (death expected within 72 hours without care) are treated at the Crow clinic (Doug Moore, IHS-Billings medical director, personal communication, April 10, 2009). In addition, few Reservation residents have alternatives to utilizing IHS. If tribal members are found to have cancer, they will receive treatment through IHS Contract Health Service (essentially insurance coverage for illness not treatable at the local clinic), but IHS does not have adequate resources to provide many necessary preventative care services. Furthermore, an actuarial analysis found that the IHS budget provides only 55% of the necessary federal funding to assure mainstream personal health care services to American Indians (Indian Health Service, 2006).

In addition, IHS medical personnel have notoriously high turnover rates, meaning that most Indian patients do not have opportunities to develop a personal relationship and rapport with a family doctor over time. In general, individuals obtain screening in part because their family physicians recommend it during a regular check-up. Regular check-ups and family physicians are a rarity among Crow people, especially men. Also, the costs associated with preventive screenings (particularly the inconvenience of the travel given the expanse of the Reservation and limited access to transportation) are barriers to participation.

With respect to their health care options, many men in the focus groups report facing a lack of confidentiality at IHS about the reasons for their visits or the care they receive (not uncommon throughout rural America where anonymity is hard to come by, for example, nursing staff or medical coders may be female or even family members, resulting in embarrassment for the men, or they may be personal or clan enemies resulting in a sense of vulnerability about the confidentiality of their health status; current Crow society is characterized by substantial unresolved interpersonal conflicts). Other barriers described by men include extraordinarily long waits despite appointment times, and personnel who do not inspire trust and confidence. Therefore, a number of factors associated with IHS have impacted Crow tribal member's access to quality care.

Theme 4. Lack of health promotion

Education was also described as a critical issue influencing health and wellness for Crow men. The level of health promotion in school was described as inadequate, with many in the younger generation simply being unaware of a host of critical health issues. This was further augmented by discussion of reported high drop-out rates and poor scholastic performance of Crow youth. In addition, misinformation among Crow men was described as common. For example, several Crow elders thought prostate cancer was treated through castration. Knowledge of risk and behavioral issues associated with diet were also described as lacking with limited options to learn more about these types of basic health issues. In addition, there was a great deal of discussion on the general lack of awareness of high success rates associated with early detection of prostate cancer and the variety of treatments that can be used to address this condition.

Theme 5. Stoicism

Another theme that emerged from the focus groups was stoicism that many men stated was an inherent characteristic of Crow men, particularly amongst the older population. Men would describe their discomfort with physical vulnerability, and that they tend to face pain or disease with stoicism. There is a common attitude held by Crow men that they do not complain, do not discuss with peers, and do not seek care unless they have very serious and immediate health issues. Many said they find it embarrassing to be touched and probed in a medical exam, particularly by a female doctor. Digital rectal exams were discussed as not fitting with a man's pride.

The term "warrior" was repeatability used by Crow men to describe a mindset that persists to the present day. Men discussed a sense of "warrior pride" and the need to not share or express their personal fears and insecurities, to both women and other Crow men. Related to this theme was the topic of self-esteem and admitted confusion over what several men questioned, "what does it mean to be a Crow man?"

Theme 6. Economic situation

Many men discussed the realities of life on the Crow Reservation and the high poverty rates and unemployment that seem to be epidemic and a relentless obstacle for Crow men. Men are seen as providers to the family and community, and to take away family resources for personal issues, such as health exams or taking time from work, were seen by some to be selfish acts if the community or family were not taken care of first.

Theme 7. Spiritual/superstitious/psychological issues

Last, spiritual, superstitious, and psychological issues were described by some as impediments to good health. Many men in the focus groups described spirituality as imbuing all aspects of their life with regular prayer conducted for those who were experiencing health problems or for themselves. Some men also used the word superstitious to explain the beliefs amongst many men on the reservation of fear of the unknown or conceptions of causation with regard to health and disease. Many men knew others or believe themselves that by meeting with a health care provider for a health check up or a disease screen in itself invites the disease. Many stories were related by men who knew of others who felt positive test outcomes resulted from the test itself. Many men recognized that various belief systems could have psychological influences and thus could be a major impediment to engaging in preventive health behaviors, particularly for more traditional members of the Crow Tribe.

Objective 2. Obtain baseline survey data

The second objective of the Advisory Council was to better understand the attitudes, knowledge and behavior of Crow men with regard to cancer. A short IRB-approved survey was jointly created and distributed to men attending the focus group meetings. While the sample was not representative of all Crow men on the Reservation, it did provide some insight into the health factors especially with elder males (average respondent age of 55.2). Table 1 provides select results from Crow Men's Health Project survey.

The results revealed that more than half of survey respondents had one or no general exams in the last five years with nearly one-third having none. Several of those receiving more than five exams explained that these were the result of dialysis or advanced diabetes treatment. Nearly half admitted to being nervous about getting health screenings. When asked specifically about prostate cancer screenings, nearly half of respondents said they had not had a screening in the last two years. Respondent's knowledge of risk seems to be quite low (e.g. over 75% responded either no or they don't know if their risk of being diagnosed with prostate cancer is low over their lifetime when in fact the risk is approximately one in six). In addition, over half of respondents were unaware of the increased risk of prostate cancer if an immediate family member had been diagnosed.

Table 1. Select results from Crow Men's health project survey (N = 64).

Number of general health exams I have received in the last five years.
0 = 32.4%   1 = 25.2%   2 = 14.4%   3 = 10.8%   4 = 10.8%   5 = 36%
I am nervous about getting health screenings.
No = 53.1%   Don't Know = 4.2%   Yes = 42.7%
I have had at least 1 screening for prostate cancer in the last two years.
No = 46.9%   Don't Know = 6.1%   Yes = 47%
My risk for being diagnosed with prostate cancer in my lifetime is very low.
No = 10.2%   Don't Know = 65.3%   Yes = 24.5%
My risk of prostate cancer increases if an immediate family member has been diagnosed.
No = 28.6%   Don't Know = 21.4%   Yes = 50%
Information about prostate cancer is easy to obtain in my community.
No = 31.6%   Don't Know = 43.8%   Yes = 24.6%
I would learn more about prostate cancer if the information was readily available.
No = 8.3%   Don't Know = 4.2%   Yes = 87.5%

Despite the fact that prostate cancer seems to be uppermost in the minds of these men (they consistently have cited it as a top concern), a large majority said that, to their knowledge, information about prostate cancer was not readily available in their communities or they were not sure.

The results from the survey, while preliminary and non-random, provide at least a preview of some of the nascent issues confronting men on the Crow Reservation. It should be noted that this sample represents men who attended the focus group meetings, and thus likely had an interest in learning about and discussing health issues. It could be inferred that this sample is perhaps more knowledgeable and concerned with health discrepancies than the greater Crow population. Follow-up surveys with a larger and more representative sample will only enhance these data and provide further insight for the Advisory Council to pursue future programs and funding options.

Objective 3. Increase an awareness of men's health

As a method of raising awareness for the project, the Advisory Council organized the Crow Men's Health Ride at the Four Dances Natural Area near the Reservation. The ceremony was a colorful and poignant event with over 70 Crow men participating, many of whom on horses in traditional dress riding bareback. The ride signified the importance of health and the need for Crow men to actively engage in promoting and protecting their health and the members of their tribe.

According to Crow narrative, this location was the site of the death of several Crow warriors in the eighteenth century who contracted smallpox and decided to sacrifice themselves by riding their horses over a cliff in order to save the Tribe from the disease. Consequently, the site holds great significance for the Crow people in general and was therefore an important area to stage this health promotion event. The event was filmed in its entirety and received a great deal of media attention. An educational documentary with interviews of men discussing health issues was completed in 2009 and has been shown to men across the Reservation. The film can be viewed in its entirety at: http://crowmenshealth.org/. Future film screenings at various locations on the Reservation and for students at the university are now being planned.

At the community meetings, health professionals were occasionally brought in to share their expertise with the men in attendance and were available to answer questions. Educational material was also distributed by the Advisory Council at the meetings. Much of this educational material was specifically crafted for a Native American audience and thus an attempt was made to provide culturally-appropriate information. In addition, other health education videos were shown at the meetings to inform attendees, promote questions and discussion, and elicit personal reflection. All of the material collected and distributed was approved and gathered with the consent of the Advisory Council.

Objective 4. Pursue future funding

The Council determined that in order for a long-term intervention to be successful, a long-term funding source would have to be identified and secured. Currently, the Council is working with university faculty on several grant proposals. The purpose of the grants is to fund a program that will increase educational outreach and cancer screening rates for Crow men and in turn increase probabilities of early stage diagnosis and ultimately survival rates. Several grant proposals are now being reviewed by federal health agencies with hopes of continuing the above objectives as well as expanding the project to include active screening opportunities through a mobile testing unit that will target men at various cultural events.

The problem at the center of this project is the low numbers of Crow men who obtain health screenings, particularly for cancer. Building on information and perspectives shared over the last two years, the grants proposals center on the many structural and cultural barriers identified through the community meetings that cause Crow men to avoid health screenings. The barriers outlined in the proposal include: (1) nervousness, embarrassment and other cultural factors that influence getting tested; (2) misinformation about risk factors, the benefits of screening and treatment options; (3) challenges in utilizing the Indian Health Service clinic on the Reservation, including perceived lack of confidentiality, and perceived lack of quality and timely service; (4) lack of a personal health care provider able to serve them consistently over time; and (5) inadequate Indian Health Service resources.

The overall intent is to increase preventive health screening behaviors among Crow men, by implementing and evaluating a collaborative strategic intervention that directly addresses the barriers identified above. The proposal describes contracting with a male Family Nurse Practitioner (FNP) chosen by the Crow Men's Health Advisory Council, and introducing targeted men's health screening events. Education will be provided at the time of the screenings by the FNP, who subsequently will follow up with each man individually regarding test results, and will thereafter serve as an advocate and facilitator (throughout the life of the grant) to assist men with health conditions that require follow-up care through Indian Health Service. Health education programming also will include community-wide publicity, a lay men's health mentoring program, and collaborations with other cancer education agencies in the area. These efforts are aimed at correcting misinformation, and also at celebrating Crow men's health, promoting the concept that proud Crow men (warriors) get preventive health screenings rather than stoically suffering ill health.

Evaluation research will involve a team of university partners and the Advisory Council members and aims to determine effectiveness of the strategy for increasing the future incidence of health screenings among Crow men. The research will use quantitative surveys and in-depth qualitative interviews with screened subjects to investigate why beliefs, attitudes and values exist or change as a result of the project. In addition, the Family Nurse Practitioner will assist with analysis of health outcomes linked to the intervention. The research team will invite IHS and other health agency representatives to engage with the team in analyzing the data that result from the impact evaluation described above. Involvement with data analysis, especially review of interview data, promotes awareness that is very different from reading a report or watching a video, leading to intimate involvement with the acquisition of knowledge. Together, the data analysts will become the voice for incorporating effective aspects of the proposed intervention into protocols within IHS.

If funded, policy options development will set the stage for dialogue sessions with Crow Men's Health Advisory Council and Lay Health Mentors, Indian Health Service offices, Montana Comprehensive Cancer Coalition, relevant County health departments, and the Crow Health Department.Dialogue meetings will explore opportunities for collaboration to institutionalize appropriate supports for future Crow men's preventive health screenings.

Implications of research outcomes

As a result of the CBPR approach used in the Crow Men's Health Project, there are several tangible outcomes to date that have important implications. While this early stage of research was meant to be descriptive and exploratory, there are several evaluative and analytical statements that can be offered in the following six areas; (1) the importance of obtaining formal support from Tribal authorities; (2) the investment in time necessary to work in this context; (3) the importance of personal relationships in establishing and building trust; (4) the difficulty of obtaining baseline data; (5), the themes identified from our focus groups; and (6) the significance of providing ownership over the process and outcome by using the CBPR approach.

First, the project has the full support of the Crow Tribe's Executive and Legislative branches of government and other key individuals and organizations in the region. The project has received formal approval and support from Tribal Chair of the Crow Nation. A Tribal Resolution passed unanimously in the Crow Legislature in the summer of 2009 endorsing the project. Partnerships within and outside of the Tribe have also been established including medical personal at area hospitals, additional faculty at both Montana State University and Little Big Horn College, and Tribal representatives across the state of Montana to garner additional support and guidance. This support and the key partnerships that have resulted have been critical to promoting the project and ensuring that the program is seen as legitimate and valid.

A second outcome has been the realization of the great effort and time that has been required to reach the four objectives. In particular, time has been the great limiting factor in building relationships, trust, and ultimately identifying and prioritizing health issues and methods to address them. Native communities take great pride in social gatherings, deliberative meetings with storytelling, and building rapport, all of which are crucial to fostering trusting partnerships. However, time has been a major factor in terms of both grant funding deadlines, and university faculty obligations to produce research findings and publish results. Indeed, as Minkler & Wallerstein (2003, p. 100) note, "The reward system of universities discourages collaboration, and community members have to make time and even money sacrifices to collaborate in research, while academics get rewards." Many of the Crow men have expressed concern that certain timelines have felt rushed. To work around this issue, the project has benefited from candid deliberations of all partners in terms of personal and professional expectations and obligations; deliberations that seemed to be more productive because of the nature of the CBPR approach.

Third, a major implication of the project has been the importance of focusing on personal relationships to establish and build trust among the partners. The relationships were built from in-depth conversations conducted in a setting that was inclusive and comfortable. The resulting trust has led to a profoundly deep connection between all partners and an ability to deliberate on very personal matters. Consequently, several men have reported that they have undergone cancer and general health screenings as a result of the trusting relationships built during this project.

Forth, the project has revealed the difficulty of obtaining baseline epidemiological data. The implications are significant in that future funding must be directed toward establishing quality baseline data, and also justifying a need for any future health intervention. Next, the themes identified from the focus groups reveal important characteristics of how the Crow men envision the current health situation. These revelations will help guide the process as the partners look for strategies to improve health care opportunities for Crow men.

Last, and perhaps most important, a significant outcome has been the recognition that the CBPR approach has led to a sense of ownership of both process and outcome. The ownership has bolstered and further legitimated the Advisory Council that is viewed as critical to the success of the project. The commitment of the Council, notably the Chair, in terms of facilitating meetings and ensuring that critical members of the community were involved and actively participated in all aspects of the project. Without the ownership engendered for the process and commitment of the Council, this project would not have accomplished the stated objectives.

Conclusions

It is clear to all of the partners involved in the Crow Men's Health Project that using a CBPR approach has been integral to accomplishing the objectives to date. This approach has allowed trust to flourish between the university community and the tribal population in a way that has fostered a deep sense of commitment to task and realization that through a concerted effort to share power and resources, a mutually beneficial relationship could result. In turn, the approach has led to endorsement by tribal leaders and elders and has therefore garnered support from the rest of the community. The CBPR approach allowed the group to obtain initial funding, hold a series of community meetings and focus groups, distribute surveys, perform educational outreach, create an educational documentary film, and pursue future funding with a high probability of success.

The importance of genuine partnerships in health research and applied interventions is critical, particularly when addressing health concerns with a population that has a long history of neglect or mistreatment in terms of both health and academic research. Using this CBPR approach has been instrumental in establishing trust, building relationships and ultimately, identifying and beginning the long road of addressing health issues for men of the Crow Indian Nation.

Acknowledgement

The project described was supported by Award Number P20MD002317 from the National Center on Minority Health and Health Disparities. The content is solely the responsibility of the authors and does not necessarily represent the official views of the National Center on Minority Health and Health Disparities or the National Institutes of Health.

References

Baldwin, J., Johnson, J., & Benally, C. (2009). Building partnerships between indigenous communities and universities: Lessons learned in HIV/AIDs and substance abuse prevention research. *American Journal of Public Health*, 99(1), 77–82.

Beil, M., Evans, S., & Clarke, P. (2009). Forging links between nutrition and healthcare using community-based partnerships. *Family and Community Health, 32*(3), 196–205.

Burhansstipanov, L. (1998). Lessons learned from Native American cancer prevention, control and supportive care projects. *Asian American and Pacific Islander Journal of Health, 6*(2), 91–99.

Burhansstipanov, L., Christopher, S., & Schumacher, A. (2006). Lessons learned from community-based participatory research in Indian Country. *Cancer, Culture and Literacy, 12*(2), 70–76.

Cargo, M., & Mercer, S. (2008). The value and challenges of participatory research: Strengthening its practice. *Annual Review of Public Health, 29,* 325–350.

Centers for Disease Control and Prevention. (2009). Retrieved October 12, 2009, from http://www.cdc.gov/cancer/colorectal/basic_info/index.htm.

Christopher, S., Watts, V., Knows His Gun McCormick, & Young, S. (2008). Building and maintaining trust in a community-based participatory research partnership. *American Journal of Public Health, 98*(8), 1398–1406.

Christopher, S. (2005). Recommendations for conducting successful research with Native Americans. *Journal of Cancer Education, 20*(1), 47–51.

Dixon, M., & Roubideaux, Y. (2001). *Promises to keep: Public health policy for American Indians & Alaska Native in the 21st Century.* Washington, DC: American Public Health Association.

Fisher, P.A., & Ball, T.J. (2003). Tribal participatory research: Mechanisms of a collaborative model. *American Journal of Community Psychology, 32*(3–4), 207–216.

Foster, J., & Stanek, J. (2007). Cross-cultural considerations in the conduct of community-based participatory research. *Family and Community Health, 30*(1), 42–49.

Furshong, G., & Wamsley, M. (2009). Colorectal Cancer Screening – the Basics. Presentation at the Montana Cancer Control Programs Meeting (September 24), Montana Department of Public Health and Human Services, Helena, MT.

Hampton, J.W., Keala, J., & Luce, P. (1996). Overview of National Cancer Institute networks for cancer control research in Native American populations. *American Cancer Society, 78*(7), 1545–1552.

Holkup, P.A., Tripp-Reimer, T., Salois, E.M., & Weinert, C. (2004). Community-based participatory research: An approach to intervention research with a Native American community. *Advances in Nursing Science, 27*(3), 162–175.

Holkup, P.A., Rodehorst, T.K., Wilhelm, S.L., Kuntz, S.W., Weinert, C., Stepans, M.B., Salois, E.M., Hand Bull, J.L., & Hill, W.G. (2009). Negotiating three worlds: Academia, nursing science, and tribal communities. *Transcultural Nursing, 20*(2), 164–175.

Indian Health Service. (2006)Retrieved October 12, 2009, from http://info.ihs.gov/Files/DisparitiesFacts-Jan2006.pdf

Israel, B.A., Eng, E., Schulz, A.J., & Parker, E.A. (2005). *Methods in community-based participatory research for health.* San Francisco, CA: Jossey-Bass.

LaVeaux, D., & Christopher, S. (2009). Contextualizing CBPR: Key principles of CBPR meet the indigenous research context. *Pimatisiwin, 7*(1), 1–25.

Mail, P.D., Conner, J., & Conner, C.N. (2006). New collaborations with Native Americans in the conduct of community research. *Health Education & Behavior, 33*(2), 148–153.

Minkler, M., & Wallerstein, N. (2003). *Community-based participatory research for health.* San Francisco: Jossey-Bass.

Montana Cancer Control Coalition. (2006). *Montana Comprehensive Cancer Control Plan 2006–2011.* Helena, MT: Montana Disability and Health Program.

Montana Department of Public Health and Human Services. (2008). Cancer Prevention and Control Central Tumor Registry. Cancer among American Indian Residents of Montana. Helena, MT: DPHHS. Retrieved October 22, 2009, from http://www.dphhs.mt.gov/PHSD/cancer-control/documents/FAQsAboutCancerinAmericanIndiansinMontana_001.pdf

Partin, M.R., Rith-Najarian, S.J., Slater, J.S., Korn, J.E., Cobb, N., & Soler, J.T. (1999). Improving cancer incidence estimates for American Indians in Minnesota. *American Journal of Public Health, 89*(11), 1673–1677.

Potkonjak, M. (2004). Tribe sues ASU for $50M. *Scottsdale Tribune, March 17,* A6.

Rhoades, E.R. (2003). The health status of American Indian and Alaska native males. *Research and Practice, 93*(5), 774–778.

Strickland, J. (2006). Challenges in community-based participatory research implementation: Experiences in cancer prevention with Pacific Northwest American Indian tribes. *Cancer Control, 13*(3), 230–236.

Swan, J., & Edwards, B.K. (2003). Cancer rates among American Indians & Alaska natives. *Cancer, 98*(6), 1262–1272.

Watts, V., Christopher, S., & Smith, J. (2005). Evaluation of lay health advisor training for a community-based participatory research project in the Apsáalooke community. *American Indian Culture and Research Journal, 29*(3), 59–79.

The role of community-based strategies in addressing metropolitan segregation and racial health disparities

Malo André Hutson* and Sacoby Wilson

This paper is a conceptual analysis of the effects of racial residential segregation, which is a major contributor to racial and ethnic health disparities. Metropolitan segregation has had adverse health consequences for economically disadvantaged and minority populations because they are exposed to higher levels of environmental pollutants and have limited opportunities to gain a quality education, access to healthcare, and increase their economic opportunity. Based on our empirical and theoretical analysis we provide a holistic framework that takes an ecological systems approach to understand the affects of urban health and health disparities. We contend that in order to improve the urban/environmental health conditions for the most vulnerable urban populations, it will require comprehensive community and regional focused strategies that link local community development efforts to larger macro-level metropolitan regional strategies.

Metropolitan segregation and health disparities

Where a person lives and grows up can have a significant impact on their life-chances and quality of life. This is especially the case within the United States where the health status of an individual or group of individuals can vary widely depending on the block, neighborhood, or metropolitan area in which they reside (Fitzpatrick & LaGory, 2000). In the US federal, state, and local policies along with institutionalized racism have contributed to inequitable development across metropolitan areas, resulting in widening racial/ethnic and class divisions and unequal social and economic opportunities for economically disadvantaged residents (Dreier, Mollenkopf, & Swanstrom, 2004; Frug, 1999; Lopez, 2004; Williams & Collins, 2001). Moreover, inequitable metropolitan development results in the concentration of unhealthy living conditions and environments, which contributes to racial and ethnic health disparities.

According to the latest National Center for Health Statistics mortality data, racial and ethnic health disparities between blacks and whites and Hispanics and whites are significant (see Table 1).

---

*Corresponding author. Email: mhutson@berkeley.edu

Table 1. Age-adjusted death rates by for black, Hispanic and white ratios for the 10 leading causes of death, United States 2007.

Rank	Causes	Black to white ratio	Hispanic to white ratio
	All causes	1.3	0.7
1	Heart disease	1.3	0.7
2	Cancer	1.2	0.6
3	Stroke	1.5	0.8
4	Pulmonary disease	0.7	0.4
5	Accidents	0.9	0.7
6	Alzheimer's disease	0.8	0.6
7	Diabetes	2.1	1.5
8	Flu and pneumonia	1.2	0.8
9	Kidney disease	2.2	0.9
10	Blood poisoning	2.2	0.8

Note: Taken from Centers for Disease Control (2010).

Blacks have an overall mortality rate that is 1.3 times that of whites and Hispanics have a lower overall mortality rate than whites at 0.7. In analyzing the top 10 leading causes of death for 2007, the disparity in mortality ratio between blacks and whites was the highest for kidney disease (2.2) and blood poisoning (2.2), followed by diabetes (2.1), and stroke (1.5). Hispanics had a higher mortality ratio between whites only for diabetes (1.5). Although it appears that Hispanics have overall lower mortality ratios compared with whites it is worth noting that this could be for several reasons. According to David Williams and others, a high number of non-black minorities are classified as white on the death certificate, which leads to an underestimate of the death rates for Hispanics (Hahn, 1992; Sorlie, Rogot, & Johnson, 1993; Williams, 1999). In addition, a high proportion of Hispanics are foreign-born, thus reflecting the fact that immigrants tend to have better health status than the native-born population (Hummer, Rogers, Nam, & LeClere, 1999; Singh & Yu, 1996; Williams, 1999).

Perhaps one of the biggest factors contributing to differences in racial and ethnic health disparities has been residential segregation (Acevedo-Garcia, Osypuk, McArdle, & Williams, 2008; Corburn, 2009; Massey, 2004; Williams & Collins, 2001). Racial residential segregation directly impacts ethnic minorities' socioeconomic status (SES) at the individual, household, and community levels, which can negatively influence their health status (Ahmed, Mohammed, & Williams, 2007; Corburn, 2009; Massey & Denton, 1993; Williams & Collins, 2001). Lower socioeconomic and racially segregated minority communities and neighborhoods tend to have limited access to necessities such as quality housing, education, medical care, healthy foods, and economic opportunities – all of which are important determinants of health, especially economic opportunities. Sociologist William Julius Wilson describes the effects of deindustrialization and racial residential segregation on the economic opportunities for blacks in Chicago. He argues that highly concentrated urban poor communities "offer few legitimate employment opportunities, inadequate job information networks, and poor schools," all of which lead to the disappearance of work (Wilson, 1996, p. 52).

In addition to limited employment opportunities, poorer racially segregated communities within urban metropolitan communities offer less access to a broad range of services provided by municipal governments (Alba & Logan, 1993; Hutson, Kaplan, Ranjit, & Mujahid, 2011; Williams, 1999). A recent study that analyzed the largest 171 metropolitan areas within the United States according to metropolitan jurisdictional fragmentation and racial segregation found that metropolitan areas that were highly fragmented based on the number of governmental jurisdictions had higher overall black white mortality ratios compared with metropolitan areas with less jurisdictional fragmentation (Hutson et al., 2011).

Residential segregation also limits minorities' access to medical care and exposes them to neighborhood environments with higher levels of social disorder, violence and environmental toxins, all of which influence health (Ahmed et al., 2007; LaVeist, 1993; Massey, 2004; Morello-Frosch & Lopez, 2006; Williams, 1999; Williams & Jackson, 2005). In terms of access to medical care, the Institute of Medicine (2002) report *Unequal Treatment: Confronting Racial and Ethnic Disparities in Healthcare* found that some evidence suggests that bias, prejudice, and stereotyping on the part of healthcare providers may contribute to differences in care (2002, p. 195). Lower SES also contributes to lower levels of health insurance for poor, minority residents, resulting in fewer visits to the doctor and less access to preventive medicine (Williams & Jackson, 2005).

Highly racially segregated neighborhoods also tend to have higher exposures to environmental toxins and industrial land uses. For example, within New York City, Julie Sze argues that the most manufacturing zone increases over the years have occurred in the Bronx, an area with the highest concentration of poor and minority residents while Manhattan has experienced the greatest decreases in manufacturing zoning (Sze, 2007). Sze argues that the high level of zoned land for manufacturing within the Bronx exposed its residents to a disproportionate amount of environmental toxins compared with other communities within New York City. The Bronx, like many other poor communities of color, are exposed to unhealthy land uses and industrial production that over time can have an adverse impact on their quality of life and the overall health (Massey, 2004; Morello-Frosch & Lopez, 2006).

It is clear that racial residential segregation indirectly impacts individuals' SES, resulting in a number of deleterious influences that impacts the health status of poor, minority individuals. This raises very important questions. What can be done to address the current racial and ethnic health disparities gap that exists in the United States? What community-based strategies are most effective in addressing metropolitan segregation and racial health disparities?

Conceptual framework to address community development issues and health disparities

We should employ a comprehensive framework that considers ecologic features of the built and social environment to enhance community development in unserved and underserved communities hurt by health disparities. This framework (see Figure 1) incorporates elements of community development, urban planning, and the public health perspectives to categorize communities at different levels including neighborhoods, towns, cities, and metropolitan areas as human ecological systems, whereby the overall health of the human ecological system influences health and the degree of health disparities within and between human ecosystems (Wilson, 2009). This approach focuses on understanding how context, place, and local socio-environmental conditions impact the health of populations and individuals (Wilson,

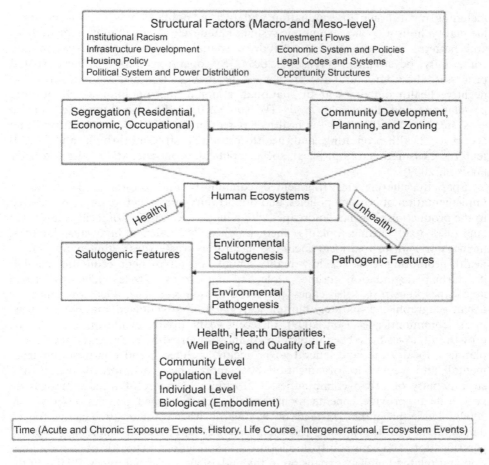

Figure 1. Ecologic framework to address development issues and health disparities.
Note: Figure taken from Wilson (2009).

2009). By modifying the health and quality of our human ecosystems, we can positively impact the lifestyles, health behaviors, health outcomes, and quality of life of populations who reside, work, or play in different ecosystems particularly disadvantaged, historically marginalized, and underserved populations (Wilson, 2009).

The framework builds upon an emerging area of environmental justice research that has explored the contribution of neighborhood stressors, structural factors, neighborhood-level resources, and the built environment to community health and the creation of health disparities (Brulle & Pellow, 2006; Gee & Payne-Sturges, 2004; Morello-Frosch & Lopez, 2006; Payne-Sturges & Gee, 2006; Payne-Sturges, Gee, Crowder, et al., 2006; Soobader, Cubbin, & Gee, 2006; Wilson, 2009), particularly disparities in asthma, adult mortality, infant mortality, cancer, obesity, cardiovascular disease, diabetes, and crime-related health outcomes. Figure 1 shows a conceptual framework that illustrates the role that different fundamental factors and spatial drivers of community context have in how human ecological systems are developed and maintained. The primary structural factors shown in Figure 1, including institutional discrimination and racism, political power, socioeconomic inequality, housing policy, economic systems and development, and investment flows and patterns, operate through and drive spatial processes of segregation and community development (Wilson, 2009). By operating through these spatial processes, these structural factors act as the main determinants of positive and negative health outcomes at the national, regional, metropolitan, neighborhood, population, and individual levels (Wilson, 2009). We can categorize human ecosystems as "healthy" or "unhealthy" based on the number and quality of and access to health-promoting and health-restricting structural (built and social) features measured across physical, social, political, economic, and spiritual spheres (Wilson, 2009).

Spatially uneven and fragmented community and economic development, implementation of housing policies, and opportunity infrastructure have contributed to the production of urban landscapes with a high concentration of locally unwanted land uses (e.g. chemical plants, factories, heavily-trafficked highways, landfills, incinerators, waste treatment facilities, hazardous waste sites), limited number of health-promoting resources, low-quality schools, unemployment, economic instability, urban degradation, crime, violence, and drugs. These unhealthy urban landscapes known as "riskscapes" (Morello-Frosch & Lopez, 2006) or unhealthy urban geographies disparately burden segregated, disadvantaged, and marginalized urban communities (Wilson, 2009). In recent years, urban revitalization and smart growth initiatives have been implemented and supported by community developers, planners, local, state, and federal governments, architects, and non-profit environmental and economic organizations as approaches to improve health and sustainability of urban communities. Unfortunately, many of these initiatives do very little to provide benefits to historically disadvantaged populations (Wilson, 2009). These programs, instead of having positive community benefits for all demographic groups in our cities and towns, may lead to more segregation, gentrification, and community development inequities characteristic of suburbanization and related highway expansion in the mid-1950s and urban renewal later in the 1970s and 1980s (Wilson, 2009).

Fortunately, the new ecosystems approach to human health presented in this paper may allow us to holistically assess, understand, and improve health by using community development to change socioenvironmental conditions. Human ecosystems with negative socioenvironmental conditions can lead to adverse health outcomes, drive bad health behaviors, and result in unhealthy lifestyles for populations within the ecosystems. On the other hand, living in human ecosystems with positive socioenvironmental conditions may lead to good health outcomes, health behaviors, and lifestyles, and improve individual-level, population-level, and community-level quality of life. The integration of the health promotion and prevention approach in community development and planning may catalyze a change in the life-course trajectory of at-risk and vulnerable populations and human ecosystems (Wilson, 2009). Therefore, the use of community development and planning initiatives and environmental health policies that help foster salutogenic (health-promoting) social and built environments may have important implications for public health in human ecosystems, particularly for disadvantaged, underserved, and marginalized populations who are disparately burdened by both environmental (i.e. landfills, incinerators, environmental hazards, air pollution, water pollution) and psychosocial (i.e. crime, violence, poverty, racism) stressors (Wilson, 2009).

Salutogens and pathogens in human ecosystems

City and regional planners and community developers may be able to use this ecological framework to improve the health of populations who reside in human ecosystems by tracking the number of and quality of the ecologic features present in the built and social environments (Wilson, 2009). Salutogens are ecologic features of the built and social environments that decrease a population's vulnerability to illness and adverse health outcomes (Antonovsky, 1987; Gee & Payne-Sturges, 2004; MacDonald, 2005; Payne-Sturges, Gee, Crowder, et al., 2006). Salutogens buffer at-risk and susceptible populations from the negative effects of pathogenic environmental exposures and increase opportunities for improvements in health, resiliency, vitality, and social capital (Wilson, 2009). There are several features of human ecosystems that we classify as salutogens, including good housing stocks, parks, medical facilities, schools, open space, supermarkets, recreational facilities, sewer and water infrastructure, equitable and just transportation networks, community gardens, farmers' markets, churches, dentists, and social service organizations (Wilson, 2009). The spatial density, distribution and quality of the salutogens are important indicators of human ecosystem health and points of intervention for improving historically disadvantaged, marginalized, and underserved communities, particularly environmental justice communities. Salutogens constitute the strengths, assets, and resources found in human ecosystems that community development professionals and advocates can use as the foundation for health promotion and prevention in the nation's efforts to eliminate racial/ethnic, socioeconomic-related, and geographic-related health disparities (Wilson, 2009).

Ecologic pathogens are features of the local built and social environments that enhance a population's vulnerability to negative health outcomes (Antonovsky, 1987; Gee & Payne-Sturges, 2004; MacDonald, 2005; Payne-Sturges, Gee, Crowder, et al., 2006), and drives negative health behaviors and lifestyles in a human ecosystem (Wilson, 2009). Ecologic pathogens act as stressors in the neighborhood environment and limit the overall health, sustainability, vitality, and quality of life and levels of social, economic, political, resource and spiritual capital in human ecosystems (Wilson, 2009). There are different categories of pathogens. These pathogens include environmental pathogens or pollutogens (e.g. landfills, incinerators, coal-fired electrical plants, hazardous waste sites, urban blight, locally unwanted land uses, heavily trafficked transportation networks, Superfund sites, waste transfer facilities, industrial corridors), social pathogens (i.e. poverty, structural racism, crime, violence, drug environs), resource pathogens (e.g. poor housing stock, low-quality medical infrastructure, poor sewer and water infrastructure, poor quality roads, fast food restaurants, liquor stores, convenience stores), and economic pathogens (e.g. quick loan facilities, pawn shops, payday lenders) (Wilson, 2009).

In conclusion, the use of this place-centric systems approach will allow us to focus our community development efforts in places with the most need and in the places where the most vulnerable or disadvantaged "reside, work and play" to eliminate disparities in burden, health, well-being, and quality of life. We can use community development programs and initiatives to modify features of the built environment to increase connectivity between different neighborhoods, decrease social isolation, improve neighborhood cohesion, and expand capital. In addition, modification of the built environment and salutogenic infrastructure may increase the accessibility of populations to resources (e.g. parks, medical facilities, grocery stores, churches, social service organizations) within and across spatially-related and unrelated human ecosystems (Wilson, 2009). This is particularly important for marginalized, disadvantaged, and underserved populations (e.g. low-income, persons of color, segregated, elderly, medically vulnerable, immigrants) who may have limited access to health-promoting infrastructure in urban environments and who have been disparately impacted by environmental, economic, and institutional racism and discriminatory policies and laws across multiple generations (Wilson, 2009).

The following case studies provide specific examples of how community-based strategies aim to reduce health disparities by addressing the pathogens described above. These case studies may share a similar goal but are very different with regards to their strategies, collaborations and local context.

Community-based strategies to address health disparities

Jamaica Plain Neighborhood Development Corporation: an effort to improve the economic opportunities of neighborhood residents and diversify of the healthcare workforce

Boston, Massachusetts is a city that suffers from a high level of racial and ethnic residential segregation. Despite slight decreases in the level of segregation over the past decade, approximately 92% of Boston's black population still lives in just seven of the city's 16 neighborhoods (Boston Public Health Commission, 2005). In order to evenly distribute ethnic and racial diversity throughout the city, 76% of blacks and 60% of Latinos would have to move from their current census tracts (The Boston Disparities Project, 2005).

The high level of racial residential segregation has had a negative impact on Boston's minority neighborhoods and its residents. According to the Mayor's Task Force Blueprint report, of the 22 waste sites in Boston, one-half are in the neighborhood of Roxbury where blacks and Latinos make up the majority of the population (Boston Public Health Commission, 2005). In addition, the Mayor's Task Force Blueprint report stated that lead poisoning is concentrated in the predominately minority communities of Dorchester, Mattapan, and Roxbury. The disproportionate exposure to environmental pollutants has had an effect on poorer children in the City of Boston. Researchers found that, between 1998 and 2002, children under the age of 5 years who lived in Roxbury were nearly twice as likely to be hospitalized for asthma as children in all other neighborhoods of the city (Boston Public Health Commission, 2005). Overall, Latino and black children were 50% more likely to be hospitalized for asthma than whites in this neighborhood (Boston Public Health Commission, 2005).

Racial and ethnic segregation has also no doubt had an effect on the economic opportunities of minority residents. According to The Boston Foundation's (2007) *Boston Indicators Report 2004–2006* there is still a significant amount of disparity in income between whites and racial/ethnic minorities. For example, in 2005 whites had a median household income of $56,627 compared with $31,331 for blacks, $23,424 for Asians, and $20,830 for Latinos (The Boston Foundation, 2007). Household income varied greatly by neighborhood. Residents living in predominately minority neighborhoods such as Roxbury, Dorchester, East Boston, and Mattapan all had household incomes well below the city-wide median of $39,629 (The Boston Foundation, 2007). Unemployment is also high in these neighborhoods. According the 2000 US Census, the neighborhood of Roxbury had an unemployment rate of 11.6% compared with the city, which had an overall employment rate of 7.2% (US Census Bureau, 2000).

The disparities in income and lack of economic opportunity inspired the Jamaica Plain Neighborhood Development Corporation (JPNDC) and its collaborators to develop a grassroots strategy that focuses on training low-wage residents residing in the Boston metropolitan's underserved neighborhoods for jobs within the healthcare sector. JPNDC and their partners formed the Boston Health Care and Research Training Institute (Training Institute), a training model that is focused on two primary goals: improving the educational and employment opportunities of low-wage adults in the healthcare and research industry; and improving the diversity and quality of care of Boston's healthcare institutions. The Training Institute officially began in 2002 as a partnership between eight major employers in the healthcare and research sector. The original partnership included the Boston Private Industry Council, a labor union, four community organizations, and two community colleges. Since its inception, the Training Institute has evolved to include more partners. In just four years the workforce intermediary grew to include 28 partners across the Boston metropolitan area – 11 employers (including all the largest healthcare employers within the Longwood Medical and Academic Area [LMA][1]), 17 organizations of higher education, a healthcare industry association, a labor union, the Boston Private Industry Council (PIC), social service agencies and community organizations. Initially managed by JPNDC in partnership with the Fenway Community Development Corporation (FCDC) and the Mission Hill Network (in February 2008, the Training Institute merged with the Jewish Vocational Service of Boston), the Training Institute provides workforce development training, education and social service support to under-skilled, economically disadvantaged individuals who reside primarily in the Fenway, Jamaica Plain, Mission Hill, and Roxbury neighborhoods of Boston and others from surrounding communities. More specifically, the Training Institute provides education and training programs to individuals who fall into one of the following categories:

- pre-employment job seekers with limited English or education;
- entry-level and mid-level workers lacking the language skills, education, and training needed to move into higher paying healthcare occupations; and
- hospital supervisors who would like assistance in learning how to improve their management skills.

Over the years the Training Institute has worked hard to increase the diversity of Boston's healthcare workforce and increase the economic opportunities of neighborhood residents, especially residents residing in Boston's poorest neighborhoods. Working closely with healthcare administrators, city and regional agencies, local elected officials, community residents, educational institutions, and social service providers, JPNDC and their partners have been successful in placing hundreds of low-wage residents in jobs within Boston's healthcare sector. The Training Institute has also worked with educational institutions and healthcare institutions to form career ladders in administration, patient care, and in technician positions. Most of these jobs pay a livable wage and include healthcare benefits enabling residents to not only improve their income but to gain access to better medical care. Since its inception the Training Institute, with an operating budget of approximately $1 million, has been successful in obtaining hundreds of thousands of dollars in the form of donations and grants from federal, state, and local foundations, government agencies, and the private sector (Boston Social Innovation Forum, 2005).

The early efforts by JPNDC and its collaborators are having a positive impact across the Boston metropolitan area. The Training Institute has become a fixture within the healthcare and research institutions across the Boston metropolitan area as it works to increase the diversity of the workforce and improve the quality of patient care, especially for underserved and minority populations. Moreover, the Training Institute has also focused a significant proportion of its resources reaching out to low-wage, low-skilled residents in an attempt to increase their economic and educational opportunities. These efforts have resulted in the Boston Redevelopment Authority (BRA) to require all developers or healthcare institutions planning development within Boston's LMA to make "an assessment of current and projected workforce needs, and to work with the BRA and the Office of Jobs and Community Services (JCS) staff to formulate a workforce development plan to address those needs" as part of the development review process (Boston Redevelopment Authority, 2003). The BRA's LMA Interim Guidelines specifically mention that it is expected that LMA institution's workforce development plans would include an increased investment in the Training Institute (Boston Redevelopment Authority, 2003). This strategy of tying development to community benefits (in the form of economic, educational, and access to medical care) helps to ensure that the poorest and least healthy residents residing in the Boston metropolitan area will have some opportunities to improve their quality of life.

In 2005 the City of Boston under the leadership of Mayor Menino released several reports and data documenting racial and ethnic disparities in the city and discussed recommended strategies to address those disparities. The initiative known as The Disparities Project is an effort to reduce racial and ethnic health disparities and to bring Boston's institutions and organizations together in order to promote fairness, equality and good health for all residents (Boston Public Health Commission, 2005; National Association of County and City Health Officials, 2011). Improving the diversity of the healthcare workforce is one of the major goals of the initiative. In an effort to improve the quality of healthcare and address workforce diversity, The Disparities Project has included the Training Institute as one of its local best practices (currently The Disparities Project oversees the implementation of 33 hospital and community-based projects in all neighborhoods in Boston) (National Association of County and City Health Officials, 2011). The hope is that, with time, efforts such as the Training Institute will be effective in diversifying the Boston metropolitan area's healthcare workforce, which will result in more culturally competent care and an overall improvement in service delivery for patients. Although a comprehensive analysis of the Training Institute's impact at increasing the economic opportunity of lower-skilled, economically disadvantaged residents has not been completed, and nor has one documenting the increases in diversity of Boston's healthcare workforce and its impact at reducing health disparities, it is clear that under the direction of JPNDC and its collaborators it has been able to begin making a difference at the local, city-wide, and regional level – only time will tell of how much of a difference it has made.

ReGenesis: an environmental justice organization's revitalization efforts in South Carolina

The City of Spartanburg is located in northwest South Carolina and has population of 40,000 with 50% black and 50% white (US Environmental Protection Agency [USEPA], 2003, 2006). This former "textile town" has undergone a transformation from its revitalized downtown to the high concentration of international business firms within the city limits (Fleming, 2004; USEPA, 2003, 2006). However, the Arkwright and Forest Park neighborhoods, two predominantly black neighborhoods with a combined population of almost 5000 residents located just beyond the City's downtown, have not benefited from these revitalization efforts (Fleming, 2004; USEPA, 2003, 2006). The closing of local mills and plants and the lack of zoning regulations and land-use controls (Fleming, 2004; Habisreutinger & Gunderson, 2006; USEPA, 2003, 2006) have left the population poor (25% in poverty), underemployed (10% unemployment) (USEPA, 2003, 2006) and negatively impacted by environmental injustice, underdevelopment, and limited access to health-promoting resources.

The residents live in a riskscape made of several environmental pathogens including the 40-acre International Mineral and Chemicals (IMC) fertilizer plant (a Superfund site), the Arkwright dump, the 30-acre former municipal landfill (a Superfund site), Rhodia chemical plant (in operation), Mt. Vernon textile mill (in operation), and six brownfields (Fleming, 2004; Habisreutinger & Gunderson, 2006; ReGenesis, 2008; USEPA, 2003, 2006). Approximately 4700 residents lived within one mile of the IMC site, 200 live within a quarter of a mile of the landfill, and several residents live adjacent to the Rhodia plant (Fleming, 2004; ReGenesis, 2008; USEPA, 2003, 2006). Due to these exposures, there is a high rate of cancer, particularly bone, colon, and lung cancer; high rates of respiratory illnesses, adult mortality, infant mortality, miscarriages, and birth defects; and in 2000 alone over 60 people died (ReGenesis, 2008; USEPA, 2003, 2006). In addition to these problems, neighborhood residents had poor transportation infrastructure, limited sewer and water services, lack of access to medical care, public safety issues, few economic opportunities, and declining property values (USEPA, 2003, 2006).

In 1997, Harold Mitchell, a resident concerned about the environmental contamination in his community, personally impacted by the loss of family members and his own health issues, and passionate about revitalizing his community, began organizing community meetings and forums to discuss environmental justice and health issues in the community (Fleming, 2004; ReGenesis, 2008; USEPA, 2003, 2006). These meetings began to empower local residents and motivate efforts by the government and industry to clean up the contaminated Superfund sites and brownfields, and later the community-driven collaboration became known as the "ReGenesis Project." In 1998, ReGenesis evolved into an environmental justice organization with official 501c3 status under the leadership of Harold Mitchell (Fleming, 2004; ReGenesis, 2008; USEPA, 2003, 2006). ReGenesis built an environmental justice partnership with the City of Spartanburg, Spartanburg County, EPA Region 4 Office of Environmental Justice, the South Carolina Department of Health and Environmental Control, Spartanburg Housing Authority, Spartanburg County's Community and Economic Development Department, local industry, and the University of South Carolina Upstate based on collaborative problem-solving principles to address the impacts of the brownfields, Superfund sites, and other environmental pathogens on local health and adopt strategies that could be employed to revitalize the Arkwright–Forest Park neighborhoods (USEPA, 2003, 2006).

With help from EPA Region 4, ReGenesis was designated one of the first 15 national demonstration projects of the Federal Interagency Working Group on Environmental Justice in 2000, which gave ReGenesis access to financial resources ($20,000) and technical experts and information (USEPA, 2003, 2006). With this designation, new funding was made available and local, state, and federal agencies began to understand that immediate action was needed in the Arkwright–Forest Park neighborhoods to save and improve lives (USEPA, 2003, 2006). The County of Spartanburg was awarded $200,000 through the EPA's Brownfield Initiative to perform site assessments of the brownfields on behalf of ReGenesis (Habisreutinger & Gunderson, 2006; ReGenesis 2008; USEPA, 2003, 2006). The brownfields assessment found contamination and led to government agencies providing additional funding to clean up the sites for redevelopment (Habisreutinger & Gunderson, 2006; ReGenesis, 2008; USEPA, 2003, 2006). For example, the South Carolina Department of Health and Environmental Control provided a $490,000 grant for brownfields redevelopment (ReGenesis, 2008; USEPA, 2003, 2006). HUD provided a $650,000 grant to ReGenesis and the City to clean up the brownfields and blighted properties and to help with neighborhood redevelopment efforts (ReGenesis, 2008; USEPA, 2003, 2006). In addition, the City of Spartanburg signed a cooperative agreement with the EPA to assess the nature and extent of contamination at the Arkwright Dump site, review the human and environmental health risks, and examine clean-up alternatives (Habisreutinger & Gunderson, 2006; ReGenesis, 2008; USEPA, 2003, 2006). The City of Spartanburg received $1.2 million dollars and used it to conduct water quality monitoring and remediation at the site (ReGenesis, 2008; USEPA, 2003, 2006). Eventually, the industrial owner of the property provided nearly $3 million in funding to the EPA for oversight, assessment, and remediation of the site (ReGenesis, 2008; Habisreutinger & Gunderson, 2006; USEPA, 2003, 2006).

The success of ReGenesis in working with its collaborative partner for assessment, cleanup, and redevelopment of brownfields and other industrial sites as part of the community revitalization efforts led to additional efforts to improve the salutogenic infrastructure in the Arkwright–Forest Park neighborhoods. ReGenesis received a US Department of Transportation (DOT) appropriation for $2 million dollars for road design and construction in order to connect the Arkwright–Forest Park neighborhoods to the greater Spartanburg community and improve access to emergency care services (ReGenesis, 2008; USEPA, 2003, 2006). ReGenesis also received $102 million dollars in HOPE VI funding to build energy-efficient, affordable housing and improve safety in the community (ReGenesis, 2008; USEPA, 2003, 2006). One of ReGenesis' greatest successes is the establishment of its Community Health Center (CHC) in 2003 through a $645,000 grant from the Department of Health and Human Services (ReGenesis 2008; USEPA, 2003, 2006). This health center provided the only source of care when it was established for many residents in the medically underserved community. The CHC is one of only 19 federally approved community health centers in the state of South Carolina and currently provides a medical home for approximately 14,000 patients (USEPA, 2003, 2006). The CHC is at the core of the long-term development and revitalization plans for the community.

Due to the collaborative effort of more than 200 agencies who contributed to the Environmental Justice partnership, the ReGenesis project has acquired $141 million in funds as of 2006 (USEPA, 2006). ReGenesis has expanded its community development and revitalization efforts to pediatric health, development of minority-owned businesses and job training through the ReGenesis Economic Development Organization, and urban greenways (ReGenesis 2008; USEPA, 2003, 2006). ReGenesis' use of the collaborative problem-solving framework has been celebrated by the EPA, who named it a model community-based environmental justice organization (ReGenesis, 2008; USEPA, 2003, 2006). Harold Mitchell has taken ReGenesis' community development and revitalization agenda to the South Carolina House of Representatives, where he has authored several affordable housing bills and environmental justice legislation to help improve the lives of underserved South Carolinians (ReGenesis, 2008).

The West End Revitalization Association: a story of success in North Carolina

Mebane, NC, is a small town located between Burlington and Chapel Hill, North Carolina. In this small community, black residents are concentrated in four historic neighborhoods (West End, White Level, Buckhorn/Perry Hill, and East End) (Heaney, Wilson, & Wilson, 2007; West End Revitalization Association [WERA], 2002, 2008; Wilson, Bumpass, Wilson, & Snipes, 2008; Wilson, Heaney, & Wilson, 2010; Wilson, Wilson, Heaney, & Cooper, 2007/2008). The WERA is a community-based organization fighting against environmental injustice, inequities in community development and planning, built environment insults, and health disparities in West End, White Level, and Buckhorn/Perry Hill (Heaney et al., 2007; Wilson, Bumpass, Wilson, & Snipes, 2008; Wilson, Heaney, & Wilson, 2010; Wilson, Wilson, Heaney, & Cooper, 2007). These neighborhoods have many low-income and elderly residents who are descendants of slaves and own land and property in Mebane passed down across multiple generations (Heaney et al., 2007; WERA, 2002, 2008; Wilson, Bumpass, Wilson, & Snipes, 2008; Wilson, Heaney, & Wilson, 2010; Wilson, Wilson, Heaney, & Cooper, 2007). The West End community hosts an old garbage dump, city landfill, and Mebane's sewage treatment plant (WERA, 2002, 2008). The West End community had been denied access to municipal sewer and water services even though residential health had been impaired by foul odors and air pollution from the sewage treatment plant, garbage dump, landfill, and a 50–100% failure rate of backyard septic systems (Heaney et al., 2007; WERA, 2002, 2008; Wilson, Bumpass, Wilson, & Snipes, 2008; Wilson, Heaney, & Wilson, 2010; Wilson, Wilson, Heaney, & Cooper, 2007). In addition, these neighborhoods are disparately impacted by a closed furniture production factory and underground storage tanks leaking carcinogenic compounds (e.g. benzene, xylene) (Heaney et al., 2007; WERA, 2002, 2008; Wilson, Bumpass, Wilson, & Snipes, 2008; Wilson, Heaney, & Wilson, 2010; Wilson, Wilson, Heaney, & Cooper, 2007).

The WERA was founded in 1994 as a community development corporation and incorporated as a North Carolina 501(c)3 non-profit in 1995 when the North Carolina Department of Transportation (NCDOT) released plans to construct the 119-bypass through two African-American communities (West End and White Level) (Heaney et al., 2007; WERA, 2002, 2008; Wilson, Bumpass, Wilson, & Snipes, 2008; Wilson, Heaney, & Wilson, 2010; Wilson, Wilson, Heaney, & Cooper, 2007). NCDOT plans to extend the 5-mile 119-bypass from I-85/40 north into the planned 27-mile interstate eight-lane highway corridor through White Level to Dansville, Virginia (Heaney et al., 2007; WERA, 2002, 2008; Wilson, Bumpass, Wilson, & Snipes, 2008; Wilson, Heaney, & Wilson, 2010; Wilson, Wilson, Heaney, & Cooper,

2007). Through right-of-way acquisition and displacement, the NCDOT planned to pay from $25,000 to $52,000 for houses regardless of their replacement value. Century old churches, small businesses, and a Masonic Temple would not be compensated. For over 15 years, local governments and the NCDOT planned the project without community knowledge or input (Heaney et al., 2007; WERA, 2002; Wilson, Bumpass, Wilson, & Snipes, 2008; Wilson, Heaney, & Wilson, 2010; Wilson, Wilson, Heaney, & Cooper, 2007). Community involvement and public hearings were held on the 119-bypass after WERA and African-American residents filed a joint Environment Justice Executive Order 12898 and Title VI of Civil Right Act complaint in 1999 at the US Department of Justice. In 1999, the NCDOT transportation corridor was placed on moratorium by the Federal Highway Administration until mitigation and corrective actions were implemented (Heaney et al., 2007; WERA, 2002; Wilson, Bumpass, Wilson, & Snipes, 2008; Wilson, Heaney, & Wilson, 2010; Wilson, Wilson, Heaney, & Cooper, 2007).

To address environmental justice, community development and planning, built environment, and health disparity issues, the WERA moved from being just a community development corporation to a community-based environmental protection organization and developed the community-owned and managed research (COMR) approach in order to empower WERA board, staff, members, and residents and use research to obtain redress for issues to impact WERA neighborhoods (Heaney et al., 2007; Wilson, Bumpass, Wilson, & Snipes, 2008; Wilson, Heaney, & Wilson, 2010; Wilson, Wilson, Heaney, & Cooper, 2007). The COMR approach is an evolved version of the community-based participatory research framework that focuses in parity in management of scientific research and equity in research funding. The use of COMR has increased community awareness and understanding of research related to public health, promoted public and civic engagement, enhanced public trust in community facilitation of research and ownership of databases, increased scientific literacy and community-driven research on environmental issues, and empowered community members (Heaney et al., 2007; Wilson et al., 2007).

In addition to the development of the COMR approach, the WERA developed a long-term multi-stakeholder collaborative partnership based on the EPA's environmental justice collaborative problem-solving principles (Heaney et al., 2007; Wilson et al., 2007). This partnership includes partners from the government, universities, health sector, community development and revitalization professionals, non-profits, environmental justice communities, and funders (Heaney et al., 2007; Wilson et al., 2007). These partners worked together on several workgroups using conflict resolution, resource leveraging and mobilization, consensus building and other collaborative principles (Heaney et al., 2007; Wilson et al., 2007) and other initiatives to address built environment, development, and health issues in WERA neighborhoods. These partners have been instrumental in sustaining the collaborative partnership over a period of 10 years and improved WERA's ability to address issues in WERA communities and other historically marginalized, disadvantaged, and underserved communities in Mebane, North Carolina, and nationally.

WERA's COMR research was funded by three grants: an EPA Environment Justice Small Grant ($15,000), University of North Carolina (Chapel Hill) EXPORT health disparities grant ($10,000), and EPA's Office of Environmental Justice Collaborative Problem-Solving grant ($100,000) (Heaney et al., 2007; Wilson et al., 2007). The experience, knowledge, and skills gained have helped the WERA leverage reduction and removal of hazards that create disproportionate and adverse public health risks under EPA's Safe Drinking Water Act, Clean Water Act, Clean Air Act, Solid Waste Disposal Act, and Toxic Substance Control Act (Heaney et al., 2007; Wilson et al., 2007). WERA's research on basic amenities (e.g. sewer and water infrastructure) documented Escherichia coli and fecal coliforms in residential well water, municipal drinking water, and surface waters that exceeded EPA's Safe Drinking Water Act and Clean Water Act standards (Heaney et al., 2007; WERA, 2002, 2008; Wilson, Bumpass, Wilson, & Snipes, 2008; Wilson, Heaney, & Wilson, 2010; Wilson, Wilson, Heaney, & Cooper, 2007). The efforts of the collaborative-problem solving partnership to obtain basic amenities led to the first-time sewer line installation for 91 homes in the West End community for only $75 per unit funded by block grants and City of Mebane matching, the connection of many WERA households to municipal water services, first-time paving of neighborhood streets, installation of gutters, removal of dilapidated and blighted housing, and leveraging of resources to continue the moratorium of the 119-bypass construction and changing of the highway plans that no longer disproportionately impact a large number of low-income black residents (Heaney et al., 2007; WERA, 2002, 2008; Wilson, Bumpass, Wilson, & Snipes, 2008; Wilson, Heaney, & Wilson, 2010; Wilson, Wilson, Heaney, & Cooper, 2007). WERA's collaborative environmental justice partnership, community-driven research, and use of Title VI of the Civil Rights Act to obtain compliance with environmental laws and public health statutes and basic amenities is a great model for other communities burdened by environmental injustice, uneven development, planning inequities, and health disparities.

Conclusion

Numerous research studies up until now have documented the deleterious impacts of racial residential segregation within metropolitan areas across the United States. Residential segregation more often than not creates neighborhoods of poverty that lack access to first-rate medical care, affordable housing, quality education, healthy food, and adequate infrastructure. Instead, poorer and minority residents forced to live in segregated communities are often left to reside in communities that are unsafe and have high levels of environmental pollutants. The persistent exposure to negative social, economic, and environmental conditions leads to poorer health outcomes for disadvantaged and minority populations, thus contributing to racial and ethnic health disparities.

If we as a nation are going to close the racial and ethnic health disparities gap that currently exists in this country, this will require a comprehensive framework that considers ecologic features of the built and social environment to enhance community development in unserved and underserved communities hurt by health disparities. As we have already mentioned, this approach must focus on understanding how context, place, and local socioenvironmental conditions impact the health of populations and individuals. A large portion of this work, as demonstrated by our community development cases, must be done at the grassroots community level. Community organizations and institutions are well-equipped to understand the challenges, assets, concerns, and potential opportunities that exist in local neighborhoods and are positioned to begin improving and modifying the health and quality of our neighborhoods.

An example of a place-based strategy that works to create healthy neighborhoods by using such a comprehensive approach is The Building Healthy Communities program. Launched in 2010 by The California Endowment, the largest health foundation in the state, the Building Healthy Communities program is a 10-year, $1 billion program to invest in 14 communities in both urban and rural areas across California.[2] The goal is to improve the health of these underserved and vulnerable communities by "improving employment opportunities, education, housing, neighborhood safety, unhealthy environmental conditions, access to healthy foods and more" (The California Endowment, 2010). A key goal of the Building Healthy Communities program is for it to be community-driven; it ultimately seeks to create communities for children where they are healthy, safe and able to learn (The California Endowment, 2010).

In addition to comprehensive place-based strategies such as The California Endowment's Building Healthy Communities program, a number of communities have also begun to rely on health impact assessments (HIAs) in order to improve neighborhood or community health. HIAs bring together public input, available data and a range of quantitative and qualitative methods to understand the potential health consequences of a proposed program, project or policy (Health Impact Project 2011[3]). In San Francisco, California, the University of California at Berkeley Health Impact Group, with funding from the Centers for Disease Control and through the federal HOPE VI program, completed a public draft of a retrospective HIA of the redevelopment of two public housing sites (Bernal Dwellings and North Beach Place). The HIA was interested in how redevelopment of public housing impacted the health of residents of two public housing sites in San Francisco (UC Berkeley Health Impact Group, 2009).

Finally in an effort to create healthier communities, a number of cities across California are using their general plan update process to transform their land use and built environment. Some cities, such as the cities of Anderson, Chino, and Richmond, California, are including a separate health element in their general plan and other cities are adding health goals and policies in various general plan elements (Healthy Eating Active Living Cities Campaign, 2011). These efforts are the first step towards what is needed to build healthy communities and reduce the level of health disparities.

As the institutions behind these programs and strategies recognize, real change in our communities requires that community institutions and local residents in partnership with public health agencies, planning institutions, social service agencies, government, non-profit organizations, and the private sector to confront the institutionalized racism and discrimination that creates disadvantaged communities across our metropolitan areas with unequal access to economic, educational, and social opportunities. In addition, addressing institutional racism and discrimination can lead to improved neighborhood environments with more equitable development and planning so that poorer residents are not exposed to an unjust amount of environmental pollutants and land uses. Only a comprehensive community-centered strategy is capable of positively impacting the lifestyles, health behaviors, health outcomes, and quality of life of populations who reside, work, or play in disadvantaged, historically marginalized, and underserved communities.

Notes

1. The Longwood Medical and Academic Area is located on 213-acre site with 24 institutions and has 15.4 million square feet of development. Each day more than 40,000 employees and 18,200 students provide medical care, conduct research, teach, attend school, or support these functions (Medical Academic and Scientific Community Organization, 2008).

2. See http://www.calendow.org/healthycommunities/
3. The Health Impact Project, a collaboration of the Robert Wood Johnson Foundation and The Pew Charitable Trusts, is a national initiative designed to promote the use of HIAs as a decision-making tool for policy-makers. See http://www.healthimpactproject.org/

References

Acevedo-Garcia, D., Osypuk, T.L., McArdle, N., & Williams, D.R. (2008). Toward a policy-relevant analysis of geographic and racial/ethnic disparities in child health. *Health Affairs*, *14*(2), 321–333.

Ahmed, A.T., Mohammed, S.A., & Williams, D.R. (2007). Racial discrimination & health: Pathways & evidence. *Indian Journal of Medical Research*, *126*, 318–327.

Alba, R.D., & Logan, J.R. (1993)Minority proximity to whites in suburbs: An individual-level analysis of segregation. *American Journal of Sociology*, *98*, 1388–1427.

Antonovsky, A. (1987). *Unravelling the mystery of health: How people manage stress and stay well*. San Francisco, CA: Jossey-Bass.

The Boston Disparities Project. (2006). *Boston Public Health Commission*. Boston, MA. Retrieved from http://www.naccho.org/topics/modelpractices/database/practice.cfm?practiceID=318

Boston Public Health Commission. (2005). *Mayor's Task Force blueprint: A plan to eliminate racial and ethnic disparities in health*. Retrieved from http://www.bphc.org/director/disp_blueprint.asp

Boston Redevelopment Authority. (2003). *LMA Interim Guidelines*. Boston, MA. www.bostonredevelopmentauthority.org/pdf/.../LMA_Int_Guidelines.pdf

Boston Social Innovation Forum. (2005). *Boston Health Care and Research Training Institute Prospectus*. http://www.rootcause.org/performance-measurement/profiles/boston-health-care-and-research-training-institute

Brulle, R.J., & Pellow, D.N. (2006). Environmental justice: Human health and environmental inequalities. *Annual Review of Public Health*, *27*, 103–124.

Center for Disease Control. (2010). *National vital statistics reports* (Vol. 58, No. 19). Atlanta, GA: Centers for Disease Control.

Corburn, J. (2009). *Toward the healthy city: People, places, and the politics of urban planning*. Cambridge, MA. MIT Press.

Dreier, P., Mollenkopf, J., & Swanstrom, T. (2004). *Place matters: Metropolitics for the twenty-first century* (2nd ed., rev.). Lawrence, KS: University of Kansas Press.

Fitzpartick, K., & LaGory, M. (2000). *Unhealthy places*. London: Routledge.

Fleming, C. (2004). When environmental justice hits the local agenda: A profile of Spartanburg and Spartanburg County, South Carolina. *PM Magazine*, *86*(5), 1–10.

Frug, G.E. (1999). *City making: Building community without building walls*. Princeton, NJ: Princeton University Press.

Gee, G., & Payne-Sturges, D. (2004). Environmental health disparities: A framework integrating psychosocial and environmental concepts. *Environmental Health Perspectives*, *112*(17), 1645–1653.

Habisreutinger, P., & Gunderson, D.E. (2006). Real estate reuse opportunities within the ReGenesis project area: A case study. *International Journal of Construction Education and Research*, *2*(1), 53–63.

Hahn, J.A. (1992). The state of Federal health statistics on racial and ethnic groups. *JAMA*, *267*, 268–271.

Healthy Eating Active Living Cities Campaign. (2011). *HEAL homepage*. Retrieved March 7, 2011, from http://www.healcitiescampaign.org/index.html

Heaney, C.D., Wilson, S.M., & Wilson, O.R. (2007). The West End Revitalization Association's community-owned and -managed research model: Development, implementation, and action. *Progress in Community Health Partnerships: Research, Education and Action*, *1*(4), 339–350.

Hummer, R.A., Rogers, R.G., Nam, C.B., & LeClere, F.B. (1999). Race/ethnicity, nativity, and U.S. adult mortality. *Social Science Quarterly*, *80*, 136–153.

Hutson, M.A., Kaplan, G.A., Ranjit, N., & Mujahid, M. (2011). Metropolitan fragmentation and health disparities: Is there a link? *Manuscript submitted for publication*.

Institute of Medicine. (2002, March). *Unequal treatment: Confronting racial and ethnic disparities in healthcare.* Washington, D.C.: National Academies Press.
LaVeist, T.A. (1993). Separation, poverty, and empowerment: Health consequences for African Americans. *Milbank Quarterly, 73*(1), 41–64.
Lopez, R. (2004). Income inequality and self-rated health in US metropolitan areas: A multi-level analysis. *Social Science & Medicine, 59,* 2409–2419.
MacDonald, J.J. (2005). *Environmental for health: A salutogenic approach.* Sterling, VA: Earthscan.
Massey, D. (2004). Segregation and stratification: A biosocial perspective. *Du Bois Review, 1*(1), 7–25.
Massey, D.S., & Denton, N.A. (1993). *American apartheid: Segregation and the Making of the underclass.* Cambridge, MA: Harvard University Press.
Medical Academic and Scientific Community Organization. (2008). Retrieved from http://www.masco.org/thelma/about-lma
Morello-Frosch, R., & Lopez, R. (2006). The riskscape and the color line: Examining the role of segregation in environmental health disparities. *Environmental Research, 102,* 181–196.
National Association of County and City Health Officials. (2011). *NACCHO model practices.* Retrieved March 8, 2011, from http://www.naccho.org/topics/modelpractices/
Payne-Sturges, D., Gee, G.C., Crowder, K., Hurley, B.J., Lee, C., Morello-Frosch, R., et al. (2006). Workshop summary: Connecting social and environmental factors to measure and track environmental health disparities. *Environmental Research, 102,* 146–153.
ReGenesis. (2008). *Environmental justice demonstration project: Community revitalization through partnerships.* Retrieved May 20, 2008, from http://www.regenesisproject.org/
Singh, G.K., & Yu, S.M. (1996). Adverse pregnancy outcomes: Differences Between U.S. and foreign-born women in major U.S. racial and ethnic groups. *American Journal of Public Health, 86,* 837–843.
Soobader, M., Cubbin, C., & Gee, G.C. (2006). Levels of analysis for the study of environmental health disparities: the role of place and social theory. *Environmental Research, 102,* 172–180.
Sorlie, P.D., Rogot, E., & Johnson, N.J. (1993). Validity of demographic characteristics on the death certificate. *Epidemiology, 3,* 181–184.
Sze, J. (2007). *Noxious New York: The racial politics of urban health and environmental justice.* Cambridge, MA: MIT Press.
The Boston Foundation. (2007). *The Boston indicators project report 2004–2006.* Retrieved from http://www.bostonindicators.org/uploadedFiles/Indicators/Indicators2006/Homepage/2004-06_IndicatorsRpt.pdf
The California Endowment. (2011). *Building Healthy Communities program.* Retrieved March 7, 2011, from http://www.calendow.org/healthycommunities/
UC Berkeley Health Impact Group. (2009, November). *HOPE VI to HOPE SF, San Francisco public housing redevelopment: A health impact assessment.* Berkeley, CA: University of California. Retrieved from http://www.hiacollaborative.org/case-studies
US Census Bureau. (2000). Retrieved from www.uscensus.gov
US Environmental Protection Agency. (2003). *Towards an environmental justice collaborative model: Case studies of six partnerships used to address environmental justice issues in communities* (EPA/100-R-03-002). Washington, DC: USEPA.
US Environmental Protection Agency. (2006). *EPA's environmental justice collaborative problem-solving model* (EPA 300-R-06-002). Washington, DC: USEPA.
West End Revitalization Association. (2002). *Failing septic systems and contaminated well waters: African-American communities in Mebane, North Carolina* (Final Report No. EPA #4EAD/EJ). Washington DC: US Environmental Protection Agency.
West End Revitalization Association. (2008). *WERA homepage.* Retrieved May 27, 2008, from http://www.wera-nc.org/
Williams, D.R. (1999). Race, socioeconomic status, and health: The added effects of racism and discrimination. *Annals New York Academy of Sciences, 896,* 173–188.
Williams, D.R., & Collins, C. (2001). Racial residential segregation: A fundamental cause of racial disparities in health. *Public Health Reports, 116*(5), 404–416.
Williams, D.R., & Jackson, P.B. (2005). Social sources of racial disparities in health. *Health Affairs, 24*(2), 325–334.

Wilson, O.R., Bumpass, N.G., Wilson, O.M., & Snipes, M.H. (2008), The West End Revitalization Association (WERA)' s right to basic amenities movement: Voice and language of ownership and management of public health solutions in Mebane, North Carolina. *Progress in Community Health Partnerships*, 2(3), 237–243.

Wilson, S.M. (2009). A holistic framework to study and address environmental justice and community health issues. *Environmental Justice*, 2(1), 1–9.

Wilson, S.M., Cooper, J., Heaney, C.D., & Wilson, O.R. (2008). Built environment issues in unserved and underserved African-American neighborhoods in North Carolina. *Environmental Justice*, 1(2), 63–72.

Wilson, S.M., Heaney, C.D., & Wilson, O.R. (2010). Governance structures and the lack of basic amenities: Can community engagement be effectively used to address environmental injustice in underserved black communities? *Environmental Justice*, 3(4), 125–133.

Wilson, S.M., Wilson, O.R., Heaney, C.D., & Cooper, C. (2007). Use of EPA collaborative problem-solving model to obtain environmental justice in North Carolina. *Progress in Community Health Partnerships: Research, Education and Action*, 1(4), 327–338.

Wilson, S.M., Wilson, O.R., Heaney, C.D., & Cooper, J. (2007/2008). Community-driven environmental protection: Reducing the P.A.I.N. of the built environment in low-income African-American communities in North Carolina. *Social Justice in Context*, 3, 41–58.

Wilson, W.J. (1996). *When work disappears:The world of the urban poor*. New York: Knopf.

THE ECONOMIC AND FISCAL IMPACTS OF THE ELDERLY ON A SMALL RURAL REGION

By Martin Shields, Judith I. Stallmann, and Steven C. Deller

ABSTRACT

Recruiting retirees is a popular economic development strategy for rural communities. Previous research finds positive economic and fiscal impacts in communities, but it tends to assume that the elderly are homogeneous and to concentrate on planned retirement communities. At the same time, concerns are expressed that older and low-income retirees will be a burden for local government. Using a quasi-experimental design, the economic and fiscal impacts of various groups of retirees classified by age and income on a rural region in Wisconsin are simulated. All groups have positive economic benefits for the region. The impacts of the different groups of elderly vary by their income and the size of their households. Contrary to the expectations of some, all groups of retirees provide positive net fiscal impacts for local governments.

INTRODUCTION

Recruiting retirees as a rural development strategy has been extensively documented in this *Journal*. Although initially controversial, this strategy has been largely vindicated by applied research showing that in-migrating retirees have significant positive economic impacts on the rural communities to which they migrate. Over the past 20 years, retirement counties as identified by the USDA-ERS[1] have experienced above average population and income growth (Cook & Hady, 1993; Deller, 1995; Walzer & Deller, 1996). Because the number of retirees is expected to increase as the baby boom generation ages, attracting retirees seems an even more promising strategy for the future. As a result, both states and individual communities have initiated programs to attract retirees (Fagan & Longino, 1993; Reeder, Hopper, & Thompson, 1995).

While previous research shows in-migrating retirees benefit rural communities, the literature has focused primarily on the impacts of younger, newly retired, affluent individuals who move permanently to planned-retirement

---

Martin Shields (corresponding author), Department of Agricultural Economics and Rural Sociology, Pennsylvania State University, Armsby Building, University Park, PA 16802. Judith I. Stallmann, Department of Agricultural Economics, 231 Gentry Hall, University of Missouri-Columbia, Columbia, MO 65211-7040. Steven C. Deller, Department of Agricultural and Applied Economics, 521 Taylor Hall - 427 Lorch Street, University of Wisconsin-Madison, Madison, WI 53706.

The Wisconsin Agricultural Experiment Station, University of Wisconsin under Hatch Project #3657 provided support for this work.

communities. However, concentrating research efforts on this segment of the population neglects the fact that retirees differ substantially among themselves. Stallmann and Jones (1995) point out that retirees are not only heterogeneous but also attracted to different types of communities. The ramification of this diversity is that the economic and fiscal impacts may differ by both the type of retiree and the type of community (Stallmann & Siegel, 1995). To date, this topic has been largely ignored in the literature.

Another shortcoming of previous research is the concern that the positive economic and fiscal impacts of in-migrating retirees hide longer-run increased health care and costs of human services, a phenomenon that Longino (1988) has dubbed the "gray peril." Longino points out that while the issue is often raised, "Nowhere is the direct impact of such migration on government expenditures estimated. Nor are there studies that compare the aggregate or per capita impact of younger and older migrant households on different types of government expenditures..." (p. 453).

OBJECTIVES

In this paper, we use an economic and fiscal impact model to investigate the differential impacts of heterogeneous retiree populations. Specifically, we examine how different "types"—characterized by age and income—of retirees uniquely affect local employment, income, and government expenditures and revenues. Our objective is to expand the knowledge-base concerning how impacts can vary according to the retiree characteristics. This information should be useful to communities as they try to assess the range of potential impacts of retiree recruitment.

Our first contribution is the explicit recognition of heterogeneity among retirees and providing comparisons among groups of retirees. As noted above, previous research treats retirees as homogeneous or focuses on a particular group of retirees without a comparison. Nevertheless, it is of particular interest to know how differences in expenditure patterns among different groups— characterized by age and income—affect the economic and the fiscal impacts. By making comparisons and contrasts among types, as we do in this applied research, we can observe the influence heterogeneity has on the direction and magnitude of impact.

The second contribution we make is to incorporate "working retirees" into the analysis. To date, research assumes that the elderly have no labor force attachment. Yet, national data show that many retiree households have a member in the labor force who often works part time (BLS, 1997). For reasons highlighted below, the fact that some retirees remain in the labor force can have important impacts on the magnitude of the economic impact.

Our third contribution is to take a more holistic approach than past efforts. The model we offer here explicitly recognizes that changes in one part of a local economy will affect other parts. Using the terminology of economic impact analysis, the model estimates the direct, indirect, and induced economic impacts on a number of indicators — primarily jobs, income, retail sales, and housing. Recognizing that this activity also influences local governments, this information is then used to estimate local fiscal impacts (i.e., local government expenditures and revenues). Finally, our analysis contributes to policy issues by explicitly discussing the types of retirees that each of the age and income groups most closely resembles.

Our study accomplishes these objectives using an economic model. In one set of scenarios, we compare the potential impacts of high- and low-income retirees on a community. When examining income differentials, conventional wisdom suggests lower-income migrants will generate less tax revenues and demand a different mix of public services than higher-income retirees will. This conventional wisdom, however, has not been examined in a systematic way. One important aspect of the research here is that we can examine the notion that low-income retirees are a fiscal drain on the local government while high-income retirees are not.[2]

Our model also facilitates a comparison of younger and older retirees. This allows us to predict economic impacts of a variety of scenarios, such as those changes experienced by a retirement community as young in-migrants age, or those community changes resulting from a resident population aging-in-place. By following this approach, the estimated impacts of older retirees also can be used as an indication of the potential impacts of recruitment strategies geared toward assistance-seeking retirees.

For most sectors of the local economy, it is expected that older retirees will generate lower economic impacts than younger retirees because older retirees have lower incomes. Older retirees, however, are also expected to generate higher demand for medical goods and services and personal and household services than younger retirees are, so that their economic effects in these particular sectors may be higher. The research here offers us a chance to see which effects are larger on balance. In addition, as above, the research also allows us to investigate whether older retirees are a fiscal drain on the resources of the local government. Together, these findings should help communities understand better the potential impacts of retiree recruitment.

REVIEW OF PREVIOUS IMPACT RESEARCH

A large amount of literature examining retiree migration can be found. Because our research focuses on the economic and fiscal impacts of retirees who migrate to rural communities, our review focuses on the issues that have not been addressed in the economic and fiscal impact literature. For our purposes, the economic impacts of retirees include their impacts on jobs and income in the community, while the fiscal impacts refer to the impacts on local government revenues and expenditures.

Most early studies only estimated direct economic impacts of retirees who migrated to rural areas (Happel, Hogan, & Pflantz, 1988; Happel, Hogan, & Sullivan, 1983). As economic impact software and data have become more readily available, recent studies have estimated direct, indirect, and induced effects (or the multiplier effects) (Woods et al., 1997). While this literature generally shows positive economic impacts on communities from retiree in-migration (i.e., moving into a community), most of the work has concentrated on planned retirement communities (Barkley & Henry, 1993; Miller, 1993; Siegel & Leuthold, 1993). Unfortunately, because these new communities are typically designed specifically to appeal to affluent retirees, the impacts documented by these studies may not apply to all types of retirees (Stallmann & Jones, 1995).

The limited research on retirees in other types of retirement communities has also shown positive economic impacts. In this *Journal,* Henderson (1994) compared expenditures of independent-living and assisted-living retirees in an Ohio community of 5,000 residents, finding that the assisted living residents had higher economic impacts. Other work with similar conclusions includes that of Woods and Allen (1993), Rowles and Watkins (1993) and Jones, Whitehorn and Wyse (1993).

While previous research has quantified the economic impacts of select scenarios, it has not typically quantified fiscal impacts (Voth, Miller, & Cluck, 1993). Even in studies where fiscal impacts are reported, the analysis is often partial, so that the net fiscal impacts on the community cannot be estimated. For example, Jones, Whitehorn, and Wyse (1993) report only the additional tax revenues generated by the in-migrating retirees, neglecting the public expenditures necessitated by the in-migrants. Still some other studies recognize the additional costs of services to the new retirement community. For example, Barkley and Henry (1993) and Miller (1993) document net fiscal impacts by comparing increased tax revenues generated by the new residents with changes in estimated government costs. However, these studies fail to account for the indirect and induced effects, hence rendering them somewhat incomplete.

Two exceptions directly tie the fiscal analysis to a complete economic impact analysis. In the first study, Siegel and Leuthold (1993) estimate the economic and fiscal impacts on the county of a planned retirement community in Tennessee. Because of the multiplier effect, additional jobs and additional in-migration are created. This leads to fiscal impacts not only by the retirees, but also by the multiplier effect that they create. The study finds positive fiscal impacts directly from the retirees, negative fiscal impacts from the indirect and induced effects, and overall positive net fiscal impacts. This is a study of a new planned-retirement community, and the authors note that the community is already trying to shift some costs from the homeowners' association to the local governments, a shift which would lower the positive fiscal impacts.

In the second study, Deller (1995) estimates the economic and fiscal impacts of retiree in-migration for the state of Maine. That study does not show the same level of positive fiscal impacts as the Siegel and Leuthold study; rather, it finds that demand for public services increases in proportion to the increase in population. Deller suggests further that the difference between the studies may be because of the level of analysis—state versus local. The state analysis includes the state revenues and the demands on state-government services, including medical costs, which are not a cost to the county and would not be included in a county fiscal analysis.

While the majority of retirees who migrate from urban to rural areas are newly retired and affluent, low-income retirees also migrate. To date, however, little work has been done examining the impacts of low-income retirees on the communities to which they migrate. One exception is the Apache Junction, Arizona, study of trailer parks that cater to low-income retirees (Happel, Hogan, & Pflantz, 1988). The study, unfortunately, does not include a complete economic and fiscal analysis. In addition, without a comparison group of higher-income retirees, the differential impact of income levels cannot be determined.

Retirees who age-in-place are also overlooked by current research. These are types of retirees who tend to have lower incomes than retirees who migrate. Their characteristics and needs also tend to differ from those of migrating retirees, thus they may require a different set of services and policies (Glasgow & Beale, 1985). Finally, communities with a high percentage of retirees aging-in-place tend to differ from communities with high in-migration (Reeder & Glasgow, 1990). Still, because of similarities in income, low-income retirees and retirees who age-in-place may have similar impacts on a community.

Older retirees generally tend to be in poorer health than younger retirees tend to be. Their incomes often are lower because they have begun to draw down their assets and/or because they entered retirement with fewer assets than the younger generation of retirees (Hurd, 1989). In addition, it is not uncommon for retirees to make another move as they age, are widowed, and/or as their health declines, in order to be nearer to family and medical services (Litwak & Longino, 1987). There is little research on the economic and fiscal impacts of older retirees who have different needs and different income levels, and therefore, different spending patterns than younger retirees have.

Contrary to popular perceptions, not all elderly retire from the labor force; many work part-time for either personal or financial reasons. Data from the Bureau of Labor Statistics show that it is not uncommon for an elderly household to have one member in the labor force, often part-time (BLS, 1997). The research literature on retiree households also confirms this. For example, Haas and Serow (1997) found that among in-migrant retirees in Western North Carolina, 30 percent of the households had someone in the labor force. Cockerham (1997) observes that the percentage of persons over age 65 remaining in the workforce is steadily declining, but the proportion of part-time workers increases at retirement age. Many of the elderly work part-time because they want to continue some work, or they work part-time to avoid having Social Security benefits reduced (Kahne,

1985). Cox (1993) further contends that low-income, unmarried [widowed], retired women are "very likely" to work at least part-time to supplement social security payments. Professional persons who are more affluent and likely to migrate, and who are the target audience of communities seeking retirees, may remain in the workforce as private consultants.

SCENARIOS, MODEL, AND DATA

For policy makers interested in retiree recruitment, some relevant questions may be asked. "What will our economy look like with a higher retiree population, and how does that compare to the status quo?" Impact analysis, which can be thought of as "with and without" analysis, is one useful tool for addressing these questions. The input-output framework can examine the potential economic impacts of a policy by comparing predictions of how the economy will evolve under various scenarios.

An important aspect of good impact analysis is a reasonable and accurate baseline against which to compare the scenario. This involves describing the baseline conditions if the local economy is not substantially altered (i.e., no new households, or the status quo). Then, the comparison scenario is simulated and compared to the baseline scenario. The difference between the comparison and the baseline scenario is the impact. When describing these effects, analysts typically present the baseline and comparison cases side-by-side in a series of tables.

In this applied research, the Wisconsin Economic Impact Modeling System, a county-level, conjoined input-output/econometric simulation model, is used to assess the impacts of subgroups of retirees on a small rural region. In conjoined models, the input-output component is used to determine industry outputs and primary factor demands. The econometric component estimates final demands, factor prices, and primary factor supplies. A graphical overview of the model is presented in Figure 1. The major modules of the model are described thus:

1. Production: uses changes in final demand to estimates changes in regional output, using IMPLAN, an input-output model.

2. Labor: uses changes in output (form module 1) to estimate changes in employment by sector, which, in turn, is used to estimate changes in wages, regional unemployment, commuting patterns, labor force, and population.

3. Demographics: uses changes in wages and employment to estimate changes in local income and income distribution (poverty).

4. Housing: uses changes in population to estimate new housing construction in the region and changes in property values caused by the increased demand for housing.

5. Local retail sales: uses changes in income and population to estimate changes in regional retail markets.

6. *Local government:* uses changes in population, income, and other variables to estimate changes in local government expenditures and revenues.

The production module, based on IMPLAN, is an input-output model that has been used in several other studies of retiree impacts (e.g., Siegel & Leuthold, 1993; Woods et al., 1997). The remaining modules consist of stochastic econometric equations. To capture interrelationships, the modules are linked by one or more endogenous variables (Shields, Deller, & Stallmann, 2001). These modules provide information on a number of variables of interest to local policy makers and development practitioners. The model is similar to other regional models in that simulations or impacts can be broken down in detail to show direct, indirect, and induced effects. Shields (1998) provides a complete description of the model.[3]

The direct impact can be thought of as an infusion of autonomous (does not depend on the local economy) expenditures into the economy. Referring to Figure 1, in this analysis, changes in the local economy are driven by shifts in *demand for locally produced goods because of the injection of new local spending* by the in-migrants. To meet this new demand, local businesses must increase

Figure 1. The Wisconsin Economic Impact Modeling System

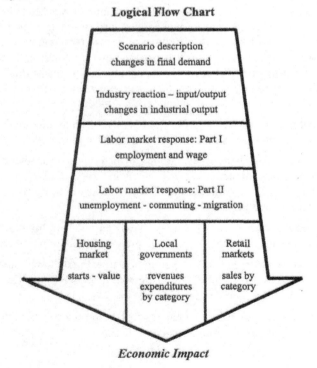

their output. In doing so, they buy more from other local firms that in turn must increase their own output and employment to meet the new demand. In turn, these firms buy more from their local suppliers who subsequently must also increase their output and employment. These resulting increases in output and employment by the suppliers are the indirect effects. The direct and indirect effects are based on the linkages between local producers as they buy and sell among themselves, and are the essence of the production module.

Nevertheless, the impacts of the new spending do not end with business purchases. The newly hired workers in all businesses also generate local economic activity by spending (at least part of) their wages locally, thus further increasing regional output and employment. In the terminology of impact analysis, the manner and extent to which the new employees spend their money in the community are known as the induced effects. Tracing these impacts through the local economy emphasizes that the economy is an integrated system characterized by a number of important local linkages.

Population and income changes drive the model's econometric modules. As new economic opportunities arise, the local population is likely to increase as job seekers move into the region. In addition to their increased spending for retail goods, these new residents may also increase the demand for housing and public goods and services while adding to local tax revenues.

In order to examine the impacts of different types of retirees, we invoke a quasi-experimental design in which the region is held constant. Because not every rural community is a potential retirement community, we focus on an area that has the potential to become a retirement destination, namely the north central Wisconsin three-county region of Oneida, Forest, and Langlade. This amenity-rich part of the state is experiencing a significant in-migration of retirees who are converting their seasonal, lakefront properties to year-round retirement homes. Thus, an existing resource amenity community is the study area rather than a new planned retirement community. Total population of the three-county region is 63,000 with a per capita income of $16,551.

In implementing the model, we constructed expenditure patterns for several types of households. Simply put, the assorted scenarios are represented by how much each group spends on a variety of goods and services (this is the infusion of new economic activity). To develop spending profiles of the various elderly household types, we draw on the U.S. Bureau of Labor Statistics' Consumer Expenditure Survey for 1994-1995.[4] In all, we document the impact of an additional 500 elderly households of each type on a small rural economy. Given that there were 17,000 recreational homes in the area in 1990, this is a reasonable number of households. Households are the unit of analysis because local services are often planned and delivered in terms of households.

In constructing scenarios, the expenditure pattern of each group, household size, and number of earners are included in the scenarios that are entered into the model. This was done by aggregating the BLS-CES expenditures by household type to coincide with IMPLAN sectors of the input-output model. Because the categories of the two do not map exactly, some BLS-CES expenditure data are "lost" to IMPLAN. The discrepancy is largest for the "entertainment" expenditures category, and the overall discrepancy is largest for the high-income group of retirees. The result is that the model will tend to underestimate the impacts in this sector.

Table 1. Select Economic and Demographic Characteristics of Elderly Households Applied to Five Scenarios

Household Characteristics	Age 65 + (comparison group)	Low income (below 20,000)	High income (above 50,000)	Age 65-75	Age 75 and over
Income before taxes ($)	22,148	10,494	91,439	25,553	18,006
Income after taxes ($)	21,068	10,152	83,146	24,205	17,252
Average annual expenditures ($)	22,249	16,241	55,202	25,277	18,572
Average number of persons in household	1.7	1.5	2.3	1.9	1.5
Average number of earners in household	0.4	0.2	1.2	0.6	0.2
Average number of vehicles in household	1.4	1.1	2.1	1.8	1.0
Percentage homeowners	79	73	91	82	76
Percentage homeowner with mortgage	14	10	24	20	8
Percentage renters	21	27	9	18	24
Estimated market value of owned home ($)	81,160	60,259	198,517	86,635	74,535
Estimated market rent of owned home ($)	530	417	971	568	484

Source: BLS Consumer Expenditure Survey (http://stats.bls.gov/csxcross.htm#y9596)

ANALYSIS RESULTS

Descriptive analysis: Elderly households differ in income, expenditures, size, and labor force participation (Table 1). The typical low-income retiree household has an after-tax income of $10,000, compared with $83,000 for high-income retirees and $21,000 for all retirees (the baseline comparison group). When looking at income by age, retirees over 75 years of age have a household income of $17,000, compared with an income of $24,000 for younger retirees. (Note that the younger retiree households also have a higher average income than the comparison group.)

On average, retiree households have 1.7 members. For our other scenario groups, the typical low-income household has 1.5 members while the high-income households have 2.3 members on average. Younger households have 1.9 members while older households have 1.5 members; the difference reflects the fact that many older retirees are widowed. The number of earners in the household also seems to be related to age and income. On average, retiree households have 0.4 earners (comparison group), while low-income households have 0.2 earners, and high-income households have 1.2 earners.

In applying these averages to the 500 in-migrant households our model examines for each scenario, we realize an additional 100 earners in the low-income scenario and 600 additional earners in the high-income scenario. Not surprisingly, the younger households have more earners (0.6 per household) than older households have (0.2 per household). Thus, 500 younger retiree households results in 300 new earners while the older retiree scenario adds only 100 earners.

Overall impacts: In all cases, the elderly have positive local economic and fiscal impacts compared with the baseline representation of the local economy. As one might expect, the magnitude and nature of impacts are generally in proportion to household size and income level. However, our results do provide some interesting differences when comparing and contrasting various groups of elderly to the commonly assumed "homogeneous elderly," which in this case is defined as the average of all persons 65 and older. The scenarios discussed below illustrate these comparisons.

Table 2 shows the extent each of the five scenarios leads to different community impacts. In each case, 500 elderly in-migrating households were added to the population of the three counties and their total impact on the baseline was assessed. The comparison group—an average mix of elderly households—leads to a population growth in the three county area of 960 persons, in part because they would leverage additional jobs that would attract new households to the local economy. As expected, 500 elderly in-migrating households in the high income scenario would attract more population growth (1,416) than 500 low income migrating households. In-migrating households age 65-75 would lead to a total population increase of 1,075, compared to only

Table 2. Simulated Population and Labor Force Impacts of 500 Elderly Inmigrating Elderly Households: By Type

	Baseline Value	Age 65 and over (comparison group) Impact	Per Household	Low income (below 20,000) Impact	Per Household	High income (above 50,000) Impact	Per Household	Age 65-75 Impact	Per Household	Age 75 and over Impact	Per Household
Population	63,210	960	1.92	819	1.64	1,416	2.83	1,075	2.15	842	1.68
Local labor force	31,780	264	0.583	139	0.28	754	0.75	373	0.75	153	0.30
Local unemployed	1,837	-40	-0.08	-22	-0.04	-113	-0.11	-56	-0.11	-24	-0.05
Net out-commuters	951	-2	0	-15	-0.03	93	0.19	-2	0	-4	0
Employed new residents (non-retiree)		45		27		4		41		45	

842 for a similar group of immigrants whose age is over 75. Table 2 also shows the per household increase to the three counties.

The local labor force increases under all scenarios. This increase includes both the retiree households as well as current residents who decide to enter the labor force. While the number of local unemployed residents decreases in all scenarios, the decline is less under the low-income and older retiree scenarios than it is in the comparison group scenario (Table 2).[5] In contrast, the high-income retirees produce the largest decrease in the number of unemployed. Overall, because unemployment is measured by place of residence, this means that some unemployed residents have taken jobs. Still, these impacts are mitigated by the fact that new, working-age migrants also join the local labor force to fill some of the new employment opportunities (shown as "employed new residents" in Table 3). Note that the "employed new residents" impact is highest in the low-income and older retiree scenarios where the number of household members in the labor force is lowest. The low-income and older retirees' scenarios have lower population impacts than the comparison group has (Table 3). This is mainly because of smaller household size in these groups.

Employment Impacts: As we show in Table 3, *introducing* high-income and young retirees to our 3-county retirement area generates higher employment in every sector relative to an average comparison group. In contrast, low-income and older retirees create less employment in every sector of the local economy than the comparison group creates. For example, the 500 high-income retiree households generate a total of 810 jobs, while 500 low income retiree households generate only 156 jobs. The average is 287 jobs created by 500 additional retiree households (comparison group). In all cases, the major employment impacts are in the trade and services sectors. Government and construction also show notable employment impacts, while employment impacts in other sectors are minor.

As noted above, retirees take a number of the additional jobs shown in Table 3 because these households have members (i.e., earners) in the labor force. An important implication is that the retiree labor force participation requires that the scenario construction reflect sectors in which the retirees are employed. For simulation purposes, these workers were evenly distributed across the trade and service sectors, an assumption that is consistent with the literature (e.g., Gunter & McNamara, 1990; Kahne, 1985).

Income Impacts: Given that they create fewer jobs than households of the comparison group, it is not surprising that the low-income and older retirees also create less total earnings than the comparison group creates (Table 3). Under all scenarios, earnings per worker fall relative to the baseline, but they fall less in the low-income and older-retiree scenarios than in the comparison group. In fact, earnings per worker are lowest in the scenarios with the higher-income groups—the young and high-income retirees. The decline in earnings per worker indicates that the new jobs tend to pay lower wages than existing jobs. The

Table 3. Simulated Employment and Wage Impacts of In-migration by Elderly Households

Sector	Baseline Value	Age 65 and over (comparison group) Impact	Per Household	Low income (below 20,000) Impact	Per Household	High income (above 50,000) Impact	Per Household	Age 65-75 Impact	Per Household	Age 75 and over Impact	Per Household
Total Employment	33,312	287	0.57	156	0.31	810	1.62	399	0.80	173	0.35
Agriculture	1,604	0	0	0	0	0	0	0	0	0	0
Mining	121	0	0	0	0	0	0	0	0	0	0
Construction	1,806	3	0	2	0	6	0	4	0	3	0
Manufacturing	5,289	0	0	0	0	1	0	0	0	0	0
TCPU*	1,581	3	0	2	0	5	0.01	3	0	2	0
Trade	8,343	145	0.29	78	0.15	404	0.81	203	0.41	85	0.17
FIRE**	1,343	5	0.01	4	0.01	7	0.01	5	0.01	4	0
Services	8,966	114	0.23	56	0.11	352	0.70	166	0.33	63	0.13
Government	4,259	17	0.03	13	0.02	34	0.07	18	0.04	15	0.03
Earnings per worker	$9,662	-$24	-0.12	-$12	-0.06	-$71	-0.36	-$35	-0.18	-$13	-0.07
Total earnings ($)	54,971,430	4,824,526	0.74	2,651,848	0.40	13,509,324	2.06	6,657,345	1.02	2,948,706	0.45

*TCPU Transportation, communications and public utilities
**FIRE Finance, insurance and real estate
Baseline data are actual current employment and earnings in the 3-county area (population 63,210)

lower earnings per worker in the latter two scenarios may be because of two factors: (1) the larger number of part-time workers in these households relative to the comparison group and to the other two groups; and (2) the proportionately larger increase in jobs in the retail and service sectors, which historically are lower paying jobs.[6]

As noted above, the direct and indirect changes in income and population are the model's main drivers. In Tables 4-6, we explore the retail and fiscal impacts of the changes for each of the scenarios. We report the aggregate impacts, which are derived by multiplying the per capita impacts for each scenario by their respective total change in population. This information is useful in that it shows the magnitude of the differences in impacts for the various scenarios. In some cases, the scenarios may have fairly similar total impacts, whereas in others they may differ significantly. For practitioners, one potential use of these results would be to estimate the "impacts per migrant," which could be used as a multiplier when estimating potential impacts in a community. This information is provided in the tables.

Retail Impacts: The impacts of 500 new elderly households to the 3-county area vary across the scenarios (Table 4). The average comparison group would increase local retail sales by more than $7 million per year. While this is a large amount, it is only about 1.2 percent of the total baseline sales ($545 million). If the in-migrants were low-income, however, the increase is estimated at only $4.6 million; by comparison, the high-income households would increase total retail sales by $21 million.

It is informative to look at the per household impacts. Here, we see that total retail sales will increase by $14,178 per new household in the comparison specific impacts among the scenarios. For example, when looking at health care, older retirees increase total local government health care expenditures relative to the baseline, while expenditures decrease for all other groups, including the low-income retirees.

The retail sectors most impacted are autos, food stores and general stores, accounting for more than 50 percent of all retail impacts.

Local Government Impacts: Total government expenditures increase in all scenarios relative to the baseline (Table 5). In the comparison group, total non-education expenditures increase by about $669,000. In the low-income scenario, total expenditures increase by $538,688, whereas total expenditures increase by $1.28 million in the high-income case. In the age 65-75 case, total expenditures are expected to increase by $733,477 and in the age 75+ case, total local expenditures are predicted to increase by about $598,000. In general, the relative increase or decrease in total expenditures is a function of the increase in population under each scenario. Nevertheless, there are some differences in specific impacts among the scenarios. For example, when looking at health care, older retirees increase total local government health care expenditures relative to the baseline, while expenditures decrease for all other groups, including the low-income retirees.

Table 4. Simulated Retail Impacts of In-migration by Elderly Households

Retail Sector	Baseline Value ($)	Per Capita	Age 65 and over (comparison group) Impact	Per Household	Low income (below 20,000) Impact	Per Household	High income (above 50,000) Impact	Per Household	Age 65-75 Impact	Per Household	Age 75 and over Impact	Per Household
Total Retail Sales ($)	544,859,743	8,619.83	7,088,765	14,178	4,577,967	9156	21,007,090	42014	8,007,115	16014	6,016,548	12033
Furniture	14,437,945	228.41	194,120	388	146,204	292	441,349	883	213,746	427	171,798	344
Autos	123,280,613	1,950.33	1,708,683	3,417	808,043	1616	6,925,513	13851	2,021,821	4044	1,339,123	2678
Building	31,587,661	499.73	474,943	949	365,798	732	966,579	1933	538,341	1077	406,945	814
Apparel	18,766,967	296.90	336,622	673	326,032	652	208,778	418	377,021	754	298,788	598
Drug stores	13,483,658	213.32	220,568	441	162,677	325	481,701	963	255,821	512	182,992	366
Food stores	100,484,868	1,589.70	1,118,364	2236	784,397	1569	3,049,504	6099	1,206,486	2413	1,006,480	2013
General	66,612,533	1,053.83	1,118,390	2236	783,383	1567	2,711,231	5422	1,308,356	2617	914,097	1828
Eating and drinking	53,924,431	853.10	702,414	1404	522,314	1045	1,624,135	3248	779,162	1558	615,542	1231
Miscellaneous	73,588,949	1,164.20	574,237	1148	110,817	222	3,739,090	7478	612,510	1225	495,996	992
Gasoline	48,692,119	770.32	640,426	1280	568,302	1137	859,210	1718	693,851	1388	584,787	1170

Baseline data are actual current retail sales in the 3-county area

Looking at the per household impacts, we see that total non-education expenditures will increase by $1,338 per new household in the comparison group case. In the high-income case, total expenditures are expected to increase by $2,545 per new household, whereas per new household expenditures will increase by only $9,156 in the low-income scenario. In the age 65-75 case, per new household expenditures will increase $1,466, while expenditures will increase by $1,195 per new household aged 75+.

One important consequence of these findings is that simply applying per capita government expenditures based on baseline data, as some studies have done, can give misleading results for specific expenditure categories. For example, in the low-income scenario, road expenditures per new household are expected to increase by $160, while road expenditures per new high-income household are predicted to increase by $735. In part, this reflects the different population effects in the two scenarios, but it also suggests a greater demand for roads due to higher income.

Education: The additional (non-retiree) working-age migrants to the area increase the number of school-aged children. The increase, however, is lower than in previous studies because retirees – rather than working-age in-migrants – take most of the new jobs.

Total expenditures increase in all scenarios relative to the baseline (Table 5). In the comparison group, total education expenditures increase by about $731,000. In the low-income scenario, total expenditures increase by $1.56 million, whereas total expenditures increase by $1.40 million in the high-income case. In the age 65-75 case, total education expenditures are expected to increase by $802,737 and in the age 75+ case, total local expenditures are predicted to increase by about $652,135.

Looking at the per household impacts, we see that total education and expenditures will increase by $1,462 per new household in the comparison group case. In the high-income case, total expenditures are expected to increase by $2,792 per new household, whereas per new household expenditures will increase by $3,114 in the low-income scenario. In the age 65-75 case, per new household expenditures will increase $1,605, while expenditures will increase by $1,304 per new household aged 75+.

Revenues: Non-educational revenue is divided into property tax revenue inter-governmental revenue. All subgroups of retirees increase total non-educational revenues relative to the baseline. Total non-educational revenues increase for the younger and higher-income retirees relative to the comparison group (Table 6). This pattern in repeated for property tax revenues and intergovernmental revenues. Residential property tax revenues increase for several reasons: (1) new homes are built by the retirees or by residents who can sell their existing homes; (2) conversion of recreational homes to year-round homes; and (3) a general increase in demand for housing, which increases housing prices. Inter-governmental revenues increase when property tax revenues

Table 5. Simulated Local Government Expenditure Impacts of In-migration by Elderly Households

	Baseline		Age 65 and over (comparison group)		Low income (below 20,000)		High income (above 50,000)		Age 65-75		Age 75 and over	
	Value	Per Capita	Impact	Per Household	Impact	Per Household	Impact	Per Household	Impact	Per Household	Impact	Per Household
Total non-education expenditures ($)	51,431,000	814	669,064	1338	538,668	1077	1,272,799	2546	733,477	1467	597,956	1196
Health	12,991,000	206	123,067	246	122,234	244	114,088	228	119,888	240	125,788	252
Government	9,409,000	149	175,035	350	145,556	291	250,197	500	205,736	411	144,296	289
Safety	12,025,000	190	127,947	255	101,572	203	277,688	555	133,334	267	120,514	241
Roads	10,564,000	167	125,843	251	80,170	160	367,283	735	145,101	290	104,019	208
Waste	2,545,000	40	55,130	110	40,314	81	140,311	281	60,138	120	49,145	98
Amenity	3,897,000	62	62,044	124	48,822	98	123,233	246	69,280	139	54,194	108
Total education expenditures ($)	75,599,192	1196	731,090	1462	1,557,179	3114	1,396,015	2792	802,737	1605	652,135	1304

Baseline data are actual current government and education expenditures in the 3-county area

Table 6. Simulated Local Government Revenue Impacts of In-migration by Elderly Households

	Baseline		Age 65 and over (comparison group)		Low income (below 20,000)		High income (above 50,000)		Age 65-75		Age 75 and over	
	Value	Per Capita	Impact	Per Household	Impact	Per Household	Impact	Per Household	Impact	Per Household	Impact	Per Household
Total non-education revenues ($)	96,521,670	1,527	1,403,177	2806	1,160,897	2322	2,354,892	4710	1,563,725	3127	1,233,911	2568
Intergovernmental	27,496,350	435	352,320	705	282,321	565	683,101	1366	385,326	771	315,577	631
Property tax	69,025,320	1,092	1,050,857	2102	878,576	1757	1,671,791	3344	1,178,399	2357	918,334	1837

Baseline data are actual current government revenues in the 3-county area increase because the Wisconsin system rewards communities that are willing to tax themselves.

Net Fiscal Impacts: Under all scenarios, the net fiscal impact of non-educational revenues and expenditures is positive (Tables 5 and 6). The magnitude of the net fiscal impact is, not surprisingly, higher for the high-income and younger retirees than it is for the comparison group. While low-income and older retirees do increase per capita local government spending on health care, they decrease per capita spending in other areas. Thus, we do not find evidence that they are a burden on local government.

While the in-migrating retirees increase property tax revenues, it was not possible to calculate impacts on all educational revenue sources (i.e., not property based) because state rules surrounding educational revenues are in transition. For this reason, the net fiscal impact on education cannot be calculated. We suspect, however, that the impact would show that total revenues would increase more than total expenditures for three reasons: (1) an increase in property tax revenues themselves; (2) increased intergovernmental revenues (a reward to communities who tax themselves in Wisconsin); and (3) low in-migration and few new children in the school system because "empty nest" retiree households take most of the new jobs.

CONCLUSIONS AND IMPLICATIONS

This research contributes to the literature on retiree migration by relaxing the traditional assumption that the elderly are a homogeneous group. Using a quasi-experimental design, we introduced groups of retirees characterized by age and income into the same community and compared their impacts. Each retiree group has particular economic and fiscal impacts that differ from those of the other groups of retirees and from the comparison group that represents the traditional assumption of a homogeneous elderly population. All of the scenarios showed positive economic impacts on the community and positive net fiscal impacts on the non-educational portion of local government, showing that retirees, no matter their age or income, are not a fiscal burden to the community. Net fiscal impacts for education were not estimated.

Of particular interest are the impacts on local government healthcare costs for low-income and older retirees. In the literature, concern about the impacts of these two groups on local healthcare costs has been called the "gray peril." While total healthcare costs increase because of population increase, we find no evidence to support the gray peril health care concern for local governments. Our study, however, does not address the possibility of a gray peril for federal and state governments, which bear the main public costs of healthcare for the elderly. It is important to note that this finding for local governments could change if the policy or rules on health-care funding for retirees change.

The differences in population change among the scenarios are mainly because of the variation in the number of persons in the retiree households. Our findings show that fewer working-age families migrate to the area to take jobs than the previous literature suggests because the elderly will supply some of the labor demand created by their own spending. This will result in less in-migration, lower demands on the educational system, and a smaller impact on housing demand if the elderly were not in the labor force.

Lower per worker wages relative to the comparison group are an unexpected outcome of the scenarios for younger and higher-income retirees. This can be explained in part by the number of part-time workers in these retiree households who enter the local labor market. These results point out the importance of including the labor force participation of retirees in impact analysis, which has not been done in previous research. Given recent changes in Social Security rules whereby benefits are not reduced when earnings exceed a certain level, labor force participation of retirees may increase.

The differences in impacts between the younger and older retirees scenarios may be useful to communities that have in the past attracted younger retirees, as it can help communities plan for changes as these retirees age. Even though differences in total and per household impacts are not as large as between other groups, there are important differences in impacts for specific sectors. For example, per household sales in specific retail sectors and per capita government expenditures in specific categories differed greatly for these two groups relative to the comparison group. This suggests shifts in the local economy and in local government spending as retirees age. The older-retirees scenario might also be used by communities that tend to attract older retirees who are making a second move for health reasons. This research shows that aging clearly changes the demand mix for both the private and public sectors.

Some communities have a high percentage of retirees not because of in-migration, but because of retirees aging-in-place. Communities may want to plan for the needs of these citizens. For policy purposes, the lower-income retirees can be thought of as similar in economic characteristics to retirees who age-in-place. Even low-income retirees have positive economic impacts, but not as large as younger and wealthier retirees. Low-income retirees increase total retail sales, but not to the same extent as high-income and younger retirees increase them. In addition, low-income retirees require a different mix of government services than the comparison group of retirees requires; in particular, they require more health services.

Low-income retirees have positive net fiscal impacts on the non-educational portion of local government. This finding is significant because we used the lowest income level in this scenario to provide a conservative estimate of the impacts of low-income retirees. The finding runs counter to fears that low-income retirees may be a fiscal burden on the community.

High-income retirees make the highest demands on local government expenditures. The areas with the largest increases are waste, roads, and amenities.

If a community plans to attract retirees, it makes sense for that community to target particular groups of retirees based on how their demands and impacts fit with the community and its goals. For example, the largest increase in per capita government amenity spending is in the high-income scenario. A community that does not wish to increase public funding of amenities might be advised not to recruit high-income retirees.

A community may wish to develop programs that will keep retirees, who might otherwise migrate, in the community. Information provided here also can be interpreted as to what the community would lose if such retirees were not retained, and it could be used to develop programs that would retain them. In addition, many communities have a mix of young, old, poor, and well-off retirees. The needs of these varied groups will not be met by a "one-size-fits-all" set of services for the elderly.

It is also important to recognize that the economic and fiscal impacts of retirees will change as state and national policies change. For example, a community bears very few medical costs for retirees, and the medical spending of retirees generates jobs in the community. A policy change in the funding of Medicare and Medicaid will affect local health care costs and the economic and fiscal impacts of retirees. It should also be pointed out that this analysis cannot be generalized to the state level because the state bears a different set of costs and has different revenue streams than local governments bear (Deller, 1995; Stallmann & Siegel, 1995). The state, for example, incurs medical costs for retirees eligible for Medicaid. Therefore, retiree migration that generates a positive fiscal impact at the local level could result in a negative impact at the state level.

NOTES

1. Specifically, nonmetropolitan counties with a net in-migration of at least 15 percent by persons aged sixty and over (Bender et al., 1985).

2. In this model, the high-income retirees serve as a proxy for retirees who migrate to rural areas for lifestyle and recreational opportunities. In comparison, the low-income retirees serve as a proxy for two groups: (1) low-income retirees who migrate to lower their living costs (Happel, Hogan, & Pflantz, 1988); and (2) retirees who age-in-place. In the latter case, the results can be interpreted as what the community would lose if retirees who age in place would choose to leave (a counterfactual).

3. Our model closely resembles a plethora of regional models constructed for policy simulations, for example Kort and Cartwright (1981) for U.S. states; Conway (1990) for Washington State; Coomes, Olson and Glennon (1991) for Louisville; Treyz, Rickman and Shao (1992) for user-defined regions; Rey (1997) for San Diego; Swenson and Otto (forthcoming) for Iowa counties; and Johnson, Scott and Ma (1997) for Missouri communities.

4. One concern might be the use of national expenditure data to approximate actual local spending. It must be remembered that these are urban retirees migrating to rural areas. In this particular case, many are from Chicago and Milwaukee. Thus, their consumption patterns are likely to match national patterns. This may be less true for rural retirees who age in place, but no other data source is available.

5. Table 2 measures employment by place of work, that is, jobs in the region. Table 3 measures the labor force, that is, persons. The labor force is smaller than the number of jobs because some people hold more than one job.

6. Because secondary data on employment do not distinguish between a full and a part-time job, we cannot model the number of new full and part-time jobs. In "Employment Impacts," we cite research evidence about the part-time employment of the elderly.

REFERENCES

Barkley, D. L., & M. S. Henry. 1993. Economic Impact of Savannah Lakes Village on McCormick County South Carolina. Little Rock: University of Arkansas Cooperative Extension Service.

Bender, L. D., B. L. Green, T. F. Hady, J. A. Kuehn, M. K. Nelson, L. B. Perkinson, & P. J. Ross. 1985. The Diverse Social and Economic Structure of Non-Metropolitan America. Rural Development Research Report No. 49. Washington, DC: Agriculture and Rural Economy Division, Economic Research Service, United States Department of Agriculture.

Bureau of Labor Statistics (BLS). 1997. Consumer Expenditure Survey, 1994-1995. http://www.bls.gov/cex.

Cockerham, W. C. 1997. *This Aging Society.* Prentice-Hall.

Conway, R. 1990. The Washington projection and simulation model: A regional inter-industry econometric mode. *International Regional Science Review* 13(1-2): 141-165.

Cook, P. J., & T. F. Hady. 1993. Updating the ERS County Typology: A View From the 1980s. Staff Report No. AGES9327. Washington, DC: Agriculture and Rural Economy Division, Economic Research Service, United States Department of Agriculture.

Coomes, P., D. Olson, & D. Glennon. 1991. The inter-industry employment demand variable: An extension of the I-SAMIS technique for linking input-output and econometric models. *Environment and Planning A* 23(7): 1063-1068.

Cox, H. G. 1993. *Later Life: The Realities of Aging.* Englewood Cliffs, NJ: Prentice Hall.

Deller, S. C. 1995. Economic impact of retirement migration. *Economic Development Quarterly* 9: 25-38.

Fagan, M., & C. F. Longino. 1993. Migrating retirees: A source for economic development. *Economic Development Quarterly.* 7: 98-106.

Glasgow, N., & C.L. Beale. 1985. rural elderly in demographic perspective. *Rural Development Perspectives* 2: 22-26.

Gunter, L., & K. T. McNamara. 1990. The impact of local labor market conditions on the off-farm earnings of farm operators. *Southern Journal of Agricultural Economics.* 22: 155-165.

Happel, S. K., T. D. Hogan, & E. Pflantz. 1988. The economic impacts of elderly winter residents in the Phoenix area. *Research on Aging.* 10: 119-133.

Happel, S. K., T. D. Hogan, & D. Sullivan. 1983. The social and economic impact of Phoenix area winter residents. *Arizona Business.* 30: 310.

Haas, W. H. III, & W. J. Serow. 1997. Retirement migration decision making: Life course mobility, sequencing of events, social ties and alternatives. *Journal of the Community Development Society* 28(1):116-130.

Henderson, D. 1994. Estimates of retirees spending in the retail and service sectors of a community. *Journal of the Community Development Society* 25(2): 259-276.

Hurd, M. D. 1989. The economic status of the elderly. *Science.* 244: 659-664.

Johnson, T. G., J. K. Scott, & J. Ma. 1997. The Community Policy Analysis System (COMPAS). Web-published paper: http://www.cpac.missouri.edu/library/papers/compas-021997.html.

Jones, L. L., N. C. Whitehorn, & A. J. Wyse. 1993. Economic and Social Impacts of Retirees Migrating to East Texas. DIR 93-2. College Station, TX: Texas A&M University System, Texas Agricultural Experiment Station.

Kahne, H. 1985. The Concepts of part-time work: The old and the new. In *Reconceiving Part-Time Work—New Perspectives for Older Workers and Women.* Totowa NJ: Rowman and Allanheld.

Kort, J. & J. Cartwright. 1981. Modeling the multiregional economy: Integrating econometric and input-output models. *The Review of Regional Studies* 11(1): 1-17.

Litwak, E., & C. F. Longino, Jr. 1987. Migration Patterns among the elderly: A developmental perspective. *The Gerontologist* 27: 266-72.

Longino, C. F. Jr. 1988. The Gray Peril Mentality and the impact of retirement migration. *The Journal of Applied Gerontology* 7(4): 448-455.

Miller, W. P. 1993. Economic and Fiscal Impact of Bella Vista Village Arkansas. Little Rock, Arkansas: University of Arkansas Cooperative Extension Service, 1993.

Reeder, R., & N. L. Glasgow. 1990. Nonmetro Retirement Counties Strengths and Weaknesses." *Rural Development Perspectives.* 6: 12-17.

Reeder, R., R. Hopper, & C. Thompson. 1995. Rural retiree attraction: Recent trends and strategies. In R.P. Wolensky and E.J. Miller (eds.), *The Small City and Regional Community*, Vol. 11. 1994. Conference Proceedings, University of Wisconsin-Stevens Point, Center for Small Cities.

Rey, S. 1997. Integrating regional econometric and input-output models: An evaluation of embedding strategies. *Environment and Planning A.* 29(6): 1057-1072.

Rowles, G. D., & J. F. Watkins. 1993. Elderly migration and development in small communities. *Growth and Change* 24: 509-538.

Shields, M. 1998. *An Integrated Economic Impact and Simulation Model for Wisconsin Counties.* Unpublished Ph.D. Dissertation, Department of Agricultural Economics, University of Wisconsin-Madison.

Shields, M., S. C. Deller, & J.I. Stallmann. 2001. Comparing the impacts of retired versus working-age families on a small rural region: An application of the Wisconsin Economic Impact Modeling System. *Agricultural and Resource Economic Review* 30(1): 20-31.

Siegel, P. B., & F. O. Leuthold. 1993. Economic and fiscal impacts of a retirement/recreation community: A study of Tellico Village, Tennessee. *Journal of Agricultural and Applied Economics* 25: 134-147.

Stallmann, J. I., & L. L. Jones. 1995. A typology of retirement places: A community analysis. *Journal of the Community Development Society* 26(1): 1-14.

Stallmann, J. I., & P. B. Siegel. 1995. Attracting retirees as an economic development strategy: Looking into the Future. *Economic Development Quarterly* 9: 372-383.

Swenson, D. & D. Otto. (forthcoming). The Iowa economic/fiscal impact modeling system. *Journal of Regional Analysis and Policy.*

Treyz, G., D. Rickman & G. Shao. 1992. The remi economics demographic forecasting and simulation model. *International Regional Science Review* 14(3): 221-253.

Voth, D. E., W. P. Miller, & R. E. Cluck. 1993. Retirement In-Migration Study Benton County, Arkansas. Little Rock, Arkansas: University of Arkansas Cooperative Extension Service.

Walzer, N., & S. C. Deller. 1996. Rural issues and trends." In N. Walzer (ed), *Community Strategic Visioning Programs*. Westport, CT: Praeger.

Woods, M., & C. Allen. 1993. Economic and Social Impacts of Retirees Migrating to Tahlequah and Cherokee Counties. Agricultural Economics Reports 9321. Stillwater, Oklahoma: Oklahoma State University, Department of Agricultural Economics.

Woods, M. D., W. Miller, D. Voth, B. Song, & L. Jones. 1997. Economic impacts of in-migrating retirees on local economies. *Journal of Community Development Society* 28(2): 206-224.

Bowling Alone but Online Together: Social Capital in E-Communities

James K. Scott and Thomas G. Johnson

In this paper, we present a non-technical overview of new forms of voluntary association called online (or e-) communities and explore the implications they present for community development theory and practice. E-communities are groups of people with common interests that communicate regularly, and for some duration, in an organized way over the Internet (Ridings et al., 2002). They are designed to provide users with a range of tools for learning, personal development, and collective action—all embedded in a complex, continuing, and personally enriching network of social relations. We pose several fundamental questions, including these: a) what are the key features of online communities? b) how do they compare to (offline) communities of place? c) how are they designed and developed? and d) how do e-community members use them to affect collective action? We define key terms related to online communities, place them in the context of broader Web cultural practices, and review emerging literature in online community development. We present findings from case studies of four very different active online communities. Social interaction in these communities was extensive, and surprisingly civil. Web site managers use a variety of community development practices to attract and retain members, and to establish community norms, trust, and collective resources.

Several years ago Robert Putnam captured the attention of many social scientists, policymakers, and community leaders with one simple observation: membership in bowling leagues in the United States was declining (Cf., Putnam, 2000). Statistics showed that bowling remained a very popular leisure activity. However, people were less inclined to participate in the context of more or less formal voluntary associations we call leagues. When considered in isolation, this observation seems quite inconsequential. However, Putman and others have skillfully linked it with data that show a steady and rather steep decline in American participation in voluntary associations generally for the past fifty years. Along with many other social theorists before them, Putnam and colleagues argued that broad participation in voluntary associations was a chief source of the norms, trust, and collective resources (labeled *social capital*) that are essential to community life.

Putnam's research has inspired thousands of scholars and practitioners around the world to investigate and debate the current state of voluntary associations and their importance to community development. A review of this remarkably vital and productive dialogue is beyond the scope of this paper.[1] However, as scholars and practitioners debate key concepts and research methods, collect and analyze data, and publish research findings about social capital

---

James K. Scott and Thomas G. Johnson are at the Truman School of Public Affairs, at the University of Missouri-Columbia.

and community development, something very interesting is happening. Even as membership in bowling leagues, service clubs, parent teacher associations, etc. declines, participation in new forms of voluntary associations called *online* (or *e-*) communities appears to be rapidly increasing. Online communities are groups of people with common interests that communicate regularly, and for some duration, in an organized way over the Internet (Ridings et al., 2002). These Web-based associations are typically less proximal than community networks or tele-community centers, which have been the focus of recent productive community development research and practice (Cf., Hampton & Wellman, 2000; Gurstein, 2000; Pigg, 2001). E-communities are typically more comprehensive in scope than other computer-mediated-communication technologies, such as discussion lists, chat rooms, Web-based conferencing, or collaboration systems. They are designed to provide users with a range of tools for learning, personal development, and collective action—all embedded in a complex, continuing, and personally enriching network of social relations.

As we will see below, some of the most heavily visited sites on the World Wide Web are, at least in part, platforms for large and active online communities. E-communities are widely used to support online retail and other commercial ventures,[2] and to facilitate learning and communication for professional development and for sports or hobby enthusiasts. They are attracting increasing attention from information and social scientists and philosophers (Cf., Feenberg & Barney, 2004; Shane, 2004; Ciffolilli, 2003; Shoberth et al., 2003). In this paper, we present a non-technical overview of online communities for a wider audience and pose several fundamental questions. What are the key features of online communities? How are they similar to and different from (offline) proximal communities? Why are they attracting new members? How are they designed and developed? What are their strengths and limitations? What implications do they present for (offline) community development theory and practice?

This paper reviews trends in online community development and invites scholars and practitioners to pursue further investigation and dialogue. It is developed in four sections. First, we define key terms related to online communities, place them in the context of broader Web cultural practices, and review emerging literature in online community development. We then propose research questions and describe the methodology employed to investigate them in four different active online communities. Next, we present research findings. Finally, we review lessons learned and discuss the implications of this research for community development research and practice.

INTRODUCTION

For purposes of this paper, we define community as *a group of people sharing common rights, privileges, or interests, or living in the same place under the same laws and regulations*. Members of community also share, at least to some degree, a sense of common identity as well as the desire or need for at least occasional collective action. This definition can apply to members of a religious community, tenants in a cooperative apartment complex, or residents of a municipality or region. An online community is simply one whose members interact primarily through computer-mediated communication—particularly in a Web environment. In the following paragraphs, we briefly compare the attributes of communities of place and e-communities.

Online community encourages extensive interaction through a variety of means (often bundled together on the same Web site) such as chat rooms, asynchronous discussion forums, Web logs (or Blogs) (Blood, 2000), and Web-based collaboration systems called wikis (Leuf & Cunningham, 2001).[3] People involved in online communities can use these tools to join or start conversations (or projects) whenever they choose. However, a key feature of online community building—and what makes this approach unique—is its use of software such as reputation systems[4] to augment members' abilities to filter through information, build personal connections, and affect collaborative or collective action. Case and colleagues (2001) argue that online community sites must regulate the amount of communication and information flow intelligently, so that the burdens of membership do not outweigh its benefits. They also contend that to foster community spirit, these sites should allow members to build relationships with members that share particular interests (Case et al., 2001, p. 64). On e-community sites, members' identities are typically persistent. Users can know one another by reviewing more or less elaborate member profiles, and by relying on emerging Web-applications called reputation systems (Resnick, 2004; Masum & Zhang, 2004; Hitlin, 2004). In e-communities, users can distinguish members from visitors. Members are typically assigned greater privileges (such as enhanced access to site features and more influence in community decisions or governance) as well as greater responsibilities. They agree to follow a set of discussion rules or guidelines. In effect, the technologies that filter information, connect potential collaborators, and establish and enforce standards of community conduct represent a *de facto* system of community governance (Shirky, 2003a).

Little is known about the demographics or the motivations of e-community members (Ridings et al., 2002; Horrigan & Fox, 2001; Hitlin, 2004; Nonnecke & Preece, 1999). However, evidence suggests that participation in online communities is clearly compelling to many Internet users. In Table 1, we show a list of popular Web sites that are designed to foster such user involvement. The Web sites are selected to illustrate the range of commercial, non-commercial, recreational, and socio-political purposes that can be pursued. The table reports data available from Alexa— a firm that analyzes continuous usage of the World Wide Web.[5] The table reports: 1) the date when each community site first appeared online; 2) the number of sites that currently link to it; 3) the number of people per one million Internet users that visit this site—based on a rolling average daily use over the preceding ninety days; and 4) the current ranking of each site in terms of overall user traffic, in relation to over four million Web domains monitored by Alexa.

Table 1. Selected Online-Community Site Usage Patterns: October, 2004*

Online Community Site	Description	Online Start Date	Links	Visitors per 1 Million Internet Users	Website Traffic Rank
http://www.eBay.com	Online auction portal	8/14/95	31,955	24,605	15
http://www.fool.com (The Motley Fool)	Personal finance and investment	6/26/95	12,136	572	1,791
http://www.geocaching.com	Recreation and outdoor adventure involving GPS	7/3/00	2,811	52	12,560
http://www.Ethepeople.org	Political discussion and action site	4/8/96	1,545	7.1	184,937**
http://www.friendster.com	Find old and new friends.	3/22/02	1,068	1,275	115
http://.www.meetup.com	Arrange off-line meetings on topics of common interest	8/20/98	1,098	236	3,700
http://www.Slashdot.com	News and alternative views on new technology	2/1/00	33,994	804	1,607
http://www.iVillage.com	News and conversation for topics of interest to women	7/26/95	12,211	1,110	836
http://www.Epinions.com	Consumer reviews on goods and services	2/12/99	13,398	1,009	970
http://www.Wikipedia.org	Designed to generate a dynamic comprehensive reference through collaborative writing.	1/12/01	6,849	2,015	450

*Traffic data gathered from alexa.com on October 13, 2004

**Due to data limitations, Alexa is unable to verify the accuracy of traffic rankings over 100,000.

In a highly competitive, rapidly expanding Web environment, several of these sites have existed for nearly ten years. In a study of user behavior at large retail Web sites, Brown et al. (2002) found that the users who participated in the site's online communities were nine times more likely to visit the site often, and twice as likely to purchase items. A recent case study on the popular iVillage site found that 93 percent of its members regard the site content to be "very useful" in their everyday lives (Figallo, 2002).

Theoretical Perspectives on E-Community Development

Sociologist Peter Kollock is one of several social scientists to investigate communities in cyberspace (Cf., Kollock, 1998; Smith & Kollock, 1998). He draws on foundational works by Axelrod (1984) and Ostrom (1991) about cooperation and community conflict to build theoretical principles that guide his analysis. These principles, he argues, are keys to the success of online communities.

Axelrod is particularly interested in the social origins and processes of cooperation. He argues that cooperation among people is most likely when: 1) the people have met or are likely to meet in the future; 2) they are able to identify each other; and 3) they are able to assess each other's capacity to contribute to mutual interests and their trustworthiness (See also Ridings et al., 2002). In e-communities, Axelrod's first condition for cooperation often does not hold—although some large communities such as eBay and geocaching.com now facilitate events where members can meet in person. However, many e-communities are designed explicitly to meet conditions two and three in ways that often greatly extend the members' range of individuals with whom cooperation is possible.

Ostrom (1991) is concerned with the management of community conflict, and the classic problem of governing the Commons. Kollock (1998) sees online communities as an emerging form of Commons and extracts four main observations from Ostrom, which are listed below.
1. Communities that share a common resource must have boundaries (e.g., distinctions between members vs. visitors or strangers). Such explicit distinctions make clear who can access and use collective resources and protect the commons from external takings.
2. Rules governing the collective use of resources are geared to the needs of members.
3. Sanctions are appropriate—and wherever possible, enforced by members.
4. Some conflict is inevitable. Community members must be able to access low-cost tools for conflict resolution.

According to Kollock, each of these principles is important in the design and implementation of successful e-communities (Kollock, 1998). Along with these, he proposes at least one other elemental feature, which he applies for both on- and offline communities. He argues that communities exist around some manifestation of scarcity and/or risk. For example, they facilitate some sort of exchange or (virtual) economy. He argues that apart from risk, there are few incentives for people to collaborate, and there is little need for interpersonal trust. The element of risk encourages the formation of clubs or groups to spread and share risk.

Online versus Offline Community Characteristics

One way to assess the utility of these principles is to compare the features of on- and offline communities of place. Table 2 compares key attributes relevant to community development theory and practice between online and (offline) communities of place, organized by six different features: community membership, personal identity, norms, communication, respect, and social capital. Following Woolcock and Nayaran (2000), we define *social capital* simply as: *the norms and networks that enable people to act collectively*.

In communities of place, an individual's membership is, in some sense, automatic and arbitrary—determined by the individual's location of residence or other long-term association with the place (e.g., business operator, property owner, etc.). Community residents may or may not be aware of,

Table 2. Characteristics of Online Communities Versus Communities of Place

	Communities of Place	Online Communities
Membership	Automatic–based on location of residence and social interaction.	Individual choice–based on common interest and contractual agreement.
Personal Identity/ Anonymity	Legal. Locatable. Actions are sometimes anonymous.	Extra-legal. Not locatable. Actions are rarely anonymous.
Norms	Formal and informal. Relative and multiple sanctions.	Formal and informal. Fairly absolute and single sanctions.
Authentic Communication	Enabled by interactions at multiple levels. Constrained by congestion, time and space.	Overcomes space-time limits through technology. Constrained by Internet access and lack of media "bandwidth."
Respect or Status	Not readily apparent. Episodic and emergent. Specific or categorical. Earned by positive contribution and association.	Readily apparent. Cumulative. General. Earned by positive contribution and peer review.
Social Capital	Combined with many other resources to affect collective action.	One of a few resources to affect collective action.

or agree with local shared purposes or expectations. They may or may not contribute meaningfully to collective action. Still, they are *de facto* members of their community. Membership in online communities is not tied to proximity. People who wish to enroll in online communities typically register as members, provide information about personal interests, select a name (by which they can be known), and agree to a code of community values or conduct. Membership can be terminated at any time by the individuals or the online community (Web site) managers.

A second important difference between proximal and online communities involves the potential for anonynmity and personal identification. Contemporary debates about security and privacy policies underscore the legal and ethical issues associated with personal identity. Marx (2001) illustrates the importance of these issues for social relations as well. In proximal communities, it is relatively easy for members to establish another member's legal identity, locate, and contact that person whenever they want. On the other hand, sometimes people in proximity may be able to act with anonymity (e.g., when outside their normal social or professional circles). People may use this anonymity to donate to a local charity or to violate a personal or professional trust. In any event, anonymous actions are difficult to trace, and thus, difficult for other members to consider as they work to affect personal or collective goals. In online communities, these conditions are reversed. Community rules and procedures make it difficult or impossible for members to establish a person's legal identity, or to locate and contact them directly unless that person grants them such permission. However, unlike many Internet chat or game rooms, e-community systems typically encourage members to establish persistent identities. Every action within the e-community is recorded and attributed to the particular individuals involved. Every contribution by a member to the life of the community—and others' response to it—becomes part of that member's profile and is available for inspection by any interested member. In that sense, anonymity is difficult to achieve.[6] The incentives for individual members are clear. They can develop strategies to participate according to their interests, assess the contributions and reputations of others, and manage their own. Actions that violate (formal or informal) community standards can be attributed to individuals, and often, violators are quickly "punished" with ostracism or other sanctions. This unique social setting has significant implications for the theory and practice of community development. In proximal community settings, actors seeking to enlist or mobilize others toward collective action often have very limited information about others' history and identification with community life. (Typically, this information comes from personal experience or recollection, and/or from third party recommendations.) In online communities, members can monitor the exact history of others' community participation and commitment. In many communities, they can also assess members' community influence or effectiveness.

Both types of communities are governed by formal and informal rules or codes of conduct; but they vary by the nature and scope of sanctions used to enforce them. In localities, rules are established and enforced in a broad context of social relations. Individual members can be rewarded or sanctioned in numerous ways, accounting for all sorts of relative circumstances. Penalties and rewards in online communities are much more limited—in part, because their authority is limited. Nevertheless, members of online communities who violate codes of conduct can either be shunned by other members or banished from community life by site managers. Decisions to sanction members are often arbitrary, absolute, and independent of community member input.

Communication is central to community life. Because of their proximity, local residents can interact and associate in multiple, often overlapping settings of work, service clubs, special purpose projects, or informal social settings. Place thus offers the potential of rich communication networks and strong social bonds. Of course, as Putnam (2000) and others have argued, the quality of communication in communities is constrained by congestion, and the challenges of finding common space and time to meet (Cf., Wheatley & Kellner-Rogers, 1998). Such barriers to communication may explain in part the rapid growth of online communities (Nonnecke & Preece, 1999). In addition, in proximal communities, particular members often control the flow of relevant information—either through one-on-one communications, or one to many broadcasts. This control of information can affect or impede collective action. From a normative perspective, it can lead to negative outcomes, such as misunderstandings, social exclusion, or reduced community capacity. E-communities use Web technology to help members overcome the barriers of space and time, and pursue more direct and democratic "many-to-many" communication.

Clearly, e-communities can provide venues for rich and sustaining personal communication. For example, a recent study found that eBay hosts 1.5 billion unique Web site visits per month, and the average member of eBay's online community spends one hour and 48 minutes per visit (Fan & Dierkes, 2004). Two key challenges to authentic communication remain for online communities. The first involves filtering through huge volumes of interaction to find personally relevant conversations. Most e-community Web sites use knowledge management and/or different types of intelligent agents continuously to learn about members' individual preferences, and thereby direct them to content they will find of interest. The second relates to what Feenburg and Bakardjieva (2004) call the narrow "bandwidth" of communication options. Most interaction is limited to the (remote) use of text or graphics—stripped of information derived from body language, human contact, "pregnant pauses," and other sensory perceptions. To address this limitation, many online communities are creating offline activities and events. Nevertheless, Web technology will not replace or fulfill the need for intimate human interaction.

Perhaps the most interesting comparison between online and proximal communities relates to the process for acquiring respect and social capital, and the relative criticality of that resource for community life. In online communities, measuring and comparing members' reputations is essential in affecting individual and community objectives (Ridings et al., 2002). When members register on these sites, they are asked to create a more or less standard user profile. Through accessible profile databases, users (and site managers) can monitor and evaluate members' community participation. Each member question, comment, or action can be evaluated by interested and qualified[7] members. These evaluations are quantified by various means, and real time '"reputation" scores are readily available for all members. The scores are then used by members to determine the trustworthiness of other members and filter through messages to view the contributions that others consistently find of value. In effect, the scores are measures of each individual's reputation or social capital within the community. This quantified reputation is one of the only assets individuals can use to pursue recognition and personal or community interests. Member reputation scores are powerful incentives. They are a tangible measure of an individual's current value to community life. Since these scores are readily accessible to all, many members work hard to manage their scores. They therefore tend to present themselves as intelligent, friendly, fun, and practical to other members, and eager to collaborate in common interest.[8] Since the scores are presented as perhaps the best and only way to evaluate the trustworthiness and capabilities of others, assessments of member contributions related to a few particular topics of interest may be generalized to all fields of competence. Pursuit of higher scores becomes—for some—both fun and relentless. In a way, these scores measure each member's access to social capital, which is a real, tangible resource they can use to affect individual or collective action within the e-community[9] (Resnick et al., 2004).

Reputation in proximal communities is measured and applied much more subtly and fluidly. Members' reputations are not readily apparent. They must be assessed subjectively. Our experience suggests that typically, in proximal communities, reputations are measured in episodes— not cumulatively. Reputations are assigned by personal experience, trusted recommendations, and by association. (People are often known by the company they keep). Finally, although relationships and reputation are very important, they are not the only resources available to affect individual and collective action.[10] Financial assets and social status and position are also of great practical value. When investigating power structure and influence in proximal communities, we are often advised to "follow the money." To study power and influence among online community members, we can simply follow their reputation scores.

It is important to note that the vast majority of e-community members rarely posts messages or contributes directly to community life. Research by Preece (2000) and colleagues (Nonnecke & Preece, 1999; Schoberth et al., 2003) estimates that for every active community poster there are as many as 100 who regularly monitor (or *lurk*) on community sites. Most reputation systems essentially ignore this passive listening. As a result, a large proportion of e-community members have low reputation scores. These members, therefore, may have limited influence within the online community. However, they may gain valuable insight from "listening" to community discussions (Resnick, 2004).

Design Principles for Online Community Development

To build user interest, online community site developers adopt simple but elegant principles of Web design, based on theories of social psychology (Cf., Beenan et al., 2004, Karau & Williams, 1993; Thompson et al., 2002), the use of various types of social software (Shirky, 2003a; 2003b), and the development of knowledge management and reputation systems (Resnick, 2004; Masum & Zhang, 2004). Some of the design principles—summarized and illustrated in a very practical, recent guide by Kim (2000)—are listed below. Although the similarities are not directly acknowledged, we suggest that the principles are quite consistent with good practices in (offline) community development work.

- Define and articulate the site's purpose. Communities come to life when they fulfill an ongoing need in people's lives. Remember why and for whom the online community is being built. This vision needs to be expressed in the design, technology, and policies of the online community.
- Build flexible, extensive gathering places, such as discussion threads, chat rooms, blogs, and wikis. Allow members to join or start discussions as they choose. Encourage fun, and informal as well as formal conversation. Help members find lively conversations by organizing them topically, and by posting information about the most popular or most recent postings.
- Create meaningful and evolving member profiles. This helps online community builders learn about site members and helps them to know each other. Profiles can help build trust, foster relationships, and infuse community with history and identity.
- Design for a range of community roles. Address the needs of newcomers without alienating the regulars. Guide newcomers, and offer recognition, involvement, "member in good standing" privileges, and other incentives to regulars.
- Establish a strong leadership development program. Members should have opportunities

to learn and accept more responsibility as they wish. Leaders should welcome newcomers, answer questions, advise site managers on content and policies, and help address any potential "problem" members or troublemakers.
- Encourage appropriate community etiquette. Conflict can be civil and invigorating for the community. Post clear ground rules for participation.[11] Set up systems that allow enforcement and evolution of standards.
- Promote cyclic events. Use the online community site to promote on- and off-line events, such as conferences, chats with leaders, etc.
- Integrate the rituals of community life. Celebrate community milestones or common holidays. Provide easy access to the history of the online community. Acknowledge personal transitions or successes of members.
- Facilitate member-run subgroups.

Every online community is unique—a product of the vision, technologies, and policies of its builders, as well as the chemistry and participation of its members. There are no standard methods, and certainly no guarantees of community viability. However, the basic software needed to support online communities is readily available. Much of it is accessible to local community groups in open source format, or as free or low-cost services on existing Web sites. Results in online community projects depend in part on the purpose and overall vision of the builders. Application of these principles in proximal community development projects could facilitate significant new public involvement.

METHODOLOGY

To investigate the practical application of online-community principles further, we studied the design and daily activities on four different Web communities. Selection of these sites was designed to reflect the diversity of history, purpose, community social and technical design features, content, overall size or scale, and user activity represented by this approach. Though nascent, much of the research on e-communities to date focuses on their use in e-commerce (Cf., Resnick et al., 2004). We wanted to compare these sites with online communities that are essentially non-commercial in nature. With that in mind, the four communities selected include two commercial sites (eBay.com and The Motley Fool), a recreational site (geocaching.com), and a site designed to promote (U.S.) political and public dialogue (E the People).

The authors registered as members on the sites, participated in and observed community discussion, and monitored how each site applied the design principles described above. This research was conducted independently and compiled during October and November 2004.

RESULTS

Analysis of these e-communities is presented as individual case studies below, and summarized in Table 3.

eBay (http://www.ebay.com)

By far, the largest online community site on the World Wide Web is eBay. Founded in 1995 at the beginning of the dot.com era by two entrepreneurs in San Jose, California, Pierre Omidymar and Jeff Stool (Gomes-Casseres, 2001), its purpose was to create a marketplace on the Web for individual buyers and sellers of goods and services. Since its inception, growth at eBay has been phenomenal. For example, in 1997, the site had 340,000 registered users, and totaled approximately $40,000,000 in sales. In FY 2004, the company topped $24 billion in sales and over 95 million users.[12] It is the first—and by far, the largest—auction site on the Web. The site sells everything from airplanes to art work, collectibles, travel, and other services, helping affect trades by individuals and companies around the world. In August 2004, the site had the fifth most unique visitors on the Web—over 48 million (Fan & Dierkes, 2004). The site now averages 1.5 billion unique page views per month.

One of the keys to eBay's success has been its clear commitment to developing a sense of community. To maintain its market leadership and to add value, eBay has to attract and retain millions of buyers and sellers to its site. To do that, they must affect satisfactory buyer-seller exchanges. Satisfactory exchange requires mutual trust—usually between individuals who have never met. One of the ways that eBay fosters trust is through an extensive reputation system (Cf., Lampe & Resnick, 2004; Resnick, 2004). Prospective buyers can learn much about sellers by viewing their member profiles, which include their selling history and ratings or comments from people who purchased items from them in the past. This rating system not only offers buyers and sellers more information, but also rewards them for affecting efficient and reliable transactions. Presumably, individuals who have acquired poor reputations can also be weeded out of the marketplace, thus adding value to the eBay experience.

However, eBay does much more than track the reputation of buyers and sellers. It also wants to help them achieve their objectives, and enroll them to use the site regularly. To do that, eBay creates a site that provides information and satisfactory transactions, along with opportunities for learning, personal development, fun, and relaxation. This includes e-newsletters, lots of tips for new users, and assistance for experienced buyers and sellers as well. The site also sponsors eBay University, where users can enroll in specific e-learning workshops taught by eBay staff and by experienced users. In addition, eBay encourages users to communicate with one another on individual "about me" pages, and in discussion forums, chat rooms, and topical workshops. Registered users can monitor and join existing forums or start their own. They are expected to follow simple rules relating to discussion and to adhere to a set of simple community values.[13]

Despite the size of the eBay community and the extensive volume of communication it affords, the tone of interaction on the site is surprisingly civil, productive, and *fun*. Users can track and participate in discussions, and they are encouraged to share their feedback or their ideas about how to improve the site—and anyone who wants can review and respond. eBay illustrates the strategies proposed by Kim (2000) and the social psychological framework described by Beenan et al. (2004). For example, eBay responds to user input and makes sure individuals have the opportunity for recognition and reward. The site also provides content for users at various stages in the *life cycle* of the e-community. Visitors, novices, active participants, and expert users all have opportunities to contribute to community life. Users can also assume varying levels of leadership responsibility in the online community. For example, they can help "police" discussion forums, give advice or assistance to new community members, propose, plan or manage eBay events (either on or off line), or participate in eBay University Web courses (as students or teachers). All of this is supported by a staff of technicians, moderators, and educational and community development specialists. The content, the access to a vast market—and the community experience attracts strong user interest. In August 2004, the average user stayed on the eBay site for one hour and 48 minutes (Fan & Dierkes, 2004)—the longest duration of any destination on the Web.

The Motley Fool (http://www.fool.com)

The Motley Fool is a somewhat smaller, more specialized e-community. Motley Fool was founded in 1993 by Tom and David Gardner, with the catch phrase, "to educate, amuse and enrich individuals"—particularly about personal finance and investments.

The site averages two million user visits per month, with over 150,000 registered users. The Motley Fool estimates that twenty-five percent of all (U.S.) Web users have visited their site at least once.

The Motley Fool site offers expert advice columns on several key topics in personal finance. It also offers comparison charts for various financial service providers, as well as decision aid tools, such as 401k management and retirement calculators. However, the key to the site's traffic—and value—is in the user discussion boards. Registered users can choose forums on dozens of topics, related to both personal finance and personal enrichment. Users find the boards useful in learning how to manage investments and identify with the "fool" community.

Table 3. Comparing Online-Community Characteristics and Strategies

	eBay.com (http://www.ebay.com)	The Motley Fool (http://www.fool.com)	E the People (http://www.ethepeople.com)	Geocaching.com (http://www.geocaching.com)
Purpose	Facilitate the world's largest online marketplace.	Inform, amuse and enrich people interested in personal finances and investment.	Facilitate conversation about political and social issues.	Facilitate the global sport of geocaching.
Member Profiles	Detailed summary of members, designed to give entire history of members activity. Optional member photo.	Excellent summary of members. Fun, informative. Optional interview.	Brief summaries available on hyperlinks of member postings. Standard questions. Optional links to member Web page.	Optional profiles of members, which may include photos, personal information, contact information.
Gatherings	Thousands of forums on eBay Community, product topics and entertainment. Local meetings.	Hundreds of discussion boards. "Folly groups" in 50 states.	Members and guests can join dozens of ongoing conversations.	A few dozen forums based on topics and locations. Real gatherings (event caches) are held occasionally.
Education and Personal Development	eBay University, extensive learning opportunities, success stories.	Topical newsletters. Expert recommendations. Wide range of services.	N/A	Extensive learning opportunities. Geocaching University.
Roles	Extensive services for newcomers, expert users, "neighborhood watch," people who host local meetings, and paid "community development" people.	Extensive services for newcomers, expert users, people who host local forum members, local coordinators, meetings, and paid "community development" people.	Background materials for newcomers.	Services for newcomers, services for premium users, and cache owners.
Incentives for Trust and Community Development	Detailed member reputation system. The reputation allows for appeals process. Member spotlights. Calendar of events. Encourages buyers and sellers to contribute to charity. Inactive member accounts deleted.	Provides tools for members to manage "favorite boards and favorite fools." Profiles offer strong indirect incentives for users to contribute. Inactive member accounts deleted. Established fun experience.	Clear presentation of community core values. Relevance Scores for each original post. A list of people who are online at any moment. Regular e-newsletter to summarize conversation. Inactive member accounts deleted.	Based on honor system. Cache owners may delete inaccurate or indecent Web logs. Inactive member accounts deleted. Members' statistics are automatically reported. Informal competition among users to get finds, hides, and complementary logs. On-line form for rating caches.

Table 3 cont'd. Comparing Online-Community Characteristics and Strategies

	eBay.com (http://www.ebay.com)	The Motley Fool (http://www.fool.com)	E the People (http://www.ethepeople.com)	Geocaching.com (http://www.geocaching.com)
Etiquette and Protection	Explicit policies that are readily accessible. Five basic eBay community values inform all policies. Clear rules and user agreements. Member privacy and security safe guarded.	Excellent disclaimer. Terms of service. Direct support if user has been violated. Users can also block further input from individuals they find annoying.	The site reserves the right to block or terminate. The forums are filtered (and sometimes edited), based on user feedback and a set of dialogue standards.	Terms of participation. Site reserves the right to remove Web logs. Joint responsibility of users to police other members. Members may send e-mail through intermediary to protect identity of both parties.
Events and Rituals	Annual eBay community conference. Local and regional offline events.	Fools radio, syndicated newspaper. Fools conferences and events. Annual member- selected fool award.	N/A	Event caches organized by individuals. Developing geocaching jargon. Geocachers create unique calling cards, Web log styles, and create tagged trinkets.
Outcomes	World-wide. Average site visit –1 hour, 48 min. – longer than any other Website.** 102,000 links to site.***	Preeminent source for analysis and advice re: personal finance and investments. 9,500 links to site.***	Community stats on conversation page shows number of members, postings and visitors. 96 links to members, 800,000 posts.	190,000 caches in 217 countries. 138,000 web logs per week.**** 4,350 links to site.***

** Source: Nielsen Net Ratings. September, 2004. *** Source: http://www.google.com. Accessed October 8, 2004. **** Source: Geocaching.com, August, 2005.

The site sets a relaxed environment for discussion, and provides a number of tools to help users evaluate the quality of information they receive, and the trustworthiness of other community participants. For example, the site suggests that users evaluate advice from strangers in discussion boards as if they were meeting them at a party. In other words, they should listen for information, but verify with their own research. Users can also recommend comments to others, or file user comments in their favorite fools or ignore them in the future.

Geocaching (http://www.geocaching.com)

Geocaching.com is an online community that supports a rapidly growing adventure sport called geocaching. In this activity, participants use global positioning systems (GPS) data and receivers to hide caches filled with mementos and a logbook. They then post the coordinates of the cache on the Web site, along with details on the location, size, type, degree of difficulty, and original contents of the caches. Other geocachers will visit the Web site, register, and search for caches in a given area. Armed with the details provided about the cache, members pursue, and sometimes, find the cache. Each time a cache is discovered, participants are encouraged to take one or more items from its contents and are encouraged to leave items of equal or greater value, novelty, or interest. They record comments in the logbook and replace the cache to its exact location. Then, participants go back to the Web site and post results from their search, along with their thoughts on the cache, its condition, its location, and anything else they wish to record.

The new sport was started in May 2000 among a small group of friends. In September 2000, the Web site went public. People joined this e-community, mostly by word of mouth, communicating through a Newsgroup. Soon, a private company called Groundspeak, Inc. was created to own and operate geocaching.com. As of this writing, the Web site records approximately 124,000 active geocaches in 210 countries. On average, about 10,000 Web logs are added to the Web site each day. The site does not report how many active geocachers there are in the world but the number is clearly in the hundreds of thousands from all over the globe.

Geocaching.com offers a series of guidelines for siting and hiding caches in ways that make them safe, sustainable, environmentally responsible, respectful of landowners, and enjoyable for participants. Most caches are hidden on public property with the permission of the appropriate agency. Each geocacher is allocated a Webpage that can be designed as desired but which includes a record of the tally of finds, links to all the geocacher's Web logs, a tally, and links to the caches each has hidden, and links to any photos each has placed on the site.

Geocaching's copyrighted motto is, "The sport where YOU are the search engine." In its short existence, geocaching has evolved significantly by the actions of its members. Geocachers have invented new variations on the caches, organized group-caching events, formed clubs, encouraged official local policies, and even offered classes on geocaching. The sport was started as a non-commercial activity, and even today it is more a user-directed activity than a commercial venture. For most, there is no charge for membership, although users must register to have access to the full Website. There is a premium service that costs $20 per year that offers additional services such as larger storage space and alerts participants about new caches.

The success of geocaching seems to stem from its appeal to peoples' interest in discovery and attraction to place. It is ironic that a technology whose strength is its virtual and ubiquitous presence should develop an e-community whose essence is place. Yet, one of the key attractions of geocaching is that finding and hiding caches allow people to visit interesting places, share their impressions, and compare them with others who have also visited.

The geocaching.com community provides a venue through which members can develop guidelines and rules for the sport.[14] Locally, park services, state governments, and agencies have established policies and rules to regulate geocaching activities within their jurisdiction.[15] Many voluntary leaders have emerged among geocachers to organize event caches (caches where a time component is added to the latitude and longitude and cachers can meet face to face), to create local clubs, and to petition local and state governments to sanction geocaching.

Geocaching has turned out to be fertile ground for innovators and entrepreneurs. Many different variations have been generated on the basic cache idea, including multi-caches, virtual caches, locationless caches, Webcam caches, and moving caches. The owners of the geocaching.com site moderate some of these innovations in an attempt to maintain the quality of the experience and to maintain ethical and safety standards, but they have generally been very permissive. Entrepreneurs have started to produce and sell trinkets to leave in caches such as geocoins, buttons, compasses, and other things. Others have developed companion businesses such as Geocacher University.[16] Competitive sites such as navicache.com have emerged but do not rival the size and interest level of geocaching.com. Sponsors, including manufacturers of GPS receivers and recently DaimlerChrysler Corporation, have teamed with the owners of geocaching.com to create contests to promote their products. Touristic agencies, such as the Canadian Province of Ontario, have developed and promoted geocaches in their regions as a means of generating more visits.

And, of course, there are deviants. Caches are sometimes stolen, destroyed, or plundered in the language of geocachers. However, this behavior is rare, and the affected caches are usually quickly reestablished in a nearby location. Anyone can register, find a cache, and take what they wish, but rather than degrading, the cache trinkets often improve over time. Geocachers frequently perform routine maintenance, or even replace other people's caches when they are plundered or damaged. Other deviant behavior such as putting dangerous materials in caches is rarely observed and quickly reported or corrected.

E the People (http://www.ethepeople.com)

E the People is a site designed to foster and facilitate honest and open conversation mainly about (U.S.) politics and public issues. It is part of the Democracy Project—a not-for profit organization established by Michael Weiksner and Scott Reents in 1999.[17] The purpose of this site is to encourage civic participation and to use the Web as a way to involve as many different views from different people as possible. E the People attracts significantly less traffic than the examples of e-community described above attract. It is supported not by advertising or user fees, but through contributions from individuals and foundations. Users of the site can: 1) propose, review, and sign electronic petitions; 2) email letters to elected representatives; 3) respond and review real-time results on opinion polls; and 4) participate in e-conversations on dozens of topics.

E the people uses online community building principles to stimulate conversation among users and to build user interest and loyalty (Table 3). For example, forum participants must create a (free) member account and login before they can post comments. Members are asked (but not required) to answer a few brief questions, which then form the basis of a brief member profile. Users can review the profiles of all who contribute to forum discussions. Members use this information to get to know other participants and to help filter through conversations of interest. Member posts are organized by topics and by date. Recent posts are given added visibility on the site. Members are encouraged to respond to posts and to evaluate each post they read as either a positive or a negative contribution. A real-time tally of this information, as well as the total volume of site posts, is presented to encourage lively conversation.

As with other online communities observed, it is surprising how "civil" the community discussion seems.[18] Since it is focused on political issues, clearly, the potential for ugly disagreement exists. The site posts clear guidelines for civil conduct. On occasion, the site filters and/or blocks individual comments. However, in general community members police inappropriate actions. The use of member profiles and the tracking of positive and negative feedback for each post provide incentives for members to guard their reputations and to stimulate further positive conversation.

SUMMARY/CONCLUSION

This paper reports results from exploratory research on how four different Web-based e-communities seek to facilitate social trust and collective action among their users. It is designed to stimulate further study and dialogue regarding the theory, practice, and effects of online community development. The study was designed to provide a descriptive survey for scholars and practitioners interested in e-community development. Our findings suggest that online community Web sites can support rich, compelling, and sustainable social settings and genuine, sustainable communities (Cf., Etzioni, 2004). We see opportunities for dialogue between site developers and community development professionals that could advance both disciplines in unexpected ways—in terms of both applications and research.

Applications in Community Development

Online communities offer a number of intriguing possibilities for collective action and community development initiatives, primarily because of their convenience, accessibility, and capacity to facilitate collective action or collaboration. According to Horrigan and Fox (2001), roughly one-third of all U.S. Internet users rely on the World Wide Web as a key source of information about their local community. Roughly, the same percentage of users indicated that the Internet helped them deepen their existing ties to their hometown. Nearly thirty percent of survey respondents reported that the Internet helped them build a connection with people of different race, ethnic, or economic background. Though research on the demographics of online communities is limited, one study suggests that members generally represent an audience that is otherwise difficult to reach in community development initiatives. They are younger, more urban, more ethnically diverse, less educated, and have lower incomes than the general Internet user population (Hitlin, 2004). A carefully-targeted online community project could provide these and other interested stakeholders with a new way to participate in public dialogue. It could become a means for people to learn more about critical professional or public issues. Community leaders and facilitators can also learn more about stakeholder views through e-communities. Because they can monitor use of discussion forums and chat rooms historically and continuously, community development practitioners can gain a richer and more dynamic understanding of community members' perspectives and concerns than they can with more conventional data collection strategies, such as the use of surveys or focus groups. Community development professionals can not only learn people's views on particular issues, but also learn how people respond to others' perspectives. More importantly, if allowed to discuss in safety and security, people gathering in local online communities might generate new ways to address public opportunities and challenges that would otherwise not have been considered. Online communities can support public events or activities at minimal cost. Using social networking software or the existing technology found at sites such as http://www.meetup.com, community development leaders can assist participants directly in building networks or can schedule meetings with interested stakeholders on specific topics. If online community environments are well-planned, users can even have *fun* and be productive at the same time. In short, online communities offer the potential to complement and support a wide range of ongoing community development tasks.

Expanding Community Research

The proliferation of online communities as new social forms and virtual voluntary associations (Ciffolilli, 2003) also offers important opportunities to advance community development research—in terms of both theory and method. The Web-based technology makes comprehensive records of these voluntary associations readily accessible. Community development scholars can pursue both qualitative and quantitative studies of the design, use, and effects of online communities for collective action. To date, we have found no studies of online communities designed exclusively to foster and support place-based community development initiatives. Identification and documentation of such cases would represent an important contribution to the field.

Research on e-communities could help advance our theoretical understanding of (offline) community development as well. In essence, the design and functionalities of online community sites represent Web site managers' embodied, observable, coherent, and systematic theories of community development processes. Research is needed to articulate and compare the theories that underlie various online communities and to assess their performance and effects. Results may affect the theory and practice of offline community development. In particular, we plan to investigate the policies, technologies, and motivations and incentives that help *govern* virtual communities, and seem to support a level of online civility that we did not anticipate at the beginning of the current research. We plan to study further the relationship between members' awareness of online reputations, and the strategies and tactics they use in the accumulation and use of social capital. We plan to compare the attributes and effects of various reputation systems, and to investigate how reputation scores affect interactivity and relative member influence within communities. Finally, it is important to note that our research focuses on the principles, structures, and processes employed in four selected community sites. Subsequent research could provide a broader survey of e-community sites, and more in-depth case studies of individual e-communities (Cf., Shade, 2004). Further research is also needed to measure the perceptions, intentions, and attitudes of e-community developers as well as e-community members (Cf., Ridings et al., 2002).

NOTES

1 For a useful review of the social capital literature, see Portes, 1998.

2 For an interesting account of the commercialization of two online community projects, see Shade, 2004.

3 A wiki is "...a freely expandable collection of interlinked web pages, a hypertext system for storing and modifying information. (It is) a database, where each page is easily editable by any user with a forms-capable Web browser client." (Leuf & Cunningham, 2000, p. 14). Developed by Ward Cunningham at the Portland Pattern Repository, it is software designed to host collaboration spaces on the Web. The term "wiki" derives from a Hawaiian static verb (wikiwiki), which means "to hurry or hasten." In practice, wikis are used by online communities to organize and share their collective knowledge on topics of interest. Wiki users do not need to understand the underlying mechanisms or storage models in a given wiki. They can collaborate to edit or add pages to the community knowledge by simply using their browser. Since every user has exactly the same capabilities, the software is inherently democratic. Wikis are typically based on open source software, so they are easily accessible to interested organizations. They are applied widely in business, in research and educational environments. To review interesting wiki (or wiki-like applications), see http://www.wikipedia.org and http://everything2.com, as well as a useful site for wiki developers at http://c2.com/cgi/wiki.

4 Online reputation systems (also known as recommender or feedback systems) collect feedback from members of an online community regarding past experiences with other members of that community. They are designed to assist e-community members in filtering information, building relationships with members of interest, and inducing good behavior and civil interaction. Systems encourage members to rate others' actions or ideas within the community, aggregate feedback from others, analyze the feedback data, and make results available to the community in the form of member *reputation profiles* (Dellarocas, 2003, p. 3).

5 For more information about how Alexa generates these data, see http://pages.alexa.com/prod_serv/traffic_learn_more.html. Accessed October 15, 2004.

6 In e-communities, even a member's silent observation (what some participants call 'lurking') is recorded in member profiles.

7 Some online communities, such as http://www.everything2.com, do not allow members to evaluate others' contributions until they have reached a particular level of tenure and status in the community.

8 The use of reputation scores encourages members of online communities to behave in ways that are contrary to conventional wisdom on social practices of the Internet. Without such scores, individuals act in anonymity, so they are tempted to violate moral and ethical interpersonal communication standards.

9 For an empirical study of the (economic) value of reputation in the eBay online community, see Resnick et al., 2004.

10 As others have noted (Cf., Portes, 1998), powerful actors such as organized crime leaders also accumulate and use social capital to affect collective action that may not always coincide with public interests. Their social capital is maintained and increased, in part, by the presence of information asymmetries. To the extent that they control information flows, they also affect collective action. In theory, web applications such as e-communities can multiply information flows, reduce information asymmetries, and change processes for accumulating and using social capital.

11 For an excellent example of discussion guidelines for an online community, see http://builder.com.com/2001-6741-0.html. Accessed November 18, 2004. For an example of discussion guidelines for active web-based community forums managed on local government sites, see http://www4.co.honolulu.hi.us/idealbb/register/register.asp?mode=&uid=&username=&sessionID= {F36316DF-37E7-4273-97AF-4B357AEB6DE5}. Accessed November 18, 2004, or http://www6.indygov.org/cgi-bin/ubb/Ultimate.cgi?action=agree. Accessed November 18, 2004.

12 (http://www.a1auctions.com/ebayfacts.htm). Accessed October 8, 2004.

13 (http://pages.ebay.com/community/people/values.html). Accessed October 8, 2004.

14 (http://www.geocaching.com/faq/). Accessed October 6, 2004.

15 (http://geocachingpolicy.info/). Accessed October 6, 2004.

16 (http://www.geocacher-u.com/). Accessed October 6, 2004.

17 For a useful background and history of the E the People project, see http://www.e-thepeople.org/about/fullstory. Accessed October 8, 2004.

18 Civility in online communities is not guaranteed. For a counter example, see the history of LamdaMOO, http://www.cc.gatech.edu/classes/AY2001/cs6470_fall/LTAND.html, as cited in Shirky, 2003a). Accessed on November 30, 2004.

REFERENCES

Axelrod, R. 1984. *The Evolution of Cooperation.* New York: Basic Books.

Bakardjieva, M. 2004. Virtual Togetherness: An Everyday Life Experience. Pp. 121-142 in A. Feenburg & D. Barney (eds.), *Community in the Digital Age: Philosophy and Practice.* Lanham, MA: Rowman and Littlefield.

Beenan, G., K. Ling, X. Wang, K. Chang, D. Frankowski, P. Resnick, & R. Kraut. 2004. *Using Social Psychology to Motivate Contributions to Online Communities.* Paper presented at the 2004 Computer-Supported Collaborative Work, Chicago. November.

Blanchard, A., & T. Horan. 2000. Virtual communities and social capital. Pp. 6-22 in G. D. Garson (ed.), *Social Dimensions of Information Technology: Issues for the New Millennium.* Hershey, PA: Idea Group Press.

Blood, R. 2000. Weblogs: A History and Perspective. *Rebecca's Pocket.* September 7, 2000; September 26, 2004. http://www.rebeccablood.net/essays/weblog_history.html. Retrieved on October 6, 2004

Bowman, S., & C. Willis. 2003. *We media: How audiences are shaping the future of news and information.* http://www.hypergene.net/wemedia/weblog.php?id=P37. Retrieved on October 6, 2004.

Brown, S., et. al. 2002. The Case for Online Communities. *The McKinsey Quarterly* 1. http://www.healthyplace. com/Advertise/story_communities.asp. Retrieved on May 13, 2005.

Case, S., N. Azarmi, M. Thint, & T. Ohtani. 2001. Enhancing E-Communities with Agent-Based Systems. *Computer* July: 64-69. http://ieeexplore.ieee.org/iel5/2/20203/0093505.pdf. Retrieved on December 9, 2004.

Ciffolilli, A. 2003. Phantom Authority: Self-selective recruitment and retention of members in virtual communities: the case of Wikipedia. *First Monday* 8(12). http://firstmonday.org/issues/issue8_12/ciffolilli/index.html. Retrieved on February 22, 2005.

Dellarocas, C. 2003. The Digitization of Word-of-Mouth: Promise and Challenges of Online Reputation Systems. MIT Sloan Working Paper No. 4296-03. http://papers.ssrn.com/sol3/papers.cfm?abstract_id=393042. Retrieved on February 22, 2005.

Di Maggio, P., et.al. 2001. The Internet's effect on society. *Annual Review of Sociology* 27: 306-327.

Etzioni, A. 2004. On Virtual, democratic communities. Pp. 225-237 in Feenburg, Andrew and Darin Barney (eds.), *Community in the Digital Age: Philosophy and Practice.* Lanham, MA: Rowman and Littlefield.

Evans, P. 1995. *Embedded Autonomy: States and Industrial Transformation* Princeton, NJ: Princeton University Press.

Fan, J., & M. Dierkes. 2004. San Diego, Phoenix and Detroit Lead Broadband-Wired Cities, according to Nielsen/Net Ratings. September 15. http://www.nielsen-netratings.com/pr/pr_040915.pdf. Retrieved on September 19, 2004.

Feenburg, A. & M. Bakardjieva. 2004. Consumers or Citizens? The Online Community Debate. Pp. 1-29 in A. Feenburg and D. Barney (eds.), *Community in the Digital Age*. Lanham, MA: Rowman and Littlefield.

Feenburg, A. & D. Barney (eds). 2004. *Community in the Digital Age: Philosophy and Practice*. Lanham, MA: Rowman and Littlefield.

Figallo, C. 2002. iVillage: Investing in Community and Banking on Trust. *Econtent* 25(6): 52-53. http://www.econtentmag.com/Articles/ArticleReader.aspx?ArticleID=988&Query=iVillage. Retrieved on December 9, 2004.

Gomes-Casseres, B. 2001. eBay: A Concise Analysis. http://www.cs.brandeis.edu/~magnus/ief248a/eBay/index.html. Retrieved on September 19, 2004.

Granovetter, M. 1973. The Strength of Weak Ties. *American Journal of Sociology* 78: 1360-80

Gurstein, M. 2000. *Community Informatics: Enabling Communities with Information and Communications Technologies*. Hershey, PA: Idea Group Publishing.

Hampton, K. & B. Wellman. 2000. Examining Community in the digital neighborhood: early results from Canada's wired suburb. In I. Toru and K. Isbister (eds.), *Digital Cities: Technologies, Experiences and Future Perspectives*. Berlin: Verlag-Springer.

Hitlin, P. 2004. *The Use of Online Reputation and Rating Systems*. Pew Internet Project Data Memo. Pew Internet and the American Life Project. October. http://www.pewinternet.org/pdfs/PIP_Datamemo_Reputation.pdf. Retrieved on November 29, 2004.

Horrigan, J. 2004. *How Americans Get in Touch with Government*. A Pew Internet and the American Life Report. May 24. http://www.pewinternet.org/reports/pdfs/PIP_E-Gov_Report_0504.pdf. Retrieved on May 25, 2004.

Horrigan, J., K. Garrett, & P. Resnick. 2004. *The Internet and Democratic Debate*. Pew Internet and the American Life Project Report. October 27. http://www.pewinternet.org/pdfs/PIP_Political_Info_Report.pdf. Retrieved on November 29, 2004.

Horrigan, J., & S. Fox. 2001. *Online Communities: Networks that Nurture Long Distance Relationships*. Pew Internet and the American Life Report. October 31, 2001. http://www.pewinternet.org/pdfs/PIP_Communities_Report.pdf. Retrieved on November 29, 2004.

Karau, S. & K. Williams. 1993. Social loafing: a meta-analytic review and theoretical integration. *Journal of Personality and Social Psychology* 65(4): 681-706.

Kim, A. J. 2000. *Community Building on the Web*. Berkeley, Peachpit Press.

Kollock, P. 1998. Design Principles for Online Communities. *PC Update* 15(5): 58-60.

Lampe, C., & P. Resnick. 2004. *Slash(dot) and Burn: Distributed moderation in a large online conversation space*. http://www.si.umich.edu/~presnick/papers/chi04/LampeResnick.pdf. Retrieved on October 6, 2004.

Leuf, B., & W. Cunningham. 2001. *The Wiki Way: Quick Collaboration on the Web*. Boston: Addison Wesley.

Locke, E. A., & G. P. Latham. 2002. Building a practically useful theory of goal setting and task motivation: a 35 year odyssey. *American Psychologist* 57(9): 705-717.

Masum, H., & Y. C. Zhang. 2004. Manifesto for the Reputation Society. *First Monday* 9(7). http://www.firstmonday.dk/issues/issue9_7/masum/. Retrieved on October 5, 2004.

Marx, G. 2001. Identity and Anonymity: Some Conceptual Distinctions and Issues for Research. In J. Caplan and J. Torpey (eds.), *Documenting Individual Identity*. Princeton: NJ, Princeton University Press. http://web.mit.edu/gtmarx/www/identity.html. Retrieved on February 22, 2005.

Nalbandian, J. 1999. Facilitating Community, Enabling Democracy: New Roles for Local Government Managers. *Public Administration Review* 59(3): 187-197.

Nonnecke, B., & J. Preece. 1999. *Shedding Light on Lurkers in Online Communities*. http://www.ifsm.umbc.edu/~preece/Papers/SheddingLight.final.pdf. Retrieved on May 13, 2005.

Notess, G. 2002. *Search Engine Statistics: Database Total Size Estimates*. December 31, 2002. http://www.searchengineshowdown.com/stats/sizeest.shtml. Retrieved on November 11, 2004.

Ostrum, E. 1991. *Governing the Commons: the Evolution of Institutions for Collective Action*. New York: Cambridge University Press.

Papacharissi, Z. 2004. Democracy online: Civility, politeness, and the democratic potential of online political discussion groups. *New Media and Society* 6(2): 259-283.

Pigg, K. 2001. Applications for Community Informatics for Building Community and Enhancing Civic Society. *Information, Communication, & Society* 4(4): 507-527.

Portes, A. 1998. Social Capital: Its Origins and Applications in Contemporary Sociology. *Annual Review of Sociology* 24: 1-24.

Preece, J. 2002. *Online Communities: Designing Usability, Supporting Sociability*. New York: Wiley & Sons.

Proxicom, Inc. 2001. Nine Myths of E-Community Building. *Destination CRM*. February 28. http://www.destinationcrm.com/articles/default.asp?ArticleID=1674. Retrieved on September 16, 2004.

Putnam, R. 2000. *Bowling Alone: The Collapse and Revival of American Community*. New York: Simon and Schuster.

Putnam, R. 1995. Tuning In, Tuning Out: The Strange Disappearance of Social Capital in America. *PS: Political Science and Politics* December: 664-683

Resnick, P. 2004. *Impersonal Sociotechnical Capital, ICTs and Collective Action Among Strangers*. http://www.si.umich.edu/~presnick/papers/xforment/chapter.pdf. Retrieved on April 20, 2004.

Resnick, P., et.al. 2004. *The Value of Reputation on eBay: A Controlled Experiment*. Working Paper. http://www.si.umich.edu/~presnick/papers/postcards. Retrieved on February 5, 2005.

Rheingold, H. 1993. *The Virtual Community*. Cambridge, MA: MIT Press.

Ridings, C. M., et.al. 2002. Some antecedents and effects of trust in virtual communities. *Strategic Information Systems* 1(1): 271-295.

Rogers, B., & E. Robinson. 2004. *The Benefits of Community Engagement*. London, Active Citizenship Centre. May. http://www.active-citizen.org.uk/files/downloads/Reports/Benefits%20of%20Community% 20Engagement.pdf. Retrieved on September 18, 2004.

Schoberth, T., et.al. 2003. Online Communities: A Longtitudinal Analysis of Communication Activities. *Proceedings of the the Hawaii International Conference on Systems Sciences*. January 6-9. Big Island, Hawaii.

Shade, L. R. 2004. Gender and the Commodification of Community. Pp. 143-160.143-160 in A. Feenburg and D. Barney (eds.), *Community in the Digital Age*. Lanham, MA: Rowman and Littlefield.

Shane, P. (ed.). 2004. *Democracy Online: The Prospects for Political Renewal Through the Internet*. New York: Routledge.

Shirky, C. 2003a. Social Software and the Politics of Groups. *Networks, Economics and Culture Newsletter*. March 9, 2003. http://www.shirky.com/writings/group_politics.html. Retrieved on November 16, 2004.

Shirky, C. 2003b. A Group Is Its Own Worst Enemy. *Networks, Economics and Culture Newsletter*. July 1, 2003. http://shirky.com/writings/group_enemy.html. Retrieved on November 16, 2004.

Singh, S. 2004. B*uilding E-Community: Increasing Stakeholder Participation Using Information and Communication Technology, Asian Development Bank Institute at the Asian Institute of Technology.* http://www.adbi.org/scripts/download_file.php?file=2004.07.24.cpp.building.ecommunity.paper.pdf. Retrieved on September 16, 2004.

Smith, M., & P. Kollock. 1998. *Communities in Cyberspace*. New York: Routledge.

Thompson, L. F., J.P. Meriac, & J. Cope. 2002. Motivating Online Performance: the influences of goal setting and Internet self efficacy. *Social Science Computer Review* 20(2): 149-160.

Wenger, E. 1998. *Communities of Practice: Learning, Meaning and Identity*. New York: Cambridge University Press.

Wenger, E., R. McDermott, & W. Snyder. 2002. *Cultivating Communities of Practice: A Guide to Managing Knowledge*. Boston: Harvard Business School Press.

Wheatley, M., & M. Kellner-Rogers. 1998. The Paradox and Promise of Community. In F. Hesselbein, et.al (eds.), *The Community of the Future*. San Francisco: Jossey-Bass.

Woolcock, M. & D. Narayan. 2000. Social Capital: Implications for Development Theory, Research, and Policy. *World Bank Research Observer* 15(2).

Zhang, Y. C. 2001. Happier world with more information. *Physica A*. Proceedings of the NATO ARW on Applications of Physics in Economic Modeling. February. http://arxiv.org/pdf/cond-mat/0105186. Retrieved on October 6, 2004.

Can community interventions change resilience? Fostering perceptions of individual and community resilience in rural places

Marianna Markantoni, Artur Adam Steiner, and John Elliot Meador

ABSTRACT
Governments move away from their roles as providers and take on roles as facilitators and enablers. Such transformations provide opportunities for individuals to play an active role in improving the resilience of their communities. However, the effects of such transformations may not be experienced by all communities equally. In the light of the emerging enabling state, which entails a more proactive type of community, this article examines whether community projects can enhance the resilience of hard-to-reach rural communities. Analysis from 345 interviews with rural residents from six communities shows that successful completion of community projects can positively change perceptions of resilience, whereas uncompleted projects negatively affect perceptions of resilience. We conclude that for some hard-to-reach communities, in order to build their resilience, continuous funding support needs to be in place. To enhance the resilience of rural communities, the state must also create opportunities for effective community participation.

Introduction

The livelihoods of communities all over the world are increasingly undergoing transformations that often amplify social, cultural, environmental, and economic vulnerabilities (Gray, 2002). The combined effects of national and local stressors such as economic, social, and natural hazards mean that central governments will no longer be able to achieve their goals on their own. Prolonged austerity measures (Pierson, 2001) require welfare states of affluent societies to make their localities more sustainable. The need to mobilize diverse community actors working together is widely acknowledged as a means to address socioeconomic and environmental challenges (Marinetto, 2003; Zebrowski & Sage, 2016).

In recent decades, society has been experiencing a sociocultural shift in which it is moving away from being passive and dependent on the state to being more active and self-reliant. This shift is articulated in many policy and community interventions seeking to strengthen resilience and foster community-led development (Wright, 2016).

CONTACT Marianna Markantoni marianna.markantonis@gmail.com

In the wake of the enabling state, Cope, Leishman, and Starie (1997) argue that we need a state "able to enable," one that creates opportunities for engagement at the level of communities, neighborhoods, families, and individuals. Expanding this argument, Elvidge (2014) talks about a new role for government as facilitator and enabler rather than provider and manager. Zebrowski and Sage (2016) take a more critical stance and note that local communities have emerged as a principal target of contemporary empowerment and resilience programs, with such policies going beyond community preparedness and aiming to "responsibilize" individual citizens for the future of their locality.

The policy focus on fostering community-led development continues in the context of reduced public expenditure. Many scholars (e.g. Shortall, 2008) highlight the need for inclusive civic engagement that ensures that community participation does not only favor the well-resourced and affluent communities. Shucksmith (2010, p. 215) further argues that marginalized communities are less likely to participate in local development processes "unless explicit attention is given to their inclusion." Communities with well-established partnerships and networks are more often successful in pursuing their development goals (Shucksmith, 2010). While the role of the state in public service provision is weakening, more affluent communities with greater institutional capacity defend their interests and pursue their objectives by taking advantage of remaining government schemes (Wright, 2016). So does this mean that more opportunities are offered to those who experiment while others fall behind? Or should we help release the potential to innovate in hard-to-reach[1] communities where local people are less engaged in community development?

In light of the transition toward the enabling state, the purpose of this study is to evaluate resilience outcomes of a rural capacity-building program. The aim of this article is to examine whether externally funded interventions can change or influence perceptions of community and individual resilience among rural residents in hard-to-reach communities. A better understanding of how local residents' perceptions of resilience change over time can help shed light on the type of interventions needed to foster rural resilience. In other words, do rural communities with low levels of civic engagement need externally funded program to improve their resilience?; and what type of support, if any, is required to enhance resilience at individual and community levels? This article answers the above questions by evaluating the Capacity for Change (C4C) community intervention in Dumfries and Galloway region in the south-west of Scotland. C4C was facilitated by the European Union (EU) funding scheme for rural development called LEADER. C4C ran over a two-year period (2011–2013) and aimed to enhance community resilience and to build the capacity of hard-to-reach rural communities (see the forthcoming *Is LEADER in line with an enabling state?* section for details).

For the purpose of this study, we developed an analytical tool to examine how the implementation of a local community project affects residents' perceptions of individual and community resilience in three main domains according to Wilson (2012a): social, environmental, and economic. The tool measures community and individual resilience based on multiple indicators under the three domains from Wilson (2012a). In this article, we compare the difference between resilience indicators for communities that completed and those that did not complete their projects.

An enabling type of Scottish government

In the wake of welfare state restructuring, policies in the UK and Scotland in particular, are shifting from paternalistic passive approaches toward citizen participation in the co-design and co-production of services (Christie, 2011; Steinerowski & Woolvin, 2012). Increasingly, governments consider participation and local initiatives in the delivery of services to be key instruments for making communities and regions resilient (Farmer, Hill, & Munoz, 2012).

Scotland has been supporting an asset-based approach to community development and renewal of its public services. The "Scottish model" advocates a collectivist approach to public services (Markantoni, Steiner, Meador, & Farmer, 2018). This includes the abolition of departmental structures, the agreement between the Convention of Scottish Local Authorities (COSLA) and the Scottish government to focus on Single Outcome Agreements for all 32 Local Authorities, and the development of Community Planning Partnerships which are an expression of direct engagement for communities in setting local priorities (Carnegie UK Trust, 2013; Scottish Government, 2016).

This Scottish approach to public policy creates opportunities for strengthening local democracy and shifting the focus to more asset-based and place-based community action. The Scottish Government (2016) is aiming to achieve positive change by tapping into local resources and knowledge of local people. The birth of the Scottish Rural Parliament in 2014 is also a manifestation of representation for rural Scotland to influence "big policies" on rural community empowerment and to strengthen local democratic structures in rural locations.

In light of the preceding discussion, one question that arises is whether Scotland can restructure its public policies toward a more inclusive and enabling state and abolish a "command and control" approach (Edwards, 2009). Is it fair and realistic to rely solely on communities to solve their own problems and make them accountable and responsible for local development? Within this transformative transition, the state does not shoulder the main responsibility of supporting resilience in communities but, instead, relies heavily on people on the ground (Edwards, 2009). Coaffee, Murakami-Wood, and Rogers (2008, p. 3) are critical of this development and argue that:

> Resilience cannot simply be left to communities themselves but requires steering, not rowing, from state level in some form of collaborative alliance to be successful. Arguably, the building of such resilience will be most effective when it involve[s] a mutual and accountable network of civic institutions, agencies and individual citizens working in partnership towards common goals within a common strategy.

In the following sections, we examine this issue of "responsibilizing" and discuss whether communities (especially the hard-to-reach ones) can enhance their resilience on their own or whether external support in the form of community interventions is needed to enhance their capacity.

Multiple understandings of community resilience

Multiple dimensions of resilience

Resilience is described in many different ways and as "different kinds of things" (Anderson, 2015, p. 60). The concept is interdisciplinary and is evident in geography, economy, sociology, psychology, ecology, physics, engineering, and disaster and natural hazard studies (Coaffee et al., 2008; Porter & Davoudi, 2012; Wilkinson, 1991). Despite the popularity of the concept of resilience, scholars have not yet answered the fundamental question of what makes some communities more resilient than others (Steiner, 2016; Wilson, 2010). This is especially the case when applied to people and their environments; resilience is not easily captured or described in a single definition (Norris, Stevens, Pfefferbaum, Wyche, & Pfefferbaum, 2008). Definitions of the term therefore vary widely according to the contexts and disciplinary fields in which it is deployed. There are divergent voices regarding resilience among policymakers, academics and practitioners, as well as contingencies in the performance of resilience in everyday life.

There is however a strand of recent literature that, rather than attempting to pin down a singular definition of resilience, has sought to understand how a multiplicity of "resiliences" articulates different forms of governance and socioeconomic assemblages. Walker and Cooper (2011, p. 144) argue that resilience is more than one thing, suggesting that there may be various types or forms of resilience at a time in which it has become "a pervasive idiom of global governance." While there is much merit in the various articulations of defining resilience, in this paper we adopt the view that there are multiple resiliences and that resilience is not a singular or a fixed entity.

The concept of resilience is also gaining currency in the field of community and rural development studies (Amir, Ghapar, Jamal, & Ahmad, 2015; Fischer & McKee, 2017; Kulig, Edge, Townshend, Lightfoot, & Reimer, 2013; Magis, 2010; Matarrita-Cascante, Trejos, Qin, Joo, & Debner, 2017; Steiner & Markantoni, 2014). Still, Imperiale and Vanclay (2016) call for more research into how resilience comes about in rural areas.

Conceptualizing and operationalizing community resilience

Community resilience is generally perceived to promote greater wellbeing (Aked, Marks, Cordon, & Thompson, 2010) by creating common objectives and encouraging community members to work together for the common good of their place. In this context, rural community resilience is often defined as both a "personal" and a "collective" capacity to respond to change (Rennie & Billing, 2015; Steiner & Markantoni, 2014). This understanding of resilience links with the definition offered by Magis (2010, p. 402) who suggests that "members of resilient communities intentionally develop personal and collective capacity that they engage to respond to and influence change, to sustain and renew the community and to develop new trajectories for the communities' future." Magis introduces a new understanding of community resilience by including human agency (collectively and individually), proactivity, and social capital. Although the literature is still inconclusive about what resilience really means, to operationalize the concept of resilience in this study, we adapt Magis's (2010) definition.

In addition to individual and collective levels of understanding of rural community resilience (Magis, 2010), Wilson (2012b, p. 123) argues that community resilience is best conceptualized on the basis of "how well the critical triangle of economic, social, and environmental capital is developed in a given community and how these capitals interact." Wilson (2014, p. 7) explains in his conceptual model that "the strongest resilience is achieved when all three critical capitals are equally well developed, i.e. multifunctional communities that incorporate several social, economic, and environmental 'functions' simultaneously and that do not rely on only one capital asset." The concepts of resilience and capitals are, therefore, interlinked and should be discussed together as one influences the other.

We recognize there are arguably many types, dimensions, and models of resilience. For the purpose of this paper, we explore economic, social, and environmental dimensions of self-reported resilience (based on Wilson, 2012b, 2014) at community and individual levels (based on Magis, 2010). Building on the conceptual framework for measuring community resilience developed by Steiner and Markantoni (2014), Figure 1 depicts the analytical approach used in this study. Social resilience is measured with the level of community participation, feeling part of the community, and the ability of a community to succeed in improving the village. Environmental resilience is measured with the utilization of green spaces and appreciation of the natural environment and whether local residents maintain and care for the natural resources. Economic resilience is measured by the utilization of local skills and knowledge in the village, whether the current services meet community needs, if community groups work together to generate income for their village and whether local communities attempt to improve their economic situation. The set of indicators applied in this research have been co-developed together with LEADER staff working with the communities in this study.

Several key dimensions have been empirically found to enhance the resilience of rural communities. For instance, a person's connection with the land, the feeling of "I belong to this community" (McManus et al., 2011, p. 21), the ability of community members to work together in difficult times (Schwarz et al., 2011), and the presence of diverse types of businesses and employment opportunities (Steiner & Atterton, 2015) all define elements of thriving local communities.

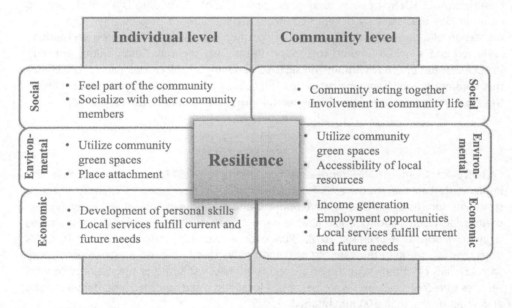

Figure 1. Components of resilience (adapted from Steiner & Markantoni, 2014).

Is LEADER in line with an enabling state?

LEADER approach to community development

To be successful, rural communities build on networks within and beyond their locality. These networks should include a variety of actors at different governance levels (Bock, 2016; Wright, 2016). The role of the state as enabler and facilitator is crucial in creating opportunities for communities to take part in networked developments (Shucksmith, 2012).

To that end, the LEADER approach is increasingly recognized as a networked development enabling active public engagement and participatory governance: "joining together local aspiration with assets within and beyond the territory in a process of mobilisation of place, space, and democratic decision-making" (Shucksmith, 2012, p. 12). LEADER (a French acronym meaning links between actions for the development of the rural economy) is a European Union initiative that supports rural development and revitalization at the local level. The program was introduced in 1991 and since then it has provided funding to thousands of community-development projects across EU countries, bringing together public, private, and civil-society stakeholders. The aim of LEADER is to find innovative solutions to rural economic and social challenges which best suit specific areas, and to serve as a model for developing rural areas elsewhere (Shucksmith, 2010).

Over the last 20 years, the LEADER approach to Community-Led Local Development (CLLD) has helped rural actors capitalize on the potential of their locality and it has assisted the delivery of development policies in rural Europe (European Commission [EC], 2014). The aims of CLLD are to (i) encourage local communities in developing bottom-up approaches, (ii) build community capacity and stimulate innovation, (iii) promote community ownership, and (iv) assist multi-level governance. These features are consistent with the overarching aims of an enabling state model and LEADER philosophy guiding the building of community resilience.

Although LEADER supports rural development, LEADER funding is available only to communities that skillfully develop community-development project ideas. The implementation of a project takes place when a community project application is successfully reviewed and a match-funding to support the project secured. Communities applying for LEADER funding but without the skills to generate a project idea cannot qualify for this community-development program. This leaves less capable communities without the support and opportunities for generating local development (Steiner, 2016).

Capacity for change

Capacity for Change (C4C) represents one of the LEADER-funded projects that was implemented in the southwest of Scotland. C4C was developed to identify effective strategies for sustainable rural development and to address potentially widening disparities between "strong and capable" and "weak and less capable" communities (Steiner, Woolvin, & Skerratt, 2018). Run over a two-year period (2011–2013), C4C's objective was to build the capacity of communities that (i) had no engagement history with LEADER or other major funding streams, (ii) had lost some or the majority of local services in recent years and were perceived locally as disadvantaged, and (iii) were rural and small (fewer than 500 inhabitants).

Through direct financial investments and the engagement of the LEADER project manager, C4C aimed to enhance inclusivity and resilience and, as a consequence, empower selected communities. As opposed to other LEADER initiatives, C4C guaranteed financial and mentoring support to C4C communities: communities were offered up to £20,000 to develop local projects and the assistance of a project manager to facilitate the implementation of a community project idea. C4C funding regulations stipulated that all projects had to be completed within a 2-year period.

C4C could be seen as one response to a critique of LEADER: that it is the most privileged who are able to win funding, since they already have a greater capacity to act (building on previous successful applications). C4C was designed to address some of the challenges associated with the current UK and Scottish policies, investigating whether the policy for "responsibilizing" communities is a realistic one. We present findings that highlight aspects of dependency culture, community empowerment and resilience.

Methods and research approach

Study context

Implemented in Dumfries and Galloway, a rural region in the south-west of Scotland, the C4C project took place in six communities whose population density was approximately one-third of the Scottish average, and whose Gross Value Added[2] per head of population was below the national average. The area is characterized by regional decline, and an aging and dispersed population. According to the Scottish Index of Multiple Deprivation (Scottish Government, 2017), one of the communities lies in the 20–40% range of the most deprived areas in Scotland, and the remaining communities are in 40–60% group of the most deprived areas. These features suggested that selected locations could benefit from the C4C program. The names of the villages are not mentioned due to confidentiality issues.

Data collection and analysis

The evaluation of C4C consisted of a longitudinal mixed methods research approach in which selected community members were interviewed twice – before and after the C4C intervention, with an additional qualitative sub-sample of interviews to assess in more detail the complexities of C4C community-development process. Firstly, and before the C4C intervention took place, we conducted interviews and gathered quantitative and qualitative baseline data from participating C4C communities. The formulation of our interview questions was based on the community resilience literature review and refined through discussions with rural community members and regional community-development officers.[3] Respondents provided answers using the Likert scale from 0 (very negative) to 10 (very positive). In addition, respondents gave qualitative information explaining their numeric responses. The interviews aimed to identify self-reported level of individual and community resilience and the questions referred to social, economic, and environmental dimensions. Secondly, when community projects were sufficiently developed, we conducted in-depth interviews with C4C community members on *how* change happens, *who* facilitates the community-development process, and *why* it is/is not possible. This helped to reveal aspects of people's motivation and willingness to support projects such as C4C. Finally, after the implementation of C4C, we applied our baseline interview questions to as many interviewees as possible from the initial sample. This longitudinal approach enabled us to measure self-reported changes in the level of community resilience.

To identify C4C community respondents, snowball sampling was adopted. The initial respondents were randomly selected from a list of potential interviewees provided by the C4C project manager. Interviewed C4C community members were those involved in the development of, or who could benefit from, the C4C project. In each C4C community, we collected views from approximately 10% of the local population and our data analysis aimed to identify patterns across the data. The sample frame consisted of community members with diverse sociodemographic characteristics (including age distribution, gender, education, employment, health, marital status, origin background, length of stay in a community, and access to a vehicle).

In total, 345 face-to-face interviews with community members were conducted. Interviews lasted 40–60 min and were recorded, with consent, and subsequently transcribed. All respondents were ensured anonymity in research outputs. Field notes were also collated and observations recorded. All data were coded, categorized, and analyzed using the constant comparison method and analytic induction. This formed the basis for systematic analysis of transcripts using the N-Vivo qualitative data analysis software program. Statistical information was analyzed using SPSS quantitative data analysis software. For the purpose of our data analysis, the communities were divided into two groups: (1) communities which *completed* and finalized the program within the two-year time frame (labeled as C1, C2, C3), and (2) *uncompleted* communities which did not manage to finalize the program within the two-year time frame (labeled here as U4, U5, U6). After data cleaning, the "completed-project communities" group included the responses of 81 community members, and 56 community members in the "uncompleted-project communities" group. The analytical framework presented in Figure 1 was used to conduct data analysis focused on 10 resilience questions (see Table A1). The questions helped to assess social, economic, and environmental dimensions of self-reported resilience at community and individual levels.

Analysis and findings

Resilience change in completed and uncompleted C4C projects

Community members who participated in C4C identified a variety of ideas for their local projects. These included a community garden with a seaside view (Figure 2), a kitchen facility in a village hall, enhancement of a heritage trail, design and development of a local statue symbolizing characteristics of the village, and a forest-path linking two villages. While some communities successfully completed their projects within the C4C lifetime, other struggled to do so. Here we present findings that show whether community interventions can change or influence perceptions of community and individual resilience among rural residents in hard-to-reach communities.

Table 1 presents the change in resilience levels for each resilience variable between the two stages of the study (i.e. before and after C4C intervention). Firstly, a Shapiro–

Figure 2. Opening a new community garden with school pupils helping with the planting
(source: *The Galloway Gazette*, 2013).

Table 1. Mean changes in level of social, environmental, and economic resilience.

Type of resilience	Questions asked	Completed (n = 163) Before	After	Change	Uncompleted (n = 112) Before	After	Change
Social community	a. To what extent do you engage with other members of your community?	7.1 (1.9)	7.4 (2.2)	0.3	6.9 (2.2)	6.8 (1.9)	−0.1
	b. To what extent do you feel part of this community?	7.3 (2.2)	7.8 (1.8)	0.5*	7.5 (2.0)	7.4 (2.0)	−0.1
Social individual	c. To what extent do you think your community succeeds in developing and improving this village?	6.2 (2.0)	6.7 (2.0)	0.5	5.5 (2.5)	5.3 (2.7)	−0.2
	d. To what extent are all members in the community encouraged to be involved in community life?	7.1 (1.7)	6.8 (2.3)	−0.2	6.7 (2.3)	5.7 (2.5)	−0.9*
Environmental individual	e. How much do you use green spaces and appreciate the natural environment in your community?	7.1 (2.9)	8.1 (2.0)	1.0**	8.7 (1.4)	8.3 (2.4)	−0.4
Environmental community	f. To what extent do your community members utilize, maintain, and care for existing natural resources in the village?	7.3 (1.7)	6.9 (2.0)	−0.3	6.7 (2.0)	5.8 (2.5)	−0.9*
Economic community	g. To what extent do you use your skills and knowledge you have in your village?	5.0 (3.2)	6.4 (2.6)	1.4***	5.4 (2.7)	5.4 (2.7)	0
	h. To what extent do services and infrastructure in your village meet your current and likely future needs?	5.2 (2.6)	5.7 (2.4)	0.5	6.3 (2.4)	5.6 (2.3)	−0.7
Economic individual	i. To what extent do community groups work together to generate income for the village?	5.4 (2.8)	6.0 (2.5)	0.6*	5.4 (2.7)	4.6 (2.4)	−0.8*
	j. To what extent do you think your community makes most of what it has to improve its economic situation?	4.1 (2.5)	5.3 (2.3)	1.3*	5.1 (1.9)	4.7 (2.3)	−0.4

*$p < .05$; **$p < .01$; ***$p < .001$; based on chi-square distribution.
Standard deviations are represented in parenthesis.

Wilks test of normality was conducted on each variable in addition to a visual inspection of the distribution of each variable using density plots. This test indicates whether a variable is normally distributed or not. The Shapiro–Wilks test and a visual test of each variable's distribution indicate that, while most variables appear to be normally distributed, a chi-square test is an appropriate measure of difference. Chi-square tests of significance were performed for each variable presented in Table 1. The *p*-values are indicated with asterisks using the conventional approach.

Table 1 grouped our results according to *completed* and *uncompleted* projects as well as the change in a particular dimension between stages for each group. Overall, the self-reported resilience scores of communities which completed the C4C projects increased across the board, except for the Social Individual question: "To what extent are all members in the community encouraged to be involved in community life?" and the Environment Community question: "To what extent do your community members utilize, maintain, and care for existing natural resources in the village?" Neither of these are statistically significant at alpha level 0.05. Respondents of uncompleted community projects reported a decrease or no change in all variables. There are statistically significant changes in the questions: "To what extent are all members in the community encouraged to be involved in community life?"; "To what extent do your community members utilize, maintain, and care for existing natural resources in the village?"; and "To what extent do community groups work together to generate income for the village?" The mean score of each of these variables lowered between the two stages.

Table 2 shows the reliability score for each resilient type and a 95% confidence interval for the test statistic. Both community and economic resilience have scores over 0.60, with a score of 0.67 and 0.65 respectively. Environmental resilience has Cronbach's alpha score of 0.22, which is too low to indicate any reliable scaling, thus it should not be considered a scaled resilience type in its current form. It is likely that the number of variables included (2) is too low to be considered for scaling in the same way that community resilience and economic resilience are (Brown, 2014).

One conclusion from these initial findings suggests that only completed community C4C projects lead to an increased level of self-reported level of resilience. Communities that do not complete their projects decreased or maintained their level of reported resilience. However, to further interpret the results and understand how community interventions can change or influence perceptions of community and individual resilience among rural residents, we present findings from the qualitative component of the C4C study. These are summarized in the following sections as social, environmental, and economic resilience at both the community and individual levels.

Table 2. Item reliability analysis.

Scaled item	Cronbach alpha	95% Confidence interval Lower bound	95% Confidence interval Upper bound
Community	0.67	0.61	0.73
Environmental	0.22	0.15	0.30
Economic	0.65	0.59	0.72

Note: Environmental resilience type has only two factors.

Social resilience

Measuring change and the wider impact of the C4C program, the study found that individual perceptions of social community resilience showed a statistically significant increase in the communities that successfully completed their C4C projects. The biggest change (and statistical significant at p .05) was seen in the social community question: To what extent do you feel part of this community?

However, in uncompleted community projects, all self-reported social resilience variables at both community and individual levels decreased over time (Table 1). The largest decrease occurred in the variable: "To what extent are all members in the community encouraged to be involved in community life?" This question had a decrease of about 0.9 and is statistically significant. It is worth noting the already high levels of social resilience of both completed and non-completed projects. Still, with this high level of overall social resilience, completed projects saw an increase in perceived social resilience, while uncompleted projects saw a decrease.

To understand the phenomenon of resilience in more depth, besides measuring changes between the two stages of the study, the self-reported social resilience of respondents from all participating communities were examined. Respondents were asked to elaborate on their perception of social resilience by discussing their everyday experiences of how they engaged and socialized with other community members. Respondents from both types of communities (completed and uncompleted C4C projects) mentioned that on a daily basis they visited and helped neighbors (especially the elderly), some volunteered, while others actively participated in local events and in community council meetings. However, in two villages (U4, U5) which did not complete their C4C projects, respondents elaborated on the tendency "not to get too involved" and "to preserve some distance" from the other community residents. One interviewee mentioned that "going into my neighbor's house was something I generally tried to avoid" (U4-12). It is interesting to note that in these villages, it was also emphasized that those people who volunteered to support local community centers often created what was described as "closed circles" and that they did not interact with all members of the community, which could have made the other villagers reluctant to participate in wider community affairs.

In general, across both types of communities with completed and uncompleted C4C projects, the main obstacles hampering participation in community life were the lack of time and busy life schedules, with some expressing a preference for staying at home in the evenings rather than engaging in community life (C1). This approach could be problematic in the long-term, because it can lead to the isolation of individuals. The level of solidarity in both types of communities, however, is interesting, especially in relation to caring for the elderly residents. Helping neighbors in times of an emergency, such as power cuts or bad weather conditions (e.g. flooding), and ensuring that everyone in the community is supported and safe, seemed natural to most of the respondents.

Moving our discussion to the level of social community resilience, the findings show a more complex picture. For the question regarding the extent to which a community succeeds in developing and improving its village, we found that the self-reported level of resilience increased across communities with completed C4C projects and decreased across communities with uncompleted projects. However, the extent to which members of the community felt encouraged to get involved in community life saw a decrease in all participating communities in our study. This decrease was small and not found to be statistically significant in completed projects. Whilst, for uncompleted projects, the decrease was substantial and significant (about 0.9); overall, completed projects have a higher overall mean between both rounds as compared to uncompleted projects. This suggests that even capacity-building projects, such as C4C, do not necessarily help to integrate all community members but only subgroups within communities. Those who do not participate in local projects might be under the impression that there is no external encouragement to be actively involved in community life.

Environmental resilience

Results of the self-reported change in environmental resilience at the individual level show that only communities that successfully completed their C4C projects scored high in the question concerning the utilization of green spaces and appreciation of the natural environment (Table 1); this increase is statistically significant at alpha level 0.01. These findings were to be expected especially because some C4C projects were related to connecting communities with nature (e.g. a community garden and a forest-path linking two villages). However, the changing dimensions of environmental resilience at the community level are less evident.

At the environmental community level, the findings indicate that the extent to which community members utilized, maintained, and cared for existing natural resources in their villages decreased in all communities studied (both completed and uncompleted C4C projects), although the decrease in this component of self-reported resilience was lower in the former communities (i.e. 0.2), than in the latter communities (i.e. 0.9). The negative change observed in communities with completed C4C projects suggests that implementation of a local project does not guarantee that all community members will utilize and/or care about its outputs.

When respondents were asked to elaborate on how community members helped to improve the environment, it was mentioned that in general residents "keep the village tidy, maintain community grounds and play areas for children well, and help to create an attractive environment for visitors and residents" (U4-20). In one of the communities that did not complete the C4C project, the community council managed to secure money to purchase land for a recreation ground for kids (U4-23), which shows that creating outdoor space is important to local residents. The following quote from a respondent of the same community is illustrative:

> Such efforts continue to inspire [us] to improve other facilities in the village ... but it depends if we got finance for it. We can try to generate income but we need sponsors (U4-19).

Results from the qualitative data show that for both types of communities, with completed and uncompleted C4C projects, the local environment and nature were highly valued and that all communities strived to enhance the surroundings of their communities by securing finance to buy community-owned land, maintaining community gardens and creating an attractive place to live in.

Economic resilience

The self-reported economic resilience, at both the community and individual levels, increased in the communities which completed the C4C projects and decreased or stayed the same in the communities which did not complete C4C projects (Table 1). Although C4C helped to develop small-scale projects that did not aim directly at economic revitalization, it seems that C4C brought hope for positive economic change. At the same time, individual participants' perceptions and attitudes related to resilience for uncompleted C4C projects had a negative impact on the economic resilience. It is interesting to note that respondents from completed C4C community projects scored higher in the question of utilizing skills in their village, when compared with respondents from uncompleted community projects. The mean increase is 1.4 and statistically significant. This is the largest increase in any measured variable for both completed and uncompleted projects. It might be that C4C helped community members to utilize their skills during the setting up and development of local projects such as utilizing financial or project management skills. Indeed, respondents from communities with uncompleted C4C projects indicated a need for more diverse ways to increase their skills within the villages (see Table 3). This could mean that more tailored support, such as training opportunities and financial incentives, would be beneficial to economic resilience.

The fact that there are limited services in some communities was not always considered problematic. Respondents claimed that even though they would like to have more shops and facilities in their village, they realized that it was not feasible due to rurality and low population density. Respondents acknowledged that there were good services near their communities, highlighting the importance of interconnectedness for rural locations. While others accepted the loss of the local shops, they also expressed the need for a meeting point in the community to catalyze social interactions. Hence, economic aspects, as suggested, are linked to social resilience.

Respondents from both types of communities (with completed and uncompleted C4C projects), talked about ways in which local services could be improved. However, many services such as digital infrastructure, transport and connectivity services, road infrastructure, and access to healthcare are traditionally provided by regional and national governments, which suggests a continuous need for a high level of state support.

Table 3. What would encourage community members to use their skills more widely?

Completed community projects	Uncompleted community projects
• Better health conditions • Availability of time (some are already involved in many community initiatives) • Financial incentives • Apprentice-type opportunities • More confidence	• Better health conditions • Availability of time • Financial incentives • More community-type projects (e.g. gardening) • Job opportunities in the local area • Training opportunities • Childcare facilities in the village to enable local employment • Participation in a local committee • A formal way of identifying needs and skills • Willingness from others to engage and be engaged e.g. Someone asking me/Someone making the first move/Knowing whether people actually needed my skills

Discussion

This research adds to the current knowledge base of community resilience by developing an understanding of the effects of community interventions, whether such interventions can change or influence perceptions of community and individual resilience among rural residents in hard-to-reach communities. We examined whether the C4C program influenced aspects of social, environmental and economic resilience at individual and community levels.

Our findings show that, despite being tailored to support the development of skills and building the capacity of communities to empower them, C4C succeeded in half of the C4C communities. Those belonging to "the glass is half full" camp might view this as a success story; others might argue that investments in development projects in hard-to-reach communities are too risky and not financially sustainable.

The results from the self-assessment of resilience by rural residents in six communities where C4C was implemented show that, overall, based on the individual participants' perceptions and attitudes related to resilience, communities that completed their projects increased their resilience scores. On the other hand, communities with uncompleted projects self-reported a decrease or no change of resilience in all evaluated variables. We conclude that successful implementation of community projects is an indicator of how communities perceive social, environmental, and economic resilience at individual and community levels. We note that the initial self-reported social resilience scores across communities with uncompleted projects were much lower than in the communities with completed projects. This lower and decreasing score could be explained by the fact that in the communities with uncompleted C4C projects we observed difficulties with social inclusion and community participation; for instance, respondents talked about "closed circles" that made some of them reluctant to participate. It would appear, therefore, that the culture of inclusiveness and openness might influence the outcomes and perception of community-development projects.

Interestingly, individual participants' perceptions related to economic resilience at both community and individual levels increased in communities that completed their C4C projects and decreased in communities that did not complete their projects. It appears that successful completion of C4C-type projects can contribute to creating a positive economic change. Caution is therefore needed when designing and implementing community interventions and care should be taken to ensure their timely completion.

Conclusion

The study presented has provided a better understanding of how individual participants' perceptions and attitudes related to resilience change over time with regard to community interventions in hard-to-reach communities. Especially in communities with little or no engagement as collectives, support is needed not only in financial terms to initiate community projects, but also to mentor and facilitate the process of project implementation. Any challenging issues faced by community members who run local projects should be resolved in the early stages to prevent problems from escalating. As evidenced in the C4C study, the engagement of a project officer who facilitates implementation of the project might not be sufficient. Consequently, "enabling" strategies might not always work and more on-going direct state support might be essential to ensure the development of resilient communities.

The state and external funders have a challenging task of navigating between encouraging and facilitating communities to take ownership of local projects and the potential risk of their failure if projects are not completed. Especially in the era of welfare retrenchment, communities where projects are not completed may not only experience the effects of these failures but also encounter an ever-shrinking safety net for the most vulnerable. Although helpful, public grants and support from experienced community-development program such as LEADER do not guarantee the success of projects. Hence, there is a need to work with hard-to-reach communities, to exercise care when designing community interventions, and to set up a contingency plan in case of a project failure. Such a plan could help boost community confidence and remedy any negative effects.

We agree with Elvidge's statement (2014) that the state must take on its new role by empowering communities, families, and individuals to play a more active role in improving their own wellbeing. Although the rhetoric behind community engagement and empowerment is positive, capacity building within communities might require both greater state funding and long-term (and therefore costly) interventions. Hence, in times of limited public budgets, rather than saving finances, a higher spending can be anticipated.

While it is useful to assess how the C4C changed the perceptions of resilience among rural residents in hard-to-reach communities, this does not reveal the long-term impacts of the intervention. It may be that communities that did not succeed in finalizing their C4C projects still learned something new, drawing relevant and useful conclusions from negative experiences that could influence their future projects. At the same time a critical question arises as to what happens when the project support is gone and the project is finalized. It is possible that communities with completed C4C projects might not be able to run their future projects independently. Secondly, although new policies might not necessarily lead to a more sustainable system, it is hoped that the empowerment agenda will lead to a fairer state. However, as suggested by our findings, power can go to certain subgroups within communities rather than entire communities, causing alienation and lack of integrity in the communities concerned.

Our study generates a number of questions, indicating that there is an on-going need to find better ways of empowering communities, especially hard-to-reach communities. The C4C approach represents one of many approaches. This is not surprising, as empowerment processes are complex (Skerratt & Steiner, 2013) and can take place only by creating common objectives and encouraging community members to work together (Aked et al., 2010). The state should not absolve itself from its responsibilities under the banner of neoliberal governmentality (Zebrowski & Sage, 2016) but instead it should design interventions in partnership with communities (Coaffee et al., 2008).

Concluding, we argue that the process of moving toward resilient communities seems to require a set of appropriate mechanisms at the local level with the right support (financial and others) to build the capacity that enables communities to act and successfully complete their community projects. If we are to redesign the role of the state, then we must create opportunities for meaningful and effective community participation that enhances the resilience of rural communities as well as develop a better understanding of the appropriate level of state support at the local level.

Although relevant to policy, research, and practice, there are limitations in the findings presented. Our study was conducted in a specific type of community (i.e. small and with no previous engagement in LEADER or other major funding initiatives) in rural Scotland. Also, our quantitative findings are based on an analytical framework that has not been tested before. We therefore encourage researchers in the field to test the framework and aspects of community resilience in other community settings.

Notes

1. The term "hard-to-reach" relates to communities with no history of engagement as collectives.
2. Gross value added is a measure of the increase in the value of the economy due to the production of goods and services.
3. A detailed description of the C4C methodology is presented in Steiner et al. (2018).

Disclosure statement

No potential conflict of interest was reported by the authors.

Funding

This research took place within the Scottish Government-commissioned Strategic Research Programme, "Governance and Decision-Making for Community Empowerment" (2011–2016).

References

Aked, J., Marks, N., Cordon, C., & Thompson, S. (2010). *Five ways to wellbeing*. The New Economics Foundation. London: Creative Commons.
Amir, A.F., Ghapar, A.A., Jamal, S.A., & Ahmad, K.N. (2015). Sustainable tourism development: A study on community resilience for rural tourism in Malaysia. *Procedia – Social and Behavioral Sciences, 168*, 116–122. doi:10.1016/j.sbspro.2014.10.217
Anderson, B. (2015). What kind of thing is resilience? *Politics, 35*, 60–66. doi:10.1111/1467-9256.12079
Bock, B. (2016). Rural marginalisation and the role of social innovation; A turn towards nexogenous development and rural reconnection. *Sociologia Ruralis, 56*, 552–573. doi:10.1111/soru.12119
Brown, T.A. (2014). *Confirmatory factor analysis for applied research*. New York, NY: Guilford Publications.
Carnegie UK Trust. (2013). *The enabling state in Scotland*. Dunfermline: Author.
Christie, C. (2011). *Commission on the future delivery of public services*. Edinburgh: APS Group Scotland.
Coaffee, J., Murakami-Wood, D., & Rogers, P. (2008). *The everyday resilience of the city: How cities respond to terrorism and disaster*. London: Palgrave/Macmillan.
Cope, S., Leishman, F., & Starie, P. (1997). Globalisation, new public management and the enabling state. Futures of police management. *International Journal of Public Sector Management, 10*, 444–460. doi:10.1108/09513559710190816
Edwards, C. (2009). *Resilient nation*. London: Demos. Retrieved from https://www.demos.co.uk/files/Resilient_Nation_-_web-1.pdf
Elvidge, J. (2014). *A route map to an enabling state*. Dunfermline: Carnegie UK Trust.
European Commission (EC). (2014). *Community-led local development. Cohesion policy 2014-2020*. Brussels: Author.

Farmer, J., Hill, C., & Munoz, S.-A. (2012). *Community co-production. Social enterprise in remote and rural communities.* Cheltenham: Edward Elgar.

Fischer, A., & McKee, A. (2017). A question of capacities? Community resilience and empowerment between assets, abilities and relationships. *Journal of Rural Studies, 54*, 187–197. doi:10.1016/j.jrurstud.2017.06.020

Gazette, G. (2013, July 8). Drummore's gateway garden opens. Retrieved from http://www.gallowaygazette.co.uk/news/drummore-s-gateway-garden-opens-1-2993176

Gray, J. (2002). *False dawn: The delusions of global capitalism.* London: Granta Books.

Imperiale, A.J., & Vanclay, F. (2016). Experiencing local community resilience in action: Learning from post-disaster communities. *Journal of Rural Studies, 47*, 204–219. doi:10.1016/j.jrurstud.2016.08.002

Kulig, J.C., Edge, D.S., Townshend, I., Lightfoot, N., & Reimer, W. (2013). Community resiliency: Emerging theoretical insights. *Journal of Community Psychology, 41*, 758–775. doi:10.1002/jcop.21569

Magis, K. (2010). Community resilience: An indicator of social sustainability. *Society & Natural Resources, 33*, 401–416. doi:10.1080/08941920903305674

Marinetto, M. (2003). Who wants to be an active citizen? The politics of practice and community involvement. *Sociology, 37*, 103–120. doi:10.1177/0038038503037001390

Markantoni, M., Steiner, A., Meador, E., & Farmer, J. (2018). Do community empowerment and enabling state policies work in practice? Insights from a community development intervention in rural Scotland. *Geoforum, 97*, 142–154. doi:10.1016/j.geoforum.2018.10.022

Matarrita-Cascante, D., Trejos, B., Qin, H., Joo, D., & Debner, S. (2017). Conceptualizing community resilience: Revisiting conceptual distinctions. *Community Development, 48*, 105–123. doi:10.1080/15575330.2016.1248458

McManus, P., Walmsley, J., Argent, N., Baum, S., Bourke, L., Martin, J., ... Sorensen, T. (2011). Rural community and rural resilience: What is important to farmers in keeping their country towns alive? *Journal of Rural Studies, 28*, 20–29. doi:10.1016/j.jrurstud.2011.09.003

Norris, F.H., Stevens, S.P., Pfefferbaum, B., Wyche, K.F., & Pfefferbaum, R.L. (2008). Community resilience as a metaphor, theory, set of capacities, and strategy for disaster readiness. *American Journal of Community Psychology, 41*, 127. doi:10.1007/s10464-007-9156-6

Pierson, P. (2001). *The new politics of the welfare state.* Oxford: Oxford University Press.

Porter, L., & Davoudi, S. (2012). The politics of resilience for planning: A cautionary note. *Planning Theory & Practice, 13*, 329–333. doi:10.1080/14649357.2012.677124

Rennie, F., & Billing, S.-L. (2015). Changing community perceptions of sustainable rural development in Scotland. *Journal of Rural and Community Development, 10*, 35–46.

Schwarz, A., Béné, C., Bennett, G., Boso, D., Hilly, Z., Paul, C., ... Andrew, N. (2011). Vulnerability and resilience of remote rural communities to shocks and global changes: Empirical analysis from Solomon Islands. *Global Environmental Change, 21*, 128–1140. doi:10.1016/j.gloenvcha.2011.04.011

Scottish Government. (2016). *How community planning works.* Edinburgh: Author.

Scottish Government. (2017). Scottish index of multiple deprivation. Retrieved from http://www.gov.scot/Topics/Statistics/SIMD

Shortall, S. (2008). Are rural development programmes socially inclusive? Social inclusion, civic engagement, participation, and social capital: Exploring the differences. *Journal of Rural Studies, 24*, 450–457. doi:10.1016/j.jrurstud.2008.01.001

Shucksmith, M. (2010). Endogenous development, social capital, and social inclusion: Perspectives from LEADER in the UK. *Sociologia Ruralis, 40*, 208–218. doi:10.1111/1467-9523.00143

Shucksmith, M. (2012). *Future directions in rural development?* Dunfermline: Carnegie UK Trust 2012.

Skerratt, S., & Steiner, A. (2013). Working with communities-of-place: Complexities of empowerment. *Local Economy, 28*, 320–338. doi:10.1177/0269094212474241

Steiner, A. (2016). Assessing the effectiveness of a capacity building intervention in empowering hard to reach communities. *Journal of Community Practice, 24*, 235–263. doi:10.1080/10705422.2016.1201561

Steiner, A., & Atterton, J. (2015). Exploring the contribution of rural enterprises to local resilience. *Journal of Rural Studies, 40*, 30–45. doi:10.1016/j.jrurstud.2015.05.004

Community Development and Community Resilience:
An Integrative Approach

Alex Zautra, John Hall, and Kate Murray

Throughout history, communities and civilizations have sought to enhance the quality of community life and the well-being of its people. However, more recently there has been greater interest in attending to the details of community development by capitalizing on the improved ability to capture community well-being and successes scientifically. That interest invites greater attention to the development of indicators that can quantify those qualities of life that lead to strong and healthy communities. The selection of meaningful indicators is dependent upon several factors including a process that stimulates meaningful involvement of community stakeholders, but the single most important is the identification of an underlying model to guide the work. Indicators do not have meaning in themselves. For these measures to provide a coherent assessment of the community, an integrative approach to understanding what constitutes a healthy and strong community in a dynamic environment is required. A resilience perspective serves that purpose and provides a framework that is broad, neutral, and conceptually strong enough to structure development of significant sets of indicators. Exemplary community indicator processes across the nation, particularly recent efforts in the Phoenix, Arizona region, provide evidence supporting the value of indicator development for community building.

> *"Growth" has been a buzzword in our society. More is better. But are more people, more highways, more factories, more consumption intrinsically better? Cancer, too, is growth - growth out of step with the body, the larger system it depends on. A co-intelligent community, conscious of its internal and external interconnectedness, would not seek endless growth of its material "standard of living." Rather, it would seek sustainable development of its "quality of life," as manifested in the welfare of its members, the vitality of its culture and the health of the natural environment in which it was embedded.*
>   *- From: http://www.co-intelligence.org/S-sustainableSeattle.html*

Alex Zautra, John Hall, and Kate Murray: Resilience Solutions Group, Arizona State University; Contact information: Alex Zautra, Kate Murray: Psychology Department, Arizona State University, Tempe Arizona,USA (atajz@asu.edu; kate.murray@asu.edu); John Hall: School of Public Affairs, Arizona State University, Tempe Arizona, USA (john.hall@asu.edu). The authors wish to acknowledge the dedication and diligence of Billie Sandberg in preparation of this article. Order of authorship for the first two authors who were equal contributors to this article was determined by the toss of a coin.

Overview: Resilience, Community Indicators, and Community Development

Throughout history, communities and civilizations have sought to enhance the quality of community life and the well-being of its people. However, more recently we have seen greater interest in attending to the details of community development by capitalizing on the improved ability to define, measure and extend community well-being and successes to all residents. With that interest has come attention to the development of indicators of the threat of loss and progress in furthering well-being in the community. In this article an integrative model is proposed for the identification and use of community indicators to quantify those qualities of life that lead to strong and healthy communities.

Communities are vibrant, ever-changing, and challenging social worlds, a thoughtfully crafted comprehensive community index can inform us about the direction, negative or positive, of growth and change in those communities. A glance into the community indicator literature uncovers a formidable list of attempts by organizations and communities to tackle this daunting task. Each attempt aims to capture a picture of the functioning and status of their community, reducing the complex phenomenon of community life into a few quantifiable mileposts for the purposes of evaluation and informing policy and programming. As with any measure, an indicator must outline the target phenomenon or condition and the specific goals and desired outcomes for which it is being developed. The need to link community vision, goals, outcomes and indicators within a community resilience framework requires attention to processes as well as outcomes.

Cities are vibrant and dynamic and the measures used to capture them should be able to capture the breath and movement of a city. A snapshot of any scene can provide a number of important details about what may be happening, such as the race, gender, or approximate age of the participants. However, it does not tell a story where people may have been or where they are heading. Longitudinal research is an essential component of any community indicator program. The positive impact of programming and developments may not be seen in a matter of weeks, or certainly not in a one time assessment of life in a community.

A community that is building capacity is one that plans for positive growth as well as decline, integrates economic and social goals, and fosters connections across diverse groups within its borders. For these lofty ambitions to be more than pipe dreams, the community needs methods to chart its progress on social and economic goals using real data. The 21st century metropolis that stays tuned in to a range of risk and resource factors rather than relying solely on a model of risk not only bucks the current and long-standing trends but is one that is moving toward a model of governance that provides a greater capacity to sustain quality of life for its members.

The selection of meaningful community indicators is dependent upon several factors, but the single most important is the identification of an underlying model to guide the work. As Kurt Lewin once admonished, "Nothing is as practical as good theory." Indicators do not have meaning in themselves. In order for these measures to provide a coherent assessment of the community, an integrative approach to understanding what constitutes a healthy and strong community needs to be selected. Otherwise, the data that arise from a set of indicators is more likely to be subject to interpretative whim and fancy. A strong model of what is important for our community is essential in order to correctly focus and interpret the data to judge the extent and even the direction of positive change resulting from ambitious community programs.

Resilience has been chosen as the key construct with which to build a model that informs the choices of community indicators. To inquire about the resilience is to ask two fundamental questions about human adaptation. First is recovery: how well do people bounce back and recover fully from challenge (Masten, 2001; Rutter, 1987)? People who are resilient display a greater capacity to quickly regain equilibrium physiologically, psychologically, and socially following stressful events. Second and equally important is sustainability: The capacity to continue forward in the face of adversity (Bonanno, 2004). To address this aspect of resilience it must be asked, How well do people sustain health and meaningful positive engagement within a dynamic and challenging environment? Healthy communities are those that confer these capacities for resilience to their constituents.

A community's resilience is best understood by applying ecological principles to the analysis of social systems in terms of these two defining features of resilience: recovery and sustainability. With a focus on recovery, Black and Hughes defined resilience as "the ability of systems to cope with shocks and bounce back" (Black & Hughes, 2001, p. 16). Another definition Fiksel offered in terms of sustainability is "the capacity of a system to tolerate disturbances while retaining its structure and function" (quoted from Fiksel, 2006, p. 16). Folke et al. (2002, p. 438) integrated these two properties when they identified three elements of resilience: (1) "the magnitude of shock that the system can absorb and remain within a given state;" (2) "the degree to which the system is capable of self-organization;" and (3) "the degree to which the system can build capacity for learning and adaptation."

In 1987, the U.N. World Commission on Environment and Development (also known as the "Brundtland Commission") defined sustainable development as "development that meets the needs of the present without compromising the ability of future generations to meets their own needs" (Sustainable Pittsburgh, 2004, p. 82). Folke et al. (2002, p. 439) point out, when resilience is synthesized in the context of sustainable development, at least three general policy recommendations can be drawn: (1) "the first level emphasizes the importance of policy that highlights interrelationships between the biosphere and the prosperous development of society;" (2) "the second stresses the necessity of policy to create space for flexible and innovative collaboration towards sustainability;" and (3) "the third suggests a few policy directions for how to operationalize sustainability in the context of social-ecological resilience." The authors of this study agree with Hancock (2000): A healthy community must also perforce be a resilient community, one that has the systems of governance and social capital needed to rebound from difficult times and sustain that which is most positive about its identity for its current and future inhabitants.

In sum, a resilience portfolio can help inoculate communities against potential threats and crises, but it requires new perspectives, actions and measures. Operationally this means a focus on identifying, conserving and investing in the human, social, intellectual, and physical capital, rather than expending large parts of that capital and energy of its leadership in short term, narrow programs, activities and services (Churchill, 2003). Investment in valid indicators of social progress in keeping with a resilience perspective provides the kind of feedback needed to build more vibrant and sustainable communities. By taking the broad view of human and community health, and focusing on qualities that promote resilience, the task of identifying yardsticks for community resilience becomes a challenging one. However daunting the complexities that underlie this approach, to attempt anything less would be to shortchange community potential, and diminish chances of building on the positive forces of sustainable growth and development.

II. Indicators in Action

According to The World Health Organization (WHO), a social indicator is a "variable, which helps to measure change" (as cited in Boothroyd & Eberle, 2000). Innes (1990) defines an indicator as "simply a set of rules for gathering and organizing data so they can be assigned meaning."[1] To enrich definition, analogies are often used to illustrate the concept. For example, a report from the Sustainable Seattle project likens indicators to "gauges and dials of an aircraft's instrument panel" (cited in Phillips, 2005). This is a metaphor with meaning for the Seattle community, the home of Boeing and one of greatest concentrations of engineers in the United States. Review of the substantial community indicators literature shows that many analogies have been applied to clarify the meaning of indicators, and that indicators have been used to serve different overlapping primary functions shown in Table 1 and including description, simplification, measurement, trend identification, clarification, communication, and catalyst for action (Phillips, 2005). Indicators also have great practical power. As noted in Health in a New Key, "what gets measured gets done" (St. Luke's Health Initiatives, 2003, p. 17). Since much of what has been measured to date focuses on risk rather than resilience, targets for action are often reactive and defensive, designed to avoid deeper problems rather than increase capacities.

Table 1. Functions of Community Indicators

Function	Description	Answers the question...
Description	Describe conditions or problems; Increase general understanding	'What are things like?'
Simplification	Simplify complexity; provide a representative picture with significance extending to a larger phenomena of interest	'What's the big picture?'
Measurement	Measure characteristics of quality of life; measure performance of activities or services	'How much?'
Trend Identification	Establish baseline data; identify trends or patterns; show direction, improvement, disintegration, plateaus. Two types: 1) Past-orientation. Indicators are chosen in light of their 'historical trend-identification properties' (MacLaren 1996, p.9) i.e. showing how dimensions of a identified phenomenon have been changing; 2) Future-orientation. The indicator is a 'forward-looking instrument' (MacLaren 1996, p.9), used as a predictive, forecasting device.	'How did we do?' / 'Where are we headed?'
Clarification	Clarify analytical issues or long-term goals; highlight areas of concern or improvement	'What's most important?'
Communication	Translate data into terms understandable by wide range of users	'How do we explain...?'
Catalyst for Action	Stimulate public, stakeholder and political awareness, as well as interest and will to work towards change	'What next?'

Indicators of community life derive in part from the work of social scientists on the broader domain of social indicators. This work, begun in the later half of the past century, focused on the development of measures of social progress that would parallel the gathering of data to provide "economic indicators" of the vitality of regions of the country. It was evident then, and subsequently reinforced by numerous observations of the uneven growth and decay of quality of life even in economically flourishing communities, that a balanced approach is needed to charting progress in regional community development (Swain, 2002). Indeed, the founding fathers acknowledged the importance of gathering data on the social condition of our nation by including in the United States Constitution the requirement that the government conduct a periodic census of its people. Although the original U.S. Census of 1790 consisted of a mere 6 questions about the number race and age of people, living in each household, the Census has evolved as the most comprehensive national data set detailing the nation's demographic, social, and economic conditions and change. Social researchers have relied heavily on these data to interpret quality of life trends, progress, and challenges of the society.

Of interest as well has been the concern for inclusion of indicators of quality of life that include the perspectives of the community members themselves as well as urban planners and social scientists. Researchers have constructed inventories to examine the individual's perceptions of their own health and well-being (Andrews & Withey, 1976; Campbell & Converse, 1972). In these efforts, individuals are asked to rate their well-being and satisfaction with their own lives. Interestingly, this work uncovered distinct differences between perceptions of quality of life as defined by the subject in contrast to those defined by social indicators. The disconnect between the two sets of findings suggests the need to incorporate ways of estimating both the social and psychological well-being with community indicators.

One of the major advancements in the field of social indicators has been the study of environmental issues. Cobb & Rixford (1998) highlight that this area of emphasis has made extraordinary advances in theory development. The ecological framework has advanced the indicator movement beyond solely descriptive statistics to examining theoretical frameworks of change and developing a future orientation. By looking to the future, environmental indicators can identify the impact of current systems and practices and develop alternative means for enhancing future outcomes in the ecosystem.

Many Types of Indicators. The number of indigenous community indicator programs has grown in recent decades. Dluhy & Swartz (2006) identified over 200 community based indicator projects in the U.S. alone. The recent community indicators movement has employed largely bottom-up planning, where each community has set its own goals and monitored its own changes. This stands in contrast to previous efforts primarily by governmental bodies to examine national trends. Indeed democratic theory dictates that to some extent the desired outcomes and the important dimensions to evaluate will vary across communities. However, one key limitation of a bottom up community-based approach is the lack of a unified conceptual framework with which communities of location and interest can work together for the benefit of the whole region. An effective response to this limitation would be a universal conceptual framework with the flexibility to adapt to take local characteristics and circumstances into account.

Ongoing social and community indicator programs. There are a number of U.S. communities that are setting the pace for developing community indicators of resilient processes and incorporating those indicators into on-going community building efforts. Table 2 below describes some of the leaders in this emerging field.

Table 2: Examples of Exemplary U.S. Community Indicator Projects

Sustainable Pittsburgh

Committed to affecting regional decision-making processes so that regard for sustainability in economic, environmental, and social ventures alike is incorporated, the nonprofit organization Sustainable Pittsburgh developed and produced a set of performance indicators in 2002. This set of indicators proved to be only the beginning for Sustainable Pittsburgh, for they have led the organization to develop Affiliate Network Topic Teams, through which action items are developed by participating community members in order to move the region closer to its goals of creating a sustainable environment and economy, and sustainable system of social equity. For more information, log onto www.sustainablepittsburgh.org.

Community Indicators Initiative of Spokane

Harnessing the resources of partners like Eastern Washington University, the City of Spokane, and the Spokane County United Way, the Community Indicators Initiative of Spokane, Washington has been able to engage its community toward the lofty goal of democratizing data in the name of improving communities. From these indicators, which culminated in a comprehensive report in 2005, local organizations and community-based groups are able to glean data for making organizational and community decisions. For more information, log onto www.communityindicators.ewu.edu.

Jacksonville Community Council, Inc.

The Jacksonville Community Council, Inc. (JCCI) is a pioneer in the field of community indicators. For more than twenty years, the JCCI has collected and disseminated information on the quality of life in the Jacksonville area of Florida by utilizing a comprehensive list of more than 100 indicators in nine areas of interest, which include arts and culture, education, public safety, and health. The JCCI—comprised of expert staff and citizen volunteers—is able to produce comprehensive reports, for use by government, business leaders, and other citizens in making decisions and taking action to improve the community's state of being. For more information, log onto www.jcci.org.

Sustainable Seattle

For more than fifteen years, the nonprofit organization Sustainable Seattle has sought to enhance the quality of life in the Seattle area by providing communities with information to make choices that will lead to a more sustainable future. As part of this effort, in the mid-1990s, the organization began the process of developing a set of regional indicators through an inclusive process of community participation that drew on citizens' values and goals. While pleased with early efforts, which led to the publication of multiple reports of indicators for community use, Sustainable Seattle reassessed its indicator project in the early part of the 21st century, with an eye toward making the product more effective and beneficial to the community. This has led the organization to develop neighborhood-based indicators (to complement the ongoing system of regional indicators), and to develop a comprehensive plan for moving the indicators from assessment to action to garner sustainability for the Seattle area in the long-term. For more information, log onto www.sustainableseattle.org.

Truckee Meadows Tomorrow

Based in Reno, Nevada, the nonprofit organization Truckee Meadows Tomorrow is dedicated to providing information that will lead decision-makers to create positive change within communities. Working with a set of 33 indicators of the quality of life in northern Nevada, Truckee Meadows Tomorrow publishes an annual Community Well-being Report, which highlights not only the area's current state of being, but also policies and programs that are actively working toward counteracting negative trends in the community. But their work does not end there. They actively encourage community members to take a personal interest in changing their community's status by personally adopting an indicator as a tool to drive advocacy and service efforts, by participating in their online forum to discuss issues with like-minded community members, and by joining their organization. For more information, log onto www.truckeemeadowstomorrow.org.

Table 2. Cont'd.

City of Santa Monica

In the mid-1990s, the City of Santa Monica heeded the community's concern that their current progress might be coming at the price of future generations' well-being, by developing and adopting a plan to base citywide decisions on the premise of sustainability. In short, they keep an eye to the future when making decisions about the present. The City of Santa Monica does so through the assistance of its Sustainable City Plan—a set of goals and indicators for all segments of the community that were developed by city staffers and a group of community stakeholders who operated under an agreed-upon set of ten guiding principles of sustainability. This plan for the City of Santa Monica has over time become embedded within the fabric of its decision-making processes, to the extent that the city finds itself not only meeting its targets, but (in many instances) exceeding them. For more information, log onto www.smgov.net/epd/scp/index.htm.

Boston Indicators

The Boston Foundation, Greater Boston's community foundation—grant maker, partner in philanthropy, key convener, and civic leader—coordinates the Boston Indicators Project in partnership with the City of Boston and the Metropolitan Area Planning Council. The Project relies on the expertise of hundreds of stakeholders gathered in multiple convenings to frame its conclusions, and draws data from the wealth of information and research generated by the region's excellent public agencies, civic institutions, think tanks, and community-based organizations. For more information, log onto www.bostonindicators.com

Perhaps because of its relative longevity, the Jacksonville Community Council, Inc. (JCCI) is repeatedly cited as one of the leading efforts and was highlighted in the well known book, *Smart Communities: How Citizens and Local Leaders Can Use Strategic Thinking to Build a Brighter Future*, by Suzanne Morse (2004). JCCI was established in 1975 and has consistently worked to increase the dialogue of Jacksonville's current state and functioning and the future it hopes to attain for itself. Their mission statement is to engage "diverse citizens in open dialogue, research, consensus building and leadership development to improve the quality of life and build a better community in Northeast Florida and beyond" (as stated on their website http://www.jcci.org/about/missionstatement.aspx). As is the case with many other indicator mission statements, the leaders of this nonpartisan civic organization proclaim the importance of indicators in opening a civic dialogue on the current status and functioning of their communities.

Although each of the cases mentioned in Table 2 has adopted different approaches, they share important common elements. To begin, they are each fully collaborative ventures, incorporating ideas and resources from many sectors of the community including governments, universities, nonprofits, private firms, and the general citizenry. They have all developed extensive processes to help derive and use key indicators. A major part of the process work focuses on stimulating and sustaining genuine grass-roots participation, while at the same time including various community "experts" and policy makers in the processes. The result is that while indicators and goals chosen differ by community, there is substantial overlap of concepts and measures. In addition, these examples show significant signs of sustainability and impact on community dialogue, and, in some cases, policy actions.

Two potential flaws are also identifiable in looking at these examples. The first is that they often identify many indicators which raise questions about community priorities and focus. The second is that it is difficult to determine policy and theoretical accountability for some indicators. If the community group finds indicator(s) moving in an undesirable direction they must determine why the change and who is likely to respond. Depending on the indicator, this can be a difficult assignment.

The Phoenix Citistate as a new urban laboratory. The many diverse communities within the booming Phoenix region represent natural experiments for understanding and measuring resilience in response to the major challenges of the future. Phoenix and its surrounding cities and suburbs are growing together, with great degrees of economic, social, and physical interdependence, hence the designation "Citistate" (Peirce, Johnson & Hall, 1993).

Some of the Citistate issues include the impact of increased immigration and diversity, scarcity of resources and environmental erosion, decreasing emphasis on community in exchange for sprawl and individuation (characteristics for which the Wild West has long been known). According to the U.S. Census, Phoenix is the fastest growing American metropolitan region of the past decade. The challenges it faces are similar to issues that other countries and communities across the U.S. will increasingly face if they are not already. Phoenix faces a fundamental paradox: How do you build a community within a city of transients (Long, 1991)?

The issues of immigration and diversity are faced every day in Phoenix and they will only continue to demand attention in communities around the globe. As a border state, Arizona faces the unique challenges of being at the front end of the changing face of modern forms of immigration (e.g. "illegal immigration" and human trafficking) and rapid growth. With the substantial improvements in transportation and communication over the last decades, residents of Phoenix often encounter next door neighbors representing people from around the globe. In an increasingly diverse society, there are even greater cultural gaps between the individuals and groups that are coming in contact today than yesterday. How communities respond to this diversity will have short- and long-term implications for the future of any community. The role of government and public policy in these trajectories are critical.

In addition, environmental degradation and the impact of rapid growth and expansion are other issues in which Phoenix provides a model laboratory. Given the ongoing efforts to build and expand within the desert landscape, Phoenix faces unique challenges that are global issues for the long-term. The limitations of existing natural resources place a strain on the environmental impact of growth and development. Increased driving times and the reliance on traditional forms of energy have raised levels of pollution which undeniably impact health and well-being. The social characteristics and ramifications of such growth are also apparent. Changes in daily interactions and the goals or expectations of neighbors and communities are of increasing interest to social scientists and of concern to city planners. The impacts of growth on individual well-being and health are only beginning to be realized.

Within this context, there is clear need to cultivate vision for a sustainable and resilient future. Some efforts such as the Phoenix Futures Forum have been launched and found partially successful in developing greater public involvement in developing goals, strategies and progress measures for the region's future (Hall & Weschler, 2005). In addition, Metro Phoenix has had significant experiments in the large scale collection of data of great potential for local public policy and an informed citizenry. The now defunct Data Network for Human Services was a massive effort to chart cost and outcomes of wide range of public services. Based on periodic questionnaire data from local service delivery agencies for over a decade, the effort eventually became too costly and was subject to increasing criticism about its utility and cost effectiveness (Hall, Jones, Snook, & Springer, 1998).

A current effort involves the development of Arizona Indicators. Similar in design to Boston Indicators, the Arizona Indicators Project aims to offer a one-stop data research tool that tracks Arizona's economic, social and environmental trajectory. In 2007, Arizona State University began this initiative to produce community indicators. A series of initial projects are the first steps toward producing a comprehensive set of indicators that are maintained and updated on an ongoing basis. These are initial efforts, with enhancements and improvements intended to be developed over time. Foreshadowing the importance of the effort, production of the first set of indicators was coordinated by the Office of the President at ASU. Broad-ranging indicators, with a geographic focus on the Phoenix area, were produced by experts throughout the university. The project has evolved into a collaboration among A.S.U., the Arizona Republic newspaper, the State Department of Commerce, and the Arizona Community Foundation. Indicators will be updated regularly and are available to all residents and interested parties by simply checking the project's web site dashboard (www.Arizonaindicators.org).

These are admirable attempts to infuse the Metro Phoenix public policy process with greater rationality and provide access to important community information, but like many other community data collection examples these falter because they lack a unifying framework. Questions about what is most important, how indicators are connected or not related, are minimized or sometimes avoided entirely as data are collected. What differentiates large quality of life or community betterment data collection efforts from most of the "Exemplary Cases" listed in Table 2 is degree of conceptual clarity and focus. In addition, most exemplary cases have evolved from a heavily collaborative, sustained process including grass roots dialogue and involvement.

A more targeted approach to developing community resilience and appropriate indicators is now underway in Phoenix as a part of new and significant effort called Health In a New Key (HNK). Developed by St. Luke's Health Initiatives, an Arizona Community Foundation, HNK is a five year, multi-million dollar program that blends the concept of resilience with strength-based community development (Kretzman & McKnight, 1993). This initiative awards community organizations that develop new partnerships to implement resilience-based interventions that focus on assets, not deficits. The effort is defined as "a way of identifying, framing and responding to issues that focuses first on existing strengths and assets...and avoids the pervasive culture and model of deficits and needs" (St. Luke's Health Initiatives, 2008). This innovative program marks an important step in providing funds to move beyond threat and response paradigms to funding resilience and assets-based research and interventions that can be sustained within communities.

As a part of the overall deployment of HNK, Arizona State University's Resilience Solutions Group (RSG) is engaged in designing community tools for developing resilience indicators including a process for generating stakeholder involvement in the selection of the best Community Resilience indicators. A community resilience indicators Workbook (Zautra & Hall, 2008) is being piloted among communities of the Phoenix Citistate presently and is organized around workshops that cover several domains of community life, including critical resilience capacity areas of Social Domain, Physical Infrastructure, Civic Infrastructure, Economic Domain, Environmental Domain, Human Development, and Health and Well being.

Although this work is in progress and it is too early to formally evaluate progress of the HNK effort, it is clear that this work on asset-based strategic planning, community development, and indicator based evaluation is changing the way in which many local organizations are thinking about their mission, their connection to other community entities and policies, and critical mission determinants such as the difference between "human development" and "human services" in the traditional sense. Early "emerging lessons" reported in a new article (Hughes, 2008) about HNK underscore this change:

1. Resilience is enhanced by connecting civic and political institutions
2. Resilience is enhanced by community wells of information, services, and social connections
3. Resilience is enhanced by leveraging local culture
4. Resilience is enhanced through strong feedback loops

These notable community information experiments and processes have great potential for theory and practice. A logical first step toward achieving that potential involves reviewing these cases with an eye to understanding how they may collectively reflect on exiting theories, definitions, hypotheses and policies that swirl around the question of the place of community resilience in community development. That is the objective of the final section of this article.

Analysis and Implications

Healthy Communities

A take-off point for the development of community resilience indicators anywhere is an understanding of the operational meaning of community. Community has many definitions, and debate among social scientists and philosophers on the fine points of what a community is, and is not, will likely carry on indefinitely. Nevertheless, there are many common threads with which a working definition can be woven together useful for the purposes of informing the development of Community Resilience Index (CRI). In essence a community is defined by the presence of sustained and substantial positive social interaction among people who share common ground. Past definitions focused on the patterns of social engagement bounded by geographic areas such a neighborhoods, towns, and school districts, or what Black and Hughes (2001) refer to as "communities of location." In addition, social networks of people with shared identities and purposes define what Black and Hughes (2001) refer to as "communities of interest." These clusters of people are bounded by common values rather than by geography, but are no less important in our understanding of community. A focus on community, then, embraces both the shared geographic and the conceptual spaces that constitute what social scientists have referred to as "weak ties" (Granovetter, 1973). These webs of social interconnection determine the extent of civic engagement and social capital. From the perspective of resilience, a key domain of interest is how communities further the capacities of their constituents to develop and sustain well-being, and partner with neighboring communities of location and interest to further the aims of the whole region.

The definition of health as the absence of disease has held sway in public policy debates for the greater part of the 20th Century. This narrow view has been gradually overtaken by a broad and more comprehensive approach that includes the capacity for quality of life as well as the absence of pathology[1]. In terms of physical health this transition has led to greater attention to functional capacity and less on prevalence estimates of "caseness." In mental health a similar transformation has taken place in referring to disablement as the criterion for poor mental health rather than a diagnosis of mental disorder (Diagnostic and Statistical Manual (DSM-IV): APA, 1994).

Inquiries into the processes that allow for resilience in physical and mental health lead in this study to a deeper appreciation of human capacities than are found in the standard paradigms that underlie the clinical research and practice. Paradigms within the clinical sciences have focused so much on revealing hidden pathologies that the natural capacities of people, even those who are ill, to resolve problems, bounce back from adversity, find, and sustain energy in the pursuit of life's goals have been ignored. Instead of focusing on the attributes of people and their social worlds that confer risk, ideas like recovery and sustainability invite examination of the qualities of the person and his/her social and community environments that confer optimism, hope, purpose, positive and lasting social ties, self and collective efficacy. These are qualities that permit flourishing within dynamic, challenging even threatening environments that characterize rapidly changing metropolitan areas.

In parallel fashion, the quality of life within a community is often defined by the absence of crime, safe streets, convenience to stores selling everyday commodities, and a relatively unfettered path from home to work, and back again. People need the structure of a coherently organized physical environment that affords them basic goods. They want to live within communities that support their needs for social connection and psychological growth. Resilient community structures build on peoples' hopes as well as provide a means of circling the wagons to provide a "defensible space." We need definitions that go beyond the absence of problems: not just risk, but also capacity, thoughtfulness, planning, and a forward-leaning orientation including attainable goals and a realistic vision for the community as a whole.

Boothroyd and Eberle (1990) defined a healthy community: as one in which all organizations, large and small, formal and informal, work together successfully to enhance the quality of life of all its members. The authors agree. From the resilience perspective, health refers to not simply the attending to levels of illness, pain, and psychological disturbance, but also a social accounting of balance of opportunities for an enrichment in work, family and civic life, the qualities that sustain well-being for individuals and build vibrant communities that can sustain healthy lifestyles for generations.

A Community Resilience Index (CRI)

By taking the broad view of human and community health, and focusing on qualities that promote resilience, the task of identifying yardsticks for community resilience is made a challenging one. However daunting the complexities that underlie that effort, to attempt anything less would be to shortchange the communities studies, and diminish the chances of preserving the local resources that provide for sustainable growth and development.

One temptation is to embrace the conceptual foundations outlined thus far, but stop short of completing the difficult work of operationalization. In so doing, one only "talks the talk," leaving behind the legacy of an academic exercise, or, worse yet, a framework so open to interpretation, that all efforts, or lack there of, are justifiable. Community indicators integrated into an index of resilience provide a means of making tangible progress toward shared goals, yielding critical feedback on the success of our efforts. Efforts at strengthening community can then be evaluated in terms of resilient processes and outcomes, providing information about what works and what programs need to be reexamined in light of the data.

Advancing beyond existing methodologies. Indicator development to date has laid substantial groundwork from which to begin to build a Community Resilience Index. However, there are several opportunities to improve on existing indicators and to further the thinkin, measurement and analysis of community resilience. Thus far, indicators have largely relied on descriptive statistics without a guiding theory. Also, the social issues that the indicators aim to address remain vague and ambiguous. For example, the health of constituents may be boiled down to the number of hospital visits and infant mortality rates. This type of data serves as a crude estimate and tells little about the physical functioning of individuals. In turn, such information has little impact on the community receiving such information and how it should inform their daily behaviors and understanding of community health.

Resilience theory provides a framework to enhance existing indicators, which have tended to take a singular approach to measurement. That is, most have examined what it takes to constitute a healthy or an unhealthy community without attention to the underlying structure that defines the two constructs. A bi-dimensional framework of resilience suggests that resilience factors are not simply qualities found at the positive end of a single continuum of risk. Models that contain at least two separate dimensions, one that estimates vulnerabilities, and another, strengths (Zautra, 2003) together confer unique advantages in the prediction of health not accounted for by one-dimensional assessments of relative risk.

When examining individuals, this two-dimensional approach is superior because it more accurately represents the complexity of human motivations. At the core of human striving lie two fundamentally different motivational processes: The need to protect and defend against harm, and the need to move forward, and to extend one's reach toward positive aims (Bernston, Caccioppo, & Gardner, 1999). These processes infuse a two-dimensional meaning structure to emotion, cognition, and behavioral intention (Canli et al., 2001; Reich & Zautra, 1991; Sutton & Davidson, 1997; Watson, Wiese, Vaidya, & Tellegen, 1999). Social relations have similar bifurcated structures (Finch, Okun, Barrera, Zautra, & Reich, 1989; Stone & Neale, 1982). When investigators have constructed separate indices of positive and negative aspects of the person and/or social relations, they have uncovered surprising currency for positive aspects in prediction of health and illness unaccounted for in measures taken of negative affective dimensions (Cohen, Doyle, Turner, Alper, & Skoner, 2003; Moskowitz, 2003; Russek & Schwartz, 1997; Seeman et al., 1995).

This two-factor approach makes obvious the point that the absence of negative experiences does not *pari passu* imply the presence of positive ones. Conversely, the absence of positive experiences does not necessarily imply the presence of negative ones. Proceeding without an awareness of the distinct quality and meaning of positive versus negative aspects of mental health and social relations, however, leads to shortsightedness in the selection of measures and the construction of predictive indices of health, resulting in shortfalls in predicting differences between groups in health and wellbeing. Further, the confusion that comes from mixing together disparate (and unrelated) indicators leads to lack of specificity in identifying active ingredients of the processes (social, cultural, interpersonal and physiological) that could direct the design of preventive interventions, and build theory (Castro, Cota, & Vega, 1999; Steptoe & Marmot, 2003). Communities are complex, and capturing their assets as well as their liabilities extends the two-dimensional approach of resilience properly to identification of indicators to chart progress toward greater health and well-being at the level of community.

Another limitation to existing indicator selection has been the very practical constraints of data availability and the cost of new data acquisition. At first glance, there seem to be fountains of information from various public, nonprofit and private organizations, state local and national, so much information that many sound alarms about information overload. But not all information from the vast fields of websites and official reports is uniformly available for all communities. It is often possible to augment existing data with new research to provide the best set of indicators for a particular community. Indeed, when community members are brought together to talk about the best measures of progress for their neighborhood, town, region, they are likely to suggest new measures that require individual data collection through surveys, focus groups, and other approaches. This is all well and good as a community involvement and planning process, but also expensive.

There are many different types of communities and the definitions used in indicators remain varied and vague. Communities have complex and dynamic features that the statistical measures and research questions are only beginning to appreciate. Sophistication in design and methods of inquiry in addition to good theory is essential for understanding them. Issues of how to define a community, measure its direct and indirect effects, and tease apart the relative importance of individual, family, and community level factors are only beginning to be addressed. Advances in research over the last ten years have begun to identify the impacts of neighborhood characteristics on individual health and well-being (Folland, 2007). These improvements in community research provide methodologies to successfully move social indicators beyond an era of descriptive statistics to making and testing predictions regarding what constitutes a resilient community.

Distinguishing processes and outcomes. The articulation of a conceptual framework for community resilience requires attention to processes as well as outcomes. The final test of resilient outcomes comes when the community faces a formidable challenge. The assessment of progress toward resilience requires attention to those intermediary processes that increase the likelihood of resilience. Black and Hughes (2001) provide the diagram shown in Figure 1 of the relationship among key sets of variables. Resources such as human and financial capital provide the raw materials for healthy communities. These and other factors influence the development of resilient processes, such as social capital and collective efficacy. Those processes lead to resilient communities. The model has feedback as well. Communities that demonstrate resilience further develop their capacities for resilience.

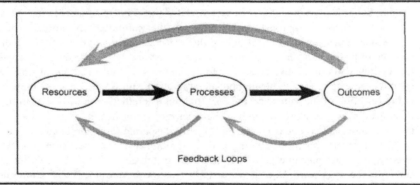

Figure 1. Diagram of Analytical Framework of Community Resilience (from Black & Hughes, 2001, p. 33)

Time is of the essence. Cities are vibrant and dynamic and the measures used to capture them should be able to capture the breath and movement of a city. Different histories, cultures, experiences, plans and contexts are what differentiate communities. A resilient community is one that examines the long-term changes within the society, warding off ill outcomes before they arrive and enhancing quality of life over previous generations. Longitudinal research is an essential component of any community indicator project. The positive impact of programming and developments may not be seen in a matter of weeks, or certainly not in a one time snapshot of life in a community.

Longitudinal analyses provide the opportunity to begin to understand causal processes which can not be assessed in cross-sectional data. That is, it can help to decipher the programming that is facilitating positive change and that which is not. Statistical analyses are rapidly evolving and the opportunities to use longitudinal growth and dynamic systems modeling are improving by the day. Although many indicators have been consistently collected over time, there has been minimal examination of growth and trajectories within those data sets. In addition, little is known about models of change within communities.

Developing CRI's. An accurate depiction of community resilience requires a mix of strategies. First, a social accounting would rely on existing indicators with which to map and monitor trends in community resourcefulness and potential vulnerabilities. These indicators, if carefully chosen, may be used to capture resilient outcomes of communities following unplanned events that challenge its adaptive capacity. For example, the proportion of residents with four or more years of higher education provides one indicator of work force flexibility in the event of an economic crisis. Second, a direct appraisal of key elements of resilience processes is needed to assess key dimensions of resourcefulness not detected with existing methods, and to capture emergent strengths that do not yet register on global outcome indices of social and economic progress. The extent of resident knowledge of and participation in community forums and other means of active engagement in collective decisions that affect their lives provides information about the degree of social connection and resident commitment to furthering the quality of life in their communities. Third, the social ecology of sustainability and recovery cannot be ignored. Along with measures of job growth and household income, for example, budgets for family time, and impacts of income disparity on community civility must be assessed.

To illustrate, consider the following list of attributes of resilient processes for communities of location reproduced in Table 3. These are key elements of community resilience theory that should be monitored for degrees of change in communities that aspire to develop greater resilience capacity.

Table 3. Fundamentals of neighborhood resilience

Resilient Communities...

1. have neighbors that trust one another. (Kawachi, Kennedy, & Glass, 1999; Kawachi, Kennedy, & Glass, 2005; Sampson, Raudenbush, & Earls, 1997; Subramanian, Kim, & Kawachi, 2002)

2. have neighbors that interact on a regular basis. (Berkman & Syme, 1979; Bolland & McCallum, 2002; Unger & Wandersman, 1985)

3. have residents who own their houses and stay for awhile. (Bures, 2003; Galster, 1998; Temkin & Rohe, 1998)

4. have residents who have a sense of community and cohesion. (Brodsky, O'Campo, & Aronson, 1999; Chavis & Wandersman, 1990; Cutrona, Russell, Hessling, Brown, & Murry, 2000; Farrell, Aubry, & Coulombe, 2004; Sarason, 1974)

5. have residents who work together for the common good and are involved in community events and affairs. (Duncan, Duncan, Okut, Strycker, & Hix-Small, 2003; Hyyppa & Maki, 2003; Perkins, Florin, Rich, Wandersman, & Chavis, 1990; Price & Behrens, 2003; Sampson et al., 1997)

6. have formal and informal civic places for gathering. (Oldenburg, 1991; Sharkova & Sanchez, 1999)

There are indicators that are routinely collected which may "stand in" as valid indicators for many of the qualities of community life depicted here, but not all of them. The measurement of "trust", for example, is a critical dimension that requires direct assessment. Household surveys have been used for this purpose, and are the best methodology currently available. The cost of this method is prohibitive although the innovative use of web-based technologies may make large samples for citizen interviews affordable in the near future. The authors of this study advocate a complimentary, at times, alternative approach to acquiring information about community reliance. Citizen panels, constituted by leaders and other concerned citizens who are members of the communities studied could be developed to identify unique characteristics of their constituent areas that deserve close attention. These citizen panels can fill the gaps left by social accounting and address directly problems and prospects for community resilience. With care in selection of the citizen panel to assure it is representative of those most informed and concerned, the group may be enjoined to meet periodically to review the status of their communities, follow a well facilitated, carefully designed uniform framework for analysis, suggest new and better indicators of progress, and provide early warning to downturns in quality of life that is likely to leave their communities less resilient in the future.

In their discussions with our Resilience Solutions Group about community resilience indicators for the Phoenix project, community leaders frequently emphasized the need to make qualitative assessments of many descriptive measures that appear frequently in community indicator projects. Beyond public park acreage for example, they have asked for ways to measure the trend in development of safe and useable parks. They raised questions like, "What is the quality of organization (or social) contributions to neighborhood development?" and "How well and how frequently are organizations collaborating?" These and many other good qualifications were suggested to add shape and meaning to suggested indicators. Citizen Panels could focus on these and many other qualitative issues associated with determining direction and pace of community resilience processes and outcomes.

Conclusion

In sum, if the goal is to uncover indicators of resilient communities, the challenges of measuring change are readily apparent. A city that plans and is future-oriented, connected, not segmented, and focuses resources as well as risk factors bucks the current and long-standing trends. However, considerable effort is needed to generate such dramatic shift in attention to community resourcefulness. Despite these challenges, there are reasons to believe that critical steps can be taken to move to more resilient governance with substantial and sustainable gains in community well-being as a result. A "tipping point" in which the benefits outweigh the investment costs is required. To reach this critical point in community development requires resourceful people with keen insights and strong leadership skills, coupled with accurate data that can persuade the skeptics and reassure supporters that the path they have chosen is the correct one. An effective model depends on good data, high quality feedback, leadership willing to listen and act, and a citizenry that is informed and involved. The resilience model is no different in this regard. Resilience fundamentals applied through civic engagements that further "learning governance" provide a path to community development that strengthens prospects for a sustainable future for all.

Notes

1   In 1984, the World Health Organization (WHO) first extended the concept of health from the individual level to both of the individual and group level. It says: "Health is defined as the extent to which an individual or group is able, on one hand, to realize aspirations and satisfy needs; and, one the other hand, to change or cope with the environment. Health is, therefore, seen as a resource for everyday life, a dimension of our 'quality of life,' and not the object of living; it is a positive concept emphasizing social and personal resources, as well as physical capabilities" (cited in Boothroyd and Eberle, 2000, p. 3).

References

American Psychiatric Association. (1994) *Diagnostic and statistical manual (DSM-IV)*. (IV ed.). Washington, D.C.: Author.

Andrews, F. M., & Withey, S. B. (1976). *Social indicators of well-being: Americans' perceptions of life quality*. New York: Plenum Press.

Berkman, L. F., & Syme, S. L. (1979). Social networks, host resistance, and mortality: a nine-year follow-up study of Alameda County residents. *American Journal of Epidemiology, 109*(2), 186-204.

Bernston, G. C., Caccioppo, J. T., & Gardner, W. L. (1999). The affect system has parallel and integrative processing components: Form follows function. *Journal of Personality and Social Psychology, 76*, 839-855.

Black, A., & Hughes, P. (2001). *The identification and analysis of indicators of community strength and outcomes*. Canberra, ACT: Department of Family and Community Services.

Bolland, J. M., & McCallum, D. M. (2002). Neighboring and community mobilization in high-poverty inner-city neighborhoods. *Urban Affairs Review, 38*(1), 42-69.

Bonanno, G. A. (2004). Loss, trauma, and human resilience: Have we underestimated the human capacity to thrive after extremely aversive events? *American Psychologist, 59*(1), 20-28.

Boothroyd, P., & Eberle, M. (1990). *Healthy communities: What they are, how they're made*. Vancouver, BC: UBC Centre for Human Settlements.

Bowen, D. J., Morasca, A. A., & Meischke, H. (2003). Measures and correlates of resilience. *Women & Health, 38*(2), 65-76.

Brodsky, A. E., O'Campo, P. J., & Aronson, R. E. (1999). PSOC in community context: Multilevel correlates of a measure of psychological sense of community in low-income, urban neighborhoods. *Journal of Community Psychology, 27*(6), 659-679.

Bures, R. M. (2003). Childhood residential stability and health at midlife. *American Journal of Public Health, 93*(7), 1144-1148.

Campbell, A., & Converse, P. E. (1972). *The human meaning of social change.* New York: Russell Sage Foundation.

Canli, T., Zhao, Z., Desmond, J. E., Kang, E., Gross, J., & Gabrieli, J. D. (2001). An FMRI study of personality influences on brain reactivity to emotional stimuli. *Behavioral Neuroscience, 115*(1), 33-42.

Castro, F. G., Cota, M. K., & Vega, S. C. (1999). Health promotion in Latino populations: A sociocultural model for program planning, development, and evaluation. In R. M. Huff & M. V. Kline (Eds.). *Promoting health in multicultural populations: A handbook for practitioners* (pp. 137-168). Thousand Oaks, CA: Sage.

Chavis, D. M., & Wandersman, A. (1990). Sense of community in the urban environment: A catalyst for participation and community development. *American Journal of Community Psychology, 18,* 55-81.

Churchill, S. (2003). Resilience, not resistance. *City, 7*(3), 349.

Cobb, C. W., & Rixford, C. (1998). *Lessons learned from the history of social indicators.* San Francisco, CA: Redefining Progress.

Cohen, S., Doyle, W. J., Turner, R. B., Alper, C. M., & Skoner, D. P. (2003). Emotional style and susceptibility to the common cold. *Psychosomatic Medicine, 65*(4), 652-657.

Cutrona, C. E., Russell, D. W., Hessling, R. M., Brown, P. A., & Murry, V. (2000). Direct and moderating effects of community context on the psychological well-being of African American women. *Journal of Personality and Social Psychology, 79*(6), 1088-1101.

Dluhy, M., & Swartz, N. (2006). Connecting knowledge and policy: The promise of community indicators in the United States. *Social Indicators Research, 79,* 1-23.

Duncan, T. E., Duncan, S. C., Okut, H., Strycker, L. A., & Hix-Small, H. (2003). A multilevel contextual model of neighborhood collective efficacy. *American Journal of Community Psychology, 32*(3-4), 245-252.

Eckersley, R. (2000). The state and fate of nations: Implications of subjective measures of personal and social quality of life. *Social Indicator Research, 52,* 3-27.

Farrell, S. J., Aubry, T., & Coulombe, D. (2004). Neighborhoods and neighbors: Do they contribute to personal well-being? *Journal of Community Psychology, 32*(1), 9-25.

Fiksel, J. (2003). Designing resilient, sustainable systems. *Environmental Science and Technology, 37*(23), 5330-5339.

Fiksel, J. (2006). Sustainability and resilience: Toward a systems approach [Electronic Version]. *Sustainability: Science, Practice, & Policy, 2,* 14-21. Retrieved on June 26, 2007 from http://ejournal.nbii.org/archives/vol2iss2/0608-028.fiksel.html.

Finch, J. F., Okun, M. A., Barrera, M., Jr., Zautra, A. J., & Reich, J. W. (1989). Positive and negative social ties among older adults: measurement models and the prediction of psychological distress and well-being. *American Journal of Community Psychology, 17*(5), 585-605.

Folke, C., Carpenter, S., Elmqvist, T., Gunderson, L., Holling, C. S., & Walker, B. (2002). Resilience and sustainable development: Building adaptive capacity in a world of transformations. *AMBIO: A Journal of the Human Environment, 31*(5), 437-440.

Folland, S. (2007). Does "community social capital" contribute to population health? *Social Science & Medicine, 64*(11), 2342-2354.

Galster, G. (1998). *An econometric model of the urban opportunity structure: Cumulative causation among city markets, social problems, and underserved areas.* Washington, D.C.: Fannie Mae Foundation.

Granovetter, M. (1973). The strength of weak ties. *American Journal of Sociology, 78*(6), 1360-1380.

Hall, J.S. & Weschler, L. (2005). The Phoenix Futures Forum creates vision and implants community: Case study plus. (reprinted from the *National Civic Review,* Spring 1991 at http://www.cpn.org/topics/community/phoenix.html).

Hall, J.S., Jones P.M., Snook, M. & Springer, C.G. (1998). The information partnership: Planning a community information-sharing network for metropolitan Phoenix. Funded by the City of Phoenix and the Arizona Department of Economic Security.

Hancock, T. (2000). Healthy communities must also be sustainable communities. *Public Health Reports, 115*(2-3), 151-156.

Hughes, R. A. (2008). Health in a new key: Fostering resilience through philanthropy. In J.W. Reich, A. J. Zautra & J.S. Hall, *Handbook of adult resilience: Concepts, methods, and applications*. Guilford Publications Inc. Manuscript in preparation.

Hyyppa, M. T., & Maki, J. (2003). Social participation and health in a community rich in stock of social capital. *Health Education Research, 18*(6), 770-779.

Indicators of Sustainable Community. (1998). Seattle, WA: Sustainable Seattle. Retrieved on July 16, 2007 from http://www.sustainableseattle.org/Programs/RegionalIndicators/.

Innes, J.E. (1990). *Knowledge and public policy*. New Brunswick, NJ: Transaction Publishers.

Ives, A. R. (1995). Measuring resilience in stochastic systems. *Ecological Monographs, 65*(2), 217-233.

JCCI. (2005). Quality of life progress report: A guide for building a better community. Jacksonville, FL: Jacksonville Community Council, Inc.

Kawachi, I., Kennedy, B. P., & Glass, R. (1999). Social capital and self-rated health: A contextual analysis. *American Journal of Public Health, 89*(8), 1187-1193.

Kretzmann, J. P., & McKnight, J. (1993). Building communities from the inside out: a path toward finding and mobilizing a community's assets. The Asset-Based Community Development Institute, Institute for Policy Research, Northwestern University. Chicago, IL: ACTA Publications.

Long, N. E. (1991). The paradox of a community of transients. *Urban Affairs Quarterly, 27*(1), 3-12.

Lynam, D.R., Milich, R., Zimmerman, R., Novak, S.P., Logan, T.K., Martin, C. et al. (1999). Project DARE: No effects at 10-year follow-up. *Journal of Consulting and Clinical Psychology, 67*(4), 590-593.

Mallak, L. A. (1998). Measuring resilience in health care provider organizations. *Health Manpower Management, 24*(4), 148-152.

Masten, A. S. (2001). Ordinary magic: Resilience processes in development. *American Psychologist, 56*(3), 227-238.

Morse, S. W. (2004). *Smart communities: How citizens and local leaders can use strategic thinking to build a brighter future*. San Francisco: Jossey-Bass.

Moskowitz, J. T. (2003). Positive affect predicts lower risk of AIDS mortality. *Psychosomatic Medicine, 65*(4), 620-626.

Mueller, B. (2003). Building community sustainability indicator reports. Paper presented at the Georgia Basin/Puget Sound Research Conference.

Neubert, M. G., & Caswell, H. (1997). Alternatives to resilience for measuring the responses of ecological systems to perturbations. *Ecology, 78*(3), 653-665.

Office of Public Health Assessment. (2004). Utah community health indicators report. Salt Lake City, UT: Utah Department of Health.

Oldenburg, R. (1991). *The great good place*. New York: Marlowe & Company.

Peirce, N., Johnson, C.W., & Hall, J.S. (1993) *Citistates*. Washington, D.C.: Seven Locks Press.

Perkins, D., Florin, P., Rich, R., Wandersman, A., & Chavis, D. M. (1990). Participation and the social and physical environment of residential blocks: Crime and community context. *American Journal of Community Psychology, 18*, 83-115.

Phillips, R. (2005). Community indicators measuring systems. Aldershot, England: Ashgate.

Price, R. H., & Behrens, T. (2003). Working Pasteur's Quadrant: harnessing science and action for community change. *American Journal of Community Psychology, 31*(3-4), 219-223.

Reich, J. W., & Zautra, A. J. (1991). Experimental and measurement approaches to internal control in older adults. *Journal of Social Issues, 47*, 143-188.

Russek, L. G., & Schwartz, G. E. (1997). Perceptions of parental caring predict health status in midlife: A 35-year follow-up of the Harvard Mastery of Stress study. *Psychosomatic Medicine, 59*(2), 144-149.

Rutter, M. (1987). Psychosocial resilience and protective mechanisms. *American Journal of Orthopsychiatry, 57*(3), 316-331.

Santa Monica Sustainable City Plan. (2006). Santa Monica, CA: City of Santa Monica.

Sampson, R. J., Raudenbush, S. W., & Earls, F. (1997). Neighborhoods and violent crime: a multilevel study of collective efficacy. *Science, 277*(5328), 918-924.

Sarason, S. B. (1974). *Psychological sense of community: Prospects for a community psychology.* San Francisco: Jossey-Bass Inc.

Sawicki, D. S. (2002). Improving community indicator systems: Injecting more social science into the folk movement. *Planning Theory and Practice, 3*(1), 13-32.

Sawicki, D. S., & Flynn, P. (1996). Neighborhood indicators: A review of the literature and an assessment of conceptual and methodological issues. *Journal of the American Planning Association, 62*(2), 165-183.

Seeman, T. E., Berkman, L. F., Charpentier, P. A., Blazer, D. G., Albert, M. S., & Tinetti, M. E. (1995). Behavioral and psychosocial predictors of physical performance: MacArthur studies of successful aging. *Journal of Gerontology Series A: Biological Sciences & Medical Sciences, 50*(4), M177-183.

Sharkova, I. V., & Sanchez, T. W. (1999). *An analysis of neighborhood vitality: The role of local civic organizations.* Portland, Oregon: Center for Urban Studies, Portland State University.

Social Indicators 2001. (2001). Missoula, MT: United Way of Missoula County.

St. Luke's Health Initiatives (2003). *Resilience: Health In a New Key.* Phoenix, Arizona: Author.

St. Luke's Health Initiatives (2008). *Health In a New Key.* Retrieved on September 4, 2008 from http://www.slhi.org/new_key/index.shtml.

Steptoe, A., & Marmot, M. (2003). Burden of psychosocial adversity and vulnerability in middle age: associations with biobehavioral risk factors and quality of life. *Psychosomatic Medicine, 65*(6), 1029-1037.

Stone, A. A., & Neale, J. M. (1982). Development of a methodology for assessing daily experiences. In A. Baum & J. E. Singer (Eds.), *Advances in environmental psychology: Environment and health.* Hillsdale, NJ: Lawrence Erlbaum.

Subramanian, S. V., Kim, D. J., & Kawachi, I. (2002). Social trust and self-rated health in US communities: a multilevel analysis. *Journal of Urban Health, 79*(4 Suppl 1), S21-34.

Sustainable Development: National Indicators. (July 31, 2006). Retrieved on April 19, 2007 from http://www.sustainable-development.gov.uk/progress/national.index.html.

Sustainable Pittsburgh. (2004). *Sustainable Pittsburgh: Southwestern Pennsylvania regional indicators report.* Pittsburgh, PA.

Sutton, S. K., & Davidson, R. J. (1997). Prefrontal brain asymmetry: A biological substrate of the behavioral approach and inhibition systems. *Psychological Science, 8,* 204-210.

Swain, D. (2002). *Measuring progress: Community indicators and the quality of life.* Jacksonville, Florida: Jacksonville Community Council Inc.

Temkin, K., & Rohe, W. M. (1998). Social capital and neighborhood stability: An empirical investigation. *Housing Policy Debate, 9*(1), 61-88.

2006 Quality of Life Progress Report. (2006). Jacksonville, FL: Jacksonville Community Council Inc.

Unger, D. G., & Wandersman, A. (1985). The importance of neighbors: The social, cognitive, and affective components of neighboring. *American Journal of Community Psychology, 13*(2), 139-169.

Victor, P. A. (1991). Indicators of sustainable development: Some lessons from capital theory. *Ecological Economics, 4,* 191-213.

Watson, D., Wiese, D., Vaidya, J., & Tellegen, A. (1999). The two general activation systems of affect: Structural findings, evolutionary considerations, and psychobiological evidence. *Journal of Personality and Social Psychology, 76*(5), 820-838.

Zautra, A. J. (2003). *Emotions, stress and health.* New York: Oxford University Press.

Zautra, A. J. & Hall, J.S. (2008). *Working Toward the Good Life: Creating Indicators of Community Resilience.* Phoenix: Resilience Solutions Group. Workbook in preparation.

HEALTHY COMMUNITIES: THE GOAL OF COMMUNITY DEVELOPMENT

By Alvin S. Lackey, Robert Burke and Mark Peterson

ABSTRACT

A concept of community health is presented as the goal of community development. The four attributes used to define community health are: (1) attitudes and values, (2) capacities, (3) organizational structures and (4) leadership. The implications of using community health as a variable in measuring program success and for the training of community development practitioners are spelled out. Future steps necessary for the construction of scales to measure community health are indicated.

INTRODUCTION

This article presents a concept of community health as the goal of community development. What is meant by health, however, is different from the ordinary medical or public health use of this term. Community health, as defined in this paper, does not refer to environmental sanitation, disease or death rates. Furthermore, it does not refer to the physical appearance of a community. Community health is used as a sociological and developmental concept defined by the possession of four attributes. These attributes are: (1) attitudes and values, (2) capacities, (3) organization and (4) leadership. It is proposed that the goal of community development is to assist communities in obtaining, maintaining and/or improving these attributes of community health.

The purposes of this paper are to define the concept of community health and to show how it relates to the practice of community development, the evaluation of community development programs and the training of community development practitioners.

Dr. Alvin S. Lackey is a Professor of Community Development at the University of Missouri–Columbia (UMC); Robert Burke is a Graduate Student at UMC's Department of Community Development; Mark Peterson is a Community Development Specialist in Warrenton, Missouri. Special thanks are extended to Marian Ohman for her excellent editorial assistance. This paper is a revision of the one presented by Robert Burke to the annual meeting of the Community Development Society on August 4, 1983.

Literature relating to community health suggests three important positions: (1) agreement on the need to define community development goals (Sanders, 1953; Schoenberg and Rosenbaum, 1980; Luloff, 1980a, 1980b; Cottrell, 1983; Warren, 1983); (2) proposals for defining community health according to community members' attitudes, functions and capabilities rather than the physical characteristics or services within a community (Sanders, 1953; Kaufman, 1959; Iscoe, 1974; Goudy, 1977; Schoenberg and Rosenbaum, 1980; Cottrell, 1983; Warren, 1983); and (3) proposals that emphasize how people subjectively perceive their community (Luloff, 1980A, 1980B; Moore, 1980; Deseran, 1980).

Various authors have employed terms similar to that of a "healthy community." Sanders (1953), Kaufman (1959) and Warren (1983) use the term "good community" while Cottrell (1983) and Iscoe (1974) use the concept of "competent community." Glick (1983) describes a state of "community well-being" and Schoenberg and Rosenbaum (1980) employ the term "viable neighborhoods" to describe characteristics of neighborhoods that work. More important than the terms these authors use are the characteristics they deem essential for their idealized communities. These traits include: (1) local groups with well developed problem solving skills and a spirit of self-reliance (Kaufman, 1959); (2) a broad distribution of power in decision-making, commitment to the community as a place to live, and broad participation in community affairs (Warren, 1983); (3) leaders with community-wide vision and residents with a strong sense of community loyalty (Sanders, 1953); (4) effective collaboration in defining community needs and the ability to achieve a working consensus on goals and priorities (Cottrell, 1983); (5) citizens with a broad repertoire of problem solving abilities who know how to acquire resources when faced with adversity (Iscoe, 1974); (6) commitment to the community and a government that provides enabling support for the people (Glick, 1983); and (7) a formal or informal mechanism for exchange among conflicting groups (Schoenberg and Rosenbaum, 1980).

Goudy (1977), Paulson (undated), Rutter (1981), Hinds (1983), Blackwell (1954), Wilkerson (1979), Tumin (1958) and Fanslow (1982), and all support the contention that the above characteristics are essential attributes of a "healthy community." Goudy (1977) operationalized Warren's (1983) nine characteristics of a good community and included them on a list of thirty-two variables in a community satisfaction study. Because these nine characteristics are closely associated with the American values of community life, they were better predictors of community satisfaction than the physical aspects of the community or the existence of community services. Rutter (1981), writing from a futuristic perspective, suggests that local governments increasingly will become dependent upon the skills, knowledge and capabilities of local residents in order to meet community needs and to foster interaction between government and the people.

Luloff (1980A, 1980B), Moore (1980) and Deseran (1980) have engaged in an interesting exchange concerning the definition and measurement of the "good community." This series of short papers provides ample evidence of the confusion and lack of agreement on what a "good community" is and the need for additional conceptualization, theory and research.

DEFINING COMMUNITY HEALTH

The essential attributes of a healthy community are: (1) attitudes and values, (2) capacities, (3) organization and (4) leadership. Each of these attributes is elaborated below.

Attitudinal/Value Orientations

Attitudes and values exert strong influences on behavior, including the degree to which citizens participate in community affairs. The most important attitudes and values of a healthy community are listed below. Healthy community members will have higher ratings on these items than members of less healthy communities.

- *Esprit de corps:* Citizens are proud of their community. This includes community self-esteem and a positive self-image.
- *A positive vision of the community's future:* Within the context of the larger society, citizens share a common vision of what they want their community to become.
- *Acceptance of the values and norms of the larger society:* The most pertinent universal values and norms agreed to by members of the United Nations are taken from the United Nations Declaration of Universal Human Rights (1948) as follows:
  - The inherent dignity and worth of the human person.
  - Equal and inalienable rights of all members of the human family including the right to life, liberty and security of person.
  - Equality before the law.
  - Freedom of thought, conscience, religion, opinion and expression.
  - The right to participate in government.

- The right to have a freely elected government which derives its authority from the will of the people.
- Everyone has duties to the community in which alone the free and full development of (one's) personality is possible.
- No one has the right to destroy the rights or freedoms of others.
- Tolerance, understanding, friendship and peace.
- *Commitment:* Citizens are planning to stay in the community indefinitely and are predisposed toward working toward community improvement.
- *"Can do," achievement orientation:* Community members believe that they can do a lot toward the resolution of community problems with the use of outside assistance when and if needed. This dimension includes self-reliance and confidence.
- *Cooperation:* People are predisposed toward working together. This does not preclude conflict but suggests that the community has found ways to resolve conflict constructively. It further suggests that negative elements are dealt with in a positive curative sense. This assumes that meaningful opportunities to participate in decision-making functions as well as to contribute to the implementation of community-wide activities are open to all who are interested.
- *Nurture:* Community members care about each other's welfare, and are open and friendly toward each other. Newcomers are welcomed and given opportunities to participate in community endeavors. All citizens accept each other without unjust discrimination or bias.

Capacities

In order for community members to identify and resolve community problems, they must be able, in some collective sense, to perform certain *functions* which in essence define the community development process. To perform these functions, a number of *tasks* must be completed that, in turn, must employ one or more *techniques.* For community members to implement these techniques they must have the necessary *knowledge* and *skills.* Thus, the capacities that must exist within a community form a hierarchy which may be conceptualized as shown in Figure 1.

An example of this hierarchy would occur when community members have the necessary *knowledge* and *skills* for selecting and implementing the most appropriate *techniques* for the *tasks* they need to perform in carrying out the planning, implementation and evaluation *functions* required for identifying and resolving community problems.

THE CAPACITY HIERARCHY

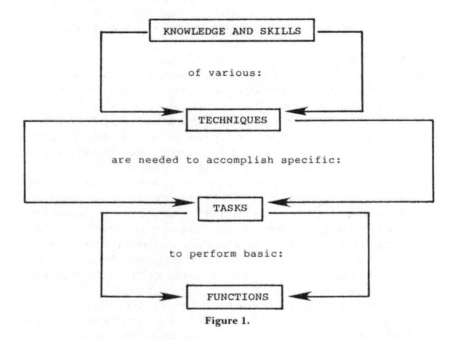

Figure 1.

As elaborated below, the capacity hierarchy specifies what the members of a healthy community need to know. Within the context of fostering community health, it also identifies important educational objectives of a community development professional. Within the same time context, it suggests useful curriculum content for pre-service and in-service training of community development professionals. In addition, it is suggestive of the kinds of knowledge and skills that should be incorporated into a standard community development job description. Finally, if this concept of a healthy community is accepted as the goal of community development, the capacity hierarchy would indicate a number of objectives that community development practitioners could include in yearly work plans. In so far as a community's health is low, a work objective would consist of raising it to an acceptable level.

The elements of each component of the capacity hierarchy are detailed below. It will be noted that the hierarchy can be read from top to bottom or from bottom to top. In order to perform the functions, a base of knowledge and skills must exist. Therefore, the discussion below starts with the functions to be performed and ends by identifying the knowledge and skills necessary to carry them out.

Functions. Communities will rank high on a community health scale to the degree to which citizens and community organizations can perform the following community development functions which are basic to the community development process:

- Identify and obtain agreement on broad, long term community goals.
- Identify community-wide problems and establish objectives instrumental to goal attainment.
- Identify the interrelationships among identified problems.
- Determine the influence of historical, external and other relevant factors, both positive and negative, on each identified problem or problem set.
- Assign priorities and a timetable to each objective and goal.
- Identify community and external human, physical and financial resources available for goal achievement.
- Develop and implement action plans for goal achievement.
- Assess and evaluate progress and adjust action plans based on findings.
- Resolve conflict among competing interests.

Tasks, techniques, knowledge and skills. As the capacity hierarchy indicates, accomplishing functions listed above requires that a number of tasks be performed. For each task one or more techniques may be employed. Community members need to know which techniques are most appropriate and have the required knowledge and skills to employ them. For example, to perform the goal setting function the task of conducting a needs assessment would have to be accomplished. This task could be performed by any number of different techniques such as a questionnaire, the nominal group process or delphi surveys. Knowing which technique(s) are the most appropriate under different circumstances and possessing the technical and other abilities to implement them constitute the knowledge and skills required.

Communities are more or less healthy to the extent to which a number of individuals within community organizations have the knowledge and skills to implement the most appropriate technique(s) to perform these tasks. (It is assumed here that unorganized individuals will not be effective in performing these tasks and that healthy communities will have organizational structures through which individuals can work.) Although the number of people who should be able to perform these tasks or employ these techniques cannot be specified, a larger number would be better than a smaller number, all other things being equal. Some important tasks and associated techniques that community members should be able to perform are provided below.

Conduct a needs assessment. The ability of a community to examine itself is one of the most essential tasks community members must be able to perform (Beal, 1964). Needs assessment is a logical first step in any development process for defining broad, long range goals (Witkin, 1984). Several needs assessment techniques are available such as community surveys and self-surveys, participant observation, case studies, the nominal group process, the delphi technique and various techniques for analyzing statistical and/or census data, including economic base analysis and population shifts. For example, Butler and Howell (1980), Kaufman (1977) and Witkin (1984) provide references for the appropriate use of different needs assessment techniques. Croll and Tharp (1984) provide a workbook for performing economic base studies. Warren (1955) is a valuable guide for conducting community surveys.

Analyze and prioritize problems. This task of a healthy community is related closely to the first two citizen capabilities of Cottrell's (1983) "competent community": collaborating in identifying problems and needs and achieving a working consensus. Techniques needed for this task include such things as the nominal group process, task forces, community forums, key informants, the delphi technique and advisory groups. The paired comparison or paired weighting technique permits one to rank any list of items from least to most important and thus is a useful technique for establishing priorities (Altschuld et al., 1980; Arnot et al., 1985).

Develop a comprehensive goal statement and plan of action, including proposed activities and projects. This plan should include the community's goals, the proposed activities and projects, plus the data base on which these decisions were made. Techniques for performing cost analyses such as cost-effectiveness, cost-feasibility, cost-benefit and cost-utility are important for decision-making at this point. Thompson (1980) and Levin (1983) are useful references for these techniques. Force field analysis, which aids in identifying the hindering and helping forces affecting goal achievement, is a valuable technique for selecting activities and projects with good possibilities of success (Arnot et al., 1985).

Develop project objectives, budgets and timetables. In order to assess progress on community projects or activities, a statement of measurable objectives needs to be made. A timetable for reaching each objective also would be required, along with a proposed budget and source of funding. Techniques enumerated in Craig's (1978) *Hip*

Pocket Guide to Planning and Evaluation, and the Logical Framework approach of the Agency for International Development (undated) would be applicable here. Knowing how and where to obtain information about legal procedures that need to be followed and the laws or regulations governing the specific activity(ies) being proposed is important at this stage in order to avoid difficulties or legal roadblocks during the implementation phase.

Implementation. The skills needed by community members in order to implement a plan of action are determined largely by the nature of the project or activity being undertaken. In general, managerial and administration skills are important. Cox et al. (1977, Chapter V) present a number of articles on program administration. Techniques such as the Program Evaluation and Review Technique (PERT), Critical Path Analysis and Gantt Charts are useful. Mulvaney (1984), Moder et al. (1983) and The Federal Electric Corporation (1963/4) provide guidelines for learning these techniques.

Evaluate and reassess activities and plans. Essential to any plan of action or development process are evaluation procedures that permit assessment of progress during the implementation phase (process evaluation) and the assessment of accomplishment after project completion (summative evaluation). Good evaluation depends upon sound project planning, clearly set goals, the formulation of specific objectives and proper implementation (Rutman, 1980). Citizen participation, understanding and decision-making concerning project design and redesign is fostered when community members conduct their own evaluations of their own projects. To do this, citizens need to know how to gather baseline data, build project monitoring aspects into their plans, and interpret the results of the data they gather. In addition to quantitative measures, qualitative approaches, including community impressions and opinions regarding the progress and outcomes of projects, also are important in evaluating projects. "Blue Ribbon Panels," community surveys, personal testimonies and written documentation are additional evaluation techniques. Useful references for how to conduct program evaluations may be found in Rutman (1980), Posavac and Carey (1985) and Rossi and Freeman (1985).

Resolve conflicts and create cooperative attitudes. Negotiating, bargaining, consensus building and compromise are important techniques in resolving conflicts and creating cooperative attitudes. Established procedures or mechanisms for bringing about accommodation, as Cottrell (1983) suggests, contribute to the healthy community. Skills related to human relations, group process, interpersonal community and other interactional skills are important here. Marc (1982) and Robinson and Clifford (1976) provide material on conflict resolution.

Identify and utilize resources, both internal and external. A thorough knowledge of local resources and how to tap them, as well as the knowledge of where outside resources are available and how to acquire them, are essential capacities for making the best use of existing resources. Resources include the human, physical and financial requirements for problem resolution.

Fundraising is of obvious importance in acquiring needed resources. Fundraising techniques take many forms. Mail, telephone and door-to-door soliciting are three major techniques for raising funds directly. Sales of various types—rummage sales, ticket sales, raffles, entertainment, and formal dinners—are common fundraising techniques at the grass-roots level. To solicit funds for a community project a group should be able to articulate the benefits of its project, investigate the legal requirements and implications, keep financial records, maintain bank accounts, develop a list of prospective funding agencies and develop expertise in grant writing. Flanagen (1980) is a good reference for fund raising techniques at the community level. Murphy (1977) is a useful reference for techniques related to resource identification and utilization.

Share information concerning community issues, activities and plans publicly and openly with all community members. Public speaking ability, the ability of a group to articulate its position, knowledge of media coverage and how to work with the media are important skills related to this task. Tropman and Alvarez (1977) cover some beneficial suggestions on effective writing techniques.

Understand and influence legislation and administration. Community members should have a good understanding of the legislation, laws and regulations which impinge on community functioning and know how to initiate or change them. Techniques such as organizing referenda, initiatives and submitting petitions are relevant here. Techniques related to the enforcement of legislation are also important. Cox et al. (1977, Chapter IV) deal with techniques for exerting influence on power structures and other population groups.

Organizational Requirements

Most communities have single or limited purpose organizations, such as civic clubs, churches and chambers of commerce, which may perform the functions listed above within their own organizational context. Healthy communities, however, also have the capability to perform these functions on a holistic, community-wide basis. That is, they will have an organizational structure that does needs assessments, problem analysis and goal setting, comprehensive planning and related functions on a community-wide basis, in which elected officials, governmental agencies, clubs and organizations and individual citizens may be included. Such an organizational structure may be formal or informal and will vary from community to community. Nevertheless, some form of community-wide or at least neighborhood-wide organization, in which citizens volunteer their time over and above the formal structure of official government, must be present in a healthy community. Spergel (1979) is a useful reference for organizing local communities.

Because full, meaningful participation in this process by all interested community members is essential, healthy communities will contain mechanisms to insure that community or neighborhood-wide organizations include opportunities for all people and groups—including youth, aged, race, ethnic minorities and the disabled—to participate and to develop participation and leadership skills. Equally important is the psychological perception within the community or neighborhood that meaningful opportunities to participate do, in fact, exist. Other characteristics such an organizational structure should have will parallel those of the healthy community itself. This is a vitally important, although frequently overlooked requirement. Many agencies are engaged in what they call the participatory approach to development, but since they are not organized on a participatory mode internally, they are unable to implement such programs effectively (Zevenbergen, 1984; Leger, 1984). Thus the community-wide organization not only needs to exercise democratic participation but it should: (1) have a positive vision of the future, (2) nurture its members, (3) have a problem solving outlook and capacity, (4) engage in the development of leadership and membership abilities through training programs and (5) establish productive links with other organizations and agencies within and outside the community. Furthermore, its leadership should reflect and promote these attributes.

Leadership Requirements

Leadership in healthy communities may be characterized using a community and individual dimension. From the community perspective, healthy communities are characterized by broad based leadership in which many people have opportunities to perform leadership roles. This includes people of different ages, ethnic backgrounds, race, sex and abilities. These leaders in turn have a broad view of the community and the interrelated segments that make up the whole. Such communities also have mechanisms for providing inexperienced people with leadership opportunities, experience and education. These mechanisms include such things as adult education courses in leadership and management, election of new people to head committees and task forces and youth groups which permit young people to take on meaningful leadership roles. Through these mechanisms they are continually renewing their leadership through education and the democratic process. Leadership training and renewal are essential to ensure that the total community's resources are being used effectively, to introduce new ideas, to maintain vigor and excitement in the development process and to avoid the natural tendencies toward oligarchy (Michels, 1959).

The individual perspective refers to the competence, abilities and style of leaders. The more competent leaders would possess traits such as organizational ability, creative imagination, innovativeness, enthusiasm, the ability to involve, encourage and stimulate others to do their best and the capacity to engender respect. Such leaders would have warm, positive, and nurturing interpersonal relationships with other members of the community. They also would have an abundance of energy and drive. Their achievement orientation, however, would be balanced by an understanding of the need to cultivate the human relations and process variables. Both left and right brain functions would be combined into a working whole. The style of leadership in a healthy community is one that fosters democratic participation along the lines of McGregor's Theory Y (1960) and Ouchi's Theory Z (1981). An additional dimension of the competent community leader is that such leaders maintain active participation in a network where they relate to other leaders and influential persons both within and outside the community.

The community and individual dimensions of leadership are closely interrelated. A community in which leadership functions are shared broadly obviously will be less dependent upon one or two individuals who have these characteristics.

SUMMARY AND IMPLICATIONS

A healthy community is one in which the members have a positive self-image. They have a "can do" attitude, coupled with a realistic sense of their own capabilities. The value structure stresses the inherent dignity and equal rights of all persons. It fosters freedom of thought, participatory democracy and democratic decision-making. Healthy community citizens possess the knowledge and skills necessary to perform the tasks related to the community development functions of needs assessment, goal setting, planning, implementation, evaluation and conflict resolution. Healthy communities have community-wide or neighborhood-wide organizational structures and leadership capabilities which permit those who want to participate in community affairs to do so.

The Measurement of Community Health

Each characteristic of community health, as elaborated within the text, may be formulated into scales. These scales provide operational definitions of the four attributes of community health, namely: (1) attitudes and values, (2) capabilities, (3) organization and (4) leadership. Once definitions are made, questionnaires can be constructed for measuring communities on each attribute. Samples or other surveys of communities can result in community profiles which can be used for community self-analysis and program planning purposes. Community health profiles also can be used to compare communities of similar characteristics. When used repetitively over a large number of similar communities, it is possible to establish some standardized measures of community health.

Implications of the Definition

The adoption of the concept of community health as a goal of community development has major implications for the profession. It implies that the success of a community development effort would be measured, in large part, by the extent to which the attributes of community health have been incorporated within a community. This involves an assessment of the capacities that community residents have obtained and a determination of the kinds of organizational structures and leadership capabilities that have been developed within the community.

The degree to which positive attitudes and values have been instilled within the community would be another area for examination in measuring success. An essential requirement then would be the conduct of base-line studies to determine the initial position of the community on the four community health attributes. These four attributes could be incorporated within community self-studies along with other information about the community. The resulting community health profile would indicate areas of strength and weakness for each attribute. Such a profile would be helpful in establishing community needs which a trained community development professional can help resolve. The profile, in turn, provides a base-line for evaluation studies aimed at measuring progress toward better community health.

Another implication of adopting the community health concept as the goal of community development pertains to the training of community development professionals. Professional training programs would have to provide the knowledge and practical skills to produce practitioners who are adept at applying the various techniques associated with task accomplishment as spelled out in the body of this article. Because the role of the community development professional would include the training of community members to give them the knowledge and skills required for conducting their own needs assessments and preparing their own plans, training programs would be oriented heavily toward adult education skills. Of special importance would be gaining proficiency in the necessary skills for working with people, especially with adult volunteers in a learning situation. The training curriculum would include instruction and practical exercises on how to conduct formal as well as informal educational experiences. An understanding of the social sciences and human behavior including how adults learn would constitute important knowledge areas within a professional curriculum. A competent professional would understand the role of attitudes and values on behavior and ways of encouraging attitudinal and value change. Counseling and value clarification skills would be useful for this purpose. Organizational skills as well as interpersonal communication and conflict resolution skills also would feature strongly in the preparation of a professional community development practitioner. Techniques for developing broad based democratic leadership with a holistic viewpoint would constitute another training need. While these topics would not constitute the entire curriculum or educational needs of a community development professional (which also would include such things as theory, research, history of the field and other topics ordinarily covered in community development training programs), this subject matter should comprise an essential part of the curriculum.

Finally, it is felt that adopting the community health concept would go a long way toward giving more concrete and substantive content to the definition of community development.

NEXT STEPS

This paper has attempted to define the concept of community health and to show how it is related to the field of community development. Several steps are necessary, however, before this concept can be put into operational use. The definition of community health is still subject to revision, elaboration and refinement. It is contended, however, that the human attributes, as presented in this paper, are more fundamental to community health than a community's physical attributes or appearance. Physical attributes are but symptomatic correlates of community health that, because of changing economic circumstances beyond community control, do not always reflect the state of community health.

The next steps for making this concept and its measurement useful for practitioners and researchers alike would include (1) the construction of scales with operational definitions of each community health attribute, (2) the design of sample questionnaires that may be used or adapted by interested practitioners and/or researchers to obtain some preliminary measurements, (3) the refinement of the questionnaires for administration in a number of communities, (4) the construction of norms or standards that can be used to compare different communities and/or to establish program objectives and (5) the development of research projects that will investigate the correlates of community health.

One correlate of community health, as herein defined, may be stated in terms of an untested hypothesis. The authors hypothesize that communities that score high on the community health variable also would score low on the incidence of various social problems and forms of anti-social behavior. Thus a community with a high health score should have a low incidence of such problems as substance abuse, alcoholism, crime, violence, juvenile delinquency, rape, vandalism and mental health illnesses. The theory supporting this hypothesis states that as people become more involved in their community they become invested in it and protective of it. They also develop greater prestige and have a more positive self-image. Their level of self-confidence and self-acceptance also increases. This combines to prevent self-destruction, anti-social behavior and mental illness. Evidence for this theoretical proposition comes from a study by Leighton and Stone (1974) in which community development was characterized as a therapeutic force in overcoming mental illness.

REFERENCES

Agency for International Development, State Department, Washington D.C. *The Logical Framework*.
No date

Altschuld, Al, Taylor, James & Canelos, W. D. Classifying needs assessment strategies
1980   for teaching purposes. Presentation at the annual meeting of the Evaluation Network and the Evaluation Research Society. Baltimore, Md.

Arnot, Marie, Cary, Lee J. & Houde, Mary Jean. *The Volunteer Organization Handbook*.
1985   Blacksburg, Va.: Center for Volunteer Development, Cooperative Extension Service, Virginia Polytechnic Institute and State University.

Beal, George M. Social action: Instigated social change in large social systems. In James
1964   H. Copp (ed.), *Our Changing Rural Society: Perspectives and Trends*. Ames: Iowa State University Press.

Butler, L. M. & Howell, R. E. *Coping with Community Growth: Community Needs Assessment*
1980   *Techniques*. Oregon State University, Western Rural Development Center (44).

Blackwell, G. W. A theoretical framework for sociological research in community
1954   organization. *Social Forces* 33:57–64.

Cottrell, L. S. The competent community. Pp. 401–411 in Roland L. Warren (ed.),
1983   *New Perspectives on the American Community*. Homewood, Ill.: Dorsey Press.

Cox, Fred M., Erlich, John L., Rothman, Jack & Tropman, John E. *Tactics and Tech-*
1977   *niques of Community Practice*. Itasca, Ill.: F. E. Peacock Publishers, Inc.

Craig, Dorothy P. *Hip Pocket Guide to Planning and Evaluation*. Austin, Texas: Learning
1978   Concepts.

Croll, John & Tharp, John. *Foundations of an Economic Base Study: A Workbook*. Columbia,
1984   Mo.: Department of Community Development, University of Missouri, Columbia, Mimeo.

Deseran, F. A. Comment: Behavioral patterns and subjective worlds in the good
1980   community. *Newsline* July, 8(4):48–49.

Fanslow, Alyce M. Knowledge and skills needed by community members. *Journal of*
1982   *the Community Development Society* 13(2):43–52.

Federal Electric Corporation. *A Programmed Introduction to PERT*. New York: John
1963/4   Wiley & Sons.

Flanagen, Joan. *The Grass Roots Fundraising Book: How to Raise Money in Your Community*.
1980   Chicago: Contemporary Books.

Glick, I. *Factors of Community Well-Being As Identified by Residents of A Resource Town*.
1983   Edmonton, Alberta, Canada: Doctoral Dissertation, University of Alberta.

Goudy, W. J. Evaluations of local attributes and community satisfaction in small towns.
1977   *Rural Sociology* 42(3):371–382.

Hinds, David G. New directions: The socio-technical future of community develop-
1983   ment. *Community Development Society, Wisconsin Chapter Newsletter* April: 4–6.

Iscoe, I. Community psychology and competent community. *American Psychologist* 29(8):
1974   607–613.

Kaufman, Roger. A possible taxonomy of needs assessments. *Educational Technology*
1977   November.

Kaufman, Harold F. Toward an interactional conception of community. *Social Forces*
1959   October 38:8–17.

Leighton, Dorothea C. & Stone, Irving T. Community development as a therapeutic
1974   force: A case study with measurement. In Paul M. Roman and Harrison M. Trice (eds.), *Sociological Perspectives on Community Mental Health*. Philadelphia: F. A. Davis.

Leger, Ronald. The challenge to donors: Learning from experience. *Development: Seeds*
1984   *of Change* (2).

Levin, Henry M. *Cost-Effectiveness: A Primer*, New Perspectives in Evaluation, Volume
1983   4. Beverly Hills, Calif.: Sage Publications.

Luloff, A. E. The good community: A rural sociological perspective. *Newsline* July, 8(4):
1980a   44–48.
1980b   The good community revisited. *Newsline* July, 8(4):53–56.

Marc, Robert. *Managing Conflict from the Inside Out*. Austin, Texas: Learning Concepts.
1982

McGregor, Douglas. *The Human Side of Enterprise.* New York: McGraw-Hill.
1960
Michels, Robert. *Political Parties.* New York: Dover.
1959
Moder, Joseph J., Phillips, Cecil R. & Davis, Edward W. *Project Management with CPM,*
1983   *PERT and Precedence Diagramming,* Third Edition. New York: Van Nostrand Reinhold Company.
Moore, Dan E. A good community by definition? *Newsline* July, 8(4):51–52.
1980
Mulvaney, John E. *Analysis Bar Charting: A Simplified Critical Path Analysis Technique.*
1984   Washington, D.C.: Management Planning and Control Systems.
Murphy, Michael J. Community resources: How to find and use them. In Fred M.
1977   Cox, John Erlich, Jack Rothman and John Tropman (eds.), *Tactics and Techniques of Community Practice.* Itasca, Ill.: F. E. Peacock Publishers, Inc.
Ouchi, William G. *Theory Z.* New York: Avon Books.
1981
Paulson, B. *A Model for Community Analysis: Steps in Planning the Total Health of a Community.* Unpublished, undated manuscript.
Posavac, Emil J. & Carey, Raymond G. *Program Evaluation: Methods and Case Studies.*
1985   Second Edition. Englewood Cliffs, N.J.: Prentice-Hall.
Robinson, J. W., Jr. & Clifford, R. C. *Conflict Management in Community Groups.* North-
1976   Central Regional Extension Publication No. 36-5, Revision 1. Urbana, Ill.: University of Illinois, April.
Rossi, Peter H. & Freeman, Howard E. *Evaluation: A Systematic Approach.* Third Edition.
1985   Beverly Hills, Calif.: Sage Publications.
Rutman, Leonard. *Planning Useful Evaluations: Evaluability Assessment.* Beverly Hills,
1980   Calif.: Sage Publications.
Rutter, Laurence. Strategies for the essential community: Local government in the
1981   year 2000. *Futurist* June:19–28.
Sanders, Irwin T. *Making Good Communities Better.* Lexington, Ky.: University of Ken-
1953   tucky Press.
Schoenberg, S. P. & Rosenbaum, P. O. *Neighborhoods That Work: Sources for Viability in*
1980   *the Inner City.* New Brunswick, N.J.: Rutgers University Press, Chapter 3.
Spergel, I. Organizing the local community: The social stability approach. In Fred M.
1979   Cox et al. (eds.), *Strategies of Community Organization,* Third Edition.
Thompson, Mark S. *Benefit-Cost Analysis for Program Evaluation.* Beverly Hills, Calif:
1980   Sage Publications.
Tumin, Melvin M. Some requirements for effective community development. *Com-*
1958   *munity Development Review.* Number 11:1–40.
Tropman, John E. & Alvarez, Ann Rosegrant. Writing for effect: Correspondence,
1977   records, and documents. In Fred M. Cox, John L. Erlich, Jack Rothman and John E. Tropman (eds.), *Tactics and Techniques of Community Practice.* Itasca, Ill.: F. E. Peacock Publishers, Inc.
United Nations. *United Nations Universal Declaration of Human Rights.*
1948
Warren, Roland L. *Studying Your Community.* New York: Russell Sage Foundation.
1955
1983   The good community: What would it be? In Roland L. Warren and Larry Lyon (eds.), *New Perspectives on the American Community.* Homewood, Ill.: The Dorsey Press (Reprinted from the *Journal of the Community Development Society,* Vol. 1, No. 1, Spring, 1970).

Wilkerson, Kenneth P. Social well-being and community. *Journal of the Community*
1979 *Development Society* 10(1):5–16.
Witkin, Belle Ruth. *Assessing Needs in Educational and Social Programs.* San Francisco:
1984 Jossey Bass.
Zevenbergen, W. Official development assistance and grassroots action: A delicate
1984 relationship. *Development: Seeds of Change* (2).

Index

ability, organization's 176, 179, 222
academics 2, 6, 14–15, 242, 308
action plans 9, 206, 345, 347
active citizenship 80, 83
active online communities 287
adjacent counties 130, 139
administrators 172, 174–175, 178, 180
affluent communities 306
African Americans 65, 122, 124–130, 132, 134–136, 138, 177, 215
age 65, 80, 83–86, 88, 95–96, 234, 236, 265–266, 268, 272, 274, 276, 278, 280
agencies 6, 13, 18–19, 28, 30, 109, 111, 297, 307, 347, 349
Alexander, E. R. 160
amenities 42–44, 51, 125, 139, 184, 281–282; environmental 44, 186
American Indians 231–232, 234–235, 237
Apsaalooke Nation 231, 234
Arlington County 193–194
Arnstein, S. 114, 212, 218
arts 9, 13, 41–45, 215, 327
aspirations 156, 159–161, 164
assessment 104, 112, 116–117, 150–151, 227, 231, 254, 256, 327, 332, 334, 345–348, 350–352
attitudes 59, 79–82, 86, 97–98, 126, 229, 239, 241, 317–318, 340–342, 351–352; political 79, 82, 98; and values 241, 340, 342, 351–352
attraction, ratio of 203–204
attributes 287, 300, 331, 335, 340, 342, 349, 351
autonomy 150–151, 175

barriers 62, 66, 70, 72, 74–75, 132, 177, 235–238, 241, 291
Beck, Roger 18, 40
black leaders 106, 201–206
black leadership group 204
black members 130–132, 135–136, 203
black residents 130, 257
block parties 212, 219, 222
Blueprint Project 195
Bockmeyer, J. L. 213–214

Boston 209, 252–254, 328
Boston Public Health Commission 252, 254
Building Healthy Communities program 260
business development projects 37
business location decisions 43

cancer 231, 234–237, 239–242, 249, 255; prostate 234, 238–240
capacity building 62, 74–75, 104, 147–148, 150, 319, 323
capacity hierarchy 344–345
capacity of communities 310, 318
capitals 5–6, 8, 22, 30–31, 37–38, 41, 45–46, 116, 251, 308–309, 324
categories of projects 34–35
CBPR approach 231–233, 242–243
CDCs 46, 106, 114, 209–210, 212–223, 234; in Detroit 106, 215–217; Detroit's 209, 214–215, 217, 222–223
charrettes 189, 192–194
churches 65, 69, 71, 97, 109–110, 113, 130, 176, 251–252, 348
citizen participation 105, 170–173, 180, 185, 187–189, 192–195, 209–214, 216–219, 223, 307, 347; role of 184, 209, 214; scope of 209–210, 215
citizen participation continuum 209–210, 212–213, 217–223
citizen participation processes 184, 193, 212
citizens 63, 79–80, 82, 154, 156–161, 177, 184–185, 187–188, 191–196, 212–213, 218–219, 327, 341–343, 345, 347
city governments 26–27, 176
collective action 67, 70, 72–73, 104, 108–109, 113, 115–117, 228, 287, 290–292, 299–300
Commission members 127, 136
communities: affluent 306; capacity of 310, 318; empowering 319; existing 186; general 205; good 341–342; hard-to-reach 306, 312, 318–319; host 122–124; low-income 171, 177; low-wealth 72; marginal 124; offline 289; under-resourced 63, 73

community-based development projects 33–35, 37
community-based organizations 170–172, 176, 180, 209–214, 223, 328; empowerment-oriented 176–177
community developers 2, 4, 9–10, 152, 171, 250–251
community development 2–10, 12–15, 17–20, 103–115, 123–124, 146–147, 149–150, 199, 227–229, 248, 250, 257–259, 286–287, 299–300, 306–307, 323, 330–331, 336, 340, 352–353; corporations 41, 45–46, 106, 114, 209, 217, 257–258; goal of 229, 340, 344, 351–352; initiatives 9, 63, 74, 299; online 287, 299; organizations 18, 57, 59; practice 2, 4, 6, 13, 104, 108, 111, 117, 146–148, 151–152, 227–228; practitioners 4–5, 38, 41, 104, 106, 108–109, 148, 150, 199–200, 206–207, 340, 344; process 4–5, 9–10, 13, 103, 213–214, 223, 300, 343, 345; professionals 2, 251, 299, 344, 352; projects 11–12, 124, 214, 222; theorists 200
Community Economic Development 217, 223
community groups 17, 38, 45, 63, 73, 151–152, 156, 159, 165, 220–221, 328
community health 229, 249, 260, 324, 332, 340–341, 344, 351–353
community leaders 2, 6, 17, 41, 79, 84–86, 88, 91, 96–98, 201, 203–204; perceptions of 86, 95–97
community life 31, 113, 160, 201, 286, 290–292, 294, 314–316, 323, 330, 341
community meetings 70–71, 221, 228, 233–234, 236, 240–241, 243
community members 2–3, 62–64, 73–74, 103, 184, 191–192, 232–233, 287, 289, 308–309, 311–312, 314–319, 326–327, 343, 345–348; leadership capacity of 2, 103
community organizations 28, 56–57, 59, 117–118, 173, 176, 253, 345
community projects 229, 311, 318–319, 346, 348
community residents 4, 46, 53, 105, 110, 171–173, 176, 178, 184, 196, 253; low-income 170–171
community resilience 229, 305–308, 310–312, 314, 318, 320, 331–333
competency 85–86, 88, 91, 96
completed projects 190, 315–316, 318
conflict of interests 151–152
costs 24, 29–32, 35–37, 48, 72, 186, 220, 235, 237, 265, 267–268
Council, Advisory 133, 233, 236, 239–241, 243
county, Arlington 193–194
courthouse 129, 131–133, 137–138
critiques 154–157, 192, 213–214, 311
cultural differences 122, 135–136

Dalton, R. J. 83, 88, 91
decision-making processes 12–13, 63, 66, 75–76, 111–112, 114, 171–174, 178–179, 184, 187–189, 193–196, 218, 220, 223–224, 346–347
Deller, Steven C. 228, 264
democratic leadership 18, 58
Detroit 106, 213–217, 223
Detroit's CDCs 209, 214–215, 217, 222–223
development approaches 186, 194
development process 2, 12, 14, 18–19, 41–42, 184–185, 189–190, 194, 218, 346–347, 350
development projects 123, 184, 188–189, 191–194, 318; community-based 33–35, 37; local business and industrial 34–35
development tourism 124
diabetes 235–236, 247, 249
dimensions of participation 210, 212–213
disciplines 2–3, 7–8, 103, 107, 109, 227, 299
Disparities Project 254

e-communities 286–291, 293–294, 297, 299; research on 293, 300
e-community members 288, 292, 300
economic impacts 149, 265–267
economic opportunities, of neighborhood residents 252–253
economic resilience 309, 314, 317–318
education 14, 42–43, 80, 83–85, 88, 94–96, 149, 152, 177–180, 238, 241, 253, 278, 280, 350; public affairs 147, 149
educational tourism 124
efficacy 81, 85–86, 91, 95–96, 178
employment 41, 44, 47, 50, 97, 130, 162, 179, 269, 271, 274
empowerment 45, 62–64, 68, 70, 105, 154, 158–159, 170–180, 319
empowerment-oriented approaches 172–173
empowerment-oriented community-based organizations 176–177
environmental amenities 44, 186
environmental justice 109, 255–256, 258
environmental justice communities 251, 258
environmental resilience 309, 314, 316
EPA 185, 187, 189, 194–195, 256–258
ethical principles 104, 146–147, 152
ethnic group members 165, 175
ETMC 125–128, 130–139; members 126–127, 132–133, 135–136
expenditures 151, 266–267, 270, 272, 276, 278, 280; total local government health care 276

families 62, 69, 109, 114, 130, 133–136, 160–161, 173, 238, 332–333, 342
family members 237–239, 255
federal programs 7, 29
fiscal analysis 267–268

INDEX

fiscal impacts 228, 265–268, 273, 276, 280–282; positive 267–268, 282
Flora, Cornelia 17
Flora, Jan L. 17
focus group participants 66, 68–69
focus groups 65–66, 68, 70, 75, 218–219, 222, 228, 233–234, 236, 238–239, 242–243
Forester, J. 156
Friedmann, J. 154, 159

general leaders 201–205
general leadership group 204
government, Scottish 307, 311
grassroots 106, 209, 212, 215–216, 219–221, 223
grassroots organizations 212, 223
grassroots participation 106, 209–210, 212–214, 221–223
Green, Gary P. 17
group members, ethnic 165, 175
group process, nominal 345–346
groups 5, 10–12, 17–18, 26–27, 56, 58–59, 63, 109, 113–116, 131–132, 149, 151–152, 161–167, 203, 212–213, 220–224, 273–274, 276, 280–281, 348–349; informal 109; new 165–166; oppressed 155, 158; public interest 83
group's life 162–164
groups of residents 73, 75, 220
groups of retirees 228, 265, 280
group structure 203

hard-to-reach communities 306, 312, 318–319
health 13–14, 227–230, 233–236, 239–241, 243, 247–249, 251, 256, 259–260, 325–327, 329–333, 340; and resilience 14, 227
health disparities 228, 232–233, 246, 248–249, 252, 257, 259–260
health issues 228, 233–234, 238, 240, 255, 258
health project 227, 231, 233, 235, 242–243
Health Project Advisory Council 233–234
health project survey 239
health screenings 239, 241
health services, Indian 231, 233–235, 237, 241
healthy communities 8, 13, 17, 229–230, 260, 323–324, 332, 334, 340–342, 344–351
heritage tourism 126, 130, 135
high-income retirees 266, 272, 274, 281–282
historic preservation projects 33–35, 37
host community 122–124
households 42–45, 79, 85, 247, 268, 271–274, 276, 326; new 269, 273, 276, 278
Howe, E. 146
human ecosystems 248–252
Hutson, Malo Andre 228

ICMA 185–186, 188, 192
ideology 154, 156–158, 160

income 22–23, 37, 40–41, 43–44, 48, 83–85, 88, 95–96, 252–253, 265–266, 268–270, 272, 280, 314, 316; growth 43–44, 48, 50, 264
Indian Health Service (IHS) 231, 233–235, 237–238, 241
indicators 14, 229, 266, 309, 318, 323, 325–330, 332–336; Boston 328–329
individual participants 317–318
industrial development projects 34–36
informal groups 109
informal networks 105, 170, 175–176, 178, 180
informants 30–31, 36, 127–128, 201–202, 214
instrumental goals 218–219, 222
instrumental participation 210, 212, 219, 223
interpersonal skills 165
Interpretive research 126
interviews 127–128, 134, 136–137, 201, 214–215, 218, 240, 311–312

jobs 17–18, 22–23, 28–29, 35–37, 41, 46–47, 49, 175–176, 184–185, 187, 253–254, 266, 274, 276, 281–282; professional 35, 37; service industry 48–49
JPNDC 253–254
justice 6, 12–13, 103, 106, 122–124, 147–148, 152, 258

Kaufman, J. 146
knowledge 2, 4, 8, 11, 57, 59, 75, 156, 158, 164, 166, 239–241, 307, 309, 348; and skills 124, 344–345, 350, 352

labor force 265, 268–269, 274, 281
labor force participation of retirees 274, 281
lack of trust 64, 67–68, 72–73, 91, 96–97, 232
leaders 18–19, 56–59, 69–71, 79, 91, 113, 115–116, 201, 203–206, 306, 310–311, 319–320, 326, 328, 349–350
leadership 10–12, 17–20, 56–57, 59, 69–70, 151–152, 175, 178–179, 254–255, 336, 340, 342, 349–351; capabilities 351; democratic 18, 58; development 6, 10–12, 56, 62, 74–75, 328, 349; nominations 201, 204; opportunities 11–12, 18–19, 350; roles 10, 18–19, 177, 349; skills 59, 63, 74, 172, 349; stable 215
leadership group 201, 203–205; black 204; general 204; total 202, 204
local communities 36, 38, 98, 170, 299, 306, 309–310, 349
local development organizations 33
local economy 26, 29, 97, 186–187, 265–266, 269–271, 273–274, 281
local election 81, 85, 91, 95–96, 189
local governments 22, 27, 29–31, 36–37, 45–48, 75, 184, 188–189, 191–196, 228, 266–267, 270, 280–282

INDEX

local organizations 22, 38, 115, 170, 176, 178, 212, 327, 330
local projects 311–312, 316–319
local residents 29, 36, 131, 133, 138, 210, 255, 260, 306, 309, 316
logistic regressions 95–96
low-income communities 171, 177
low-income retirees 266, 268, 276, 281
low-income scenarios 273, 276, 278
low-wage residents 253
low-wealth communities 72

managers 56–59, 140, 173–175, 290, 306
marginalized communities 75, 306
marginalized groups 116, 124, 171–172, 174, 177, 179
material, educational 240
McAdam, D. 112
medical care 14, 235, 237, 247–248, 254–255
member profiles 288, 294, 298
members 64–66, 116, 124–125, 127, 130, 132–140, 164, 171, 173–176, 191–192, 202–204, 272, 287–293, 297–300, 314–315, 342, 349–350; black 130–132, 135–136, 203; e-community 288, 292, 300; family 237–239, 255; individual 114, 176, 290–291; tribal 233, 236–237
members of marginalized groups 174, 177
mental health 331, 333
minority residents 19, 248, 252, 259
Mississippi 108, 125, 127–128, 131, 133, 138
mistrust 62, 67, 72, 191
models of practice 104, 110, 112, 157, 172
modes of participation 218

National Congress for Community Economic Development 217
neighborhood-based organizations 218, 220
neighborhood residents 45, 65–66, 73–74, 188, 255
neighborhoods 64–66, 68–75, 184, 186–187, 189–190, 192–194, 215, 217–218, 220, 246–248, 250–252, 254, 257, 259, 331
nominal group process 345–346
nominations 201, 203–205
non-governmental organizations 186
nonleaders 202–204
nonprofit corporations 18, 40–41, 43–45, 47–53
non-profit organizations 11, 18, 50, 52, 170–172, 176, 178–179, 195, 260, 327; community-based 170, 173, 176
nonprofits 11, 18, 40, 42–48, 50–53, 105–106, 210, 212, 214, 217, 223; local 106, 223–224; social service 50
nonprofit sector 41, 49, 52–53

obstacles 9, 24, 31–32, 34–36
offline communities 289

older retirees 266, 268, 272, 274, 276, 280–281; scenarios 273–274, 281
online communities 228, 287–294, 297–300; active 287; effects of 228, 300
online community development 287, 299
openness to transformation 67, 71–72, 74
oppressed groups 155, 158
organizational capacity 222
organizational efforts 23, 155
organizational form 114
organizational resources 179, 220, 222
organizational staff 175
organizational structures 58, 105–106, 113–114, 175, 180, 345, 348–349, 351
organizations 11, 17–18, 23–24, 26–27, 31, 38, 63–64, 71–72, 104–105, 108–115, 117, 170–180, 210–223, 253–254, 327, 349; civic 97, 109; Development 23, 56; farm 17, 33, 37; grassroots 212, 223; local 22, 38, 115, 170, 176, 178, 212, 327, 330; neighborhood-based 218, 220; new 215, 223; nongovernmental 110, 112; non-governmental 186; nonprofit 11, 18, 50, 52, 195, 327; private 52, 333; strategy 221

participant observation 163, 346
participants 38, 41, 43, 64–66, 71–74, 113–114, 165–166, 170, 173–174, 176–177, 187, 189–190, 192, 195, 297–299
participation 5–6, 8–9, 12–13, 63, 79–81, 83, 96, 103–106, 112–114, 130–132, 170–174, 177–180, 209–210, 212–214, 217–220, 222–224, 232–233, 287–288; dimensions of 210, 212–213; instrumental 210, 212, 219, 223; process 212–213
people-centered approach 105, 161–162, 164, 167
people-centered community planning 105, 154, 158–160, 164, 167
people-centered planning 154, 158–159, 161–162, 165–166
permissive leadership 58
personal communication 235, 237
petition 19, 83, 85, 88, 91, 95–96, 178, 298
planned retirement communities 267
planning, people-centered 154, 158–159, 161–162, 165–166
planning document 65–66, 69–71
planning practice 155–157
planning process 68, 70, 74, 105, 158–162, 164–167, 188, 190, 218, 333
policy development 6, 9–10, 156
political action 81, 172–173, 176–178
political activity 19, 80, 82–83, 88, 91, 96, 157
political attitudes 79, 82, 98
political behavior 79–80, 82, 96
political campaign 81, 85, 91, 95–96, 178
political-economic constraints 104, 108, 111

political engagement 19, 63, 81–82, 84–86, 91, 95–98
political participation 79–81, 83, 85–86, 97, 170, 177–178
political power 105, 173–174, 178–180, 206, 250
population 4, 7, 85, 129–130, 159, 195, 215, 217, 228, 231–232, 248, 250–252, 255, 268–270, 276; urban 98
population growth 188, 273
positive fiscal impacts 267–268, 282
preservation projects, tourism and historic 35, 37
presidential elections 80–81, 177
problems, wicked 219–220
producer services 48–49
professionals 157–161, 163, 165
program areas 216, 220
programs: federal 7, 29; redistributive 47, 52–53
projects 11–12, 17–19, 21–28, 30–38, 131–133, 138–139, 187–190, 192, 207, 210, 216–220, 232–234, 240–243, 310–312, 314–319, 346–348; completed 190, 315–316, 318; disparities 254
prostate cancer 234, 238–240
proximal communities 287, 290–292
psychological empowerment 172–175
public affairs education 147, 149
public housing sites 260
public interest groups 83
public involvement processes 189–190
public services 31, 42–43, 113, 266, 268, 307, 329

quality of care 237, 253
quality of life 6–7, 9–11, 14, 185–186, 227, 229, 246, 248, 251, 254, 326–328, 331–332, 335; improvements in 13

racial reconciliation 125–128, 130–133, 135
racial residential segregation 246–248, 252, 259
ratio of interests 203–204
reconciliation 73, 104, 124–126, 131–140
reconciliation tourism 104, 125, 131, 139–140
redevelopment projects 44–45
redistributive programs 47, 52–53
ReGenesis Project 255–256
regret, statement of 133–134, 137
relationships 68–69, 79, 81–83, 85–86, 97–98, 114, 116, 123, 126, 138–139, 159–160, 164, 166, 242–243
representatives, tribal organizational 232
reputations 136, 290–292, 294, 298
reputation systems 287–288, 292, 294, 300
research design 64, 215, 232
research on e-communities 293, 300
research process 66, 232
research projects 124, 353
research team 64, 241

residence 79, 81, 83–85, 91, 97, 130, 274, 289, 330
resident engagement 61, 76
residential segregation 247–248, 259; racial 246–248, 252, 259
residents 5, 8–14, 17, 19, 31, 63–76, 85, 97–98, 122, 129–132, 134–135, 138–140, 186–187, 190–196, 210, 214–215, 218–222, 252–256, 329–330; current 71, 274; disadvantaged 7, 246, 254; elderly 257, 315; existing 68, 71–72, 74, 97; groups of 73, 75, 220; involving 17, 88; link 172–173, 176; low-wage 253; minority 19, 248, 252, 259; rural 97, 306, 312, 314, 318–319; small numbers of 218; urban 79, 81, 97; voices of 73, 75; ways for 12, 104; white 122, 128, 130, 132, 134, 138
resilience 6, 14, 227, 229–230, 306–309, 311, 314–315, 317–318, 322–325, 330–334; environmental 309, 314, 316; individual 306, 312, 314, 318
resilience change 306, 312, 318
resilience of rural communities 229, 309, 319
resilient communities 6, 13–14, 73, 117, 227, 229, 308, 319, 324, 333–334, 336
resource mobilization 104, 108, 113, 115, 222
resources 10–11, 63–64, 80, 105–106, 109–111, 113–115, 158–159, 175–176, 179–180, 186–187, 213–214, 220, 223, 251, 291–292, 327–329, 348; organizational 179, 220, 222
retail impacts 276
retiree households 265, 268, 272, 274, 280–281
retiree impacts, economic and fiscal 266, 282
retirees 228, 264–269, 271–272, 274, 278, 280–282; economic and fiscal impacts of 266, 282; groups of 228, 265, 280; high-income 266, 272, 274, 281–282; labor force participation of 274, 281; particular groups of 265, 282
retirement communities 228, 266–267; planned 267
revenues 29–30, 36, 44, 50, 265–266, 270, 278
Robinson, J. 11
role models: effective 236–237; lack of 236
role of citizen participation 184, 209, 214
Rothman, J. 62
rural communities 4, 7, 21–22, 31, 36, 81, 223, 228–229, 264, 266, 271, 306, 309–310; characteristics of 81
rural residents 97, 306, 312, 314, 318–319

SACOG 195
Schmidt, Frederick E. 17, 21
scope of citizen participation 209–210, 215
Scottish Government 307, 311
segregated communities 247, 259
self-development 22, 24, 29, 31, 37–38; activities 24, 27–32, 36; cases 25–27, 31; efforts 22–23, 29, 36, 38; process 38; projects 17, 22–33, 35–37; strategies 26, 28, 31

self-efficacy 172–173, 179
service delivery 52–53, 173, 179, 254, 307
service sectors 48, 274, 276
Shields, Martin 228
Silverman, R. 106, 174, 214
small business emphasis 5
smart growth approaches 185–186, 188–189, 192–193, 195
Snavely, Keith 18
social actors 109, 111–117
social capital 5
social cohesion 62–63, 75
social indicators 325–326, 333
social isolation 62–63, 80, 251
social justice 5, 12–13, 42, 103–104, 122, 140, 146–148, 151–152, 154, 161
social movements 103–104, 108–111, 113, 115–116
social policies 152, 170
social resilience 309, 315, 317
social service nonprofits 50
social service organizations 171, 251–252
solidarity 13, 109, 115–116, 315
Southside neighborhood 190
staff members 170–172, 174–175, 178–180, 215
stakeholders 65, 105, 184–185, 187–192, 194–195, 299, 328
Stallmann, Judith I. 228
statement of regret 133–134, 137
Sumner 128–129
supervisors 129–130, 133–134, 138
sustainable communities 62, 75, 299, 324
sustainable tourism industry 138, 140
synoptic planning 154–157, 167

Tallahatchie County 125, 127–130, 132–140
technical assistance 3, 7, 35, 104, 108, 110, 112, 116, 147–148, 150
techniques 5, 12, 111, 117, 126, 343, 345–348, 352
teleological ethics 147, 150
Till, Emmett 130–136, 138–140
total education expenditures 278
total expenditures 276, 278, 280
total leadership group 202, 204

tourism 11, 33–35, 37, 104, 122–126, 128, 131, 134, 138–139; educational 124
tourism industry 122–123, 126, 131, 134, 138; sustainable 138, 140
tourism planning 104, 133
transformation, openness to 67, 71–72, 74
tribal members 233, 236–237
tribal organizational representatives 232
tribe 235–236, 240, 242
trust 12, 19, 66–68, 71–72, 74–75, 79, 82, 85–86, 91, 95–97, 227, 232–233, 242–243; connected 68; lack of 64, 67–68, 72–73, 91, 96–97, 232
trust and efficacy, perspectives on 85–86, 96
trust and mistrust 67, 72
trustworthiness 66, 289, 291–292, 297

uncompleted C4C projects 312, 315–318
uncompleted projects 314–318
under-resourced communities 63, 73
urban population 98

variables 41, 74, 85–86, 94, 97, 192, 270, 314–315, 325, 334, 341; dependent 95–96; independent 94–95
villages 309, 311–312, 314–317
voluntary associations 286–287, 299
voter registration 177–178, 180
voter turnout 80–81
voting rights 112, 177–178
vulnerability, population's 251

Warren, Roland L. 341, 346
web site 288
WERA 257
white members 132, 134–137, 139
white residents 122, 128, 130, 132, 134, 138
whites 135, 234, 246–247, 252
wicked problems 219–220
Williams, H. 114
Wilson, Sacoby 228
work groups 57–59

younger retirees 266, 268, 272, 280–281